T0355211

USEFUL ENEMIES

NOEL MALCOLM

USEFUL ENEMIES

Islam and The Ottoman Empire in Western Political Thought, 1450–1750

OXFORD
UNIVERSITY PRESS

OXFORD
UNIVERSITY PRESS

Great Clarendon Street, Oxford, OX2 6DP,
United Kingdom

Oxford University Press is a department of the University of Oxford.
It furthers the University's objective of excellence in research, scholarship,
and education by publishing worldwide. Oxford is a registered trade mark of
Oxford University Press in the UK and in certain other countries

First Edition published in 2019

Impression: 2

Published in the United States of America by Oxford University Press
198 Madison Avenue, New York, NY 10016, United States of America

British Library Cataloguing in Publication Data
Data available

Library of Congress Control Number: 2018957358

ISBN 978–0–19–883013–9

Printed and bound in Great Britain by
Clays Ltd, Elcograf S.p.A.

*This book is dedicated to the memory
of Mark Whittow*

Contents

Preface

In 1999 I received an invitation to give the Carlyle Lectures in the history of political thought at Oxford in the year 2001. The Carlyle Lectures are a long-running and distinguished series; this was an honour which I had no hesitation in accepting. However, when the Carlyle electors suggested that I speak about the political philosophy of Thomas Hobbes, I asked if I might give the lectures instead on a different subject which had interested me for some time: Islam, the Ottomans, and 'Oriental despotism' in Western political thought from the Renaissance to the Enlightenment. My proposal was accepted very graciously, but also, as it seemed to me, with slight puzzlement. The unspoken question, I sensed, was whether any audience would be interested in coming to hear lectures on such an out-of-the-way topic.

I gave the lectures in February and March 2001. Six months later, on 11 September, the world changed. Friends and colleagues then urged me to turn my lectures into a book as quickly as possible, as there was now a hunger for works that might cast some light on the history of relations between Islam and the West. But I had more than one reason for demurring. I did not want to exaggerate the topical relevance of my work; while it was obviously true that present-day Western assumptions about Islam and the Islamic world have very long histories, which require careful examination, I thought it would be wrong to present any account of early modern theorizing (of the kind sketched in my lectures) as a 'key' to understanding relations with the modern phenomenon of political Islamism. In any case, I had some other books waiting to be written or edited, which had to take priority. And most importantly, I knew that the contents of my six lectures, if transferred to the page without substantial additions, would yield only a short and unsatisfactory book. My general subject matter was a huge one, ranging over at least three centuries, and I wanted more time to explore it in depth.

That time has passed. I may have strained the patience of the Carlyle electors, who impose no formal obligation to publish, but are understandably glad to see the lecture series turned into books, as they almost always

are; nevertheless, I am glad that I did not rush into print. I feel sure that the
work which I have now written is less unsatisfactory than it would have
been seventeen years ago, even though I am very conscious of the fact that
it gives a summary account of various interesting and important matters,
compressing some things that I do know, and, doubtless, leaving out others
that I do not. Specialists in particular topics will be conscious of my con-
tractions and omissions, and of innumerable nuances which I have not had
space to explore (to say nothing of all the detailed references to their own
writings which I have failed to make; I have had to adopt a fairly minimalist
approach to such reference-giving, having many topics to cover and no
wish to clog the pages unnecessarily with bibliographical material). But
I hope they may also feel that there is some benefit to be gained from placing
their special topics in a broader perspective and a longer narrative.

   Arranging that narrative has not been easy; here too I must ask for some
indulgence. While the overall treatment is chronological, from the fifteenth
century to the eighteenth, it has been necessary to devote individual chapters
to particular themes or traditions. Sometimes—especially when covering
the sixteenth century, when so many significant intellectual developments
took place—I must follow one of these subjects for a hundred years or so,
and then double back chronologically to pick up the story of the next one.
None of these topics and traditions existed in a watertight compartment,
of course, and some writers (such as Jean Bodin) feature in my accounts of
more than one of them; a certain amount of referring back and referring
forwards is unavoidable, therefore. But I am certain that the alternative,
a single onward-moving account of everything in mere chronological order,
would have been much less helpful to the reader.

   The title of the book requires a little elaboration on several points. First,
the word 'enemies': I seriously hesitated over using this term, as I did not
and do not want to give the impression that enmity was the only essential
relationship between the Ottoman and Islamic worlds and the West
European Christian one. As my previous book *Agents of Empire* makes clear,
the spectrum of interactions between the two did include various kinds of
positive collaboration and cooperation in the early modern period. But the
subject matter of this book is not the entire historical reality of relations
between them, but rather the mental world of those in the 'West' who
wrote in a political way about the 'East'. A degree of enmity was built
into the assumptions of the overwhelming majority of them; and even
when writers praised Islam or the Ottoman system, as a significant number

of them did, they could assume that this would have all the more impact (as part of a critical argument about their own society) precisely because Western readers took them to be praising an inimical religion and an enemy state.

Secondly, the dates used in the title have been chosen merely as round figures. For practical purposes 1450 is a proxy for 1453, the year of the Ottoman conquest of Constantinople; and 1750 is close enough to 1748, the date of publication of Montesquieu's *De l'esprit des lois*—a work which took the long-standing tradition of theorizing about Ottoman 'despotism', developed it further, and, by means of the reactions which Montesquieu provoked to his most extreme claims, helped to bring about its end.

Thirdly, 'Western' is used here primarily in contradistinction to the Ottoman world, and more specifically to refer to Western Christendom. Writings by Orthodox Slavs and Orthodox Greeks are not considered here; some of the former and most of the latter were, in any case, living under Ottoman rule. And while 'Western political thought' was certainly no monolithic entity, my focus has to be mostly on tendencies in the overall development of political thinking in Western culture. This is not a history of everything that was thought, in political terms, about Islam and the Ottomans by anyone living in 'the West'. The Ottoman history written in Hebrew by the sixteenth-century rabbi Elia Capsali, for example, is a text of great intrinsic interest, written in a territory which can be described as 'Western' (the island of Crete, under Venetian rule); but that work, like some other little-known Hebrew texts, played no role in the development of Western thought more generally, so it is not discussed here.[1]

Fourthly, I should emphasize that the phrase 'political thought' in the title has been deliberately chosen in preference to 'political philosophy' or 'political theory'. The ideas of several major theorists and philosophers are discussed in this book, but its scope is not confined to any canon of abstract theoretical works. Many different sorts of material contributed to the development of political thought, in a broader sense: descriptive writings by travellers, speeches by diplomats, polemical pamphlets, millenarian treatises, and so on. Although my coverage of them cannot be systematic, I have tried to do justice to the range of forms in which political thinking about, or in

---

1. On Capsali and his work see the recent monograph by Aleida Paudice, *Between Several Worlds*, esp. pp. 1–2, 79–86, 99–127.

relation to, Islam and the Ottoman Empire took place in the culture of early modern Europe.

Yet I must immediately add—again, emphatically—that this is only a history of political thought, broadly conceived, not a general cultural history of Western Europe's experience of the Ottoman and Islamic worlds. (This point is also relevant to the choice of source materials: playwrights, for example, may often have reflected cultural assumptions about 'the Turk' in interesting ways, but that is not the same as making original contributions to Western political thought.) To discuss all the ways in which early modern Europe absorbed and reacted to Islam and the Ottoman Empire would require a book of much greater length, and of a much more capacious character. Where Islam is concerned, the history of Western religious thought about it in this period extends far beyond the political or politically related aspects that I discuss here; major areas of theological debate have to be left aside in this account. And as for the actual human interactions, the experiences of Muslim slaves in Europe, Christian captives in Muslim territories, Moriscos in Spain, missionaries in the Ottoman Empire, and others: I discussed these topics in another lecture series, the Trevelyan Lectures, which I gave at Cambridge in 2010. That was a very different project, and will lead, in due course, to a very different book.

On one other point I should emphasize what this book is not. It is a study of Western political thinking about Islam and the Ottoman Empire in the early modern period, not a study of Islam and the Ottoman Empire in their own right. There is a wealth of scholarly writings on the Muslim and Ottoman historical realities; I have benefited greatly from reading such works, and refer to them in many places in this book. Nevertheless, their value to the argument of this work is mostly indirect or supplementary. Historians of the Ottoman Empire do not write directly about the history of Western political thought, and I do not write directly here about the history of the Ottoman Empire.

Finally, a few linguistic points. All material from foreign-language sources is given in translation in the text, with the original supplied in the notes; the translations are mine, unless otherwise attributed. In early modern texts in most West European languages the word for 'Turk' ('turc', 'turco', etc.) was seldom used with the ethnic-linguistic or national meaning that it now has; the usual sense was either 'Ottoman' or 'Muslim', and I have translated it accordingly. Similarly, phrases meaning 'the Turk' or 'the great Turk', and versions of the formula 'le grand Seigneur', were used to mean 'the Sultan', which is how I have translated them. Standard English forms of Ottoman terms are used where they exist: 'Janissary', 'pasha', 'vizier', and so on. Other Ottoman words—in their modern Turkish forms—are given in italics, and explained on their first appearance (which can be located using the index). More generally, I should point out that some of the Western comments on Islam and Muhammad which are quoted or summarized in this book are of a kind that would be felt to be unpleasantly crude, or worse, if made by politicians or journalists today; but they were made hundreds of years ago, and are an essential part of the story that I tell here. To understand the present we must understand the past, and we cannot do that properly if we try to force the past to conform to the standards of the present.

I am extremely grateful to the Carlyle electors for their original invitation, especially to their presiding genius, George Garnett. While I gave the lectures I was also given hospitality at All Souls College on my weekly visits to Oxford; I particularly want to say what a kind welcome I received from the late John Davis, then Warden of the College. (From time to time thereafter he would ask me when I was going to write 'the Carlyle Lectures book'; it is a source of particular sadness to me that he did not live to see it published.) One year later it was my very good fortune to join the College as a Fellow; it has been not only an ideal place of work, but also, even beyond collegiality, a place of real friendship, and I thank all my colleagues, past and present, for that.

I am very grateful to the staffs of all the libraries and archives in which I have done preparatory reading for this book. Sixteen are listed in the List of Manuscripts at the end of the book; to those I would add the Biblioteca Marciana, Venice; Cambridge University Library; the Codrington Library, All Souls College, Oxford; the Herzog August Bibliothek, Wolfenbüttel; the Houghton Library, Harvard University; the National Library, Valletta; the Newberry Library, Chicago; the Österreichische Nationalbibliothek, Vienna; the Sackler Library, Oxford; the School of Oriental and African Studies, London; the School of Slavonic and East European Studies, London; the Skilliter Centre for Ottoman Studies, Cambridge; the Taylor Institution Library, Oxford; and the Warburg Institute, London.

Over the years, some fragments of the original Carlyle Lectures have been turned into articles or chapters and published separately. For permission to reuse some of that material here I thank Ashgate (for 'Positive Views of Islam and of Ottoman Rule in the Sixteenth Century: The Case of Jean Bodin'); the British Academy (for 'The Crescent and the City of the Sun:

Islam in the Renaissance Utopia of Tommaso Campanella'); and the Oxford University Press (for 'Alberico Gentili and the Ottomans': this text was first printed in the proceedings of a conference on Gentili organized by Professor Diego Panizza, to whom I am also extremely grateful).

This book is dedicated to the memory of Mark Whittow, a brilliant scholar as well as a deeply valued friend. He attended the original lecture series, and after my arrival in Oxford he and Helen enriched my life with their hospitality and many kindnesses. His untimely death is a source of great sadness for so many reasons; the fact that he would have read this book with interest, raising all kinds of original points in response to it, is absolutely the least of them, though it still matters to me.

All Souls College,
February 2018

ONE

The fall of Constantinople, the Turks, and the humanists

On the morning of 29 June 1453 a ship arrived at Venice, bearing the news that Constantinople had been conquered by the Ottoman Sultan Mehmed II. Letters describing the fall of the city, written by officials in some of the Venetian possessions on the coast of Greece, were read out to a shocked Senate in the Doge's Palace. On the following day the Venetian government sent a messenger to Rome to implore the help of the Papacy; he arrived there eight days later, where his news caused dismay in the Vatican and panic in the streets. In Florence, Cosimo de' Medici described the loss of Constantinople as the most tragic event the world had seen for centuries; in Naples, King Alfonso V called for unity and military action. As the fate of the Byzantine capital became known further afield, in Spain, Portugal, France, Burgundy, the Netherlands, Germany, Denmark, and England, the reaction was similar: consternation and mourning, mingled, in many cases, with a call to arms. On all sides it was understood that this was an event of huge historical and geopolitical significance.[1]

At first sight, there is something puzzling about the importance attributed to this one city. By 1453 the 'empire' of which it was the capital was a very paltry affair. The main territory belonging to it (at least nominally) was the Despotate of the Morea, covering southern Greece; but the rulers of that territory, themselves shaken by recent Ottoman attacks, had not sent any troops to assist in the defence of Constantinople, and would shortly ask

---

1. Setton, *Papacy and Levant*, ii, pp. 138–40; Schwoebel, *Shadow*, pp.1–4. For the first reactions see Pertusi, *La caduta*; for reactions in the Eastern Orthodox world see Dujčev, 'La Conquête turque'. Franz Babinger comments that 'Everywhere it was felt that a turning point in history had been reached... With good reason the year 1453 has been designated as the dividing line between the Middle Ages and the modern era' (*Mehmed*, p. 98).

for Ottoman help in suppressing their own rebels. During the previous century large parts of the Balkans had been taken over by the Ottomans, who had seized Thrace and Bulgaria, reduced Serbia to vassal status, conquered Salonica from the Venetians, taken control of most of Albania, and intervened repeatedly in the kingdom of Bosnia.[2] In purely strategic terms the capture of Constantinople was a mere mopping-up operation. Nor had the Western powers that mourned the loss of the Byzantine capital made much effort to save it. One Genoese commander did supply a contingent of soldiers at the start of the campaign; but thereafter both Venice and Genoa, the major commercial powers (and fierce rivals) that operated in Constantinople and the Black Sea, stayed their hands until it was almost too late, finally sending or loaning small groups of ships that could make no difference to the final outcome. The Pope had sent a more or less symbolic contingent of 200 armed men in 1452, and his modest naval contribution in April 1453 was also too little, too late.[3] Other Western powers, to whom the last emperor, Constantine Palaeologus, had sent desperate requests for help, had done even less.

To some extent, therefore, the sense of dismay and grief expressed by many Italian and West European rulers may have been quickened by a feeling of bad conscience. (This was perhaps especially true at the papal Curia, where the official policy for several decades had been to insist that the Byzantine authorities fulfil their pledges of ecclesiastical union with Rome as a condition for any help.[4]) Another factor contributing to the emotional reaction was the nature of some of the early reports, which were filled with stories of atrocities—stories which, in turn, were taken up and amplified by those activists in the West who wished to galvanize their rulers. It was claimed that 40,000 men had been either blinded or killed by the Ottomans, that nuns and virgins had been raped on church altars, that monks had been hacked to death, and that rivers of blood had flowed through the streets.[5] Acts of violence, desecration, looting, and killing certainly took place during the three days of plunder which Mehmed granted to his army. This was standard procedure for a city which had resisted calls to surrender, and overall the devastation may have been less severe than that inflicted on the city by its Catholic, West European invaders 249 years earlier. The population

2. See Fine, *Late Medieval Balkans*.
3. Weber, *Lutter contre les Turcs*, p. 131 (papal contribution).
4. Ibid., pp. 128–30.   5. Schwoebel, *Shadow*, pp. 3, 7–9, 12–13; Meuthen, 'Der Fall', pp. 4–6.

was indeed seriously depleted, not by mass murder but by the carrying away of captives for sale as slaves. But Mehmed took quick action to secure the future of Galata, the neighbouring city dominated by Western merchants; within less than a year he also appointed a new Greek patriarch and guaranteed the essential rights of his Church, to reassure the Orthodox population, and concluded a treaty with Venice, granting it full trading privileges in the Ottoman Empire.[6] Within a fairly short time, therefore, those West European powers that had direct commercial links with Galata and Istanbul would have been aware that the Sultan was a rational, pragmatic ruler, keen to promote prosperity and stability in his new possession, not a monster driven by fanaticism and a thirst for blood. And yet the tendency to portray the fall of Constantinople as a cataclysmic event continued unabated.

Part of the reason for this was symbolic. Although there was little Western interest in the history of the Byzantine Empire—which would remain a curiously neglected subject until the last part of the sixteenth century—there was of course a general understanding that Constantinople was the city of Constantine, the son of St Helena (finder of the True Cross) and the first emperor to favour Christian worship throughout the Roman Empire.[7] It was the 'New Rome', which had maintained the Roman imperial tradition after the barbarian invasions of Italy and the Western Empire, and it was the seat of the patriarch of a major Christian Church, albeit a schismatic one. These facts gave Constantinople a historico-symbolic importance of a kind that a city such as Salonica could never attain. When Niccolò Sagundino, an experienced Greek official in Venetian service, addressed an admonitory 'oration' to King Alfonso V of Naples at the beginning of 1454, he explained that Mehmed II was influenced 'by certain prophecies and preachings that promise him the conquest of the kingdom of Italy and the city of Rome; he has said that the seat of Constantine was granted to him by heaven, and that that seat is not Constantinople but Rome, and that it seems to him both just and very appropriate that, having taken the daughter-city by force, he may also take the mother-city.'[8] As we shall see, the notion that Ottoman sultans

6. Babinger, *Mehmed*, pp. 101–5.
7. On the slow development of Western interest in Byzantine history see Pertusi, *Bisanzio e i Turchi*, pp. 3–66.
8. Pertusi, *La caduta*, ii, p. 132 ('vaticiniis et praedicationibus quibusdam quae sibi regnum Italiae et urbis Romae expugnationem promittunt; ait sibi concedi coelitus Constantini sedem, hanc vero Romam esse, non Constantinopolim, videri aequum valdeque congruere, quasi filiam vi ceperit, hanc etiam matrem capere posse'). On Sagundino see ibid., ii, p. 126, and Meserve, *Empires of Islam*, pp. 106–12.

might claim the historic rights of the Roman emperors would trouble a number of Western writers over the next century and a half.

The main fear, though, arose simply from contemplating the power of the Ottoman military machine and the likely direction of its future attacks. Although the defence of Constantinople had been thin in terms of man-power, the city's massive fortifications had posed a challenge which any Western army of the period might have found insuperable. Mehmed's army, estimated at more than 200,000 men, was of a size that none of the West European powers could possibly match; and his mastery of the latest artil-lery technology equalled that of the best of them. With the seizure of this city, he consolidated his position in the Balkans (making it easy to pick off other minor Christian outposts to the east, on the Crimean coast and at Trebizond); his future advances, once the south of Greece was fully con-quered, were naturally assumed to be westward. Twice in the previous sixty years European powers had mounted large campaigns against the Ottomans, fighting them at Nicopolis, on the lower Danube, in 1396, and at Varna, on the Black Sea coast, in 1444. Both had ended in heavy defeats for the Catholic Christians, but in each case this happened only after an offensive by a crusading force which had penetrated deep into the Balkans. Now all the indications were that in future the offensive campaigns would be launched in the opposite direction, by the Ottoman Sultan against Catholic Europe. It was military reality, much more than any concern about the revival of imperial rights, that made Western thinkers and rulers so suddenly fearful and, for the first time, so very defensive. A fundamental shift in the balance of power had taken place—or rather, had finally become impossible to ignore. Soon after the fall of Constantinople, the Venetian chronicler Languschi wrote of Mehmed II that 'he now says that the times have changed, so that he is to move from east to west, just as the westerners went eastwards in the past.' As Enea Silvio Piccolomini, the future Pope Pius II, wrote to Leonardo Benvoglienti in September 1453: 'the Italians used to be the masters of the world; now the empire of the Turks is beginning.'[9]

For people whose historical understanding was, at its deepest levels, shaped by religious belief, such a momentous change had to have a theo-logical explanation. The easiest way to account for the fall of Constantinople

---

9. Pertusi, *La caduta*, ii, pp. 64 (Piccolomini: 'Fuerunt Itali rerum domini, nunc Turchorum inchoa-tur imperium'), 70 (Languschi: 'Hora dice esser mutato le saxon [*sic*: for 'stagioni'] di tempi, sì che de oriente el passi in occidente, come gli occidentali in oriente sono andati').

was to blame the sins of the Greeks, who had been viewed as schismatics since the eleventh century, and most recently had rejected the pledge given by their own representatives at Florence in 1439 to accept union with the Roman Church. This approach chimed with a longer tradition of anti-Greek feeling in the West, as exemplified to a rather startling degree by the poet Petrarch, who, in the mid-fourteenth century, had denounced the Orthodox Greeks as the worst sort of heretics and had called repeatedly for a crusade against Constantinople.[10] Such attitudes also helped to shape some of the earliest Western attempts to account historically for the rise of Islamic power in the East at the expense of the Byzantine Empire: writing in the 1430s, when attempts to pressure the Greek Church into union with Rome were at their most intense, the Augustinian friar Andrea Biglia had concluded that the Eastern Christians had lost control over so many of their territories as a punishment from God for the heresies into which they had fallen.[11]

One of the earliest accounts of the conquest of Constantinople, by the eyewitness Leonardo Giustiniani, Catholic Archbishop of Mytilene, confidently ascribed the Ottoman victory to the fact that God had withdrawn his support for the Greeks when they refused to implement the union with Rome agreed in 1439.[12] (Soon afterwards, the Orthodox Metropolitan of Moscow based the same conclusion on the opposite premise: God had punished the Byzantines for having agreed to union with Rome in the first place.[13]) The prominent humanist scholar Poggio Bracciolini, writing in 1455, accused the Byzantine Greeks of sabotaging the Crusades, reneging on their promises of union, and, for good measure, being so avaricious and so lazy that they refused to spend their own immense wealth on the defence of their city, preferring to beg for help from the Papacy instead. Their defeat occurred, he concluded, 'not by chance, but by divine judgment'.[14] Other writers agreed: Ubertino Puscolo, a humanist scholar from Brescia who was studying in Constantinople at the time of the conquest, wrote that if an angel had appeared, promising to drive away the Ottoman forces so long as the Greeks agreed to union with Rome, they would have accepted Ottoman rule instead. (The question of union had in fact bitterly divided the Greek churchmen, and it was true that some preferred the temporal rule of the

10. Bisaha, *Creating East and West*, pp. 120–1.   11. Webb, 'Decline and Fall', p. 207.
12. Meserve, *Empires of Islam*, p. 30.   13. Strémooukhoff, 'Moscow', p. 88.
14. Meserve, *Empires of Islam*, p. 30 (Giustiniani); Bisaha, *Creating East and West*, p. 126 (Poggio).

sultan, under whom their Church could retain its nature, to the ecclesiastical primacy of the Pope.) Puscolo also gave a very jaundiced account of the Constantinopolitans, portraying them as lazy and corrupt people who had lost all Christian virtue; for their sins, they were at last abandoned by God.[15] This view became commonplace. Writing a travelogue in the 1480s, the Franciscan friar Alessandro Ariosto (who went to the Levant on a papal mission to the Maronite Arab Christians) devoted several pages to denouncing the Greeks, explaining that they had been conquered and scattered as a divine punishment for their 'impietas'.[16] And in the 1520s Ludovik Crijević Tuberon, a Benedictine humanist scholar from Dubrovnik, would solemnly declare: 'as the outcome showed, God had foreordained the destruction of the Greeks, not only because they had rejected the authority of the Roman Pontiff, but also because they had completely abandoned the true rite of the Christian religion.'[17]

Such a view, though focused in this case primarily on the 'schism' of the Orthodox Church, belonged to a larger pattern of theological thinking in which the Ottomans functioned as the 'scourge of God'. The underlying template for all such theological interpretation was to be found in the many passages of the Old Testament where the children of Israel were subjected to defeats, enslavements, and other tribulations, at the hands of human oppressors but in a way that expressed God's corrective wrath. Some of the possible implications of this manner of thinking would take time to emerge, being elaborated much more fully in the religious literature of the sixteenth century: for example, the idea that the Ottomans' lack of virtue proved that their success had a divine cause, not a human one, or, alternatively, that their role as instruments of divine punishment was confirmed by the fact that they did possess precisely those virtues that the sinful Christians lacked.[18] And there is a more basic reason why the 'scourge of God' theme became

---

15. Schwoebel, *Shadow*, pp. 17–18; Filelfo, *Amyris*, p. 7. On Greeks preferring the sultan to the Pope see Evert-Kappesova, 'La Tiare ou le turban'. On humanists blaming the Greeks for the fall of Constantinople see also Hankins, 'Renaissance Crusaders', pp. 131–2.

16. Ariosto, *Itinerarium*, pp. 137–42.

17. Crijević Tuberon, *Commentariorum libri XI*, p. 220 ('Destinauerat enim Deus, vt rei euentus affirmauit, Graecorum nomen delere: propterea, quod non modo ius Romani spreuerant Pontificis, sed etiam a recto Christianae religionis ritu iam fere defecerant'). He also emphasized that it was the Byzantine Greeks who, for their own short-sighted purposes, had first invited the Ottoman Turks into Europe (pp. 220–1). On Crijević ('Crieva', 'Cerva') Tuberon ('Tubero'), who had studied in Paris before returning to his native Dubrovnik, see Pertusi, 'Giovanni Battista Egnazio', pp. 486–7; Rezar, 'Dubrovački humanistički historiograf'.

18. For the former view see Andreas Osiander, quoted below, p. 86. For the latter, see Theodore Bibliander, *Ad socios consultatio*, sigs. d8r–e2r.

prominent only at a later stage: the biblical template implies that the victims of this divine punishment are, after all, God's chosen people. This implication, a source of consolation as well as a spur to moral and spiritual renewal, could be deployed very effectively by Western and Central European writers addressing their own populations when they came under Ottoman attack, but would not appeal to Catholic writers dismissing the sufferings of Orthodox Greeks as condign punishment for their schism.[19] The first significant use of the 'scourge of God' argument in fifteenth-century Catholic Europe emerged among Hungarian writers, after Mehmed II's large-scale (but ultimately unsuccessful) campaign to seize the key Hungarian stronghold of Belgrade in 1456: it was employed both by the humanist Archbishop of Esztergom, János Vitéz, and by the Hungarian-Croatian poet Janus Pannonius (János Cseszmiczei, Ivan Česmički), whose poem 'De inundatione' portrayed the Hungarians as suffering a physical flood as a punishment for the sins of all Christians.[20]

So long as the divinely sanctioned role of the Ottomans was confined to punishing a schismatic Church, there was no difficulty whatsoever in thinking that, for Catholic Christians, the appropriate response to any Ottoman advances was to go to war against them. All theological interpretation of the Ottoman threat began with the fact that these were non-Christians and, in some obvious sense, enemies of Christianity. The medieval crusading tradition—or, at least, the tradition of thinking in terms of crusades, planning them and declaring them—was still alive and active in fifteenth-century Europe; it was a papal bull of 1443, formally proclaiming a crusade against the Ottomans, that had launched the campaign which ended so disastrously at Varna in 1444. So, within three months of learning the news of the fall of Constantinople, Pope Nicholas V issued a crusade bull, describing Sultan Mehmed as a fierce persecutor of Christianity and identifying him with the seven-headed dragon of the Book of Revelation. He called on all the rulers of Europe to defend the Christian faith, and offered a full indulgence to all those who would take part in the campaign.[21]

19. Orthodox Greeks, on the other hand, did use the 'scourge of God' argument after the fall of Constantinople: see Giombi, 'La cristianità', pp. 171–3.
20. Kiss, 'Political Rhetorics', pp. 143–4. In the sixteenth century this line of thought would be taken up in Hungary by both Protestant and Catholic writers, sometimes with an explicit parallelism between the Hungarians and the Jews: see Fodor, 'View of the Turk', p. 118; Jankovics, 'Image of the Turks', p. 268; and Őze, *Apocalypticism*, pp. 121–3.
21. Schwoebel, *Shadow*, p. 31; Housley, *Crusading and Ottoman Threat*, p. 18.

One ruler at least did respond enthusiastically. The Duke of Burgundy, Philip the Good, who had been a zealous supporter of anti-Ottoman and anti-Mamluk crusading projects for many years, organized an elaborate festivity in Lille in early 1454 in order to enlist his entire nobility in the cause.[22] Otherwise, however, the international response to the papal call to arms was unsatisfactory. The Holy Roman Emperor, Frederick III, summoned three imperial diets in 1454–5, at which the assembled princes were harangued by one of the greatest Latin orators of the age, Enea Silvio Piccolomini (the future Pope Pius II); yet, by the second of these, as Piccolomini himself later recorded, 'the Germans had changed their minds: none of them now favoured the idea of a crusade... It was a fine trick, [they said,] to swindle the Germans of their treasure by proclaiming a crusade against the Ottomans.'[23] King Alfonso of Naples expressed enthusiasm to begin with, but, counterproductively, kept up his own intra-Italian offensives, even as Nicholas V and his successor, Calixtus III, were trying to unite the Italian states in this common cause. Meanwhile Venice had signed its own peace treaty with the Sultan. A further crusading bull was issued by Calixtus in 1455; and when he was succeeded by Pius II in 1458, several more years of intensive papal effort followed, culminating—though that is hardly the right word—in Pius's attempt to muster a crusading army at Ancona in 1464. Carried on a stretcher to the port, the sick and prematurely ageing pope died there, but not before most of the ill-disciplined forces he had assembled had melted away.[24]

Since the crusading tradition went back several hundred years, it may seem easy to assume that to announce a crusade was to equip oneself automatically with a familiar and solid set of justificatory arguments. Yet this was not the case; and what to modern eyes might appear to be the simplest and most secure justification—that Christians had a basic religious duty to fight infidels—was the least solid of them all. Some such principle had been at work in the eleventh century during the papacy of Gregory VII, whose ideas about holy war helped form the background to the First Crusade; according to him, soldiers dying in such a righteous cause would be freed

22. Paviot, Les Ducs de Bourgogne, pp. 127–35.
23. Pius II, Commentaries, i, pp. 134–5 ('Mutati erant Theutonum animi, nec cuiquam placebat expeditionem in Turchos fieri... pulchrum id esse aucupium, expeditionem in Turchos decernere ut a Germanis aurum subtili ingenio... extrahatur'). On his speeches to the diets see Helmrath, 'Pius II. und die Türken', pp. 92–5.
24. Göllner, Turcica, iii, pp. 50–1.

automatically of all their sins.[25] But even then the argument was not entirely straightforward, involving as it did both the idea of warfare as an act of penance and the aim of helping those Christians who were under Islamic rule. Thereafter, penance and charity remained important justificatory elements, but another important concern was added to them: putting the Holy Sepulchre under Christian control was seen as a way of restoring the correct pattern of sacred world history.[26] Later medieval arguments in favour of crusading ranged more widely; one common theme was 'recuperatio'— 'recovery' or 'restitution', a legal concept loosely applied here to the previous Christian 'ownership' of the Holy Places or the Holy Land. But there were various other justifications, including the religious conversion of infidels.[27]

According to the influential writings of the canon lawyer Sinibaldo Fieschi, who became Pope Innocent IV (r. 1243–54), infidels had to be allowed to own property and to exert governmental powers, as these were rights and capacities that inhered in all human beings, not just in Christians. No Muslim ruler could be attacked and deposed, therefore, merely because he was a Muslim. Thanks to an ongoing and fruitful interaction between scholastic natural law theory and canon law, this became the dominant view. But it was not uncontested; one of Innocent's most prominent students, Henry of Segusio, known as Hostiensis, did argue that 'with the coming of Christ...all lordship and jurisdiction was taken from every infidel lawfully and with just cause and granted to the faithful through Him who has the supreme power and cannot err'—that is, the Pope. The implications of Hostiensis's argument were in practice moderated by his claim that only the Pope, not ordinary Christian rulers, could organize the deposition of infidel rulers, and by his assumption that the first step should always consist of sending missionaries, not soldiers. And whereas his argument was toned down in these respects, Innocent IV's was stepped up, in a way that took it some distance beyond the initial refusal to interfere in states ruled by non-Christians. According to Innocent, the Pope did exercise, on behalf of Christ, a general moral jurisdiction over all peoples, with the right to inter-vene and punish them for gross breaches of natural law—which included idolatry. He also argued that the Pope had not just the right but the duty to send missionaries, and that if an infidel ruler blocked them the Pope would

25. Villey, *La Croisade*, pp. 26–9; Brundage, 'Holy War', pp. 104–5.
26. Tyerman, *God's War*, pp. 47–9, 66–9.   27. See Kedar, *Crusade and Mission*.

then be justified in organizing a military invasion of that ruler's territory.[28] (This argument, which would have a long subsequent history, conveniently permitted the use of force in support of a programme of conversion, while scrupulously preserving the principle that conversion itself must be voluntary and peaceful.) In practice, however, Innocent's justification of crusading activity was based on the claim that the Muslims had unjustly seized the Holy Land from its original Christian inhabitants, and on a more general idea that Christ's special connection with the Holy Places had created a kind of right over them which must inhere in Christ's followers (as represented by the Pope).[29] In broad terms, therefore, it was legal or quasi-legal considerations—the right to expel a usurper, and a kind of 'recuperatio' involving a special variety of ownership—that predominated in this, one of the most influential statements of the justification of the Crusades.

Two centuries later, these traditional crusading considerations, which related specifically to the Holy Land, were still at work. In April 1452, just over a year before the fall of Constantinople, Enea Silvio Piccolomini addressed an oration to Pope Nicholas V and the Emperor Frederick III, passionately advocating an expedition to the Holy Land. The humanist scholar and papal employee Flavio Biondo, writing an address to King Alfonso V of Naples at the end of July 1453, urged him to mount an anti-Ottoman campaign that would also include the conquest of Jerusalem. Nicholas V's successor, Calixtus III, called for such a crusade in 1456, and continued to harp on this theme—in his more optimistic moments, at least—over the following two years. And in the great speech given by Piccolomini (now Pope Pius II) to the special congress he had summoned to Mantua in 1459, there was a strong emphasis on the idea that the Muslims had unjustly seized the Holy Land, and an explicit defence of the notion of 'recuperatio': if the ancients had believed that it was just to act for the recovery of your possessions ('pro repetendis rebus'), what cause could possibly be juster than this?[30] It is sometimes claimed that during the mid-fifteenth century the general pattern of pro-crusading argument turned decisively away from previous concerns with the Holy Places. Of course the new focus on Constantinople (a long way from Jerusalem) and on the Ottomans (a different power from the Mamluks, who ruled the Holy Land) did involve

28. Muldoon, *Popes, Lawyers and Infidels*, pp. 6–18 (quotation: p. 16).   29. Ibid., p. 6.
30. Helmrath, 'Pius II. und die Türken', p. 89 (1452); Biondo, *Scritti inediti*, p. 46; Housley, *Crusading and Ottoman Threat*, pp. 27–8 (1456); Weber, *Lutter contre les Turcs*, pp. 125–7 (optimistic moments); Pius II, 'Cum bellum hodie', p. 401 (1459).

a significant shift of emphasis; but it would be wrong to suppose that Jerusalem and Bethlehem disappeared entirely from either the rhetoric of would-be crusaders or their long-term plans. Whilst the formal crusading bulls of the popes quietly dropped their references to the Holy Land after the late 1450s, contemplating this ultimate goal did remain part of the culture, not least because of the eschatological vision of history that lay behind so much thinking about anti-Ottoman and anti-Muslim wars. In the years that followed the conquest of Granada in 1492 by Ferdinand II of Aragon and Isabella I of Castile, and their capture of the Algerian port of Oran in 1509, there was a flood of publications predicting or hoping that their victories over Muslim forces would continue all the way to the Holy Land; and in 1525 Alfonso de Valdés, secretary to the Chancellor of the Holy Roman Emperor, Charles V, would confidently write that God intended the Emperor's armies to 'recover the empire of Constantinople and the holy house of Jerusalem'.[31] (By this stage, after the destruction of the Mamluk regime by Sultan Selim I in 1516–17, the Ottoman Empire did also include the Holy Places.) Calls for a crusade to the Holy Land would be revived by anti-Ottoman writers towards the end of the sixteenth century, and in the second decade of the seventeenth there would be a serious attempt to set up a new anti-Ottoman and crusading order, the 'Christian Militia', which had the recovery of the Holy Places as its final aim.[32]

What is undeniably true is that after the terrifying display of the Ottomans' military might at Constantinople in 1453, and in view of the rolling sequence of their westward advances, there was a new emphasis on self-defence, or mutual defence, as a major justification for anti-Ottoman warfare; here there was a real departure from the medieval crusading tradition. The person who did most of all to propagate this line of argument was Enea Silvio Piccolomini. Writing to his friend Cardinal Nicholas of Cusa at the end of July 1453, he warned that Mehmed II could soon mount an invasion of southern Italy from the Albanian coast: 'the sword of the Turks is now threatening our own necks.' Such fears were widely shared during 1453–4, and were strengthened by the advice of knowledgeable informants such as

31. Haran, *Le Lys et le globe*, pp. 73–5 (after Granada and Oran); Bosbach, '*Imperium Turcorum*', pp. 177 (after Granada), 180 (de Valdés: 'cobrar el imperio de Constantinopla e la casa sancta de Jerusalem'). On such Spanish-focused prophecies in this period (by, among others, Christopher Columbus) see Reeves, *Influence of Prophecy*, pp. 359–60, 446–7.
32. Anonymous text of 1585 in Ventura, ed., *Tesoro politico*, fo. 100v; Ammirato, *Orazioni*, p. 104 (oration to Clement VIII, delivered in the period 1592–8); Göllner, 'La Milice Chrétienne', Dedouvres, *Le Père Joseph*, pp. 417–26, and Humbert, 'Charles de Nevers' (Christian Militia).

Niccolò Sagundino. Warnings of an impending invasion of Italy featured prominently in Pius II's great speech at Mantua in 1459; they were repeated by his successor-but-one, Sixtus IV, in 1471; and in 1480 they were dramatically corroborated by the Ottoman seizure of the city of Otranto, on the Apulian coast, in what was clearly intended as a campaign of territorial expansion, not mere raiding.[33] The special focus on the threat to Italy, which appears in several of Pius II's writings, seems to have been a matter of practical strategic thinking: only 50 miles of sea separated the Apulian coast from the Ottoman-ruled Albanian port of Vlorë. According to one modern historian, Pius II's interest in uniting the Italian powers against a common threat connects his thinking with that of the humanist scholar Lampo Birago, whose treatise on fighting the Ottomans singled out Italy as the repository of those ancient Roman virtues that needed to be revived in order to guarantee military success. Yet in his earlier pronouncements, such as his great speech at Mantua, Pius's argument about mutual or collective defence had ranged much more widely, referring to Ottoman attacks on Hungary and addressing the whole of Catholic Christendom; and his crusading bull of 1463 was promulgated throughout Western Europe, drawing in volunteers from as far afield as the Netherlands, Spain, and Scotland.[34]

Indeed, one of the achievements sometimes credited to Pius II is that his anti-Ottoman speeches and writings helped to develop a new consciousness of 'Europe' as a social and political entity. He popularized the term 'Europaei' (Europeans) and, addressing the Imperial Diet at Frankfurt in 1454, famously exclaimed: 'but now we are being assaulted and murdered in Europe, that is, in our fatherland, our own home, our own residence.'[35] It is true that some humanists did consciously revive the notion of 'Europe', as an ethnocultural as well as a geographical entity, which they found in the texts of classical geographers. Flavio Biondo, for example, confidently declared that 'those who know ancient history easily understand that Europe has always exceeded the other parts of the world in its virtues and its strength', and

33. Pertusi, *La caduta*, ii, p. 58 ('Imminet iam nostris cervicibus Turchorum gladius'); Mureşan, 'La Croisade en projets', pp. 276–7 (widely held; Sagundino); Helmrath, 'Pius II. und die Türken', p. 96 (1459); Housley, *Crusading and Ottoman Threat*, p. 19 (1471); Setton, *Papacy and Levant*, ii, pp. 343–5, and Fonseca, ed., *Otranto 1480*.
34. Damian, 'From "Italic League"' (modern historian); Pius II, 'Cum bellum hodie', pp. 399, 402 (1463); Göllner, *Turcica*, iii, p. 50 (1463).
35. Mertens, 'Europäischer Friede', p. 50(n.) ('Europaei', 'nunc vero in Europa, id est in patria, in domo propria, in sede nostra percussi caesique sumus'); Céard, 'L'Image de l'Europe', pp. 50–4 (from Strabo).

various arguments for European superiority, drawn mostly from the ancient Greek geographer Strabo, would become commonplace in sixteenth-century treatises.[36] Seen in this perspective, Pius II's use of the term might be regarded as part of a general humanist tendency to shift from a Christian world view to a classical one. Yet his actual usage does not bear out such an interpretation: glossing the term 'Europaei' (Europeans), he explained it as 'those who are described as Christians'. Another humanist politico-religious orator, Ivan Stojković (John of Ragusa), addressing the Emperor Frederick in the 1430s, had used the phrase 'nostra Europa' (our Europe) to encourage a sense of underlying identity between Latin and Greek Christians when warning of the encroachment of Ottoman power: 'see how our Europe is also partly occupied by the infidels.'[37]

When Pius II set out the basic justifications for fighting the Ottomans in his oration at the Congress of Mantua in 1459, the first was 'that, avenging the injuries that have been suffered, we recover what has been lost'; the 'we' here were Christians, or 'the Christian religion', which, as he explained, in the age of Constantine had extended from India to Spain. Sorrowfully listing the areas that had been lost to infidel powers, he concluded: 'these are your boundaries, Christians; this is how you are surrounded; this is how you are forced into a corner, you who were once extremely powerful lords possessing the world.'[38] So whilst Europe was now the 'corner' that had to be defended, its significance was that it was all that remained of a larger Christian world. When he called for a crusade in 1452, he had emphasized 'commiseratio', pity for those Christians who had fallen under Muslim rule; again, the primary consideration was a shared Christian identity.[39] Such concerns were echoed by his friend and colleague János Vitéz, the Archbishop of Esztergom, at the Imperial Diet of Wiener Neustadt in 1455, when he insisted on the duty to help the oppressed Christians of the Eastern Church, and also implored his listeners: 'Believe the signs: this enemy is trying not merely to harm one part of the Christian world ['cristianae societatis'], but

36. Biondo, *Scritti inediti*, p. 32 ('Europam semper ceteras orbis partes virtutibus potentiaque superasse faciliter intelligunt qui veteres norunt historias').
37. Mertens, 'Europäischer Friede', pp. 50(n.) ('ecce...nostra Europa eciam pro parte a...infidelibus occupatur'), 52 ('qui nomine Christiano censentur'). Stojković was sent on a mission to Constantinople by the Council of Basel, and was an active promoter of closer relations with the Greek Church: see Tomljenović, 'Dubrovčanin Ivan Stojković'.
38. Pius II, 'Cum bellum hodie', pp. 399–401 ('ut susceptas injurias ulciscentes, res amissas recuperemus', 'christiana religio', 'Hi sunt termini vestri, o christiani; sic circumdati estis; sic in angulum coartati, potentissimi quondam domini et orbis possessores').
39. Helmrath, 'Pius II. und die Türken', p. 89 (commiseratio).

to tear up the very foundations of the Catholic religion.'[40] In accordance with this line of argument, writers such as Vitéz promoted the idea that a state such as Hungary was an 'antemurale christianitatis', an outwork or protecting wall of Christendom—the implication being that in defending itself against Ottoman expansion, it was at the same time defending the larger community of Christians, and thus deserved their support. The metaphors of 'antemurale', 'propugnaculum' (rampart or bulwark), and 'arx' (citadel) were not entirely new; they had been used in Central Europe from the thirteenth century onwards, to describe defensive warfare against raids by Mongols and Tatars. But now they received a fresh ideological impetus, especially in Hungary and Poland; and during the sixteenth century phrases such as 'bulwark of Christendom' would be commonly applied by European publicists to a whole succession of strategically important outposts, from Belgrade to Rhodes, Corfu, Malta, and Cyprus.[41]

Pius II's 'European' rhetoric expressed an essentially religious viewpoint, relating to the entity of Christendom and the rights and duties of Christians. But its practical purpose was, by invoking a special kind of collective identity, to strengthen collective action. The nature of that identity could, for some purposes, embrace those Christians who had fallen under Ottoman rule; on this basis it was possible not only to act out of 'pity' for them, but also to take on the role of reclaiming their rights. Mostly, however, Pius was concerned with persuading Catholic rulers to abandon their mutual rivalries and conflicts, and unite in a common cause. All through the period of the Crusades, the desirability of peace within Christendom had been a standard theme; the Papacy had always had its own interest in pressing this point, which gave it a reason for intervening as an arbiter in many political disputes.[42] Yet, given the many conflicts between Catholic rulers in the fifteenth century, especially on the Italian peninsula, it was in any case a natural and genuine reflex on Pius's part. In one of his earliest letters commenting on the fall of Constantinople he ruefully observed that 'when I consider the

---

40. Vitéz de Zredna, *Orationes*, pp. 17 (duty to help), 19 ('Crede indicibus, non porcionem aliquam solam cristian[a]e societatis, hostis ipse ledere conatur, sed ipsa catholice religionis fundamenta conuellere').

41. Kiss, 'Political Rhetorics', p. 143 (Vitéz); Terbe, 'Egy európai szállóige életrajza', pp. 299–301 (Hungarians, variant terms); Srodecki, '*Validissima propugnacula*' (medieval usage, Hungarians, Poles); Housley, *Crusading and Ottoman Threat*, pp. 40–50 (Hungarians, also Venetians); Poumarède, *Pour en finir*, pp. 75–6 (Belgrade, Rhodes, etc.).

42. Weber, *Lutter contre les Turcs*, pp. 61–2.

failure to act of our rulers and the mutual enmities of our peoples, it seems to me that I am looking at our destruction; we are all agents of the Sultan, all paving the way for Mehmed II.' (On this point he did briefly invoke the 'scourge of God' argument, saying that the Ottoman successes were a divine punishment—the sin for which punishment was imposed being that of disunity.)[43] His friend Cardinal Bessarion, a Greek scholar who had joined the Roman Church and risen to high office, similarly emphasized the need for harmony in Christendom; this would become a standard homiletic theme among religious writers on warfare against the Ottomans.[44]

A more specific purpose, in advocating collective action, was to persuade those states that were not directly threatened by Ottoman military advances to come to the assistance of those that were. In his Mantuan speech the second main justification for an anti-Ottoman campaign put forward by Pius was 'to avoid future dangers'; there was a need for anticipatory or pre-emptive action, and the logic of this applied not only to the war as a whole but also to the participation in it of individual states.[45] Among humanist lobbyists for a crusade against the Sultan, it became common practice to invoke the lines from one of Horace's Epistles, 'For when your next-door neighbour's house is burning, that is your concern; and fires usually gather strength when they are neglected.'[46] This would become a very long-lasting trope. The Ragusan poet Marko Marulić used it in 1522, warning the Papacy not to think only of the security of Italy; in August 1529, as a large Ottoman army marched towards Vienna, the Archduke Ferdinand I published a 'Manifesto to all Christendom' declaring that 'the roof of your closest neighbour is burning, your own safety is in danger, all your property is threatened'; and in 1576 the Flemish Imperial diplomat Ogier Ghiselin de Busbecq would write, in his 'Exclamatio, sive de acie contra Turcam instruenda consilium', that 'if a fire starts in a city, there is no one who will not leave his affairs and

43. Pertusi, *La caduta*, ii, p. 62 ('Cum vero nostrorum principum desidiam privatasque populorum inimicitias intueor, videre videor sterminium nostrum. Omnes Turchi procuratores sumus, Maumetho viam omnes preparamus').
44. Schwoebel, *Shadow*, p. 158.
45. Pius II, 'Cum bellum hodie', p. 399 ('ut futura...pericula evitemus').
46. Epistles, I.18, l. 84 ('Nam tua res agitur, paries cum proximus ardet, | et neglecta solent incendia sumere vires'); Housley, *Crusading and Ottoman Threat*, p. 35. Pius II himself seems not to have used this in his oratory, but cf. his remark that the Emperor Frederick decided not to attend the Diet in Regensburg in 1454 and stayed instead in Austria, 'fearing that the flames next door in Hungary would finally set his own house alight' (Pius II, *Commentaries*, i, pp. 28–9: 'veritus ne vicina Hungariae flamma suam domum incenderet').

rush to help put it out.'[47] But whereas this particular metaphor implied a prudential requirement to join in collective defence, the basic argument about pre-emptive defensiveness could be used also to justify an offensive war. Writing to King Alfonso soon after the fall of Constantinople, Flavio Biondo advised going on the offensive against the Ottomans, and actually gave as one of his reasons the observation that 'in our provinces of Christendom' rulers did not take war seriously unless it affected their own territory directly, with the unfortunate result that they could be picked off one by one.[48]

Such were the fundamental justificatory reasons for going to war given by Pius II in his Mantuan oration. Like so many other humanist writers on this subject, he also added a variety of other inducements and incitements. These thinkers were all students of classical rhetoric, who knew that there were many different ways in which to work on both reason and the passions; as the texts they produced were mostly works of rhetoric, not legal or theological treatises, it would be wrong to try to squeeze all their arguments into a single logical structure. Addressing the Diet at Frankfurt in 1454, for instance, Piccolomini (as he then was) spoke at length not only about the 'justice' of an anti-Ottoman crusade, but also about its 'easiness' and its 'profitability'. Expanding on this at Mantua five years later, he insisted that the Ottomans were much easier to defeat than common report would have it (citing recent victories over them by the Hungarian–Romanian commander János Hunyadi or Ioan de Hunedoara, and by the Albanian Gjergj Kastrioti, known as Skanderbeg), and listed the profitable consequences of a successful campaign: the acquisition of weapons, gold, slaves, and slave-girls, as well as 'eternal fame' and a heavenly reward.[49]

References to fame attract the attention of modern historians, who are especially alert to classical influences on the minds of these humanist writers. Yet, as this speech shows, human fame was just part of a spectrum of benefits that ranged from material goods to rewards in the life to come—the last of these being, self-evidently, the most important. Writing in the same year,

47. Albrecht, *Das Türkenbild*, p. 161; Kohler, *Ferdinand I.*, p. 219 ('es brennt das Dach eures nächsten Nachbars, in Gefahr steht euer eigenes Heil, euer ganzes Besitztum wird bedroht'); Busbecq, 'Exclamatio', p. 114 ('In vrbe si quod ortum est incendium; nemo est qui non relictis rebus ad restinguendum concurrat'). For examples from the following century see Crucé, *Le Nouveau Cynée*, p. 57 (1623); Anon., *Tisch-Reden*, sig. A3r (1663); Olearius, *Türckenfall*, p. 44 (1664).
48. Biondo, *Scritti inediti*, pp. 42–3 ('in nostris Christianorum provinciis').
49. Helmrath, 'Pius II. und die Türken', p. 93 (1454: 'justitia', 'facilitas', 'utilitas'); Pius II, 'Cum bellum hodie', pp. 404–11 (p. 411: 'famam aeternam').

1459, Cardinal Juan de Torquemada listed the four main motives that should impel Christian princes to war against the Ottomans: devotion to Jesus, love of Christendom, 'honour and glory', and the spiritual rewards promised to all who fought in such a campaign.[50] Where mere earthly fame was concerned, such writers were just as likely to single it out as a motive for the Ottoman Sultan: thus Pius portrayed Mehmed II as driven by this desire, and Bessarion wrote that Mehmed was determined to imitate Alexander the Great and equal him in his glory.[51] On the Christian side of the argument, however, 'fame' might specifically involve appreciation of one's exploits as a defender of the true faith: urging on the King of Poland and Hungary in his fateful Varna crusade of 1444, the humanist Francesco Filelfo wrote that he would earn 'an immortal, splendid reputation' by defeating the Sultan, conquering the Holy Land, and then outdoing Alexander by spreading Christianity all the way to India.[52] Generally, when humanist writers of this period put forward glory as a motive for anti-Ottoman warfare, it supplemented or was combined with other aims and values, always including religious ones. In the 1480s the German counsellor Ludwig von Eyb (adviser to the Elector of Brandenburg, and brother of the well-known humanist writer Albrecht von Eyb) wrote a memorandum on going to war against the Sultan which began with three justifications: it was honourable (implying that it would confer fame), pious (meaning that it would lead to heavenly rewards), and necessary (for self-defence). The humanist historian Jakob Wimpfeling argued very similarly in 1505 that such warfare would achieve three ends: glory, the service of Christ, and the protection of the fatherland.[53]

Perhaps the most outspoken defence of 'glory' was offered by the Spanish classical scholar and publicist Juan Ginés de Sepúlveda in his treatise *Gonsalus seu de appetenda gloria dialogus* of 1523, which distinguished the quest for glory from mere 'ambition' and concluded: 'I would think nothing in human affairs to be worth seeking or choosing other than virtue and glory'; the

50. Torquemada, *Tractatus*, fo. 54r ('honor et gl[or]ia').
51. Helmrath, 'Pius II. und die Türken', pp. 111–13; Carretto, 'Bessarione e il Turco', p. 261. Cf. Ludovik Crijević Tuberon, writing in the 1520s about Sultan Selim I: 'he had such a lust for rule that he thought that the greatest and almost the only glory consisted in having the largest possible empire; for that purpose, he was more eager to get a great reputation than a good one' (*Commentariorum libri XI*, p. 356: 'Eam autem dominandi libidinem habuit, vt maximam et solam fere gloriam, in maximo imperio sitam esse putaret; et ob id studiosior erat magnae famae, quam bonae').
52. Meserve, *Empires of Islam*, p. 86.
53. Thumser, 'Türkenfrage', p. 85 (von Eyb); Mertens, '"Europa, id est patria"', p. 46 (Wimpfeling).

link with virtue was essential to his argument, and in a later dialogue, *Democrates* (1535), he went out of his way to explain that a proper desire for glory was entirely compatible with the Christian faith, citing St Augustine in support of this claim. As the latter work began as a celebration of Habsburg military actions against the Sultan, with much praise of the Christian piety of those Spanish noblemen who volunteered to take part in anti-Ottoman campaigns, Sepúlveda's views were very much in tune here with those of his contemporary Paolo Giovio, who wrote that a new crusade against the Ottomans should be motivated by two things: glory and religion.[54]

Another theme that seems to give the anti-Ottoman writings of the humanists a particularly classical or classicizing slant is that of outrage at the destruction of learning and culture. One of the shocking things about the looting which followed the fall of Constantinople was the treatment of books and libraries: according to the Cretan Venetian Lauro Quirini, who spoke to some of the first refugees from the city, more than 120,000 manuscript volumes were destroyed. 'That body of literature which had illuminated the whole world has perished', he wrote.[55] Writing to Pope Nicholas V, Piccolomini similarly bemoaned the loss of 'innumerable' books, 'still unknown to Western Christians'. This passage came immediately after a comment on the desecration of churches, and he concluded: 'I see both faith and learning eliminated at the same time.' Similarly, in a letter to Nicholas of Cusa he discussed the profanation of churches, including the Hagia Sophia, and then referred to that ancient learning of which Constantinople was still the home: his list moved seamlessly from pagan philosophers and historians to Church Fathers, from Plato, Aristotle, Demosthenes, Xenophon, and Thucydides to Basil, Dionysus the Areopagite, and Origen.[56] Classical literature mattered deeply to him, but it did so not least because it helped to form the foundations of Christian culture.

It is certainly true that such writers borrowed classical terms and concepts in order to distinguish as strongly as possible between their own high culture and the presumed savagery of the Ottoman invaders: the latter were described as 'barbari' (barbarians), 'saevi' (wild or savage people), and

54. Sepúlveda, *Gonsalus*, pp. 229 ('praeter honestatem et gloriam nihil ex rebus humanis mihi vel quaerendum vel optandum putarem'), 231 ('ambitio'); Sepúlveda, *De conuenientia*, pp. 12–22 (military actions, Spanish noblemen), 214 (glory, faith, Augustine); Pujeau, *L'Europe et les Turcs*, p. 378 (Giovio).

55. Pertusi, *Testi inediti*, p. 74 ('Illae litterae pereunt, quae orbem universum illustraverunt').

56. Pertusi, *La caduta*, ii, pp. 46 ('innumerabiles, nondum Latinis cogniti', 'Video simul et fides et doctrinam deleri'), 52 (list).

'immanes' (monstrous, inhuman).[57] Piccolomini's letter to Nicholas of Cusa remarked that the fall of Constantinople was very different from the conquest of ancient Athens by the Romans, as this new aggressor was an empire 'of extremely savage men, enemies of good conduct and of letters'.[58] Since texts that were intended to galvanize Western rulers into action against the Ottomans naturally put great emphasis on the atrocities committed by them, the destruction of cultural heritage could easily be incorporated in a general list of their outrages, in a way that resonated with ancient Greek and Roman ideas about barbarian peoples. But classical influences were not the only ones at work here; for on this topic, as on most others, humanists were not so much importing a completely new intellectual agenda as adapting and developing certain aspects of the mental world that they had inherited. Among medieval writers on the Crusades, the term 'barbarae nationes' had been in standard use from the beginning. Papal documents had normally employed the adjective 'barbarus' in a religious context, in phrases such as 'barbari infideles'; the implication was that such people were barbarian not in some prior cultural or ethnographic sense, but because they had rejected the true faith and were now in the service of the Devil. As one modern historian has commented, 'for most of the faithful, "barbarian" had a religious meaning, referring to non-Christian peoples.'[59] And according to some writers, the barbarian qualities of Muslims could be specifically traced to the teachings of Muhammad: thus the Florentine historian Benedetto Accolti, writing in 1463–4 about the origins of Islam, observed that 'nothing could be more inimical to a sham religion than virtue and knowledge of the arts and sciences, and so men turned to debauchery and idleness.' It became common practice to refer to all Muslim peoples as barbarians, regardless of their particular cultural characteristics.[60]

Closely linked to the characterization of the Ottoman Turks as 'barbarians' was a Renaissance debate about their historical and ethnic origins. When Lauro Quirini passed on the news of the fall of Constantinople, he denounced the conquerors as 'a barbarous people, a wild people, of no fixed standards and no laws, leading their lives in a free-living, unsettled, and arbitrary

57. See Tateo, 'L'ideologia umanistica', pp. 162–7; Hankins, 'Renaissance Crusaders', pp. 121–3; Bisaha, Creating East and West, pp. 59–75.
58. Pertusi, La caduta, ii, p. 54 ('bonorum morum atque litterarum hostium').
59. Weber, Lutter contre les Turcs, pp. 463–4 ('Pour la majorité des fidèles, "barbare" avait une signification religieuse et désignait les peuples non chrétiens').
60. Black, Benedetto Accolti, p. 265; Bisaha, Creating East and West, p. 78.

way'; whilst he did not go into detail about their origins, he was clearly conjuring up an image of primitive nomadism.[61] In the hands of Enea Silvio Piccolomini, and with the help of Nicolò Sagundino, whose treatise on the origins of the Turks (1456) was written at Piccolomini's request, a strong tradition was established of identifying them with the Scythians who, according to ancient writers, had led a wild, nomadic life on the steppes to the north and north-east of the Black Sea. Blending details from the classical accounts with his depiction of modern Turks, Piccolomini wrote that the Scythians were primitive and wicked people, eaters of unclean foods (not just horse meat and vultures, but aborted human foetuses too), and guilty of 'all kinds of rapes', who had moved via the Caucasus into Asia. He also argued that the Turks, like the Tatars, were just the most recent of a long succession of barbaric Scythian invaders of Europe, going back to the Huns, Vandals, and Goths.[62]

Here, at least, some humanist writers did adopt an ethnocultural approach to identifying certain peoples as barbarous. Possibly Sagundino should be given credit for being one of the first to develop an 'ethnographic' style of argument that looked for resemblances in the customs and behaviour of different peoples. Thus he wrote that the descent of the Turks from the Scythians was confirmed by 'the similarity of their way of life and behaviour, their physical appearance and comportment, their method of riding and shooting arrows, and overall by a certain shared, ancestral training in military matters—as well as the resemblance in language and in ways of speaking'. (This approach would later be taken up by Paolo Giovio, one of the most influential sixteenth-century writers.)[63] For Piccolomini himself, however, the purpose of the exercise was not an academic enquiry of an anthropological nature, but rather an attempt to paint the Turks in the worst possible colours, and to characterize them as ancestral enemies of Western Europe. Nor was the 'Scythian' theory about the origins of the Turks the product of new research by Renaissance classical historians. As recent

---

61. Pertusi, *Testi inediti*, p. 76 ('Gens barbara, gens inculta, nullis certis moribus, nullis legibus, sed fusa, vaga, arbitraria vivens').
62. Pertusi, *La caduta*, ii, p. 54 ('in cunctis stuprorum generibus'); Meserve, *Empires of Islam*, pp. 68–9, 99–101 (primitive, unclean foods), 107–11 (Sagundino writing for Piccolomini); Terbe, 'Egy európai szállóige életrajza', p. 310 (Huns, etc.).
63. Pertusi, 'I primi studi', p. 473 ('vitae morumque similitudo, habitus cultusque corporis, equitandi sagittandique ratio et omnino rei militaris communis quaedam et patria disciplina; et...linguae ipsius ac usus loquendi cognatio'). Cf. the very similar remarks in Giovio, *Commentario*, p. 73 (developed, in turn, in Esprinchard, *Histoire des Ottomans*, fos. 1v–2r).

scholarship has demonstrated, some of its key sources were not classical texts at all, but familiar products of medieval culture, such as the twelfth-century chronicle of Otto of Freising. And, what is more, the medieval literature was influenced by a Christian legend, going back at least in part to Saint Jerome, according to which the monstrous tribes that had poured forth from the Caucasus were the descendants of Gog and Magog, the savage war leaders from Ezekiel who were given an eschatological role in the Book of Revelation.[64] The association of Scythians with depravity and barbarism was well established, long before Renaissance writers began to explore the accounts of the Scythians in classical texts; and the most important ancient source, Herodotus, seems to have been generally ignored until the sixteenth century.[65]

While this theory quite quickly became the dominant one among historical writers, its implications did not always conform to the darkly negative stereotype that Pius II intended. Some classical sources portrayed the nomadic Scythians as noble savages, leading lives of admirable simplicity and martial virtue, and this might occasionally interact with positive accounts of the Turks' way of life and military behaviour. Even Pius II himself, in one highly untypical text (written as a conciliatory letter to Mehmed II), wrote that since the Sultan's origins were Scythian, he was warlike and brave, unlike the 'effeminate Egyptians and unwarlike Arabs'.[66] The contrast made here was in line with some broader assumptions, themselves of ancient origin, about the characteristics of peoples from different latitudes or climates: Aristotle, for example, had written in his *Politics* that those who lived in a cold climate and in Europe were 'full of spirit', good at retaining their own freedom though incompetent when it came to ruling others, whereas Asians were 'intelligent and skillfull, . . . but lack[ing in] spirit, so that they are in continuous subjection and slavery.'[67] Thus, while the 'Scythian' theory about the Turks made use of some classical assumptions where wild barbarians were concerned, it distanced them from other classical stereotypes involving effete, corrupt, and servile Asiatics.

---

64. See Meserve, *Empires of Islam*, esp. pp. 76–9 (Gog, Magog), 104–6, 113–14 (Otto). These issues have all been greatly clarified by Meserve's book.
65. Ibid., pp. 152–3. Herodotus would be invoked, e.g. by Philip Melanchthon in the 1530s (Reddig, *Reise zum Erzfeind*, p. 35) and Nicolas de Nicolay in the 1560s (*Dans l'empire*, p. 140).
66. Meserve, *Empires of Islam*, pp. 72–4; Pius II, *Epistola*, p. 74 (on this text see below, pp. 42–4).
67. *Politics* VII.6, 1327b24–29, pp. 565–7.

The entire historical sequence of 'Scythian' invaders, beginning with Huns, Vandals, and Visigoths, was seen as representing a flow of active, martial, freedom-loving peoples from northern latitudes. Of those, the Huns were accepted by Renaissance writers as the ancestors of the Hungarians, while the Visigoths were understood to have founded the first Spanish kingdom; and from the latter part of the fifteenth century onwards the recently discovered text of Tacitus' *Germania* gave German scholars new ways of celebrating the martial qualities and political independence of their own ancestors, whom the Romans had regarded as fierce barbarians. So a curious conjunction now came into play between the celebratory foundation myths of various Christian European peoples and the condemnatory portrayal of the Turks as descendants of Scythians. In Hungary, King Matthias Corvinus (r. 1458–90) was happy to be described as 'the second Attila', and the tradition of identifying the Hungarians with 'Scythian' Huns, already present in the writings of earlier Hungarian chroniclers but greatly strengthened in his reign, would continue for hundreds of years. Having fought vigorously against the Ottomans in the 1470s, Matthias wrote to Mehmed II in 1480 saying that he would prefer friendly relations with him 'because the same blood is flowing in our veins'; whether this referred to common Scythian origins, or to a fanciful story that Mehmed's mother was a kidnapped member of Matthias's family, is not clear.[68] The Italian humanist historian Antonio Bonfini, who went to Budapest and wrote a history of the Hungarians at the behest of Matthias and his successor, Vladislaus II, constructed a great world-historical sequence of 'translationes imperii' (transfers of empire): from Assyrians to Persians, then Macedonians, Carthaginians, Romans, Goths, Huns, Vandals, and Avars, and finally to the Hungarians.[69] Whilst the Ottoman Turks were not part of this sequence, the overall idea was curiously close to some of the claims made by, or attributed to, the Ottoman Sultans. In Spain, the 'Scythian' link took longer to emerge in the minds of writers; only by the early seventeenth century did it become a common assumption. In 1624 Julián del Castillo argued, in his *Historia de los Reyes Godos*, that after the Flood Scythia had been divided into two parts, one European and the other Asian: the former had produced the Goths, who were ancestors of the Spanish, and from the latter had come the Turks, ancestors of the Ottomans. His contemporary Lope de Vega had a character

68. Fodor, 'View of the Turk', pp. 112–13 ('second Attila', 'same blood'); Péter, 'Das skythische Selbstbewusstsein' ('Scythian' tradition). See also Birnbaum, 'Attila's Renaissance'.
69. Havas and Kiss, 'Die Geschichtskonzeption Bonfinis', p. 292.

exclaim in one of his plays that no one should be surprised that the Turks were noble people, as they were 'Scythians, from whom the Goths were descended'.[70]

As for the Germans: sometimes the Scythian connection was made via speculations about biblical ancestry, as in a 1561 treatise by the visionary French oriental scholar Guillaume Postel, which claimed that Noah's grandson Gomer was the ancestor of the Scythians, who were sometimes called Germans (and added for good measure that Gomer's son Togarmah was the ancestor either of the Germans or of the Turks). Other lines of argument were also possible; one later scholar, Marcus van Boxhorn, developing some elements of what would eventually be called Indo-European philology, combined linguistic evidence with the study of the early barbarian invasions to conclude that the original Germans were of Scythian origin.[71] As late as 1692, the polymathic philosopher Gottfried Wilhelm Leibniz would write that 'all appearances suggest that the Germans themselves, as well as the Slavs, Hungarians, Huns, and Turks, came out of Scythia.'[72] Swedish writers, for their part, had developed elaborate theories about the Goths (their own presumed ancestors); the early sixteenth-century writer Johannes Magnus, beginning his account of the dynamic role played by the Goths in world history, claimed that Noah's family settled in Scythia after the Flood, from where his son Magog took his own people, the Goths, to live in Scandinavia.[73] Meanwhile sixteenth-century Polish historians were tracing the origins of the Poles to the free, warlike people of Sarmatia, an area north of the Black Sea overlapping with, or at least adjoining, Scythia: the 'Sarmatian' theory would become an important part of the self-image of the Polish nobility for several centuries to come. Explicit links with the Turks were not normally made in these latter cases, but in general what might be called the 'alienation effect' of categorizing the Turks as descendants of ancient Scythians could only be weakened by the existence of so many parallel claims of Scythian or quasi-Scythian ancestry.[74]

70. Mas, *Les Turcs*, ii, p. 191 (del Castillo, *Historia*; Vega: 'son citas...de quien descienden los Godos').
71. Postel, *Cosmographicae disciplinae compendium*, pp. 19 (Gomer), 26 (Togarmah); Hultsch, *Der Orient*, p. 15 (Boxhorn).
72. Leibniz, *Sämtliche Schriften*, ser. 1, viii, p. 139 (Letter to Landgraf Ernst of Hesse-Rheinfels, 30 July 1692: 'toutes les apparences sont que les Allemans memes, aussi que les Esclavons, Hongrois, Huns, et Turcs sont sortis de la Scythie').
73. Johanneson, *Renaissance of the Goths*, pp. 89–90.
74. See Kersken, 'Geschichtsbild und Adelsrepublik', and Daiber, 'Sarmatismus', pp. 31–4, 44–50; on the geographical ambiguities of Sarmatia see Jaroszewska, 'À la découverte'. Occasionally, Polish nobles did associate their 'Sarmatian' ancestors with some aspects of Turkish culture, to emphasize the difference between them and Western Europeans: see Niedźwiedź, 'Orientalizm'.

Although the Scythian hypothesis about the origins of the Turks became the most widely accepted view, it was not the only theory available. Arguments from biblical ancestry could easily be combined with it, and Togarmah was a popular candidate for the Ur-ancestor of the Turks (thanks not only to the first syllable of his name, but also to a passage in Ezekiel referring to 'the house of Togarmah of the north quarters' joining the army of Gog and Magog); yet according to one of the several theories adopted by Postel, the Turks were in fact descended from the Lost Tribes of Israel, who in their distant exile had turned into Tatars and had then adopted the 'Scythian' language.[75] Another oft-cited derivation was taken from an influential late-medieval text, the *Flos historiarum terrae orientis* (or *Liber historiarum partium orientis*), written in France at the beginning of the fourteenth century by an Armenian nobleman, Hayton or Hetoum of Korikos. This book, which circulated widely in manuscript before undergoing many printings in the sixteenth century, was concerned mostly with the 'Tartari' (a term used by Hayton for the Mongols, whom he was keen to present as potential allies in a future crusade); but it also discussed the 'Turci', explaining that their name came from 'Turquestan', the area they first inhabited.[76] While the exact location of that area may have been unclear to many readers, it was understood by some to be a different place from Scythia— which opened up the possibility that they might have some non-Scythian characteristics. The Venetian writer Donado da Lezze, beginning his 'Historia turchesca' in the second decade of the sixteenth century, set out three competing theories about the origins of the Turks, of which one was that they came from Scythia, and another was that they migrated from the territory of 'Turquesten'.[77]

The third theory put forward by that writer, though quite outlandish to modern eyes, was rich in historical, poetic, and moral resonances for the

75. Ezekiel 38: 6; Postel, *Histoire et consideration*, pp. 21–7. Postel's 'Lost Tribes' theory about the Tatars (which had medieval precedents: see Bezzola, *Die Mongolen*, pp. 102–3, and Connell, 'Western Views') was not widely accepted, but more than 50 years later the English geographical and historical writer Edward Brerewood thought it worth devoting 15 pages to its refutation (*Enquiries*, pp. 94–108); in 1709 it was revived by another English writer, Aaron Hill (*Full and Just Account*, pp. 330–1). For a typical text by a mainstream Protestant writer accepting the derivation of 'Turk' from 'Togarmah' see Bibliander, *Ad socios consultatio*, sigs. f5v–f6r.

76. Hayton, *Liber historiarum*, fos. B3v–D4v. On Hayton see Bundy, 'Hetᶜum's *La Flor des Estoires*' Meserve, *Empires of Islam*, pp. 163–8.

77. da Lezze, *Historia turchesca*, pp. 1–2. On this text, which contains some material copied from works by Giovanni Maria Angiolello and is sometimes misattributed to him, see Ion Ursu's 'Introducere' (ibid., pp. v–xxxvii), and MacKay, 'Content and Authorship'.

Renaissance reader: the claim that the Turks were directly descended from the ancient Trojans. Like some of the apparently classicizing theories mentioned above, this theory had medieval origins. A seventh-century text known as the 'Chronicle of Fredegarius' stated that after the fall of Troy some of the exiled Trojans chose a king named 'Francio', and wandered through Europe, eventually populating what became the homeland of the Franks. During their travels, a group of them separated under a leader called 'Torquotus', and these became the ancestors of the 'Torci' or 'Turqui'—who were assumed, by later readers of versions of the story, to be the Turks.[78] This theory was at least reported, though not directly endorsed, by some authors in the Middle Ages, such as the encyclopaedist Vincent of Beauvais.[79] Thanks to the popularity of the latter's work it became a widely available idea, even if it was never the dominant one. Thus, for example, the French soldier of fortune and royal counsellor Philippe de Mézières, writing in the late fourteenth century, claimed that the Turks themselves believed that 'the Turks and the French [or 'Franks'] had once been brothers, at the time of the destruction of Troy'; and the full Trojan story was reproduced, as reliable information, in the pilgrimage narrative of the Swiss Dominican friar Felix Fabri, written in the 1480s. In the lavishly illustrated world chronicle by the German humanist Hartmann Schedel, printed in Nuremberg in 1493, this theory was also presented, though with the final qualification that 'others say they originated in Scythia'; but Fabri had already shown how to reconcile those alternatives, by saying that the Trojans under 'Turcus' had settled in Scythia, where they 'led their life in a bestial way'. This solution was also adopted by the Spanish Benedictine abbot Gonzalo de Arredondo y Alvarado, in a work published in 1528 and reprinted 36 years later.[80]

Two other factors promoted this Trojan hypothesis. One was the tendency of some humanist writers, from the late fourteenth century onwards, to use the word 'Teucri' as the Latin for 'Turks': this pleasingly similar classical

78. Heath, 'Renaissance Scholars', p. 456; Asher, *National Myths*, pp. 9–10; Meserve, *Empires of Islam*, pp. 49–51.

79. Meserve, *Empires of Islam*, p. 58.

80. Pippidi, *Visions*, p. 12 (Mézières: 'les Turcs et les Francoys jadis, a la destruction de Troyes, furent freres'); Fabri, *Evagatorium*, iii, pp. 236–9 (p. 237: 'more bestiarum vitam duxerunt'); Meserve, *Empires of Islam*, p. 59 (Schedel: 'Alij eoru[m] origine[m] ex Scythia referunt'); Arredondo y Alvarado, *Castillo inexpugnable*, fo. 28r. In ascribing this belief to the Turks, Mézières was combining the Trojan story with the tradition, reported by an anonymous history of the Crusades at the end of the 11th century, that the (Seljuk) Turks believed that they and the Franks came from the same martial stock (see Meserve, *Empires of Islam*, pp. 56–7).

name was the one commonly used for the Trojans in Virgil's *Aeneid*.[81] The other was the idea that the Ottoman Turks warred against the Greeks of Byzantium—and, indeed, took such pains to conquer their capital city—because they sought revenge for the sufferings of their Trojan ancestors at the hands of the ancient Greeks. One popular text, which circulated both before and after the fall of Constantinople, purported to be a letter to the Pope from a Turkish potentate called 'Morbisanus', who declared his wish to subjugate the Greeks in order to avenge the blood of his ancestor Hector. It was widely assumed to be genuine; only the most recent scholarship has established that it was in fact a version of an Italian anti-Venetian propaganda text, written in the 1340s to oppose an alliance between the Papacy and Venice against the ruler of Smyrna, Umur Pasha ('Umur Bassanus': 'Morbisanus'). Thanks above all to the influence of this imaginative and entirely spurious text, the idea of Trojan revenge was quickly introduced by various writers into accounts of the fall of Constantinople in 1453; one description of that event, for example, had Sultan Mehmed raping a Greek woman in the church of Hagia Sophia in order to avenge the rape of Cassandra.[82] The revenge motif seems to have appealed particularly to poets, such as Giovanni Maria Filelfo (son of the humanist pro-crusading writer Francesco Filelfo), who composed a Latin poem in the 1470s in praise of Mehmed II: its opening section included a rousing speech addressed to the young Mehmed by the war goddess Bellona, in which the need to avenge the murder and humiliation of his ancestors at the fall of Troy took pride of place.[83] Few serious historical writers adopted this peculiarly pointed version of the theory of Trojan origins. Nevertheless, the Trojan hypothesis, in some form or other, had gained a place in Western thinking about the Turks, and would prove curiously hard to dislodge. It reappeared in several German publications of the sixteenth century; in 1540 Christophe Richer, who was in French royal service, cited the Trojan and Scythian theories with equal respect, refusing to adjudicate between them; and seven years later the

---

81. Runciman, 'Teucri and Turci'; Meserve, *Empires of Islam*, pp. 26–32 (noting that many used 'Teucri' without implying Trojan ancestry); Weber, *Lutter contre les Turcs*, p. 45 (recording the alternating use of 'Turchi' and 'Teucri' in 15th-century papal documents).

82. Meserve, *Empires of Islam*, pp. 35–7; again, it is Meserve's painstaking research that has clarified this whole issue.

83. Filelfo, *Amyris*, pp. 67–74 (Bk I, ll. 407–554). This poet's apparent Turcophilia is to be explained by the fact that the work was commissioned by an Italian merchant who cultivated good relations with the Ottoman court (see ibid., p. 20); it was later reconfigured by the poet, after that merchant's death, as an anti-Ottoman work.

Spanish soldier, priest, and playwright Vasco Díaz Tanco solemnly reported that the Turks 'hold themselves to be true Trojans, and therefore they say that as they are the heirs of the Trojans the empire of the West belongs to them, since it was conquered by the Trojan people with Aeneas and other military leaders'.[84]

To attribute any such reasoning to the Ottoman Turks must seem, to modern eyes, fanciful indeed—the sort of explanation of their actions that would have satisfied only a poet or littérateur, not a serious political analyst. Yet many Western thinkers, for whom classical history was a significant part of their mental world, found it easy to ascribe such motives to the Ottomans, as they believed that the sultans were almost as deeply interested as they were in the history of ancient Greece and Rome. In his oration addressed to Alfonso V in early 1454 Niccolò Sagundino wrote that Mehmed II had two physicians, one Greek and one West European, from whom he obtained knowledge of the classical world; he had learned about the history of Sparta, Athens, Rome, and Carthage, 'but above all he picked out Alexander of Macedon and Julius Caesar as people he wanted to imitate, and had the story of their deeds translated into his language.' The account given by the Venetian chroncler Languschi was even more specific: 'every day', two Italians would read to him 'histories of the Romans, and of others', including 'Diogenes Laertius, Herodotus, Livy, Quintus Curtius, and chronicles of the popes, the Holy Roman Emperors, the kings of France, and the Lombards'.[85] Mehmed's grandson Selim I (r. 1512–20) was likewise described as employing someone to read to him 'the deeds of famous men, especially Alexander the Great'; Paolo Giovio wrote that Selim studied histories of Alexander and Caesar; and Selim's son Süleyman the Magnificent was also said to read histories of Alexander.[86] (These recurrent references to works about Alexander may have had some factual basis, as versions of the

84. Göllner, Turcica, iii, pp. 234–5 (German texts); Richer, De rebus Turcarum, pp. 5–7; Bunes Ibarra, La imagen, p. 70(n.) (citing Díaz Tanco's Libro intitulado Palinodia, de la nephanda y fiera nacion de los Turcos (Orense, 1547), fo. 2r: 'se tienen por verdaderos troyanos e por tanto dizen que como sucessores de troyanos les toca el imperio de poniente, el qual las troyanas gentes con Eneas y otros capitanes señorearon').

85. Pertusi, La caduta, ii, pp. 130–2 (Sagundino: 'Alexandrum Macedonem et C. Caesarem praecipue sibi imitandos delegit, quorum res gestas in linguam suam traduci effecit'); Babinger, 'Maometto', p. 440 (Languschi: 'Ogni dì', 'historie romane et de altri', 'Laertio, Heródoto, Liuio, Quinto Curtio, Cronice de i papi, de imperatori, de re di Francia, de Langobardi'). Some early accounts even described Mehmed as proficient in Greek and Latin, but this is very unlikely: see Patrinelis, 'Mehmed II'.

86. Crijević Tuberon, Commentariorum libri XI, p. 357 ('gesta illustrium virorum, praesertim Magni Alexandri'); Pujeau, L'Europe et les Turcs, p. 82 (Giovio); Bassano, Costumi, fo. 51v (Süleyman).

'Alexander Romance' in Persian and other Eastern languages were popular in Ottoman culture; but that was a fabulous fictional work, not an account of classical history.[87])

For Western Europeans who studied these accounts, the main point was simply that the Ottoman Sultans were seeking to emulate the most devastatingly successful military commanders of the ancient world. But, given the special achievements and status of Alexander and Julius Caesar, some larger implications were also present. When Sagundino wrote that Mehmed wished to imitate those two, he immediately went on to say that he wanted 'to claim for himself the empire of the world'. Piccolomini, picking up on this theme, warned the Imperial Diet at Regensburg in the summer of 1454 that Mehmed often said to his close advisers: 'why shouldn't I conquer the whole of the West? When Alexander, son of Philip, had acquired only Macedonia, he crushed the whole of the East.'[88] The concept of universal empire, which had a special history (connected with the claims of the Papacy) in the West, would receive increasing attention in debates about the Ottomans during the sixteenth century, when a Habsburg universal empire seemed a real possibility. And, more specifically, sixteenth-century writers did worry about the notion that the Sultans were claiming to have inherited the historic rights of the Roman emperors—an idea first expressed, as we have seen, by Sagundino soon after the fall of Constantinople. 'I have heard from trustworthy people', wrote Paolo Giovio about Süleyman the Magnificent in 1532, 'that he often says that the Empire of Rome and of the whole of the West belongs to him by right, as he is the legitimate successor of the Emperor Constantine, who transferred the Empire to Constantinople.' Eighty years later, an eminent legal theorist such as Alberico Gentili would still think it worth devoting some trouble to refuting this dangerous notion.[89]

Dismissing the Ottoman Turks as wild barbarians from Scythia was a tactic of argument that added emotional force to any calls to arms against them—not least by intensifying Westerners' fears about falling under

87. Note, however, that the surviving catalogue of the library of Bayezid II, Selim's father, includes not only several of these but also a history of Alexander translated from the Greek (Maróth, 'Library of Sultan Bayazit II', pp. 120, 131); and Mehmed's library apparently included a Greek manuscript of Arrian's *Anabasis* (Raby, 'Mehmed', p. 6).

88. Pertusi, *La caduta*, ii, p. 132 ('imperium orbis vindicare sibi'); Gaeta, 'Sulla "Lettera"', pp. 153–4(n.) ('Cur non ego mihi totum Occidentem armis acquiram … quando Alexander Philippi cum solam Macedoniam obtineret, totum calcavit Orientem').

89. Giovio, *Commentario*, p. 156 ('Ho inteso da uomini degni di fede che spesso dice che a lui tocca di ragione l'Imperio di Roma e di tutto Ponente per essere legittimo successore di Costantino imperatore quale transferì l'Imperio in Constantinopoli'); A. Gentili, *De iure belli* I.23, p. 181.

Ottoman rule. Yet, as we have seen, it did not in fact mean that this invading people was categorized in Western minds as a completely alien entity. The Scythian theory—which itself permitted ancestral connections to be made with various Christian European peoples—coexisted in popular culture with the theory of Trojan origins, and it was widely believed that the Sultans' designs on Western Europe were bound up with ideas about the rights of the Roman emperors. When humanist writers set out the reasons why it was justified and necessary to go to war against the Ottomans, they did not base their arguments on the barbarian otherness of the Turks; rather, they used a variety of mostly traditional lines of reasoning, concerned above all with two things: self-defence (pragmatically extended to embrace pre-emptive measures), and reclaiming historic rights to territory. The one thing that gave these arguments a special colouring, distinguishing them from the points that might have been made against any other aggressor, was the fact that in this case Christians had lost territory to, and were at risk of attack by, non-Christians. Of course, the fact that the Ottomans were 'infidels' did not—any more than that they were 'barbarians'—automatically justify any war of conquest against them; that point was already well established in the mainstream theological and legal tradition. But the religious difference did make possible, on the Christian side of the argument, a broader idea of mutual self-defence, and a more capacious notion of 'recovering' lost rights and lost territory. It also encouraged the interpretation of human political and military events in terms of a divine plan—perhaps even, as we shall see, God's plan for the end of the world. Whilst it was not too difficult for Western intellectuals to incorporate these invaders, one way or another, into a familiar schema of human history dating back to the ancient world, it was even more important to know what their role in sacred history might be. And for that reason it was necessary to understand what kind of religion these 'infidels' professed and followed.

TWO

Views of Islam
Standard assumptions

Early modern Europe inherited from the Middle Ages a large body of ideas about Islam, of which some were broadly correct, some fanciful, some innocently uncomprehending, and some wilfully false and defamatory. They had been generated and developed in three main areas of Christian–Muslim interaction: Byzantium, the Levant, and Spain. From the eighth century onwards, Byzantine theologians had constructed detailed refutations of Islam, out of which some account of Muslim belief and practice necessarily emerged. During the period of the Crusades, various Western writers who visited or resided in the Levant—including some who acquired a knowledge of Arabic—learned about Islam and wrote about it, again with polemical intent. And over several centuries the presence of a cultural and political frontier between Islam and Christianity in Spain stimulated anti-Muslim writings of various kinds by Christians, including not only Western scholars who learned Arabic, but also 'Mozarabs' (Christians under Muslim rule) who knew Arabic well, and some converts from Islam to Christianity.

It was in Spain that the two major medieval Latin translations of the Koran were written: the first, made by the English scholar Robert of Ketton at the request of the Abbot of Cluny, Peter the Venerable, in 1142–3, and the second, by Mark of Toledo, nearly 70 years later. Both were conscientious attempts to convey the meaning of the text, but on rather different assumptions about the nature of the translator's task; Robert of Ketton's approach was to produce something like an eloquent paraphrase, rather than the sort of literal version at which Mark of Toledo aimed. It was Robert's translation that was most widely circulated in manuscript, and became the first Western version of the Koran to be printed, in 1543. However conscientious his general approach may have been, Robert of Ketton's paraphrase technique did make possible the insinuation of his own prejudicial assumptions into the text of the Koran; but this was as nothing compared with the other negative features of the manuscript transmission, which filled the margins of the translation with denunciatory comments on the text, and supplemented it with translations of other works, of which the most important was an Arabic Christian refutation of Islam attributed to an author called al-Kindi. Within such a framework, study of Islam's holy book on its own terms was not really possible; the Koran was used as a series of pegs on which to hang preconceived criticisms of Islam on grounds of doctrinal error, absurdity, and immorality. And these criticisms were linked, in a satisfying system of mutual reinforcement, with polemical claims of many kinds about the life and actions of Muhammad, drawn from the whole range of previous Christian writings on Islam. During the course of the Middle Ages a considerable amount of new information did become available about Islamic belief and practice; but, as one modern scholar has written, 'time and again, the new data failed to modify the writers' preconceptions; on the contrary, the preconceptions dictated the extent to which the data were absorbed.'[1]

The focus on Muhammad is understandable enough. Since it was axiomatic for all Christian writers that Islam was a false religion, it followed that it must be a human creation. And as Muhammad was the supreme prophet of Islam, and the proclaimer—in Christian eyes, the author—of the Koran, it seemed clear that any understanding of Islam's real nature must depend on an analysis of his motives and actions. From the earliest phase of Christian anti-Muslim polemics, therefore, it was generally assumed that this was a religion invented and imposed for essentially secular purposes. (The only possible alternative to this view was the idea that its creation was inspired by the Devil; but Satanic guidance was understood to be quite compatible with the ordinary motivation of sinful humans.) Pious Christian writers thus developed an approach to the understanding of a major religion which, as we shall see, would eventually be turned by more radical thinkers within Western culture into a possible critique of other religions, including Christianity itself.

1. Kedar, *Crusade and Mission*, p. 87 (quotation). For general studies see d'Ancona, *La leggenda di Maometto*; d'Alverny, 'La Connaissance de l'Islam'; Southern, *Western Views of Islam*; Khoury, *Polémique byzantine*; Daniel, *Islam and the West*; Hoyland, *Seeing Islam*; Tolan, *Saracens*; Akbari, *Idols in the East*; on the translations see d'Alverny, 'Deux traductions'; Bobzin, *Der Koran*, pp. 52–60; Burman, *Reading the Qur'an*.

The master idea was that of 'imposture'—lies and deception, 'imposed' on an audience for the impostor's own ulterior purposes. In every Christian account, Muhammad was a pseudo-prophet who had bamboozled people into believing that he spoke with angels or with God, and had passed off his own effusions as divine revelation. Tricks of all kinds were attributed to him: he trained a pigeon to take grains of corn from his ear, so that it would seem to be a heavenly messenger communicating with him; he trained a bull or an ox to come at his call, bearing the Koran on its horns; he persuaded an accomplice to secrete himself in a well, cistern, or hole in the ground, from which to call out in an unearthly voice that Muhammad was a prophet of God, after which Muhammad encouraged his followers to throw stones into that space, thereby eliminating the only person who might ever have revealed the trick. These products of the medieval Christian imagination persisted for an extraordinarily long time in Western writings; the story of the pigeon was repeated, for example, by the English traveller George Sandys in 1615 and the scholar Hugo Grotius in 1627, and that of the man in the well was solemnly related by Jean Coppin, a former French consul in Egypt, in 1686.[2] For almost every Western thinker until at least the latter part of the seventeenth century, deception was simply intrinsic to the origins and nature of Islam.

Various motives could be used to explain Muhammad's promulgation of a new religion. One widely held view was that he invented his conversations with the Angel Gabriel in order to avoid the embarrassment of explaining to his wife that he suffered from epileptic seizures. But the dominant idea, from Byzantine writers such as John of Damascus and Niketas onwards, was that he was driven by personal ambition of a more or less political kind: it was known, from the Koran itself, that he gathered a large popular following, becoming a military and political leader, so it was assumed that his actions in proclaiming a new religion had all been aimed at winning the obedience of the people.[3] According to the thirteenth-century Franciscan writer Thomas of Pavia, Muhammad and his key adviser, a heretical Christian monk,

> began to consider how they might be accepted by some population and obtain rule over it. They had no hope of being able to deceive the Roman people, as

2. Sandys, *Relation*, p. 53; Grotius, *De veritate* VI.5, p. 283; Coppin, *Le Bouclier*, pp. 224–6. On the medieval myths see Daniel, *Islam and the West*, p. 32; Tolan, *Saracens*, p. 141; Ajello, *La croce e la spada*, pp. 129–30.
3. Khoury, *Polémique byzantine*, pp. 88 (John), 128–32 (Niketas).

they were mostly Christian, and extremely wise; and they did not dare tackle the Persians in this matter...So, by mutual agreement they turned to the Arabs, who were simple people, and they began to preach to them about religion and how to live.[4]

The Dominican Riccoldo da Monte Croce, whose treatise against Islam, written at the beginning of the fourteenth century, would have a large influence in sixteenth-century Europe, had a simpler account of Muhammad's political ambition: 'having become a prince of thieves, he broke out into such pride that he wanted to become king of the Arabs too. But since they did not accept him, because he was of low birth and low reputation, he pretended that he was a prophet.'[5]

Some of the basic features of Islam could be explained in terms of ingenious tactics devised to gain acceptance by, and influence over, the Arab population. That Islam contained elements drawn from the Jewish as well as the Christian tradition was noted by medieval Western writers, but mostly just as confirmation of its artificial nature as a mere pseudo-religion. For some later writers, however, this could also be used as evidence of Muhammad's secular ambition. As the Huguenot theologian Pierre Viret put it in 1565:

> seeing that people were very troubled and disturbed on all sides, both by the quarrels and wars in the [Byzantine] Empire and by the heresies, sects, and divisions in religion, he put forward this new form of religion, taken from all those that were in dispute, in order to combine them in a single form, so that he could more easily attract to it at least a large number of those who professed one or other of them.[6]

4. Thomas of Pavia, 'Gesta Imperatorum', p. 493, ll. 12–18 ('cogitare ceperunt, quomodo possent alicui genti preferri eiusque dominium obtinere. Verum Romanam gentem se posse decipere desperabant, eo quod christiani pro maxima parte forent essentque nimium sapientes. Persas autem attentare super hoc non audebant...Itaque de communi consensu Arabes tamquam simplices homines sunt aggressi et de religione et moribus sermones inter eos seminare ceperunt').
5. Riccoldo da Monte Croce, Confutatio Alcorani, p. 136 ('princeps latronum factus in tantam prorupit superbiam, ut et rex Arabum fieri voluerit. Sed quia ipsi non suceperunt eum, quia de genere et opinione vilis erat, finxit se esse prophetam'). A similar account was given by the mid-15th-century writer Dionysius Carthusianus: see Malvezzi, L'Islamismo, p. 159. On Riccoldo see George-Tvrtković, Christian Pilgrim; on his influence see Göllner, Turcica, pp. 206–7; Mérigoux, 'L'Ouvrage', pp. 43–58; Riccoldo da Monte Croce, op.cit., pp. 15–22.
6. Viret, L'Interim, p. 35 ('voyant...que les hommes estoyent fort troublez et esbranlez de toutes parts, tant pour les dissensions et guerres qui estoyent en l'Empire que pour les heresies et sectes et divisions qui estoyent en la religion, il a mis en avant celle nouvelle forme de religion, prise de toutes celles qui estoyent en different, pour les conjoindre en une afin qu'il attirast plus facilement à icelle, pour le moins, une grande partie de ceux qui faisoient profession de quelqu'une des autres'). For a similar analysis, probably influenced by Viret, see Mornay, De la vérité, p. 830. On the medieval view see Daniel, Islam and the West, p. 188.

Once this new form of faith was fixed, however, Muhammad had allegedly secured adherence to it by forbidding any kind of argument about its contents. This claim was based on a somewhat prejudicial reading of several verses in the Koran; worked up into a polemical argument by Peter the Venerable (who had commissioned Robert of Ketton's translation), it would become a stock part of the Western anti-Muslim repertoire. While the main point here was to suggest that Muhammad realized that his new-fangled religion could withstand neither comparison with the Bible nor the application of logical argument, the implication was that he had taken special care, by this means, to consolidate his power over his followers. The German humanist ethnographer Johannes Boemus noted that Muhammad had decreed the death penalty for all who disputed his 'law'; Pierre Viret described the ban on disputation as one of the defensive 'fortresses' with which Muhammad had surrounded his new creation.[7]

A more central part of the traditional argument, however, was the idea that Muhammad had cleverly adapted the contents of his religion to the frailty of human nature, thus making it something that passionate, sinful people would naturally choose in preference to the more demanding creeds of Judaism or Christianity. The argument concentrated here on the theme of sensuality and lust—above all, on the allowing of polygamy, divorce, and concubinage, and the apparent promise of sensual pleasures in Paradise. Much was made of this last point, as it gave Western writers the opportunity to combine moral superiority with salacious interest: the French traveller Pierre Belon reported, for example, that each copulation in the Muslim Paradise would last for 50 years.[8] As the Franciscan missionary Alessandro Ariosto put it in 1481, the reason why Islam had expanded so successfully was that 'they say, and preach to the common people, that man's supreme and everlasting good consists of bodily pleasure.' And whilst this message was assumed to have a universal appeal, it was thought to be especially well adapted to the nature of the Arabs, who, as a southern race, had a particularly sensual nature.[9] (That Islam banned wine, and also imposed a strenuous one-month fast every lunar year, was a detail passed over in most of these

7. Kritzeck, *Peter the Venerable*, pp. 166–71, 237–43; Boemus, *Omnium gentium mores*, p. 115 ('lex'); Viret, *L'Interim*, p. 37 ('forteresses'). On the medieval use of this argument see Bisaha, *Creating East and West*, p. 169.
8. Daniel, *Islam and the West*, pp. 135–52; Belon, *Voyage*, p. 457.
9. Ariosto, *Itinerarium*, pp. 237 ('summum et sempiternum hominis bonum corporis voluptatem dicunt ac vulgo predicant'), 241; Bunes Ibarra, *La imagen*, p. 104 (Arabs).

accounts; but Pius II dealt with this problem by explaining that fasting was a way of enhancing the pleasure of eating, and that wine was harmful in hot countries, where there was more pleasure to be had from cold watery drinks.[10]) Being hot-blooded, sensual creatures, the Arabs had also been greedy and cruel; Muhammad had likewise taken advantage of these tendencies by preaching holy war and promising booty from conquests. And according to some Western accounts of the early history of the Turks, it was the licence to conduct wars of conquest and expropriation that had first persuaded them to convert to Islam.[11]

Violence and coercion had a more central role than that, however, in medieval and early modern writings about the religion founded by Muhammad. Islam was seen as a faith propagated and maintained by 'the sword'—in contrast to Christianity, which, despite the frequent resort to violence by Christian authorities in order to enforce orthodoxy, was portrayed as a religion of peace which had spread by preaching and persuasion. This view of Islam was often combined with the argument about Muhammad's forbidding of religious disputation: as Peter the Venerable put it, 'he took up arms as a substitute for reason and, in the manner of madmen, giving no reply to anyone who questioned him, resorted to stones, sticks, or swords. Muslims, that is the way—so just, so reasonable!—in which your prophet Muhammad brought disputations to an end.'[12] Some writers also adduced the Islamic doctrine of holy war, noting that Muhammad had enjoined his followers to spread his faith by the sword. Overall, therefore, the argument developed that the Muslim faith was essentially dependent on violence. In his letter to Sultan Mehmed, written in 1461, Pius II quoted the prophet of Islam as saying that 'I have not been sent except with the strength of the sword.'[13] Twenty years later one of the most influential early accounts of life in the Ottoman Empire, by the writer known as George of Hungary, observed that the Muslims 'try to defend their sect in the manner of beasts, not by reasons or arguments but by swords and weapons, because, they say, their law orders them to do so'. In 1529 Martin Luther similarly argued that Islam was dependent on 'the sword', and that 'they are instructed in their law that it is a good and godly deed to rob and murder'; the French orientalist

10. Pius II, *Epistola*, p. 75.   11. Bunes Ibarra, *La imagen*, pp. 73, 104.
12. Kritzeck, *Peter the Venerable*, p. 241 ('pro ratione arma assumpsit, et furiosorum more, nullum dans interroganti responsum ad lapides, fustes, uel gladios se conuertit... Talem, tam iustum, tam rationabilem disputationibus finem uester propheta Mahumeth o Agareni imponit').
13. Daniel, *Islam and the West*, pp. 123–5 (holy war); Pius II, *Epistola*, p. 90.

Guillaume Postel would declare, fifteen years later, that 'Muhammad based
his system on the sword and power.'[14]

All of these arguments combined to characterize not only the prophet of
Islam as an evil man, but also Muslims generally as practitioners of a wide
range of vices, from sensuality to murderous violence. Yet, at the same time,
some Western writers did note the presence of positive virtues in Muslim
societies. A few medieval observers were quite emphatic about this. In his
Itinerarium, recounting his travels in the near East and his prolonged stay in
Baghdad, Riccoldo da Monte Croce exclaimed: 'Who will not be astounded,
if he carefully considers how great is the concern of these very Muslims
for study, their devotion in prayer, their pity for the poor, their reverence for
the name of God and the prophets and the Holy Places, their sobriety in
manners, their hospitality to strangers, their harmony and love for each other?'[15]
As more information became available about life in Muslim territories
in the fifteenth and early sixteenth centuries, such accounts multiplied.
The former captive Johann Schiltberger, writing in the 1430s, praised the
Muslims' strict regard for social justice in the marketplace, and noted that
'before the sermon, their priests [*sc.* imams] always tell them to be helpful to
one another and to obey authority, and that the rich should show humility
towards the poor.' George of Hungary particularly commended the piety of
Muslim worship. 'It would take a long time', he wrote, 'to describe in detail
the order, virtuous behaviour, silence, and devotion which they maintain in
their church. But in brief I say this: when I consider the silence of the
Muslims in their church and the disorder of the Christians in theirs at times
of prayer, I begin to feel great wonder.'[16] As the sixteenth century progressed,
yet more positive descriptions emerged—as we shall see—of the virtues,
social as well as religious, of Muslim society within the Ottoman Empire, to
the point where a Protestant theologian such as Theodore Bibliander (a keen

14. George of Hungary, *Tractatus*, p. 368 ('more bestiarum sectam suam non rationibus seu argu-
    mentis, sed gladiis et armis defendere contendunt, eo quod in lege sua sic se habere dicunt in
    precepto'); Luther, 'Vom Kriege', p. 123 ('das schwerd', 'es wird yhn ynn yhrem gesetz gebot-
    ten als ein gut Göttlich werck das sie rauben, morden'); Postel, *De orbis terrae concordia*, p. 174
    ('Ratio Muhamedis est in gladio & potentia posita'; the translation here is approximate, as
    'ratio' could mean both 'method' and 'justification').
15. Quoted in Daniel, *Islam and the West*, p. 196.
16. Schiltberger, *Reisen*, p. 132 ('Och sagent in ir priester allweg voran ir predig, das sie hilfflich
    aneinander sigent vnd iren obersten vnderthänig. Vnd die richen gegen den armen demüntig');
    George of Hungary, *Tractatus*, pp. 260–2 ('De ordine autem, honestate et silentio, quam habent
    in ecclesia, et deuotione longum foret narrare per singula. Hoc tamen breuiter dico, quod,
    quando Turcorum in ecclesia eorum silentium et Christianorum in sua ecclesia tempore
    orationis tumultum considero, magna mihi admiratio generatur').

reader of such accounts, and the editor of Robert of Ketton's translation of the Koran) could exclaim in 1542: 'those virtues which are prescribed by our master and ruler Jesus Christ are more favourably nourished and cultivated among those who go along with the superstition of Muhammad than they are among our feigned Christians.'[17]

For many or indeed most writers, the primary purpose of giving such a positive account of Muslim virtue was not to praise it absolutely, still less to commend Islam itself, but to castigate their own Christian societies by showing how far they fell short of the standards current in the infidel world. As Riccoldo put it very explicitly, 'We refer here briefly to some of the works of perfection of the Muslims, rather to shame the Christians than to commend the Muslims.'[18] That was the rationale of a famous passage in the popular travel-book ascribed to Sir John Mandeville, in which the narrator purported to describe a private conversation with the Mamluk Sultan of Egypt. Setting out a severe and painfully accurate criticism of Christian society, the Sultan declared: 'your priests serve not God duly in good living, as they do . . . Ye should be simple, meek and soothfast . . . as Christ was in whom ye say ye trow. But it is all otherwise. For Christian men are so proud, so envious, so great gluttons, and so lecherous'. The narrator reflected: 'methought great shame that Saracens, which have nowhere right belief ne perfect law, should thus reprove us of our imperfectness and keep their vain law better than we do the law of Jesu Christ . . . they are right devout in their law and right true and well keep the commandments of their Alkaron.'[19] Such a method of castigating Christian society was common in religious texts, where it had a clearly homiletic aim; but use of the Muslim counter-example could equally be made by secular writers, such as the satirist Pietro Aretino, who complained in 1534 that virtues such as piety and courtesy had fled from the cities of Europe and were now to be found only in Istanbul, or the playwright Ludovico Dolce, writing seven years later, who portrayed the Turks as possessing the virtues of sobriety and solidarity which the Christians had lost.[20] Comments of this kind are sometimes hailed by

17. Bibliander, *Ad socios consultatio*, sig. a5v ('uirtutes à magistro et Imperatore IESV CHRISTO praescriptas, apud superstitionis Mahumeticae complices . . . benignius foueri & coli, quàm apud fucatos Christianos').

18. Quoted in Daniel, *Islam and the West*, p. 196.

19. Letts, ed., *Mandeville's Travels*, i, pp. 97–9; 'soothfast' = truthful, faithful; 'Alkaron' = Koran. As Letts points out, the conversation was adapted from an early 13th-century work, the *Dialogus miraculorum* by Caesarius of Heisterbach.

20. Olivieri, *Immaginario*, p. 91 (Aretino); Giombi, 'L'umanesimo', p. 201 (Dolce).

modern scholars as expressions of 'Turcophilia', or of admiration for Islam; but in the great majority of cases that is a misleading way of representing the intentions of the author. (The misunderstanding is not a new one; Paolo Giovio was accused by one critic of being 'an admirer of the Turkish nation' because of his technique of holding up examples of virtuous behaviour by Ottomans as a reproach to his Christian readers.[21]) Inducing shame, rather than dispensing praise, was the primary purpose. So central was this whole style of argument to so much early modern commentary on Islam and the Ottomans that it deserves a name of its own: 'shame-praising' may be the simplest way to describe it.

For shame-praising to have its effect, it was at least necessary to give some positive value, if only a relative one, to the virtues practised by the Muslims. Only the most resolute of theological thinkers were prepared to reject this idea. Martin Luther showed how it might be done: in his 'Heerpredigt' or military sermon against the Ottomans he noted that while the Muslims prayed 'with such decency, silence, and fine outward comportment', it was much better to be an ill-behaved Christian with true beliefs. And in the preface he wrote to a translation of George of Hungary's treatise, he commented on the author's portrayal of the 'modesty and simplicity' of the Turks, as well as their religious piety, suggesting that their virtues were essentially ostentatious—vitiated, therefore, by the sin of pride.[22] The underlying argument here was the hardline Augustinian one that virtues unaligned with love of the true God were not real virtues at all, but 'splendida peccata', shining sins. And yet even Luther himself, in his first major writing on the Turks, had conceded: 'When people talk about how the Turks are faithful and friendly to one another, I am happy to believe that, and I am sure that they possess other fine virtues too. There is no one so wicked that he does not have some good in him.'[23]

For those who were not hardline Augustinians, the simplest way to account for the virtues of the Muslims was to suppose that they were the

21. Price Zimmermann, *Paolo Giovio*, p. 122 (citing the *Antijovio* of Gonzalo Jiminez de Quesada: 'aficionado a la nación turquesca').

22. Luther, *Eine Heerpredigt*, p. 187 ('mit solcher zucht, stille und schönen eusserlichen geberden'); Luther, 'Vorwort', p. 206 ('modestia et simplicitas').

23. Luther, 'Vom Kriege', p. 127 ('Das man aber sagt, wie die Turcken untereinander trew und freundlich sind... das wil ich gerne glauben Und halt, das sie noch wol mehr guter feiner tugent an sich haben. Es ist kein mensch so arg, Er hat etwas gutts an sich'). On Augustine's position, which contained both hard and moderate elements, see T. Irwin, 'Splendid Vices?', and Marenbon, *Pagans and Philosophers*, pp. 34–41. The phrase 'splendida peccata' was popularized by Reformation theologians, but was not used by Augustine himself.

products of natural reason, which made it possible for any human being to work out some of the basic principles of ethical behaviour. Luther's follower Philipp Melanchthon took this line, commenting that Islam retained the fifth and seventh commandments, against murder and theft, 'for utility's sake'. (More generally Melanchthon viewed Islam as a religion cleverly adapted to natural reason, claiming that Muhammad had abolished the doctrine of the Trinity, for example, 'because he knew that difficult articles of faith, which cannot be judged by reason, give rise to quarrels'; this is another example of the nature of Islam being explained in terms of an ultimately political purpose.)[24] That all human beings were endowed with sufficient reason—and/or innate awareness of good and evil—to be able to act morally was a standard scholastic view, so there was no difficulty in assuming that non-Christians could, to some extent at least, engage in virtuous behaviour. But Muslims were non-Christians of a peculiar kind: it was well understood that their faith included elements drawn from Christian doctrine as well as Judaism. Even Melanchthon, who was keen to distance them from Christianity (comparing them to Plato and other pagans, on the grounds that the God they worshipped was not the true God), felt obliged to note: 'Muslims do retain a particle of [true] doctrine: they say that God exists and that he will resurrect and judge the dead, giving the righteous eternal life.' The word 'retain' there was crucial: Islam was in some way an inheritor from Christianity, and this opened the possibility that some of the positive aspects of Muslim life might flow, ultimately, from Christian sources. As Melanchthon conceded in another remark, 'the Muslims retain something else: they say that Christ was a wise teacher, who gave good laws.'[25]

The fact that Muslims venerated Jesus was widely understood in the West from the Middle Ages onwards. Riccoldo da Monte Croce was happy to point out that Muhammad commended both Jesus and the Gospels, and to affirm that the Koran said more positive things about Jesus than it did about Muhammad himself. Cardinal Nicholas of Cusa, writing an analysis of Islam at the request of Pius II, cited several passages from the Koran in praise of Jesus, and of Christians, and argued that there were numerous truths in the

---

24. Köhler, *Melanchthon und der Islam*, pp. 34 ('quia sciebat dissidia oriri de difficilibus articulis, qui non iudicantur ratione'), 35 ('utilitatis causa').

25. Ibid., pp. 49 (Plato), 50 ('Mahometistae retinent particulam doctrinae; dicunt esse Deum et esse eum iudicaturum et resuscitaturum mortuos, daturum iustis vitam aeternam'), 51 ('Turci etiam aliquid retinent; dicunt Christum fuisse sapientem doctorem, dedisse bonas leges').

Koran that must derive from the Gospels, including its 'love of virtue'.[26] The point was confirmed not just by Western students of the Koran, but by many of the early reports of life in the Ottoman Empire: George of Hungary noted that Muslims accepted as great prophets Moses, David, and Jesus as well as Muhammad; the French traveller Pierre Belon wrote in detail about the praise of Jesus in the Koran; his contemporary the French Knight of Malta Antoine Geuffroy declared that 'they greatly revere our Lord Jesus Christ...and they say the Lord's Prayer just as we do, translated word for word into Arabic'; and the former captive Luigi Bassano described popular veneration not only for Jesus but also for a variety of Christian saints.[27]

It was thus possible to describe Muslims as in some sense partial Christians—perhaps even, in the phrase advanced rather daringly by Erasmus in 1530, semi-Christians. There were several possible implications to be drawn from this, some positive, some negative. One positive view was that Islam had its place in a divine providential plan, as a stepping stone away from paganism in the direction of the true faith. On this basis the success of Islam in world history might been seen as validated by God—which was, however, a troubling idea for those who now felt threatened by Ottoman power. George of Hungary complained of 'certain learned men' who argued that 'the reason why that sect has lasted longer than other sects and heresies is that it abhors idols and worships one God.'[28] He did not say who those learned men were, but another text from the late fifteenth century identifies one candidate. After a lengthy discussion of Islam in his popular pilgrimage narrative, Bernhard von Breydenbach asked why God had permitted it to last so long. He began his answer with a summary of the opinion of a learned man, a convert to Christianity from Judaism, who had put forward three reasons: Islam was free of idolatry, which was the one sin God punished most severely and most quickly; it did not force Christians to perform Muslim worship (differing thereby from the practice of previous pagans ruling over Christians); and it did not revile Christ, venerating him instead

26. Riccoldo da Monte Croce, *Confutatio Alcorani*, pp. 166 (more positive), 172 (praise by Muhammad); Nicholas of Cusa, *Cribratio Alkorani*, in *De pace fidei*, pp. 94 (love of virtue), 97–8 (praise of Christ, Christians).

27. George of Hungary, *Tractatus*, pp. 256–8; Belon, *Voyage*, p. 446; Geuffroy, *Briefve description*, sigs. e2v–e3v ('Ils ont notre seigneur Iesuchrist en grande reuerence...Et dient le pater noster comme nous, translaté en langue Arabique quasi de mot a mot'); Bassano, *Costumi*, fo. 11v. The claim about saints was correct, unlike that about the Lord's Prayer.

28. George of Hungary, *Tractatus*, p. 256 ('quidam de sapientibus', 'causam durationis illius secte super alias sectas et hereses...quia ydola detestatur et unum deum colit').

as a very holy man. The ex-Jewish author was Paul of Burgos (Pablo de Santa Maria), who served as Archbishop of Burgos from 1415 until his death in 1435; his *Dialogus* or *Scrutinium scripturarum*, from which these points were taken, went through several editions after its first printing in *c.*1470, and his argument on this topic can only have been propagated further by Breydenbach (despite the lengthy refutation of it which he immediately put forward), whose own book was one of the great publishing successes of the late fifteenth and sixteenth centuries.[29]

Yet although these ideas were widely circulated, full-blown adoption of a providentialist view of Islam was—understandably enough—a rarity in this period. The only major writer to advance such a theory was the maverick orientalist Guillaume Postel, at least in his later writings. (In an early work he specifically argued that the scale and success of the early expansion of Islam did not prove that it had the blessing of divine Providence, as the Persian ruler Chosroes had obtained an equally large empire 'without any religion'.) In his general history of the Muslim peoples, published in 1560, Postel declared that all evils permitted by God lead to greater goods, and that 'one must conclude that the good brought in by the Muslims when they destroyed idolatry is infinitely greater than any evil that they have brought into the world.'[30] While such a providentialist argument was not widely accepted, many writers felt that it had to be refuted, not simply ignored; thus Philippe de Mornay insisted very firmly that the huge success of Islam in the world had been accomplished purely 'by human means'.[31]

Another, more obviously positive, implication of the partly Christian nature of Islam was that it might prove easier to convert Muslims to Christianity than members of other faiths. Grand designs to convert Muslim populations had been current in Western thinking for a long time; sometimes this aim had been given as a justification for the Crusades, though there was also a minor but vocal tradition of argument, represented by

29. Breydenbach, *Peregrinatio*, pp. 380–95 (summary of opinion), 396–407 (refutation); Paul of Burgos is not named, but his work is cited as the *Scrutinium* (pp. 401–2). On the publishing history of Breydenbach see Gomez-Géraud, *Le Crépuscule*, pp. 305–6, and Ross, *Picturing Experience*.
30. Postel, *De orbis terrae concordia*, p. 107 (anti-providentialist: 'sine ulla religione'); *Histoire et consideration*, p. 44 ('il faut conclure que le bien, lequel ont en detruisant l'idolatrie introduit les Musulmans soit infiniement plus grand, que quelque mal qu'ils ayent introduit au monde'); he also noted (p. 45) that Islam preserved much Christian theology, and that without it many parts of Asia and North Africa would have lost this heritage altogether. See also the comments in Lestringant, 'Guillaume Postel', pp. 286–7.
31. Mornay, *De la vérité*, p. 830 ('par moyens humains').

thinkers such as Roger Bacon and (in some of his works) Ramon Llull, which said that the use of military force was an obstacle to true conversion.[32] In the fifteenth century this tradition was maintained by an influential churchman, Juan of Segovia, whose long intellectual engagement with Islam included commissioning a trilingual version (which unfortunately does not survive) of the Koran in Arabic, Latin, and Spanish. In his treatise 'De mittendo gladio Divini Spiritus in corda Saracenorum' he argued that 'the conversion of infidels is seldom or never brought about by the terror of war.' His alternative strategy involved developing peaceful relations, intensifying cultural contacts, and then engaging in theological debate. But the key to it all was his confidence that Muslims could be converted, not least because they already accepted as authoritative many books of the Old Testament, and the Gospels.[33] This view was shared by his colleague and friend Nicholas of Cusa, whose short treatise of 1453 'De pace fidei' argued that every non-Christian religion—paganism, Judaism, and Islam—contained some element of truth, and that the infidels' rejection of Christian doctrine was based only on misunderstandings, which could be dispelled by patient and rational explanations. The main emphasis here was on reason, but Muslims clearly emerged as the best candidates for conversion because, as Nicholas put it, they were already closer to recognizing the truth about Jesus than the Jews were. In another treatise, 'Cribratio Alcorani', written at Pius II's request seven years later and devoted specifically to Islamic doctrine, Nicholas took a more hostile line, especially where the motives of Muhammad were concerned; but while his confidence in the power of reason seems to have waned somewhat in this work, he put all the more emphasis on the presence within the Koran of passages which, he believed, could be used to persuade Muslims of the divinity of Jesus Christ.[34]

These writings form part of the background to one of the strangest documents of this entire period, the letter, addressed by Pius II to Sultan Mehmed in 1461, in which the Pope invited this great foe of Christendom to convert to Christianity. If you accept baptism, he wrote, 'we will call you ruler over the Greeks and the East; what you now hold by force and injustice,

32. See Kedar, *Crusade and Mission*, esp. pp. 186–7, 198–9.
33. Cabanelas Rodríguez, *Juan de Segovia*, pp. 117–18 (strategy), 139–60 (new translation), 271 ('terrore belli vix aut nunquam infidelium fit conversio'), 301 (accepted Old Testament, Gospels).
34. Nicholas of Cusa, *De pace fidei*, pp. 55 (closer than Jews), 104–12 (passages in Koran). On the relations between the ideas of Nicholas of Cusa and Juan of Segovia see Álvarez Gómez, *Über die Bedingungen*; Sanz Santacruz, 'Juan de Segovia'.

you will rightfully possess.' (And, what was more, the Pope would then happily turn to Mehmed for help in forcing the schismatic Eastern Christians back into the true Catholic fold.) At the start of the text Pius insisted that the sultan had no historic right to rule Italy, and that Christendom would unite if Italy were attacked; there would always be wars between Christians and Turks, he warned, so long as the latter were Muslims, but if they converted to Christianity—as they all would, 'if you alone nod'—it would become possible to establish a general peace. And at the end he took his argument one step further, raising at least the possibility of rule over Western lands: 'you cannot attain glory and power among Christians, which you seem to want, especially over Europeans and people of the Occident, if you remain in your religion. But if you are willing to be initiated into Christian rites, we can hold out to you ample hope for power and glory.'[35] In between, the main body of the letter was devoted to explaining the intrinsic superiority of Christianity over Islam. Some points were conciliatory in tone, emphasizing some initial areas of agreement (monotheism, belief in an immortal soul, acceptance of much of the Old Testament, respect for Jesus), but the bulk of the argument consisted of strong criticism of many Islamic theological positions, and denunciations of Muhammad for having based his new religion on 'artifice and fraud'.[36] While some elements of this text suggest the influence of Juan of Segovia and Nicholas of Cusa, the prime debt was to the more combative, refutatory treatise written by Cardinal Juan de Torquemada two years earlier; indeed, Pius borrowed entire passages from that work.[37]

What exactly Pius's intention was in writing this letter has been a matter of unending scholarly debate. There is no evidence that it was ever sent to Istanbul, and a veil of silence descended on it in Pius's later autobiographical writings; yet his authorship of it has never been contested, and it did circulate widely in the West (at least 94 manuscript copies survive). Some historians have dismissed the text as a fantasy, an academic exercise, or an unconventional 'meditation'.[38] It has been pointed out that the personal

35. Pius II, *Epistola*, pp. 12–13 (Italy), 18–19 (baptism, forcing schismatics), 20 (peace), 101 (final quotation).
36. Ibid., pp. 29 (monotheism, soul), 37 (Old Testament), 41 (Jesus), 43–70, 77–8 (criticism), 75 (Muhammad; cf. 88–90).
37. See Gaeta, 'Sulla "Lettera"', pp. 163–73.
38. Helmrath, 'Pius II. und die Türken', p. 126 (94 MSS, 'Nachdenken'); Babinger, 'Pio II', p. 6 (fantasy: 'un'impresa...fantastica'); Schwoebel, *Shadow of the Crescent*, p. 66 (academic exercise). Göllner suggests that it may have been sent (*Turcica*, iii, p. 48), but acknowledges the lack of evidence. On the alleged reply to it by 'Morbisanus' see the reference to Meserve, above, ch. 1, n. 82.

compliments that Pius scattered in Mehmed's direction here contrast with his descriptions of the Sultan elsewhere as a bloodthirsty tyrant, and it has been argued that the Pope would never seriously have invited someone, as he appears to do in this text, to regard baptism as the acceptance of just 'a little bit of water'. Yet the flattery would make most sense, surely, if we assumed that Pius did intend the letter to be read by the Sultan, and so too would the offhand description of baptism, as that is how the sacrament would have appeared to a Muslim reader, not a Christian one.[39] The idea that a whole population could be turned to Christianity by converting its ruler was deeply rooted in Christian history; on various occasions, from the eleventh century onwards, popes had written personal letters to infidel rulers in the hope of bringing that about. Attempts to convert Muslim potentates, in particular, were nothing new: in 1219 St Francis of Assisi had even obtained an audience with the Mamluk Sultan for that purpose.[40] And a few years after Pius wrote his letter, the Cretan–Venetian scholar George of Trebizond would travel to Istanbul with the genuine intention of converting Mehmed II to Christianity.[41] It is not biographically implausible that Pius might, by 1461, have entered a temporary state of despair about the possibility of assembling a viable coalition of Christian powers against the Ottomans: after the fall of the great Serbian fortress of Smederevo in 1459, the severe tensions between the Holy Roman Emperor and the King of Hungary, the suspension of Skanderbeg's anti-Ottoman campaigning in 1460, and the inconclusive ending of the Congress of Mantua late that year, and with the increasing Ottoman threat to the mainly Catholic kingdom of Bosnia, whose king died in the summer of 1461, Pius may well have toyed, if only for a short while, with the idea of a radically different solution to the geopolitical threat posed by Sultan Mehmed.[42] It is possible to assume, therefore, that the letter did express a genuine hope—but a hope which was born of despair under extreme conditions, and turned out to be quite transitory.

In any case, Pius did not create a precedent. It is true that (as we shall see) apocalyptic and millenarian currents of thinking would long nurture the

39. Bisaha, *Creating East and West*, pp. 149–52 (contrast over Mehmed; baptism phrase (a point emphasized by Babinger, 'Pio II', p. 4); concluding that 'it was clearly not intended for a Muslim audience').

40. Weber, *Lutter contre les Turcs*, pp. 52–6 (tradition, papal letters); Lemmens, 'De sancto Francisco' (St Francis).

41. Monfasani, *George of Trebizond*, pp. 131–2.

42. For the political and biographical context see Matanic, 'L'idea e l'attività', pp. 387–92.

idea that the Last Days would be preceded by the conversion of the infidels—especially the Muslims—to the Christian faith. Well into the seventeenth century, adventurous individuals with such thoughts in their heads, such as the Quaker Mary Fisher in 1658 or the German mystical poet Quirinus Kuhlmann twenty years later, would set off for Istanbul in the hope of performing the personal conversion of the sultan; but the underlying beliefs and assumptions of these people were very different from those of Pius II. That individual pashas and viziers might be 'turned' by bringing them to Christianity was also a dream of Western strategists at various times of Christian–Ottoman conflict; that notion depended, however, on the fact that most of them were 'renegades', converts to Islam from Christianity, in the first place.[43] The idea that a final, grand geopolitical settlement could be achieved simply by persuading the sultan, by means of reasonable arguments, to embrace Christianity would have no lasting history in the real world of early modern politics.

While the visible overlap between Islamic and Christian doctrine led some Western Europeans to think more positively about the possibility of converting Muslims, a more common reaction was to associate Islam with damnable heresy. One traditional view, indeed, was that Islam itself should be classified as a heretical form of Christianity. The earliest major Byzantine critique of Islam, by John of Damascus, called it a 'haeresis' or heresy (though in the broader sense of 'false belief'), and some other Byzantine writers treated it as a Christian sect. Peter the Venerable admitted: 'I cannot clearly decide whether the Mohammedan error must be called a heresy and its followers heretics, or whether they are to be called pagans', telling his readers that they should choose for themselves, and that, on balance, he chose to call them heretics.[44] This approach was still current in the fifteenth and sixteenth centuries: the scholar and philosopher Marsilio Ficino, writing in the 1470s, observed that 'the Muslims seem to be, in a certain manner, Christians, albeit heretical ones—followers of the Arians and the Manichaeans', and in 1543 Theodore Bibliander invoked John of Damascus's broad categorization in order to explain: 'for that reason we shall very correctly classify the Koran

43. Villani, *Tremolanti*, pp. 50–2 (Fisher); on Kuhlmann see below, p. 270. For examples of Western ambitions to 'turn' senior Ottoman officials see Malcolm, *Agents of Empire*, pp. 236–7, 242, and Graf, *Sultan's Renegades*, pp. 189–91.
44. Hoyland, *Seeing Islam*, pp. 485–6 (John—though noting also uncertainty about the authorship of this work); Göllner, *Turcica*, iii, p. 200 (Byzantine writers: sect); Kritzeck, *Peter the Venerable*, pp. 39, 143–4 (quotation: p. 143).

as heretical doctrine.'[45] But this view coexisted with the idea that Muslims were infidels ('infideles' was a term commonly used by humanist writers), to be classed with pagans and idolaters rather than Christians. The association with idolatry seems at first sight strange, given Islam's well-known icono-clastic tendencies and fierce hostility to idol worship. There may have been some residue in Western culture of the popular medieval notion that the 'Saracens' were polytheists and idol worshippers, and the idea that Muslims prayed to Muhammad was a persistent one (affirmed, for example, by Thomas Tenison as late as 1678).[46] But generally a more sophisticated theo-logical argument was at work: as Calvin implied, any false god was an idol, and since Muslims denied the divinity of Christ, the god they worshipped must have been a false one. Or, in the words of the influential Swiss Protestant Heinrich Bullinger, 'even though the Muslims do not make images of God, and do not possess or venerate any images, their hearts are nevertheless full of the horrible idols of a false faith.'[47] In the end, whether or not the concept of idolatry was invoked, the general view in the sixteenth and seventeenth centuries was that Muslims were infidels, whose false faith happened to incorporate, in mostly or entirely heretical form, some borrowed fragments of Christian doctrine.

The basic idea of a link between Islam and Christian heresy was present in the minds of almost all Western writers about it, thanks to a claim made in every version of the biography of Muhammad that was available to them: that he had been guided, while devising his new religion, by a disaffected Christian priest or monk. The remote origin of this notion was the tradition, deriving from some early Islamic writings on the life of the Prophet, that the young Muhammad had met in Syria a Christian monk called Bahira, who had immediately recognized his divinely appointed role. Medieval

45. Ficino, De religione christiana, fo. 15r ('Maumethenses christiani quodammodo esse videntur: quamuis heretici: arrianorum manicheorumque sectatores'); Bibliander, 'Apologia', sig. α5v ('Qua ratione Alcoranum inter doctrinas haereticas rectissimè constituemus', citing the De haeresibus but misattributing it to Epiphanius).

46. Bisaha, Creating East and West, p. 162 ('infideles'); Tenison, Of Idolatry, p. 146 (also claiming that Muslims worshipped Muhammad's tomb). Tenison would become Archbishop of Canterbury in 1694. On the popular medieval notion see Daniel, Heroes and Saracens, pp. 121–78; Akbari, Idols in the East, pp. 200–7.

47. Calvin, Institutes II.vi.4, i, p. 298 ('the Turks...who...though proclaiming...that the Creator of heaven and earth is their God, yet, by their rejection of Christ, substitute an idol in his place'); Bullinger, Der Türgg, sig. A7v ('ob glych wol die Türggen / Gott weder verbildend / noch einiche bilder habe[n]d / oder vererend / stäckend doch ire herze[n] vollen greulicher götzen falsches gloubens'). Calvin's view was shared by later Jesuit writers: see Colombo, 'Jesuits and Islam', p. 337.

Christian writers in the Middle East transformed the monk's name into 'Sergius', identified him as a heretic (usually either an Arian or a Nestorian), and gave him a larger and more sinister role as an instructor who helped Muhammad to form the whole body of Islamic doctrine.[48] (This legend was very persistent: Guillaume Postel pointed out as early as 1544 that there was no trace of such a person in the Koran, but more than eighty years later the respected historian Michel Baudier would still confidently explain that Sergius, a Nestorian, had fled to Arabia, where Muhammad had 'subjected his opinion to that of this false monk, who was learned in the Holy Scriptures, having been a professor of them in Constantinople'.[49]) In any case, while Sergius was usually described as an adherent to just one standard heresy, Christian writers were happy to identify many different heresies—thereby, incidentally, displaying their own erudition in the history of the early Church—in Islamic doctrine. Thus Riccoldo da Monte Croce found that Muhammad combined the erroneous beliefs of Sabellius, Arius, Ebion, Carpocrates, Macedonius, the Manichaeans, the Donatists, and the Anthropomorphites; Theodore Bibliander went through a long list of Muslim beliefs and practices, arguing that each matched an earlier heretical position— the Arians had approved of religious coercion, the Severians had prohibited wine, and so on.[50]

While scholars and theologians continued to identify particular elements of Islamic belief with Christian heresies, the fact that Muslims were gener- ally categorized as 'infidels' was of real importance where their treatment in practice was concerned. Muslims of several kinds could be found living under Christian rule: a large population in Spain and a more recently settled one (of Tatars) in Poland and Lithuania; significant numbers of slaves in Italy, Sicily, Malta, and the Iberian peninsula (with a few in the south of France, and small numbers scattered through the Holy Roman Empire); and visiting merchants in various Mediterranean ports and central European cities. Had they been viewed, in formal terms, as Christian heretics, the full weight of ecclesiastical law—and public policy—would have been directed against

48. See Roggema, *Legend of Sergius*; on the adoption of the name 'Sergius' see Öze, *Apocalypticism*, p. 187.
49. Postel, *De orbis terrae concordia*, pp. 144–5 (and cf. his *De la république des Turcs*, p. 85); Baudier, *Histoire generale*, p. 12 ('asseruit son opinion à celle de ce faux moine, sçauant aux Sainctes lettres, desquelles il auoit esté professeur à Constantinople').
50. Riccoldo da Monte Croce, *Confutatio Alcorani*, pp. 38–42; Bibliander, 'Apologia', sigs. β1v–β3r.

them: excommunication, prosecution by the Inquisition, and so on. Their status as infidels saved them from this.

General accounts of the development of religious toleration in Christian Europe often give the impression that thinking about the need to tolerate religious difference was first prompted by divisions within Christianity, and that the tolerationist principles so formed were extended at some later stage to non-Christian religions; but this is somewhat misleading. One of the most basic presuppositions of religious toleration was set out by Thomas Aquinas in his *Summa theologiae* (though not for the first time—it goes back to Church Fathers such as Lactantius). Posing the question 'ought infidels to be compelled to believe?', he replied that heathens and Jews should not be compelled, because belief is by its nature voluntary. It is true that he immediately went on to condone some other actions against infidels, saying that they should be compelled not to hinder Christianity by means of their blasphemies, persuasions, or persecutions; but still he placed them in a very different category from that of Christian heretics and apostates from Christianity, to whom compulsion could properly be applied. As he put it, 'taking a vow is a matter of free will, yet keeping it is a matter of obligation.' So whilst Christians who were straying from their 'vow' could be coerced into obeying it, no one should be forced to become a Christian in the first place.[51] This was a fundamental idea, which can only have been reinforced by the constant denunciation, in medieval and early modern Europe, of Islam itself for being propagated by the sword.

Not forcing people to convert was one thing; granting them full toleration was, of course, another, and it is unsurprising that that did not follow in medieval European practice. Later in the same section of the *Summa theologiae* Aquinas asked the question, 'Are the rites of the infidels to be tolerated?', and answered by invoking the general principle that 'although infidels may sin in their rites, they may be tolerated on account of some good that results or some evil that is avoided.' The Jews (classified here simply as infidels) were to be tolerated because the practice of their religion contributed a kind of good to the Christian world, by enacting a prefiguration of the Christian faith. As for Muslims and pagans: 'the rites of other infidels, which are neither truthful nor profitable, are by no means to be tolerated, except perhaps to avoid some evil, for example the scandal or disturbance that might ensue, or some hindrance to the salvation of those of them who, if

---

51. Thomas Aquinas, *Summa theologiae* IIa IIae, qu. 10, art. 8, resp., p. 538 (ad 3: 'vovere est voluntatis, reddere autem est necessitatis').

they were unmolested, might gradually be converted to the faith.'[52] Those last concessive qualifications left the door ajar for some pragmatic policy-making; visiting Muslim merchants, for example, would not be molested for the discreet performance of ritual ablutions, prayers, and fasts.

A broadly similar attitude was to be found expressed in Catholic canon law. One of the medieval 'glosses' on Gratian's *Decretum* said that if the Muslims were peaceful, 'we should not molest them', and 'we may eat at their table'—the latter being a significant point, in comparison with excommunicated heretics.[53] The basic rules of canon law tended to lump Muslims together with Jews. Under a decretal of Innocent III, both categories of people were required to wear some distinctive clothing; the main purpose of this was to reduce the chances of Christians entering unknowingly into sexual relations with them, and it was partly for that reason that canon law forbade Christians to live in their midst. Both Jews and Muslims were under some legal disabilities: while they could bring actions at law, they could not be prosecution witnesses against Christians. On underlying theological grounds, canon law was more hostile to Jews, seeing them as people who had been given their promised Messiah and had refused to recognize him. So, whereas one provision forbade Christians to attend the 'feasts' of the Jews, as submitting to Jewish dietary rules after the coming of Christ would be sacrilegious, there was no equivalent law against dining with Muslims.[54] However, at the Council of Vienne (1311–12) a stern decree was issued against some Muslim religious practices: the call to prayer was forbidden, and Christian princes were ordered to stop the visits by Muslims to the tombs of their holy men. This was a 'scandal' which, rulers were told, they should 'remove' from their territories. (The later gloss on this decree would misinterpret the reference to tomb-visiting as meaning the pilgrimage to Mecca, and would also misunderstand the passage about removing the scandal, taking it to require the physical removal of both Muslims and Jews.)[55]

---

52. Ibid. IIa IIae, qu. 10, art. 11, resp., p. 539 ('quamvis infideles in suis ritibus peccent, tolerari possunt vel propter aliquod bonum quod ex eis provenit, vel propter aliquod malum quod vitatur', 'aliorum vero infidelium ritus, qui nihil veritatis aut utilitatis afferunt, non sunt aliqualiter toleranti, nisi forte ad aliquod malum vitandum, scilicet ad vitandum scandalum vel dissidium quod ex hoc posset provenire, vel impedimentum salutis eorum, qui paulatim, sic tolerati, convertuntur ad fidem').
53. Bussi, 'La condizione giuridica', p. 461 ('nullam debemus facere molestiam', 'ad mensam eorum comedere possumus').
54. Ibid., pp. 462, 465–9.
55. Ibid., pp. 479–80 ('auferant…opprobrium'), 487–8 (later gloss). The decree was general, but it was primarily concerned with Muslim practice under Spanish Christian rule. The interpretation

Many years after the formation of the classic corpus of canon law, a papal bull of 1442 tightened the screw a little against both Jews and Muslims, ordering Christians not to eat, live, or bathe with them, renewing the rules about their distinctive dress, extending the list of occupations which they were not allowed to perform in Christian society (such as estate managers, brokers, and midwives), and forbidding them to employ Christian servants. Much of this was repeated by Calixtus III in another bull in 1456. Writing less than three years after the fall of Constantinople, he took what had been primarily an anti-Jewish measure and made sure that all of its provisions applied against Muslims too; and when dealing with the subject of usury (where the Jews were certainly the prime target) he decreed that confiscated profits should be put to the use of 'the most holy expedition [*sc.* the crusade] against the Ottomans'.[56] One might expect that anti-Muslim animus would remain the norm thereafter in official papal pronouncements, at least until the waning of the Ottoman threat two and a half centuries later; yet pragmatic interests could and did overcome religious zeal. In 1573 Gregory XIII issued a decree to protect all the Levantine merchants—Jews, Muslims, and Orthodox Christians—who traded in the papal port of Ancona. Not only did he forbid the local Christians to molest them in any way, but he also endowed them with solid legal immunities and privileges. At one point, in an ambiguously worded part of the decree, he even opened the possibility of the Muslim merchants erecting their own mosque on papal soil: the passage referred to building 'one school or synagogue', which suggests that it was concerned only with Jews, but it began by extending this privilege to 'the said Jews, Muslims, Greek Orthodox, and other Levantines'.[57]

Possibly it was with this sort of permissive practice in mind that the great Jesuit theologian Francisco Suárez, in a text first composed in Rome in 1583, later revised, and finally published posthumously in 1621, gave a new twist to Thomas Aquinas's argument about the two different kinds of infidel worship.

requiring physical removal may have provided some background justification for the later Spanish expulsions. On the general provisions of canon law see also Gilles, 'Législation'.

56. Tomassetti et al., eds, *Bullarum diplomatum*, v, pp. 67–70 (1442), 127–30 (1456; p. 129: 'expeditionem sanctissimam contra Turcas').
57. Ibid., viii, pp. 32–9 (p. 33: 'unam scholam seu synagogam', 'dictis Hebraeis, Turcis, Graecis et aliis Orientalibus'). Remarkably, this bull is dated 23 February 1573, before the end of the war between the Holy League (of which the Papacy was by now the most fervent member) and the Ottoman Empire. On the special papal interest in protecting its Anconitan trade see Poumarède, *Pour en finir*, pp. 342–50; see also Delumeau, 'Un ponte'; Bonazzoli, 'Ebrei italiani'.

As we have seen, Aquinas had distinguished between the (permissible) rites of the Jews and the (mostly impermissible) worship by other infidels, including Muslims. Suárez completely reconfigured the distinction, turning it into one between rites that did not go against natural reason, even though they fell far below Christian standards, and rites contrary to natural reason (which it was the duty of a Christian ruler to suppress). The former, he wrote, 'are indeed superstitious in comparison with the Christian faith and its precepts, but not because they are intrinsically evil in themselves or contrary to natural reason. Such are the rites of the Jews, and perhaps also many rites of the Muslims, and of similar infidels, who worship only the one true God.'[58]

In these various ways theological and legal principles, and actual practice, were able to find a *modus vivendi* for those Muslims who lived within Christian societies. They were absorbed, so to speak, into ordinary life. And yet, at the same time, Christian culture nursed an utterly different way of thinking about Muslims—a hostile vision which drew on a certain kind of prophetic or apocalyptic biblical theology, and implied that the followers of Islam had a role in God's plan that was much more negative than that of the Jews. On this view, Muslims were not just ordinary heretics or infidels; they were agents of cosmic evil, and the divine pattern of world history would not reach fulfilment until they were either converted or totally destroyed.

There were two main traditions in medieval Western Europe, each of which had been generated, in the first place, by a reaction to Islamic military power. The first stemmed from a text which was known as the *Apocalypse* of Saint Methodius; that attribution was false, so the anonymous author is known to modern scholarship as Pseudo-Methodius. This work was originally written in Syriac by a Mesopotamian Christian soon after the Arab conquests, some time in the second half of the seventh century.[59] Via Greek, it was turned in eighth-century France into a Latin version, which was widely distributed thereafter in Western Europe, coming into print as early

58. Suárez, *Selections*, i, pp. 483 (citing Aquinas, *Summa theologiae* IIa IIae, qu. 10, art. 11), 484 ('sunt superstitiosi quidem per comparationem ad Christianam fidem, & praecepta eius, non verò quia per se sint intrinsicè mali, vel contrarii rationi naturali, vt sunt ritus Iudaeorum, & fortasse multi etiam ritus Sarracenorum, & similium infidelium, qui vnum tantùm verum Deum adorant').
59. Alexander, *Byzantine Apocalyptic Tradition*, pp. 13–29 (dating to 650s); Reinink, 'Der "Pseudo-Methodius"' (dating to early 690s); Möhring, *Der Weltkaiser der Endzeit*, pp. 75 (dating to 680s), 101 (Latin translation), 321–2 (distribution).

as 1470. The author adapted an earlier tradition, derived partly from the so-called prophecy of the Tiburtine Sibyl (a text composed probably in fourth-century Constantinople), which foretold that a heroic Greek emperor would defeat all the pagan barbarians assailing the Christian world, including the terrible army of Gog and Magog that would be unleashed from its mountain strongholds in the Caucasus, and he would then go to Jerusalem to hand over his earthly authority to God; after that, the Antichrist would appear, only to be defeated by divine power, and the Second Coming of Christ would follow. The main change to this story made by Pseudo-Methodius was to turn the pagan hordes into something much more specific: the 'sons of Ishmael', by which he meant Muslim Arabs. (Popular tradition identified the Arabs with the descendants of Ishmael, Abraham's son by his maidservant Hagar; both 'Ishmaelite' and 'Hagarene' or 'Agarene' were commonly used terms for Arabs and Muslims.) In the seventh and final millennium of world history, Pseudo-Methodius wrote, these merciless invaders would be unleashed as a chastisement for the moral failings of the Christians; in vivid detail he described how they would conquer all Christian territories, massacring many of their inhabitants and reducing the rest to slavery, until a great 'king of the Greeks, that is of the Romans' would rise up and defeat them.[60] Then the 'gates of the North' would be opened, and the nations hitherto enclosed there would pour forth, people who 'eat unclean things' including human foetuses. God would send his own commander to defeat them, and the king of the Greeks would then retire to Jerusalem and surrender his rule. At this point the Antichrist would appear, deceiving the world with false miracles; and he in turn would be overthrown at the Second Coming of Christ.[61] Thus this tradition contributed one positive element to Christian apocalyptic thinking—the idea of a heroic 'Last World Emperor'—while emphasizing the roles of not one, but three, negative elements: the Ishmaelites, who would themselves subdue the entire Christian world; the disgustingly barbaric nations of the North, led by Gog and Magog; and the Antichrist. The first of these were explicitly identified as Muslims; the second would easily become associated (as we have already seen) with the 'Scythian' Turks; and the third would soon find a role to play in Western thinking about Muhammad, Islam, and the Ottoman Empire.

60. Pseudo-Methodius, *Apocalypse*, pp. 36–56 (Ishmaelite conquest), 56 ('βασιλεὺς Ἑλλήνων ἤτοι Ῥωμαίων'), 58–60 (defeat of Ishmaelites).
61. Ibid., pp. 60–2 (nations of the North), 62–8 (Antichrist).

The other major prophetic tradition that influenced Western Christianity was the one founded by the twelfth-century Calabrian abbot and biblical exegete Joachim of Fiore. Joachim's vision of world history was based on the Trinity: first the age of the Father, then that of the Son, and finally that of the Holy Spirit. The ultimate transformation of the world would depend on 'spiritual men'; he looked forward not to a Last World Emperor but to a spiritual leader who might be described as an Angelic Pope. Indeed, the total and final defeat of the Roman Empire by rulers from the East was to be a proper punishment for its moral corruption. Like Pseudo-Methodius, Joachim was influenced by the role of Islam in contemporary political events: in this case, the campaigns of Saladin against the Crusaders, culminating in the humiliating defeat of the latter in 1187 and the surrender of Jerusalem. Unlike Pseudo-Methodius, Joachim based his prophecies on citations from a wide range of biblical texts. Above all he concentrated on the Book of Revelation, with its sevenfold patterning involving the book of the seven seals (Rev. 5–6) and the beast with seven heads (Rev. 13: 1–10); these were made to correspond with a sequence of historical oppressors and tribulations. The exact equivalences lined up by Joachim vary from work to work, but Muslim elements are always present. In one work the 'Saracens' are the pale horseman, Death, unleashed on the world under the fourth seal (Rev. 6: 8); in another work the fifth period, represented by the beast's fifth head, is that of persecution by 'Meselmutus', to which the explanation is added that 'the Moors are commonly called Meselmuti' (a garbling of some version of the Arabic word 'muslim'); and the sixth head of the beast is also identified as Saladin.[62] Ominously, while he notes that the Saracens have so far absorbed under their rule only Orthodox people, not Roman Catholics, Joachim adds: 'this will be so until that time which is near, of which the psalmist said: "Thou makest darkness, and it is night: wherein all the beasts of the forest do creep forth." '[63] Nevertheless, the spiritual Church will eventually prevail, and there will be rule by the saints on Earth for a thousand years until, at the end of history, Satan inspires 'the nations which are in the four quarters of the earth, Gog and Magog' (Rev. 20: 8) to attack the

---

62. Joachim of Fiore, *Liber de concordia*, p. 300 (fourth seal); Reeves, *Influence of Prophecy*, pp. 8 ('Mauri qui vulgo dicuntur Meselmuti'), 305 (Saladin).
63. Joachim of Fiore, *Liber de concordia*, p. 367 ('Erit autem hoc usque ad tempus illud quod prope est, de quo dicit psalmista: "Posuisti tenebras, et facta est nox, in ipsa pertransibunt omnes bestie silue" ' [Ps. 104: 20]).

Church; they will be destroyed by fire from heaven, ushering in the Second Coming, the resurrection of the dead, and the Last Judgment.[64]

In the uses that could be made of them, the most obvious difference between these two major traditions was that one was pro-imperial, while the other saw the Roman Empire and its successor, the Holy Roman Empire, as part of the problem, not the solution. Yet the two shared enough common material to make it possible for later writers to combine them in various ways. For example, the fourteenth-century Franciscan Jean de Roquetaillade (Johannes de Rupescissa) foretold that whereas Antichrist would appear in the West as a cruel and heretical Emperor, the King of France would take over the Holy Roman Empire and cooperate with the Angelic Pope: 'by means of those two, the whole world will be restored, and they will destroy the entire religion and tyrannical power of Muhammad.'[65] Here was a Joachimite vision which, conveniently, could still give the French King a role equivalent to that of the Last World Emperor. An enduring tradition of French Joachimism developed along these lines, with the King of France destined by sacred history either to eliminate the Holy Roman Empire or to extend his rule over it; Guillaume Postel would still be arguing passionately in this way in the mid-sixteenth century.

Not surprisingly, the anti-Muslim and anti-Ottoman aspects of these prophetic traditions became much more prominent in the decades after the fall of Constantinople. A group of Dominicans compiled a collection of prophecies, printed as *Tractatus de Turcis* in 1474, which cited Joachim himself and various writers in the Joachimite tradition. Statements made by one of Joachim's followers, the Dominicans gloomily noted, 'seem to speak very explicitly of some devastation of Italy that will be brought about by the Turks'. Nevertheless, they were confident that the destruction of the Muslims would soon be accomplished by a Christian king—not the Holy Roman Emperor, but perhaps Mathias Corvinus, King of Hungary.[66] Six years later the Italian Dominican Annius of Viterbo published a commentary on the Book of Revelation which, in a similar vein, predicted the defeat of the Muslims and the unification of all Christian Churches, to be achieved by a pope and a temporal ruler—not the emperor—working in harmony together. 'The pope and the future prince', he wrote, 'will induce those

---

64. Joachim of Fiore, *Sull'apocalisse*, pp. 322–4.
65. Cited in Reeves, *Influence of Prophecy*, p. 323 ('per illos duos totus orbis reparabitur et ab eis destruetur tota lex et tyrannica potentia Mahometi').
66. Ibid., pp. 335–7 (p. 335(n.): 'expressissime videntur loqui de quadam devastacione Ytalie fienda per Turcos').

Christians who live under the Turks to rebel against them, and will forbid merchants to trade with them'—the latter point suggesting an anti-Venetian agenda. That text would undergo multiple reprintings.[67] And in 1481, just a year after Annius's initial publication, the first printing took place of George of Hungary's account of conditions under Ottoman rule; this work, which would enjoy a wide circulation throughout Europe, cited Joachim more than once and ended with a chapter entitled 'This is Abbot Joachim's opinion about the sect of Muhammad.' Here a long quotation was given from Joachim's commentary on Revelation, comparing Islam with both the seven-headed beast of Revelation 13 and the fourth beast in the vision of Daniel (Dan. 6: 7–26). Joachim wrote that Muslim rule was worse than all the other oppressions suffered by Christians; and of Muhammad himself he declared: 'just as Moses, the lawgiver, preceded Christ by a long time, so that purveyor of lies prepared the way for Antichrist.'[68] George of Hungary was also a Dominican, having joined the order immediately after his captivity; it is clear that the Joachimite prophetic tradition, which had been strongest among the Franciscans in previous centuries, now had this order in its grip. Another Dominican, the fiery preacher Girolamo Savonarola, addressing the people of Florence in the 1490s, also outlined a Joachim-derived sequence of future events, including the recovery of Jerusalem and the conversion of the Muslims.[69] But there were plenty of prophetic writers outside the ranks of the friars. One of the most influential was the court astrologer to the Emperor Frederick III, Johann Lichtenberger, whose *Prognosticatio* of 1488 combined Pseudo-Methodian and Joachimite themes, focusing not on Frederick but on his son Maximilian as the prince who would defeat the Muslims and begin the process of spiritual *renovatio* on Earth. Again, this work would prove highly popular, being reissued at least 42 times in Latin, German, Italian, and French during the following quarter-century.[70]

67. Annius, *Glosa*, ch. 18, sig. e3v ('pontifex et princeps futur[us] inducent christianos existe[n]tes sub turcis ad rebellione[m] et mercatoribus prohibebu[n]t com[m]ercia cu[m] eis'). The first edn. (1480) was produced at Genoa, with the government of that republic among the dedicatees; hence, no doubt, the anti-Venetian animus. Later edns. were at Louvain (c.1481), Gouda (c.1481–2), Nuremberg (c.1485), Cologne (1482; 1497; 1507), and Paris (n.d.). On this text see also Deny, 'Les Pseudo-prophéties', p. 216, and Reeves, *Influence of Prophecy*, p. 354. Annius is now best known for his forgeries of ancient historical texts.

68. George of Hungary, *Tractatus*, pp. 173, 306 (citations), 416 ('Hec est opinio abbatis Joachim de secta Mechometi'), 418 ('Ut enim Moyses legislator [et] longo ante precessit Christum, ita et iste lator mendacii parauit itinera Antichristi').

69. Reeves, *Influence of Prophecy*, pp. 435–6.

70. Ibid., pp. 347–52; Kurze, *Johannes Lichtenberger* (pp. 81–6: list of edns.). On Lichtenberger's large influence in Italy see Fava, 'La fortuna', and Niccoli, *Prophecy and People*, pp. 137–8.

This whole style of thinking would remain a formative influence on many people's ideas about Islam and the Ottoman Empire, not only throughout the sixteenth century but also, where some religious writers were concerned, well into the seventeenth. In one significant way the implications for the Ottoman Empire became stronger in the sixteenth century: after Selim I's campaign against the Mamluk Sultanate of Egypt and Syria in 1516–17 the Holy Places fell under Ottoman rule, so that any scenario involving the enactment of eschatological events in Jerusalem necessarily required the defeat of the Ottoman sultan. The Reformation period would generate a heightened sense of religious crisis, on both sides of the confessional divide, with more frequent recourse to identifications of Antichrist, and more common assumptions that the tribulations experienced by the faithful (of whichever variety) were signs that the Last Days were rapidly approaching. In this whole pattern of thought and feeling, fear of Ottoman power found its own natural place. For the Ottoman Empire was to be seen not only as a threat in ordinary, temporal terms, but also as a special kind of infidel power endowed with a peculiar, God-given significance. In the minds of any Western Christians who were touched by the prophetic tradition, Islam could not be regarded with the degree of religious indifference that might have been applied to Hinduism or Buddhism, had knowledge of those been generally available. Islam, together with its apparent political embodiment, was identified as having a special—and negative—role to play in God's plan for the entire history of humankind.

THREE

Habsburgs and Ottomans
'Europe' and the conflict of empires

In September 1520 Sultan Selim I was succeeded by his highly ambitious and energetic son, Süleyman I, who would be called Süleyman 'Kanun', the law-giver, by his subjects, and would become famous in the West as Süleyman 'the Magnificent'. Within less than a year he seized the military stronghold of Belgrade, in northern Serbia; in 1522 he besieged and conquered the island of Rhodes, expelling the military-religious Knights of St John; four years later he inflicted a crushing defeat on the Kingdom of Hungary at the Battle of Mohács, where the young King Lájos met his death; and by 1529 Süleyman's troops were at the gates of Vienna. All this in less than one decade—and there were many decades of East–West conflict to follow in the contested territories of central Europe.

The Sultan's counterpart, on the Western side, was Emperor Charles V. Thanks to good fortune and the dynastic planning of his Habsburg grandfather, Emperor Maximilian I, Charles became not only Duke of Burgundy (1506) and King of Spain (1516) but also Archduke of Austria (1519). In the summer of 1519 he was elected Holy Roman Emperor, succeeding his grandfather; two years later he passed the Archduchy of Austria to his younger brother Ferdinand. Thereafter, while Charles's overall responsibility for the Empire was not in doubt, it was Ferdinand who prepared and directed operations in central Europe. Charles's own anti-Ottoman interests were directed primarily at the 'Barbary corsairs' of North Africa, who were allies and nominal subjects of the Sultan. After the disaster at Mohács Ferdinand's involvement in conflict with the Ottoman Empire would become much more intense, as he tried to impose himself on Hungary as its new king; the Hungarian nobility chose instead the Prince of Transylvania, who was forced by Ferdinand's military intervention to turn to Süleyman for support. Ferdinand's renewed efforts to claim Hungary after that Prince's death in 1540 would lead to a full-scale Ottoman occupation of most of the kingdom.

In all the standard histories of the German and Austrian lands, this is the period most strongly associated with the famous 'Türkenfurcht', the general 'fear of the Turks' or 'Turkish terror'. The term refers not so much to the kind of apocalyptic religious feeling discussed in the previous chapter, as to a widespread concern about the military and political threat posed by Ottoman expansion. That some people had reasons to be fearful is certainly true: the southern flanks of the Austrian territories (Styria, Carinthia, and Carniola) had been subject to frequent Ottoman raids since the late 1460s. But modern scholarship has found that the extent of this raiding was significantly exaggerated at the time; in one case, a famous repulsed Ottoman attack of 1492 (involving the death of 10,000 Ottoman soldiers and the liberation of 15,000 Christian captives), it seems that the entire episode was retrospectively invented by local worthies keen to burnish their credentials as Habsburg loyalists.[1] As for a general opinion that the Sultan's armies posed an existential threat to all the Christian lands of central or Western Europe: in a period when almost any powerful state, Christian or non-Christian, was inclined to extend its territories at the expense of its neighbours, some fear of further Ottoman expansion was no doubt reasonable, especially in view of the sheer quantities of manpower and resources that Süleyman could muster. In practical military terms, however, Ottoman campaigning in this period still involved a long march out from Istanbul or Edirne in the spring and a long march back in the autumn, with the time available for active campaigning becoming shorter and shorter, the further the army travelled; this was already beginning to set some limits on what was feasible. But the most important mental adjustment that modern readers need to make is to rid themselves of the automatic assumption that in every case a passive Western power was experiencing a wave of gratuitous attacks by a remorselessly aggressive Eastern one. Such a view ignores the fact that after 1526 a two-sided contest was taking place for the control of the Hungarian territories; for Süleyman's campaigns of 1529 and 1532 were, to a large extent, responses to the Habsburg expeditions into Hungary of 1527 and 1530.[2]

---

1. Neumann, 'Die Türkeneinfälle', esp. pp. 88–98 (invented); Jug, 'Turški napadi', pp. 11–12 (exaggerated); Vilfan, 'Die wirtschaftlichen Auswirkungen', pp. 177–82 (exaggerated).
2. For a valuable corrective to the standard assumptions see Höfert, *Den Feind beschreiben*, esp. pp. 51–5.

Already under Maximilian I, efforts had been made by the Empire's publicists to create a sense that the Habsburg Emperor acted, vis-à-vis the Ottomans, as representative or champion of the whole of Christian Europe. Maximilian encouraged such rhetoric because he needed the Imperial Estates to grant him a 'Türkensteuer' or 'Türkenhilfe', a subsidy against the Ottomans—not least because he was spending so much, in the last two decades of his reign, on intra-Christian warfare in northern Italy. (The fact that in 1510 he tried to initiate negotiations for a Habsburg–Ottoman alliance against Venice was, understandably enough, kept as secret as possible.)[3] Under his successors Charles and Ferdinand, the rhetoric of defending Christendom or Europe—the two being still rather interchangeable terms— was ramped up further, not only because Süleyman was much more active on the central European front than his father had been, but also, after 1526, for one particular reason: Hungary was not part of the Holy Roman Empire. When a component of the Empire was under attack, strong and simple arguments could be made to require the other Imperial territories to contribute to its defence; but this was not the case with the Hungarian lands, which were seen rather as presenting an opportunity for Habsburg dynastic self-aggrandizement. (So, for example, when Charles and Ferdinand pleaded with the Imperial Diet for money as the Ottoman army approached in 1532, Bavaria said that it would contribute only if German territories were attacked, not Hungarian ones.[4])

The Habsburg line about defending the more general entity of Europe found some eloquent proponents. In January 1543, for example, in the great hall of the University of Cologne, the Spanish humanist physician Andrés Laguna performed what he called a 'mournful declamation' in the form of an extended dialogue with a female figure identified as 'Europe'. (Elsewhere in the text the terms 'the whole Christian world' and 'the Christian commonwealth' were also used.) 'Miserable and pitiable, I am everywhere attacked by the same foreign and extremely barbarous enemy', she exclaimed, mourning the loss of 'her' cities of Constantinople, Salonica, Durrës, and Belgrade; at the end of her speech she gave high praise to Ferdinand, 'who, with his unceasing, tireless virtue, seeking to break the forces of my enemies

3. Ibid., pp. 106–7 (publicists), 108 (negotiations). On the use of print media to gain support for Maximilian's anti-Ottoman policies see also Füssel, 'Die Funktionalisierung'.
4. Aulinger, 'Kundschafterberichte', p. 169.

and to give me sweet freedom, leaves nothing unattempted'.[5] In the latter part of the sixteenth century, again, serious efforts were made by the Habsburgs to produce political messages along these lines, directed largely at the political classes represented in, or connected with, the Imperial Estates, and emphasizing both the severity of the Ottoman threat and the importance of their own role as defenders of a larger Christian–European community.[6]

Political arguments of this kind were not all directed from above. There were many writers and intellectuals who, whether from dismay at Ottoman successes or from a desire to gratify important political patrons (or a combination of the two motives), were keen to promote the anti-Ottoman policies of Charles V and Ferdinand I. In 1529 the classical scholar Juan Ginés de Sepúlveda, who had recently been appointed historiographer to Charles V, published a short 'exhortation' to war against the Ottomans, addressed to the Emperor. He painted a lurid picture of the misery and oppression suffered by those who lived under the Sultan's rule, and argued that an offensive campaign, aimed at conquering the entire Ottoman Empire, would be both justified and feasible.[7] Early in the following year, the humanist writer Paolo Giovio met Charles V at the long-delayed coronation of the Emperor by Pope Clement VII in Bologna; Giovio was working as an adviser to the Pope. On his return to Rome Giovio began collecting information on the Ottoman Empire, in order to compile a treatise that would inform Charles and his counsellors about the enemy and encourage them to go on the offensive. This was his *Commentario de le cose de' Turchi*, completed in early 1531, published—with a dedication to the Emperor—in 1532, and frequently reprinted thereafter. (There were at least 23 editions by the end of the century.)[8] Also in 1531, the German humanist scholar and natural philosopher George Agricola (Georg Pawer or Bauer), who had recently been appointed historiographer to Prince Maurice of Saxony, published a short work dedicated to Ferdinand I, *Oration, Anred und Vermanung*; seven years later he issued a slightly enlarged Latin translation of it, under the title

5. Laguna, *Europa heautentimorumene*, pp. 77 ('totus Christianus orbis', 'Respublica Christiana'), 120 ('declamatio lugubris'), 146 ('undique ab externo eodemque immanissimo hoste misera atque miseranda concutiar'), 156 ('qui heroica atque indefessa uirtute cupiens meorum hostium uireis confringere meque in dulcem libertatem asserere...nihil intentatum relinquit'). On this Habsburg propaganda line see also Prosperi, 'Un'Europa' (emphasizing its use against France).
6. Vocelka, 'Das Türkenbild', esp. pp. 23–4; Vocelka, *Die politische Propaganda*, esp. pp. 84–90, 239–79.
7. Sepúlveda, *Ad Carolum V.*, esp. sigs. a3v–a6r (misery), c2v–c4v (offensive campaign).
8. Giovio, *Commentario*, p. 64 (editions); on the background to its composition see Price Zimmermann, *Paolo Giovio*, p. 121.

Oratio de bello adversus Turcam suscipiendo. He set out a range of arguments in favour of making war on the Ottomans, emphasizing—like Sepúlveda—the misery of life under their rule, commenting proudly on the resources and warlike qualities of the Germans, and invoking divine providence as the ultimate guarantee against defeat by infidel forces. Nor did this scholarly man, who had never been on a battlefield in his life, forbear to give detailed advice about how to deploy infantry and artillery to counter the Ottomans' military tactics.[9]

To some extent these three writers were following in the footsteps of another eminent humanist, the Valencian scholar Juan Luis Vives. In October 1526, soon after he had heard the news of the disaster at Mohács, he had written a pamphlet in the form of a dialogue in the underworld about the 'quarrels of Europe' and the Ottoman war: *De Europae dissidiis et bello turcico dialogus*.[10] For Vives, the defeat of the Hungarian army came as a terrible admonition about the weakening of Christendom by its own internal conflicts—most recently, the wars in northern Italy which had led to the defeat and capture of the King François I of France by the Emperor at the Battle of Pavia in 1525, and the 'Peasants' War' in Germany later that year. There was thus a strongly homiletic and moralizing element in his argument: war against the Ottomans would never be successful unless Christians reformed their own behaviour and learned to live in peace among themselves. (This chimed with the well-known views of another great humanist, Erasmus, which will be discussed in the next chapter.)

One of the speakers in the dialogue, however, was the great Roman military commander Scipio Africanus, and to him Vives gave a series of positive arguments—structured in accordance with the standard humanist rhetorical triad of 'just', 'profitable', and 'easy'—for going on the offensive against the Ottomans: it is just to fight the Turks because they seek to destroy Christianity; there will be rich booty; Ottoman soldiers who were forcibly converted to Islam will welcome the chance to rejoin the Christian faith, and Asians have always lost their wars against Europeans, as is demonstrated by the Trojan War, the conquests of Alexander the Great, and the Roman campaigns in the Near East, because Asians are by nature soft,

---

9. Agricola, *Oratio*, esp. sigs. A4v–B2v (misery), B2v–B4v (Germans), C1v (providence), D1v–D2r (tactics); see also the discussion in Pujeau, '*Conseils*', pp. 304–8.
10. On the background to its composition see Margolin, 'Conscience européenne', pp. 107–9.

timorous, and unsuited to warfare.[11] These arguments are not opposed by
any of the other speakers; but the final word is given to Tiresias, the ancient
prophet and personification of wisdom, who concludes that the Christian
Europeans must reform themselves before they can take on the Ottoman
foe. 'The only weaponry, the only fortress of Christians is the protection of
their Christ. If He accepts them, there is no nation or people that will be
able to conquer them or harm them. But if He rejects them, what else can
they become but prey? So let them say prayers to Christ, begging Him for
peace and pardon.'[12] Given this conclusion, and the open, dialogic nature of
the work, commentators have described this either as an essentially 'pacifist'
text or as one that yields no clear message.[13] Yet Vives can surely be credited
with setting up a very particular structure of argument, in which the judgment of Tiresias correctly expresses the fundamental nature of the need for
moral and spiritual reform, but the arguments of Scipio are also allowed to
be valid. The recommendations of the latter would work, however, only if
the requirements of the former were satisfied. Thus, in a subtle rhetorical
manoeuvre, those worldly people—the majority of readers, perhaps, and
very probably most of the political class—who would be motivated primarily by Scipio's promises of earthly success were given self-interested reasons
for adopting an intrinsically non-self-interested programme of moral and
religious renewal.

In the texts by Sepúlveda, Giovio, and Agricola, this Erasmian emphasis
on the prior need for reform was toned down (Christian disunity was
treated more as a problem of politico-military organization than as a sin that
must be purged) or removed altogether, while the arguments of Vives's
Scipio were further developed. All were in favour of offensive war. Sepúlveda
proposed a conquest of the entire Ottoman Empire, both European and
Asian.[14] Giovio mentioned that 'some people' preferred to fight a defensive
war, for logistical reasons, but he said that that advice would be valid only
if—as was patently not the case—all Christian princes were willing to

11. Vives, *De Europae dissidiis*, sigs. E6r–F1r. The argument of a previous speaker, Basilius Colax,
that war should be undertaken for glory (sig. E5r), was rejected.
12. Ibid., sig. F3r ('vnica Chr[ist]ianorum arma, solum praesidium...est Christi sui tutela. si is eos
recipiat, inuicti, inuiolabiles cunctis erunt nationibus ac gentib[us]. sin rejiciat, quid aliud fuer-
int, quam praeda?...Pacem & veniam a Christo peta[n]t, ac prece[n]t'). 'Peace' here means
intra-Christian peace.
13. See for example Margolin, 'Conscience européenne' (pacifist); Colish, 'Vives on the Turks'
(no clear message).
14. Sepúlveda, *Ad Carolum V.*, sigs. c2v–c3r.

contribute their forces as soon as news arrived of an Ottoman attack.[15] And
for Agricola the traditional defensive policy of building fortresses on the
frontier was 'useless'; either the forts were small, and could be overrun, or
else they had to be massive and well stocked, in which case their expense,
over time, would be ruinous.[16] In their attempts to boost confidence in the
chances of success, both Sepúlveda and Agricola renewed Vives's arguments
about the inferiority of Asian people, emphasizing the successes of Greeks and
Romans over Persians and other Asiatics, and dismissing Asian men as 'soft' and
'unwarlike'. For good measure, the weapons and armour of the Europeans
were also said to be greatly superior to those of the Ottoman troops.[17]
It followed that the victories achieved hitherto by the Ottomans must be
attributed to luck, or cunning, or the strategic disunity of the Christians.

On this point, however, a very different note was struck by Paolo Giovio.
Alone among these authors he emphasized those ways in which the
Ottoman troops were not merely as good as the Western ones, but actually
superior to them. Writing about the Janissaries (the Sultan's standing army
of infantry), he observed that they were promoted on the basis not of
patronage but of pure merit—'which makes them become so valiant, as
they have always turned out to be on the battlefield'. He also noted that in
their camps they lived 'in unbelievable tranquillity and concord'; the reason
for this was that 'The Ottomans manage military discipline with such justice
and severity that one can say that they exceed that of the ancient Greeks
and Romans... every slightest offence is punished with death.'[18] Here by
'military discipline' he just meant the prevention of violence, theft, and
other wrongdoing among the ranks. But the term could have a wider meaning, concerning the whole body of teaching or training in military matters;
and it was evidently with that sense in mind that Giovio wrote: 'this troop
of Janissaries is no different from the Macedonian phalanx with which
Alexander the Great subdued all the East, and it seems that the Ottomans,
as successors of the Empire, are also imitators of the military discipline of

15. Giovio, *Commentario*, pp. 171–2 (p. 171: 'alcuni').
16. Agricola, *Oratio*, sig. C2v ('inutile').
17. Sepúlveda, *Ad Carolum V.*, sigs. c1r (weapons, armour), c3r ('molles & imbelles'); Agricola,
    Oratio, sigs. C1r ('imbelles'), D1r (weapons, armour).
18. Giovio, *Commentario*, pp. 164 ('che è cagione de fargli riuscire sì valenti come sempre son
    riusciti nelle battaglie', 'con una incredibile quiete e concordia'), 169 ('La disciplina militare è
    con tanta giustizia e severità regulata da Turchi che si può dire che avanzino quella de gli
    antichi Greci et Romani... ogni minimo delitto si punisce con la morte').

the ancient kings of Macedonia.'[19] Summing up his findings, he wrote: 'The Ottomans are better than our soldiers for three reasons. The first is their obedience; one finds little of that on our side'. The second factor was their religious fatalism, which enabled them to go into battle without fearing death; and the third was their ability to live not on the pleasant victuals that Western soldiers required, but just on water and small amounts of rice. This degree of austerity was also typical, Giovio noted, of the soldiers of ancient Rome.[20] In a later text, written in 1538 to advise Charles V on how best to fight the Ottomans, Giovio did claim that the Christian armies had better infantry, better weapons, more skill in fortification and siege warfare, and general superiority at sea. But he also gave a slightly revised version of his three points about Ottoman superiority: 'they have huge numbers, they are extremely obedient, and they put up with more discomfort and hunger than our soldiers.' And he insisted even more strongly on the need for discipline (in the narrower sense) in the Christian ranks, demanding ferocious punishments for all breaches of order: any who told lies should be paraded naked through the camp, persistent blasphemers should have holes bored through their tongues, anyone who wounded another man was to have his left hand cut off, and any soldier who killed a colleague should be quartered alive.[21]

The main difference between Giovio's 1532 text and the writings of the other humanists was that his was not merely an exhortatory work, but an attempt to summarize existing knowledge about the Ottomans and their military and political organization; and there were many positive comments about the quality of the Ottoman military in the previous literature. As early as 1396 the Florentine humanist Coluccio Salutati had praised the Janissaries' training methods, which inured them to heat, cold, and poor food; Niccolò Sagundino had made similar comments about the Ottoman system of training; George of Hungary had remarked on the admirable peace and silence that prevailed in their armies; and Giovanni Albino, writing in the 1490s about the Ottomans' Otranto campaign of 1480–1, noted the extraordinary

19. Ibid., p. 165 ('né altro é questa banda de Iannizzeri che la falange macedonica con la quale Alessandro Magno debellò tutto il Levant, e par che li Turchi come successori dell'Imperio siano ancora imitatori della disciplina militare de gli antichi re di Macedonia').

20. Ibid., pp. 169–70 (p. 169: 'Sono li Turchi per tre ragioni migliori de nostri soldati: prima per l'obbedienza, qual poco si trova fra noi').

21. Giovio, 'Consiglio', pp. 91 ('sono gran moltitudine, son di grandissima obedienza, et soffrono più disagi, & la fame, che i nostri soldati'), 92 (better infantry etc.), 99 (discipline, punishments). On the background to this text see Pujeau, *L'Europe et les Turcs*, pp. 207–8.

obedience and efficiency of the Ottoman forces, and exclaimed: 'given such discipline ('disciplina'), no one should be surprised that their rule over Asia was consolidated so quickly.'[22] The historian of Venice Marcantonio Coccio, known as Sabellicus, included a rhapsodic passage on the qualities of the Ottoman soldiery in his widely read *Enneades* of 1498. 'Nothing about these people is more to be wondered at than the speed with which they act, their constancy when in danger, and their obedience to their commands', he wrote. Their encampments were free of all noise, tumults, and conflicts; during the night they would even allow captives to slip away rather than disturb the silence of the camp by raising the alarm. 'In short: of all the people in the world, these are the ones that go to war in the proper way.'[23]

To an informed reader in the early sixteenth century, then, the idea that the Ottoman military was peculiarly well disciplined and effective was already familiar. Such a person would have discounted claims that the Ottoman soldiers were 'soft' Asiatics, not only because the evidence of their prowess disproved it, but also because it was known that the Janissaries themselves, and many of the other troops fighting alongside them, were Europeans.[24] But what was more unusual about Giovio's account was his emphasis on the idea that the Ottomans were 'imitators' of ancient military techniques. A few early writers had said something similar; Coluccio Salutati had remarked that their 'customs, life and institutions' resembled those of 'the mighty Romans', and Andrea Biglia, in his manuscript treatise written in the early 1430s, went so far as to portray the Turks as inheritors of Hellenic civilization and classical virtue.[25] Yet such linkages were rarely made until Giovio's work conveyed the idea to a European audience.

Thereafter, it quickly spread. The French traveller Nicolas de Nicolay, in a widely read description of the Ottoman Empire written in 1555 (but not published until 1567), borrowed Giovio's remark about the Turks being 'imitators of the military discipline of the ancient kings of Macedonia', before developing a further classical comparison by suggesting that the

22. Bisaha, *Creating East and West*, p. 56 (Salutati); Pertusi, 'I primi studi', p. 475 (Sagundino); George of Hungary, *Tractatus*, p. 222; Gualdo Rosa et al., eds., *Gli umanisti*, pp. 58–60 (Albino: 'Qua disciplina, et si Asiae imperium tam brevi coaluerit, nemini mirum esse debet').
23. Coccio, *Opera omnia*, ii, col. 1049 ('Sed nihil est quod in ea gente magis mirari possis, quàm celeritas in agendo, in periculis constantia, obseruatio imperij', encampments, captives, 'ut breuiter dicam, hi ex omni mortalium numero hodie legitimè militant').
24. Vives was aware of this fact, but dealt with it by saying that these soldiers, having been forcibly converted from Christianity, would melt away at the approach of a Christian army (*De Europae dissidiis*, sigs. E6v–E7r).
25. Bisaha, *Creating East and West*, p. 58 (Salutati); Meserve, *Empires of Islam*, pp. 169, 179 (Biglia).

Ottoman Empire was already beginning to parallel the decline of the Roman one. In 1560 the popular historian Francesco Sansovino wrote that the Ottomans had inherited the military discipline, obedience, and fortune (i.e. success) of the ancient Romans.[26] The focus of most military comparisons shifted from Macedonia to Rome: the report on the Ottoman Empire written by the Venetian bailo (representative in Istanbul) Marcantonio Barbaro on his return to Venice in 1573 remarked of the Janissaries that 'this infantry greatly resembles the ancient Roman legions', and a popular printing of his report would transmit this idea to a very wide audience.[27] In the latter part of the sixteenth century comparisons between Ottoman and Roman military practice became commonplace. They can be found, for example, in one of the letters of the Imperial diplomat Ogier Ghiselin de Busbecq (published in 1589): 'it was by confidence in their experience of arms, though with a training quite different from our system, that the Romans in ancient times brought their wars to a triumphant conclusion, and the same reason will account for the uniform successes of the Turks in modern days.'[28] Even after the outbreak of the 'Long' Ottoman–Habsburg war in 1593, when Western writers strained every sinew to prove that the Sultan could be defeated, such comparisons continued to be made. The classical scholar and moral theorist Justus Lipsius, in his book about the Roman army (1596), noted Ottoman–Roman parallels concerning military camps, punishments, and the use of shields, even though he protected his argument with the general dismissal: 'Away with you, Ottomans, with your Janissaries, who usurp a certain resemblance—though a false one—to the army of the ancients.'[29] Three years later the Venetian diplomat and political writer Paolo Paruta remarked, more wistfully, that 'in our age Christian rulers do not have a strong, well disciplined, well ordered army, maintained with permanent salaries, as the Ottomans do, and as the Romans did before.'[30] And in 1600 Scipione Gentili, professor of law at the University of Altdorf, published a comparison between Roman and Ottoman military practice, noting various similarities

26. Nicolay, *Dans l'empire de Soliman*, pp. 156 ('imitateurs en la discipline militaire des antiques rois de Macédoine'), 157–8 (decline); Yerasimos, *Hommes et idées*, p. 56 (Sansovino).

27. Albèri, ed., *Relazioni*, ser. 3, i, p. 305 ('questa fanteria s'assomiglia molto alle antiche legioni romane'); Ventura, ed., *Tesoro politico*, fo. 82r.

28. Forster and Daniell, *Life and Letters*, i, p. 224.

29. Lipsius, *De militia romana*, pp. 115, 228, 243–5, 246 ('Abite Turcae, cum Ianizaris vestris, qui imaginem aliquam vsurpatis militiae priscae, sed falsam').

30. Paruta, *Discorsi politici*, p. 615 ('Non hanno i Prencipi Christiani à questa età milita ferma, ben disciplinata, ben ordinata, & trattenuta con stipendij perpetui, comme hanno i Turchi, & come già hanno hauuto i Romani').

and singling out the Ottomans' imitation of Roman 'severitas': 'hence the discipline of the Janissaries, which is admired by all of us Christians.'[31]

To make particular comparisons on practical points was one thing, but to suggest that the Ottomans were acting as 'successors' of the Macedonian Empire, or that they had 'inherited' the qualities of the ancient Romans, was a different matter, potentially with more troubling implications. For it was thought that there were some larger Ottoman claims of imperial right, which might seem to be reinforced by the existence of underlying cultural or institutional continuities between the classical empires and the contemporary Ottoman one. As we have seen, soon after the fall of Constantinople Sagundino and Pius II had discussed the notion that the Sultans claimed to have inherited the rights of the Eastern Roman Empire; it was a worrying thought, and it did not go away. 'I have heard from trustworthy people', wrote Paolo Giovio about Süleyman the Magnificent in 1532, 'that he often says that the Empire of Rome and of the whole of the West belongs to him by right, as he is the legitimate successor of the Emperor Constantine, who transferred the Empire to Constantinople.'[32] More than sixty years later, during the Ottoman–Habsburg war (in which the Papacy was strongly involved in support of the Habsburgs), the political writer Scipione Ammirato would repeat this in an oration addressed to Pope Clement VIII: 'the Ottomans claim that, because of the unbroken, uninterrupted succession of the Empire in Constantinople, they are the true successors of Caesar, the founder of the Roman Empire, and so they declare that the Empire of Rome, and of Italy, belongs to them by right.'[33] And as late as 1612 the jurist Alberico Gentili (Scipione's more eminent brother) would still think it worth taking some trouble to refute this idea. 'As for the Ottomans', he insisted, 'they do not form the Roman Empire, nor do they retain its name... They took possession of part of the Roman Empire, but not of the Empire itself.'[34]

31. S. Gentili, *Orationes*, p. 45 ('Hinc illa, quam omnes Christiani miramur, disciplina Ianizerorum').
32. Giovio, *Commentario*, p. 156 ('Ho inteso da uomini degni di fede che spesso dice che a lui tocca di ragione l'Imperio di Roma e di tutto Ponente per essere legittimo successore di Costantino imperatore quale transferrì l'Imperio in Constantinopoli').
33. Ammirato, *Orazioni*, p. 104 ('pretendendo gli Ottomani per la succession dell'Imperio non mai spezzata, ne interotta in Constantinopoli di esser veri successori de Cesare fondatore del Romano Imperio, affermano di ragione appartenersi loro l'Imperio di Roma, & d'Italia').
34. A. Gentili, *De iure belli* I.23, p. 181 ('Atque ad Turcas quod attinet... non esse eos Romanum imperium, qui nec nomen Romani imperii tenent... De Romano imperio acceperunt, sed no[n] Romanum imperium').

Whether Sultan Süleyman himself placed much weight on these arguments is far from clear. One report from 1531 claimed that 'he detests the Emperor, and his title of *Caesar*, he, the Ottoman, causing himself to be called *Caesar*'; but it is hard to tell what legal claims, if any, lay behind this. The idea that Europe had formed part of the empire of Alexander the Great, which was now inherited by the Ottomans, and the suggestion that in conquering Constantinople the sultans had become successors to the Roman Empire, can be found in some Ottoman literary–historical works of the 1540s and 1570s. Yet before those texts were written, Ottoman imperial pretensions had gone, in any case, much further than that. Selim I, Süleyman's father, had used the title 'world-conqueror'. And among Süleyman's formal titles was 'Sultan of the Two Continents'; Ottoman geographers regarded Europe as one continent and Asia–Africa as the other, so this implied rulership over the known world.[35]

For Christian Europeans, the idea of an Ottoman drive for universal empire was more powerfully troubling than any apparent legal claims. In 1531 Archduke Ferdinand I wrote to his brother Charles V, pleading for more financial and military help, and warning that if Hungary fell the Ottomans would threaten the Holy Roman Empire, the rest of central Europe, and Italy: the Sultan was aiming 'to extend his lordship and to place the whole world under him'. More than forty years later, the Venetian bailo Marcantonio Barbaro would regard it as not unthinkable that the Ottoman Empire might become 'a universal monarchy'.[36]

These ideas resonated, not only because there was a long history of theorizing about universal monarchy in the medieval West, but also because the territories of the Habsburgs and the Holy Roman Empire, as united under the rule of Charles V and his brother, were themselves the closest thing that anyone had seen to a pan-European empire since the Roman period. And this empire was hugely augmented by Spanish possessions in the New World; so even after Charles divided his Austrian and Spanish domains between his successors in the 1550s, the Spanish Empire would still be seen as having global range and universal potential. Universal empire, or universal monarchy, was an idea positively promoted by some of the publicists

35. *Calendar of State Papers, Venice*, v, p. 620 (report by the Venetian ambassador to France, 8 May 1531, giving a phrase quoted by King François I from 'advices [*sc.* 'avvisi', news reports] from Constantinople'); Nyitrai, 'Third Period', pp. 164–6 (titles), 170–4 (literary–historical works).
36. Kohler, *Ferdinand I.*, pp. 211–12 (p. 212: 'de estender su señorio y poner a todo el mundo debaxo de sy'); Albèri, ed., *Relazioni*, ser. 3, i, p. 301 ('una monarchia universale').

and promoters of both Charles V and his son Philip II of Spain. Nor was this simply a matter of propagandistic phrase-making; proponents included intellectuals such as the canon lawyer Miguel de Ulçurrum and the Benedictine writer Gonzalo de Arredondo y Alvarado, as well as Charles's grand chancellor Mercurino Gattinara, who was his most influential counsellor in the early part of his reign. In 1522, for example, Gattinara was seriously advising the Emperor on how to attain 'monarchy of the world'.[37] And while such arguments usually had a religious character, they took place against a background of much broader acceptance, by writers with a classical training, of the whole idea of empire—modelling the victories of Charles V, actual or prospective, on those of the Roman Empire in its heyday.[38]

To those who entertained such ideas on the Habsburg side, then, talk of Ottoman desires for universal empire was not just empty phrase-making; it seemed to describe a possibility in the real world, and thus a genuine danger. But the implications could be more awkward than that. The Sultan's ambition to extend his empire ever further was easily denounced in moralistic terms, as an expression of the 'libido dominandi', the lust for rule, which Augustine had identified as a fundamental cause of human evil. Might not the same criticisms apply equally to the Habsburgs, if their own ambitions were ultimately on the same scale? Domingo de Soto, the influential theologian and moral-legal theorist, apparently thought so; in his *De iustitia et iure* he wrote that however great the empires of the ancient East may have been, or that of Rome, their justification for expansion—sheer power, the right of conquest—would not be good enough for a Christian emperor.[39] And the point was made repeatedly by French writers, in their constant struggle to undercut Habsburg pretensions. The French diplomat Guillaume du Bellay declared in 1536 that in his campaigns against the Ottomans Charles V was 'motivated only by a greed for glory, and by a rivalry which he and the Sultan seem to have taken up, each against the other, for the monarchy of the world'; in the following year King François I sent a formal message to the Estates of the Holy Roman Empire, claiming that Charles

---

37. See Bosbach, *Monarchia universalis*, esp. pp. 23–40 (medieval theorizing), 41–75 (Charles), 43 (Ulçurrum), 63–6 (Gattinara), 77–104 (Philip); Arredondo y Alvarado, *Castillo inexpugnable*, fos. 58r, 59r; Headley, 'Habsburg World Empire', p. 102 (1522 advice).
38. See Dandelet, *Renaissance of Empire*, esp. pp. 74–134.
39. Soto, *De iustitia* IV.iv.2 ('Vtrùm Imperator sit dominus orbis'), p. 282. He accepted the idea of an emperor of all Christians, but not of all the world; where the Ottoman Empire was concerned, however, he argued (p. 283) that such an emperor could claim those territories which had previously been Christian.

fought the Ottomans only out of a lust for power.[40] More than 50 years later, the French diplomat Arnaud d'Ossat would tell the Pope that the worst possible scenario would involve the King of Spain conquering other Christian states and then going to war against the Sultan, 'so that these two Turks, who agree in various matters and differ on nothing more than the external appearance of their religion, would share out Christendom between them, if not by agreement then at least *de facto*, enslaving it and making it captive'.[41] A doctrine of equivalence between the two forms of imperialism, Habsburg and Ottoman, also became commonplace among Protestant writers. Alberico Gentili, for instance, writing in 1598, expostulated: 'Wouldn't it be absolutely right for everyone to resist both the Ottomans there and the Spanish here, given that they are planning and working towards imposing their rule everywhere?'[42]

On balance, however, the idea that the Sultan was seeking world domination was more of an asset than a liability for Habsburg publicists. So formidable was the threat, it could be said, that only a Christian emperor endowed with the greatest possible power and authority would be able to overcome it. There was thus a duty, on the part of all other Christian Europeans, to unite under the leadership of the Habsburgs. Discussing in his *Commentario* (addressed to Charles V) the immense wealth and power of the Sultan, Paolo Giovio was content to accept the parallelism of the situation as a positive sign from God:

> just as Your Majesty has under your sceptre more kingdoms than any other Western emperor has ever had, so Süleyman's empire exceeds, in its power and extent, all those foreign kingdoms that are recorded in history; and it seems that God wishes to guide the affairs of the world towards the ancient form of monarchy in order to make Your Majesty, with a single victory, just like Caesar Augustus.[43]

40. du Bellay, *Double d'une lettre*, sig. D4v ('seulement meu de cupidite de gloire, & dune co[n]-tention quil semble que lesdictz Empereur, & Turcq ayent prinse lung contre lautre pour la monarchie du monde'); Bosbach, *Monarchia universalis*, p. 70 (François I).
41. Le Guay, *Alliances du Roy*, p. 112, citing a letter from d'Ossat in Rome, undated but probably from the period of his negotiation for the papal recognition of Henri IV, which was achieved in 1595 ('Tellement que CES DEUX TVRCS symbolisans en plusieurs choses, & n'ayans point plus grande difference entre eux, que l'APPARENCE exterieure de la Religion, se partageroient la Chrestienté entre eux, sinon par co[n]tract, au moins en effect, l'asseruissant & la captiua[n]t').
42. A. Gentili, *De iure belli*, p. 103 ('Turcis illinc, Hispanis hinc, meditantibus vbique dominatum, & molientibus, non obsisterent omnes iustissimè?'). On the Protestant argument, which lasted well into the 17th century, see Headley, '"Ehe Türkisch als Bäpstisch"'.
43. Giovio, *Commentario*, p. 158 ('sì come Vostra Maestà ha sotto il suo scettro più regni che nessuno altro Imperadore occidentale abia mai avuto, così Solimanno di potenza e d'amplitudine

Often there was a strong religious colouring to this argument; and such attitudes were not confined to theological writers sitting in their studies, being present in the general culture much more widely. In 1520, for example, responding to the news of Charles V's initial coronation as Holy Roman Emperor at Aachen, the town council of Barcelona issued a proclamation saying that he was another Charlemagne who would use their city to launch expeditions for the recovery of Jerusalem; he would defeat the Sultan, unite the eastern and western empires, unify all Christian Churches, and usher in the golden age.[44] Gonzalo de Arredondo y Alvarado, who dedicated his treatise to Charles, wrote that there were divine reasons why the empire of the world had been given to Rome, and that Charles's election as Holy Roman Emperor was also arranged by God. Noting that Spain was the best place from which to launch a crusade for the Holy Land, he then invoked the prophecies of Pseudo-Methodius: the Christians would defeat the Muslims, the 'King of the Romans' would rule, 'and there will be great tranquillity and peace on earth, the like of which there has never been before and will never be again'. Charles would defeat all the enemies of Christianity because, 'apart from the highest vicar of Christ [the Pope], your marvellous Celsitude is, according to the laws, lord of the world and prince of the whole globe.'[45] Similar exhortations and predictions were produced by many scholars and intellectuals, including the Franciscan scholar Pietro Galatino in 1524, Friedrich Nausea, the future Bishop of Vienna, in 1532, and Wolfgang Lazius, a professor of medicine and court historian to Ferdinand I, in 1547.[46]

Apocalyptic and prophetic writings continued to exert a powerful hold on the popular imagination during the sixteenth century. One of the most widely cited was the prophecy of a certain Antonio Torquato or Arquato, printed for the first time in 1534. The author to whom this work was attributed was apparently a Ferrarese astrologer of the late fifteenth century; but the text itself, which claimed to have been composed in 1480, was

d'Imperio avanza tutti quelli Re esterni di che se n'ha memoria per l'istorie e pare che Dio voglia condurre le cose dell'universo alla antica Monarchia per far Vostra Maestà con una sola vittoria, così in effetto come [u]n Cesare Augusto').

44. Headley, 'Habsburg World Empire', pp. 99–100.
45. Arredondo y Alvarado, *Castillo inexpugnable*, fos. 22r (Rome), 23r (election), 55r–v (crusade), 58r (Pseudo-Methodius: 'el rey delos romanos', 'y sera gran tra[n]quilidad y paz sobre la tierra la qual nunca fue antes ni sera despues semejable'), 59r ('despues del summo vicario de christo es v[ues]tra admirabile celsitud / segu[n] las leyes / señor del mu[n]do / y principe de todo el orbe'). He also cited Joachim da Fiore: fo. 56v.
46. Reeves, *Influence of Prophecy*, pp. 366–7 (Galatino), 369–72 (Lazius); Niccoli, *Prophecy and People*, pp. 186–7 (Nausea); Lerner, *Powers of Prophecy*, pp. 172–3 (Lazius).

clearly a later forgery, written in 1534 in order to bolster Charles V's prestige, especially in relation to his impending campaign for the conquest of Tunis.[47] For those who took the 1480 date at face value, the accuracy of some of Torquato's predictions would have felt quite electrifying: he said that the Ottomans would conquer Rhodes and Belgrade, that a great 'heresiarch' would arise in northern Europe, and that discord among the Europeans would become so severe that some Christians would even beg the Ottomans to help them—a stinging reference to the policy of François I. Anti-French animus was a powerful element in this work; the 1544 printing would bear, on its title page, an engraving of an imperial eagle with a cockerel ('gallus' in Latin, a standard symbol for France) in its claws. It predicted first the victory of the Emperor over France, and then an Ottoman civil war following the death of the Sultan, whereupon 'all Christians, with a single intention and a single action, will rapidly cross the sea . . . then you will see the Turks flocking to the Christian faith.'[48] So comforting was this text for the Imperial side that, after many later printings, it was reissued in 1591 by the writer on Ottoman history Joannes Leunclavius (Hans Löwenklau) in a new version, with predictions of an abortive Ottoman invasion of Germany to take place in 1594 or 1595, and the death of the Sultan dated 1596 at the latest. A Spanish version of the prophecy would be printed in Madrid as late as 1626.[49]

Examples could be multiplied of other prophecies in the Pseudo-Methodian and Joachimite traditions throughout this period: to give just one, in 1570 the Croatian scholar, encyclopaedist, and hermeticist Pavao Skalić wrote that the Muslims would conquer many Christian territories, including Italy, until a universal emperor arose who would restore unity to the Church, end all fighting, convert the Muslims, and recover the Holy Land.[50] A new development, however, in the middle part of the sixteenth century was the introduction of prophecies said to be current among the Ottomans themselves. In his advice for Charles V, written in 1538, Paolo

47. See Deny, 'Les Pseudo-prophéties', pp. 207–14; Cantimori, 'Note', pp. 344–6; Battaillon, 'Mythe', p. 453.

48. 'Torquato', *Prognosticon*, sigs 2v (begging Ottomans for help), 5r (Rhodes, Belgrade), 7v ('heresiarcha'), 9v (victory over France), 11r (death of Sultan), 11v (civil war, 'Christiani omnes vno animo vnóque impetu alacres mare transibunt . . . Tunc videbis Turcas ad fidem Christi conuolare'). This author's use of the term 'Europa' is probably also indicative of the line taken by pro-Habsburg publicists in the 1530s.

49. Leunclavius, *Historiae musulmanae*, cols. 842–4; Battaillon, 'Mythe', p. 455.

50. Skalić, *Miscellaneorum libri septem*, fo. 170r–v. On Skalić see Secret, 'La Tradition'; Čvrljak, *Filozofija*.

Giovio reported that among the Ottomans there was a belief, derived from a dream of Sultan Murad I, that Süleyman would be the last sultan. Cannily, Giovio concluded that the prediction, however bogus in itself, would prove self-fulfilling, because 'when they come to battle, most of their Muslim soldiers, convinced by this prophetic illusion, will fight half-heartedly.'[51] In some other cases the Ottoman prophecy, being so agreeable to Western hopes, was accepted with very little demur. What became the most famous prediction of that kind was the one reported by a former captive, Bartolomej Djurdjević, whose brief but influential accounts of life under the Ottomans were published in the 1540s. In his *Prognoma, sive praesagium mehemetanorum* (1545) he printed a prophecy, both in Turkish and in Latin translation, which declared that the Sultan would conquer the land of the infidel, including the 'red apple', and hold it for up to twelve years, after which he would be driven out by the sword of the Christians. There is other evidence that some such prophetic references to the 'red apple' did circulate among the Ottomans at this time; for them, the term seems to have meant the citadel of Buda at first, and then Vienna, though Djurdjević believed that it was a name for Constantinople. Bizarrely, however, the origins of the phrase are to be found in the prophetic work published by the Imperial astrologer Johannes Lichtenberger in 1488; it was in fact a reference to Cologne, the place where, according to Lichtenberger, the Ottomans would finally be defeated. The most likely explanation is that a version of this prophecy had been transmitted to the Ottoman world by Christian captives or renegades.[52] Retransmitted back to the West as an authentic 'Turkish prophecy' via Djurdjević's work, which was widely circulated in many editions and translations, it could only strengthen the view, already held by many on the Habsburg side, that some sort of divinely guided scenario was about to take place, with the Emperor playing a central role in it.

Writers who placed the two great empires, Eastern and Western, side by side in their accounts were often pursuing a theological–prophetic argument. But some wrote in reaction to such tendencies; and others adopted a more simply factual approach, as they marshalled the available information in order to make geographical and political comparisons. The French legal and political theorist Jean Bodin, in his very influential work on historiography, the *Methodus* (1566), ridiculed the popular interpretation of the vision of Daniel

---

51. Giovio, 'Consiglio', pp. 99–100 (p. 100: 'venendo à giornata il più de' loro Turchi, persuasi da questa profetica imaginatione, combatteranno con due cuori').
52. See Yerasimos, 'De l'arbre à la pomme', esp. pp. 170–9.

which, identifying Daniel's fourth and final empire as the Roman Empire, saw it as having a continuous subsequent history as the Holy Roman (or, as he called it, 'German') Empire. In one of the most outspoken appraisals of the greatness of the Ottoman Empire ever written in this period, he exclaimed:

> what has Germany to oppose to the sultan of the Turks?... This fact is obvious to everyone—if there is anywhere in the world any majesty of empire and of true monarchy, it must radiate from the sultan. He owns the richest parts of Asia, Africa, and Europe, and he rules far and wide over the entire Mediterranean and all but a few of its islands. Moreover, in armed forces and strength he is such that he alone is the equal of almost all the princes.[53]

Troubled by such comparisons, the Messinese astronomer and geographer Giuseppe Moleti wrote a treatise in 1580 comparing the extent of the Ottoman and Spanish empires (and other territories, such as those of the King of Abyssinia). People were convinced that the Sultan was 'the greatest ruler holding sway in the world today', but he was able to disprove this— thanks above all to the Spanish possessions in the New World. His calculations showed that whereas the Sultan ruled over 1,023,219 square miles, King Philip II's domains came to 7,266,160, 'from which, then, we can conclude that it is not the size of the Sultan's state, nor the prowess of his army and soldiers, nor his military science that makes him to be feared, but the fatal inclination of the heavens, or the will of God, which, as a penitence for our sins, makes him seem terrible, horrible, and invincible.'[54] In spite of those grim remarks, Moleti's work was clearly meant to fortify the resolve of those who were prepared to fight against the Ottomans; and it was in a similar spirit that the traveller, soldier, and geographer Filippo Pigafetta wrote a treatise in 1593, proving that the Roman Empire, at its height, had been much larger than the present-day Ottoman one.[55]

---

53. Bodin, *Method*, p. 292 (*Methodus* (I cite the 1572 edition, which incorporates some minor revisions by Bodin), p. 463: 'quid habet Germania quod principi Turcarum opponat?...patet hoc quidem omnium oculis. si enim est vsquam terrarum vlla maiestas imperij ac verae monarchiae, in eò profecto elucet. occupat enim opulentissimas Asiae, Africae & Europae partes, totóque mari mediterraneo & insulis omnibus, exceptis admodum paucis, latè regnat. armis autem ac viribus tantus est, vt vnus omnibus ferè Principibus par esse possit').

54. Biblioteca Ambrosiana, Milan, MS P 145 sup., item 4, fos. 2r ('il maggior Prencipe ch'hoggi nella Terra domina', 'da doue poi si potra credere non la grandezza dello stato del Turco, non la virtu del suo essercito et de suoi soldati, non la scienza militare sia quella che fà temerlo, mà ò fatal dispositione de' Celi, ò uoler Diuino per penitenza de nostri peccati fà parerlo spauentuole, horribile et inuincibile'), 3v (statistic), 6v (statistic). On this work see Revelli, 'Un trattato'.

55. Biblioteca Nazionale Centrale, Florence, MS II. II. 140 (formerly Magl. XXIV. 134), fos. 101r–112r: 'Che gli Imperatori Romani à q[ua]lche tempo ebbero Imperio di gran lunga

In 1590 Moleti's short treatise was published as an appendix to the Italian translation of a widely read French book (itself first printed in 1588), René de Lucinge's *De la naissance, durée et chute des estats*.[56] Lucinge himself did not attempt a quantitative comparison, but he did discuss the Spanish and Ottoman empires in a way that made it very clear that the latter was more coherent and better constructed. In a barely veiled criticism, he wrote that Philip II's empire (which, from 1580, included all Portuguese-ruled territories) was so scattered over Europe, Africa, Asia, and America that 'there is, in the fact that it is held together, more of a miracle than a sign of human planning and prudence. For, in truth, to rule so many peoples, so far removed one from another, different in their religions, customs, and languages, without ever moving from Spain—isn't that a heavenly achievement, not one of human wisdom and reason?' Whereas the Ottomans had shown themselves to be 'more judicious', allowing no motives of short-term advantage to tempt them into 'leaping forwards unwisely, or throwing themselves into any distant undertaking'. So, unlike the Spanish, 'they have marched step by step from country to country.' And that was the reason why they had enjoyed 'the good fortune of so many victories, the benefit of such great and rich conquests, and also the consequence that it is easy for them to maintain and preserve what they had acquired'.[57] Whether or not the Ottoman Empire was physically larger than the Spanish one, it remained a formidable power, with special strengths of its own—of which territorial coherence was just one—that had to be understood, if it was ever to be decisively defeated.

maggiore di Sultan Amorath hodierno Prencipe de turchi', dedicated to Grand Duke Ferdinand of Tuscany. A copy is in Biblioteca Ambrosiana, Milan, MS R 125 sup., fos. 67r–74r.

56. The translation was Lucinge, *Dell'origine* (fos. 93r–101v: Moleti text, attributed to 'Horatio Malaguzzi'). Moleti's work was later printed in the *Tesoro politico*: see Balsamo, '"Une parfaite intelligence"', pp. 311–12.

57. Lucinge, *De la naissance*, p. 106 ('il y a en cette conservation plus de miracle que de conseil et de prudence humaine. Car à la verité, regir tant et tant de peuples, et si esloignez l'un de l'autre, differents de religion, de meurs et de langues, sans se bouger toutesfois d'Espagne, n'est-ce-pas oeuvre celeste, non de sapience et de discours humain?', 'plus judicieux', 'sauter indiscretement, ou se jeter en aucune entreprise loingtaine', 'ils ont marché pied à pied de païs en païs', 'du bon heur de tant de victoires, le bien de si grandes et riches conquestes, la suitte aussi de la facilité de maintenir et conserver ce qu'ils avoyent acquis').

FOUR

Protestantism, Calvinoturcism, and Turcopapalism

Attempts by the Habsburg rulers to drum up support for warring against the Ottomans met, as we have seen, with scepticism and hostility of various kinds: reluctance on the part of some Germans to contribute to what they saw as Habsburg self-advancement; moralistic arguments about wars for empire; and more cynical attempts to equate Imperial or Spanish intentions with those of the Sultan himself. But the Habsburgs were not the only ones advocating anti-Ottoman warfare. The Papacy was also actively involved in such efforts during much of the sixteenth century—beginning with Alexander VI sending a papal legate to preach the crusade in the Holy Roman Empire in 1500–3, and continuing with Pope Leo X's strenuous attempts to organize a crusade in the period 1517–21. One might imagine that these initiatives, at least, would have escaped censure: the motive was patently altruistic—religious, indeed—and the call to arms came from what was generally regarded as the highest moral authority in Western Christendom. And yet the most powerful criticism, and the most momentous in its long-term effects, was directed at these papal efforts, not at the Imperial ones as such.

A moral and religious reaction against the intra-Christian warfare of the first two decades of that century set the tone. Various currents of thought and practice in Western Christianity contributed to such a reaction, including the Joachimist yearning for a 'renovatio' of the Church, to be introduced by a new kind of spiritual Christian, and the growing influence of pietistic movements of lay spirituality such as the Brethren of the Common Life. One person strongly influenced by the latter (though not at all by the former) was the Dutch humanist scholar Desiderius Erasmus. His *Enchiridion militis christiani* of 1503 presented, in the form of an advice book, an in-depth moral portrait of the good Christian, combining Stoic moral precepts with the even more demanding requirements of the Sermon on the Mount; its title, 'Handbook of the Christian Soldier', was resolutely metaphorical, as this exemplary Christian's life would involve a rejection of all the worldly motivations and qualities traditionally associated with war. In 1515 Erasmus published a greatly enlarged version of his collection of classical proverbial sayings, the *Adagia*. Here the entry under the saying 'Dulce bellum inexpertis' ('War seems sweet to those who have not experienced it') was a long and passionately argued essay on the evils of war. The main focus was on the waging of wars by Christians against their co-religionists; but anti-Ottoman warfare did not go unmentioned. 'To me', Erasmus wrote, 'it does not even seem recommendable that we should now be preparing for war against the Ottomans. The Christian religion is in a bad way, if it depends on this sort of defence. Nor is it consistent to make good Christians under these auspices. What is taken by the sword is lost by the sword.' If you want to 'win the Ottomans to Christ', he told his readers, you should display a blameless life and 'the wish to deserve well even from your enemies ... [and] let them hear that heavenly doctrine which is in accordance with this kind of life. These are the best arms with which to defeat the Ottomans.' Anyone who invoked religious motives for war was, in Erasmus's eyes, already suspect: 'we have cloaked our disease with respectable titles. I am really hankering after the riches of the Ottomans, and I cover it up with the defence of religion.'[1]

Within the next few years, this line of argument was developed further by Martin Luther. The call for spiritual and moral renewal on the Christian side remained the dominant theme, but Luther added two elements that were not present in Erasmus's essay: a strong, explicit criticism of the Papacy for its fundraising efforts, and an ominous invocation of the idea that the Ottomans were the 'scourge of God'. (In fact the first of these was also present in Erasmus's mind; in a private letter to a friend in 1517 he repeated, with barely veiled approval, the comments of Swiss friends who said that the Pope's recently announced crusade was just a pretext

---

1. Erasmus, *Adages*, pp. 344, 349 (emended) (*Adagiorum chiliades*, fos. 278v–279r : 'Mihi sanè ne hoc quidem adeo probandum uidetur, quod subinde bellu[m] molimur in Turcas. Male profecto agitur cu[m] religione Christiana, si illius incolumitas à talibus pendet praesidiis. Neq[ue] consentaneum est, his initiis bonos gigni Christianos. Quod ferro paratum est, ferro uicissim amittitur', 'Turcas ad Christum adducere', 'studiu[m] benemerendi etiam de hostibus ... audiant coelestem illam doctrinam, cum huiusmodi uitam congruentem. His armis optime subiuguntur Turcae', 'morbu[m] nostrum honestis titulis praeteximus. Inhio Turca[rum] opibus, & obtendo religionis defensionem'). On Erasmus's near-pacifism see Adams, *Better Part of Valor*, pp. 93–109.

for collecting money.[2]) The sale by papal representatives of 'indulgences', grants of remission of the penance that was due for sins, raised large sums from the Holy Roman Empire in the late fifteenth and early sixteenth centuries, and one of the commonest purposes proclaimed for the whole operation was the financing of war against the infidels.[3] But the practice of getting people to buy indulgences ran so contrary to Luther's vision of true Christianity based on faith, not works—here was a 'work' that seemed to involve no effort at all, other than spending money—that it became one of the main targets of the famous Ninety-Five Theses that he advertised for debate in 1517. Writing in defence of those theses in the following year, he complained of the Pope's foolish arrogance in thinking that he could drive away 'the Turks and Tatars and other infidels whom every single Christian knows to be the whips and rod of God.' Indeed, the Pope was one of 'many great people in the Church' who 'dream of fighting a war against the Sultan, that is, they plan to war against the punishment for iniquity and not against the iniquities, and to struggle against God, who says that He uses that rod to punish our sins, as we do not punish them ourselves'.[4] When Pope Leo X issued his bull of condemnation against Luther, *Exsurge domine*, in 1520, one of the heretical 'articles' he cited was that 'to war against the Ottomans is to struggle against God, who uses them to punish our iniquities.' With characteristic pugnacity, Luther quickly published a defence of all his articles of belief, including this one. It was, he wrote, an obvious statement of the truth, for two reasons. The first was that all anti-Ottoman attempts hitherto had ended in failure. And the second was the ignominious fact that for years Europe had been infested with 'impostors and Roman legates, so many times selling indulgences and licenses, most shamelessly, for an anti-Ottoman war'. Giving full rein to his rhetoric, Luther referred to these people as 'fiercer, more cruel, and more insatiable Turks', describing the Ottomans, in comparison, as 'the better Turks'.[5]

---

2. See Pippidi, *Visions*, p. 80.

3. See Winterhager, 'Ablasskritik'; Housley, *Crusading*, pp. 174–210.

4. Luther, *Resolutiones*, p. 535 ('Turcas et Tataros aliosque infideles quos esse flagella et virgam dei nemo nisi parum christianus ignorat', 'plurimi…magni in ecclesia nihil aliud somnient quam bella adversus Turcam, scilicet non contra iniquitates sed contra virgam iniquitates bellaturi deoque repugnaturi, qui per eam virgam sese visitare dicit iniquitates nostras, eo quod non visitamus eas').

5. Luther, *Assertio*, pp. 140–1 ('Praeliari adversus Turcas est repugnare deo visitanti iniquitates nostras per illos', 'impostores et legatos Romanos, toties ad Bellum Turchicum indulgentiis ac facultatibus impudentissime venditis', 'truculentiores, cruentiores, insatiabiliores Turcas', 'meliores Turcas').

Clearly Luther was tapping into some popular feelings here. Not only were the activities of the indulgence-sellers disliked by many, but there was also a long tradition of scepticism in the German lands about calls to fight the Ottomans. (As we have seen, as early as 1455 Enea Silvio Piccolomini had encountered complaints at the Imperial Diet about 'a fine trick to swindle the Germans of their treasure by proclaiming a crusade against the Ottomans'.[6]) Reluctance to go to war for Hungary was also strong in the 1520s—until the siege of Vienna in 1529 created a much more powerful feeling that the Empire itself was under attack. What is more, as Luther's doctrines spread during that decade, winning over some important rulers of German territories, a new religio-political dynamic developed in which the Protestant leaders sought a trade-off between their cooperation with the Habsburgs over the Ottoman issue and the granting of concessions on the religious question. So, for example, when the Imperial Diet met at Speyer in 1526, Charles V's recent refusal to call a council of the Church to discuss reform caused such hostility that a significant part of the Diet said they would not give Ferdinand the help against the Ottomans that he demanded, until the request for a council was granted; Ferdinand then promised a council within eighteen months—against his brother Charles's express instructions—and allowed them the freedom to decide the religious arrangements in their own territories in the mean while. (Only then, in late August, did they agree to send a force to fight the Ottomans in Hungary—too late to help the Hungarian army, which was destroyed on 31 August at Mohács.) The eighteen-month moratorium helped to enable the leading Protestant rulers, of Hesse and Saxony, to consolidate Lutheranism in their territories. And this was not the only such episode: similar trade-offs took place again in 1529, 1532, and 1540.[7] It would be an exaggeration to say that the success of the Reformation depended simply on the Ottoman threat; the most important factor was clearly the personal conviction and commitment of the German Protestant rulers. Yet the underlying dynamic here was not hard to see, and this did contribute to a desire, on the part of exasperated Catholics, to link Protestants with 'the Turk'. For Protestant writers and theologians, on the other hand, the fact that their cause benefited in some way from the Ottoman threat was a thoroughly inconvenient matter; various responses and reactions were possible, of which the easiest was to ignore it.

6. Above, p. 8.
7. See Fischer-Galaţi, *Ottoman Imperialism*, pp. 22–9 (1526), 32–3 (1529), 51–5 (1532), 80–2 (1540).

Martin Luther's thinking about anti-Ottoman warfare underwent a development of its own during this period. And although he seems not to have been influenced by tactical calculations about bargaining for concessions at the Diet, thoughts about the actual political situation did evidently play a role. Above all, he did not want to encourage in any way the idea that the Emperor—or any secular ruler—should use military force for a religious agenda, since such an agenda, as directed from Rome, might very soon have the Protestants in its sights. In late 1528 he wrote a treatise (published in the following year) on the question of anti-Ottoman warfare, *Vom Kriege widder die Türcken*. Referring at the outset to his controversial 'article' of 1520, he explained rather defensively: 'above all, what concerned me was that people were proposing to fight against the Ottomans in the name of Christ, which is clean contrary to Christ's teaching.' This did not mean, he insisted, that Christians were forbidden absolutely to take up weapons in the service of their ruler.[8] (In recent years Luther had been obliged to make this point explicitly, in order to distinguish his position from that of radical Anabaptists.[9]) He continued to argue that the primary response of any Christian should be 'penitence, tears, and prayers'; the Sultan was so powerful that only a 'miracle' from God could ensure his defeat, and the Germans would not qualify for such divine intervention until they improved their spiritual state. Nevertheless, if the Imperial territories were attacked, the Emperor could respond by waging a defensive war. But he should do so neither as a crusade, nor for the purpose of converting the Muslims, nor for any worldly motive beyond the sole legitimate one of defending his subjects. Here Luther disagreed openly with a significant part of the standard humanist position, insisting that all the traditional earthly incitements to warfare—glory, plunder, territory—must be strictly excluded.[10]

His calls for moral and spiritual purification, on the other hand, did represent an overlap between Luther's views and those of pious humanists such as Juan Luís Vives and Desiderius Erasmus. When the latter published his own 'most useful advice' on waging war against the Ottomans in 1530, *Utilissima consultatio de bello Turcis inferendo*, major parts of the argument

---

8. Luther, *Vom Kriege*, pp. 111 ('uber alles bewegte mich, das man unter Christlichem namen widder den Türcken zu streiten für nam...Welchs ist stracks widder Christus lere'), 112 (not forbidden).

9. See especially the instructions he issued in 1528, *Unterricht der Visitatorn*, pp. 228–9. On the general development of Luther's justification of military service in the 1520s see Francisco, *Martin Luther*, pp. 71–4.

10. Luther, *Vom Kriege*, pp. 129 ('busse, weinen und gebet', 'wunderzeichen'), 130–1 (Emperor, motives).

chimed closely with Lutheran themes. The Ottomans have won victories not through their own virtue, he wrote, but because of our lack of it; we must not oppose them by acting on the same vicious motive—the lust for dominion—that drives them, and if we seek merely to conquer their state and rule it we shall become just like them.[11] Erasmus's scathing remarks in this work about the past history of papal fundraising for crusades aligned him quite closely with Luther: 'the money which was gathered remained, it is said, stuck to the hands of the popes, cardinals, monks, generals, and princes' and so on. Like the German reformer, he did allow the possibility of a just war against the Ottomans, so long as it was waged not for land or riches but for defence and the restoration of peace and tranquillity. The fact that—despite these various similarities—he directly criticized Luther in this text, for saying that it was wrong to oppose the Ottomans as they were a punishment from God, has sometimes been taken to be significant. (Erasmus's argument was that illness may also be visited on us by God, but that does not make it wrong to use a doctor.)[12] All it really indicates, however, is that Erasmus did not have a detailed knowledge of Luther's recent writings, relying instead mostly on the papal condemnation of the Protestant theologian's 'article', and on Luther's own defence of it.

Nevertheless there were some divergences in approach between these two works. The emphasis in Erasmus's text on the ultimate aim of peaceably converting the Ottomans—it was here that he described Muslims as 'semi-Christians', a point on which he would elaborate further in the 1533 edition of his *Adagia*—was quite distinctive, for example. And at a deep level the two authors had very different views of the relationship between temporal power and religion. Whereas Erasmus wrote that it was legitimate to fight the Ottomans in order to defend 'the tranquillity of the Christian community', Luther insisted that the Emperor did not and could not fight on behalf of Christendom as such; he was only a secular ruler, whose duty was to defend his particular subjects. An unyielding Augustinian, Luther distinguished sharply between the spiritual realm, under God, and the temporal realm, where secular power was used, albeit with divine sanction, for secular reasons—above all, for the control of those

---

11. Erasmus, *Utilissima consultatio*, pp. 38 (not through virtue), 52 (same motive), 62 (become like them).

12. Ibid., pp. 54–8 (Luther; p. 58: doctor), 64 ('Pecunia inquiunt collecta haesit in manibus pontificum, cardinalium, monarchorum, ducum ac principum'). For an exaggerated view, see Margolin, 'Erasme', pp. 24–5; for a more balanced one, see Giombi, 'La cristianità', pp. 198–9.

violent and criminal impulses that were inherent in fallen mankind. So
there could be no correlation between the 'Christian community' (which,
for Luther, would have meant the universal priesthood of all believers) and
the authority of any given ruler.[13]

One important corollary of this approach was a strong doctrine of non-
resistance to the secular authority. Romans 13: 1—'Let every soul be subject
unto the higher powers. For there is no power but of God: the powers that
be are ordained of God'—was, for Luther, always a key text. If the ruler
commanded a subject to commit sinful acts, the only proper response was
passive disobedience, refusing to commit the act and then accepting the
punishment for such refusal. Did this mean that if the Ottomans succeeded
in conquering German lands, the inhabitants should thereafter behave as
positively obedient subjects of the sultan—or at most, occasionally, as pas-
sively disobedient ones? Luther was understandably reluctant to draw that
conclusion in explicit terms, for all his early boldness in arguing that it was
wrong to oppose God's punishment. Once (in 1519) he did grasp the nettle
to the extent of saying that all existing Ottoman subjects should obey their
ruler as a divinely instituted authority.[14] The full implication, for those who
might be conquered in the future, must therefore have seemed hard to
avoid. Luther's close follower Johannes Brenz (Brentius), writing in 1531,
made the essential point almost inadvertently, while encouraging German
Protestants to serve their Catholic ruler Charles V in a defensive war against
the Ottomans. 'Even if the [Holy] Roman Emperor were personally a pure
heathen,' he wrote, 'all the people who belong to the Empire would still be
obliged to obey him in those matters which an emperor, *qua* emperor,
commands, and which are not against God.'[15] That point would surely apply
to the sultan too. Indeed, Protestants who were already facing persecution
in some Catholic territories could easily have thought that the Ottoman
government, which generally did not suppress Christian beliefs or practices
and had no overall policy of forced conversion to Islam, might be less likely
than some Western European ones to command things 'against God'. Luther
himself was clearly troubled by this, and in his 1528–9 treatise *Vom Kriege*

13. Erasmus, *Utilissima consultatio*, pp. 52 ('semichristianos'), 58 ('reipublicae christianae tranquillitas');
      Cargill Thompson, *Political Thought of Luther*, pp. 36–78, 116–17.
14. Buchanan, 'Luther and the Turks', p. 150 (1519).
15. Brenz, *Wie sich Prediger halten sollen*, sig. A2r ('wenn schon die person des Römischen Keysers
      eyn lauter heyde were / so sind doch alle / so ins reych gehören / schuldig / solchem Keyser
      vnterthenig zu seyn / in denen stücken / die ein Keyser als ein Keyser zu gebieten hat / vnd
      nicht wider Got sind').

widder die Türcken went out of his way to deny the possibility of leading a normal Christian life under Ottoman rule. 'Although some people praise the Sultan's rule on the grounds that he lets all people believe what they want, and merely wishes to be the temporal ruler, such praise is nevertheless untrue. For in fact he does not allow Christians to assemble together in public, and everyone is forbidden to acknowledge Christ publicly.'[16]

That point was made as part of a larger pattern of argument in Luther's writings in the years 1528–30, as he sought to find ways of demonstrating that the Ottoman Empire was not a normal temporal power operating on the ordinary principles of human motivation and behaviour; rather, he insisted, it was an unusually evil entity, animated by peculiarly anti-Christian feelings. He emphasized that the Sultan had no justification for offensive war, and was acting instead like a highway robber. What distinguished the Ottomans from other earthly powers, according to Luther, was that they were driven by Islam, a religion dependent on 'the sword'.

> For they are told by their law [*sc.* religion] that it is a good, godly work to rob and kill...For that reason it [*sc.* the Ottoman Empire] is not a godly, orderly authority like others, keeping the peace, protecting the pious, and punishing the wicked; rather, it is, as I have said, the sheer wrath of God, His rod and punishment meted on the unbelieving world.[17]

But although he repeated here his standard line about a punishment from God, Luther's sense of the significance of the Ottoman Empire in the divine scheme of things was undergoing a change. Early in this treatise he described the Sultan as not only 'God's rod' but also 'the Devil's servant'; a little later he wrote that 'the spirit of lying' inspired the Sultan, the Papacy, and the Anabaptist leader Thomas Müntzer; and then he added that 'as the Pope is the Antichrist, so the Sultan is the Devil incarnate.' Introducing the Devil (and, for good measure, the Papacy) changed things. To resist God's punishment, as Luther had put it in his early article, was one matter; but to fight

---

16. Luther, *Vom Kriege*, p. 120 ('wie wol ettlich sein regiment darynn loben, das er yederman lest gleuben was man wil, allein das er weltlich herr sein wil, So ist doch solch lob nicht war. Denn er lest warlich die Christen öffentlich nicht zu samen komen Und mus auch niemand öffentlich Christum bekennen').

17. Ibid., pp. 116 (no justification), 123 ('das schwerd', 'Denn es wird yhn ynn yhrem gesetz geboten als ein gut Göttlich werck das sie rauben, morden...Darumb ists nicht ein götlich ordenliche öberkeit wie andere, den fride zu handhaben, die frumen zu schützen und die bösen zu straffen, Sondern wie gesagt ein lauter Gotts zorn, rute und straffe uber die ungleubige welt').

against the Devil was another—even if, in this case, both descriptions were applied in tandem—and was surely the duty of every true Christian.[18]

This change of direction in Luther's argument received a powerful stimulus from the work of two of his friends and colleagues on a particular biblical prophecy. In the second half of 1529 Philip Melanchthon and Justus Jonas prepared a short text on the interpretation of the vision described in chapter 7 of the Book of Daniel; it was published, under Jonas's name and with additional material by him on Islam, the Ottomans, and the need to fight them, in 1530.[19] Daniel had seen four great beasts emerging from the sea; the fourth was 'dreadful and terrible, and strong exceedingly', differing from the other three. It had ten horns on its head; 'and behold, there came up among them another little horn, before whom there were three of the first horns plucked up by the roots: and, behold, in this horn were eyes like the eyes of man, and a mouth speaking great things.' Then God appeared and made his judgment; the beast was killed and consigned to the flames, and 'one like the Son of man' was given everlasting dominion over all of mankind. In his vision Daniel asked a bystander to explain the meaning of all this, and was told that the beasts were four great kings; the fourth would 'devour the whole earth', and

> the ten horns out of this kingdom are ten kings that shall arise: and another shall rise after them...and he shall subdue three kings. And he shall speak great words against the most High, and shall wear out the saints of the most High...and they shall be given into his hand...But the judgment shall sit, and they shall take away his dominion, to consume and to destroy it unto the end.[20]

According to Jonas and Melanchthon, the fourth beast was the Roman Empire, and the ten kingdoms were those that had emerged from the break-up of that Empire: Egypt, 'Asia' (Anatolia and Syria), Greece, Italy, Germany, France, and so on. The little horn was the Ottoman Empire, which had 'plucked up by the roots' the first three on that list; its 'mouth speaking great things' was the preaching of Muhammad's doctrine in the Koran. Islam was thus the last heresy to appear on Earth, and 'the final raging of the last furious wrath of the Devil before the Last Day'. The fourth great kingdom, the

18. Ibid., pp. 116 ('Gottes rute und des Teuffels diener'), 125 ('lügergeist'), 126 ('wie der Bapts der Endechrist, so ist der Türck der leibhafftige Teuffel').
19. Jonas, *Das siebend Capitel*; on the preparation see Köhler, *Melanchthon*, p. 20; Wengert, 'Biblical Commentaries', pp. 57–8 (also pointing out that Melanchthon had himself been preparing a commentary on Daniel earlier in that year).
20. Dan. 7: 3–26.

Roman Empire, had fallen (though a remnant of it continued in Germany), and there would not be a fifth. The little horn had conquered three other horns, and 'the other horns are all to remain, and will not be overthrown.' Since the little horn made war against the saints, even getting some of them (in Daniel's words) 'into his hand', it was the duty of the remaining saints to repel its attacks; and indeed, the Sultan would soon be defeated, since 'the lord Christ will certainly come soon.'[21]

Here was a way of elaborating, with a vengeance, on Luther's argument that the Ottoman Empire was not like other earthly powers: unlike every other government in human history, it was essentially diabolical. Justus Jonas included a long section developing this theme, in which he not only expatiated on the evil of Islam, but also took trouble to refute those who had written that the Ottomans exhibited virtues of various kinds, including the protection of female honour and abstinence from drink and gambling. In fact, he said, they dishonoured marriage in their own society, and in their conquests they were merciless towards women, children, the sick, and the old.[22] Many of the same points were taken up in the following year by Johannes Brenz, in another text to which Melanchthon also contributed: the Ottoman Empire was the diabolical 'little horn' described by Daniel, the Sultan's attacks on neighbouring territories made him nothing better than a murderer and a robber, albeit one acting on the commands of a false religion, and Ottoman conquests were followed by rape and butchery. The Ottoman Empire was thus doubly unlike other states: it broke the ordinary rules of natural law, as well as being driven by a peculiarly anti-Christian— and therefore devilish—religion.[23]

Indeed, after the siege of Vienna there seems to have been an organized programme of publications by Luther and his immediate circle, propagating the message that there was a special divine warrant for taking up arms against any Ottoman attacks. Luther's own contribution was a 'military sermon', prepared in 1529 during and after the Ottoman campaign, and

21. Jonas, *Das siebend Capitel*, sigs. C3v (fourth beast, ten kingdoms, little horn), E3v ('das letzte wueten der letzte grimmige zorn des teuffels vor dem Jungsten tag'), H2r (fourth fallen, no fifth, three conquered, 'die andern horner sollen alle bleiben / vnd werden nicht vmbgestossen'), H3r ('Darumb wird der Herr Christus gewis bald komen').

22. Ibid., sigs. E1v–F4v, esp. F1r (exhibiting virtues), F2r (conquest), F3v (dishonouring marriage).

23. Brenz, *Wie sich Prediger halten sollen*, sigs. A2r (Daniel), A3v (murder, religious commands, conquest), A4r (natural law), B1v (little horn). Brenz was based in Swabia, but had been present with Luther, Melanchthon, and Jonas at the Marburg Colloquy in early October 1529, while the siege of Vienna was in progress.

printed towards the end of that year. In the opening section he set out the
Jonas–Melanchthon interpretation of Daniel's vision, 'from which it appears
that the Ottoman Empire is to be destroyed by Heaven'. Luther too paused
to consider the apparent virtues of the Turks, noting their piety, abstinence,
and obedience, but insisting that such things were meaningless without faith
in Christ, and that in any case terrible vices ('Italian and Sodomitical'—the
two terms being synonymous) lurked underneath. His main argument was
that anyone who fought against the Ottomans was fighting 'an enemy of
God'; and the implication he drew from this must have been, to anyone
who had followed his statements at the beginning of the 1520s, quite surprising. If you die in this fight, he told his military congregation, 'Heaven
is yours, without any doubt.'[24] From denouncing the impiety of resisting
God's punishment, Luther had moved all the way to presenting an argument
for holy war. This quickly became the standard view among his followers.
In his 1531 pamphlet Johannes Brenz wrote that preachers should urge the
rulers of Imperial territories to resist the Ottomans, and should tell the
general population that they must serve obediently in their rulers' armed
forces: 'and this obedience is a good, holy deed, so that if anyone loses his
life in doing so, he should not doubt that he dies in obedience to God, and
so long as he truly believes in Christ, he will undoubtedly be saved.'[25] In a
popular work published eleven years later (soon after Süleyman's final
conquest of most of Hungary), Andreas Osiander resumed the standard
argument that Ottoman successes had been permitted by God as a punishment for sinful Christians, but he did so not only to enjoin penitence and
prayer but also to explain that there was no natural cause of Ottoman
victory: the Sultan did not possess any special wisdom, and the great size of
his army was of no account as they were all 'effeminate people'. His conclusion was that the Ottomans would lose all their strength the moment God
withdrew his permissive support; then Christians would be able properly to
fight them, and those who died in doing so would be blessed, 'not only
because they would be found to have performed a good Christian work of

24. Luther, *Eine Heerpredigt*, pp. 171 ('Aus dem es scheinet, das des Türcken reich von hymel
    gestörtzt werden sol'), 173 ('einen feind Gottes'), 175 ('Der hymel ist dein, das hat keinen
    zweifel'), 187–90 (apparent virtues), 191 ('Welsch und Sodomisch'). On the dating see
    Buchanan, 'Luther', p. 156.
25. Brenz, *Wie sich Prediger halten sollen*, sig. A3r ('Vnd diser gehorsam ist ein gut heylig werck / das
    ob schon eyner darinn vmb kummet / sol er nicht zweyffeln / er sterbe in Gottes gehorsam /
    vnd so er sunst an Christum warhafftigklich glaubet / wirt er on zweyfel selig').

obedience and defence of the fatherland, but also because they had been willing to shed their blood, above all, for Christ's name'.[26]

There had always been an apocalyptic element in Luther's thinking on these matters. When commenting on the Psalms in 1513–15 he had compared the Ottoman Empire to the beast with two horns in Revelation 13: 11–18 (explicating those horns on the basis that Islam made false use of both the Old and the New Testament).[27] One particular influence on him was a commentary on Daniel by Johannes Hilten, a fifteenth-century Franciscan with, it seems, Joachimite tendencies; a copy of this text was sent in late 1529 to Luther and Melanchthon, both of whom studied it with care. Luther may have felt especially flattered by Hilten's prophecy that a great reformer of the Church would arise in 1516. He certainly agreed with the Franciscan writer that the Turks were the people of Gog and Magog referred to in Ezechiel 38 and Revelation 20 (though that identification was already a common one); later both he and Melanchthon seem also to have accepted Hilten's more sombre prediction that most of Italy and Germany would be overrun by the Sultan in 1600.[28] But what developed significantly in Luther's thinking about these issues was something that Hilten himself could not have supplied: a parallelism between, and occasional near-identification of, Muhammad, Islam, the Turks, or the Sultan on the one hand and the Papacy or the Roman Church on the other. Luther's remark in 1529 that 'as the Pope is the Antichrist, so the Sultan is the Devil incarnate' has already been noted; that became his normal position, with some latitude about the precise devilish status of the Sultan. On occasion, he was happy to imply a closer parallelism between them: in a letter of November 1529, celebrating the Ottoman retreat from Vienna, he wrote about the imminent destruction of 'both Gog the Sultan, and Magog the Pope, the former being the political enemy of Christ, and the latter, the ecclesiastical one'. Generally, however, he reserved the title of 'Antichrist' for the Pope, not just because of the papal

26. Osiander, *Unterricht und vermanung*, sigs. A3r (no wisdom), A3v ('weybische leut'), C2r–v (loss of strength, Christians could fight properly), C3r ('Als die nit allein / inn eim [*sic*] guten Christlichen werck des gehorsams / vnd beschutzung des vaterlands erfunden würden / Sonder auch ir blut / fürnemlich vmb Christus namen willen / vergossen hetten'). The scholar and theologian Andreas Osiander was the leading Lutheran figure in Nuremberg.
27. Ehmann, *Luther*, p. 195.
28. On the sending of the text in 1529, and for what little is known of Hilten, see Clemen, 'Schriften'. On its influence see Köhler, *Melanchthon*, pp. 73–5; Pfister, 'Reformation', p. 362; Schulze, *Reich und Türkengefahr*, p. 43; Francisco, *Martin Luther*, pp. 22–3. On its Joachimism see Reeves, *Influence of Prophecy*, p. 234(n.); on the 1600 prediction see also Kaufmann, '1600', pp. 91–108.

claims of special status in Christianity, but because Luther regarded the Pope as fundamentally more harmful than Muhammad or the Sultan.[29] It was Melanchthon who developed a theory of the 'double Antichrist', a historico-theological composite of both the papal Antichrist and the Islamic one. And although diehard Lutherans would eventually reject Melanchthon's views on some important theological points, the hardliners under Flacius Illyricus (Matija Vlačić) who compiled the huge historical work known as the 'Magdeburg Centuries' (1559–74) were happy to incorporate the double Antichrist into their account. In particular, they were pleased to find a historical correlation between two events in the early seventh century: the rise of Muhammad, and a decree of the Emperor Phocas (dated by them to 606) which declared that Pope Boniface III was the head of all Christianity. This linkage between Islam and Roman Catholicism would become the standard view of generations of Lutheran theologians.[30]

In Luther's own writings the connection was not just that both were, broadly speaking, diabolical; he was interested in some more specific resemblances. Indeed, one of the noteworthy things about Luther's whole approach to Islam and to the Ottoman Empire is his appetite for detailed knowledge about them. Placing them in a category of apocalyptic and diabolical evil did not diminish his interest in the human *actualité*, and this was an attitude that would be shared by many other early Protestants. In *Vom Kriege widder die Türcken* Luther wrote that 'I have some parts of Muhammad's Koran; if I have time, I should translate it into German, so that everyone can see what a rotten and infamous book it is.' That hope was never fulfilled, but in 1542 Luther did issue his own German translation of Riccoldo da Monte Croce's *Confutatio Alcorani*, and when the Swiss Protestant theologian Theodore Bibliander published an edition of the medieval Latin translation of the Koran (by Robert of Ketton) in 1543 it included—in some copies, at least—a preface by Luther.[31] That edition of the Koran was supported also by Melanchthon, and by many Swiss theologians, including Bullinger.

29. Francisco, *Martin Luther*, p. 84; Segesvary, *L'Islam*, pp. 114 (more harmful), 218, n. 88 ('Gog Turcam, et Magog Papam utrumque, illum politicum, istum Ecclesiasticum hostem Christi').

30. Flacius et al., *Ecclesiastica historia*, i, 1st pagination, 1st century, cols. 399, 440 (double Antichrist), iv, 2nd pagination, 7th century, cols. 21–2 (Boniface, Muhammad); on Melanchthon's double Antichrist see Seifert, *Der Rückzug*, pp. 13–14, 21. The Magdeburg Centuriators may have been influenced by a pamphlet by Andreas Musculus, *Beider Antichrist* (1557), which made the historical correlation in an approximate way (sigs. B2v–B3v). For an early use of this (1565), following the Centuriators, see Göllner, *Turcica*, iii, p. 179.

31. Luther, *Vom Kriege*, pp. 121–2 ('Ich habe des Mahometes Alkoran etlich stück. Hab ich zeit so mus ichs ia verdeudschen, auff das ydermann sehe welch ein faul schendlich buch es ist');

(Although it was accompanied by a plethora of Christian texts refuting the Koran and denouncing Muhammad, it would be seized on by Catholic writers as evidence of scandalous pro-Muslim tendencies among their Protestant opponents.) Luther also wrote a foreword to an edition of George of Hungary's book about life under the Ottomans, and in 1537 Justus Jonas published a translation of Giovio's *Commentario*, with a preface by Melanchthon. Such interest in Islam and the Ottoman world was stimulated by various factors, including a desire to extend the Reformation to areas close to or under Ottoman rule; but the general principle was 'know your enemy', and for Luther this always included studying the resemblances between Islam and Roman Catholicism.[32]

The key point here was that Islam was a religion of 'works', not faith: as he put it in his *Vom Kriege widder die Türcken*, 'the Turk' (meaning here a generic Muslim) was 'papistical, because he believes that holiness and salvation come through works'. Luther's dismissal of the virtues shown by Muslims in their daily lives was based on this; he was happy to say that they did more good works than Catholic monks, as he was confident that neither category could be saved thereby. Similarly, a comment in his *Table-Talk* places Muslims, Catholics, and Jews on the same level, all trusting in 'works' without the saving faith in Christ. And in addition, Luther felt able to point to a pernicious effect of this resemblance between Roman Catholicism and Islam: many Catholics had found it easy to convert to the religion of Muhammad, because they were already trained by Catholic teaching to put all their trust in works.[33] Other Protestant theologians took up the general line. Melanchthon made just the same comparison between Islam, Catholicism, and Judaism; Theodore Bibliander noted that Roman Catholicism resembled Islam in its 'invocations of saints, pilgrimages to holy places, and trickery offered as miracles'; Heinrich Bullinger observed that Islam offered salvation to 'a person who fasts, prays, gives alms, and fights bravely [for Islam], just as some popes have promised indulgences to those who are

Riccoldo da Monte Croce, *Confutatio*; Bobzin, *Der Koran*, pp. 95–7 (Riccoldo), 209–11 (preface to Koran); Segesvary, *L'Islam*, p. 166 (preface to Koran).

32. Luther, 'Vorwort' (to George of Hungary); Price Zimmermann, *Paolo Giovio*, p. 121 (Jonas translation). On the 1543 Koran and accompanying texts see Segesvary, *L'Islam*, pp. 161–99; Bobzin, *Der Koran*, pp. 159–275; on Protestant missionary interests see Benz, *Wittenberg*, pp. 141–208; Rupel, *Primus Truber*.

33. Luther, *Vom Kriege*, p. 129 ('Papistisch, Denn er gleubt durch werck heilig und selig zu sein'); Segesvary, *L'Islam*, pp. 136 (Muslims, Catholics, Jews), 224 (monks); Francisco, *Martin Luther*, pp. 1–2 (monks), 89 (easy to convert).

killed in wars waged on behalf of the Roman Church', and that 'Muhammad
too has his monks and priests, and derives salvation from their merits; for he
attributes salvation not to faith, but to the merit of works.'[34]

Given the long-standing tendency in Western culture to interpret the rise
of Islam in terms of Muhammad's purely temporal ambitions, it is not
surprising that Protestant writers also made connections between that presumed aspect of Islam and what they saw as the lust for power of the Papacy.
As Melanchthon put it, 'Muhammad and the Pope developed idolatrous
religious practices for the sake of empire.' The French Protestant polemicist
Pierre Viret, picking up on the linkage with Pope Boniface III, explained:
'If you consider when the Roman See was built up and extended its lordship over all of Christianity, you will find there almost all the same things
that I mentioned when talking about the time when Muhammad built up
his rule and his religion.'[35] Yet, given also the traditional emphasis on Islam
being a religion spread by, and dependent on, 'the sword', it was hard for
these Protestant writers to take this parallelism all the way. In his pamphlet
of 1557 comparing the two Antichrists, Papistical and Muslim, the Lutheran
Andreas Musculus admitted that whereas Muhammad had used physical
violence from the outset, the Papacy 'grew and arose, to begin with, without
any external force or use of the sword, using only trickery'. But the Pope
was playing a clever game: 'at first he did not make it so obvious that he was
also planning to gather worldly power for himself, seeking instead only
authority and power over the Churches; but when he had seized the latter,
he immediately grasped after the former.'[36] In this way the parallel with the
other Antichrist was still maintained. Yet in any case, Luther had found

34. Köhler, *Melanchthon*, p. 95; Bibliander, *Ad socios consultatio*, sig. c4r ('diuoru[m] inuocationes, peregrinationes ad loca religiosa, miraculorum... praestigiae'; the contemporaneous English translation added 'Romyshe pardons' to the list: *Godly Consultation*, fo. 35v); Bullinger, *Der Türgg*, sig. A6r ('wenn der mensch faste / bätte / allmüsen gäbe / ritterlich stryte... Glych wie ettlich Bäpst ablass der sünden denen verheissen habend / die in kriegen von wägen der Römischen kirche[n] erschlagen werdend. So hat Machomet ouch sine münch vnd pfaffen / setzt in deren verdienst das heil. Dann er gibt die säligkeit zu nit dem glouben... sunder dem verdienst der wercken').
35. Köhler, *Melanchthon*, p. 32 ('Mahometh, Papa propter imperia excogitarunt idolatrices cultus'); Viret, *L'Interim*, p. 40 ('Si tu considere... quand le siege romain a esté dressé et a estendu sa seigneurie sur toute la Chrestienté, tu y trouveras presques toutes les mesmes choses que j'ay touchees, parland du temps auquel Mahomet a dressé son regne et sa religion').
36. Musculus, *Beider Antichrist*, sigs. C1r (Muhammad, 'wechst vnd steiget erstlich vnd anfenglich ohn alle eusserliche gewalt vnd Schwerdt / allein durch betrug'), C3r ('hat in her erst sich nit so grob lassen mercken / das er auch das Weltlich Regiment gedechte an sich zu ziehen / sonder hat allein die oberhand vnd gewalt gesucht / vber die Kirchen... Do er aber das eine hat erschnapt / hat er als bald nach dem andern auch gegriffen').

another way to manage the argument, shifting attention from the early development of Islam to the actual practice of the contemporary Ottoman Empire. Ever happy to portray Catholicism as the greater of the two evils, he emphasized that the Catholic Church was actually more willing than the Ottoman regime to use coercive power in religious affairs: 'for the Pope is much worse than the Sultan in this matter: the Sultan never forces a Christian to renounce Christianity and join his religion.'[37]

When one reads these comparisons, it is sometimes difficult to locate the dividing line between real theological conviction and an opportunistic use of apparent resemblances for rhetoric's sake. The same can sometimes be true of the equivalent arguments that were directed by Roman Catholics against the Protestants. An anonymous pamphlet of 1527 made a series of lurid comparisons, mostly of an opportunistic kind: 'the Turk' demolished churches, and Luther destroyed monasteries; the Turk forbade Christian preaching, and Luther abolished Christian ceremonies; the Turk abused women, and Luther enticed nuns into contracting false marriages; and so on.[38] In the summer of 1529 the Catholic humanist scholar Johann Drobneck, who published under the name Johannes Cochlaeus, issued a lengthy attack on Luther, concentrating on his shifting opinions about the legitimacy of fighting against the Ottomans. Chapter 6 of this work was entitled 'Luther's doctrine conforms to that of the Koran.' Seizing on a critical remark which Luther had made in one of his publications about the word 'homousios' ('of one substance') in the Nicene Creed, Cochlaeus argued that he undermined belief in the divinity of Christ, just like Muhammad; he also observed that, like the Muslim Turks, 'many of the Lutherans today desire nothing more than wars, the killing of priests and monks, and the seizure of property.' Luther's notorious acceptance of bigamy was deftly assimilated to the approval of polygamy in Islam, and his 'blasphemies' against the Virgin Mary, the Cross, and many of the ceremonies of the Church were said to be worse than anything in the Koran.[39] Three years later, another prominent opponent

---

37. Luther, *Eine Heerpredigt*, p. 195 ('Denn der Bapst ynn dem stück viel erger ist, denn der Türcke. Der Türcke zwinget doch niemant Christum zu verleugnen und seinem glauben anhangen'). This may be technically compatible with Luther's argument (see above, n. 16) that Christians did not enjoy the freedom to practise their religion properly under Ottoman rule.

38. Bohnstedt, *Infidel Scourge*, p. 27 (citing *Ein Sendbrieff darjnn angetzeigt wird vermeinte ursach warumb der Turck widder die Hungern triumphirt und obgelegen hab* (Dresden, 1527)).

39. Cochlaeus, *Dialogus*, fos. 10r ('Lutheri doctrinam Alcorano co[n]formem esse'), 10v ('Nec hodie aliud desyderant magis plaeriq[ue] Lutheranoru[m] qu[am] bella caedesq[ue] sacerdotu[m] & monachorum rerumq[ue] direptio[n]es'), 11r (bigamy, blasphemies).

of Luther, Johann Eck (who had challenged him in a famous public disputation in 1519), published a set of sermons on the Ottoman threat in which some connections with Protestantism were also made. Developing the standard argument that the Ottomans owed their success partly to the internal divisions of the Christians, he emphasized the role of 'Lutheranism' in causing that disunity; and he even declared that since the Lutherans and Zwinglians (Swiss Protestants) were blaspheming, robbing monasteries, and committing other crimes, 'it would be better to live among the Turks than among those apostate and faithless Christians.'[40]

The first really thorough attempt to link Protestantism and Islam together was made by the oriental scholar and maverick Catholic Guillaume Postel, in a short book published in 1543: *Alcorani seu legis Mahometi et Evangelistarum concordiae liber*. Using his intellectual authority as an Arabist who had read the original text of the Koran, Postel produced a list of 28 'axioms' of Islam, each of which could be matched by Protestant doctrine or practice: for example, 'there should be no images of saints in the temples', or 'there is no dignity involved in priesthood, and the choice of religion should be decided by the secular power'. Whereas Muhammad had taught the common people to dismiss the traditions of their forefathers—an essential move, Postel noted, for anyone founding a new religion—the Protestants had similarly rejected long-standing traditions, writing new liturgies of their own. And where the founder of Islam had wanted the authority of his muftis and *kadi*s to depend not on any process of ordination by 'holy magistrates' but simply on 'the sword', the Protestants had their ministers appointed directly by kings and princes.[41] Despite Postel's rather marginal position in Catholic intellectual life, many of the points he made here would percolate, over time, into the mainstream of anti-Protestant polemical writing.

Where there was some plausibility in these comparisons—for instance, on the question of venerating images—Protestants could use them to argue that at least the Muslims were not as badly corrupted in their beliefs and practices as the Catholics were. Occasionally this might generate a more

---

40. Eck, *Sperandam esse victoriam*, sigs. A3r ('Lutheranismus'), C2r ('adeo ut satius esset inter Turcas uiuere, quam inter apostantes istos & perfidos Christianos'). This work is notable also for the influence on it of Pseudo-Methodius, Joachim, and Lichtenberger.

41. Postel, *Alcorani et Evangelistarum concordiae*, pp. 21 ('Nullas sanctorum imagines haberi in templis debere'), 22 ('Nil habere dignitatis sacerdotes & religionis arbitrium à potentia saeculari regi debere'), 43–4 (rejecting traditions), 59 ('à sacris magistratibus', 'a gladio'). *Kadi*s were judges, and muftis were senior legal experts, superior to *kadi*s. Early modern European writers generally thought of muftis as the Islamic equivalent of bishops; but Postel's apparent assumption that a *kadi* was a religious minister was less common.

positive appreciation of Islam as a religion that shared the Protestant distaste for Catholic 'superstitions'. Melanchthon told the story of a conversation about Luther which took place in 1539 between the Polish diplomat Hieronim Łaski and Süleyman the Magnificent, in which the Sultan had said: 'Whoever he is, he is a great man, but he has not yet arrived at the enlightenment which we enjoy.'[42] From there it was only a short step to thinking that, in territories under Ottoman rule, Protestantism might perhaps be regarded more favourably by the authorities than Roman Catholicism. The historical evidence is unclear about this; in Ottoman Hungary, when rival Christian congregations laid claim to the same church building, the local pasha did sometimes stage a Protestant–Catholic disputation, awarding the church to whichever side he judged to be the winner, but it seems that no systematic preference was at work. Nevertheless, in 1542 Melanchthon was able to inform one of his correspondents about a recent episode in which the pasha of Buda had asked the Protestant minister what he was telling his flock: the minister said he instructed them that the fate of the Church was independent of any temporal political arrangements, and that they should obey the powers that be—whereupon the pasha praised him, and promised to act in favour of the Protestants.[43] One of Melanchthon's Hungarian correspondents, the Transylvanian Zsigmond Torda, assured him in 1545 that the Ottoman conquest was a special blessing of God, designed to encourage the spread of Protestantism. Six years later Torda sent him a notably positive account of conditions in Ottoman Hungary. 'The Ottomans do not force anyone to convert to Islam', he wrote.

> In the churches they allow the Word of God to be taught, and permit the use of pious ceremonies, so that, indeed, quite a few people [*sc.* Catholics] are accepting our profession of faith. Our rulers were going to use their weapons and armies to fight against the glory of Christ [*sc.* Protestantism]; that is why God brought in the Ottomans, who permit the free profession of heavenly doctrine. In this way people are coming to recognize the true God.[44]

42. Köhler, *Melanchthon*, p. 50 ('Est magnus vir, quisquis est, sed nondum pervenit ad istam lucem, in qua nos sumus').
43. Gragger, 'Türkisch-ungarische Kulturbeziehungen', pp. 8–9 (disputations), 12 (Melanchthon letter about Buda); Unghváry, *Hungarian Protestant Reformation*, p. 117 (no preference).
44. Gragger, 'Türkisch-ungarische Kulturbeziehungen', p. 7 (Torda, 1545); Melanchthon, *Epistolae*, pp. 322–3 ('Turcae neminem cogunt ad Machometismum... In templis permittunt doceri Verbum Dei et concedunt usum piarum Ceremoniarum. Quin etiam plerique nostram professionem amplectuntur... Nostri Principes armis et castris erant oppugnaturi gloriam Christi, propterea Deus adduxit Turcas, qui concedunt libere doctrinae coelistis Confessionem. Quo fit, ut populus ad veri Dei agnitionem veniat'). On Torda see Fraknói, *Melanchtons Beziehungen*, pp. 24–32; Okal, 'La Vie'.

The Swiss theologian Heinrich Bullinger, who believed in the possibility of
a general conversion to Protestantism of the Hungarian population under
Ottoman rule, would publish a short work in 1559 instructing the Protestants
there to pray for their enemies, the 'Turks'. While his providentialist view
was much less positive than Torda's, he did remind his Hungarian readers
that it was God who had placed them under the Ottomans, and he urged
them to earn 'tranquillity' there by means of good deeds, avoiding all 'tricks,
conspiracies, or seditions'.[45]

During the second half of the sixteenth century, the positions taken by
Protestants and Catholics accusing each other of being like Muslims became
more polemical and unyielding. Where Protestant writers were concerned,
factors contributing to this included the activities of the newly established
Roman Inquisition, the growing 'Black Legend' of the Spanish Inquisition,
and the outrages committed during the French Wars of Religion and the
Dutch Revolt. On the Catholic side there was a special critical focus on
the way in which Protestantism was developing in more radical directions,
generating sects which might be portrayed as more comparable to Islam, the
more remote their beliefs were from those of Catholicism. The Zwinglian
and Calvinist doctrine of the Eucharist, which viewed it as a merely com-
memorative or symbolic act (denying both the Catholic idea of transubstan-
tiation and the Lutheran doctrine of the Real Presence), could with a little
effort be represented as a step towards the Muslim belief that Jesus was only
a holy man; already in 1543 Postel included this Eucharistic opinion in his list
of Islamic 'axioms'.[46] But the most significant development was the growth
of anti-Trinitarianism, a movement which drew its strength from the
Protestant principle of 'sola Scriptura' (basing doctrine only on what was
stated in the Bible), and which did in one obvious way adopt a theological
position closer to Islam. Anti-Trinitarianism spread rapidly in Transylvania in
the 1560s, acquiring a degree of official protection there in 1571; there was
no direct causal link between the status of Transylvania as an Ottoman vassal
state and the flourishing of this movement there, but some indirect connections did exist, such as the fact that Transylvanian anti-Trinitarians could
arrange for works to be printed in nearby Ottoman Hungary.[47] At least one

45. Pfister, 'Reformation', p. 375 (belief in conversion); Bullinger, 'Brève et pieuse institution',
   pp. 283–4 ('Turcs', 'des ruses, des machinations ou des séditions', 'la tranquillité').
46. Postel, *Alcorani et Evangelistarum concordiae*, p. 22.
47. Generally see Pirnát, *Die Ideologie*; L. Binder, *Grundlagen*; Balázs, *Early Transylvanian Antitrinitarianism*.
   For an example of printing in Ottoman Hungary see Borsa, 'Die Buchdrucker', p. 15; Rother,
   Siebenbürgen, pp. 93–4.

Transylvanian, Markus Benkner, is known to have progressed from a Lutheran family background, via anti-Trinitarianism, to becoming a Muslim convert in Istanbul in 1572 (though the role played by theological argument in that last decision is, as in almost all such cases, quite obscure).[48] The person with whom he travelled to Istanbul, and who also converted to Islam, was a well-known Calvinist theologian from Heidelberg, Adam Neuser, who had become convinced that the traditional doctrine of the Trinity was false. Neuser's case became a *cause célèbre*—a source of deep shame and embarrassment to Calvinists, and a gift to Catholic polemicists.[49]

Radical sects had been troublesome for mainstream Protestants almost from the beginning. Depicting them as similar in some way or other to Muslims or Turks was a common tactic. As we have seen, Luther had joined together the Sultan, the Papacy, and Thomas Müntzer's Anabaptists as representatives of the 'spirit of lying'. He likened the radical Protestant 'attackers of pictures' to the image-hating Muslims; and he also compared the Anabaptists to the Ottomans where their rejection of social hierarchy was concerned. The Sultan, he wrote, 'is just like Müntzer too, for he roots out all superior authority, and permits no hierarchy of temporal estates (such as princes, counts, lords, noblemen, and other vassals), being instead lord over everything in his territory.'[50] Anti-Trinitarianism shocked Lutherans and Calvinists alike; it was, after all, Calvin himself who had the Spanish anti-Trinitarian Miguel Servet (Servetus) burnt at the stake in 1553. (The articles of accusation against Servet charged him with favourizing Jews and Muslims by 'excusing' their rejection of the Trinity, demanded to know whether he had studied the Koran, and required him to denounce it as 'a wicked book full of blasphemies'.)[51] As the rejection of the Trinity spread in central Europe, the prominent Calvinist Andreas Volanus (Andrzej Wolan) warned those who held such views that if they persisted they would 'fall into Judaism

---

48. On Benkner see P. Binder, 'Transylvanian Saxons', pp. 399–401; Müller, *Franken in Osten*, pp. 217–19; Müller, *Prosopographie*, vii, pp. 153–6 (evidence of anti-Trinitarianism); Graf, *The Sultan's Renegades, passim* (as 'Penckner').

49. On Neuser see Burchill, *Heidelberg Antitrinitarians*, pp. 85–124; Motika, 'Adam Neuser'; Mulsow, 'Fluchträume'.

50. Above, n. 18 (spirit of lying); Luther, *Vom Kriege*, p. 128 ('bilden sturmer', 'ist auch gar Müntzerisch, Denn er rottet alle Oberkeit aus und leidet keine ordnung in weltlichem stande (als Fürsten, Graven, Herrn, Adel und ander lehenleute) sonder ist alleine herr uber alles yn seinem lande').

51. Pannier, 'Calvin', p. 281 ('excusant', 'ung meschant livre plein de blasphèmes'). See also below, p. 317.

or Islam.'[52] Yet, overall, it was the Calvinists who were most commonly stigmatized—by both Catholic and Protestant opponents—as tending theologically towards Islam. Commenting on Adam Neuser in 1594 (eighteen years after Neuser's death), the Lutheran theologian Konrad Schlüsselburg wrote that he had passed 'via Arianism [sc. anti-Trinitarianism] to Islam, with not a few other Calvinists'. According to Schlüsselburg, a recent Ottoman envoy to the King of Poland had said that the Sultan was hoping that the Holy Roman Emperor would expel all the Calvinists and send them to Ottoman territory, on the grounds that 'if that happens, it will soon be possible to propagate the religion of the Turks more widely, as it so much agrees with the doctrine of the Calvinists, with the exception of a few articles.'[53]

By far the most impressive work along these lines was written by an English Catholic convert, William Rainolds, a former Fellow of New College, Oxford, who became a Catholic priest, taught at Douai and Rheims, and died in Antwerp in 1594. The long text on which he had been working was edited and completed by another Englishman who taught theology at Rheims, William Gifford, and was published in 1597 under the title *Calvino-Turcismus*. It is primarily a dialogue between two Englishmen: Michaeas, an English Protestant who has converted to Islam, and Samuel, a minister of the Church of England. This takes place in Istanbul in the house of a French Catholic, Ludovicus, who joins the discussion at certain points and provides an authoritative conclusion. One of the remarkable things about this book is the even-handed way in which the Muslim and Protestant speakers are dealt with: they are presented throughout as arguing in good faith, and each is allowed to make some valid points. Michaeas begins by bemoaning the irreligious spirit that now prevails in Christendom. If the Church had kept its original purity, he says, 'our Muhammad would never have written his Koran, and God would never have let him seize so many kingdoms and provinces from the Christians.' Samuel admits that disunity is the great failing of Christianity, but tells Michaeas that 'your mutual agreement and unity are founded in servitude, and in the terror exerted over you by the Koran.' Muhammad forbade people to dispute about Islam, which shows that he was aware of its intellectual weakness, whereas 'the harder the truth

---

52. Volanus, *Paraenesis*, p. 34 ('in Iudaismum aut Mahomaetismum prolabamini').

53. Schlüsselburg, *Theologiae calvinistarum*, fos. 9v ('per Arianismum, ad Mahometanismum vsq[ue], cum alijs non paucis Caluinistis'), 10r ('Hoc enim si fiat, Turcarum Religionem mox latiùs propagari posse. vtpote cum Caluinistarum doctrina prorsus congruentem, paucis articulis exceptis').

is shaken, the more accurately it is discussed, the more subtly one enquires into it, it maintains itself more firmly, becomes stronger, and shines more gloriously.' Michaeas responds that if it is cruel to use force against those who err in religious matters, then Moses was cruel, and so was God. Besides, the English have imposed religious uniformity by statute. Islamic law seeks to control the religious adherence only of those who were born Muslims or have voluntarily become Muslims, allowing members of other religions to practise freely, whereas the English legal system tries to make Catholics abandon their faith.[54]

One of the argumentative strategies of this book, therefore, is to draw comparisons between the politico-religious situations in England and the Ottoman Empire, putting the former in a worse light. On some points the Ottoman policy may receive a positive portrayal, for shame-praising purposes, but more commonly the English Protestant speaker is allowed to criticize the Muslims in a convincing way, only for it to be shown—often by the Muslim speaker—that such criticism is hypocritical, as the English are even worse. But there are other strategies too, especially where the theological contents of these religions are concerned. When Michaeas lists the doctrines of Islam, Samuel comments, like a good Protestant controversialist, that it resembles Roman Catholicism in four respects: salvation by 'works'; ceremonies and bowings-down; venerating saints; and refusing to allow its Holy Scripture to be translated into the vernacular. (He adds the practice of praying for the dead, but observes that that was a pagan custom which passed first into Catholicism and then into Islam.) Michaeas has a simple reply: the fact that we share something with the Papists does not prove that it is wrong; you Protestants share many basic Christian beliefs with them. But then he turns the tables, arguing that the Protestants resemble Muslims in more respects: divorce, simplified liturgy, hostility to images, and so on. The Muslim–Catholic resemblances are on points that are shared with all the religions of the world, whereas the similarities between Islam and Protestantism are peculiar to those two. Yes, Islam was propagated by the sword; so was Protestantism, by the soldiers of the Schmalkaldic League.

---

54. Rainolds, *Calvino-Turcismus*, pp. 4 (irreligion), 5 ('nunquam Mahometes noster Alcoranum suum scripsisset, nunquam à Deo tam multa regna, & prouincias à Christianis ereptas obtinuisset'), 25 ('vestra…concordia, & unitas fundatur in seruitute, & terrore quo vos premit Alcoranus', 'Veritas enim quo magis excutitur, quo accuratius ventilatur, quò subtilius in eam inquiritur, eò se tuetur solidius, eò consistit fortius, eò fulget gloriorius'), 29 (cruelty, uniformity), 31 (English law). The last point was a rather prejudicial description of the relevant English laws, which imposed disabilities on Catholics but did not force them to become Protestants.

You say that Islam was made of old heresies; we can show that Protestantism is made of new ones.[55]

So on some matters where Muslim practices can be aligned with those of religions in general, and therefore also with Catholicism, Rainolds feels able to write in positive terms. Michaeas tells Samuel, for example, that the holy month of Ramadan involves not only fasting but also extra prayers and alms-giving. (This information was derived from Postel.) He emphasizes that it is strictly enforced and sincerely observed; the Muslims are more religious, he says, in the sense of practising true religion—prayers, alms-giving, fasting—than the Protestants, who have rejected the Catholic fast days and Lent. On the other hand, in matters where it is possible to yoke Protestantism and Islam together, Rainolds happily does so in order to discredit the former: the Zwinglian doctrine of the Eucharist (which Michaeas compares to the feast of Bayram or Eid, commemorating Abraham's near-sacrifice of Isaac), the Protestant willingness to view parts of the Gospels as textually corrupt, the reduction of ministers of religion to quasi-lay status, and so on. And on the central issue of the Trinity, he wields the standard Catholic argument that anti-Trinitarianism flows ineluctably from the Protestant idea that all Christian doctrine must consist of things clearly stated in Scripture.[56]

Where the relation between church and state is concerned, the Muslim convert Michaeas becomes almost a mouthpiece for the Catholic point of view, even while describing the Islamic system. The Protestant Churches are badly arranged, he says, and bound to be prone to division; their rulers claim to govern them on the basis of Scripture, but have no authentic interpreter of it. Muhammad had a better design: the head of his church is a pope [sc. the Grand Mufti], not an emperor, and it is governed by the rules of the Koran. This tradition, he says, has continued without interruption, giving Islam a long history of internal peace and stability, 'free from sects'. It is left to Ludovicus, many pages later, to supply a corrective: Islam may be well organized nowadays, but in its original form, as set up by Muhammad, it was very similar to the Protestant system, with spiritual power attached to the king 'in the English way'. The true successor to Muhammad would thus be not the Grand Mufti (as in the Ottoman system) but a Caliph or

55. Ibid., pp. 145–9 (summary of Islam), 152 (four respects), 153 (prayers for dead), 156–8 (Michaeas's reply), 160 (sword), 167–72 (heresies). The Schmalkaldic League was an alliance of Lutheran princes and free cities in the Holy Roman Empire, which fought against Charles V in 1546–7.
56. Ibid., pp. 271–2 (Ramadan, more religious), 277–9 (Eucharist, Bayram), 288 (Gospels corrupted), 295–302 (ministers), 389 (Trinity).

'pope-emperor'; and the early history of Islam was full of political and religious conflict. The final conclusion, drawn by Ludovicus, is that Islam is fully reconcilable—in all its essential practices and beliefs—with Protestantism, but not with true Christianity.[57]

Within two years, a fierce reply to Rainolds was published, under the title *De turcopapismo*, by Matthew Sutcliffe, who was Dean of Exeter and a prolific polemicist on behalf of the Church of England against both Presbyterians and Roman Catholics. Sutcliffe's book was thought significant enough to merit a reprinting in Hanau (the Calvinist publishing centre near Frankfurt am Main) five years later; yet it is a rather mechanical piece of work, entirely outclassed by the subtlety and resourcefulness of Rainolds's writing. Sutcliffe runs through all the most predictable arguments one by one, starting with the claim that 'papismus' began with Pope Boniface III in 606, the very year (according to the fifteenth-century writer Breydenbach) of Muhammad's birth. Both the Papacy and the founder of Islam used tricks and simulated sanctity to gain the loyalty of the people; the Koran is an absurd farrago, enforced by law, just like the papal decretals; both profess to be against coercion in religion, but in both cases their deeds belie their words; both claim temporal and spiritual power; both try to hide the scriptures from the eyes of the common people; the Papists have mendicant friars, while the Muslims have wandering dervishes; and so on.[58]

Sutcliffe's main focus is on the use of coercive power and violence. The Muslims and the Catholics are alike in using brute force to defend and promote their faith, but the latter are distinctly worse: among other evils, he cites the Spanish Inquisition and the destruction of the Hussites 'by sword and fire'. The depiction of the Ottomans is generally very negative, but a kind of relative shame-praising does take place on some of these pages; Sutcliffe notes that the Sultan sometimes keeps his promises, and that Muslims do not rebel against their ruler, unlike Roman Catholics.[59] Above all, the 'Turks' are praised in this way for their religious toleration. Although they are a 'savage and cruel' people, they are more full of 'clemency and

57. Ibid., pp. 502–3 (badly arranged), 507 (Muhammad's better design, 'à sectis libera'), 641 (Ludovicus: 'more Anglicano', 'Imperator Ponteficius'), 644–5 (conflict), 924 (conclusion). Cf. also pp. 315–16, comparing Queen Elizabeth to the early caliphs of Baghdad, and contrasting this with the present-day relationship between Mufti and Ottoman Sultan.

58. I cite the Hanau edition: Sutcliffe, *De turco-papismo*, pp. 15–19 (Boniface, birth of Muhammad), 21 (tricks), 32, 40–1 (Koran, decretals), 48 (claim about coercion), 50 (temporal and spiritual), 51 (hiding scriptures), 75 (friars, dervishes).

59. Ibid., pp. 99 (Hussites), 100 (Inquisition), 105 (promises), 136 (alike in use of force), 138 (no rebellion).

humanity' towards Christians than the Papists. 'There are many Christians in the Ottoman kingdom, in Asia and in Europe, who freely profess the Christian religion', Sutcliffe writes, and he also notes that Ottoman policy on this point derives from the teaching of the Koran.[60] If one puts together the two books by Rainolds and Sutcliffe, the one common point that emerges most strongly is that both writers, for their own argumentative purposes, end up acknowledging in an explicit and positive way the degree of religious toleration that was such a striking feature of the Ottoman system of government. It was not part of the direct purpose of either work to praise the Ottomans—still less, to praise Islam. But the method adopted for an intra-Christian debate led to the relatively positive use of an extra-Christian model.

These two books are, as has already been noted, unevenly matched in quality. And there is a larger historical asymmetry too: while Sutcliffe's concept of 'Turcopapism' failed to embed itself in the broader culture, Rainolds's 'Calvinoturcism' did enjoy some currency, and has been picked up and developed by modern historians. The reasons for this are to be found in political developments affecting several populations of Calvinists—or, at least, Protestants in the broader 'Reformed' tradition—in the second half of the sixteenth century and the first half of the seventeenth. During the Dutch Revolt, pamphleteers harped on the fact that there was more toleration under the Ottomans than under Habsburg rule; the slogan 'Liever Turks dan paaps', 'Rather Turkish than Popish' (apparently derived from a comment attributed to Byzantine Greeks before the fall of Constantinople), was taken up with pride. Knowing that this would infuriate the Catholic Habsburgs, for whom the Ottomans were a perennial enemy, they minted symbolic coins in the form of a crescent with a version of the slogan stamped on them. One Dutch writer, describing the making of such coins during the siege of Leiden in 1574, commented: 'they regarded the Pope's tyranny as greater than that of the Sultan, who does not oppress the consciences of his tributary people.'[61] The point made here was mostly about toleration; but, given the geopolitical balance of power which aligned the Ottoman

---

60. Ibid., pp. 98 ('saeva & crudelis', 'clementiam & humanitatem', from Koran), 99 ('multi per Asiam & Europam in regno Turcico sunt Christiani, qui liberè profitentur religionem Christianam').

61. Mout, 'Turken in het nieuws' (pamphleteers); Van der Meulen, 'Liever turksch' (Byzantine origin); Westerink, 'Liever Turks', p. 76 (coins; citing Fruytiers, *Corte beschrijvinghe*, fo. 18r: 'sy achteden des paeus tyrannie grooter dan van des Turckes, die noch wel der luyder conscientien onder tribuyt onghedwonghen laet').

Empire against Spain, there was at least the potential for cooperation between the rebels and the Sultan. In 1569 William of Orange despatched a secret envoy to Istanbul; at some point the Grand Vizier sent William a letter proposing an alliance against Spain; and an Ottoman agent was sent to Holland in 1574, with a message from the Sultan which assured the Dutch rebels of his 'compassion and solicitude', even promising that 'our victorious troops will be sent from land and sea' to assist them. Although nothing concrete ever came of this, the overall alignment of mutual interests would have been obvious to observers, even without any knowledge of these particular dealings.[62]

Similarly, the balance of forces in international politics made England a natural ally of—or, at least, would-be cooperator with—the Ottoman Empire in the final decades of the sixteenth century. One crucially important factor was the papal bull of 1570 which released Elizabeth's subjects from their duty of obedience to her: thereafter the country was a potential target for conquest by Philip II of Spain (and, in 1588, an actual one). A pioneering English commercial mission to Istanbul, in 1578, led first to a charter of trading privileges granted by the Sultan in 1580, then to acceptance of an English resident ambassador in 1583, and the link so established was soon being used by Elizabeth to lobby the Ottomans for more actively anti-Spanish policies. During the 1580s there were rumours that the English were plotting to seize the island of Malta and hand it over to the Sultan, and Elizabeth's various schemes to involve the Ottomans in supporting a claimant to the throne of Portugal (which had been seized by Philip II in 1580) were said to include a promise that, once wrested from Spanish control, that country would become a tributary state of the Ottoman Empire. Both the English ambassador in Istanbul, William Harborne, and Elizabeth herself in her letters to the Sultan were happy to invoke some common Protestant–Muslim interests: addressing the Sultan, Harborne urged him to join England in destroying the King of Spain 'and all the other idolaters'.[63]

Such tactics did not escape the notice of Catholic writers. William Rainolds complained that when in 1587 the English ambassador had tried

---

62. De Groot, *Ottoman Empire*, p. 84 (1569 envoy, Grand Vizier's letter); Hess, 'Moriscos', pp. 19–21 (agent, 1574; p. 20: quotation).

63. Skilliter, *William Harborne* (early mission); Vella, *Elizabethan-Ottoman Conspiracy* (Malta); Malcolm, *Agents of Empire*, pp. 370–1 (Portugal); Bodl. MS Tanner 7, fo. 102v (Harborne to Sultan: '& tuttj altrj Idolatrj'). The term 'Protestant' is used here rather than 'Calvinist'; the Elizabethan Church of England was not narrowly Calvinist in doctrine, but it was strongly influenced by Swiss Reformed theologians, including both Calvin and Bullinger.

to persuade the Sultan to expel the Jesuits who had come to Istanbul in the Imperial envoy's retinue, he had argued that both Protestants and Muslims opposed idolatry; for good measure Rainolds also devoted some pages to discussing Elizabeth's shocking cultivation of diplomatic relations with the rulers of Morocco and Algiers. In 1592 an anonymous pamphlet, written by the Catholic polemicist Richard Verstegan, similarly protested about the English: 'yf we looke what new confederates they haue chosen . . . we shall see them to be the great *Turk,* the kinges of *Fesse, Marocco,* and *Algiers,* or other *Mahometains* and *Moores* of *Barbarie,* all professed enemies to *Christ.*' He continued: 'And the great *Turk* and his consorts, may be by the English excited to inuade some partes of Christendome, neere vnto them adioyning (as alredy vpon such perswasio[n] they haue attempted) but good vnto England they can do none, albeit the English would excha[n]ge their *Geneua Bible,* for the *Turkish Alcora[n],* because their situations are to farr distant.' Replying to this pamphlet, in a little tract which circulated widely in manuscript, Francis Bacon was happy to turn the Sultan's friendly attitude towards Elizabeth into a theological debating point against the Catholics: 'If he mean it because the Turk seemeth to affect us for the abolishing of images, let him consider then what a scandal the matter of images hath been in the church, as having been one of the principal breaches whereby Mahumetism entered.'[64]

Other cases of political alignment between Calvinists and Ottomans would develop later in central Europe. In 1604, when Transylvania had been conquered by Habsburg forces and a rigorous programme of Catholicization had been imposed, a large-scale revolt developed under the leadership of the Calvinist nobleman István Bocskai. As the 'Long' Ottoman–Habsburg war was still in progress, this put the Transylvanian Calvinists (and others who joined the revolt) on the same side as the Ottomans, from whom Bocskai sought, and received, political support.[65] By the time the Thirty Years' War broke out in 1618, another Calvinist nobleman, Gábor Bethlen, was Prince of Transylvania; he had cooperated even more closely with the Ottomans during the Bocskai revolt, and during the period 1618–27 the prospect of his helping to organize an Ottoman attack on the Habsburgs played an

64. Rainolds, *Calvino-Turcismus,* pp. 11 (ambassador's argument), 1,005–7 (Morocco, Algiers); Verstegan, *Declaration,* pp. 48–9 (quotation); Bacon, 'Certain Observations', p. 204 (emending 'branches' to 'breaches'). On Verstegan's work see Arblaster, *Antwerp,* pp. 55–6. On reactions to the Anglo-Ottoman *rapprochement* see Dimmock, '"Captive to the Turke"'; on the relationship more generally, Brotton, *This Orient Isle.*
65. Lefaivre, *Les Magyars,* i, pp. 266–76 (Bocskai revolt); Etényi, Horn, and Szabó, *Koronás fejedelem,* pp. 184–5, and Papp, 'Bocskai István török politikája' (Bocskai, Ottoman support).

important part in the strategic thinking of the Calvinist Elector Palatine and his Protestant allies. Accusations and revelations concerning these dealings would revive (as we shall see) the concept of Calvinoturcism and give it a new urgency. What had begun as an artificially constructed term of abuse in inter-confessional polemics had turned into a way of describing—no less polemically—an aspect of political reality. The slogan 'Rather Turkish than Popish' lived on; the equivalent phrase used by the Catholic theologian Johann Eck when denouncing the Lutherans, 'it would be better to live among the Turks than among those apostate and faithless Christians', was quietly forgotten.

FIVE

Alliances with the infidel

Many were shocked by the idea of Protestants allying themselves with the Ottoman Empire. Yet Protestants were not the only Europeans to adopt such a strategy. The most important alliance with the Sultan, which was active during key parts of the sixteenth century (with a slight afterlife in the seventeenth), was the one conducted by the kings of France—each of whom rejoiced in the traditional honorific description 'le roi très chrétien' or 'rex christianissimus', 'the most Christian king'. And they were not the only Catholic rulers to align themselves with, or seek assistance from, the Ottomans; there are examples of that from the fifteenth century too.

Historians of international relations have traditionally taken the view that the Ottoman Empire was very slow to join the European system of states. It has been common to assert that it was 'not part of the European international society' for most of its history, or that it was formally inducted into 'the European state system' only in 1840 or 1856.[1] Much depends here on definitional assumptions about what makes, at the international level, a 'society' or a 'system'. Debate about the former may revolve around the question of shared values, raising some complex issues; but the shared practices of a system should be easier to analyse. Here, however, too much emphasis has been given to a few formal or institutional factors, such as the sending of resident ambassadors—which, for the Ottomans, began only when they established a permanent embassy in London in 1793.[2] The significance of this particular practice is overstated. It had taken quite a long time for it to become established in early modern Europe: the fifteenth-century popes sent such representatives but did not receive them, for example, and in 1463 and 1470 Louis XI of France refused to accept a permanent Venetian ambassador.[3] In the

1. Watson, 'Systems of States', p. 101 ('society'); Naff, 'Ottoman Empire', p. 143 ('system', 1840, 1856).
2. Kürkçüoğlu, 'The Adoption and Use of Permanent Diplomacy'.
3. Yurdusev, 'Ottoman Attitude', pp. 26–7.

sixteenth century at least one major Christian state, Poland, discouraged resident ambassadors (other than papal nuncios), and as late as the seventeenth, England conducted most of its diplomatic business with Sweden—a major European power—by means of 'envoys extraordinary', sent on specific missions. While the Ottoman sultans accepted permanent representatives of the Christian powers in Istanbul, they conducted their own European diplomacy in the early modern period by means of ad hoc envoys—most frequently to Venice and Poland, but also to other Italian states, France, the Holy Roman Empire, and (occasionally) elsewhere. Until quite recently, the scale of this has been seriously underestimated. The standard modern history of Ottoman–Polish relations claimed that there were 20 Ottoman missions to Poland between 1509 and 1777; a more recent study has identified 22 of them in the period 1576–86 alone. And between 1453 and 1645, as the painstaking work of one scholar has shown, there were no fewer than 176 Ottoman diplomatic missions to Venice.[4]

Some writers, realizing that the integral role of the Ottoman Empire in the whole system of European international affairs long predated the nineteenth century, have looked to other formal criteria: the use, by the Ottomans in their dealings with Western powers, of titles implying a parity of esteem, for example (often identified as beginning with the Treaty of Zsitvatorok of 1606), or their participation in 'a general assembly of the European powers' (in the negotiations for the Treaty of Karlowitz of 1699).[5] But these again are too formal to capture the reality, which was that the Ottoman Empire was an active component of European geopolitics from a very early stage. Recognizing this, several studies have observed that it became part of the European 'concert of powers' or 'system' in the reign of Süleyman the Magnificent.[6] Arguably the starting point should be pushed back well before that.

The close relationship between Venice and the Ottomans is well known; this preceded the fall of Constantinople, with no fewer than three Venetian–Ottoman treaties signed in the quarter-century before that event. Genoa, the great trading rival of the Venetians, was no less open to cooperation

4. Kołodziejczyk, *Ottoman-Polish Diplomatic Relations*, pp. 181–2 (Poland); Pedani, *In nome del Gran Signore*, pp. 203–9 (Venice).

5. Housley, *Later Crusades*, p. 455 (Zsitvatorok, Karlowitz); Vocelka, 'Die diplomatische Beziehungen', p. 172 (Zsitvatorok). The question of parity of title-giving is not clear-cut, however: see Köhbach, 'Caesar oder imperator?'.

6. Kissling, 'Die Türkenfrage', p. 53 ('Konzert'); Bull, *Anarchical Society*, p. 14 ('system'); cf. also Komatsu, 'Die Türkei'. For a valuable survey of the whole pattern of Ottoman–European alliances, from the 14th century to the 17th, see Vaughan, *Europe and the Turk*.

with the Ottomans, hiring out ships to them for military purposes in 1425, seeking their help against the Venetians in 1431, and assisting them in their response to the Varna crusade in 1444. Commerce was the key factor here, and these were not the only Italian states adapting their international policies in order to pursue that goal in Istanbul; Florence, for example, having made a profitable trading agreement with the Ottomans in 1461, would pointedly ignore Pius II's calls for a new crusade against the Sultan two years later. But in other cases it was more general political, strategic, or military interests that made Western powers seek the cooperation of the sultans. In the late 1420s and early 1430s Filippo Maria Visconti, the ruler of Milan, used his good relations with Murad II to turn the Holy Roman Emperor in his own favour—quite possibly, in the hope of damaging Venetian interests too.[7] In 1494, when King Charles VIII of France was preparing to march on the kingdom of Naples to enforce his claim to its throne, and declaring (if only for public relations purposes) that from there he would launch a crusade against the Ottomans, it was none other than the Pope, Alexander VI, who, favouring the existing heir to Naples and fearing Charles's military power, sent an envoy to the Sultan, to warn him of this and to ask for financial help. Federico Gonzaga, ruler of Mantua, was also cultivating the favour of the Sultan; the battle cry of his troops when they fought against Charles VIII in the following year was 'Turco! Turco!' And in 1509, when a powerful league of Venice's enemies had occupied that republic's territories on the Italian mainland, there were serious discussions in the Venetian government about hiring an army of 15–20,000 men from the Ottomans. The idea was dropped, in the end, for fear of grave reputational harm; one Venetian commented that it would be like a man cutting off his penis to spite his wife. But negotiations with Istanbul continued, and small numbers of Ottoman soldiers were put to use. In 1526 the Venetians, hoping to divert the Habsburgs away from north Italy, would incite Sultan Süleyman to invade Hungary; in 1530 they would secretly encourage him to attack southern Italy.[8]

7. Hankins, 'Renaissance Crusaders', p. 126 (Venice treaties); Bitossi, 'Genova e i turchi', p. 92 (Genoa); Babinger, 'Lorenzo de' Medici', pp. 308–12 (Florence, noting also that in 1462 and 1466 Florence intercepted Venetian correspondence and sent it to the Sultan); Romano, 'Filippo Maria Visconti', pp. 595–616 (Visconti).
8. Thuasne, *Djem-Sultan*, pp. 326, 334–40 (Alexander VI); Pfeffermann, *Die Zusammenarbeit*, pp. 97–105 (Alexander VI); Kissling, *Sultan Bayezid's II. Beziehungen*, pp. 52–60 (Gonzaga); Mallett and Hale, *Military Organization*, pp. 317–18 (Venice, 1509); Finlay, 'Al servizio del Sultano', pp. 82 (Venice, 1526), 89 (Venice, 1530). A century later, in 1631, Venice would turn to the pasha of Bosnia for troops: Pedani and Bombaci, *I 'documenti turchi'*, p. 372.

As we have seen, the standard doctrine among Catholic theologians since the thirteenth century had been that 'infidels' could exercise temporal power in a perfectly legitimate way. From this it followed that they could be included in those forms of interaction that took place between secular states *qua* secular states—principally, diplomacy and trade. In the Crusading period, however, some limitations were placed on the latter activity. At the Lateran Council of 1179 a canon was issued forbidding Christians to sell arms, iron, or timber to the 'Saracens', or to pilot their ships, under pain of excommunication. Similar decrees by later popes added various other items to the category of war matériel: horses, mules, rope, and, sometimes, grain and other foodstuffs. (Nevertheless, special permission was given repeatedly to Venice to maintain its Levantine trade, where some of the sensitive commodities were concerned.) From the mid-fifteenth century onwards a formulaic statement of this kind was included in the bull *In coena Domini*, a compendium of general excommunications that was updated and promulgated every year in Rome. Canon lawyers were quick to point out, however, that this prohibition applied only to direct sales to the infidels; selling such goods to third parties who would then sell them to the Ottomans was not an excommunicable offence.[9]

Trade in inoffensive goods was permitted, and so was the sending and receiving of envoys to maintain peaceable relations. But making an alliance with non-Christians was a very different matter. The basic principle here had been laid down as early as the 870s, by Pope John VIII, when he ordered Naples, Salerno, and Amalfi to abandon their Saracen alliance. The proof-text to which he appealed was 2 Corinthians 6: 14: 'Be ye not unequally yoked together with unbelievers: for what fellowship hath righteousness with unrighteousness? and what communion hath light with darkness?' In his order he used the phrase 'impium foedus', 'unholy alliance'; and the basic theological principle to which he appealed—that Christendom was the 'mystical body' of Christ, which must not be polluted by such a connection—would exert a strong influence for many centuries. Of course an ecclesiastical prohibition of this kind did not prevent Christian rulers from making such alliances, but it did create some constraints; because of it, for example, when Frederick II

---

9. Vismara, 'Limitazioni', pp. 454–8 (canon, bull); Poumarède, *Pour en finir*, pp. 310–16 (bull); Thomas à Jesu, *De procuranda salute*, p. 749 (canon law on third parties). It is worth noting that the Ottomans operated an equivalent list of forbidden exports, for equivalent reasons: see Pedani, *Dalla frontiera*, p. 63.

concluded a treaty with the Mamluk Sultan in 1229, he went to great trouble to keep its ratification secret.[10]

Might an exception be made in the case of an alliance with one infidel power in order to weaken or defeat another infidel power? There was very little extended theorizing on this issue in the late medieval or Renaissance period, but the scenario was not an unthinkable one, and there is clear evidence of people considering it, in practice, in a very positive way. The widely read text by the early-fourteenth-century Armenian writer Hayton or Hetoum, for example, focused on the idea that the Christian powers should ally themselves to the 'Tatars' (i.e. the Mongols) in order to defeat the Seljuk Turks. In the 1440s Pope Eugenius IV sent an envoy to conclude an offensive agreement against the Ottoman Turks with Ibrahim, the powerful Türkmen Bey of Karaman; Flavio Biondo would later boast that he had drafted the text of the treaty for Eugenius. In 1500 the Greek-born Catholic bishop Alexius Celadonius wrote a memorandum urging collaboration with the Mamluk Sultan of Egypt against the Ottomans. Six years later Pope Julius II was planning an alliance with the Shah of Persia; twelve years after that, and again in the 1520s, there were contacts between Charles V and the Shah for that purpose.[11]

The most difficult case to justify, of course, would involve making an alliance with an infidel power in order to inflict harm on a Christian one— the sort of three-cornered relationship that was present in the examples of Christian–Ottoman cooperation given above, even if, in those cases, it did not go quite so far as the ratifying of a formal alliance. Defences of such an arrangement were extremely rare, and when they did occur they depended on the idea that self-defence was an absolute necessity. This was a principle more easily to be found in Roman sources than in Christian theological ones; Cicero had described self-defence as an innate law of nature, and the *Digest* asserted the basic legal principle that it was justified to use force to repel any attack.[12] In the early fourteenth century a prominent papal lawyer,

10. Vismara, *Impium foedus*, pp. 16 (John VIII), 29 (mystical body), 96–101 (Frederick II). As Vismara notes (p. 66), alliances between Christian Spanish rulers and Muslims were quite frequent from the 10th century onwards.

11. Hayton, *Liber historiarum*, sigs. S2r–S3r (ch. 60: 'De societate Christianorum, & Tartarorum'); Weber, *Lutter contre les Turcs*, p. 86 (Ibrahim); Biondo, *Scritti inediti*, p. 45 (boast); Kissling, 'Militärisch-politischen Problematiken', pp. 117–18 (Celadonius); Göllner, *Turcica*, iii, p. 69 (Julius II); Ursu, *La politique orientale*, p. 28 (Charles V, 1518); Fischer-Galaţi, *Ottoman Imperialism*, p. 16 (Charles V, 1520s).

12. Cicero, *Pro Milone* 11.30; *Digest* I.1.3, and IX.2.45.4, in Krueger et al., eds., *Corpus iuris civilis*, i, pp. 29, 162.

Oldradus de Ponte, issued the following 'consilium' or formal advice: 'May a Christian, without sinning, use the help and assistance of infidels in his own defence? It seems that he can, for what anyone does in defence of his body is considered to have been done as a matter of right, especially if he cannot otherwise protect himself... One cannot be blamed for wanting to save one's own skin in any way whatsoever.' He even added: 'Not only can we make war upon our enemies [in cooperation] with infidels and deceivers, but we can use deceit in doing so.' Self-defence was the essential point here, but, no doubt aware that his conclusion was an extreme one, Oldradus tried to buttress it with other arguments: he noted the analogous principle that 'in time of necessity we communicate with the excommunicated', and he also drew attention to biblical precedents, such as Abraham's confederacy with the Amorite Eshcol (Gen. 14: 13), or the alliances with Gentiles contracted by the Maccabees.[13]

Not many theologians were willing to go this far. In 1467 the Spanish bishop Rodrigo Sánchez de Arévalo wrote a commentary on the papal decision to depose George of Poděbrady, the Hussite King of Bohemia, in which he discussed the possibility of leagues between Christians and infidels. His view was that these were normally prohibited, being permissible only for the defence of the Catholic faith against other infidels—not for the defence of a Christian state against another Christian ruler. Later in his text he did concede, however, that if the realm of a great defender of the faith, such as the King of Spain, were at risk of destruction by another Christian prince, he could seek aid from an infidel such as the Muslim King of Granada, because the loss of such a stronghold of Catholicism would harm Christendom as a whole. But, he emphasized, this was a matter only of seeking practical assistance, not involving the kind of moral commitment that would come from a formal treaty.[14] Among the lawyers, however, there was a little more openness to the kind of argument put forward by Oldradus. The collection of Oldradus's 'consilia' was printed many times in the fifteenth, sixteenth, and seventeenth centuries, and was frequently and respectfully

13. Zacour, *Jews and Saracens*, pp. 44–5 (translation, emended), 78 ('Nunquid Christianus possit sine peccato ad defensionem suam uti auxilio sive adiutorio infidelium? Et videtur quod sic. Nam quod quis ob tutelam sui corporis fecerit iure fecisse existimatur... maxime si se aliter tueri non potest... Ignoscendum enim est illi qui qualitercunque sanguinem suum redimere voluit... Nec solum cum infidelibus et dolosis possumus inimicos impugnare, sed per dolum', 'et tempore necessitatis communicamus excommunicatis').
14. Trame, *Sánchez de Arévalo*, pp. 165–6.

cited by jurists.[15] One such writer, Decianus (Tiberio Deciani or Deciano), who lectured on civil law at Padua up until his death in 1582, wrote a consilium on the question, 'Whether secular rulers may justly enter into an alliance with infidels, and use their assistance to preserve their kingdoms and principalities'. Decianus cited Oldradus as an authority, pointing out that his argument defended the use of infidel alliances by Christian rulers even against other Christians. He also appealed to biblical examples; but his main argument was, once again, that of necessity and self-preservation: 'all laws and all *iura* [rights] allow the defence of one's body and one's possessions...therefore a ruler will be permitted to preserve the peace and tranquillity of his state by any means whatsoever, including war, and peace, and alliances, especially when his state cannot be preserved in any other way.'[16]

It was against this theoretical background that the greatest practical example of Christian–Muslim confederacy in early modern Europe developed: the alliance between France and the Ottoman Empire. Some foreshadowings of this alliance can be found in the latter part of the fifteenth century, but the beginnings of it, in practical terms, arose from the ill-judged attempt by King François I in 1521 to seize territories from the Emperor Charles V. François was soon on the defensive on several fronts, and suffered the serious loss of the Duchy of Milan, which was of central importance for his territorial ambitions in Italy. In 1522 he sent an envoy to seek help at the courts of several East European rulers, including the Ottoman vassal prince of Transylvania, John Zápolya; he also despatched an agent to persuade the 'Barbary corsairs' of North Africa to attack Habsburg territory, and was interested in encouraging the pasha of Bosnia to invade Styria and Carniola. There was no attempt to contact Istanbul directly at this stage; but that would change with the defeat of François at the Battle of Pavia in 1525, and his subsequent year-long imprisonment by Charles V. François's mother, acting as regent, sent an agent to Sultan Süleyman with a smuggled letter from François. In it, according to contemporary reports, the French King asked Süleyman for a military campaign in his support, warning that otherwise he would have to submit to all of the Emperor's demands, whereupon Charles

---

15. Zacour, *Jews and Saracens*, pp. 95–7 (list of edns.).
16. Decianus, *Responsorum*, iii, Resp. 20, fo. 63r–v ('An Principes seculares possint ex iusta causa foedus cum infidelibus inire, & eorum auxilio tueri regna, & Principatus suos', 'omnes leges, & omnia iura permittunt defensionem corporis, & rerum suarum...ergo licebit principi quocunque modo, & bello, & pace, & confoederationibus pacem, & quietem status sui tueri, praesertim cum statum suum aliter tueri non posset').

would become master of the world. Süleyman responded with general expressions of good will (in a letter which, unfortunately for François, fell into Charles's hands); nothing very concrete came of this at the time, but a foundation had been laid for future cooperation.[17]

Further diplomatic contacts between the French King and the Sultan took place in the early 1530s. François's main preoccupations were with gaining or regaining territory in Italy. Süleyman instructed the leader of the Barbary corsairs, Hayreddin Barbarossa (who had been given the status of admiral of the Ottoman navy), to collaborate with him; some corsair raiding of Italy did take place.[18] In 1535 François sent an envoy, Jean de La Forest, first to Barbarossa and then—to take up a position as a resident ambassador in Istanbul—to Süleyman; he came with a warning that Charles V was seeking 'world monarchy', and a proposal that Barbarossa attack Sicily and Sardinia, installing a French governor in the latter. A plan for coordinated French and Ottoman attacks on Habsburg territories in Italy in 1537 failed, apparently because of a lack of resolve on the French side; but by the early 1540s both parties were again keen to collaborate. In 1543 an Ottoman fleet of more than 100 galleys under Barbarossa's command, with a senior French official on his flagship, sailed to Marseille. There it was joined by a smaller French fleet, and the two then attacked Nice (a town in the territory of the Duke of Savoy, who was a Habsburg ally), where their bombardment destroyed much of the city but failed to take the fortress. In September François put the port of Toulon at the disposition of the Ottomans for the winter months, ordering most of the inhabitants to vacate their houses. One eyewitness, simultaneously shocked and impressed, would write in January 1544:'Looking at Toulon, you would say that it was Istanbul, with great public order and justice.'[19] European opinion was scandalized; even the Venetians complained, and when François sent a representative to explain his position at the Imperial Diet in Speyer the Germans would not let him enter their lands, saying that the French King was as much an enemy of Christianity as the Sultan. Barbarossa left Toulon in April 1544, pillaging Italian coasts and islands on his way, and taking a new French envoy to Istanbul. Cannily, François changed

17. Housley, *Crusading*, p. 38 (foreshadowings); Ursu, *La Politique orientale*, pp. 20–35 (events, 1520–5).
18. Ursu, *La Politique orientale*, pp. 56–65 (contacts, Italian territories), 71–2, 76, 79–80 (Barbarossa).
19. Ibid., pp. 89–91 (La Forest mission; p. 90: 'la monarchie du monde'), 99–105 (1537), 138–47 (1543); Dorez, ed., *Itinéraire*, p. 311 ('à veoir Tollon on diroit estre Constantinoble . . . avec grande police et justice'). On the occupation of Toulon by *c*.29,000 Ottoman troops and crew see Bérenger, 'La Collaboration', pp. 56–7, and Isom-Verhaaren, *Allies with the Infidel*, pp. 121–40.

his strategy to the extent of offering to use his credit with the Sultan to help broker a Habsburg–Ottoman peace settlement. In the resulting treaty, formalized in 1545, France was listed as one of the parties on the Ottoman side.[20]

François I died in 1547, but his pro-Ottoman policy was revived a few years later by his successor, Henri II. When the French ambassador in Istanbul, Gabriel Luetz, baron d'Aramon, returned to Paris in 1551, he proposed that Henri should take advantage of a new conflict between Charles V and the Sultan over North Africa: he suggested either conquering Sicily or making a coordinated attack on mainland Italy, with France invading the north while the Ottomans attacked Apulia. Henri agreed to cooperate with the Ottomans, and sent d'Aramon back to Istanbul to request a joint naval action. On his voyage there he was diverted to the Libyan port of Tripoli, which the Ottomans were on the point of seizing from the Knights of Malta; d'Aramon did in fact intercede for the lives of the Knights (whose commander, as it happened, was a Frenchman), but in a subsequent pamphlet war he was denounced by pro-Habsburg writers as complicit in the conquest of this Christian stronghold. The Sultan sent a fleet for a Franco-Ottoman campaign against the Habsburg-ruled Kingdom of Naples in the following year, and there were some joint naval actions in 1553 and 1555, but the overall effects were insignificant, and the alliance became relatively inactive after the death of Henri II in 1559.[21] It was reinstated in the 1590s by Henri IV, the Protestant King of Navarre turned Catholic King of France, who, in addition to his conflicts with French hardline Catholics, was at war with Spain from 1595. Even before that war was declared, he was asking his talented ambassador in Istanbul, Savary de Brèves, to encourage the Sultan to mount a large attack on Aragon and Valencia, in the hope of raising a revolt among the Moriscos. In December 1595 he requested that a large fleet of Barbary corsairs be sent from Algiers to help him control the port of Marseille and prevent rebel elements from handing it over to Spain; and he also suggested that if the Ottomans gave him the use of some transport ships, he could land a small French army in the territory of Naples and make trouble for the Spanish authorities there.[22]

---

20. Göllner, *Turcica*, iii, pp. 127–9 (scandalized); Ursu, *La Politique orientale*, pp. 150 (Venice, Diet), 151–4 (Barbarossa, envoy), 156–66 (strategy, treaty). For a general account of François's policy see Garnier, *L'Alliance impie*.

21. Yerasimos, 'Les Relations franco-ottomanes', and Gomez-Géraud and Yérasimos, 'Introduction', pp. 15–21 (d'Aramon, Tripoli, Naples); Guignard de Saint-Priest, *Mémoires*, pp. 45–6 (joint actions, 1553, 1555, against Tuscany, Elba, Corsica).

22. Berger de Xivrey, ed., *Recueil*, iv, pp. 90 (28 Jan. 1594: Aragon, Valencia), 475–6 (11 Dec. 1595: Marseille, Naples).

After the assassination of Henri IV by a Catholic fanatic in 1610, the French–Ottoman relationship cooled significantly. Richelieu was an anti-Habsburg realpolitiker, happy to ally France with Protestant powers in the Thirty Years' War; yet his attempts to reactivate the military alliance with the Ottoman Empire were slight and largely ineffectual. (The main example is the instruction he gave to the new French ambassador to Istanbul in 1639, which required him to ask the Sultan to authorize an attack on Imperial forces by his vassal in Transylvania, György Rákóczi, and also to send a fleet to conquer Sicily or the Kingdom of Naples; in the latter case, he was to promise that France would deploy its navy in the Mediterranean to prevent Spain from sending reinforcements.[23]) One reason for Richelieu's relative lack of interest in such strategies may be that in the 1630s, when the Ottoman army could have made a decisive difference in central Europe, the Sultan was known to be preoccupied with his long-running war against Persia; another may be found in the influence of Richelieu's adviser Père Joseph, a man whose hatred of Spanish Habsburg power was matched only by his fervent desire for a new crusade against the Sultan.[24] Père Joseph was probably in tune with French opinion more generally during this period; the contemporary pamphlet literature includes many items that were anti-Ottoman and pro-crusade, and a distinctive current of thought combined celebrations of the French medieval crusading tradition with ideas—some of them Joachimite in origin—about the kings of France having the right to inherit the Roman Empire and rule the world. Nevertheless, France still benefited from its privileged commercial relationship with the Ottomans, based on agreements drawn up in the earlier period of positive cooperation, and the special role of 'Protector' of the Holy Places in Palestine was cherished as a source of prestige for the French crown, so good diplomatic relations with Istanbul were carefully maintained.[25]

Under Richelieu's successor, Mazarin (a former papal diplomat), the official policy was similarly balanced, though behind the scenes Mazarin seems to have been more genuinely interested in supporting anti-Ottoman actions by other powers for reasons of Christian solidarity. During the prolonged Ottoman campaign to conquer the Venetian-ruled island of Crete, which lasted from 1645 to 1669, Mazarin allowed Venice to recruit soldiers

23. Avenel, ed., *Lettres*, vi, pp. 323–4 (Rákóczi), 384–6 (Sicily, Naples).
24. On Père Joseph's anti-Ottoman plans see below, p. 256.
25. Hochedlinger, 'Die französisch-osmanische "Freundschaft" ', p. 111 (public opinion); Billacois, 'Le Turc' (pamphlet literature); Haran, *Le Lys et le globe* (current of thought); Tongas, *L'Ambassadeur*, pp. 31–2 (commerce, 'Protector', diplomatic relations).

on French soil, and gave some financial help. The Venetian envoy to Paris, Giambattista Nani, was impressed by Mazarin's sympathetic attitude, but also noted that among the fixed maxims of French foreign policy 'the main one is that friendship with the Ottoman Porte is necessary and useful for trade, and as a restraint on the power of the Austrians.' It followed, he wrote, that 'all the words bandied about in public, concerning joining a league with other rulers or helping the Emperor, are just empty formalities and compliments.'[26] During the personal rule of Louis XIV (after Mazarin's death in 1661) there were moments when such words about helping the Emperor did in fact become realities—notably in 1664, when Louis contributed 9,000 soldiers to the Emperor Leopold I's anti-Ottoman campaign in Hungary. In 1686–7 Louis even sent an engineer to survey the fortifications of Istanbul and neighbouring ports, with a view to a possible French conquest of the Ottoman Empire. And yet when he launched his army against the Imperial territories of the Rhineland in 1688, he was—not unknowingly—granting a vital respite to the Ottomans, who had been close to accepting a disadvantageous peace after a string of military failures and defeats at Habsburg hands. Out of all his sets of instructions to outgoing ambassadors and envoys to Istanbul, those of 1689 and 1692 were the only ones to concentrate not on commercial or religious concerns but rather on coordinating military strategies: Louis's diplomats were to urge the Sultan to wage a major war of reconquest against the Habsburgs in Hungary. For the best part of a decade at least, until Louis signed his own peace treaty with the Emperor in 1697, a kind of Franco-Ottoman alliance existed once more, *de facto*.[27]

During this long history of cooperation—sometimes passive at most, but in some periods surprisingly positive and active—between Paris and Istanbul, public debate about the alliance never ceased. Among the critics of French policy, the main argument was very simple: it was obviously and utterly wrong for a Christian power to collaborate with an infidel one against the interests of other Christian states. The anonymous author of an 'exhortation' against François I (probably an ecclesiastic at the papal court) asked how it was possible for a Christian king to seek aid from barbarians

26. Darricau, 'Mazarin' (Mazarin's policy); Bilici, 'Les Relations', pp. 44–7 (Mazarin's policy), 54 (1664); Bibliothèque Sainte-Geneviève, Paris, MS 3366, fos. 108v–109r ('La principale è, che l'amicitia con la Porta Ottomanna sia necessaria, et utile per il commercio, e per freno alla potenza de gli Austriaci', 'siano discorsi à pompa, e parole di complimento tutte quelle, che sono corse per le Piazze, ò di unirsi con altri Prencipi, ò di prestare assistenza all'Imperatore').
27. Bilici, 'Les Relations', pp. 54 (1664), 59 (1688); Bilici, XIV. Louis (1686–7 survey); Duparc, ed., Recueil des instructions, pp. 133–42 (1689), 151–62 (1692).

who were rebels against God. Such a policy, he added, was pursued to the detriment of 'Europe'—which, as we have seen, could be used both as a synonym for Christendom and as a concept serving Habsburg purposes.[28] Nor was it only Catholic theologians who were shocked by the impiety of French policy. Contemplating the welcome given to the Ottoman fleet in Toulon, the French Protestant Guillaume Farel, a major figure in the early Reformation in Switzerland, wrote to Calvin expressing his dismay at the fact that the 'impious' religious practices of Muslims had been allowed on French soil at a time when Protestants, devoted to the true worship of God, were being 'most seriously and savagely tormented in that kingdom, under that "most Christian king"'. In comparison with such ardent theological concerns, secular arguments may have seemed much less powerful, but they were also deployed; one pamphlet of 1618, for example, warned that once the Sultan had conquered the Holy Roman Empire, France would inevitably become his next target.[29]

In defence of French policy many works were written, deploying a wide range of arguments and mingling apologetics with outright defiance. The senior diplomat Guillaume du Bellay, who had spent some years trying to rally opposition to Charles V among the German princes, published a lively text in 1536, partly in response to the Emperor's much-trumpeted conquest of Tunis in the previous year. Charles had driven out Barbarossa, who had himself taken the city one year earlier from its native ruler, the Hafsid Sultan al-Hasan; on leaving Tunis, Charles restored al-Hasan to the throne there as his quasi-vassal. Cleverly turning the tables on those who tried to associate François I with Islam, du Bellay exclaimed: 'what interest do we have in one rather than the other [*sc.* al-Hasan or Barbarossa], in whether the errors and impostures of Muhammad should be preached in Africa by a Moor or by a Turk?' It was the Emperor, he said, who preferred the friendship of a Moor to that of his own brother-in-law, the King of France. And in attacking Barbarossa, the Sultan's local representative, Charles had made war against the Ottoman Empire not in order to expand Christendom, nor for self-defence, nor even to extend his own territorial rule, but 'to restore and re-establish an infidel king', merely because he was 'motivated by a greed for glory'. In these circumstances it was only natural, observed du Bellay, that the Sultan

---

28. Pujeau, *L'Europe et les Turcs*, p. 402 (citing Biblioteca Apostolica Vaticana, MS Urb. Lat. 849, 'Esortazione a Francesco re di Francia').
29. Pannier, 'Calvin et les Turcs', p. 281 ('impia', 'gravissime et saevissime cruciantur in regno et sub rege Christianissimo'); Billacois, 'Le Turc', pp. 238–9 (1618 pamphlet).

should respond by preparing an anti-Imperial campaign. On the fundamental issue of accepting military help from a non-Christian ruler, du Bellay first set out a number of biblical examples of alliances with unbelievers (by Abraham, David, Solomon, and the Maccabees), and then declared that under canon law any Christian prince, deprived of his estate, was entitled to seek assistance, if needed, from rulers of a different faith.[30]

One of the most rhetorically brilliant defences of the Franco-Ottoman alliance was produced by another French diplomat, Jean de Monluc, who had himself acted as a personal envoy from François to Barbarossa in 1537. After the scandalous stay of the Ottoman fleet at Toulon in 1543–4, he was sent to Venice in order to explain and exculpate François's policy; the speech he gave to the Venetian Senate made a great impression there. He began with biblical and historical precedents, declaring that it was a new and false article of faith to say that a ruler could not use the help of infidels in his own defence—such a rule would condemn not only King David, and King Asa of Judaea (2 Chron. 16: 2–4), but also the Christian East Roman Emperors Constantine, Arcadius, and Heraclius. The Holy Roman Emperor Frederick II had used the help of 'Saracens' to conquer much of Italy, and quite recently the Emperor Maximilian had made efforts to encourage an Ottoman attack on Venetian territory. With these last examples Monluc had shifted from offering models of pious prudence to denouncing the Imperial side for hypocrisy; yet he immediately went on to claim, on the strength of all these precedents taken together, that 'for the King my lord, gaining assistance from the support of the Sultan is licit and allowed *for any need he may have* [emphasis added].' Sultan Süleyman had offered help, and François had accepted it in order to counter 'the insolence of the Imperial ministers'; in doing so, he had gained a position of influence over the Ottoman fleet, with the result that—unlike Imperial troops crossing Venetian territory, who pillaged and murdered as they went—those ships had passed peacefully up the Italian coast, troubling no one. From this it followed that 'our particular advantage was, in this case, united with the public benefit of all Christendom.'[31]

In the latter part of his speech, Monluc offered a much more specific justification of French policy. The King had accepted Ottoman help 'not

---

30. du Bellay, *Double d'une lettre*, sigs. C8v ('quel interestz auons nous en lung plus quen laultre, que les erreurs & impostures de Mahomet soient preschees en Africque ou par vng More, ou par vng Turc?'), D1r (preferred friendship), D3v–D4r (biblical examples, canon law), D4v ('pour restablir & remectre vng Roy infidele', 'meu de cupidite de gloire').

31. Weiss, ed., *Papiers d'état*, iii, pp. 2–3 (examples), 4 ('al re mio sig^e, ad ogni suo bisogno, l'aiutarsi dello sussidio del s^r Turcho sia lecito et concesso'), 5 ('la insolenza de' ministri imp^li', '[il] nostro utile particolare era in questa parte congiunto con il beneficio publico di tutta la christianità').

out of ambition to dominate, not to act in vindication of an injury received, not to make himself lord of other people's possessions, not to recover what had been unjustly taken from him, but only to defend himself.' The narrowing of the range here may have surprised some of Monluc's hearers, as two of the rejected lines of defence (vindicating an injury, and recovering one's property) were regarded as solid justifications in traditional 'just war' theory. But the purpose was to emphasize the extreme forbearance and political virtue of the French King, who, as Monluc went on to explain, had received many injuries from Charles V, but had responded by 'willingly and lovingly agreeing to a ten years' truce'. As for the basic theological argument that it was wrong to collaborate with an unbeliever: here Monluc found an easy target on the other side, demanding to know why the Emperor enlisted the forces of Protestant Germans, and had formed an alliance with the arch-heretic King of England, Henry VIII.[32]

Another text, produced in 1544 in the name of François I, was addressed to the members of the Imperial Diet of Speyer (summoned by the Emperor in February of that year) and was issued in Latin, thereby inviting a wider European readership. It used several of the arguments deployed by du Bellay and Monluc: for example, it noted the enlistment of Saracens by Frederick II, and cited the cases of Abraham, David, and Solomon as evidence of 'a common right of all nations'. It also emphasized both the self-restraint of François's policy in not asking Barbarossa to attack the Spanish fleet, although it was a serious threat to France, and the benefits the French had bestowed by restraining the Ottomans: they had moderated Barbarossa's conduct at the siege of Nice, and had used their influence to protect Italy from any depredations that his fleet might otherwise have inflicted—'with a degree of benefit to our friends to which almost all Italy bears witness, having given such warm greetings to Barbarossa's fleet as it sailed past'. (Evidently this rosy-eyed account was written before July, when, on its return voyage, the fleet mounted a full-scale attack on the island of Lipari, to the north of Sicily, carrying off large numbers of its inhabitants into slavery.)[33]

32. Ibid., pp. 6 ('non per ambicione di dominare, non per vendicarsi della ricevuta ingiuria, non per insignorirsi della robba d'altrui, non per recuperare quello che ingiustamente gli è usurpato, ma solo per defendersi'), 8 ('volontieri et amorevolmente la tregua di dieci anni consentì'; Germans, Henry VIII).

33. François I, *Oratio*, sigs. D4r ('com[m]uni quodam omnium gentium iure'), D4v (Frederick II, canon law), E4v (Spanish fleet), F1v (Nice), F2v ('Quanto amicorum beneficio, testis est Italia propè omnis, quae praetereuntem Aenobarbi classem tantum de littore salutauit'); Dorez, ed., *Itinéraire*, p. 126 (Lipari).

In some of the later defences of the Franco-Ottoman alliance, one senses that the essential justification was becoming simpler and more clearly focused. The *Apologie pour le Roy, contre les calomnies des Imperiaulx*, published in 1551 (after d'Aramon's involvement in the fall of Tripoli) by the humanist scholar, diplomat, and royal tutor Pierre Danes, treated the religious arguments of pro-Imperial writers as mere camouflage: those who denounced the French King simply wished, 'under the mask of religion and holiness, to confuse everything, establish a tyranny in Italy, and rob the King of his possessions'.[34] An 'Apologie' written in *c.*1605 by a M. Racauld and dedicated to one of Henri IV's counsellors, while it cited Monluc's speech and made the standard references to Abraham, David, and Solomon, put particular emphasis on 'the fine and ancient maxim of state which says that the safety of the state must take priority over all laws and all considerations'.[35] In the years since the reign of François I, the development of 'reason of state' theory had rendered such points easier to make; and yet there was still a feeling that setting out the obvious truth about French geopolitical interests vis-à-vis the Ottoman Empire was an awkward thing to do. When Savary de Brèves (Henri IV's ambassador in Istanbul) warned that any breach in the friendship between the French King and the Sultan would be seized on by the King of Spain, who would be able to cultivate good relations with Istanbul and then, freed from his fear of the Ottoman navy, 'would find it much easier than he now does to attack us and harm us, both openly and surreptitiously', he did so only in a manuscript memorandum, not in a printed text.[36] And when Louis Deshayes, the son of a later French envoy to Istanbul, published a defence of the alliance in 1624, he ran through all the traditionally avowable justifications—the French King 'is not at all motivated by his particular interests, seeking only the good and advantage of Christendom'; others, including even popes, have sought help from the Ottomans; commerce (not only French, but of other nations too, under French protection) brings

---

34. Danes, *Apologie*, sig. D5r ('soubz le masque de religion & saincté, mettre en confusion toutes choses, establir vne tyrannie en Italie, despouiller le Roy de ce qu'il y tient').

35. Bibliothèque Sainte-Geneviève, Paris, MS 3086, fos. 5r–v ('ceste belle & antienne maxime d'estat, qui dit que le salut de l'estat doibt aller par dessus toutes loix et considerations', Monluc), 11r (Abraham, etc.). This text is undated, but datable on internal grounds.

36. Bibliothèque Inguimbertine, Carpentras, MS 1777, fo. 7v ('Il luy seroit beaucoup plus facile que maintenant de nous attaquer et endommager ouuertement et par menees secrettes'). This text differs from the 'Discours sur l'alliance qu'a le Roy, auec le Grand Seigneur, & de l'vtilité qu'elle apporte à la Chrestienté', printed in his *Relation des voyages*, 4th pagination, pp. 3–10, which gives the publicly avowable justifications (commerce, protection of the Holy Places, etc.) but not this one.

great benefits; and France protects Catholics in the Ottoman Empire, as well as the Holy Places—before adding, obscurely, that there were some other reasons which could not be published.[37]

In the following year, however, a more outspoken book was produced in Paris on this topic, with a dedication to Richelieu. The author, Guillaume Le Guay, was a private individual, not a diplomat or official but a priest and doctor of laws; perhaps he did not feel as constrained by the dictates of public policy as Savary de Brèves or Deshayes. His book ran through a whole range of familiar points, from biblical examples to the hypocrisy of the Imperial side. As a theologian, he adduced some new arguments from the New Testament: for example, to show that the Law of the Gospel had not changed the rules under which Abraham and David had cooperated with unbelievers, he quoted Galatians 6: 10, 'As we have therefore opportunity, let us do good unto all men.' He also referred to canon law, citing the Spanish Dominican theorist Domingo Báñez to the effect that since infidels could themselves undertake just wars, it must be legitimate for a Christian waging a just war to enlist infidel support. Unusually, he quoted at some length the cautionary remarks made in Erasmus's essay on the saying, 'War seems sweet to those who have not experienced it' (while also explicitly rejecting Luther's warnings against resisting the instrument of God's wrath). But at a central point in his argument, Le Guay did set out the obvious truth which other writers had been chary of mentioning. France was a constant object of jealousy and aggression by its neighbours, he wrote, and when it was left at peace this was only for two reasons: its own strength, and its enemies' fear of the Ottomans, which diverted elsewhere the military forces that would otherwise be used to attack it. Everyone must realize, therefore, that 'if this fear works so much to his [sc. the King of France's] advantage, for the safety, preservation, and consolidation of his rule, he will have good cause not to be among the first of those who hasten to put an end to it.'[38]

37. Deshayes, *Voiage de Levant*, pp. 271 ('n'y est point porté pas ses interets particuliers, mais seulement pour le bien & pour l'aduantage de la Chrestienté'), 272 (popes), 273–6 (Catholics, Holy Places), 278–9 (trade, other reasons). This work, though referring to Deshayes in the third person, is traditionally attributed to him.

38. Le Guay, *Alliances du Roy*, pp. 12–17 (examples), 36–8 (Gal. 6: 10; idols, where the correct references should be 1 Cor. 8: 10–12 and 10: 20–8), 44–5 (canon law), 48 (officials), 55 (hypocrisy), 98–9 (two reasons, 'Que si cette peur tourne tant à son auantage, à son salut, conseruation & establissement, il aura grande occasion de n'estre pas des premiers à courir pour la faire cesser'), 131–3 (Luther), 163–74 (Erasmus).

One theme that emerged in several of these apologetic texts was the idea that an objective international norm required rulers to keep their promises (including ones formalized in treaties), regardless of any religious differences between them. In the pamphlet issued over his name in 1544, François I blamed the most recent Ottoman invasion and conquest of Hungary on Charles V: Süleyman had acted in justified retaliation against Charles's attack on Tunis in 1535, which had been in breach of a promise of peace. Pierre Danes, similarly, noted that Charles was reneging on a peace agreement with Süleyman when he attacked positions on the Tunisian coast in 1550. And Guillaume Le Guay emphasized that treaties or other undertakings with infidels were binding, even if they were entered into out of necessity. He gave the famous example of King Ladislas of Hungary, whose disastrous 'Varna crusade' in 1444 had been in breach of a peace agreement with Sultan Mehmed, and he also defended the Ottoman decision to enslave the defenders of Tripoli in 1551 (with the exception of the Knights of Malta for whom d'Aramon had interceded), on the grounds that those men had themselves acted in breach of promise. According to legal experts, he wrote, there is no duty to fulfil your promises towards those who break their word.[39]

To assert that promises in general, and especially treaties, should be kept ('fides est servanda', 'pacta sunt servanda') was uncontroversial. But this issue had a particular salience in writings about relations with the Ottoman Empire, thanks to a tradition of Western polemical writing which portrayed the Ottomans as deliberately and systematically untrustworthy in such matters. Cardinal Bessarion had written that they regarded all peace treaties as mere pauses for convenience; Ludovik Crijević Tuberon said that Sultan Selim I was always happy to break his promises in order to gain more territory; Juan Luis Vives declared that whereas Christians knew it was a sin to break one's word, the Ottomans regarded it as almost a duty to break theirs. The widely read history of the Ottoman–Persian war by Giovanni Tommaso Minadoi (1588) confidently stated that 'this empire [sc. the Ottoman one] is ruled so impiously and barbarously that whenever it is a matter of attempting some military action to increase its territory, it is permitted to violate a truce and break a promise', and the influential chronicler Johannes Leunclavius (Johann Löwenklau) listed 'violation of promises' as one of the

---

39. François I, Oratio, sig. E3r; Danes, Apologie, sig. A3r; Le Guay, Alliances, pp. 114 (necessity), 123–4 (Varna), 125–6 (Tripoli). Le Guay was perhaps giving a simplified version of Bodin's argument on this point: see below, p. 123.

key features of the Ottoman regime. (He was followed by the English historian Richard Knolles, who drew heavily on his works; Knolles observed that 'Their leagues...haue with them no longer force than standeth with their own profit', and that Mehmed II 'kept no league, promise, or oath, longer than stood with his profit or pleasure'.)[40] One of the strongest statements of this view was in the richly rhetorical and aptly entitled 'Exclamatio' of the former Imperial diplomat Ogier Ghiselin de Busbecq, published in order to incite Christendom to war against the Ottomans in 1581. The Sultan, he wrote, was someone

> who never cared a straw for peace or for treaties; for whom none of the shared laws of the other peoples is valid; who is restrained by no sense of shame and no intention to act virtuously; who regards breaking a promise or an oath given to a Christian person, when it suits his purposes to do so, as not only not a crime, but even a pious and holy act.[41]

Here was a double charge: in general the Ottomans failed to comply with the 'ius gentium', the law of nations, and in particular they did so under the influence of their own religion.

This whole line of argument was contested, however. Paolo Giovio, in his influential *Commentario de le cose de' Turchi*, went out of his way—for shame-praising purposes, it seems—to emphasize the fidelity of Süleyman the Magnificent. Describing the surrender of Rhodes by the Knights in 1522, he wrote that their Grand Master agreed to hand over the island in return for safe conduct for the Knights with all their possessions: 'with the highest degree of respect for religion and humanity, Süleyman kept his promise, and refrained from touching the holy objects of the Church of St John—something that our own soldiers, perhaps, would not have done.' And in the great historical chronicle which he later published, *Historia sui temporis*, he gave an example of Süleyman ordering the release of the citizens of Castro (a small town near Otranto) who, on surrendering to Ottoman forces, had been taken captive

40. Schwoebel, *Shadow*, p. 158 (Bessarion); Crijević Tuberon, *Commentariorum*, p. 356; Margolin, 'Conscience européenne', p. 123 (Vives); Minadoi, *Historia*, p. 21 ('Tanto empiamente, & tanto barbaramente si gouerna questo impero, che quantunque si tratti de tentar alcuna impresa per accrescimento di lui, sia lecito violar la tregua, & romper la fede'); Leunclavius, *Historiae musulmanae*, p. 8 ('fidei violatio'); Knolles, *Generall Historie*, sig. A5r ('Their leagues...'), p. 337 (Mehmed).
41. Busbecq, 'Exclamatio', p. 115 ('qui pacem, qui foedera, nunquam pili fecit; apud quem nullae valent communes reliquarum ge[n]tium leges; quem nullus pudor, nulla honesti ratio continet; qui fidem, qui iusiura[n]dum, homini Christiano datum, violare, vbi rationibus suis conducit, non modò nullum nefas, verùm etiam pium & sanctum putat').

in breach of a promise of safety: the Sultan was 'always extremely observant of faith and justice in his dealings with those who surrendered voluntarily'.[42] The French Knight of Malta Antoine Geuffroy, whose account of the Ottoman court (1543) was translated into German, Latin, and English, wrote that Süleyman was regarded as someone who 'keeps his faith and his word, whatever he promises'. And the description of the Ottoman Empire by the royal servant Christophe Richer, published just a few years earlier, made a broader cultural claim when discussing promises of eventual freedom made by Ottoman masters to their slaves: 'the Turks are so faithful that they keep whatever promise they make; and they trust one another so much that in their contracts they make no use of bonds, seals, or signs manual, believing in the word of the promiser.'[43]

For some writers, the way to deal with the evidence of Süleyman's faithful conduct was simply to portray him as an exceptional figure in Ottoman history. Michel de Montaigne, commenting appreciatively on the freeing of the citizens of Castro, began his account with the words, 'Süleyman, from the family of the Ottomans, a family that has paid little attention to the observance of promises and treaties'. (Picking up on a further comment made by Giovio, he added that the Sultan was calculating that breaches of promise of this kind would make it harder to conquer territories in future.) Richard Knolles also gave Süleyman credit for this action—calling him 'a most iust prince'—while retaining, as we have seen, a general condemnation of the Ottomans as treaty-violators.[44] But some authors were happy to celebrate such examples of Ottoman fidelity for more general reasons. Matthew Sutcliffe, in the course of his denunciation of 'Turcopapism', declared that the Ottomans kept their word, at least some of the time, unlike the Roman Catholics, and that they did not teach—as the Catholics did—that promises could be broken. The examples he gave included Süleyman's conduct after the siege of Rhodes, and 'after the capture of Belgrade, and in other places'.[45]

42. Giovio, *Commentario*, p. 151 ('Solimano con somma religione e umanità servò la promessa, né toccò le cose sacre del Tempio di San Giovanni il che forse non arebbero fatto i nostri soldati'); Giovio, *Opera*, ii, p. 334 (*Historia*, ch. 36) ('semper in sponte deditos fidei atque iusticiae obseruantissimus').

43. Geuffroy, *Briefve description*, sig. f3r ('gardant sa foy & parolle quoy quil promette'); Richer, *Des coustumes*, p. 19 ('les Turcs sont de telle foy, que ce qu'ilz promettent, ilz le tiennent: & se fient tant les vngs aux autres, que en leurs contracts ilz n'usent point d'obligations, ne de seaulx, ne de seigns manuels: ains croyent a la seule parolle de celuy qui fait la promesse').

44. Montaigne, *Essais*, ii, p. 633 ('Solyman, de la race des Ottomans, race peu soigneuse de l'observance des promesses et pac[t]es'); Knolles, *Generall Historie*, p. 674.

45. Sutcliffe, *De turco-papismo*, p. 105 ('capto Belgrado, & aliis in locis').

One of the fullest discussions of the whole subject of treaties and alliances was given in a lengthy chapter (V.6) of Jean Bodin's very influential political treatise *Six livres de la république* (1576). Bodin was passionate about the importance of keeping one's word: 'Seeing then that faith is the only foundation and support of iustice whereon not only Commonweales, but all humaine societie is grounded, it must remaine sacred and inuiolable in those things which are not vniust, especially betwixt princes.' The phrase 'in those things which are not vniust' was an important qualification, and he also accepted the principle that those who break their word deserve to receive the same treatment in return. But the examples he gave of such breaches of faith were all committed by Christians, including one where a papal legate had instructed the Hungarians to renege on a peace agreement with the Ottomans, with disastrous results.[46] Whilst Bodin did not make any specific references here to exemplary faith-keeping by the Ottoman sultans (though elsewhere he commended Mehmed II for his virtue and piety in extraditing to Florence the murderer of Giuliano de' Medici, who had sought refuge in Istanbul), he made it clear that he did not regard them as faith-breakers in general.[47] He dismissed with scorn Charles V's complaint against François I for making an alliance with the Sultan, pointing out that Poland, Venice, Genoa, and Dubrovnik had also made such agreements with the Ottoman Empire, and that Charles himself had entered into a treaty of friendship with the Shah of Persia.[48] Citing the case of Joshua, who had kept his agreement with the Gibeonites even when he found that they had deceived him in making it (Josh. 9), Bodin insisted that treaties must be kept with pagans and infidels. His basic principle was that 'if it be lawfull to break ones faith with infidels, then it is not lawful to giue it; but contrariwise if it bee lawfull to capitulate [*sc.* make a formal agreement] with infidels, it is also necessarie to keepe promise with them.' For that reason he was particularly

---

46. Bodin, *Six Bookes* (I cite this translation, which includes passages added in the later Latin translation by Bodin, not only because it is generally accurate but also because, in the absence of standard modern editions of the French and the Latin, it is the most widely available version of the full text), pp. 626ʳA ('Seeing...'; *Les Six Livres*, p. 802: 'Or puis qu'il est ainsi, que la foy est le seul fondement & appuy de iustice, sur laquelle sont fondees toutes les Republiques, alliances & societés des hommes, aussi faut il qu'elle demeure sacree & inuiolable, es choses qui ne soint point iniustes: & principalement entre les Princes'), 628ʳB (papal legate). I cite the French from the 1583 edn., which incorporates minor revisions by Bodin.

47. On the treatment of the defenders of Tripoli in 1551, to whom safe conduct had been promised, Bodin commented that the Ottoman commander invoked a correct principle (faith can be broken with those who have themselves broken their word), but misapplied it to the facts of the case: *Six Bookes*, p. 628ᵛF–G.

48. Bodin, *Six Bookes*, pp. 359D (extraditing), 628ʳC–D (Charles V, Poland, etc.).

scathing about the decision of the Council of Constance that permitted Catholics to break their word to 'enemies of the faith' (a view which never became the general position of the Church, but which was often attributed by Protestant writers of the late sixteenth and early seventeenth centuries, such as Sutcliffe, to Catholics in general and Jesuits in particular).[49]

In agreeing that one need not keep promises towards those who break theirs, Bodin was not only repeating a legal commonplace, but also accepting, in this context, one element of what modern theorists would call—as we have seen—a concept of 'international society'. (There could be no making of alliances in the first place with pirates and brigands, he argued, as they stood outside the 'ius gentium', the law of nations, and could not be beneficiaries of it.[50]) On this point he was in no doubt that, as a matter of fact, the Ottomans qualified as members. Those who argued most strongly on the other side—such as Busbecq—not only denied the factual premise where this particular criterion was concerned, but also portrayed the Ottomans much more generally as beyond the bounds of all civilized behaviour. One of the strongest expressions of this view was presented in a 'discourse' on alliances with Muslim powers, published in 1587, by the Huguenot writer (and military commander) François de La Noue. Amid much anti-Ottoman invective, the only specific example he gave of perfidy by a sultan was that of Süleyman's takeover of most of Hungary after the death of John Zápolya in 1540, apparently in breach of his original promise to that ruler. (This charge involved a considerable simplification of the historical circumstances of 1540–1.) But La Noue's argument rested not so much on empirical evidence as on religious conviction. He wrote that he had consulted theologians, who assured him that Muslims were represented by the 'little horn' of the fourth beast in Daniel's vision; and he noted that in the Old Testament God had forbidden alliances with the Canaanites and the Moabites, because of their 'impieties' and 'vices'.[51] Islam was full of wickedness and blasphemy, 'and their government is the most horrible and cruel tyranny that ever existed, being arranged, it seems, not to maintain laws, discipline, and virtue, but to overturn them.' The problem with Christian rulers trying to ally with

49. Ibid., pp. 628ʳA (Constance; *Six Livres*, p. 808: 'ennemis de la foy'), 628ʳC ('if it be...'; *Six Livres*, p. 809: 'si la foy ne doit estre gardee aux ennemis, elle ne doit pas estre donnee: & au contraire s'il est licite de capituler auec les ennemis, aussi est-il necessaire de leur garder la promesse'), 628ʳE–628ᵛF (Joshua).
50. Bodin, *Six Bookes*, p. 630ʳB–C (pirates, brigands).
51. La Noue, *Discours*, pp. 444 (Zápolya), 450 (little horn), 451 ('impietés', 'vices'). On the 'little horn' see above, pp. 84–5.

the Ottomans was, he insisted, not just the familiar one that occurs when less powerful states make disadvantageous alliances with stronger ones; it was fundamentally different in this case, because it involved 'destroyers and banes of the world, among whom treason, impiety, injustice, and cruelty are always present'. Therefore, he warned, it could never be right to make an alliance with them, as they would always be aiming at your enslavement and ruin.[52] Some kinds of agreement could legitimately be entered into, such as truces, peace settlements, agreements on reparations, and commercial treaties, but not alliances of mutual aid, which aimed at maintaining 'civil amity'. As for seeking their military help against other Christian powers: 'isn't this as if someone went to the woods in order to hire brigands to enter his house and kill a relative or a friend?' On the subject of the French–Ottoman alliance, La Noue added some bitter comments about the enslavement—and, even worse, conversion to Islam—of Christians by Barbarossa, observing that the international 'vituperation' caused by this had greatly reduced 'the glory and the power' of France. His conclusion was that all Christian powers were under a constant duty to make war against the Ottomans—not to convert them to Christianity (as true religion can never be propagated by force), but to counter their 'cruelty and tyranny'.[53]

The most distinguished sixteenth-century writer to address these topics after Bodin was Alberico Gentili, whose *De iure belli* (1598) is one of the foundational texts of what later came to be conceptualized as the doctrine of international law. A Protestant, he fled his native Papal States and moved to England in 1580, becoming Professor of Civil Law at Oxford in the following year. This meant that he was quite far removed from the practical politics of relations with the Ottoman Empire, though his theoretical engagement with the issue was no less strong for all that: Gentili was, or became, an outspoken advocate of anti-Ottoman warfare. (His arguments about this will be discussed in chapter 11, below.) Like most Protestant theorists in this period, he was opposed to the idea that religious difference was an adequate reason for going to war; it would not be legitimate to attack the Ottomans just for

52. La Noue, *Discours*, pp. 439 ('& leur gouuernement la plus horrible & cruelle tyrannie qui fut onques: estant dressee (ce semble) plustost pour renuerser les loix, la discipline & l'honnesteté, que pour les maintenir'), 442 ('destructeurs & fleaux du monde, chez lesquels la trahison, l'impieté, l'iniustice & la cruauté sont tousiours logees').
53. Ibid., pp. 442 (truces, etc.), 443 ('amitié ciuile'), 445 ('N'est-ce pas autant comme si quelqu'vn alloit dans les bois loüer des brigands pour tuer dans sa propre maison son parent ou son ami…?'), 446–7 (French–Ottoman alliance), 448 ('la gloire & la puissance'), 452 (duty, 'cruauté & tyrannie').

the purpose of converting them, still less because of the mere fact that they were not Christians. His more general arguments about the difference between God-related and man-related duties have led some commentators to describe him as a 'secularizing' thinker. And yet, when he came to consider the question of alliances with infidel powers, religion did play some part in his argument.

His main discussion of this came in a chapter of *De iure belli* (III.19) entitled 'Whether it is right to enter into an alliance with people of a different religion'.[54] Here he accepted that various forms of cooperation with infidels are allowed, including trade. A commercial treaty is, he argues, perfectly acceptable. Some other kinds of formal engagement are also permitted by him, so long as they are on unequal terms: thus it is lawful to make treaties that bind infidel states to you as your tributaries, and it is also permissible to enter into a contract of hire under which they agree to supply soldiers to fight on your behalf. However, Gentili insists that a treaty of alliance, in which a Christian power agrees to fight together with an infidel power against another infidel power, is not lawful—so, *a fortiori*, it must be illicit to ally with infidels to fight against Christians. Referring to the Italian Protestant theologian Peter Martyr Vermigli, he declares that 'I agree with the most learned theologian of our age, who says that it is never right to make a military alliance with infidels.' And, in accordance with this doctrine, he condemns the Franco-Ottoman alliance.[55]

This absolute rejection of alliances with infidels, even for the purpose of fighting against other infidels, is surprising for more than one reason. A late-sixteenth-century author such as Gentili who had drunk deep from the wells of 'reason of state' theory, and who admired the pragmatic and realistic approach of Bodin, should not have been overly troubled by the notion of an alliance with the Ottomans. He was himself one of the leading exponents of the theory of the 'balance of power', which was being developed during precisely this period. In his chapter on pre-emptive defence, he quoted the famous statement by Lorenzo de' Medici 'that the affairs of the rulers of Italy should be balanced by equal weights', and immediately drew the conclusion that Spanish power must be counterbalanced in Europe: 'Unless there is something that can withstand Spain, Europe will indeed

---

54. Ibid. III.19, p. 649 ('Si foedus recte contrahitur cum diuersae religionis hominibus'). What follows here is drawn partly from Malcolm, 'Alberico Gentili'.

55. Ibid. III.19, pp. 657–60 (p. 659: 'maneo cum doctissimo nostri seculi theologo: qui negat, cum infidelibus arma rectè coniungi vmquam').

fall.'[56] What could counterbalance the might of Habsburg power? Since the 1520s, the kings of France had considered that question and had found just one obvious answer. For Gentili it must have been awkward (to say the least) to realize that, of his two most feared expansionist powers, one might be positively needed to redress the balance against the other. He was, besides, a passionate Protestant who, in one of his early works, had set out to prove in great detail that the Papacy was the Antichrist predicted in the Book of Revelation; at the start of that treatise, he had rejected the claim that the Antichrist should be identified with Islam instead, pointing out that the 'priests' of the Muslims, unlike those of Rome, never imposed their law on people's consciences.[57] Here was at least a tiny germ of potential 'Calvinoturcism' in Gentili's thinking; and yet his statements about relations with the Ottomans simply ruled out any kind of strategic alliance with them, even against the Antichrist of Rome.

Much of Gentili's discussion of the issue of alliances in *De iure belli* I.19 is framed as a reply to Decianus's consilium (cited above) on the question, 'Whether secular rulers may justly enter into an alliance with infidels'.[58] Here too there is something a little surprising about the pattern of argument. Alberico Gentili, the 'secularizing' theorist, insists that it can never be right to make an alliance with infidels. Decianus, the pious Catholic jurist steeped in the canon law tradition, argues that it is sometimes permissible. And the reasoning on which Decianus depends is not some convoluted piece of peculiarly Catholic theology, which Gentili could not have accepted; rather, it is a simple principle of necessity and self-preservation, drawn from a medieval legal tradition that is rooted directly in the *Digest*. Whatever its sources or nature, one might expect Gentili to have accepted it, given his comments in several of his writings on cases where special measures were called for. In his disputation on lying, published in 1599, he defended the use of an 'officious lie' in cases of 'great necessity', and insisted that the law should be considered in the light of its ultimate aim, citing the maxim, 'Salus populi suprema lex esto' ('Let the safety of the people be the supreme

---

56. Ibid. I.14, p. 104 ('vt res Italorum principum paribus libratae ponderib. forent'), 105 ('Nisi sit, quod obstare Hispano possit, cadet sanè Europe'). Cf. Van der Molen, *Alberico Gentili*, p. 126; Sheehan, *Balance of Power*, pp. 29–33.
57. Bodleian Library, Oxford, MS D'Orville 607, fo. 5r ('Turcismus abominabilis, apostatica, magna ecclesia est Antichristus? negant etiam Scolastici Rabbini Papales, nec Apostolorum tempore uiuebat Maumetus; nec in templo Dei sedet hic, quod videbimus; nec sacerdos unus Turcis est, qui legem conscientijs ponat').
58. See above, p. 110.

law').[59] In his *De armis romanis* he declared: 'That which is not permissible by law is made permissible by necessity. Necessity has no law, but it itself makes a law. Necessity makes something approvable that was otherwise to be disapproved of.'[60] And in *De iure belli* he applied this principle, albeit under stricter conditions, to cases involving the deception of one's enemies.[61] The idea that things which were normally illicit could become licit in cases of necessity was thus perfectly familiar to him; and yet he refused to apply it to the case of an alliance with an infidel power. This requires us to look more closely at the arguments he deployed when making that stubborn refusal.

Gentili's key argument against Decianus was stated as follows. 'Such an alliance cannot be contracted with an infidel against a Christian, because it involves bringing against just enemies—who observe religion, custom, and the laws of war—those who are of an opposing religion, and who fail to observe, and are for the most part contemptuous of, every custom and every *ius* of war.'[62] Here at least was a conceptual distinction of some interest, between a 'just enemy' and an unjust one. The line of thought seems to be that although much lower standards of justice or morality apply under conditions of war (allowing, for example, forms of deception that would be impermissible in peacetime), nevertheless there is a minimum standard, that of the 'just enemy', and those who fall below that cannot be trusted in any way. This would seem to set up a purely prudential argument: if they cannot be trusted, there is no point in making any sort of alliance with them. But Gentili's argument goes further, and emphasizes the wrongness of allying with such people against Christians, whom he assumes, more or less *a priori*, to belong to the 'just enemy' category.

This extra element of Gentili's theory is not properly explained—at least, not in jural terms. Something like a psychological or descriptive explanation is offered earlier in the treatise, when he discusses the altruistic defence of subjects of other states. There he observes that the feeling of fellow-humanity on its own is seldom sufficient to move people to action on behalf of others outside their country; additional motives are needed, and, of these, religion

59. A. Gentili, *Disputationum duae*, pp. 123–210, here pp. 131 ('in magna necessitate'), 195.
60. A. Gentili, *Wars of the Romans*, pp. 115–16 ('Quod non est licitum lege, necessitas facit licitum. Non habet legem necessitas, sed ipsa legem facit. Necessitas facit probabile, quod erat aliàs improbabile').
61. A. Gentili, *De iure belli* II.3, II.4, II.5, pp. 228–49.
62. Ibid. III.19, pp. 659–60 ('Non potest contra fidelem hoc foedus cum infideli contrahi: quia contra iustos hostes, religionis, & consuetudinis, & bellicarum legum seruantes adducuntur aduersi religione, & expertes, & plurimum contemptores omnis moris, & omnis bellici iuris').

is by far the most powerful.[63] This descriptive point may well explain why it is that Christians are reluctant to enter alliances that pit infidels against other Christians; but it does not really deal with the normative question, about whether such alliances may in some circumstances be justified nevertheless. And it might be added that if Gentili's argument had been conducted essentially at the descriptive level, it might have been obliged to come, like Bodin's, to a very different conclusion—since the empirical evidence, admitted in passing by Gentili, was that Muslim rulers did sometimes act justly and morally in their external dealings (he cited the story of a king of Morocco who gave aid to the king of Castile out of a sense of common humanity), and that the Ottoman sultans did not go to war on a whim but sought 'good causes' for doing so.[64]

In the end, then, we find Gentili coming back to an essentially theological position. The argument is not that most infidels, as a matter of ascertainable fact, fail to meet the standards of the 'just enemy', which would imply that in most cases alliances with infidels are wrong. Rather, the argument is that alliances with infidels are *always* wrong, and they are wrong *because they are infidels*. The assumption, therefore, is not that various criteria should be applied to find out whether they act as members of 'international society'; they are excluded from it *a priori*. Nor does Gentili try to show that the specific doctrines of Islam require Muslims to ignore the 'customs and laws of war'; what he says here applies to all infidels, whatever their beliefs. An argument of an absolute and unconditional nature was needed to support this position, and that argument was supplied to Gentili by theology, drawing directly on Holy Scripture. The standard biblical examples of treaties made with unbelievers (by Joshua, the Maccabees, etc.) were dismissed, on the grounds that God had shown his disapproval of them; instead, Gentili referred to the severest statements in the Pentateuch about driving out the nations of unbelievers from Canaan, and quoted Exodus 23: 32, 'Thou shalt make no covenant with them'.[65] Gentili clearly thought that such theological arguments were of essential relevance, and prepared the ground for them when he announced, at the beginning of his discussion: 'This is partly a theological issue, which has been treated by theologians, and partly a civil

63. Ibid. I.15, pp. 116–17.
64. Ibid. I.6, p. 53 ('Ipsi etiam Turcae bonas quaerunt caussas, quum cogitant bellum movere'), I.15, p. 111.
65. Ibid. III.19, p. 649.

issue, which has been treated by our lawyers.'[66] But how exactly did this theological–civil combination come about in the mind of someone who, elsewhere in his writings, had distinguished carefully between the area of rights and injuries between man and God on the one hand and that between man and man on the other?[67] His reference to the theologian Peter Martyr Vermigli (cited above) was to a discussion of this question in Vermigli's *Loci communes*, which contained a strong rejection of any alliance with infidels for any purpose (even to save a Christian state in peril), and put forward just one argument: alliances of this sort might lead to the creation of mixed Christian–infidel armies, and in such an army 'the pure religion and idolatry are mixed together'.[68] Here, at least, was a clear theological argument; but it concerned idolatry, which, as Gentili had argued when rejecting the idea that the suppression of idolatry could be a just cause of war, was strictly a matter between man and God, and not a proper determinant of relations between one society and another.

So we are left with a sense that, although Gentili's separation between theology and politics was quite far-reaching by the standards of its day, it was not absolute; commitment to a strongly biblical Protestantism remained an active element in his whole pattern of thought. In this he was not an untypical figure in what modern historians may have been too eager to identify as a secularizing age.

66. Ibid. III.19, p. 649 ('est quaestio partim theologalis, tractataque theologis; partim & nostris tractata ciuilis').
67. Ibid. I.25, p. 203.
68. Vermigli, *Loci communes* IV.16.21–3, p. 943 ('religionem synceram, & εἰδωλολάτρειαν misceri').

SIX

The new paradigm

The sixteenth-century alliance between France and the Ottoman Empire had one small but significant effect on cultural and intellectual history: it stimulated, and facilitated, travel to Ottoman territory by a number of French writers. While their resulting publications differed widely, in purpose as well as in quality, several of them did add to Western knowledge about the internal conditions of the Ottoman Empire—and, in the process, contributed to a broader change of attitude towards that Empire on the part of some Western readers.

The earliest French author to benefit from these Franco-Ottoman relations was the theologian and oriental linguist Guillaume Postel, who accompanied the first ambassador, Jean de La Forest, on his journey to Istanbul in 1535, and travelled to Syria and Egypt during the following year. Postel had learned Arabic before he set out, and acquired some Turkish during his stay. This made him, on his return to Western Europe, one of the most knowledgeable Orientalists in Christendom; but he was also the most untypical. His Arabic and Hebrew scholarship was employed in various enthusiastic personal projects that set him apart from most or all of his contemporaries: proving that Jews, Muslims, and pagans could be converted to Christianity by developing principles that were common to all religions; demonstrating, on biblical grounds, that the King of France should be recognized as the rightful ruler of the world; and developing an idiosyncratic theology, based on Jewish cabbalistic texts, in which one of the primary expressions of God's spirit was incarnated in a holy woman, Zuana, whom Postel had got to know in Venice.[1] It was apparently with his conversionary purposes in mind that he spent more time in the Levant, Egypt, and Istanbul

---

1. For studies of Postel's thought see Bouwsma, *Concordia mundi*; Kuntz, *Guillaume Postel*; Petry, *Gender, Kabbalah and the Reformation* (with a valuable biographical summary, pp. 28–49); and the essays in Margolin, ed., *Guillaume Postel*, and Secret, *Postel revisité*.

in 1549–50, during d'Aramon's ambassadorship.[2] In 1560 he published three separate books relating to Islam and the Ottoman Empire: *De la république des Turcs*; *Histoire et consideration de l'origine, loy, et coustume des Tartares, Persiens, Arabes, Turcs*; and *La Tierce Partie des orientales histoires, ou est exposée la condition, puissance, & revenu de l'Empire Turquesque*. The first of these bore a royal 'privilège', for all three, dated 7 March 1547 (just a few weeks before François I's death), and a note by the printer saying that the works had been in his hands for a long time—though the point of that note may have been precisely to cover for the fact that Postel had added much new material since 1547.[3] Certainly the first and third of these works, which contained a mass of information on present-day conditions, both social and religious, gave a very different, and much more positive, account of life in the Ottoman Empire than had been contained in the few relevant pages of Postel's treatise on religious harmony of 1544, the *De orbis terrae concordia*.[4] In any case, although Postel's increasingly dubious personal reputation, and his many exalted theological and/or Gallomaniac publications, might have encouraged readers to treat him with suspicion, these factual accounts were widely read and contributed significantly to a new understanding of life under Ottoman rule.

Several other authors benefited from French diplomatic relations with Istanbul. When d'Aramon sailed from Venice as ambassador to Süleyman in early 1547, he took with him a cluster of writers: Jacques Gassot, whose brief account of the journey was published in 1550, Jean Chesneau, whose longer narrative remained in manuscript until the late nineteenth century, and the physician and naturalist Pierre Belon, whose major work, *Les Observations*, appeared in 1553. D'Aramon was already en route when François I died in late March 1547; the new king, Henri II, later sent another envoy, and he was accompanied by the writer André Thevet, whose description of his own travels, *Cosmographie du Levant*, was printed in 1554. And when d'Aramon returned to Istanbul—via Tripoli, as we have seen—for another stint as ambassador in 1551, he took with him Nicolas de Nicolay, author of what became a very popular work, *Les Navigations*, written apparently in 1555 but

2. A short text by his self-described 'disciple' Theodore Bibliander records that 'Elias Pandochaeus' (a soubriquet used by Postel) went to the Holy Land in 1549 in order to kill the prophets of Baal, having issued a 'prognosticon' for 1550, predicting the advent of the spiritual reign of Christ: Zentralbibliothek, Zurich, MS Car. I. 92, fos. 285r–312v, at fo. 285r–v.

3. Postel, *De la république*, verso of title page (privilège), and unsigned leaf before sig. a1 (printer's note).

4. Postel, *De orbis terrae concordia*, pp. 233–47 (on the negative social effects of Islam).

published in 1567. Within a decade this book was reprinted in French, and translated into Italian, Dutch, and German.[5]

It would be easy but wrong to suppose that these writers tended to project a more positive view of Ottoman life because they were in the service of, or connected to, the diplomacy of a pro-Ottoman French state.[6] The favour shown to French envoys in Istanbul no doubt had advantageous effects on these people's conditions of life there, and on their ease of travel within the Ottoman Empire; but none of them wrote as a propagandist, and several made pointedly negative comments about some of the things they saw, especially where Islamic practices were concerned. (Indeed, one historian has argued that French writers went out of their way to emphasize the negative aspects of Ottoman rule in order to bolster the main public argument in defence of the French alliance, which was that the Christians of the Levant were sorely in need of French protection; this may be true in some individual cases, but it fails to convince as a general statement.[7]) Within this whole group of writers there were differing degrees of hostility or complaisance towards the Ottoman system, with Thevet and Nicolay among the most critical, and Postel and Belon giving the most credit. There were even open disagreements between them: when Postel observed that previous descriptions, written by West Europeans who had been captured and enslaved, were slanted by those people's negative experience, Thevet tartly responded that Postel should try the experience of Ottoman slavery himself, to see how much he liked it.[8] Yet Postel's willingness to describe some aspects of Ottoman life in positive terms coexisted in his own mind with strong commitment to the idea of a crusade (which, of course, would be led by the King of France): his aim, he wrote in 1552, was that 'all Christendom, beginning with France, should willingly undertake to travel and fight against the Ishmaelites or

---

5. On these writers see Tinguely, *L'Écriture du Levant*. On Belon see Merle, 'Introduction', and Huppert, *Style of Paris*, pp. 1–20; on Nicolay see Gomez-Géraud and Yérasimos, 'Introduction'. The Nicolay edns. were German (Nuremberg, 1572), French (Antwerp, 1576), German (Antwerp, 1576), Italian (Antwerp, 1576), Italian (n.p., 1577), Dutch (Antwerp, 1577).

6. The only case in which one might suspect such an influence is that of Christophe Richer, whose little book on Ottoman life (1540) was notably non-denunciatory. Richer was a 'valet de chambre' of François I, and secretary to the Chancellor. His account was a compilation, and made no claims of first-hand experience.

7. Kaiser, 'Evil Empire?', p. 11. Kaiser writes mainly about the 18th century, but this general statement references 16th- and 17th-century works.

8. On Thevet's response (where Postel is not named, but clearly indicated), see Lestringant, 'Guillaume Postel', p. 294.

Muslims', adding that the reason why he described the riches and prosperity of the Sultan's domains was to motivate Western soldiers.[9]

Somehow, nevertheless, these writers did contribute—with Postel and Belon to the fore—to a change of view. One reason may be that this was more or less the first generation of detailed accounts that took Ottoman society, and the system of government, as an established phenomenon to be studied in its own right. Much previous Western European writing had been concerned with the Ottoman Empire as a conquering power, focusing on its nature as a military threat, the (alleged) cruelty and severity of its process of conquest, and the (alleged) sufferings of those populations that had recently fallen under it. The idea that it might be viewed and analysed as a stable regime, protecting certain ways of life and in turn being supported by them, was relatively uncommon—though, as we shall see, some of the information given in accounts by former captives did also contribute to this view.

Another reason might be described as both stylistic and attitudinal: the emphasis on direct personal experience. Postel was insistent on this point, declaring at the beginning of one of his books on the Ottoman Empire that he would not write about anything he had not seen himself (or, failing that, 'diligently sought out and heard' from reliable local informants); Jacques Gassot complained of previous accounts of Ottoman conditions by people 'who have written about them quite superficially, from hearsay'.[10] What was at stake here was more than just a claim of authority; it involved a different attitude towards the task of the writer—and hence, also, towards the reader. For more traditional authors of geographical works, exhibiting knowledge of classical sources, and thereby flattering the readers with their presumed knowledge of them too, was the thing that gave their writing real value as a literary exercise. For others, many kinds of printed sources had their own intrinsic authority, so that a basic part of the writer's task was to weave such materials together (with or without acknowledgement), in a process of what we now call 'intertextuality'. And in one major genre of writing about the Levant, the pilgrim narrative, direct description had inevitably been subordinated, in the larger scheme of things, to theological and biblical

---

9. Postel, *L'Histoire memorable*, fo. 6r ('toute la Chrestienté com[m]encant de la France entrepregne voluntiers le voyage & impugnation co[n]tre les Ismahëlites ou Turcz').

10. Postel, *La Tierce Partie*, p. 1 ('diligentement cherché & entendue'); Gassot, *Le Discours du voyage*, fo. 14r ('qui en ont escript assez legerement, & par ouy dire'). Unfortunately the detailed account which Gassot said he was preparing was not included in his published work.

concerns—although some earlier pilgrim narratives written by merchants, who had sharp eyes for matters of practical detail, broke free of such religious constraints.[11] Two of the mid-sixteenth-century French authors on the Ottoman Empire, Pierre Gylles and André Thevet, did admittedly follow a traditional approach: they were interested primarily in the classical world, using their travels to clarify points of classical learning and facts of ancient (or, for Gylles, Byzantine) history. When Thevet spoke in praise of direct observation at the start of his book, his way of defending it was to make it an adjunct to literary learning: 'a person understands and can perfectly describe what he knew from books so much better when he has carefully examined and experienced it with his own eyes.'[12] Nicolay, too, remarked in his preface that the statements of ancient authors were 'confirmed and approved by the sure sense of my own sight'.[13] But this remark was more of a pro-forma statement aimed at gaining credit with the traditional literary culture; for although his work was not free of intertextuality, it did contain much direct observation—which, together with its frequent and vivid woodblock illustrations of different types of inhabitant of the Ottoman Empire, was what ensured its popularity.

General historical claims about a sixteenth-century shift towards 'objectivity', or towards the development of an 'ethnographic' approach, have exaggerated as they have generalized. The literary and intertextual approach continued for a long time, sometimes even among writers who made a point of claiming eyewitness authority; and where direct description did take place, it often coexisted happily with strong cultural and religious bias.[14] There was no single cultural movement in the direction of objectivity; different factors were at work in different ways. Merchant culture, for example, with its privileging of factual information, influenced the style of Venetian writers such as Francesco Sansovino.[15] It also underlay the lengthy and detailed reports or 'relazioni' of the Venetian 'baili' (resident representatives in Istanbul), which, written on their return to Venice and officially secret,

---

11. On the pilgrim narratives see Ganz-Blättler, *Andacht und Abenteuer*, esp. pp. 94, 106–10 (faith in objective knowledge, intertextuality), 164–5 (merchants). For good examples of observational writings by merchants see Groote, ed., *Die Pilgerfahrt*; Heers and de Heyer, eds., *Itinéraire*.
12. Thevet, *Cosmographie*, sig. a2 ('de tant mieux l'hom[m]e entend, & peult plus parfaitement, descrire ce qu'il connoissoit par liures, l'ayant songneusement examiné & experimenté à veuë d'oeil').
13. Nicolay, *Les Navigations*, p. 51 ('confirmée et approuvée par le sûr sens de ma propre vue').
14. See Neuber, 'Grade der Fremdheit'; Höfert, *Den Feind beschreiben*, pp. 78–85.
15. On Sansovino see Bonora, *Ricerche*; on his writings on the Ottomans see Yerasimos, *Hommes et idées*, pp. 49–68; Pippidi, *Visions*, pp. 46–7.

were in fact widely circulated from the mid-sixteenth century onwards, becoming important sources of European knowledge about the structure of the Ottoman state.[16] Also in the latter part of that century a more self-conscious practice of travel-diary-writing was developed in northern and central Europe, with some attempts to systematize the gathering of empirical information.[17] There were various ways in which writing about other cultures could diverge from standard literary or theological models. But the general tendency was that, as 'high' literary works (especially ones in Latin) had a more specialized readership, it was the descriptive texts written in a plain style, in the vernacular, that obtained the widest influence.

One other category of writings contributed to the development of a new view of the Ottoman system in the mid-sixteenth century: the works of former captives. Two of these have been mentioned already: the account by the Transylvanian captive, later turned Dominican friar, known as George of Hungary, published in 1481 and frequently reprinted thereafter, and that by the Croat (or Hungarian of Croatian origin) Bartolomej Djurdjević, who, captured in his early teens at the battle of Mohács (1526), spent twelve or thirteen years in Ottoman territory, and published his work in 1544.[18] Both texts underwent many printings; the former was translated into German with, as we have seen, a preface by Martin Luther, and the latter into Italian, French, German, Czech, and Polish. Two other works were also influential. The Genoese-born Giovanni Antonio Menavino was captured at the age of twelve (in 1504) and put to work as a page at the court of Bayezid II and Selim I; after a little over a decade he returned to Italy and wrote his account, probably for the would-be crusading Pope Leo X, though it was not printed until 1548 (in a volume that also included an Italian translation of Djurdjević's work). And Luigi Bassano, a Dalmatian Slav from the Venetian-ruled city of Zadar, was a captive for several years in the 1530s; his description of Ottoman life was printed in 1545. The texts by Menavino and Bassano were widely read, thanks in part to their inclusion in the popular compilation of works about the Ottomans which was edited by Francesco Sansovino in 1560–1 and thereafter frequently reprinted.[19]

---

16. On these see Queller, 'Development'; Benzoni, 'A proposito'; on their distribution see Vivo, *Information*, pp. 57–70.
17. Stagl, 'Die Apodemik'.
18. On George of Hungary see Klockow, 'Einleitung', pp. 11–29; on Djurdjević see Jembrih, *Hrvatski filološki zapisi*, pp. 17–87; Aksulu, *Bartholomäus Georgevićs Türkenschrift*, pp. 23–34.
19. On Menavino see Bitossi, 'Genova e i turchi', pp. 109–15; on Bassano see Babinger, 'Introduzione'.

None of these works by former captives could be described as sympathetic to the Ottomans. George of Hungary, as we have seen, cited Joachimite prophecies about their impending ruin; Djurdjević had a strong religious animus against Islam (he proudly described a theological disputation he had conducted with a dervish in Transylvania), and also published an 'exhortation', dedicated to the Archduke Maximilian, calling on Christians to fight against the Sultan.[20] Menavino, having written his text originally for the Pope, then addressed it to the French King with a dedication urging him to attack the Ottomans, and Bassano's own dedication—to a Roman cardinal—called similarly for 'the destruction and final extermination of these rabid dogs'.[21] The general intention behind their detailed descriptions of Ottoman conditions could no doubt be summed up as 'know your enemy', and when they gave a positive gloss to some of the things they described, this was usually for shame-praising purposes. Yet the fact remains that they did provide some of the materials that could be used to construct a positive view of life under Ottoman rule. Their veracity on such points was not in doubt, given their obvious lack of any reason to favour the Ottomans; and the fact that they were writing, so to speak, under the pressure of involuntary experience—not having gone to the East with any ulterior literary or cultural purposes—also reinforced the factual-descriptive nature of their accounts. Yet if these had been the only available descriptions of Ottoman conditions, it is hard to believe that a positive view would naturally have emerged from reading them. Rather, it seems that the more neutral or positively appreciative accounts of writers such as Postel and Belon created a new framework of thought, into which these materials could then be incorporated. (And once that framework was in place, other descriptive texts by anti-Ottoman authors, such as those by Paolo Giovio, or the famous letters of the Imperial diplomat Ogier Ghiselin de Busbecq, could also be put to use.)

The result was the emergence of what may be called a new paradigm—a picture of Ottoman government and society as a well-ordered and stable system, in which significant aspects of civil life were better arranged than their equivalents in Western Christendom. It was a system, apparently, in which ordinary people enjoyed real material benefits, and were generally content to obey their rulers. For anyone who regarded the Ottoman Empire

---

20. Djurdjević, *Pro fide christiana* (disputation), and *Exhortatio* (exortation); on the disputation see Tommasino, 'Discussioni'.
21. Bassano, *I costumi*, sig. a2r ('la destruttione & vltimo esterminio di quelli arrabbiati Cani').

as a military threat—as almost everyone in Western Europe did, with the exception perhaps of some opportunistic French strategists—this portrayal of it carried worrying implications about its underlying strength and resilience. In that sense, the new paradigm might be seen as conveying a negative message. But at the same time it could also be taken to suggest that there were ways in which Western powers might benefit from actually imitating Ottoman practice.

What, then, were the positive features of the Ottoman system that emerged from these accounts? The least novel, for Western readers, was the order and discipline of the Ottoman army. As we have seen, this had been an object of ruefully admiring comment since the late fourteenth century. A compilatory writer such as Christophe Richer included some of the standard observations when he noted the extraordinary silence of the army encampments, and—a detail drawn perhaps from Coccio 'Sabellicus'—the willingness to allow prisoners to escape rather than disturb the camp at night.[22] Jacques Gassot, who was with his ambassador, d'Aramon, when the latter accompanied Süleyman on a military campaign against the Persians, gave his own eyewitness testimony: in the army camp, every soldier was obliged to leave his weapons in his tent, and any blows that drew blood were punished immediately with death. 'In the whole of the journey we made following the army', he wrote, 'we did not see—and this is miraculous—in a quantity of people so great that it was estimated to come to a full million, anyone draw his sword or scimitar against anyone else.' Jean Chesneau, who also travelled with d'Aramon, described a force of 3–400,000 men marching through Syria 'with a degree of order and silence that, considering the number of people, is almost impossible to believe'.[23] Postel wrote at some length on the strict discipline practised among the military ranks in general and the Janissaries in particular: where stealing was concerned, for example, the theft of a single egg was punished with a severe beating (50 blows), and taking anything that was not needed for sustaining life was punishable with death. Djurdjević—who had spent some time serving in the Ottoman army—made a similar observation about theft; and Busbecq added the piquant detail that, after a punishment beating, the offender would thank the officer

22. Richer, *Des coustumes*, p. 17.
23. Gassot, *Le Discours du voyage*, fo. 25v ('en tout nostre voyage qu'auons fait suyua[n]ts le Ca[m]p n'auons veu (par miracle) en si gra[n]d nombre de gents, que lon estime, comprenant tout vn milio[n] de personnes, tirer Espée ne Simitarre l'un contre l'autre'); Chesneau, *Le Voyage*, p. 108 ('avec un tel ordre et silence que, considerant la multitude, est quasy incroyable').

for administering it.[24] While modern readers may find such accounts very ambivalent, suggesting excessive ferocity as much as admirable order, it is clear that sixteenth-century ones (whose own penal systems made lavish provision for the death penalty) were positively impressed; the comparison they had in mind was with the outrages routinely committed by Western soldiers against the local populations, whether foreign or domestic, through whose territories they passed.[25]

The sense of peace and order extended far beyond the ranks of the military, however. According to Chesneau, 'the subjects are so highly obedient to their ruler that they take great care not to break any of his laws, living in marvellous peace and harmony, with very few quarrels or disputes, in all the towns that are subject to the Sultan.' He was particularly struck by the preservation of public order at night-time:

In the evening, everyone goes home early. And for keeping watch over the towns at night, there is just one man with a stick in one hand and a shining lantern in the other, who goes walking through the town. This man on his own, with his stick, is more feared and respected than the Captain of the Watch in Paris with all his watchmen. And the public order there is so well established, and the tranquillity so great, that it is almost incredible to see.[26]

Luigi Bassano gave a more detailed account of the system of night watchmen, who, he explained, were recruited on rotation from the men of each ward or district. He also commented on the general lack of fighting among the urban inhabitants: carrying weapons such as swords was forbidden in Ottoman towns, and the use of them to wound others was strictly punished. With one eye on the practices current in Italian society, he added: 'they are quick to forgive and put aside insults; among them you do not find ancient enmities or factions of any kind, nor do they care about being given the lie,

24. Postel, La Tierce Partie, pp. 31, 44, 47; Djurdjević, De Turcarum ritu, sig. D2r; Busbecq, Life and Letters, i, p. 294.
25. Cf. the draconian military punishments proposed, for the improvement of Christian armies, by the humanist bishop Paolo Giovio (above, p. 64).
26. Chesneau, Le Voyage, pp. 47–8 ('les subjectz rendent si grande obeissance à leur seigneur qu'ils se donnent bien garde de contrevenir à nulle de ses ordonnances, vivant en une merveilleuse paix et concorde avec bien peu de querelles et debatz en quelque ville que ce soit, subjecte au Grand Seigneur... Sur le soir, chascun se retire à bonne heure... Et pour la garde des villes de nuict, y a seulement un homme seul avec un baston en une main et une lanterne allumée en l'autre qui va se pourmenant par la ville... cet homme seul avec son baston est plus craint et redoubté que n'est le capitaine du guet de Paris avec tous ses archers. Et la police y est si bien ordonnée et la tranquilité si grande que c'est chose quasy incroyable à qui ne la voit').

or about so many points of honour.'[27] This suggested that the public tranquillity of Ottoman cities was not to be explained solely in terms of the enforcement of severe penalties; there were social values at work, which in these matters were better than those of Christendom. Pierre Belon made a similar point:

> The Turks do not define valour in the same way that we do. In Europe, if a person is always ready to fight, can roll his eyes, has a scarred face, swears, is irascible, and has successfully given the lie to someone, he is regarded as a valiant man, and praised as a fine fellow. But the Turks behave with modesty in peacetime, and leave their weapons at home, in order to live peacefully; you never see them carrying their scimitars when they are walking through the town.[28]

Another source of order, in the realm of what might be called social psychology, was the intense cult of orderliness and silence that surrounded the Sultan himself. This was not just a matter of the special internal conventions of an imperial court; it was something that was transmitted to the wider public. Nicolay was struck by conditions in the inner courtyard of the Topkapı palace when, three times a week, the *divan* (council of ministers) heard the complaints or requests of ordinary members of the public. 'However large the number of people that come there, from all quarters, there is such great silence that you would think that those present hardly dare to spit or cough.'[29] Similarly, when the Sultan made his weekly procession to a mosque in the city, it took place, according to André Thevet,

> with such fine order and silence that, were it not for the sound of the horses' hooves, you would think that there isn't a single soul in the streets—even though there is an almost infinite throng composed of different nations, watching him go past. Then all the people do reverence to him, bowing down

---

27. Bassano, *I costumi*, fos. 15v–16r (night watch), 49v ('Sono facili a perdonare e dimettere l'ingiurie. Non vi sono tra loro ne nemicitie antiche, ne fattioni di nessuna sorte, ne si fa conto di me[n]tite, ne tanti punti d'honore').
28. Belon, *Voyage*, p. 477 ('Les Turcs ne diffinent pas la vaillantise ainsi comme nous: car en Europe, si quelqu'un est toujours prêt à se battre, et sait tourner les yeux en la tête, et est balafré, jureur, et colère, et a gagné le point d'avoir démenti un autre, icelui sera mis en perspective d'un homme vaillant, loué homme de bien. Mais les Turcs en temps de paix se montrent modestes, et posent les armes en leurs maisons pour vivre pacifiquement, et ne voit-on point qu'ils portent leurs cimeterres allant par la ville').
29. Nicolay, *Dans l'empire*, p. 128 ('combien que le nombre du peuple qui y vient de toutes parts soit grand, si y a-t-il grand silence, que vous diriez qu'à peine les assistants osent cracher ou tousser'). Cf. Busbecq's account of Süleyman presiding over his ministers, officials, and Janissaries at Amasya: 'I was greatly struck with the silence and order that prevailed with this great crowd' (*Life and Letters*, i, p. 156).

their heads; and the Sultan, very pleasantly and good-naturedly, returns the same greeting to his people with a suitable gravity, nodding his head now here, now there, to those who greet him—something that is greatly to be praised in a ruler.[30]

Such a description cast a rather different light on a phenomenon—intense deference and obedience to the Sultan—which had previously been treated as a sign of either extreme fear or depravity. George of Hungary had declared, in a memorably extravagant passage, that in the Sultan's realm 'even though there is an innumerable multitude of people, no contradiction or resistance can arise; rather, they obey his sole command as if they were a single man, united in all matters and for all purposes, subjecting themselves to him and serving him tirelessly, and no one dares to undertake anything without his authority.'[31] But he had immediately gone on to say that the reason for this ultra-harmonious obedience lay not in any advantage they might obtain thereby, but rather in their own diabolical sinfulness. The travellers' accounts retained and reinforced the empirical evidence, but removed the negative explanation, and supplied some reasons for intuiting a positive one. When Pierre Belon wrote, of the conscription of galley-rowers in Ottoman Egypt, that 'they would not dare to refuse, as it is for the Sultan's service; obedience is so great among the subjects of the Sultan that no one dares to resist his will', his readers had grounds for thinking that this was a description of a well-functioning system of rule.[32]

Fear of punishment was not absent from their accounts, of course. Postel described in detail the fierce penalties that were enforced for various crimes, ranging from bastinados (beatings with a heavy stick) to impalement and being burnt alive. But he took some care to dispel any idea that these were administered in an arbitrary way; for bearing false witness, for example, one would receive precisely that punishment which, had one's false testimony

---

30. Thevet, *Cosmographie*, pp. 60–1 ('auec vn si bel ordre, & silence tel, que, hors le trac des cheu-aux, vous diriez qu'il n'y ha ame par les rues: iaçoit qu'il y ait vne multitude quasi infinie de diuerses nacions, qui le regardent passer. Lors tout le Peuple lui fait reuerence, prosternant la teste contre bas: & ledit Seigneur auec vne douceur & debonnaireté grande, rend de mesme le salut à son Peuple, auec vne fort decente grauité enclinant la teste maintenant deçà, mantena[n]t delà, à ceux qui le saluent: ce qui est grandement à louer en vn Prince').

31. George of Hungary, *Tractatus*, p. 214 ('quamuis sit innumerabilis multitudo, non potest oriri aliquid contradictionis uel repugnantiae; sed quasi uir unus in omnibus et per omnia uniti ad unicum eius imperium respiciunt, subiciuntur et indefesse famulantur, et sine eius auctoritate nemo aliquid audet presumere').

32. Belon, *Voyage*, p. 358 ('ils n'oseraient refuser puisque c'est pour le service du Grand Seigneur…L'obéissance est si grande entre les sujets du Turc que personne n'ose résister à son vouloir').

helped to convict the accused, would have been meted out to that person. And Postel was keen to insist that trials in absentia of people such as regional governors were properly conducted, and that when the çavuş (imperial messenger and officer) went to carry out the sentence, 'when it involves the death sentence, it is not suddenly carried out, without the formality of justice, as people commonly say.'[33] Both the strictness of Ottoman justice and its formal correctness were also emphasized by Bartolomej Djurdjević, who described the case of a Janissary condemned by a civil judge to be executed for stealing milk from a woman who had been taking it to market.[34]

Another common topic—remarked on, for instance, by Menavino—was the sheer speed of the judicial process. Pierre Belon was impressed by its simplicity:

> In the Ottoman Empire, you do not need an officer in order to bring someone to court. If anyone wants to take someone before the judge, he can go himself to find that person, and tell him to come before the justice of God. If there are other Muslims present, he will not dare refuse. Having gone to find the judge, who sits all day long under an awning near his house, they will debate their case in his presence, and immediately the judge will issue his sentence, as he thinks fit. So they have no need at all of solicitors, prosecutors, or barristers.[35]

Postel, likewise, praised their 'diligence' in the application of justice, contrasting the efficiency of the Ottoman system with the long-drawn-out trials and ruinous expenses of the Western one, which 'make me ashamed to describe such great diligence in these people who are proclaimed [by us] to be wicked'.[36] Such observations naturally struck a chord in the minds of readers used to particularly cumbersome judicial processes in their own countries; it is not surprising that the merits of the Ottoman justice system

---

33. Postel, *De la république*, pp. 124–5 (false witness, punishments), 127 (in absentia, çavuş); Postel, *La Tierce Partie*, p. 8 ('quant est question de mort, n'est temerairement faite execution, sans forme de Iustice, comme vulgairement on dit': the çavuş had to have recourse to the local *kadi* or judge).

34. Menavino, *I cinque libri*, p. 54; Djurdjević, *De Turcarum ritu*, sig. D3v.

35. Menavino, *I cinque libri*, p. 54; Belon, *Voyage*, p. 394 ('Il ne faut point de sergent en Turquie pour ajourner un homme. Mais quiconque voudra mener quelqu'un au juge aille lui-même trouver celui à qui il a affaire, et lui dise qu'il vienne à la justice de Dieu, alors s'il y a d'autres Turcs présents, il n'osera refuser, et allant trouver le juge qui se tient assis tout le jour dessous un appentis près de sa maison, ils débattront leur cause en sa présence, et sur-le-champ le juge ordonnera ainsi que bon lui en semblera. Parquoi ne leur faut point de solliciteurs, procureurs et avocats').

36. Postel, *De la république*, p. 127 ('diligence', 'me facent honte de reciter vne si grande diligence en gens proclamés meschants').

became the commonest pro-Ottoman theme in sixteenth-century Spanish writings about the Turks.[37]

Another point emphasized by Postel was that at the *divan* of government ministers, which he viewed as the highest court, the conduct of justice was monitored by the Sultan, who could sit in an adjacent room and observe the proceedings—while out of sight himself—through a grille or window. 'Oh, let me dare to say what I think!', he exclaimed: 'if only it could please God to let a familiar angel give the same opportunity to the King of France, to hear and see all the appeal court judges, who spin out the trials.' He also noted approvingly that the Sultan would sometimes pass incognito through Istanbul in the evening, to hear what ordinary people said—for the sake, according to Postel, of remedying injustices.[38]

Where the general administration of justice was concerned, while some Venetian and Ragusan observers commented on the use of bribes, both for obtaining false witnesses and for paying the judges directly (one Ragusan diplomat wrote in 1574 that 'justice is almost completely corrupted, as the *kadi*s and *sancakbeyi*s think only of enriching themselves'), there were many writers who gave the impression that judgments were given in an even-handed way.[39] Non-Muslims, apparently, were also beneficiaries of this: Nicolay noted that disputes could be brought before the Sultan's *divan* 'by all comers, whatever nation or religion they may belong to', and Djurdjević felt obliged to point out that Muslims and Christians went to the same judge, 'who is required to administer the law equally to all'.[40] According to Donado da Lezze (who, as we have seen, drew much of his information from Angiolello), the job of a senior judge was 'to do justice to anyone of any status whatsoever, without respecting the person of any man, however powerful, or however great a lord he might be'.[41]

37. Mas, *Les Turcs*, ii, p. 297.
38. Postel, *La tierce partie*, p. 12 ('O que je n'ose dire ce que je pense! que pleust a Dieu qu'vn ange familier peut faire la pareille opportunité au Roy Treschrestien, d'oyr & voir tous les juges souuerains, & allongeurs de proces'). Cf also his *De la république*, p. 125 (on the window, calling it a 'great and imitable precaution by the Sultan': 'Grand' & imitable cautelle du Prince').
39. Bodl. MS Rawl. D 618, fo. 108r (extracts from Francesco Gondola [Gundulić], relazione to Gregory XIII: 'La giustitia e quasi per tutto corrotta non pensando i Cadi et Sangiachi ad altro se non ad arrichirsi'); Pedani, ed., *Relazioni*, p. 110 (N. Michiel relazione, 1558: bribing judges); Albèri, ed., *Relazioni*, ser. 3, iii, p. 273 (G. Morosini relazione, 1585: false witnesses).
40. Nicolay, *Dans l'empire*, p. 128 ('à tous venants, de quelque nation ou religion qu'ils soient'); Djurdjević, *De Turcarum ritu*, sig. D3v ('qui ex aequo omnibus ius ministrare tenetur'). The legal disadvantages of Christians when bringing cases against Muslims were not noticed by these writers.
41. da Lezze, *Historia turchesca*, p. 131 ('fa giustitia a ciascuno sia di che conditione esser si voglia... non guardar in faccia ad huomo quanto fosse potente, et gran maestro').

That the Ottoman Empire did contain powerful men and great lords was not in doubt; but there was a difference in social attitudes between it and Western Christendom, which fascinated these writers. Pierre Belon was struck by the fact that all Turks, whether grand or humble, were equally content to stay in the public inns or caravanserays, accepting the three days' hospitality that was dispensed there as an act of charity. He noted that 'there is much less emphasis on family lineage': no stigma was attached to being the son of a female slave, and a man's wives might include both a daughter of the Sultan and 'one of the poorest daughters of a manual worker'. Nobility in the Ottoman Empire, he observed, 'is not like that in the other Christian lands, where sons inherit it from their fathers. Among the Ottomans, he who holds the highest office under the Sultan, without knowing his own origins or the identity of his parents, just like anyone who receives a salary from the Sultan, regards himself as no less a gentleman than the Sultan himself.' And he added, after a relativizing observation about differing attitudes to trade in Christendom (forbidden to the French nobility, but allowed to the Venetian and Florentine), a strikingly bold conclusion: 'since countries have had different opinions about the nobility of men, I assert that it is whatever you may wish it to be.'[42] Postel commented on the fact that the Sultan could raise someone from a low position to one of the highest in the land; the viziers, he noted, had been promoted 'from lower offices, by degrees, always rising and setting a good example'.[43] As we have seen, Paolo Giovio had praised the meritocratic principle as applied within the Ottoman army. For some later writers—above all, for Ghiselin de Busbecq— meritocracy extended much more widely than that: it was a basic principle of the whole Ottoman system. 'For the Turks do not measure even their own people', Busbecq wrote, 'by any other rule than that of personal merit.' In a long passage rhapsodizing on this theme he explained:

> In making his appointments the Sultan pays no regard to any pretensions on the score of wealth or rank... he considers each case on its own merits, and examines carefully into the character, ability, and disposition of the man... Each

---

42. Belon, *Voyage*, pp. 192 (inns), 404 ('n'est pas semblable à celle des autres pays des chrétiens, qui y viennent de père en fils. Mais celui entre les Turcs tiendra la première dignité après le Grand Seigneur, qui ne sait dont il est, ni qui sont ses père et mère, ains quiconque est payé de soultre du Turc s'estime être autant gentilhomme comme est le Grand Turc même', 'pource que les républiques ont eu divers jugements en la noblesse des hommes, je veux dire qu'elle est ainsi qu'on la veut estimer'), 476 ('il n'y a pas si grand lignage de parenté', 'une des plus pauvres filles d'un homme mécanique').

43. Postel, *De la république*, p. 121 ('par degrés de dignités inferieures, tousiours montant & faisant bon exemple').

man in Turkey carries in his own hand his ancestry and his position in life, which he may make or mar as he will... Among the Turks, therefore, honours, high posts, and judgeships are the rewards of great ability and good service... This is the reason that they are successful in their undertakings, that they lord it over others, and are daily extending the bounds of their empire. These are not our ideas, with us there is no opening left for merit; birth is the standard for everything; the prestige of birth is the sole key to advancement in the public service.[44]

Not only did many of the rich and powerful men in Ottoman society have humble origins; Western writers were also impressed by the fact that they used their wealth to benefit ordinary people. Menavino described the hospitals where the sick were tended free of charge, and the inns that gave three days' food and lodging free to travellers; Postel explained that these were charitable foundations whose estates were endowed like the 'commanderies' of Christian religious-military orders, but with the difference that 'there [in the Ottoman Empire] the income and alms-giving are for the benefit of needy people, whilst here [in Christian Europe] they are for the benefit of the rich.'[45] A well-informed treatise on the Ottomans by the Graeco-Venetian writer Theodore Spandounes (or 'Spandugino'), completed in 1538 and printed many times from the early 1550s onwards, explained that such foundations included hospitals, caravanserays, and even bridges; the greatest of them were set up by individual sultans, but 'these Turks, great and small, are constantly engaged on such pious and charitable works—far more so than we Christians.'[46] Pierre Belon's account added public baths to the list of institutions founded by people who, 'aiming to do great good by means of such deeds, arrange for various fine contributions to be made to the upkeep of the public good'; Bassano's also mentioned wells, fountains, and aqueducts.[47] (The *hamams* or public baths impressed many visitors; Belon wrote that the Turks were 'the cleanest people in the world'. Bassano noted that they had higher standards of public health and hygiene more

44. Above, p. 63 (Giovio); Busbecq, *Life and Letters*, i, pp. 105 ('For the Turks...'), 154–5 ('In making...'). See the discussion of this theme in Arrighi, *Écritures de l'ambassade*, pp. 299–302, noting that Busbecq was painfully conscious of his own illegitimate birth.
45. Menavino, *I cinque libri*, pp. 48–50; Postel, *De la république*, p. 59 ('là, le reuenu & aumosne est pour les indigens, ici ils sont aus riches'). Both writers (and Djurdjević: *De turcarum ritu*, sig. C1r) call these foundations *imarets*; that term referred specifically to soup kitchens that gave free food to the poor, but those were often combined in a single *vakıf* (charitable foundation) with a hospital and/or a *han* (inn, caravanseray).
46. Spandounes, *Origin of Ottoman Emperors*, p. 134 (translation emended).
47. Belon, *Voyage*, p. 191 ('Pensant donc faire un souverain bien par tels ouvrages, font faire plusieurs belles réparations au bien public'); Bassano, *I costumi*, fo. 45v.

generally, commending them for placing slaughterhouses and burial grounds outside the city, and for having a well-organized system of street cleaning.) Nicolay repeated both Bassano's admiring account of the Ottomans' public baths and Postel's praise of their humane treatment of the sick, the mad, and the indigent.[48]

What some saw as public-spiritedness, others interpreted more strictly in terms of religious obligation. Menavino gave a very positive account of the Muslim duty of alms-giving, which, he said, led rich people to seek out the poor and needy in their neighbourhoods in order to give them help; Postel's whole discussion of hospitals and soup kitchens came in a section of his book dealing with alms-giving in Islam, and he also commented that in a place with ten rich people and 200 poor ones, the former 'do not let anyone go without food'. Ottoman Muslims who visited Venice, he noted, were shocked by the sight of sick beggars in the streets.[49] Busbecq, similarly, observed that beggars in Ottoman territory were 'not so numerous as with us'.[50]

Very few of these writers theorized explicitly about the degree to which the practices they admired were caused by religion rather than by secular legislation or policy. Exceptionally, Postel did consider this point, remarking that 'the way they behave among themselves, and towards foreigners who are not of this faith, must be caused, I think, more by religion and fear of God than by the constraint of the laws.' And in his discussion of justice in the Ottoman Empire, he began by saying that in almost all societies the principles of justice are drawn from religion, and that for Muslims this involves recourse to the Koran and the *sunnah*.[51] For him these were not troubling thoughts, as he saw Islam as containing positive elements, moral as well as theological, which it shared with Christianity. But occasional comments by other writers indicated that Islamic piety might—even while producing some desirable effects—have a very different agenda. Bassano's explanation of the admirably peaceful behaviour of Ottomans within their own cities was that their religion told them to reserve their fighting for

---

48. Belon, *Voyage*, p. 506 ('les plus nettes gens du monde'); Bassano, *I costumi*, fos. 34v–35r, 36v–37r; Nicolay, *Dans l'empire*, pp. 134–40.

49. Menavino, *I cinque libri*, p. 18; Postel, *De la république*, pp. 60 ('ne laissent nul auoir faute de manger'), 62 (shocked).

50. Busbecq, *Life and Letters*, i, p. 209.

51. Postel, *De la république*, pp. 67 ('la co[n]uersation, & entr'eus, & entre les estrangers qui ne sont de cette loy, me semble plus deuoir estre faittes par religion & crainte de Dieu, que contrainte de loix'), 117 (justice). The *sunnah* is the set of records of the sayings and deeds of Muhammad, transmitted from the early period of Islam, and used as a basis for Islamic law.

infidels; Belon noted that some Ottoman women would not only be generous donors to inns and hospitals, but also 'leave their property in their wills to soldiers, to make them try harder to fight against Christians'.[52] Such observations could contribute to more general arguments which developed (as we shall see) during this period about the social or political utility of religious beliefs—arguments which were themselves concerned both with the general benefits to society and with the increase of power accruing to the ruler.

Religion was certainly not seen as the sole cause of social mores, even by Postel. Ethnic or geographical differences were also noted. In his discussion of charity he remarked that the 'Moors' (North African Muslims) were especially uncharitable, often leaving their neighbours or close relatives to die of hunger; elsewhere he praised the trustworthiness of rural Turks, especially from Anatolia.[53] While Islam was of course a constant object of interest (and, generally, distrust), many of the other writers did not pause to make any distinctions between religious influence, ethnic character, social traditions, and sultanic policy when describing the positive features of Ottoman life that caught their attention. For example, when Pierre Belon wrote that 'the slaves in the Ottoman Empire are as well treated as servants in Europe, as they have their share of happiness, in accordance with the master they serve: if they are with a good master who loves them, he treats them as he does himself', he did go on to explain the legal rights of slaves—who could ask a judge to transfer them to a different master if their present one refused to set a ransom price—but did not pause to consider whether the laws were religious or secular in origin.[54] Yet if there was an overall tendency, it was to interpret such practices as part of an effective general system of secular organization. Thus Busbecq, also commenting quite positively on slavery in Ottoman society, was content to observe: 'In Turkey the class which is likely to go astray is controlled by a master's authority, while the master is supported by the slave's labour. Both publicly and privately the Turks derive great advantages from this institution.'[55]

52. Bassano, *I costumi*, fo. 49v; Belon, *Voyage*, p. 193 ('donnent par testament ce qu'elles ont aux soldats de guerre, afin qu'ils s'efforcent mieux à combattre contre les chrétiens').
53. Postel, *De la république*, pp. 67 (Moors), 70 (Anatolia).
54. Belon, *Voyage*, p. 492 ('Les esclaves en Turquie sont aussi bien traités comme les serviteurs en notre Europe, car ils participent de la félicité selon le maître qu'ils servent. S'ils sont avec un bon maître qui les aime bien, ils sont traités comme lui-même').
55. Busbecq, *Life and Letters*, i, p. 210.

This tendency is visible also where the issue of religious toleration is concerned. Perhaps surprisingly, this was not a major theme in the body of writings under discussion here; if sixteenth-century Western Europeans became very conscious of this aspect of Ottoman life, it was thanks to the Protestant and Catholic polemicists who, as we have seen, made frequent use of it. In the works of the travellers and the captives there were occasional comments on the lack of forced conversions to Islam: George of Hungary, for example, assured his readers that 'the Turks do not compel anyone at all to renounce his faith'.[56] Postel noted that the 'Moors' were exceptional in forcing their Christian slaves to convert; he did also describe attempts by other Muslims to trick non-Muslims into saying the *shahada* (Islamic declaration of faith), but his general observation was that Muslims 'beg' people to convert, without attempting compulsion.[57] For all his willingness to do justice to the positive aspects of Ottoman rule, however, Postel's ultimate concern was to motivate Western Christians to eliminate that rule by fighting a crusading war; drawing attention to the broadly tolerable nature of Christian life under it would not have served his purposes, and there is no large-scale treatment of the toleration policy in the many pages he devoted to religious life within the Ottoman Empire. Pierre Belon, on the other hand, had no difficulty in broaching this topic, though his discussions of it were not at all lengthy. The impression given to his readers was that this was primarily a secular policy maintained for political purposes, not an application of Islamic principles. Having listed the various patriarchs of the Eastern Christian Churches, he commented: 'the Sultan lets all these patriarchs live according to their own religion, so long as he gets the tribute payment from them.' Later in the book he returned to this theme, adding a short but influential passage:

> Each of the Christian religions in the Ottoman Empire is permitted to have its own separate Church. For the Ottomans do not compel anyone to live as they do, so that it is permitted to everyone to live in his own faith. That is what has always sustained the great power of the Sultan: for if he conquers a country, it is sufficient for him that he be obeyed, and so long as he receives the tribute payment, he does not concern himself with people's souls.[58]

56. George of Hungary, *Tractatus*, p. 244 ('Turci neminem omnino cogunt fidem suam negare').
57. Postel, *De la république*, pp. 40 (tricks; 'prient'), 41 (Moors).
58. Belon, *Voyage*, pp. 135 ('Le Grand Turc laisse vivre les susdits patriarches en leur religion, moyennant qu'il en ait le tribut'), 464 ('Il est permis à toutes les religions chrétiennes vivant en Turquie d'avoir chacune son église à part. Car les Turcs ne contraignent personne de vivre à la mode turquoise, ains est permis à un chacun vivre en sa loi. C'est ce qui a toujours maintenu

To say that all these positive points, taken together, helped to fashion a new paradigm is not to imply that the old paradigm—of a malevolent and oppressive regime, inspired at least in part by an evil religion—was simply replaced thereby; it was not. But a new model did become available, a way of seeing the governmental, judicial, and civil (as well as military) conditions of Ottoman rule as features of a comparatively well-ordered system. Writers in the second half of the sixteenth century might take up and use this model for a variety of reasons, from old-fashioned shame-praising at one end of the spectrum to, at the other end, a positive programme of urging Western rulers to copy the Ottomans' methods.

One of the first people to put this new model to use was the anonymous author of the *Viaje de Turquía*. This text, dating probably from 1557, is one of the most fascinating and lively works of Spanish Renaissance literature. Written in the form of a dialogue between three speakers, it recounts the experiences of one of them, 'Pedro de Urmalas', as a captive in Istanbul earlier in the 1550s. The work circulated only in manuscript (five copies survive today, and there may well have been others); one modern scholar has suggested that its 'objective, or rather admiring' portrayal of Ottoman life had made the book 'almost unpublishable'.[59] Since its first printing in 1905 there has been much debate about its nature and the identity of its author, yet no definite conclusions have ever been reached. The two leading candidates for authorship are Andrés Laguna (the learned physician whose 'mournful declamation' about the Ottoman threat to Europe, delivered at the University of Cologne in 1543, has already been mentioned), and Juan de Ulloa Pereira, a little-known Knight of Malta who was expelled from the Order for Protestant tendencies in the late 1550s.[60] If the former proposal is correct, there can be nothing autobiographical about the text, as it is known that Laguna never visited the Ottoman Empire; the latter suggestion allows for some element of autobiography, or at least direct reportage, even though it is clear that the author borrowed much of his material from previous writers, including Menavino, Spandugino, Djurdjević, Bassano, and

le Turc en sa grandeur: car s'il conquête quelque pays, ce luy est assez d'être obéi, et moyennant qu'il reçoive le tribut, il ne se soucie des âmes'). Note, however, that while the overall analysis here is clearly political, the words 'les Turcs' and 'la mode turquoise' might also be translated as 'the Muslims' and 'the Muslim way'.

59. Salinero, ed., *Viaje de Turquía*, pp. 19–26 (5 MSS); Bataillon, *Le Docteur Laguna*, p. 68 ('objectif, plutôt admiratif', 'presque impubliable').

60. Bataillon, *Le Docteur Laguna* (Laguna); Salinero, ed., *Viaje de Turquía*, pp. 64–73 (de Ulloa Pereira). An earlier attribution to Cristóbal de Villalón has been generally abandoned.

Belon—as well as Busbecq, whose first long letter, written in Vienna after his return from Istanbul in 1555, must have been available in manuscript.[61]

Whoever he was, this author was no uncritical admirer of Ottoman life. All Muslims would go to Hell, he wrote (despite their impressive degree of piety, which exceeded that of most Christians), and he referred repeatedly, with severe disapproval, to the Ottomans' addiction to sodomy. In drawing attention to their strengths and relative virtues, his aim was the traditional one of shame-praising; comparison with behaviour and conditions in Spain, to the discredit of the Spanish, was a constant underlying theme. The Sultan's army was better organized than the Spanish one, for example, with experienced commanders and a more efficient system of recruitment. When the main speaker, Pedro de Urmalas, describes a case of summary punishment meted out by the Grand Vizier, one of his interlocutors exclaims: 'I'll be damned if any judgment at our Chancery has been as delightful and as perfectly just as that. And it makes me think: do you call these people barbarous? We are the greater barbarians, for describing them as such.' He goes on to ask: 'Do they not have law cases there lasting 30 or 40 years, as happens here?', and receives the reply that their most complicated case could not last more than one month, thanks to 'the good order which they maintain in all matters'.[62] The principal speaker has a version of the story about the Sultan's special grille or window: he sits on a throne completely hidden behind screens, from which he gives instructions to his ministers, 'and when they think that he is there, he isn't, and when they think that he isn't, he is—with the result that no one dares to do anything other than what is just.' Visits by the Grand Vizier (in disguise) to taverns and other places in the evenings are commended, as another component of an exemplary system of justice.[63] Where charity is concerned, the speaker explains that 'their bequests are no less magnificent than ours, or rather more so, and they are more generous in alms-giving during their lives... They do many other works of charity, to a

61. On the borrowings see Bataillon, *Le Docteur Laguna*, pp. 71–5; Mas, *Les Turcs*, i, pp. 136–40; Corsi Prosperi, 'Sulle fonti'; Salinero, ed., *Viaje de Turquía*, pp. 36–42. The lack of borrowing from Postel's 1560 publications tends to confirm the traditional dating of the work to the late 1550s.

62. Villalón, attrib., *Viaje de Turquía*, pp. 215 ('Ruin sea yo si de chancillería se cuente puncto de más recta justicia ni más gracioso. Y a proposito, ¿esa gente llamáis bárbara? Nosotros lo somos más en tenerlos por tales'), 216 ('¿No habrá allá pleitos de treinta años y cuarenta como acá?', 'el buen orden que en todas las cosas tienen'), 219 (sodomy), 221 (sodomy, army, recruitment), 245 (Hell).

63. Ibid., pp. 215 (taverns), 216 ('y cuando piensan que está allí no está, y cuando piensan que no está, está. Por manera que ninguno osa hacer otra cosa que la que es de justicia').

much greater extent than we do, and yet people here say they are cruel and avaricious.' The general sobriety of the Turks is also praised: they do not gamble, nor do they while away the hours with feasting, instead devoting their time to useful, serious occupations. 'In all the places I have visited', Pedro de Urmalas concludes,

> which means at least a third of the world, I have never seen people more virtuous than these, nor do I think that there are people more virtuous than these in the Indies or in the places I have not visited; I leave aside their belief in Muhammad, for which, I know, they are all going to Hell, but I am speaking about the law of nature.[64]

One later example of shame-praising may also be given, from the treatise of 1597 (discussed above) by the Catholic polemicist William Rainolds, *Calvino-Turcismus*. Rainolds had read a wide range of sources, including George of Hungary, Djurdjević, Richer, Belon, Thevet, Postel, and Busbecq. In a central part of his book he gives 'Michaeas' (the character who has converted from English Protestantism to Islam) a long and eloquent speech on the virtues to be found in Ottoman life, linking them wherever possible to the dictates of Islam. In this polity, he observes, there is more piety and less rebellion than in Christian states.

> Indeed, modesty prevents me from saying everything that could be said about the piety of our people [*sc.* Ottoman Muslims] towards God, their justice and charity towards their neighbours, their trustworthiness, truthfulness, and fair dealing towards all people in their words, promises, deeds, sales, and purchases. The reason why they excel in these virtues is partly that they are impelled by the authority of the laws of the state, and partly that they are persuaded by divine religion.[65]

He then quotes Busbecq on the marvellous orderliness and correct behaviour of the Ottoman army, and asks rhetorically: 'if our justice is so splendid

---

64. Ibid., pp. 210 ('No menos soberbias mandas hacen que nosotros, sino más, y en vida son má limosneros... Otras muchas limosnas hacen harto más que nosotros, sino que... dicen que son crueles y avaros'), 244–5 (no gambling, sobriety), 245 ('En lo que yo he andado, que es bien la tercera parte del mundo, no he visto gente más virtuosa y pienso que tampoco la hay en Indias, ni en lo que no he andado, dejado aparte el creer en Mahoma, que ya sé que se van todos al infierno, pero hablo de la ley de natura').

65. Rainolds, *Calvino-Turcismus*, p. 516 ('Pudor certè me impedit quò minus omnia dicam de nostrorum hominum pietate erga Deum, iustitia & charitate erga p[r]oximos, in dictis, promissis, factis, emptionibus & venditionibus constantia, veritate, & aequitate erga omnes, in quibus virtutibus partim legum politicarum authoritate impulsi, partim diuina religione persuasi excellunt').

in war, how much more splendid is it in peace?' Citing Thevet and Belon, he observes that Christians enjoy conditions of great security and justice in Ottoman towns; referring to Postel, he notes that Turkish merchants are famous for their honesty. And he proceeds to give a glowing account of Ottoman charity and hospitality, and of institutions such as the *hans* which offer lodgings free of charge to all travellers. The reply to this speech by 'Samuel' (the Anglican minister) is quite inadequate, offering a few counter-examples of cruel actions by Ottoman Sultans, but hardly touching on the main substance of Michaeas's argument.[66]

The primary aim of shame-praising was to provoke contrition, as a first step towards a programme of moral and spiritual reform—a programme which, once under way, might involve revivifying the existing conduct and institutions of Christian society, without necessarily remodelling them in accordance with Ottoman practice. But some writers' thoughts did turn to direct imitation. Postel himself was explicit about this: 'In order to resist such a power [as the Ottoman Empire], it seems to me that there is no better way than to copy its own methods [literally: "to beat it with its own stick"].' And his summary of those methods included 'sobriety, patience, obedience, wealth, large forces, speed of action, and having all parts of one's country well inhabited'.[67] The humanist scholar and political writer Louis Le Roy, in his influential treatise *De la vicissitude ou variété des choses en l'univers* (1575), adapted and developed Postel's list: the Ottomans had gained a great empire by means of 'sobriety, patience, obedience, concord, diligence, order, valour, abundance of men, horses, and weapons, and through the use of good military and political discipline, which they take care to observe'.[68] Le Roy was devoted to the anti-Ottoman cause, having published an oration urging the Kings of France and Spain to settle their differences permanently in order to make war against the Sultan; what interested him here about the new paradigm was not that it put the Ottomans in a better light, but simply that it suggested a whole system of interlocking policies and values which

66. Ibid., pp. 517 (Busbecq, though unnamed), 518 ('Quod si tam insignis sit iustitia nostra in bello, quanto insignior est in pace?', Christians, merchants), 519 (charity, hospitality), 520 (Samuel).
67. Postel, *La Tierce Partie*, pp. 87–8 ('Pour resister a vne telle puissance il me semble qu'il n'est tel que d'vser de son baston. Sobrieté, patience, obedience, richesse, multitude, celerité, & auoir toutes parties de son païs bien garnies de gens').
68. Le Roy, *De la vicissitude*, fo. 94v ('sobrieté, patience, obeissance, concorde, diligence, ordre, vaillance, abondance d'hommes, cheuaux, armes, & moyennant la bonne discipline militaire & politique qu'ils obseruent soigneusement'). On Le Roy see Gundersheimer, *Life and Works*.

Christians needed to imitate in order to vanquish such powerful foes.[69] In this he was (following Postel) a forerunner of a new line of political argument in the West, which pushed—as we shall see—for the adoption of various Ottoman methods, including some that had been singled out for criticism by previous Western writers.

Among all the authors of this period who were positively influenced by the new paradigm, however, one stands out: the lawyer, philosopher, and writer on politics and religion Jean Bodin.[70] His reading was very wide, encompassing many of the accounts of Ottoman life mentioned above. In his guide to the reading of history, the *Methodus* (1566), he recommended the works by Richer and Postel, as well as a number of historical studies of the Ottomans; and since he cited material included with the second edition of the medieval Latin translation of the Koran issued by Theodore Bibliander, it can be assumed that he had read the works by George of Hungary and Djurdjević which Bibliander also reprinted there.[71] It is clear that Bodin was familiar with Belon's *Observations*. Among the other sources of his knowledge, one book should be singled out for the frequent use he made of it: the treatise on northern Africa by 'Leo Africanus', a well-educated Moroccan who had been brought to Rome as a captive and had converted to Christianity.[72]

In his writings on history, politics, and society, Bodin noted many of the positive aspects of Ottoman life that were brought together in the new paradigm. He was particularly impressed by the military organization and discipline of the Ottomans, which he saw as the only system that now matched that of the ancient Romans. In his major political treatise, the *République* (1576), he wrote:

> it shall be fit to erect some legions of foote and horse according to the estate and greatnes of euery Commonweale, that they may be bred vp in martiall discipline from their youth in garrisons [and] vpon the frontires in time of peace, as the antient Romans did, who knew not what it was to liue at discre-

---

69. Le Roy, *Oratio*.

70. In what follows, I recapitulate some points made in Malcolm, 'Positive Views of Islam'. For a valuable intellectual biography see Lloyd, *Jean Bodin*.

71. Bodin, *Methodus*, p. 608. On the materials added to Bibliander's second edn. (Basel, 1550) see Bobzin, *Der Koran*, pp. 262–3. On Bodin's sources see Berriot, 'Jean Bodin et l'Islam', and Bobzin, 'Islamkundliche Quellen'.

72. Bodin, *Démonomanie*, fo. 100r ('Belon, en ses obseruations imprimees à Paris'); Turbet-Delof, 'Jean Bodin' (Leo Africanus). On Leo (Hasan al-Wazzan) see Davis, *Trickster Travels*. Bodin also gathered information from diplomats (Berriot, 'Jean Bodin', p. 172), and in his *Démonomanie* he referred to conversations with French merchants who traded in Egypt (fo. 100r).

tion, and much lesse to rob, spoile, and murther, as they do at this day, but their camp was a schoole of honor, sobrietie, chastitie, iustice, and all other vertues, in the which no man might reuenge his owne iniuries, nor vse any violence. And to the end this discipline may be obserued, as they do at this day in the Turks armie, it is necessarie that good Captaines and souldiers be recompenced... after the manner of the Romans.[73]

Earlier in that work he commented positively on the *devşirme* ('collection') system, under which Christian peasant boys were taken to Istanbul, converted to Islam, given slave status, and trained as Janissaries or officers of state. In the later Latin version he added strong praise of the Ottoman system for its meritocracy and reward of virtue:

> For as concerning the Turkes Pretorian souldiors, and those youths which are taken from the Christians as tribute, and are called tribute children, I neuer accounted them for slaues; seeing that they are enrolled in the princes familie, and that they alone enioy the great offices, honours, priesthoods, authoritie and honour; which nobilitie extendeth also vnto their [grandsons]... and all their posteritie afterward beeing accounted base, except by their vertue and noble acts they maintaine the honour of their grandfathers: For the Turkes almost alone of all other people measure true nobilitie by vertue, and not by discent or the antiquitie of their stocke.[74]

Another major theme treated in Bodin's political writings was the Ottoman practice of religious toleration. In book 4 of the *République* he observed:

> The great emperour of the Turkes doth with as great deuotion as any prince in the world honour and obserue the religion by him receiued from his

73. Bodin, *Six Bookes*, p. 613D–E (*Six Livres*, p. 780: 'qu'on establisse quelque legions de gents de pieds & de cheual, selon l'estat, pourpris & grandeur de chacune Republique, qui soyent entretenus & exercés dés leur ieunesse aux garnisons & frontieres en temps de paix auec la discipline militaire, telle qu'elle estoit entre les anciens Rommains, qui ne scauoyent que c'estoit de viure à discretion, & beaucoup moins de fourrager, voler, brigander, battre & meurtrir, comme on fait à present: ains leur camp estoit l'escole d'honneur, de sobrieté, & de chasteté, de iustice & de toute vertu, sans qu'il fust licite à personne de reuanger ses iniures, ny proceder par voye de faict. Et à fin qu'on puisse garder ceste discipline, comme fait encores l'armee des Turcs, il est besoin que les bons Capitaines & soldats soyent recompensés').

74. Bodin, *Six Bookes*, p. 44G–H (*De republica*, p. 43: 'Nam quod attinet ad Praetorianos Turcarum milites, & eos qui tributi nomine Christianis imperantur, ego illos pro seruis nunquam habui, cùm in familiam principis conscribantur, ac soli magistratibus, honoribus sacerdotiis, imperiis, nobilitate fruantur, quae nobilitas ad nepotes vsque pertinet: pronepotes verò ac posteri deinceps ignobiles habentur, nisi sua virtute ac rerum gestarum gloria dignitatem auorum tueantur: nam soli Turcae ex omnibus penè populis veram nobilitatem virtute non generis antiquitate metiuntur'). Cf. *Six livres*, p. 64: 'Car quant aux leuees des ieunes Chrestiens que fait le grand Seigneur, qu'ils appellent enfants du tribut, ie ne les tien pas pour esclaues, ains au contraire, il n'y a que ceux-là, & leurs enfans iusques à la troisieme ligne, qui soyent nobles, & ne l'est pas qui veut: attendu qu'il n'y a que ceux-la qui iouïssent des priuileges, estats, offices, & benefices.' For another passage added in the Latin on the theme of the Turks measuring nobility by virtue, see *De republica*, p. 357 (*Six Bookes*, p. 396K).

auncestors, yet detesteth hee not the straunge religions of others; but to the
contrarie permitteth euery man to liue according to his conscience: yea and
that more is, neere vnto his pallace at Pera, suffereth foure diuerse religions,
viz. That of the Iewes, that of the Christians [*sc.* Roman Catholics], that of the
Grecians, and that of the Mahometanes.[75]

The main argument which Bodin put forward here for religious toleration
was a prudential one: if a significant part of the population of a state followed a different religion from the majority, the ruler should tolerate at least
the private practice of that religion, since any policy of total suppression
might have worse consequences, reducing the minority first to atheism and
then to rebellion. For a similar reason—the danger that religious conflict
would lead to civil strife—he commended the policy of 'all the kings and
princes of Affricke and of the East', who 'doe most straitly forbid of all
men to dispute of their religion'.[76] But, as we shall later see, his reasons
for advocating religious toleration extended some way beyond the merely
prudential.

Elsewhere in the *République* Bodin commented approvingly on other
aspects of Ottoman statecraft. He recommended that kings should not show
themselves too frequently to their people, and that they should maintain a
strong sense of their 'majesty'—like 'the great kings of Aethiopia, of Tartarie,
of Persia, or of Turkie, who suffer not their subiects so much as to looke
directly vpon them'.[77] He also gave his approval to the Ottoman policy of
disarming the population, noting that 'The Turkes herein go yet farther, not
onely in punishing with all seuerity the seditious and mutinous people, but
also by forbidding them to beare armes, yea euen in time of warre, except

75. Bodin, *Six Bookes*, p. 537E (combining *Six livres*, pp. 654–5: 'Mais le Roy des Turcs, qui tient une
    bonne partie de l'Europe, garde sa Religion aussi bien que Prince du monde, & ne force per-
    sonne, ains au contraire permet à chacun de viure selon sa conscience: &, qui plus est, il entre-
    tient aupres de son serrail à Pera, quatre Religions toutes diuerses, celle des Iuifs, des Chrestiens
    à la Rommaine, & à la Greque, & celle des Mehemetistes', and *De republica*, p. 483: 'Turcarum
    quidem rex maximus summa veneratione religionem à maioribus acceptam colit, neque
    tamen peregrinas aliorum religiones execratur, sed suo quemque ritu viuere patitur, eos
    inquam, qui Romanam, qui Graecam, qui Iudaicam, qui Aethiopicam, qui Persicam sectam
    sequuntur').
76. Bodin, *Six livres*, p. 655 (main argument); *Six Bookes*, p. 536F (*Six livres*, p. 653: 'tous les Rois, &
    Princes, de l'Orient & d'Afrique, defendent bien estroitement qu'on dispute de la Religion',
    adding that the application of this principle in the Peace of Augsburg had brought an end to
    years of bitter fighting in Germany).
77. Bodin, *Six Bookes*, p. 507A (*Six livres*, p. 618: 'les grands Rois d'Ethiopie, de Tartarie, de Perse,
    & de Turquie, qui ne veulent pas mesmes que les subiects iectent la veuë droit sur eux'); this
    suggests a rather strong interpretation of Thevet's description of people 'bowing down their
    heads' as the Sultan passed.

it bee when they are to giue battell.'[78] And another feature of the Ottoman system that won his praise was the method of gathering taxes, which he portrayed as both efficient and uncorrupt. His scorn was reserved for the French method of tax-farming: 'it is a strange thing and very absurd in this realme, to see so many men giue money to their maister to pick his purse. The Emperour of Turkie doth otherwise, for he neuer sels office.'[79]

Of the various positive themes treated by the mid-sixteenth-century authors mentioned above, the only one at which Bodin appears to have baulked was that of the speedy administration of justice at the hands of an individual *kadi*. Having evidently studied Postel's account of the Ottoman judicial system, he included in his text some details of the role of the *kadi* (whom he confused, to a certain extent, with a mufti).[80] But Bodin's own *formation professionelle* as a lawyer led him to insist both that speedy justice was often bad justice ('For right hard it is for a judge pressed with choller and desire of reuenge, hasted by some, and thrust forward by others, to doe good iustice'), and that judges did better when sitting in a panel than when acting individually. In Cairo, he observed, appeals were decided by a judge sitting on his own, 'whom it is no great matter for him to winne, that standeth in his good grace, or that hath the greatest presents to giue him'. And he went on to criticize the fact that in the Ottoman Empire the judges could be dismissed and replaced, at will, by the Sultan or his senior officials.[81] This is one of the very rare points on which one finds Bodin making a general or structural criticism of the Ottoman regime.

Thus far, Bodin's views have been drawn from a political treatise in which he set out his own opinions. But some of his strongest statements about Ottoman society—and about Islam—are to be found in a more literary text, the interpretation of which is therefore less straightforward. This is the *Colloquium heptaplomeres*, one of Bodin's last works (written probably in the period 1590–2), which circulated in manuscript from the early seventeenth

78. Bodin, *Six Bookes*, p. 542F–G (*Six livres*, p. 658: 'Les Turcs y procedent encore plus estroittement, non seulement en punissant les seditieux & mutins à toute rigueur: ains aussi en defendant de porter les armes en guerre mesmes, sinon alors qu'il faut combattre').
79. Bodin, *Six Bookes*, p. 686G (*Six livres*, p. 912: 'Mais c'est chose bien estrange en ce Royaume, que tant de personnes baillent de l'argent à leur maistre pour fouiller dans sa bourse. Le Roy des Turcs fait bien tout le contraire, car il ne vend iamais office').
80. Bodin, *Six livres*, p. 374.
81. Bodin, *Six Bookes*, pp. 515C, 487E–488F (*Six livres*, pp. 629: 'car il est malaise que le Iuge pressé de colere, hasté des vns, precipité des autres, face iustice qui vaille', 596: 'qui n'est pas difficile à gaigner, à celuy qui plus a de faueur, ou de presents pour luy faire'). The suggestion about bribing judges in Cairo may perhaps have been prompted by a conversation with a merchant who traded there (see above, n. 72).

century onwards and was eventually printed in the mid-nineteenth.[82] The work is presented as a discussion on religious and philosophical themes between seven characters: a Catholic, a Lutheran, a Calvinist, two non-religious figures (who have traditionally been taken to represent 'Deism' and sceptical naturalism), a Jew, and a Muslim. The last of these, called Octavius, describes himself as a Sicilian who was seized by pirates and sold into captivity in Syria, where he converted to Islam. His fervent commendations of Muslim beliefs and practices are, therefore, those of a character in a literary work, and not necessarily those of Bodin himself; nevertheless there are significant congruences between some of his statements and the views expressed by Bodin elsewhere. Thus it is not surprising to find that the passage in which Octavius commends the religious toleration practised by Muslim rulers is followed by a more general discussion of religion and politics in which Bodin recycles material first presented in the equivalent discussion in the *République*.[83] And, in the light of Bodin's endorsement of most of the positive themes to be found in the accounts of Ottoman life by Postel and the other authors, it seems reasonable to think that Bodin agreed with the sentiments expressed by Octavius on one other major theme mentioned above, that of the Muslims' attitude to charity and welfare:

> They are amazed that Christian men are able to bear with equanimity so great a multitude of needy people, such want and poverty of their own people, since among the Muslims there are more homes for the needy and strangers than people who need them. Often you could see Turks in this city [*sc.* Venice] throwing coins freely to the poor who were chasing everywhere after the money . . . Also educated men have provided numerous homes near the shrines and very ample provisions for food. There is hardly any rich man who is not responsible for consecrating either a temple or a public lodging.[84]

Bodin's key achievement, as a writer on the Ottoman Empire, was to develop a theory of 'seigneurial monarchy' which would provide the Ottoman

---

82. Bodin, *Colloquium heptaplomeres* (translation: *Colloquium of the Seven*). Doubts have been raised (mistakenly) about whether Bodin was the author of this text; for a study of the issue see Malcolm, 'Jean Bodin'.

83. Bodin, *Colloquium heptaplomeres*, pp. 121–3 (*Colloquium of the Seven*, pp. 157–60); Bodin, *Six Bookes*, pp. 536–8.

84. Bodin, *Colloquium of the Seven*, pp. 219–20 (emended) (*Colloquium heptaplomeres*, pp. 167–8: 'Ac mirantur, Christianos homines tantam egentium multitudinem, tantam suorum nuditatem et inopiam aequo animo ferre posse, cum apud Ismaëlitas plura sint domicilia egentibus ac peregrinis vacua, quam tenues domiciliorum egentes. Saepe quidem videre potuistis Turcas in hac urbe tenuibus ubique occurrentibus nummos libenter objicere . . . Sunt etiam frequentissima domicilia a litteratis hominibus circa fana constituta et uberrimi ad alimenta reditus; vix enim est ullus opibus locuples, qui aut templum aut publicum hospitium consecrandum non curet'). 'Hospitium' here, translated by Kuntz as 'lodging', could mean either an inn or a hospital.

sultans with a distinct category—a category with, to an unusual extent, a positive value—for describing the special nature of their rule. His arguments about this will be discussed separately, below. But it seems clear that he would never have reached such a conclusion about the nature of Ottoman government in general, had he not assimilated all the particular accounts of positive aspects of Ottoman life that had come together in the new paradigm of the mid-sixteenth century.

SEVEN

Machiavelli and reason of state

There were multiple ways of making use of the new information provided by the descriptive writers of the early- and mid-sixteenth century. But the overriding aim, for almost all those who studied this material and wrote in turn about how to deal with the Ottoman Empire, was the final destruction of that enemy state. Many writers therefore tried to subject the information they had to a kind of functional analysis, seeking to work out the strengths and weaknesses of particular practices or institutions. Such a way of looking at a system of rule had to operate at some remove from ordinary moral judgement: while it was easy to describe something (the *devşirme*, for instance) as morally bad, that did not necessarily make it a cause of weakness for the Ottoman regime. Moreover, one important reason for analysing the causes of Ottoman strength was to consider whether some of those advantageous practices could be copied by Christian Europe; here too the moral status of a practice might be relegated to a matter of secondary concern, while at the same time the fact that its adoption could help Christendom to defeat the Ottomans provided a long-term justification that would act as a cover for shorter-term immorality. In the last two decades of the sixteenth century, this approach was taken very actively by writers on 'ragion di stato' or 'reason of state'. That their thinking was heavily influenced by the writings of Machiavelli has long been understood. Yet it is also well known that many of them were fervent Catholics, devoted to the principles of the Counter-Reformation, and convinced that their whole structure of argument could be justified only when set in a larger framework of religious values (a conviction which made them denounce Machiavelli sincerely and often). Nothing could have been more suited to their purposes than the great cause of anti-Ottoman warfare in defence of Christendom; indeed, it may be doubted whether reason of state theory would have been able to develop as successfully as—for a while—it did, without this overarching concern. But in order to understand the background to these later writings, it is necessary to return to the early part of the century, to consider the works of the ultimate founder of this tradition, Niccolò Machiavelli himself.

With the exception of one short chapter in *Il principe* (a work written in 1513–14, and printed in 1532), Machiavelli's writings do not contain any extended analysis of the Ottoman Empire; his main interests were intra-Italian, and the amount of detailed information available to him about the Ottoman state was in any case quite limited. Yet there is enough evidence to show that he did take some interest in the Ottoman sultans and their actions. In the *Discorsi* (written in 1513–19, printed in 1531) he mentions several episodes involving them: an assassination attempt on Bayezid II, the punishment of a pasha by Selim I for giving bad strategic advice (Machiavelli says that he has obtained this story from 'some people coming here from the Sultan's territories'), and the use of artillery by that Ottoman Sultan to defeat both the Shah of Persia and the Mamluk Sultan of Egypt and Syria.[1] Notably absent, however, from all his major works, including even his treatise on the *Arte della guerra* (written in 1519–20, printed in 1521), is any treatment of the Ottoman Empire as a significant threat to Western Christendom. His personal correspondence confirms that he was quite untroubled by this. In 1501 his friend Agostino Vespucci wrote to him contemptuously about the Pope's panic fear of an impending Ottoman attack on Rome, commenting that the Sultan would perform a much needed task if he came to Rome and purged the city of papal immorality; and in 1513 Francesco Vettori, whose friendship with Machiavelli was close enough to allow him an unbuttoned freedom of expression in his private letters, responded sarcastically to the current religious prognostications about an Ottoman conquest of Italy: 'Let the Sultan come, with the whole of Asia, and let all the prophecies be fulfilled at once!'[2] Vettori did not in fact underestimate the military power of the Sultan, but, like Vespucci, he was motivated here primarily by a fierce, moralistic anticlericalism, directed against the Papacy. As he observed later in the same letter:

> The Sultan [Selim I, who had come to the throne in the previous year]...will do something that few people now expect...Fortune is on his side, he has

---

1. Machiavelli, *Il principe* IV, pp. 14–16; *Discorsi* II.17, i, p. 49 (artillery), III.6, ii, pp. 555–6 (Bayezid), III.35, ii, p. 739 ('alcuni che vengono de' suoi paesi'). On Selim's use of artillery cf. also Machiavelli, *Arte della guerra*, fo. 65v.
2. Machiavelli, *Opere*, ed. Gaeta, iii, pp. 106 (Vespucci), 389 ('venga il Turco con tutta l'Asia, e colmisi per un tratto tutte le profezie'). In 1489 another Florentine writer, Pacifico Massimi, had similarly welcomed the prospect of the Sultan removing the Pope: see Ricci, *Appello al Turco*, pp. 82–3.

loyal soldiers in his army, plenty of money, a huge country, and nothing to stop him; and he has an alliance with the Tatar Khan. So I would not be surprised if, within one year, he had given this Italy of ours a great beating, and got these priests on the run.[3]

There is good reason to think that Machiavelli was similarly free of the usual religious scruples in these matters. In his *Istorie fiorentine* (written in 1520–5, printed in 1532) he described the First Crusade as a political ploy, cleverly devised by Pope Urban II in order to shore up his own teetering authority; and in a letter to his old friend Francesco Guicciardini in 1521 he ridiculed the popular debate stirred up by cheaply printed prophecies about 'whether the Sultan will fall, or whether these are good times for undertaking a crusade'. As for the shocking Ottoman invasion of Apulia and capture of Otranto in 1480, Machiavelli was content to portray this in his *Istorie fioren-tine* as simply an immense stroke of good luck for Florence, diverting the superior forces of the King of Naples away from that city-state at a very critical moment.[4]

At several points in his writings, Machiavelli's admiration for the military prowess of the Ottomans shines through. He praised Mehmed II for defeat-ing his neighbours (like the biblical King David) and leaving to his son, Bayezid, 'a stable kingdom'. He observed that Bayezid's son, the current Sultan Selim I, 'seems set to outdo the glory of his grandfather'—'glory' being a very positive term in Machiavelli's lexicon. He insisted that rulers ought to lead their own military campaigns, as the Roman emperors had done, and as the Ottoman sultans now did. And, looking at the whole of human history since the end of the Roman Empire, he concluded that the 'virtù' (his special term for the psychological-moral-political qualities that render a person—more specifically, a man—active, decisive, and suc-cessful) which was once concentrated in that great state had been 'dis-tributed among many countries where people have lived in accordance with virtù', singling out as examples the Frankish kingdom, the Ottoman Empire, the Mamluk Sultanate, and the modern German lands—as well

---

3. Machiavelli, *Opere*, ed. Gaeta, iii, p. 391 ('il Turco...farà qualche cosa che ora pochi vi pensano...la fortuna gli è favorabile, ha soldati tenuti seco in fazione, ha danari assai, ha paese grandissimo, non ha ostacolo alcuno, ha coniunzione con il Tartaro, in modo che non mi farei maragivlia che avanti passasse uno anno egli avesse dato a questa Italia una gran bastonata, e facesse uscire di passo questi preti').
4. Machiavelli, *Istorie fiorentine* I.17, p. 592 (crusade), VIII.20–1, pp. 953–4 (Otranto); Machiavelli, *Opere*, ed. Gaeta, iii, p. 526 ('sul Turco che debbe passare, e se fosse bene fara la Crociata in questi tempi').

as 'the Saracen sect' (Islam), whose great deeds included the destruction of the eastern Roman Empire. Even today, he wrote, among 'some part' of all those peoples, one could find the virtù 'which is desired, and which is praised with true praise'.[5]

As someone who admired successful warfare and studied the techniques and methods that made it possible, Machiavelli paid special attention to military training and discipline. It is a little surprising that he did not comment directly on the discipline of the Ottoman army; he was writing before Paolo Giovio's work highlighted this aspect of the Ottoman system, but, as we have seen, Giovio himself was able to draw on an existing body of knowledge. Machiavelli did praise the 'many exercises' of the Mamluk troops, who had been defeated by the Ottomans (while also commenting that that defeat was caused by sheer terror at the sound of the latter's artillery).[6] But his observations on discipline, which focused mostly on the Roman army, were set out in such a way that later readers, supplied with detailed accounts of Ottoman practice, would instantly have made the connection. Thus in the *Discorsi* he explained: 'in a well-ordered army, no one should do anything except in accordance with regulations. For this reason you will find that in the Roman army (which all other armies should take as their example, given that it conquered the world), no one ate, slept, or went whoring, or performed any other action, whether military or private, without the consul's order.'[7] Readers of the early accounts of Ottoman military discipline (and Ottoman justice) would also have been struck by the principle laid down in chapter XVII of *Il principe*, that a military leader should be happy to acquire a reputation for administering cruel punishments— since 'without that reputation he would never keep the army united and ready for action.'[8]

---

5. Machiavelli, *Discorsi* I.19, i, p. 121 (Mehmed II, 'un regno fermo'; Selim 'si vede costui essere per superare la gloria dell'avolo'), I.30, i, p. 152 (lead campaigns), II.Proemio, i, pp. 298–9 ('sparsa in dimolte nazioni dove si viveva virtuosamente', 'la setta saracina', 'alcuna parte', 'che si disidera e che con vera laude si lauda').

6. Machiavelli, *Discorsi* I.1, i, p. 14 ('molti esercizii'); Machiavelli, *Arte della guerra*, fo. 65v (terror). For Giovio see above, pp. 63–5.

7. Machiavelli, *Discorsi* III.36, ii, p. 745 ('in uno esercito bene ordinato, nessuno debbe fare alcuna opera se non regolato; e si troverrà per questo che nello esercito romano – dal quale, avendo elli vinto il mondo, debbono prendere esemplo tutti gli altri eserciti – non si mangiava, non si dormiva, non si meritricava, non si faceva alcuna azione o militare o domestica sanza l'ordine del console').

8. Machiavelli, *Il principe* XVII, p. 55 ('sanza questo nome non si tenne mai esercito unito né disposto ad alcuna fazione').

If readers made these connections, however, they might then have been forced to ponder the implications of an important passage in the *Discorsi*, where Machiavelli argued that good military organization was not in itself a guarantee of lasting success, even if it was combined with good fortune. When it appeared to have this effect, it was in fact merely a sign or concomitant of something deeper and more important: good 'ordine', the principle of constitutional, legal, and political order. Those who attributed Rome's success merely to its well-disciplined army 'do not realize that where there is good military organization there needs to be good order ("ordine"), and in that case it seldom happens that there is not good fortune too'.[9] Did this mean, readers might have wondered, that the Ottoman Empire, with its military discipline and many campaigns favoured by success, was also a well-ordered state? In one particular area, the treatment of newly conquered territories and populations, Machiavelli did praise Ottoman statecraft: in *Il principe* he wrote that Mehmed II was right to go and live in Constantinople after conquering it. He also commended the policy of disarming a new subject population, and, in the *Discorsi*, argued against building fortresses as a method of either external defence or internal control; on both these points, whilst he did not mention the Ottoman Empire, his advice chimed with Ottoman practice, real or perceived.[10] More generally, his insistence that a ruler 'should study no other skill than that of war' and his comment that 'it has been observed by prudent men that arms come first, and letters later' also accorded with contemporary views of the pro-military and anti-cultural nature of Ottoman rule.[11] But Machiavelli's writings do not yield any general account of the good ordine of the Ottoman state as such.

Rather, they raise some problematic issues. In the *Arte della guerra* his main speaker puts forward an important argument about how military excellence is generated. There is much more of this excellence in Europe than in Asia or Africa, he says, because Europe has several kingdoms and 'innumerable republics'. The rulers of states favour and promote virtù 'either from necessity, or from some other human passion'. Historically, there was little

---

9. Machiavelli, *Discorsi* I.4, i, p. 33 ('non si avegghino che dove è buona milizia conviene che sia buono ordine, e rade volte anco occorre che non vi sia buona fortuna').

10. Machiavelli, *Il principe* III, p. 8 (Mehmed II), XX, p. 68 (disarming); Machiavelli, *Discorsi* II.24, i, pp. 463–8 (fortresses; note, however, that the argument in *Il principe* XX on fortresses was more equivocal). It was widely believed in Western Christendom that the Ottomans set much less store by fortresses.

11. Machiavelli, *Il principe* XIV, p. 47 ('né prendere cosa alcuna per sua arte, fuora della guerra'); *Istorie fiorentine* V.1, p. 773 ('si è dai prudenti osservato come le lettere vengono drieto alle armi').

necessity for this in Asia: 'that region was all under one kingdom, in which, as it was inactive most of the time because of its size, there was no possibility of bringing forth men who excel in their exploits.' ('Inactive' here is a translation of 'ocioso' ('ozioso'), with its overtones of both leisure and idleness.) As for the role of human passions: 'more excellent men emerge from republics than from kingdoms, because in republics, for the most part, virtù is honoured, but in kingdoms it is feared.'[12] In those areas of Europe where there were many republics and principalities, such as ancient Greece and Italy, mutual distrust and fear made them cultivate military skills; but after the growth of the Roman Empire 'men of virtù began to be few in Europe, as in Asia.' And one other great historical change has subsequently taken place: 'today's way of living, with regard to Christianity, does not impose the kind of necessity of self-defence that existed in the ancient world.' In pagan times conquered land could be devastated and the people scattered or enslaved, but Christian precepts have greatly modified such behaviour. (An intriguing but entirely unspoken implication of this argument might be that it is actually good for present-day Christian states to be menaced by a powerful non-Christian one: the Ottoman threat will stimulate the production of more virtù.)[13]

The discussion of Asian states here was confined to ancient history, citing rulers such as Cyrus and Mithridates; how far Machiavelli intended it to be applicable to the Ottomans is not clear, though he must have been aware that the Ottoman Empire had not been 'inactive most of the time'. But the passage is an important one, combining as it does two lines of argument: one about the difference between a large, unitary state and a dynamic system of small ones; and one about the moral-political qualities promoted by republics and those promoted by kingdoms. (Note, however, that a further type of argument, popular among some later writers, is not present here: Machiavelli does not argue that giant, centrally ruled states are characteristically 'Asiatic', emphasizing rather that the Roman Empire followed exactly the same pattern.) On both counts, the Ottoman Empire scores badly: like any kingdom, it will produce less virtù than a republic,

12. Machiavelli, *Arte della guerra*, fo. 42r–v ('infinite Rep.', 'ò per necessita, ò per altra humana passione', 'quella prouincia era tutta sotto uno regno, nel quale, per la grandezza sua, stando esso la maggior parte del tempo ocioso, non poteua nascere huomini nelle facciende eccelenti', 'delle Rep. esce piu huomini eccellenti che de Regni. Perche in quelle, il piu delle uolte si honora la uirtu, ne Regni si teme').
13. Ibid., fos. 42v (ancient Greece, Italy), 43r ('cominciarono gli huomini uirtuosi ad essere pochi in Europa come in Asia', 'il modo del uiuere d'hoggi, rispetto alla christiana religione, non impone quella necessità di difendersi, che anticamente era').

but it will also produce less than any kingdom within the dynamic European system of states. This is not a portrayal of a state resting on good ordine.

Another basic problem was raised in chapter XIX of *Il principe*, in a discussion of standing armies. Machiavelli noted approvingly that modern European princes did not have these, and described the difficulties they caused for the later Roman emperors.

> If in those days it was necessary [for the emperor] to satisfy the soldiers more than the people, that was because the soldiers were more powerful than the people. Today it is more necessary, for all princes except the Ottoman Sultan and the Mamluk Sultan, to satisfy the people rather than the soldiers, because the people are more powerful than the soldiers. I make an exception of the Ottoman Sultan, as he always keeps 12,000 infantry and 15,000 cavalry about him, and he depends on them for the security and strength of his rule; and it is necessary that that ruler should keep them friendly to him, at the expense of any other consideration. Similarly, the Mamluk Sultan's rule is entirely in the hands of the soldiers.[14]

Here too readers were given the impression that the Ottoman Empire was an ill-constructed state; and that impression was also reinforced by a passage in the *Discorsi* pointing out that in the time of the early Roman emperors (such as Titus, Trajan, and Hadrian), 'there was no need for Praetorian soldiers or large numbers of legions to defend them, as they were defended by their habits, the good will of the people, and the love of the Senate.'[15]

Machiavelli's fullest discussion of the Ottoman Empire is given in chapter IV of *Il principe*. He begins by observing that there are two kinds of monarchical rule: in one kind, the prince rules through administrators whom he is free to select, promote, and dismiss as his 'servants'; and in the other, the administration is carried out by nobles who have their own intrinsic status, and indeed their own subjects or followers. To illustrate these two types, he compares the Ottoman Empire and the Kingdom of France.

> The whole monarchy of the Ottoman Sultan is governed by a single ruler; the others are his servants ('servi'). Dividing his kingdom into *sancak*s [large

14. Machiavelli, *Il principe* XIX, p. 66 ('se allora era necessario satisfare più a' soldati che a' populi, era perch'e soldati potevano più che e populi; ora è più necessario a tutti e principi, eccetto che al Turco et al Soldano, satisfare a' populi che a' soldati, perché e populi possono più di quelli. Di che io ne eccettuo el Turco, tenendo sempre quello intorno a sé dodicimila fanti e quindicimila cavalli, da' quali depende la securtà e la fortezza del suo regno; ed è necessario che, posposto ogni altro respetto, quel signore se li mantenga amici. Similmente el regno del Soldano sendo tutto in mano de' soldati ...').
15. Machiavelli, *Discorsi* I.10, i, p. 72 ('non erano necessarii i soldati pretoriani né la moltitudine delle legioni a difendergli, perché i costumi loro, la benivolenza del popolo, l'amore del senato gli difendeva').

military-feudal districts], he sends various administrators to them, and changes and varies them as he wishes. But the King of France finds himself in the midst of a long-established multitude of nobles, who are acknowledged in that state by their own subjects and loved by them.[16]

From these facts he draws two conclusions. The first is that the Ottoman Empire will be much more difficult to conquer than France; among the French nobility one can always find powerful, disaffected individuals who may be happy to invite and assist a foreign conqueror, but they have no equivalent in the Ottoman government. On the contrary, the Sultan's administrators,

> being all of them slaves, and under an obligation to him, are more difficult to corrupt; and even if they were corrupted, you could not hope to get much benefit from them, as they cannot draw the people after them, for the reasons already given. Therefore those who attack the Sultan must expect to find his state fully united, and must place more trust in their own strength than in any disorders on the other side.[17]

But the second conclusion is that—again, in diametric opposition to the French case—the Ottoman Empire, once successfully conquered, will be easy to hold. After the defeat of the Sultan, 'there is no reason to fear anyone apart from the Sultan's blood-relations; once they have been eliminated, there is no one left to fear, as the others have no credit with the population.'[18]

Here at least was a clear explanation of the defensive—though not the offensive—strength of the Ottoman state. Built into this account, too, was a theory which would explain why that state was well administered: its provincial governors, and other officials, were all creatures of the Sultan, with an interest in maintaining his favour and a relative inability to gain 'credit' with the people under them. But what degree of credit the Sultan himself might have had among the general population would not have been at all clear to Machiavelli's readers: perhaps very little, given that he depended on

---

16. Machiavelli, *Il principe* IV, pp. 14–15 ('servi', 'Tutta la monarchia del Turco è governata da uno signore, gli altri sono sua servi: e distinguendo il suo regno in Sangiachi vi manda diversi amministratori e gli muta e varia come pare a lui. Ma il re di Francia è posto in mezzo d'una moltitudine antiquata di signori, in quello stato riconosciuti da' loro sudditi e amati da quelli').
17. Ibid. IV, p. 15 ('sendoli tutti stiavi e obligati, si possono con più difficultà corrompere, e quando bene si corrompessino, se ne può sperare poco utile non possendo quelli tirarsi drieto e populi per le ragioni assegnate. Onde, chi assalta el Turco è necessario pensare di averlo a trovare tutto unito, e gli conviene sperare più nelle forze proprie che ne' disordini d'altri').
18. Ibid. IV, p. 15 ('no si ha a dubitare di altro che del sangue del principe: il quale spento, non resta alcuno di chi si abbia a temere, non avendo li altri credito con gli populi').

a standing army for the security of his rule, and placed the good of his army systematically above that of his people. At best, he might be the sort of ruler who was described in *Il principe* as 'making himself feared in such a way that, even if he does not acquire the people's love, he escapes their hatred'.[19] As more information emerged, in the three decades after Machiavelli's death in 1527 and the publication of most of his major works in 1531–2, about the stable and beneficial conditions of life in the Ottoman Empire, his readers would have searched for some further component that would help to explain its success—a component located, preferably, at the level of the 'people' itself. Fortunately, Machiavelli's own writings did supply such an explanation: the special role of religion. And this was capable of accounting not only for the Ottoman Empire's internal social stability, but also, to some extent, for its success in external wars of aggression.

The popular view of Machiavelli as an anti-religious writer is not correct. He was not anti-religious; he was anti-Christian—or, at least, opposed to the existing version of Christianity, characterized by him as the faith propagated by Saints Francis and Dominic, who had preached humility and obedience towards the Church. In the *Discorsi* he complained that 'our religion has glorified humble and contemplative men rather than men of action...this way of living now seems to have weakened the world, and given it as prey to wicked men.' Instead, he argued for the possibility of a different kind of Christianity: if it now seemed that Heaven had been 'disarmed', he wrote, 'this is doubtless due more to the debased nature of those men who have interpreted our religion in terms of inaction ["ozio"] and not in terms of virtù', and who have failed to understand that Christianity does permit us 'to exalt and defend our fatherland'.[20] Admittedly, there is almost no other indication in his writings of what form that true version of Christianity should take; the general comments he makes in the first book of the *Istorie fiorentine* about the Roman Church, from the conversion of Constantine onwards, are so consistently negative as to make the reader doubt whether such a beneficial form of Christianity has ever existed on Earth. But his discussion of the First Crusade, although it puts most of the

19. Ibid. XVII, p. 54 ('farsi temere in modo che, se non acquista lo amore, che fugga l'odio').
20. Machiavelli, *Discorsi* II.2, i, pp. 318–19 ('La nostra religione ha glorificato piú gli uomini umili e contemplativi che gli attivi...Questo modo di vivere, adunque, pare che abbi renduto il mondo debole e datolo in preda agli uomini scelerati', 'disarmato', 'nasce piú, sanza dubbio, dalla viltà degli uomini, che hanno interpretato la nostra religione secondo l'ozio, e non secondo la virtú', 'la esaltazione e la difesa della patria'), III.1, ii, p. 532 (SS Francis, Dominic).

emphasis on Pope Urban II's self-interested motives for calling it, does include the comment: 'many kings and many peoples contributed money, and many individuals fought without pay; so great was the effect of religion at that time on people's minds, when they were moved by the example of those who were their leaders.'[21] That religion could have such effects was a matter of keen interest to Machiavelli, and not in itself a negative thing at all. Its value was to be assessed on the principle of 'cui bono?' ('to whose benefit?'); only if the beneficiary was a corrupt, self-interested body such as the Papacy would the judgment be necessarily negative.

Machiavelli's most sustained analysis of the power of religion came in a section of the *Discorsi* (I.11–15) devoted to the beliefs and practices of the ancient Romans. Here the assessment of the functioning of religion was overwhelmingly positive. Machiavelli's hero was Numa Pompilius, the legendary second ruler of Rome (after Romulus), who, faced with the task of reducing 'a very fierce people' to civil obedience, turned to religion as 'something absolutely necessary'. All who study Roman history will observe 'how useful religion was for sending out armies, uniting the common people, keeping people good, and shaming the bad'. Indeed, religion was among the prime causes of Rome's success, since 'it caused good "ordini"', good "ordini" cause good fortune, and the success of Rome's undertakings arose from good fortune.'[22] Examples of how this causal nexus worked include the use of oracles and auspices to raise the confidence of Roman soldiers before they went into battle—'from which confidence, victory follows almost always'.[23] These comments all related to a pagan religion, not to Christianity as it was known and practised. So for any reader who might seek to apply them to the case of the success and good fortune of the Ottoman Empire, the argument could be made with very little effort: Islam, as a quasi-pagan religion devoted to action and worldly success, not to humility and contemplation, was the source of the sultans' good ordini, especially where their military operations were concerned.

21. Machiavelli, *Istorie fiorentine* I.9, p. 583 (Roman Church), I.17, p. 592 ('molti re e molti popoli concorsono con danari e molti privati sanza alcua mercede militorono; tanto allora poteva negli animi degli uomini la religione, mossi dallo esemplo di quegli che ne erano capi'). Cf. Lukes, 'To Bamboozle with Goodness', p. 273.

22. Machiavelli, *Discorsi* I.11, i, pp. 76–7 ('uno popolo ferocissimo', 'cosa al tutto necessaria'), 78 ('quanto serviva la religione a mandare gli eserciti, a riunire la plebe, a mantenere gli uomini buoni, a fare vergognare i rei'), 81 ('quella causò buoni ordini, i buoni ordini fanno buona fortuna, e dalla buona fortuna nacquero i felici successi delle imprese').

23. Ibid. I.14, i, pp. 93–6 (auspices; p. 96: 'dalla quale confidenza quasi sempre nasce la vittoria').

Machiavelli's positive view of this kind of religion did not entail thinking that any of its theological claims were true. On the contrary, he was happy to accept that it might be founded on falsehoods. Numa Pompilius 'pretended [or "simulated":"simulò"] that he had close relations with a nymph, who instructed him on what instruction he should give to the people'. Numa was forming a civil state, and his use of religion was entirely instrumental—good, in other words, insofar as its effects on the people were good. Machiavelli's argument was not about founders of religions as such, but about legislators, the makers of the basic ordini of states. And he presented it as a general historical argument which accounted for the otherwise inexplicable fact that passionate and poorly reasoning people were led, at a very early stage, to accept rules and institutions which served their long-term—but not necessarily their short-term—interests.

> There has never been a legislator who has not had recourse to God when putting people under extraordinary laws, since otherwise those laws would never have been accepted. For there are many benefits which, although they will be recognized by a prudent person, are not so self-evidently beneficial as to enable the prudent person to persuade others about them. That is why wise men, wishing to remove this difficulty, have recourse to God. Lycurgus did so; so did Solon; and so did many others.[24]

In some cases the state already existed, and the legislator set it on a new, stable basis; in others, the legislator was both the creator of the state and the designer of its fundamental laws. One of the most important examples, in the second category, was Moses, who led the people of Israel out of Egypt, created a new polity, and gave it its legislation. (Machiavelli treated Moses entirely on a par with figures from pagan history, referring, for example, to 'Moses, Lycurgus, Solon, and other founders of kingdoms and republics, who were able to form laws for the sake of the common good, thanks to the fact that sole authority was attributed to them'.[25]) However, when discussing Moses and other founders of states in Il principe, Machiavelli argued that

24. Ibid. I.11, i, pp. 79–80 ('simulò di avere congresso con una ninfa, la quale lo consigliava di quello che elli avesse a consigliare il popolo', 'mai fu alcuno ordinatore di leggi strasordinarie [sic] in uno popolo, che non ricorresse a Dio, perché altrimenti non sarebbero accettate; perché sono molti beni conosciuti da uno prudente, i quali non hanno in sé ragioni evidenti da poterle persuadere a altrui. Però gli uomini savi che vogliono tôrre questa difficultà ricorrono a Dio. Cosí fece Ligurgo, cosí Solone, cosí molti altri').
25. Discorsi I.9, i, p. 66 ('Moises, Ligurgo, Solone, ed altri fondatori di regni e di republiche, e quali poterono, per aversi attribuito una autorità, formare leggi a proposito del bene commune').

religion in itself was not sufficient to give them the power and authority they needed.

> All armed prophets have been victorious, and the disarmed ones have met with failure. For the people are fickle by nature; it is easy to persuade them of something, but difficult to keep them persuaded. Therefore one should arrange things in such a way that, when they no longer believe, one can make them believe by force. Moses, Cyrus, and Romulus would not have been able to have their ordinances obeyed for a long time if they had been disarmed.[26]

Returning to this point in the *Discorsi*, he added: 'Anyone who reads the Bible attentively will see that Moses, since he wished his laws and "ordini" to go ahead, was obliged to kill innumerable people who, motivated by mere envy, were opposing his plans.'[27]

Machiavelli himself did not apply this whole pattern of argument to the case of Muhammad and Islam. But everything he said must have seemed ready-made to fit that case, given all the standard assumptions that were held about it by Christians: that Muhammad had pretended to have communications with the Angel Gabriel (just as Numa did with his nymph-goddess), that he had not only set up new laws but also used violence to enforce obedience to them, and so on. That his laws were designed for 'the common good' would have been disputed; but their effectiveness, insofar as they were seen as embodied in the powerful and successful Ottoman Empire, was hard to deny. And it was effectiveness, at each stage of the process—from the initial 'simulation' to the final achievement of stable rule—that Machiavelli's analysis was designed to highlight, quite regardless of whether the religion involved was true or false.[28]

---

26. Machiavelli, *Il principe* VI, p. 20 ('tutti e profeti armati vinsono, e gli disarmati ruinorno. Perché…la natura de' populi è varia; ed è facile a persuadere loro una cosa, ma è difficile fermarli in quella persuasione. E però conviene essere ordinato in modo che, quando non credano piú, si possa fare credere loro per forza. Moisè, Ciro, Teseo e Romulo non arebbono possuto fare osservare loro lungamente le loro costituzioni se fussino stati disarmati').

27. Machiavelli, *Discorsi* III.30, ii, p. 710 ('chi legge la Bibbia sensatamente, vedrà Moisè essere stato forzato—a volere che le sue leggi e che i suoi ordini andassero innanzi—ad ammazzare infiniti uomini, i quali, non mossi da altro che dalla invidia, si opponevano a' disegni suoi'). The reference is to the killing of 3,000 people after the episode of the golden calf (Exod. 33: 26–8).

28. Introducing Moses to his argument in *Il principe*, he commented perfunctorily that 'one should not reason about Moses, as he merely executed the orders he was given by God', but immediately went on to emphasize that the actions and 'ordini' of Cyrus and other great pagan rulers 'will not seem any different from those of Moses' (VI, p. 19: 'di Moisè non si debba ragionare, sendo suto uno mero esecutore delle cose che li erano ordinate da Dio', 'parranno non discrepanti da quelli di Moisè').

This evident disregard for theological truth was one of the things that most enraged Machiavelli's critics. And he was not the only thinker in the first half of the sixteenth century to develop such an approach. The philosopher Pietro Pomponazzi, lecturing at Bologna University between 1512 and his death in 1525, attracted the fierce hostility of Catholic theologians for constructing a similar argument, in which religious doctrines were apparently to be assessed in terms of their social effects, not their objective truth. In his *Tractatus de immortalitate animae* (1516) he observed that while the doctrine of the immortality of the soul could not be proved by natural reason, it nevertheless served a vital purpose in human society by making wicked people fear punishments in the afterlife: 'The legislator, considering how liable men are to commit evil, and having regard to the common good, decreed that the soul is immortal, caring not about truth but only about moral goodness, with the aim of inducing people to be virtuous.'[29] 'Legislator' was the term Pomponazzi used for Moses, Jesus Christ, and Muhammad, whose three religions he referred to as three 'laws' ('leges'). The use of the term 'law' for 'religion' was not especially unusual in a comparative context: the Dominican George of Hungary had used it for Islam, for example, and later in the sixteenth century it was quite normal for a convert to Islam, being questioned by the Inquisition, to refer to 'the law of the Muslims' and 'the Christian law'.[30] But what was distinctive about Pomponazzi's use of the term was his willingness to combine the role of a founder of religion with that of a 'statesman' ('politicus') in ancient political philosophy. 'As Plato and Aristotle say', he wrote, 'the statesman is a physician of souls, and his purpose is to make human beings not so much knowledgeable as zealous to do good.'[31] One of the influences on Pomponazzi's thinking here was the twelfth-century Arab philosopher Averroes, whose commentaries on Aristotle he studied in Latin translation; it was Averroes who had insisted that laws ('leges' in the Latin version, a term embracing religions), unlike philosophical statements, are not to be interpreted in terms of the truth or

29. Pomponazzi, *Abhandlung*, p. 198 ('respiciens legislator pronitatem virorum ad malum, intendens communi bono sanxit animam esse immortalem, non curans de veritate, sed tantum de probitate, ut inducat homines ad virtutem').
30. George of Hungary, *Tractatus*, pp. 256–8 ('lex'); Archivio Storico Diocesano di Napoli, MS Sant'Ufficio 89.1075 (Anastasia of Paramythia, 1598), fo. 2r ('la legge di turchi'), 2v ('la legge christiana') (where the usage may be that of the Inquisition's scribe).
31. Pomponazzi, *Abhandlung*, p. 196 (Moses, etc., 'leges', 'ut dicunt Plato et Aristoteles, politicus est medicus animorum propositumque politici est facere hominem magis studiosum quam scientem').

falsity of what they say. And from this it followed, as Pomponazzi wrote in a manuscript commentary on Aristotle's *Physics*, that legislators, according to Averroes, were able to invent falsehoods in order to make people worship and obey God.[32] Such a line of argument might easily be combined with the idea, present in classical sources—most explicitly in a passage cited by Sextus Empiricus, in a work first printed in 1569—that all religion was invented for purposes of social control.[33]

At first sight, it is easy to suppose that this entire Machiavellian and Pomponazzian pattern of argument must have been completely objectionable to orthodox Christian thinkers. Much of it was, of course—above all, the possible implication that what was said here about religions or 'laws' could apply also to Christianity. Even if Christianity were safely set aside, there was still something troubling about the idea that a false religion, belief in which would send a person to Hell, could have beneficial effects. But on the other hand the traditional Christian view of false religions could take the line that they were mere human creations (or, at least, creations by humans under diabolic guidance), as much of the standard literature on Islam made clear. So the theory of the human invention of religion for this-worldly purposes was a usable one, so long as its use was confined to such 'infidel' faiths.

One writer who made positive use of it was Guillaume Postel, in his treatise on the underlying agreement of all religions, *De orbis terrae concordia* (1544). Discussing the origin of religion among the pagans, he set up a careful balance between two factors. On the one hand there were principles of natural theology which were available to all humans who reasoned correctly: the existence of God, his creation of the world, his supervision of mankind's earthly life, and the fact of rewards and punishments in a life after death. But on the other hand there was the state-approved religion, which, in the pagan world, 'since the true God is unknown, proceeds from wonder, fear, or love'—fear of future punishments being especially common.[34] He gave quite a detailed account of how and why religions were developed, 'either for the happiness of the people who used them, or for the advantage of the individuals who introduced them, or for both'. Fear of the (false) gods was a natural impulse, and it was equally natural that rulers should make use of it. Those who sought to found new laws or new states,

32. See Nardi, *Studi*, pp. 122–48 (Averroean influence; p. 138: MS commentary); Paganini, "'*Legislatores*'", pp. 185–9 (Averroean influence).
33. Sextus Empiricus, *Adversus mathematicos* VIII, p. 264.
34. Postel, *De orbis terrae concordia*, p. 273 ('quum verus ignoratur, admiratione, timore uel amore proficiscitur'). Postel hastens to insist that Christianity is excluded from this discussion.

knowing that innovation was usually resisted, took care to claim 'that they had familiar dealings with some god, in order to persuade the people that they had a greater, two-fold authority'.[35] He continued:

> I do not want to discuss here Lycurgus, Solon, Charondas, Zamolxis, and the others who are recorded as having been creators or introducers of laws for the great advantage of the people and for their common glory. They all established and settled their ordinances by means of oracles and a divine author. For, taking their start from religion, they needed to make use of those gods and spirits with whom they claimed to have familiar contact. But a single Arab, Muhammad, easily outdid the arts and ingenuity of all of them.[36]

Here was a fervent (though idiosyncratic) Catholic author taking up and developing a Machiavellian line of argument, and leaving open the possibility that, as the pagans' own traditions asserted, these deceptive legislators had acted for 'the great advantage of the people'. But he went further: 'In my opinion, just as people can never be made to abide by and submit to their duty except by means of a trusting belief in religion, so too that trusting belief can hardly be strengthened or maintained except by means of arms.' Ancient kings had also functioned as priestly sacrificers, 'joining both powers together', and the biblical King David 'achieved more in his capacity as a prophet than he did by his kingly power'. Machiavelli's point about the need for a prophet to be 'armed' was developed here into a general argument about the mutual dependence of religion and coercive power in the structure of a stable state—an argument which, moreover, Postel was happy to apply to a biblical prophet-king, and thus potentially to the Christian religion itself. 'For, as everyone knows, one of these [sc. religion] has the place of the spirit of the state, and the other [sc. temporal power] is like the state's body. And if the two are separated and dispersed, it is inevitable that the state will collapse.'[37]

35. Ibid., pp. 273 ('aut in foelicitate popularium ea utentium, aut in utilitate instituentis, aut in utroque'), 281 ('se consuetudinem habere cum quodam numine, ut eorum maior esset duplexq[ue] authoritas suaserunt').
36. Ibid., p. 281 ('Nolo hic Lycurgum, Solonem, Charondam, Zamolxim, & caeteros qui legum authores aut instauratores summo popularium commodo & communi gloria fuisse memorantur. Omnes enim numine authore, & oraculis constitutiones suas stabilitas firmasque fecere. Primo namque loco auspicari à religione & deorum geniorúmue, quos habere se familiares asserebant, opus fuit. Verum omnium artes & ingenium unus Arabs Muhamedes facile superauit'). Charondas was a legendary law-giver to the early Greek colonies of southern Italy; Zamolxis was said to have acted as teacher and legislator for the ancient Thracians.
37. Ibid., pp. 281 ('Meo sanè iudicio, ut homines nunquam sine religionum credulitate consistere atque retineri in officio possunt: ita credulitas sine armis uix potest augeri atque conseruari', 'utraque coniuncta potentia'), 282 ('Dauid rex prophetiae nomine plus profuit, quàm regis

Postel's own notion of the ideal state may have been a peculiar one (a French kingdom, under a saintly monarch, fulfilling its destiny to become a world monarchy); nevertheless, with these words he managed to prefigure the argument of a wide range of Catholic political theorists of the post-Tridentine Counter-Reformation. The relationship of this kind of Counter-Reformation thought to Machiavelli's claims was paradoxical and conflicted. It fully accepted the notion of the 'prophet armed', maintaining that true religion must actively guide the state, and the state must actively protect true religion. However, unlike Machiavelli, or even Postel, the later Counter-Reformation writers refused to accept the idea that an infidel religion could play a positive role in strengthening the state. What they particularly resented was Machiavelli's idea that pagan religions had been better at this than Christianity, and hence they strongly rejected his portrayal of the Christian faith as something that weakened temporal power and led to defeat and humiliation. Above all, they objected to the idea that religion should be in any way instrumentalized by politics. (A particular bugbear, arising from the French Wars of Religion, was the argument of the so-called 'politiques'—especially Jean Bodin—that heresy should be tolerated for the sake of temporal peace.) Rather, they wanted to turn that process the other way round: politics should be put to work in the service of religion. And in practical terms that also meant that it might be licit for the usual norms of political action to be transgressed for true religion's sake, in accordance with what they called 'ragion di stato' or 'reason of state'.[38]

One of the most important of these writers was Giovanni Botero, who studied under the Jesuits and then taught for many years at their colleges in Italy and France; in 1580 he entered the service of one of the leading figures of the Counter-Reformation, Carlo Borromeo, and during the 1580s he also worked for the Duke of Savoy. The composition of his first major published work, *De regia sapientia* (1583), was prompted, he said, by a recent discussion of Spanish policy towards the Dutch Revolt. Several speakers had invoked and praised Machiavelli, arguing that when kings seek to preserve

potentia', 'Nam nemo nescit, alterum animi locum, alterum ueluti corpus Reipublicae esse: quibus disiunctis atque dissipatis, statum collabi necesse est').

38. There is a large literature on this: see especially De Mattei, *Il problema*; Lutz, *Ragione di stato*; Bireley, *The Counter-Reformation Prince*. For a summary account, distinguishing between this Counter-Reformation current and a more pragmatic tradition associated with Justus Lipsius, see Malcolm, *Reason of State*, pp. 92–105. On the hostility to Bodin and the 'politiques' see Baldini, 'L'Antimachiavélisme'.

their rule, they cannot afford to follow the precepts of the Gospels. Botero profoundly disagreed. Machiavelli was 'certainly a clever person, but hardly a Christian'; and in fact, success would come only when the ruler was fully committed to practising and enforcing the true religion, as nothing could animate soldiers as strongly as Christian faith. 'Religion is the foundation of all rule', Botero announced at the beginning of his first chapter, and most of the text was devoted to a succession of biblical and historical examples of pious rulers being favoured by God, or impious ones being punished.[39] In the last part of the book he turned to what was perhaps the most glaring contemporary counter-example: the powerful and successful Ottoman Empire. The popular notion that this regime enjoyed 'diuturnitas', everlastingness, was entirely false, he argued, for 'everyone agrees that fear is a bad guardian of everlastingness, and the rule of the Ottomans depends on fear.' While issuing a cloud of invective against the evils of that empire, he fell back on the traditional homiletic argument that the success of the Ottomans was God's punishment for the impiety and disunity of Christendom. 'What is fighting against us is not the cleverness of the Ottomans, who are stupid, nor their military power, which is weak, nor their discipline, which is barbarous, but rather the force of our own crimes.'[40]

For all its rhetorical energy, this little book had almost nothing original to say. But it did play an important role, by stimulating the thinking of one of Botero's closest friends: the French soldier, diplomat, and writer René de Lucinge, who had taken Botero with him on a Savoyard diplomatic mission to Paris in 1584–5. Lucinge—who had himself engaged in anti-Ottoman warfare, serving on the Christian fleet in the Mediterranean in 1572—was fascinated by Ottoman power and determined to analyse the factors that would bring about its eventual collapse. The work he wrote on this subject (in 1586) was published in 1588 under the wide-ranging title *De la naissance, durée et chute des états*, but its focus was almost completely on the Ottoman Empire.[41]

Like Botero, Lucinge was keen to emphasize the fundamental role of religion in sustaining temporal rule. The way in which he made this point

39. Botero, *De regia sapientia*, sig. †3r (recent discussion, 'hominis sanè ingeniosi, sed parum Christiani'), p. 28 ('Religio est omnis Principatus fundamentum'). On Botero's critique of Machiavelli in this work see Vasoli, 'A proposito della "Digressio"'.
40. Botero, *De regia sapientia*, pp. 112 'malus est, omnium consensu, custos diuturnitatis metus, at Turcarum principatus metu continetur'), 113 ('Pugnant in nos non Turcarum ingenia, quae obtusa, non vires, quae infirmae, non disciplina, quae barbara est: sed facinorum nostrorum vis').
41. Lucinge, *De la naissance*, pp. 7 (composed in 1586), 183–9 (1572 campaign). On the relationship with Botero see Baldini, 'Botero et Lucinge'.

had a somewhat Machiavellian flavour to it. 'For it [sc. religion] is what rulers necessarily have to make use of in order to keep their people obedient and worshipful towards a god, whether true or false; otherwise, without it, it would be impossible for them to acknowledge a sovereign on earth, if they did not fear and acknowledge a superior power in heaven.' That was why 'Numa Pompilius, Lycurgus, Sertorius, and others' had pretended to receive divine instruction.[42] Lucinge was happy to promote this argument because it led to two comforting conclusions: first, that Ottoman rule could be undermined by a propaganda campaign, directed at its Muslim subjects, demonstrating that Islam was full of absurdities; and secondly, that any state based on Christianity was guaranteed to enjoy stability and strength. For 'there is no kind of religion that is more favourable to rulers, for the preservation and tranquillity of their state and their conscience, than the Christian one. What greater reason, or instrument, of state could one find than the one which subjects people to a perfect and full obedience?'[43]

This argument was all very well, but it did pose an obvious question about how the Ottoman Empire managed to enjoy—as it seemingly did— 'full obedience' from its own subjects. Lucinge was aware of the problematic nature of this question, having read many of those sixteenth-century descriptions of the Empire that highlighted the positive conditions of life found within it. His fundamental assumption remained, unshakably, that all Ottoman subjects were living under an oppressive tyranny; in trying to justify this assumption he played a significant role (as we shall see in chapter 9) in developing the concept of Oriental 'despotism'. So, in order to explain why the Ottoman Empire was not constantly seething with rebellion, he portrayed the whole system of rule there as a set of cunning tactics to lull the people into quiescence. He hastened to assure his readers that these were barbarous ways of governing which must be 'rejected' and 'abhorred' by Christians, and insisted that he was analysing them 'without giving any

42. Lucinge, *De la naissance*, pp. 164 ('c'est celle de laquelle il faut necessairement que les princes se servent, pour contenir leur peuple en l'obeïssance et adoration d'un dieu, soit vray ou faux; autrement, cela n'estant, il seroit impossible de recognoistre un souverain en terre, s'ils n'avoyent la crainte et la cognoissance d'un superieur au ciel'), 165 ('Numa Pompilius, Lycurgus, Sertorius et autres'). The Roman general and statesman Sertorius claimed to receive messages from the goddess Diana via a tame fawn.
43. Ibid., p. 166 ('il n'y a aucune sorte de religion plus favorable aux princes, pour la conservation et repos de leur estat et conscience, que la chrestienne . . . Quelle plus grande raison, ou instrument d'estat, sçauroit-on rencontrer que celuy qui assujectit les peuples à une parfaite et accomplie obeïssance?').

approval whatsoever to any of these methods, still less trying to describe them in order to take them as examples to be copied'.[44]

Yet on some points the need to imitate the Ottomans was plain. Borrowing from Giovio (among other sources), Lucinge praised the superior discipline of the Ottoman army; 'one has never heard of any revolt or mutiny having prevented or delayed the carrying out of their conquests.' Everything about their military organization was better. The Ottomans were always ready for war, having both a standing army and the financial reserves needed for the rapid provision of weaponry and supplies; and these advantages were combined with a remarkable speed and decisiveness of action, so that 'their promptitude and foresight have never let any opportunities escape them, without their gaining profit and glory from them.'[45]

As for the sultans' political tactics towards their opponents: here Lucinge's argumentation became strangely contorted. In a chapter entitled 'On his [sc. the Sultan's] mixing fraud with force', he began by strongly criticizing Machiavelli's recommendation of promise-breaking in chapter XVIII of Il principe, and then observed: 'Someone will say to me that the sultans have copied these bad tricks, using all kinds of ruses, deceptions, and breaches of promise towards their neighbours, and that nevertheless they have gained profit and advantage from it.' Lucinge agreed that they had, but insisted that 'the causes were different', adding that the most deceptive of the sultans were not the ones that benefited the most from such conduct.[46] Yet the only examples he gave were the stories of King Ladislas in 1444 reneging on his truce with Murad II (not the other way round) and being defeated; of Selim II breaking his peace agreement with Venice in 1570 (after which God punished the Christians for their sins, making them unable to follow up on their victory at Lepanto); and of Süleyman the Magnificent ordering his commanders to keep the promise that had been made to their captives at Castro in 1537. (This last detail was drawn from Giovio, who, as we have

44. Ibid., p. 172 ('rejettez', 'aborrez', 'sans que j'approuve nullement aucune de ces façons, ny moins que je tasche de les dire pour en former exemple recevable').

45. Ibid., pp. 131 ('leur promptitude et prevoyance n'a jamais laissé eschapper les occasions...sans en recueillir le profit et la gloire', standing army), 134–5 (financial reserves, 'Jamais on n'a ouy parler qu'aucune revolte ou mutinerie ayt empesché ou retardé les cours de leurs conquêtes').

46. Ibid., pp. 87 ('De ce qu'il a meslé le dol avec la force'), 87–90 (criticisms), 90 ('Quelqu'un me dira que les Turcs ont suivy ces mauvais artifices, et se sont servys de toutes sortes de ruses, tromperies et mauvaise foy envers leur voisins', 'les causes sont differentes').

seen, commented that the Sultan was 'always extremely observant of faith and justice in his dealings with those who surrendered voluntarily'.)[47] Of these, only the case of Selim fitted the proposed pattern of sultans gaining from their own human dishonesty for other, God-given reasons.

Towards the end of his treatise, when Lucinge put forward his own suggestions for weakening and destroying Ottoman rule, his thoughts returned to Machiavelli, but with a very different slant on his argument. Having discussed the ways in which Christian powers might corrupt and suborn people in the Ottoman Empire (both private individuals and public officials), he wrote: 'These are the methods and opportunities that must be chosen and carefully cultivated by our Christian rulers in order to bring about, gently and skilfully, the ruin of our common enemy, using—as the saying goes—the fox's skin to make up for that of the lion.' Here, while the specific allusion was to a saying attributed to Lysander by Plutarch, 'where the lion's skin does not reach, it must be patched up by the fox's', Lucinge's thoughts would inevitably have turned also to chapter XVIII of *Il principe*, where Machiavelli wrote that a ruler must imitate not only the powerful lion but also the wily fox.[48]

Lucinge's treatise was widely read, being reprinted several times in French and translated into Italian, Latin, and English.[49] It also exerted a strong influence on his friend Giovanni Botero, who was partly inspired by it to write a wide-ranging treatise on the arts of government and war, entitled *Della ragion di stato*, in 1589. Here Botero emerged as a major author, moving far beyond the narrowly religious and shrill manner of his *De regia sapientia*. His discussion ranged much more widely than that of Lucinge, drawing examples from many countries and many historical periods; but the Ottoman Empire was a constant presence in the book, which, in its enlarged 1590 edition, ended with a rousing call to Christian states, urging them to go to war against the Sultan. This work too, like Lucinge's, was conceived of as an anti-Machiavellian treatise. In his dedicatory epistle (to the Archbishop of Salzburg) Botero said that he had been shocked to hear people quoting approvingly from Machiavelli, who 'grounds reason of state on paying little

47. Ibid., pp. 90–2. For the Castro episode, and Giovio's comment, see above, pp. 121–2.
48. Lucinge, *De la naissance*, p. 254 ('Voilà les moyens et les occasions qui doivent estre choisies et soigneusement cultivees par nos princes chrestiens pour doucement et dextrement bastir la ruyne de l'ennemy commun, apportants (comme on dict) la peau du regnard au deffault de celle du lyon'); Plutarch, *Life of Lysander* VII.4; Machiavelli, *Il principe*, p. 56.
49. Lucinge, *De la naissance*, pp. 8–14, 27–9.

attention to conscience', and at the end of the 1590 edition he complained: 'I do not know why reason of state appears more hostile towards Christians than towards the Ottomans or other infidels. Machiavelli shouts impieties against the Church, but never opens his mouth against the infidels.'[50] These criticisms were of 'reason of state' as it appeared in the rather inchoate usage of current political discourse—drawn to a large extent from Machiavelli, certainly, but quite under-theorized, as the term itself had not been used by that writer. Botero's aim was to replace it with a true doctrine of reason of state, showing how and when it was legitimate for a ruler to dissimulate, simulate, and even (in wartime) engage in active deception, in order to defend and promote the true Catholic religion.

Given his dogmatic belief that a Christian state must be inherently stronger than an infidel one, Botero paid almost no attention to contemporary discussions of the superior military skills of the Ottomans. He was willing to admit that some of the sultans had benefited from studying history: it was reading about Alexander the Great and Julius Caesar that had enabled Selim I to become 'very similar to those two, both in daring and in the speed with which he undertook his military actions'. And he commended the overall Ottoman strategy of almost continuously picking off individual powers one by one, with the result that 'his armies have always consisted of veterans, and ours of novices.' But—in stark contrast to Lucinge—Botero gave little credence to reports of the Ottomans' marvellous discipline and fortitude, or their superior logistics. Mere weight of numbers was a sufficient explanation: 'the Ottomans have always achieved the greatest military undertakings more by numerical strength than by valour.' As for the famous fighting prowess of the Janissaries: German, Swiss, Italian, Spanish, or Gascon soldiers, when properly trained, were just as good, and Ottoman land victories over Christian forces were invariably due to superior cavalry numbers.[51]

The Janissaries did interest Botero, however, in a different context. He was particularly concerned to analyse the methods of pacification and control that might be applied by a ruler to a refractory territory, whether newly

---

50. Botero, *Della ragion*, pp. 3 ('fonda la Ragione di Stato nella poca conscienza'), 312 ('io non so con che giudizio la ragion di stato si mostri più nimica de' Christiani, che de' Turchi, o d'altri infedeli. Il Machiavello, esclama empiamente contra la Chiesa; e contra gli infedeli, non apre pur la bocca').

51. Ibid., pp. 58 ('similissimo all'uno e all'altro, e di ardore, e di prestezza nell'imprese, ch'egli fece'), 66 ('gli eserciti suoi sono stati sempre veterani, e i nostri sempre nuovi'), 208 ('i Turchi hanno fatto sempre imprese grandissime più con la moltitudine che col valore'), 307–8 (Janissaries, cavalry).

conquered or otherwise. (Here the problems faced by Spanish rule in the
Netherlands were uppermost in his mind.) Indeed, one of the main reasons
he gave for engaging in international warfare was that foreign campaigns
acted as safety valves, venting any turbulent tendencies in the direction of
external enemies. By means of such warfare the Ottoman sultans had 'not
only increased their empire, but also kept their subjects peaceful'. It was as
a clever pacification measure, too, that the *devşirme* system appealed to
Botero: 'No one has ever exceeded the cunning of the sultans in making
themselves sure of their dubiously loyal subjects; for they deprive their
Christian subjects of the strength of their young men, using them to fortify
their own power.'[52] Botero's main concern, throughout his lengthy discussion of how to treat disloyal subjects, was with heretics—especially Calvinists,
who, 'since they have no doctrinal justification, will defend their sect with
arms, just like the Muslims'. His advice was that such subjects should be
systematically humiliated and debased; deprived of weapons; if necessary,
transferred *en masse* to other areas; and impoverished by heavy taxation.
Mutual distrust should be stirred up among them by secret agents; their
prominent families should be prevented from intermarrying; and their
leaders should be disinherited or transported. All gatherings should also be
forbidden: after all, did not the Sultan prohibit the ringing of church bells
throughout his dominions?[53]

It was advice such as this that gave a sharp cutting edge to Botero's own
concept of 'true' reason of state. The methods were, in the general sense of
the term, Machiavellian; only the purpose they served, the defence of
Catholicism, distinguished Botero's approach here from that of the writer
whose version of reason of state he so strongly deplored. And where the
Ottomans' methods of rule were concerned, he agreed with Machiavelli on
other issues too; indeed, one could say that he was generally happy to
reproduce Machiavelli's view of Ottoman government, minus the emphasis
on its military success and the suggestion that it was strengthened by its
non-Christian religion. In a later work, the *Relationi universali* of 1595,

---

52. Ibid., pp. 110 (venting feelings), 111 ('non solamente hanno ampliato il loro Dominio,
ma...hanno...tenuto in pace i sudditi'), 151 ('nissuno con più astuzia si è mai assicurato de'
sudditi sospetti, che il Turco; perchè egli...priva i Christiani sudditi suoi del nervo della gio-
ventù, e n'arma se stesso').The use of external warfare as a safety valve was also a Machiavellian
theme: see Machiavelli, *Opere letterarie*, p. 154.

53. Botero, *Della ragion*, pp. 144 ('perchè non hanno ragione di dottrina...difenderanno la lor setta
con l'armi, a guisa de' Turchi'), 145–6 (humiliated), 151 (disarmed), 152–3 (transferred), 153
(taxed), 154 (agents), 155 (families, leaders), 155–6 (gatherings, bells).

Botero followed Machiavelli in arguing that the sultans—or rather, in his generalizing statement, all 'Muslim rulers'—were dependent not on the support of their people but on that of their soldiers; this was a grave weakness, as the soldiers 'often rise up, and make themselves masters of their rulers' states'.[54] And in *Della ragion di stato*, drawing on the comparison between France and the Ottoman Empire in chapter IV of *Il principe*, Botero declared that feudal lords were 'the bones and strength of states'; without them, the state might collapse after a single major defeat, as the common people lacked men with the leadership skills to resist an invader. 'This is what would happen in the Ottoman Empire, if it should please God to let that enemy be defeated once in battle.' Kingdoms such as France, on the other hand, containing a numerous nobility, were 'almost immortal'.[55] Whether this meant that the Ottomans' policy of eliminating the power and status of the old nobility in the European territories they conquered was wise or foolish was not a question explored by Botero (though he noted that feudal lords could also act as supporters of rebellion). But if he did think it wrong-headed, that cannot have been on account of the methods employed, as his own recommendations for the treatment by Christian rulers of suspect local dignitaries—humiliation, expropriation, transportation—made clear.

Here was a method of analysing techniques of government which looked primarily at the efficacy of the technique, reserving its normative judgment for the general nature and purpose of the rule which that technique was meant to serve. This also made it possible to recommend that Christian rulers should adopt particular methods of government used by the Ottomans. Botero himself did little of this (when advocating population transfers, for example, he did not point out that the Ottomans made use of them); but other theorists of 'reason of state' had no scruples about commending particular Ottoman practices. The political writer Girolamo Frachetta, for example, who worked as a secretary for several dignitaries, and the Spanish embassy, in Rome, praised the sultans for the secret window at which they listened to the viziers dispensing justice in the *divan*, and recommended that Christian rulers should sometimes go in disguise among their subjects—to

---

54. Botero, *Relationi*, fo. [205v] ('i Prencipe Maumettani', 'spesso si solleuano, e si fanno padroni de gli stati de' loro signori').
55. Botero, *Della ragion*, p.125 (supporters of rebellion, 'le ossa, e la fermezza degli Stati', 'si vederebbe nella Turchia, se piacesse a Dio che si rompesse una volta in campagna il nemico', 'quasi immortali').

inns at night, or, better still, to masked carnivals—in order to listen to them
expressing their opinions 'without adulation and without fear'. Frachetta
took a close, and entirely hostile, interest in the Ottoman Empire; during
the early years of the 'Long' Habsburg–Ottoman war (1593–1606) he composed several short treatises and memorandums exploring ways of bringing
about its defeat.[56]

Another writer on reason of state who was similarly active in this cause
was the commentator on Tacitus and historian Scipione Ammirato, who
worked for the Medici family in Florence. In 1598 he published a set of
'orations', urging anti-Ottoman warfare, which he had addressed to various
popes and rulers in the previous thirteen years. In the first of these, written
for Sixtus V (r. 1585–90), he gave a lengthy summary of all the ways in which
Ottoman troops were superior to their Christian counterparts: 'the marvellous obedience which they show to their ruler, their modest diet, the rarity
of fights and quarrels among them, their certain hope of rewards, the absence
of gambling among them, the fact that they have regard to no kind of
nobility other than that of virtù', and so on.[57] His reproaches towards the
Christian armies on these points were heartfelt, though they went little
beyond the traditional shame-praising rhetoric on such matters. But then he
added a practical suggestion of his own. He noted that Plato had paid special
attention to the upbringing of children, and said that the Ottomans had
rediscovered this, in the form of their training of Janissaries. He recommended 'creating seminaries of boys', especially the poor and the illegitimate (who could be taken from their parents, perhaps more benignly but just
as effectively as Christian boys in the Balkans were taken from theirs by the
devşirme), for intensive military training, which would start at the age of
ten or twelve. The aim would be to form a 'holy militia' of up to 10,000
fighting men, to go to war against the Ottomans. 'As we must renew the
ancient military "ordini"', he wrote, 'let us, moreover, give them the title
of "legionaries"'; yet it would have been clear to all his readers that what he

56. Frachetta, Il prencipe, pp. 30 ('senza adulazione, & senza timore'), 33 (window); Biblioteca
    Apostolica Vaticana, Cod. Urb. Lat. 1492, fos. 55r–68r ('Discorso de modi, che si possono tenere
    al presente per guerreggiare contra il Turco per terra'), 69r–71v ('Se l'Imperatore debba atten-
    dere alla pace col Turco o proseguir la guerra'), 73r–77v ('Discorso del modo di regolar la
    guerra d'Ungheria l'anno 1596').
57. Ammirato, Orazioni, pp. 6–7 ('l'vbbidienza marauigliosa, che essi portano al lor Principe, la
    sobrietà del mangiare, le poche gare, e contese, che sono in fra di loro . . . la speranza certa de
    premi, il non esser fra loro giuochi, il non hauer riguardo ad altra nobilità, che a quella della
    virtù'). On Ammirato's anti-Ottoman writings see De Mattei, Il pensiero politico, pp. 37–54.

really had in mind was not so much modern Roman legionaries as Roman Catholic Janissaries.[58]

The most distinctive writer in this simultaneously Machiavellian and anti-Machiavellian tradition, whose appropriation of Ottoman practices went far beyond that of Frachetta or Ammirato, was the theologian and political theorist Tommaso Campanella. The creative use to which he put such ideas was not just unusual; it was extraordinary, and deserves a separate treatment of its own.

58. Ammirato, *Orazioni*, pp. 20–1 ('far seminario di fanciulli', Plato, Ottomans), 23 (10–12, 'sacra milizia', 'douendosi rinouar gli antichi ordini militari, mettiamo pur nome di Legionarij'). It was not only political theorists that were attracted to the Janissary system. In 1578 the Ragusan Alegretto de Alegretti wrote to the Emperor Rudolf II to suggest setting up a military training centre (clearly based on the Janissary model) for Christian boys: Haus-, Hof- und Staatsarchiv, Vienna, Türkei I, Karton 36, 2nd foliation, fos. 186–7.

EIGHT

Campanella

Tommaso Campanella entered the Dominican order in his native Calabria in 1582, at the age of fourteen, and quickly began to display exceptional intellectual abilities. He read widely in the field of scholastic theology (the name 'Tommaso' was taken by him in honour of the order's most famous theologian, Thomas Aquinas), but his interests were soon captured by various kinds of new, anti-Aristotelian philosophy. The ecclesiastical authorities became suspicious of his involvement in naturalistic philosophical circles in Naples, and in 1594 Campanella was arrested in Padua and taken to the Inquisition's prison in Rome, where he was tortured and required to make an abjuration 'de vehementi'—the charge being one of a 'vehement' suspicion of heresy. While some of his philosophical ideas may have been suspect, his fervent Catholicism is apparent from at least the second half of the 1590s. Soon after leaving prison in 1595 he wrote a polemical treatise denouncing Lutheran and Calvinist doctrines; his first major political text, the *Monarchia di Spagna* (drafted in 1598, and later reworked), also displayed an enthusiasm for Counter-Reformation political activism, while at the same time bearing witness to his wide reading in the 'reason of state' tradition.[1]

In this work, Campanella advised the King of Spain first to submit fully to the spiritual authority of the Pope, and then to use every possible device (including surprise attacks, extermination, and population transfers) to extend his rule, in order to become, under the direction of the Papacy, the universal monarch. Like Giovanni Botero, whose work he had certainly read, Campanella saw himself as defending true religiously based politics

---

1. In this chapter I recapitulate some material first published in Malcolm, 'The Crescent'. For a summary of Campanella's early life, discussing the 1595 *Dialogo politico contro Luterani, Calvinisti e altri eretici* and confirming the (contested) 1598 dating of the first draft of the *Monarchia di Spagna*, see Ernst, *Tommaso Campanella*, pp. 1–65. See also Frajese, *Profezia* (esp. pp. 36, 53–7 on the 1598 dating).

against Machiavellianism, and as advancing the cause of Christianity against the infidel Ottoman Empire; like others in the Catholic 'reason of state' tradition, he was quite untroubled by the fact that some of the methods he recommended were almost identical with those of his enemies.[2]

Thus, for example, he noted that the Sultan 'has made some seminaries of soldiers, called "seraglios", in which he puts fine, strong boys from all the nations he conquers and despoils; and these boys become accustomed to recognize no other father but him, and they learn the military arts, and religion.'[3] Accordingly, a few pages later, Campanella recommended that the King of Spain should set up in his own territories

> two or four seminaries of soldiers in each place, taking all the boys of the country whose fathers are poor, and the young illegitimate boys, bringing them up together and getting them accustomed to use arms, and to recognize their King as their father...he should make another seminary for foreign nations, that is, one given over entirely to the sons of Moors or Flemings [sc. the Moriscos and the Dutch, the two populations that had rebelled against Spanish rule], train them to be soldiers, and then use them as the Sultan uses his Janissaries.[4]

And he went on to comment: 'Let no one think that these colleges or seraglios are something peculiar to the Ottomans; for it is an extremely prudent method, practised also by the apostles in the Church...and the orders of St Dominic, St Francis, and others are seminaries of apostolic soldiers.'[5]

On the question of how to deal with conquered populations, Campanella's maxim was 'spagnolare il mondo', to make all nations Spanish; he pointed out that this would involve letting them participate in the administration

2. On his attitude to Machiavellianism see Caye, 'Campanella'; Ernst, Il carcere, pp. 103–32; Frajese, Profezia, pp. 58–80.

3. Campanella, Monarchie d'Espagne, p. 130 ('si ha fatto alcuni seminarii di soldati, detti serragli, dove inchiude fanciulli belli et forti d'ogni nazione che doma e preda, e quelli s'avvezzano a non conoscere altro padre che lui, e imparano l'arte militare e la religione').

4. Ibid., pp. 136–8 ('due o quattro seminarii di soldati per luoco, pigliando tutti i fanciulli del paese che hanno i padri poveri, e li bastardelli, e nutricolandoli insieme con avvezzarli all'armi, e a conoscnere il Re loro per padre...E per le nazioni strane fare un altro seminario, cioè tutto di figli di Mori o di Fiamenghi, e allevarli alla soldatesca, e poi servirsene come fà il Turco de i giannizzeri'). The use of the term 'seminaries', and the specifying of poor and illegitimate boys, suggest that Campanella had read Ammirato, whose first 'oration' was published in 1593 (see De Mattei, Il pensiero politico, p. 39).

5. Campanella, Monarchie d'Espagne, pp. 138–40 ('Né si pensi alcuno che questi collegii o serragli son cosa da Turchi, perché è arte prudentissima, usata anche dagli apostoli nella Chiesa...e li ordini di san Domenico e san Francesco e altri son seminarii delli soldati apostolici').

and the army, 'as the Romans did, and as the Sultan is wont to do'.[6] In his general comments on government, he criticized the despotic rule of the Sultan, who, he said, inherited all his subjects' goods; yet in his own advice to the King of Spain on the treatment of conquered territories, he suggested that the people should be dispossessed of all their estates.[7] (When his *Monarchia di Spagna* was eventually published, the advice it contained on how to crush the Dutch rebels was thought to be so outrageously Machiavellian—surpassing even that of Botero—that that section of the book was gleefully extracted and published, for anti-Spanish propaganda purposes, in Italian, Dutch, German, and Latin.[8]) And discussing the relative strengths of Spain and the Ottoman Empire, he observed: 'So far as money is concerned, there is not much difference between them; but if the King of Spain were to use that absolute power which the Sultan exercises, he would greatly exceed him in this respect.'[9] Campanella's attitude towards the idea of a hereditary nobility was also ambivalent, in a way that reflected previous treatments of the issue in the 'reason of state' literature. On the one hand he commented—adhering closely to Machiavelli's argument—that the lack of 'barons' in the Ottoman system was a weakness, since, if the Sultan was defeated, the whole state might easily be occupied by his conqueror. But on the other hand, Campanella noted that the descendants of worthy ennobled men often turned out to be 'useless people', and observed that in order to remedy this ill, 'the Sultan has abolished all nobility among his people (apart from his own), and does not want the son of one of his barons to inherit either the status or the power, but rather to receive it from his lord if he is virtuous.' With some apparent regret, he stated that this remedy 'is not suitable for use by Christians'.[10]

In the final part of the book, Campanella presented his own advice on how to defeat the Ottoman Empire. Various suggestions were offered, including making a secret deal with one of the Ottoman military commanders who were renegades (converts from Christianity to Islam), a deal in which

6. Ibid., p. 108 ('deve tutte le genti spagnolare, cioè farle spagnole, e del governo farne parte e della milizia, come fecero i Romani e usa il Turco').
7. Ibid., pp. 132, 320.
8. See Firpo, 'Appunti campanelliani XXII', and Headley, 'The Reception', esp. pp. 93–4, 98.
9. Campanella, *Monarchie d'Espagne*, p. 324 ('Quanto alle monete, poco avanza l'uno l'altro, ma se re di Spagna usasse la potestà del Turco, più assai avanzerebbe').
10. Ibid., p. 118 ('disutili'; 'il Turco ha tolto via ogni nobilità, altro che la propria, de suoi, e non vuole che erediti il figlio del suo barone state né facultà, ma che lo riconosca dal suo signore se è virtuoso...ma...non comporta l'use cristiano il remedio del Turco').

that commander would use his forces against the Sultan and be rewarded by the King of Spain with a kingdom of his own; one of the candidates proposed for this role was the Italian-born Cığalazade Yusuf Sinan pasha, who was the admiral of the Ottoman fleet.[11] Campanella also recommended the introduction of printing to the Ottoman Empire, in order to get the people preoccupied with philosophical and theological disputations. Taking Machiavelli's side in the 'arms versus letters' debate, he argued that bookishness weakens a people; 'and for this reason the Sultan, who is well advised, has wanted to obtain arms, artillery, and slaves from us, but has not wanted to receive Arabic type.'[12] Campanella also recommended encouraging gambling in enemy states, in order to weaken the moral fibre of the population. At the same time, in his advice on internal policy, he proposed banning the study of Greek and Hebrew (which had led only to the proliferation of heresies and disputes), and introducing in their place the study of Arabic 'in order to be able to defeat the Muslims'.[13]

Throughout this work, then, Campanella exhibited an ambivalent relationship with the Ottoman system (as he understood it): he wished to defeat it, and therefore also in some ways to imitate it. A similar ambivalence is observable in his handling of the Machiavellian theme of religion as something founded by a 'legislator' in order to mould human behaviour on Earth. 'Every great man who has instituted a new monarchy', he wrote, 'has altered the sciences, and often religion too, in order to make himself admired by the people': his examples included Ninus, Cyrus, and Alexander the Great. 'Muhammad, aspiring to monarchy, made a new religious doctrine, suited to the taste and admiration of the people; and Caesar, with the pontificate and the use of astrology, which was little known among the Romans, and with his alteration of the Roman calendar, laid the foundations of his greatness. Therefore Spain should do something similar, as it has a great opportunity to do so.'[14] For a moment, astonishingly, he seemed to be suggesting that the King of Spain should imitate Muhammad and found a new faith.

11. Ibid., p. 330.
12. Ibid., p. 334 ('E per questo il Turco accorto ha voluto l'armi da noi e l'artiglierie e li schiavi...ma non ha voluto ricevere le stampe arabiche').
13. Ibid., pp. 98 ('per potere vincere i Macomettani'), 178 (gambling).
14. Ibid., p. 94 ('Ogni uomo grande che ha instituito monarchie nuove ha mutato le scienze, e spesso la religione, per farsi ammirabile appresso ai popoli...Macometto, aspirando a monarchia, fece nova dottrina in religione secondo il gusto e ammirazione de popoli, e Cesare, con pontificato e astrologia, poco a Romani cognita, e con mutar l'anni romani, diede principio alla sua grandezza. Dunque Spagna deve fare il simile, avendone grande occasione...').

But he quickly added that 'since it is not possible to make a new religion' (because Christianity was of course perfect), the King should confine himself to such measures as changing the names of the months to those of the twelve Apostles.[15] Campanella had thought long and hard about the identification of religion and 'law', and would return to it in several of his later works. In chapter 13 of his *Atheismus triumphatus*, and in book 16 of his *Metaphysica*, he accepted the identification as such, but attacked Averroes and the Machiavellians for arguing on the basis of it that all religions were impostures; instead, he sought to distinguish between those introducers of new laws/religions who were guided by natural reason (such as Lycurgus and Plato), those who were guided by their own cunning, or by the Devil (such as Numa Pompilius and Muhammad), and those who were guided by God.[16]

If, as the evidence suggests, the first version of the *Monarchia di Spagna* was drafted in 1598, one would expect Campanella's attitude towards the Spanish King (who also ruled the Kingdom of Naples) to have been one of unquestioning loyalty. Yet in the following year he was not just a participant in, but an intellectual leader of, an anti-Spanish revolt in his native Calabria. The reaction of the Spanish authorities to this small and ineffectual rising was rapid and draconian. Campanella and other ringleaders were arrested in early September, and at the end of the following month he was one of 156 prisoners who were taken in chains to Naples. He was now in danger, twice over: not only had he been identified as a rebel by the civil powers, but he was also wanted by the Roman Inquisition on grave charges of heresy. The Spanish authorities refused to send him to Rome, and constituted instead an ecclesiastical tribunal in Naples. But the risks were just as great in either place: since he was a heretic who had abjured his heresy once, any conviction of heresy now would make him a relapsed heretic—for which the automatic punishment was death. Hence Campanella's famous resort to the only solution left to him, the one thing that would preserve his life: pretending to be completely mad. He kept this up for fourteen months; at the end of that period, 40 terrible hours of continual torture, on 4 and 5 June 1601,

---

15. Ibid., pp. 94 ('E perché non può fare religion nuova'), 96 (months).
16. Campanella, *Atheismus triumphatus*, pp. 130–1; *Metafisica*, iii, pp. 238, 260–70. The *Metafisica* was drafted first in 1602, then in 1609; both drafts were confiscated, and it was then written in its present form in 1611–21. *Atheismus triumphatus* consisted of material about religion extracted from the *Metafisica* and reworked as a separate text in c.1605. On this 'legislator' theme in Campanella's thought see Spini, *Ricerca dei libertini*, pp. 90–108; Frajese, *Profezia*, pp. 74–80, 106–10.

failed to break through his pretence, and so his life was spared. He would spend the next 25 years of it in prison.[17]

No sooner was his life secured than he began, torrentially, to write. A succession of works on politics, metaphysics, physics, and theology poured from his pen. Some were probably reworkings of texts which he had composed before the Calabrian revolt—such as the *Monarchia di Spagna*. Others seem to have grown out of the materials he had compiled in his defence, such as the *Articuli prophetales*, a millenarian treatise which expanded on the reasons he had given for believing that a great 'mutazione' or transformation would occur in 1599 or 1600.[18] And what became the most famous of them all, *La città del sole*, written probably in 1602, was almost a retrospective manifesto for the revolt—an idealized representation, seemingly, of the sort of perfect, rational, and hierocratic state that Campanella had been hoping to establish in the mountains of Calabria.

Of all the curious features of the Calabrian revolt in 1599, none is more puzzling, or more striking, than the fact that its leaders had tried to coordinate their plans with an attack by Ottoman forces. The three key figures here were Campanella, his fellow Dominican Dionisio Ponzio, and the prominent local landowner Maurizio de' Rinaldis. One day in June 1599, when some Ottoman ships were anchored near Reggio Calabria, de' Rinaldis had taken a boat out and parleyed with the Ottoman commander, Murad Reis, asking for military help; according to de' Rinaldis (under later interrogation by the Spanish authorities), the idea of this initiative had come from Ponzio and Campanella.[19] The request was transmitted to Istanbul, where it caught the interest of the admiral of the Ottoman fleet, Cığalazade Yusuf Sinan pasha; originally named Scipione Cicala, he had been captured as a boy, had converted to Islam, and had enjoyed an immensely successful career in the service of the Sultan.[20] Indeed, the conspirators must have known of his special interest in the region: only in the previous year, Cicala had brought the Ottoman fleet to Calabria in order to visit his own mother, who was

17. For summaries of these events see Firpo, 'Tommaso Campanella', esp. pp. 375–80; Di Napoli, 'L'Eresia', esp. pp. 176–227; Headley, *Tommaso Campanella*, pp. 3–5, 19–49. For the evidence relating to the 1599 conspiracy and the subsequent trial see Amabile, *Fra Tommaso Campanella*; Firpo, *Il supplizio*.

18. For the final text (written probably in 1607–9), see Campanella, *Articuli prophetales*; for the original nucleus (of early 1600) see Amabile, *Fra Tommaso Campanella*, iii, pp. 489–98; Firpo, *Il supplizio*, pp. 129–75.

19. Amabile, *Fra Tommaso Campanella*, i, p. 172; cf. also the account in Firpo, 'Appunti campanelliani' (1962), p. 396.

20. On Cicala see Gökbilgin, 'Cığala-zâde'; Benzoni, 'Scipione Cicala'.

still living in Messina.[21] Further negotiations between the conspirators and Cicala must have followed, possibly involving a group of Calabrian 'renegades' in Istanbul. An agreement was made that he would bring 30 ships, 3,000 soldiers, and 100 artillery pieces to support the revolt; he would arrive on 10 September 1599, and would send galleys close to the shore to exchange an agreed set of signals with the rebels. Cicala did in fact keep his promise: the signals were sent, both on that day and again three days later.[22] But there was no response; by 10 September, all the leading conspirators were already under arrest.

Most modern writers on Campanella, while accepting the existence of this Ottoman dimension to the revolt, have played down its significance, treating it as little more than a desperate piece of opportunism on the conspirators' part. It has also been noted that, in his first self-exculpatory statement to the Spanish authorities, Campanella said that he had been against involving the Ottomans; and in a later letter to Pope Paul V, he claimed that he had made false admissions about the 'negozio di turchi' ('business with the Ottomans') under interrogation merely to save his life. (On the other hand, several other witnesses declared under examination that Campanella had boasted to them that he had sent an emissary to Cicala.)[23] As for the accusation, made at the start of the formal proceedings of his heresy trial, that he had claimed that 'Turkish doctrine' (i.e. Islam) was better than Christianity, this has been dismissed by one modern authority as 'insubstantial'.[24] And yet the picture which emerges from the interrogations of many of the participants in these events suggests that Campanella, together with several other conspirators, did have an interest in Islam and the Ottomans that went well beyond the requirements of tactical expediency. One witness, a Dominican, said that when Giulio Contestabile (one of the conspirators) visited Campanella in his friary, Campanella had told him to take whichever he preferred of the portraits hanging on his wall, whereupon Contestabile had taken that of the Sultan, Mehmed III. Another friar recalled Campanella questioning Muslim slaves about their practices, and praising some of their religious ceremonies. Maurizio de' Rinaldis said that he had heard

21. Hammer-Purgstall, *Geschichte*, iv, p. 301; Benzoni, 'Scipione Cicala', pp. 330–1.

22. Benzoni, 'Scipione Cicala', pp. 331–2; Firpo, 'Appunti campanelliani' (1962), p. 391.

23. Firpo, *Il supplizio*, pp. 61–2 (Campanella, 'dichiarazione' of 10 Sept. 1599); Campanella, *Lettere*, ed. Spampanato, p. 14 (letter to Paul V, 13 Aug. 1606); Amabile, *Fra Tommaso Campanella*, iii, pp. 133, 134, 138 (other witnesses).

24. Amabile, *Fra Tommaso Campanella*, iii, p. 471 (accusation); Headley, *Tommaso Campanella*, p. 47 (dismissal).

Campanella speaking well of Muslims on many occasions; the procurator fiscal was summarizing multiple testimonies when he stated that 'Campanella dared to say that the way of life of the Muslims was better than Christianity'.[25] It certainly appears that Campanella's co-conspirator and fellow-Dominican Dionisio Ponzio shared that opinion, since, after his escape from prison in October 1602, he travelled to Istanbul, converted to Islam, and took up residence in Cicala's house: the Venetian envoy in Istanbul reported Ponzio's boast that there were 300 people in Calabria, some of them men of note, who were Muslims at heart, and that Campanella would soon escape from prison and join him in the Ottoman capital.[26] And although there is no evidence to suggest that Campanella had changed his inner beliefs to those of a Muslim, there is one odd piece of evidence that he did at least try to change people's outward appearance: one of the conspirators stated that Campanella had introduced a new sort of dress for his followers, consisting of a white tunic and a piece of headgear that was tied like a Turkish turban.[27]

The white tunics (though not, understandably enough, the turbans) recur in the text of La città del sole; and they are not the only details in that work to reflect Campanella's special interest in Islam and the Ottoman Empire. Yet the standard modern studies of the meaning and significance of Campanella's best-known work have paid almost no attention to this aspect of it, preferring to treat it as a more or less rationalistic and secular exercise in political theory. This short text, written probably in 1602, subjected to some changes in 1607, and published for the first time (in Latin) in 1623, can certainly be described as a utopian work, as it is, in literary terms, a direct descendant of More's Utopia: it takes the form of a dialogue in which a traveller is questioned about his experiences on an island in the South Seas. He describes the 'city of the Sun' which he found there—a city built on a hill, in the form of seven great concentric circles—and the way of life of its people. They live in what is literally a communist system, in which all property, wives, and children are held in common; they lead a sober and virtuous existence, based on a special method of pedagogy, and ruled by wise officials

25. Amabile, Fra Tommaso Campanella, iii, pp. 230, 254, 311 ('Campanella ausus fuit dicere quod modus vivendi turcharum sit melior lege Christiana'), 337.
26. Firpo, 'Una autoapologia', p. 110(n.); Benzoni, 'Scipione Cicala', p. 335. Ponzio was later killed by a Janissary with whom he had had a casual argument: see Capaccio, Il forastiero, p. 505.
27. Amabile, Fra Tommaso Campanella, iii, p. 139 ('un coppolicchio ligato à modo di turbante di Turcho'). For the significance of the white tunics see Rev. 19: 14, 'And the armies which were in heaven followed him upon white horses, clothed in fine linen, white and clean', and the comments in Campanella, La prima e la seconda resurrezione, pp. 114–16.

(who direct them in, among other things, a programme of scientific eugenics). The supreme ruler is called 'Sol' or 'Sole' ('Sun'), and the three under him are known as 'Pon', 'Sin', and 'Mor', meaning 'Potentia' (power), 'Sapientia' (wisdom), and 'Amor' (love). Modern scholars have devoted great efforts to exploring the literary sources and models on which Campanella may have drawn; these include, in addition to Thomas More's work, the Bible (specifically, the reference to the 'City of the Sun' in Isa. 19: 18); Herodotus' account of the city of Ecbatana; Plato's republic; Diodorus Siculus' story of Iamboulos' journey to the 'islands of the Sun'; various modern accounts of the Incas and other civilizations in the New World (by Cieza de Leon, Acosta, Benzoni, and Botero); the description by Botero in his *Relationi universali* of the seven-walled city of 'Campanel' in the Indies; Alberti's architectural utopia; Ficino's *De sole*; and the model of life in a Dominican friary.[28] Some, perhaps most, of these may well have influenced Campanella's thinking. But the most important influence of all has been almost entirely neglected: the model of Ottoman society.[29]

No reader who is familiar with the sixteenth-century literature on the Ottoman Empire, and who has already observed its influence on the *Monarchia di Spagna*, can fail to be struck by one detail after another in *La città del sole*. In a general sense, the whole society resembles Campanella's vision of the 'seminaries' in which the Ottomans trained their *devşirme* boys. All undergo a communal upbringing, so that their ruler is the only person they regard as their father; their loyalty to him is therefore absolute.[30] But the resemblance is also more specific: the boys are taught military skills from the age of twelve, while the less bright ones are sent to work on farms—exactly as happened to the Ottoman *devşirme* intake.[31] And many of the details that formed the 'new paradigm' are put to work here. Gambling is strictly forbidden to the Solarians, and alcohol, while not prohibited, is allowed only in great moderation. Campanella emphasizes their frequent washing, and their use

28. See Treves, 'Title' (Isaiah); Firpo, 'Introduzione', p. xxxviii (Herodotus; Botero: Mexico); De Mattei, 'Fonti', p. 408 (Plato; Alberti); Firpo, 'La città ideale', pp. 386–7 (Herodotus; Isaiah; Diodorus Siculus; Botero: Mexico and 'Campanel'); Croce, *Materialismo storico*, p. 203(n.) (Pedro de Cieza de Leon: Peru); Ernst, *Tommaso Campanella*, p. 103 (Girolamo Benzoni: Peru); Diez del Corral, 'La città utopistica', pp. 317, 319 (José de Acosta: Quito); Crahay, 'L'Utopie religieuse', p. 380 (Ficino); Gussmann, 'Reipublicae christianopolitanae descriptio', pp. 439–40 (Dominicans).
29. The only writer to have paid any significant attention to this theme is Gisela Bock, who identifies just three Ottoman-influenced elements in *La città del sole*: absolutism, the Janissary model of education, and the lack of a hereditary aristocracy: *Thomas Campanella*, pp. 174–5.
30. Campanella, *La città del sole*, ed. Donno, pp. 84–6.   31. Ibid., pp. 58, 68.

of baths for health-giving purposes; in the Latin text he explains that these baths are 'warm ones, according to the Roman custom'—in other words, like the contemporary Ottoman *hamams*.[32] (His narrator also says that 'by these and other means they make great efforts to protect themselves against epilepsy, from which they often suffer'; and, just in case readers have not caught the significance of this, his interlocutor comments that epilepsy is a sign of 'great intelligence', and that Muhammad, among others, suffered from it.) The Solarians have their version of the Ottoman *han*: travellers are given food for three days, free of charge.[33] Their system of justice is remarkably similar to the one described by contemporary writers on the Ottomans: 'The trial is not committed to writing; rather, the accusation and the defence are uttered in the presence of the judge (and of "Potentia", the chief executive official), and the judge immediately hands down his sentence.'[34] And, of course, the entire social and political system is strictly meritocratic: there is no hereditary principle (indeed, there can be no inheritance), and the highest officials are chosen for their abilities. The Solarians, it seems, have the same concept of nobility as the Ottomans; as the narrator puts it, 'the one who learns the most skills and practises them best is held to have the greatest nobility. That is why they laugh at us when we call craftsmen ignoble and describe as noble those who learn no skill and remain idle.'[35]

The religion of the Solarians is certainly not identical with Islam, but it bears some intriguing resemblances to it—or, at least, to the version of Islam presented by contemporary writers on the Ottomans. The Solarians are monotheists; they are fiercely opposed to any form of idolatry (using the sun only as a symbol of God); they believe in rewards and punishments after death; and they also believe in good and bad angels.[36] Each morning, after they have washed, 'they turn to the east and say a very short prayer, like the Pater noster'; their priests, standing at the top of the central temple, sing

---

32. Ibid., pp. 64 (gambling), 88 (alcohol), 92 ('usano li bagni e l'olei all'usanza antica'); Campanella, *La città del sole*, ed. Bobbio, p. 147 ('Utuntur balneis, ideo et thermas habent ritu Romanorum').

33. Campanella, *La città del sole*, ed. Donno, pp. 82 (travellers), 92 ('Si forzano con questi e altri modi aiutarsi contro il morbo sacro, chè ne pateno spesso'; 'Segno d'ingegno grande, onde Ercole, Socrate, Macometto . . . ne patîro').

34. Ibid., p. 96 ('Non si scrive processo, ma in presenza del giudice e del Potestà si dice il pro e il contra; e subito si condanna dal giudice').

35. Ibid., p. 42 ('quello è tenuto di più gran nobiltà, che più arti impara, e meglio le fa. Onde si ridono di noi che gli artefici appellamo ignobili, e diciamo nobili quelli, che null'arte imparano e stanno oziosi').

36. Ibid., pp. 106–10, 112–14.

psalms to God at four fixed times each day.[37] On the wall where they display the portraits of great founders of 'laws' (i.e. religions) and sciences, they have 'Moses, Osiris, Jupiter, Mercury, and Muhammad', and in a special place of honour they have Jesus Christ and his Apostles, 'whom they hold in high regard'.[38] This is not, as some commentators have argued, a pre-Christian society; rather it is a non-Christian society, one which has acquired some knowledge of Christianity, but has never been subject to the effects of Christian revelation. Nor, for that matter, is it an Islamic society; it has an equivalent arm's-length relation to the actual figure of Muhammad. The religion of the Solarians is a natural religion, closely bound up with science, astrology, and natural magic (the priests also study the stars in order to harness their natural forces to optimum effect in their eugenics programme); it is the best possible natural religion; and it is a form of religion that coincides to a significant extent with Islam.

One other aspect of it is, however, of special importance. Although the Solarians are strict monotheists and non-Christians, they nevertheless have a kind of philosophical trinitarianism. 'You will be amazed', says the narrator, 'that they worship God in the Trinity, saying that he is the highest Power, from whom proceeds the highest Wisdom, and that from both of them proceeds the highest Love. But they do not recognize the three persons as they are distinguished and named by us.'[39] It has long been understood that Campanella was drawing here on a tradition of Christian Neoplatonism, which sought to interpret the Trinity philosophically as a triune procession of aspects of Being in God. But it has not been noticed that the source from which Campanella most probably drew this precise formulation of the argument was Book 1 of Postel's *De orbis terrae concordia*, which is devoted to explaining the methods by which Muslims can be converted to Christianity. Postel's first demonstration of the Trinity, for the benefit of Muslims, is that God, as an omnipotent creator, must have power, wisdom, and love: wisdom proceeds from power, and love proceeds from wisdom and power together.[40]

37. Ibid., pp. 90 ('fanno orazione brevissima al levante come il *Pater noster*'), 102.

38. Ibid., p. 36 ('che ne tengono gran conto'). The Latin version adds several more names to the list (including Lycurgus and Numa Pompilius), and also adds a negative comment about Muhammad, 'whom, however, they hate as a lying and sordid legislator' (Campanella, *La città del sole*, ed. Bobbio, p. 122: 'quem tamen ut fabulosum ac sordidum legislatorem oderunt').

39. Campanella, *La città del sole*, ed. Donno, p. 114 ('Qui ti stupisci ch'adorano Dio in Trinitate, dicendo ch'è somma Possanza, da cui procede somma Sapienza, e d'essi entrambi, sommo Amore. Ma non conosceno le persone distinte e nominate al modo nostro').

40. Postel, *De orbis terrae concordia*, pp. 16–17 ('So, before it [*sc.* the world] could be brought into being by God, it was necessary that power, wisdom, and love should exist in Him. Now since power comes first, not temporally but in the order of being, it is ascribed to God the Father. And since wisdom proceeds from utter power, it is called the Son, in a metaphor derived from

This clue points towards the essential purpose which *La città del sole* was designed to serve. What Campanella was describing in that work was an ideal society, embodying a perfect natural existence, cleansed of vice and filled with pure, natural pleasures—a society which, while not itself based on Islam, would correspond to many of the most positive features of Islamic practice, would appeal to Muslims, and would at the same time lead them on to something better. It was, roughly speaking, a naturalistic halfway house between Islam and Christianity, a stage through which Muslims could pass in order to join the Christians in a higher form of religion. Whether that higher religion would have corresponded to orthodox Christianity seems very unlikely; if many of the witness statements used at Campanella's trial are to be given any credence at all, his own version of Christianity was radically naturalistic, portraying Christ as just a great man (which implied that the Trinity existed *only* in an abstract, philosophical sense), denying miracles, and dismissing the sacraments as devices grafted onto the true Christian religion by Machiavellian 'legislators'.[41] This was a modified version of Christianity, and most of the modifications took it in a direction closer to Islam; when Maurizio de' Rinaldis was interrogated about Campanella's religious beliefs, he said that he had heard him describe Christ as 'a great man, who did good', and commented that 'I've heard that the Muslims say that too, and many times Fra Tommaso spoke well of the Muslims.'[42] But Campanella's starting point was in Christianity, and in Christian prophetic revelation.[43] Nothing that he believed was based on the Koran, and it would be quite wrong to portray him as a crypto-Muslim.

natural generation. But since benevolence or love proceeds from wisdom and power, it is described using the term "Holy Spirit" ' ('Opus ergo fuit, antequam à Deo in esse deduceretur, fuisse in illo potentiam, sapientiam, & amorem. Quoniam autem potentia prima in ordine, non in tempore est, patri Deo adscribitur. sapientia autem quia à summa potentia procedit, filius dicitur, metaphora à naturali generatione ducta: at quia à sapientia & potentia procedit bene-uolentia amorue, spiritussancti appellatione nuncupata est')). Campanella does not make any reference to Postel, but this is not surprising, given the notorious heterodoxy of the latter. One of the works to which he does refer, Rescius, *De atheismis*, contains a denunciation of Postel with a striking resonance: it describes him as having thought that 'a new religion should be invented, to be made by fusing together Christianity, Judaism, and Muhammad's Koran' (p. 426: 'nouam esse fingendam religionem, quae sit ex Christiana, Mosaica, & Alcorano Machometi conflanda'; for Campanella's references to Rescius see Firpo, *Il supplizio*, pp. 158, 164).

41. See the list of charges of 7 Sept. 1599 in Amabile, *Fra Tommaso Campanella*, iii, pp. 195–6.
42. Ibid., iii, p. 254 ('un grande huomo da bene . . . queste parole anco mi pare di havere inteso che le dicono li turchi, et molte volte il detto frà Thomaso hà ditto bene deli turchi').
43. It is *prophetic* revelation that must be emphasized here, as nothing in Campanella's position seems to have depended on the authority of Scripture as such—let alone the authority of the Church. He appears to have regarded prophecy too in naturalistic terms: like natural magic, genuine prophecy involved the harnessing, to an exceptional degree, of natural forces or natural powers.

Nevertheless, it is important to understand why Islam occupied such a special place in Campanella's scheme of things. The universalist tradition to which Postel belonged (together with Nicholas of Cusa, another writer who may have influenced Campanella) was no less concerned to gather people from all faiths to the true religion—not only Muslims, but also Jews, Hindus, and others. In one of the self-justificatory statements Campanella penned in prison, he wrote that he had examined Christianity in the light of 'all ancient and modern sects, and all the laws [sc. religions] of ancient peoples, and of the Jews, Turks, Persians, Moors, Chinese, Cathayans, Japanese, Brahmins, Peruvians, Mexicans, Abyssinians, and Tatars'; and his Solarians are themselves described as sending envoys throughout the world in order to learn what was good or bad in each society.[44] In some ways, it would seem in keeping with the purpose of Campanella's argument to treat the religion and society of the Solarians as a kind of syncretist naturalism, embodying the best practices of all peoples. It certainly does not bear the exclusive imprint of Islam. And yet, Islam has a special significance in it, quite different from that of any other model or influence. The explanation for this can be found in the peculiar set of beliefs—beliefs about the imminence of the Apocalypse—that had motivated Campanella's actions in the months leading up to his arrest in September 1599.

Tommaso Campanella had not merely been organizing some sort of political conspiracy. He had been preaching, and preparing for, the end of the world. All the portents were there: earthquakes, floods, eclipses, plagues, 'unheard-of changes in the stars', even the arrival in Italy of swarms of locusts. He was convinced that the end would occur in the Holy Year of 1600—or, at least, during the seven years thereafter.[45] First there would come the great war in heaven, during which the 'woman clothed with the sun' (representing probably the Church) would have to flee into the wilderness for three and a half years (Rev. 12: 1–7); then, after the pouring out of the vials, the fall of Babylon, and the destruction of Antichrist, there would be the thousand-year reign of Christ on earth (Rev. 20: 4–5). Campanella's aim was first of all to take people to the mountains, where they could survive the

44. Campanella, Lettere, ed. Spampanato, p. 15, letter to Pope Paul V, 13 Aug. 1606 ('tutte sette antiche e moderne, e con la legge delle genti antiche e d'ebrei, turchi, persiani, mori, chinesi, cataini, giaponesi, bracmani, peruiani, messicani, abissini, tartari'); Campanella, La città del sole, ed. Donno, p. 36. In a later commentary on La città del sole Campanella wrote that 'indeed we have gathered together observations, experience, and knowledge from the whole world into our Republic' ('Immò nos ex toto orbe terrarum obseruationes, & experimenta, & scientias ad nostram Remp. congregamus'): Disputationum, 3rd pagination, p. 103.
45. Firpo, Il supplizio, pp. 2, 168 ('syderum varietas inaudita'); cf. also Campanella, Lettere, ed. Ernst, p. 28, 'Memoriale al nunzio di Napoli' (1606).

turmoil of the first three and a half years (in one of his early apologias he compared this to the early Venetians retreating into the lagoon), and secondly to start building the ideal state in which people would live during the following millennium.[46] For, as he would later explain, his interpretation of this phase of the Apocalypse was both metaphorical and literal. It was metaphorical, in that he did not think this millennial kingdom would be populated only by miraculously resurrected Christian martyrs (as Revelation says), or ruled by Christ in person; rather, what would be resurrected would be the fame and spirit of holy men, and Christ would rule in the sense that his teachings would be perfectly embodied in the rule of a sacerdotal monarch. And Campanella's vision was at the same time remarkably literal: he believed that this kingdom would be a real, historical, human polity, in which human nature would be perfected in natural ways, and all spiritual and corporeal goods would be enjoyed together.[47] (The most striking feature of this was that men and women would have sex without sin.) It would, in fact, be the 'golden age' described by pagan poets, predicted by prophets such as Isaiah, and desired by all men. Defending his vision of this millennial kingdom, he wrote: 'All nations, by a natural appetite—which is not given to them by God in vain—desire an age of this sort.' Defending his *Città del sole*, he wrote: 'I say that this republic and golden age are desired by all people.'[48] The two things—millennial kingdom and *Città del sole*—may not have been identical in every detail, but the latter was at least an attempt to capture some of the key characteristics of the former. Explaining his actions in 1599 in a letter written to the King of Spain and the Pope in 1611, Campanella wrote that he had 'only wanted, in the event of the great transformation taking place, to preach and establish the republic of the Apocalypse'.[49]

Thus far, Campanella's millenarianism seems to have no special concern with Islam. It assumes, like most millenarianism, that this process will involve the gathering together of all humanity under Christ—in other words, the conversion not only of the Jews, but also of Muslims and pagans. Such universalism was certainly a feature of Campanella's thinking: the *Monarchia di Spagna* aimed at a universal monarchy for that reason, and his later treatise

46. Amabile, *Fra Tommaso Campanella*, i, p. 191.
47. Campanella, *La prima e la seconda resurrezione*, pp. 16, 44. See also the discussion of this in Ernst, 'L'alba colomba', pp. 107–11.
48. Campanella, *Articuli prophetales*, pp. 88, 94 (sex); Campanella, *La prima e la seconda resurrezione*, p. 60 ('Omnes nationes naturali appetitu, qui non datur a Deo frustra, appetunt huiusmodi saeculum'); Campanella, *Disputationum*, 3rd pagination, p. 103 ('Dico hanc Remp. & seculum aureum ab omnibus desiderari').
49. Campanella, *Lettere*, ed. Ernst, p. 50 ('solamente aver voluto che, si venia la mutazione . . . volea predicare e fare la republica dell'Apocalissi').

on the conversion of non-Christians, *Quod reminiscentur*, was equally concerned with the conversion of all of them. So wherein lies the special significance of Islam? The answer to this question can be found in the whole framework of prophecies with which Campanella supported his claims about the imminence of the end of the world. His thinking was dominated by a number of modern prophecies (by Ciprian Leowitz, Antonio Torquato or Arquato, Pavao Skalić, and the so-called Abbot Ubertino of Otranto) which asserted that the Ottomans would invade Italy and would actually conquer Rome—thus putting the Papacy to flight, like the woman fleeing into the wilderness in Revelation.[50] These were corroborated by earlier revelations, by St Bridget of Sweden and Dionysius Carthusianus, also associating a conquest of Italy by the Ottomans with the coming of the last days.[51] There was, however, one ray of light among these gloomy prognostications. According to Torquato, the Ottoman Empire would split into two; one half would then turn to Christianity, and would defeat the other half. As Campanella put it in the first full-length defence he wrote in prison, 'they were destined to be divided between two kings; one of them would join our religion *and republic*'. He also believed that this had been predicted by St Catherine of Siena.[52] Because of her closeness to the Dominicans, St Catherine was especially venerated as a prophetic authority by the Dominican order, and Campanella certainly shared that estimation of her. But there was one prophecy that concerned him in particular: her statement that the Dominicans would (as he put it) 'bring the olive branch of peace to the Muslims'.[53] Campanella believed that the Dominicans had a special missionary role to play; another saint to whom he frequently referred was the Dominican St Vincent Ferrer, who had spent years converting Muslims in Spain.[54]

50. See, for example, Firpo, *Il supplizio*, pp. 169, 171. On Leowitz see ibid., pp. 54–5(n.); on Torquato see above, pp. 71–2; on Skalić see above, p. 72 and Secret, 'La Tradition'; on the prophecy attributed to Abbot Ubertino see Firpo, 'Appunti campanelliani' (1962), pp. 364–7. As we have seen, the Joachimite tradition, which was strong in the Dominican order, had long envisaged an attack on the Church which might involve the devastation of Italy: above, pp. 53–4.
51. See Campanella, *Articuli prophetales*, pp. 196, 232.
52. Firpo, *Il supplizio*, p. 104 (emphasis added) ('dividendos esse in duos reges... et unum eorum venturum ad fidem et rempublicam'); Campanella, *Lettere*, ed. Spampanato, p. 24, to Cardinal Farnese, 30 Aug. 1606 (St Catherine).
53. Barbuto, *Il principe e l'Anticristo*, pp. 82–3 (Dominicans); Firpo, 'Una autoapologia di Campanella', p. 106 ('nos... delaturos olivam pacis ad Turcas').
54. See for example Campanella, *Legazioni ai maomettani*, p. 90.

Putting together all of these clues makes it possible to construct a plausible account of what Campanella was really trying to achieve in those heady summer days of 1599. He was expecting an Ottoman invasion of Italy, and was seeking, indeed, to hasten it. But he also believed that Cicala (Cığalazade Yusuf Sinan pasha), the admiral of the Sultan's fleet, would return to Christianity, taking half the Ottoman Empire with him, and would then fight against the other half. Cicala's return to Christianity—and that of his Muslim followers—would be accomplished, as the prophecies had foretold, by a Dominican, Tommaso Campanella. And the means of accomplishing it would be, at the same time, the means by which a group of people would at first be protected from the tribulations of the Last Days, and then be enabled to live a pure and perfect natural life on earth, the life of the golden age, in the 'republic of the Apocalypse'. When he used that phrase in his letter to the King of Spain and the Pope, he said that what he was describing had been 'expected now by St Vincent, St Catherine, St Bridget, Dionysius Carthusianus, and Serafino da Fermo'—a group of writers connected only by their interest in the conversion of the Muslims and/or the danger of the Ottomans.[55] And when he included *La città del sole* in a list of his writings which he compiled in 1607, he called it '*La città del sole*, that is, a dialogue about my own republic, in which is outlined the plan for the reformation of a Christian republic, as it has been promised by God to St Vincent, St Bridget, St Catherine of Siena, and many others'.[56] Those saints were invoked not in connection with the general reformation of the Church, but with regard to something much more specific: the conversion of the Muslims.

And how would that conversion be effected? In the second of his long self-justificatory texts, written in prison in the early months of 1600, Campanella gave his answer: 'the Muslims will come more readily to the true faith when they hear that the Paradise described by Muhammad, in

---

55. Campanella, *Lettere*, ed. Ernst, p. 50 ('aspettato mo da san Vincenzo, Catarina, Brigida, Dionisio Cartusiano, don Serafino da Fermo'). On Serafino see Ernst, "'L'alba colomba'", p. 115. In his *Breve dichiaratione*, fo. 39v, Serafino predicted that 'there will be a great struggle between the Christian and Muslim laws [*sc.* religions], and during the time of Antichrist the Church will hide while he rules in the world' ('sara gran contrasto tra la legge Christiana, & Macomettana, & nel tempo d'Antichristo la Chiesa s'ascondera per quel tempo che regnara nel mondo').

56. Campanella, *Lettere*, ed. Ernst, p. 37 ('La Città del Sole, *hoc est dialogus de propria republica, in quo idea reformandae christianae reipublicae, uti sanctis Vincentio, Brigidae, Catharinae Senensi aliisque multis pollicitus est Deus, delineatur*'). As Germana Ernst has noted, versions of this description appear as the titles of the text in two early manuscripts: Bibliotheca philosophica hermetica, Amsterdam, MS BPH M 65, and British Library, London, MS Royal 14 a XVII ('Nota al testo', in Campanella, *La città del sole*, ed. Firpo, pp. 63–101, here pp. 74, 78).

which people eat and get married, will take place not in heaven but on earth—as a sort of prelude to the heavenly Paradise, which Muhammad did not consider.'[57] In his later work *Articuli prophetales* Campanella commented as follows on Isaiah's prophecy of the golden age:

> Here Isaiah speaks about death and procreation in the way in which I described them in *La città del sole*, under propitious stars, when parents, purged of sin, will have sex in the name of God, without sin—something that will not happen in Paradise, unless in the Muslim one. Therefore the meaning of the prophet [Isaiah] is historical, and he locates these things on earth, not in heaven.[58]

Thus Muhammad's teaching had been both false and true. He deluded people with promises of a false kind of celestial life, when the life he was describing was in fact the perfect life on Earth. In one sense, therefore, he was an extreme example of a Machiavellian who manipulated religious beliefs for his own purposes; Campanella would tend, in his later, more orthodox, writings on the Apocalypse, to portray Muhammad as a diabolical figure, identifying him with the precursor of Antichrist, or the principle of Antichristianity, and declaring that the Antichrist himself would be of Muhammad's 'seed'.[59] Yet in another sense, he had been able to regard Muhammad as a near-genius, a man (as the interlocutor in *La città del sole* put it) of 'great intelligence', a 'legislator' who had devised a very effective system of life and who had harnessed people's natural desire for a perfect one. All that was needed, it seemed, was for an even greater legislator to found a new republic, to which Muslims would be irresistibly attracted. That legislator was Tommaso Campanella; and that new republic, the republic of the Apocalypse, was his City of the Sun. The combination here of the new paradigm, Machiavellianism, Renaissance naturalism, Catholic reason of state theory, and prophetic millenarianism was, just like the life-story of its author, extraordinary—indeed, it was altogether unique.

57. Firpo, *Il supplizio*, p. 152 ('Turcae promptius ad fidem venient, cum audierint quod Paradisus quem ponit Macomettus, in quo manducatur et fiunt matrimonia, non in Coelo sed in terra erit, praeludium quasi coelestis Paradisi, ab eo non considerati').

58. Campanella, *Articuli prophetales*, p. 89 ('Hic Isaias loquitur de morte et de generatione modo qualem ego descripsi in *Civitate solis* sub felicibus astris, quando parentes purgati scelere in nomine Dei coeunt, quod non erit in paradiso, nisi machometico. Ergo sensus prophetae est historicus, et in terra ponit haec, et non in coelo').

59. Ibid., pp. 215–17; *De antichristo*, pp. 36, 44–6 ('eius ex semine, hoc est Machomettico').

NINE

Despotism I
The origins

Whatever positive uses some thinkers may have made of particular aspects of the Ottoman system, the underlying assumption of the great majority of early modern writers in Western Europe was that Ottoman rule was based on oppression. And there was an obvious term for this: 'tyranny'. Most Western thinking about the nature of tyranny rested ultimately on arguments put forward in Aristotle's *Politics*, where it was explained that the commonest type of tyrant was a ruler who acted unaccountably; in his own interests, not in those of his subjects; and hence 'against the will of the subjects', given that 'no free man willingly endures such rule.'[1] In the mid-fourteenth century the legal theorist Bartolus (Bartolo da Sassoferrato) produced a useful synthesis of classical and scholastic views on this subject, explaining that there were two essential criteria for describing a ruler as a tyrant: either he lacked valid title to rule (i.e. he was a usurper) or his manner of ruling was 'not rightful' because 'his actions aim not at the common good but at the good of the tyrant himself.'[2] Drawing mainly on Aristotle's *Politics* and the late-thirteenth-century treatise on kingship, *De regimine principum*, by the Thomist Giles of Rome, he listed ten criteria for describing a ruler as a tyrant. These included 'ruining the prominent and powerful people in the state', to prevent them from leading rebellions; destroying learning; having 'many spies' within the state; making the subjects poor, to keep them occupied with their daily needs; and 'procuring wars and sending fighters outside the state, so that, as they are concentrating on those wars, they do

---

1. Aristotle, *Politics* IV.8, 1295a19–23, pp. 325–7.
2. Quaglioni, *Politica e diritto*, pp. 178 (lacking title), 196 ('opera eius non tendunt ad bonum commune, sed proprius ipsius tyranni', 'non iure').

not plan anything against him'.[3] As Western writers tried to analyse the nature of Ottoman power, from the middle of the fifteenth century onwards, such a concept of tyrannical rule provided a ready-made model. 'Tyrannis' was a standard term used about the Sultan in fifteenth-century papal texts about the Ottoman threat; and it was from those anti-Ottoman texts, apparently, that the word 'Tyrann' entered the German language.[4]

Use of the term 'tyrant' to describe the Ottoman ruler was never eliminated. But it was gradually overtaken, in the early modern period, by a different word, with a different set of connotations: 'despot'. And this is one of the most distinctive features of early modern thinking about the Ottoman sultans; for the theory of despotism was revived and developed specifically in order to describe the power they wielded. Without the presence of the Ottoman Empire on Western Christendom's borders, it must be doubted whether the notion of despotism would have gained any significant place in modern political thought.

This concept too was firmly grounded in Aristotle. In the first book of the *Politics* he discussed the different kinds of power relationships that are to be found within a household, beginning with the subjection of the household slaves to their master. The master ('despotēs' in Greek) rules his slaves in the way that the soul rules the body, merely issuing orders, and not in the way that reason rules the appetites, realigning them by a kind of persuasion. This becomes an analogy or model for the difference, in the political realm, between despotic rule on the one hand, and that of a law-bound monarch or a constitutional 'polis' on the other. For those inferior human beings whom Aristotle describes as natural slaves, it is actually in their interests to be told what to do, since, resembling animals more than free humans, they lack the ability to make the necessary decisions. In such cases, although the master aims primarily at his own interest, there is a kind of community of interests between him and his slaves, and despotic rule is appropriate. But where the enslaved people are capable of exercising human freedom, their subjection to the orders of a master is unnatural and oppressive.[5]

3. Ibid., pp. 197–8 ('excellentes et potentes homines civitatis perimere', 'multos exploratores', 'quod procurat bella et mittere bellatores ad partes extraneas, ita quod intenti ad illa non cogitent contra eum').
4. Weber, *Lutter contre les Turcs*, p. 462 (papal texts); Sieber-Lehmann, 'Der türkische Sultan', p. 23 (German).
5. Aristotle, *Politics* I.2, 1253b15–1255b23, pp. 15–29.

Aristotle returns to the issue of despotic rule in Book III, when discussing varieties of monarchical government:

> There is another sort of monarchy, examples of which are kingships existing among some of the barbarians. The power possessed by all of these resembles that of tyrannies, but they govern according to law and are hereditary; for because the barbarians are more servile in their nature than the Greeks, and the Asiatics than the Europeans, they endure despotic rule without any resentment. These kingships therefore are for these reasons of a tyrannical nature, but they are secure because they are hereditary and rule by law. Also their bodyguard is of a royal and not a tyrannical type for the same reason; for kings are guarded by the citizens in arms, whereas tyrants have foreign guards, for kings rule in accordance with law and over willing subjects, but tyrants rule over unwilling subjects.[6]

If one combines this account with other comments Aristotle makes on the relationship between masters and slaves, the key features of despotic government emerge fairly clearly: the despot's rule is legal and hereditary (i.e. he is not a usurper); although he rules as an autocrat, he does have willing subjects; and while he aims at his own benefit, the subjects also benefit in an incidental or subsidiary way. This is neither normal, law-bound kingship nor tyranny, but rather a third category which combines some of the elements of those two. But if the subjects were naturally free people, like the Greeks, not natural slaves, like the Asiatic barbarians, it would indeed count as tyranny; so in some other passages, describing the corruption of proper and beneficial forms of government, Aristotle does sometimes use 'despotic' to describe wrongful rule.

The standard medieval Latin translation of the *Politics*, made by William of Moerbeke in *c.*1260, used the adjective 'despoticus', thus helping to introduce the term to Western readers.[7] But most scholastic political theorists, having little reason to analyse Asiatic 'barbarian' rule, were content with the standard list of proper forms of government (monarchy, aristocracy, constitutional rule) and the corresponding list of their corruptions; there was little or no work for this special third category to do. Rather untypically, Ptolemy of Lucca, who completed the text of Aquinas's unfinished *De regimine principum* in *c.*1300, did divide kings into two types, regal and despotic, aligning them with, respectively, the description of a law-abiding, non-exorbitant king given by Moses in Deuteronomy 17: 14–20, and the grim warning

6. Ibid. III.9, 1285a17–27, pp. 249–51.
7. Aristotle, *Politicorum libri octo*, e.g. pp. 18, 215 ('despoticus').

about oppressive kingly rule ('He will take your sons... And he will take your daughters... And he will take your fields') given by Samuel in 1 Samuel 8: 10–18.[8] That the latter form of rule was still valid and God-given was to be explained in terms of human sinfulness and the resulting need for coercive power to govern people against their will. Ptolemy allowed that some peoples might be so virtuous that they did not need to be ruled in this way, but in those cases his argument implied that they should seek constitutional rule, not any kind of monarchy; mild, law-abiding kingship might thus turn out to be a superfluous category, for all its Mosaic authority. Here one senses the tension, so common in scholastic political theory, between Aristotelianism and Augustinianism: the former would tend to see despotic government as a minor anomaly (perhaps confined only to 'barbarians'), while the latter would make one of despotism's essential principles, the use of coercive power to rule people willy-nilly, a near-universal condition.[9] 'Despotism', as a category simultaneously significant and untypical, thus had little work to do. Even in the case of two later writers—Marsilius of Padua and William of Ockham—who did give the term a distinct and properly Aristotelian meaning, the practical use to which they put it was confined largely to anti-papal polemics.[10]

All this changed with the advent of the Ottomans. While the Sultan was a usurper where his newly conquered European territories were concerned, it was quite evident that he was a hereditary ruler over his own people, having come to power by established principles of succession. His method of government was understood to be highly autocratic, with, it was thought, no limits to the use of coercive power, and it was assumed that he ruled primarily in his own interest. Yet at the same time the Ottoman regime clearly enjoyed considerable strength and stability. One way in which the Aristotelian argument about despotism could have been developed would have been to say that Ottoman rule rested primarily on its acceptance by Asiatic barbarians— that is, the original Turks, in their Anatolian heartlands. But Western writers acquired rather little information about conditions in Anatolia, being much more interested in the growing area of Ottoman rule in Europe. There, the category of 'natural slaves' could scarcely be applied to Christian Greeks, Slavs, or Albanians. Whilst comments on the moral degeneration of the

8. Ptolemy of Lucca, *On the Government* II.9.2, pp. 123–4; III.11.1–4, pp. 177–9.
9. See Blythe, *Worldview*, pp. 142–7.
10. Koebner, 'Despot and Despotism', pp. 280–1 (Ptolemy, Marsilius, Ockham).

Greeks were common in the early period of Ottoman rule, that was a different matter; nowhere do we find writers seriously arguing that the inhabitants of south-eastern Europe were slaves by nature (as Sepúlveda did, notoriously, where the native peoples of the New World were concerned). Rather, the emphasis was placed simply on slavery as such. The master–slave relationship was after all the basis of any theory of despotic government; what Western writers found was that this was just enough—without the problematic extra claim about natural slavery—to warrant treating despotic rule as a significant category in its own right.

But in what sense could the subjects of the Sultan be described as slaves? During the sixteenth century, the idea that all Ottoman subjects had some kind of slave-like status, or slavish conditions of life, became widely held in Western Europe. This idea played an important role in the early develop-ment of the theory of Ottoman despotism, even though it rested almost entirely on confusions, textual ambiguities, and rhetorical exaggerations.

One of the most influential texts was chapter IV of *Il principe*, in which Machiavelli made his comparison between the Ottoman Empire and the kingdom of France. As we have seen, he wrote there that 'The whole monarchy of the Ottoman Sultan is governed by a single ruler; the others are his servants [or: "slaves"—"servi"].' From this, a hasty reader might easily conclude that the entire population ('the others'), apart from the Sultan himself, had been reduced to slavery. In the following paragraph Machiavelli did use the phrase 'sendoli tutti stiavi', 'being all of them slaves'; yet, as we have also seen, this was a description not of the general population but of the Sultan's senior administrators. And the same is true of the statement about 'servi': Machiavelli was describing those who governed the popula-tion on the Sultan's behalf, having just referred, in the previous paragraph, to 'Quelli stati che si governano per uno principe e per servi', 'those states that are governed by a ruler and by servants [or: "slaves"]'.[11] Machiavelli's source was most probably George of Hungary, who described how the boys taken by the *devşirme* were given the status of slaves of the Sultan, and could go on to become either Janissaries or administrators of the Empire:

> From these slaves ['servis'] of his, some are promoted, according to the virtue they have demonstrated, to the high offices of his kingdom. Whence it comes about that all his magnates and all the princes of his whole kingdom are

11. Machiavelli, *Il principe* IV, pp. 14–15 ('Quelli stati . . .', 'Tutta la monarchia del Turco è governato da uno signore, li altri sono servi', 'sendoli . . .'); cf. above, pp. 165–6.

constituted by the king as officials, and not as lords and landowners, and consequently he is the sole lord and landowner and the lawful dispenser and distributor and governor of the whole kingdom, and the others are rather executors, officials, and administrators in accordance with his will and command.[12]

This was a fairly accurate description of the Ottoman administration; and it implied nothing whatsoever about the enslavement of the general population.

That idea came, rather, from the heated rhetoric of humanist publicists, writing on behalf of the Habsburg war effort in the 1520s and 1530s. In his 'exhortation' of 1529 Sepúlveda referred repeatedly to the 'slavery' and 'servitude' suffered by all who lived under the Ottomans. The harshest rule by a Christian king was preferable, he insisted, to the lightest rule by a sultan: under the former, people keep both their Christian liberty and their civil liberty. If civil liberty is temporarily suppressed, it can be revived, since there are laws and magistrates, and the form of a royal state with free men remains; but once people are under 'the very heavy yoke of Ottoman slavery', they are without hope of freedom.[13]

It should be noted that Sepúlveda's text was addressed to those foolish Christians who, complaining of their present rulers, imagined that conditions might be better under the Sultan. This was not a flight of rhetorical fancy on his part, but a reference to a real current of popular opinion: Vives was shocked by it, Luther complained about it, the Reichstag in 1526 worried about a rumour that the Sultan was promising benign treatment to German peasants, and during the 1520s there were credible reports of people moving to Ottoman territory in the hope of a better life.[14] In a short but passionate text about conditions under the Sultan, 'De conditione vitae christianorum sub Turca', first published in 1529, Vives argued that those who imagined that life would be better under Ottoman rule were pursuing a chimerical notion of freedom:

12. George of Hungary, *Tractatus*, p. 212 ('De istis... seruis suis secundum uirtutem expertam in eis promouentur ad beneficia regni sui. Vnde fit, ut omnes sui magnates et principes totius regni quasi quidam officiales et non domini uel possessores sint a rege constituti, et per consequens ipse solus dominus et possessor et legitimus dispensator et distributor et gubernator sit totius regni, ceteri uero executores, officiales et aministratores secundum suam uoluntatem et imperium').

13. Sepúlveda, *Ad Carolum V*, sig. a4r–v ('Turcarum grauissimo seruitutis iugo'); cf. sigs. a5v ('dura seruitute'), a6r ('seruientium mancipia').

14. Margolin, 'Conscience européenne', p. 123 (Vives); Francisco, *Martin Luther*, p. 86 (Luther); Kohler, *Ferdinand I.*, pp. 218–19 (Reichstag); Göllner, *Turcica*, iii, pp. 316–17 (reports).

Some have invented a certain foolish kind of liberty, never mentioned
indeed in the ancient records of the Romans and Greeks, according to which
everyone is allowed to do as much as he likes, with impunity. And since they
have no hope of achieving this under a Christian ruler, they prefer the Sultan,
as if he would be more generous in giving them greater liberty of this kind
than the Christian. What? Is liberty really to be located in the fact that you
contribute nothing, for the public good, to the state treasury or the prince's
tax-revenues? That taxes are almost taken away? That magistrates are either
non-existent, or of such weakened and reduced authority that they hardly differ from a private individual, so that anyone can do wrong with impunity?[15]

To counter this illusion, he emphasized as strongly as he could the misery
of life under the Sultan: in fact, he wrote, 'you would have no other place
there than that of cattle ["pecudes"], raised by him purely for his own
advantage and benefit.' Ramping up his rhetoric, he asked: 'Has any people,
or indeed any person at all, ever suffered such an extreme condition of
slavery as that which is now suffered by Greece?'[16] George Agricola, for the
same reasons, painted the worst possible picture of how the Ottoman
Empire was governed: 'this is not ruling, but tyrannizing; not shearing the
sheep, but flaying them; not giving laws to the subjects, as rulers should, but
robbing them, as brigands do.'[17] These writers were engaged, after all, in an
exercise in persuasive argument, not factual description; the popular idea
that life might be better under Ottoman rule was so dangerous—precisely
because it contained a significant element of truth—that all possible rhetorical means had to be used to oppose it.

Some of this rhetoric seems to have influenced another writer, Philip
Melanchthon, who was a humanist scholar as well as a Protestant theologian; and it was Melanchthon's commentary on Aristotle's *Politics*, published

15. Vives, *De concordia & discordia*, sigs. Ii8v–Kk1r ('Alij speciem sibi quandam confinxerunt stul-
tam libertatis, ne nominatam quidem in uetustis Romanorum ac Graecorum monumentis,
nedum expressam, ut cuique impunè liceat, quantum libeat. quod quum sub Christiano con-
sequuturos se desperent, ideo uel Turcam mallent, quasi is benignior sit in largienda libertate
hac, quàm Christianus. Quid tu dicis? sita uerò est in hoc libertas, quod nihil ad publicum
bonum aerario ciuitatis pendeas, uel principis fisco? quod penitus sublata sint uectigalia? mag-
istratus uel nulli, uel autoritate debilitata prorsum & imminuta, ut à priuato non different,
quod impunè liceat cuiuis malefacere? contrà potius ea existimatur libertas summa, legibus ac
legitimis magistratibus quietè obtemperare, & bonos se ac moderatos praebere ciues').
16. Ibid., sigs. Kk6r ('non alio futuros loco, quàm pecudes, quas ad utilitates modò & fructus suos
alit'), Kk7r ('An ulla gens, aut ullus omnino hominum tam extremam est seruitutis aliquando
conditionem passus, quam nunc patitur…Graecia?').
17. Agricola, *Oratio*, sig. A4v ('Hoc non est imperare, sed tyrannidem exercere: non tondêre
oves, sed deglubere: non iura, ut magistratum decet, subditis dicere, sed eos spoliare, ut latrones
solent').

in 1530 and reprinted several times thereafter, that made the essential link between this depiction of the Ottoman Empire and the concept of 'despotic' rule. Discussing the account of the master–slave relationship in the first book of Aristotle's text, he wrote:

> The first type is called 'despotic rule', as if to say the lordship of a master over a slave, which is how the soul commands the body...From this type there arises the most harsh form of rule, in which the ruler has the power of life and death, without any fixed law. The authority of kings among the barbarians was like this in the old days, and now they say that the form of rule among the Ottomans is of this kind, where the ruler does everything at will and the subjects are forced to obey like cattle ['pecudes'] whatever the tyrant commands.[18]

The reference to 'cattle' there may well have been prompted by a reading of Vives's text. And this linking by Melanchthon of Aristotelian despotic rule, the Sultan, and the treatment of humans as if they were animals was to have a wide influence; when the popular French writer Louis Le Roy issued his own translation of, and commentary on, Aristotle's *Politics* in 1568, he copied Melanchthon almost word-for-word when dealing with this part of the text, referring to 'the form of rule of the Sultan, where he does everything as he wills, without tying himself to any fixed law, and the subjects are forced to obey him like animals, and to do whatever he commands'.[19]

That such a method of rule should produce anything like stable government, let alone successful territorial expansion, still raised some puzzling questions. Melanchthon himself did not attempt to answer them fully, but he did hint at a possible line of explanation later on in his commentary. 'As, in the treatment of diseases, sharper remedies need to be used in some regions of the world, and milder ones in others, so too there is a need for more severe forms of government where the nature of the people is more fierce [or: "wild"—"ferociora"].' Thus it was that 'in some places, the subjects are slaves; in others, the power of the kings is circumscribed by laws, and some freedom is granted to the people.' Developing the kind of biblical argument sketched by Ptolemy of Lucca, he associated the former type of

18. Melanchthon, *Commentarii*, col. 425 ('Prior species vocatur δεσποτικὸν imperium, quasi dicas herile dominium, quo modo anima imperat corpori...Ex hac specie oritur acerbissima forma imperii, in qua dominus sine certa lege tenet potestatem vitae et necis. Qualis fuit regum apud barbaros olim autoritas, et nunc ferunt talem esse formam imperii apud Turcas, ubi princeps pro arbitrio facit omnia et subditi tanquam pecudes coguntur parere, quicquid imperat tyrannus').
19. Le Roy, *Les Politiques*, p. 46 ('celle du Turc ou le Grand Seigneur fait tout à son plaisir, sans s'astreindre à certain loy: & les subiectz sont contrainctz luy obeïr comme bestes, & faire tout ce qu'il commande').

rule with the description of kingship uttered by the prophet in 1 Samuel 8, where 'the most harsh form of rule is approved'; the Holy Spirit, author of the biblical text, 'indicates that legitimate rule, however hard it may be, is nevertheless approved by God. Joseph too reduced the whole of Egypt to the most harsh slavery. So it may not be doubted that even the more wretched form of rule, so long as it does not command anything wicked, is approved by God.' The ruler must also obey the basic principles of natural law where the treatment of the subjects is concerned, but these are not very onerous: 'where there is real servitude, the masters are nevertheless not permitted to seize everything. For the law of nature and the Holy Scriptures ordain that slaves must be left with what is sufficient for life in each family.'[20] It is noteworthy that in this passage the phrase 'the most harsh form of rule' ('acerbissima forma imperii'), applied to Samuel's description, is identical with the one Melanchthon used earlier to describe the 'despotic rule' of the barbarians and the Ottomans.

Melanchthon's argument thus sketched both a causal explanation (the fierce or wild nature of people in some regions of the world) and a justification in theological and natural-law terms. Another writer who considered the nature of slavish obedience, Estienne de La Boëtie, put forward a much more psychological theory, applicable to people in any part of the world, while firmly maintaining that such a system of rule was unjustifiable. At first, he wrote, a conquered people will serve its new master under duress; 'but those who come afterwards serve without reluctance, and do willingly that which their predecessors did under coercion. That is how people born under the yoke, and brought up and raised in servitude, are happy to live as they were born, without raising their sights.' And he went on to contrast the Venetians, who had such a passionate love of freedom that not one of them would be even tempted by the idea of exercising kingly rule over the others, with the subjects of the Sultan. If an observer who had been in Venice travelled to the Ottoman Empire, and saw there 'people who regard themselves as born only to serve the Sultan, and who give up their

---

20. Melanchthon, *Commentarii*, cols. 442–3 ('ut in aliis regionibus in curatione morborum acrioribus remediis utendum est, in aliis lenioribus, ita severioribus imperiis opus est, ubi ferociora ingenia sunt', 'Alibi vere servi sunt subditi. Alibi regum potestas legibus circumscripta est, et quaedam libertas concessa populis', 'probatur acerbissima forma imperii', 'Significat...legitimum imperium, quamvis durum sit, tamen Deo probari. Et Ioseph totam Aegyptum in acerbissimam servitutem redegit. Quare dubitari non debet, quin etiam tristior imperii forma, si tamen nihil turpe praecipit, Deo probetur', 'Caeterum ubi vera est servitus, tamen non licet dominis omnia rapere. Nam ius naturae et sacrae literae iubent servis relinqui, quod ad victum in unaquaquam familia sufficiat').

lives to maintain his power', would he think that both sets of people shared the same nature, 'or rather, would he not think that, having left a city of human beings, he had entered a park full of animals?'[21]

The date at which La Boëtie wrote this text is not known with any certainty; his friend Montaigne assigned it to the late 1540s, though the early 1550s may be more likely. (La Boëtie died in 1562.)[22] Ottoman rule featured only as a minor side-issue in this polemical text, which was aimed against absolutist tendencies in the French monarchy, so it is not surprising that its author showed little interest in the new information that was emerging during the 1540s and 1550s about conditions of life in the Sultan's domains. But one person who, as we have seen, did read widely in that new body of descriptive literature was the political theorist Jean Bodin; and it was Bodin who gave new life—and, unusually, a more or less positive valuation—to the concept of despotic rule. For someone who had studied those recent accounts of conditions under Ottoman rule, it was of course much easier to see why the inhabitants there might be broadly accepting of such a political system. But Bodin also developed further the two points that had been made in outline by Melanchthon: the idea that different systems were appropriate in different parts of the world, and the underlying, but rather minimalist, requirement of adherence to some kind of law. Bodin's debt to Melanchthon—whose writings he engaged with repeatedly in the *Methodus*, sometimes critically, but with sincere praise for his universal history—was strong. Modern scholarship has ignored the German author's role in the story of the theory of despotism, portraying Le Roy as Bodin's most important predecessor instead; but while it may be true that Bodin took from Le Roy the use of the French word 'seigneurial' ('lordly') as the equivalent of 'despotic', virtually everything else that Le Roy said on this issue was already present in—and indeed directly borrowed from—Melanchthon.[23]

21. La Boëtie, *De la servitude*, pp. 96 ('mais ceus qui viennent apres servent sans regret, et font volontiers ce que leurs devanciers avoient fait par contrainte. C'est cela, que les hommes naissans soubs le joug, et puis nourris et eslevés dans le servage, sans regarder plus avant se contentent de vivre comme ils sont nés'), 97–8 (Venice, 'les gens qui ne veulent estre nez que pour le servir, et qui pour maintenir sa puissance abandonnent leur vie', 'ou plustost s'il n'estimeroit pas que sortant d'une cité d'hommes, il estoit entré dans un parc de bestes').

22. The text was printed partly in 1574 and fully in 1578: see ibid., pp. 18–20. Recent estimates of the date of composition range from 1547 (Desplat, *La Boëtie*, pp. 101–4) to 1553–4 (M. Smith, 'Introduction', pp. 10–14). The authorship has sometimes been attributed to Montaigne himself, but scholarly opinion generally inclines to the traditional attribution.

23. Bodin, *Methodus*, p. 21 (praise of Melanchthon's history, i.e. his expansion of Johann Cario's chronicle); for overestimates of Le Roy's significance see Koebner, 'Despot', p. 284;

Following the Aristotelian pattern, Bodin distinguished three varieties of kingship: 'royal' monarchy (where the king's actions were bound by the laws of nature); 'lordly' monarchy (where the king enjoyed plenary power over the lives and properties of his subjects); and tyranny. As he explained:

> Wherefore a lawfull or royal Monarchie is that where the subiects obey the lawes of a Monarque, and the Monarque the lawes of nature, the subiects inioying their naturall libertie, and proprietie of their goods. The lordly Monarchie is that where the prince is become lord of the goods and persons of his subiects, by law of armes and lawfull warre; gouerning them as the master of a familie doth his slaues. The tyrannicall Monarchie, is where the prince contemning the lawes of nature and nations, imperiously abuseth the persons of his free borne subiects, and their goods as his owne.[24]

But although the threefold patterning was Aristotelian, Bodin's argument diverged significantly from the Greek philosopher's. For Aristotle, all despotic rule was tyrannical unless it was over natural slaves: only in that case, as with the Asiatic barbarian kingdoms, could it be legal, hereditary, and over willing subjects. Bodin shifted the whole basis of the argument to Roman law categories. Slavery here was by conquest; it was legal slavery, not natural slavery, and the law in question was the *ius gentium*, the established law of nations, which in this case abridged or limited the provisions of natural law that would otherwise guarantee people their natural freedom.

Thus both a royal monarch and a seigneurial or lordly one acted under the law, but the laws in question were different, operating at different levels. The former would rule in accordance with law in two senses: according to the king's own promulgated laws, which he bound himself to observe, and according to natural law. (It was natural law that decreed, for example, that people should enjoy private property.) The seigneurial king acted as a lawful conqueror under the *ius gentium*, and this freed him from some of the applications of the natural law. In a general sense, therefore, the people under him were all in the position of slaves; they did not have civil rights that would be

Stelling-Michaud, 'Le Mythe', p. 330. In the account which follows, I recapitulate some material presented in Malcolm, 'Positive Views of Islam'.

24. Bodin, *Six Bookes*, p. 200F (*Six livres*, p. 273: 'Donc la Monarchie Royale, ou legitime, est celle où les subiects obeissent aux loix du Monarque, & le Monarque aux loix de nature, demeurant la liberté naturelle & proprieté des biens aux subiects. La Monarchie Seigneuriale est celle où le Prince est faict seigneur des biens & des personnes par le droit des armes, & de bonne guerre, gouuernant ses subiects comme le pere de famille ses esclaues. La Monarchie Tyrannique est où le Monarque mesprisant les loix de nature, abuse des personnes libres comme d'esclaues, & des biens des subiects comme des siens').

defensible against their ruler in court, and thus they could not stop him from taking their property, should he so wish. Precarious though the subjects' position might have been, however, Bodin insisted that there was a great difference between seigneurial rule and tyranny, exclaiming: 'if we will mingle and confound the Lordly Monarchie, with the tyrannical estate, we must confesse that there is no difference in warres, betwixt the iust enemie and the robber; betwixt a lawfull prince and a theefe; betwixt warres iustly denounced [sc. proclaimed], and vniust and violent force'.[25] And in each successive version of his text Bodin took increasing care to emphasize the legal basis of seigneurial rule. In the first French edition he wrote: 'for it is not unfitting that a sovereign prince, having defeated his enemies in a good and just war, should make himself lord of their goods and persons by right of war, governing his subjects as slaves, just as the head of a family is lord of his slaves and of their goods, and disposes of them as he pleases'; in the revised version of the French he added, after that last phrase, 'in accordance with the law of nations'; and in the Latin translation this passage became: 'for it is not wrong [or: "not iniquitous"] that he who has defeated and subdued men in a just and legitimate war should be the lord of their persons and goods, while he treats his subjects just as a good head of a family treats his slaves, as indeed we see to be accepted in the customs and laws of almost all peoples.'[26] (Demonstrating that the Ottoman wars of expansion had been 'just and legitimate' was, however, a challenge that Bodin silently avoided.)

Near the end of his treatise, Bodin declared that royal monarchy was best.[27] He did not argue the point in detail; but, given the emphasis on respect for 'naturall libertie' and 'proprietie' in his account of royal rule, there could be little doubt that he regarded that form of rule as preferable—even though

---

25. Bodin, *Six Bookes*, p. 204F (*Six livres*, p. 278: 'si nous voulons mesler & confondre l'estat seigneurial auec l'estat tyranique, il faudra confesser, qu'il n'i a point de différence entre le droit ennemi en faict de guerre, & le voleur: entre le iuste Prince & le brigand: entre la guerre iustement denoncee & la force iniuste & violente').

26. Bodin, *Six livres*, p. 274 ('car il n'est pas inconuenient, qu'vn Prince souuerain, ayant vaincu de bonne & iuste guerre ses ennemis, ne se face seigneur des biens & des personnes par le droit de guerre, gouuernant ses subiects comme esclaues, ainsi que le pere de famille est seigneur de ses esclaues & de leurs biens, & en dispose à son plaisir, par le droit des gents' (cf. p. 235 in the Paris, 1576 edition)); *De republica*, p. 190 ('Neque enim iniquum est, vt qui homines iusto ac legitimo bello fregerit ac domuerit personarum ac rerum dominus sit: dum subditis, non aliter quàm bonus paterfamilias, seruis vtatur, vt quidem gentium ferè omnium moribus ac institutis receptum videmus'). While emphasizing his claims about the *ius gentium*, Bodin seems to have been retreating somewhat from the position he took on the natural character of lordly rule in the *Methodus*, when he wrote that it was 'not contrary to nature or to the law of nations' (*Method*, p. 204; *Methodus*, p. 313: 'neque enim contra naturam est, aut contra ius gentium').

27. Bodin, *Six livres*, p. 972; *Six Bookes*, p. 721C.

there is nothing like a worked-out theory of natural-law jurisprudence (still less a theory of natural rights) to be found in the *République*. Nevertheless, while the superiority of royal over seigneurial rule seems clear, in Bodin's theory, where the abstract categories are concerned, it would not be such a simple task to judge between the actual nature of the Ottoman state, as Bodin understood it, and the nature of the contemporary monarchical states in Western Europe. For he appears to have believed that in many ways the objectionable features of lordly rule had, in the Ottoman case, been modified and rendered tolerable.

Where slavery was concerned, Bodin did not of course deny that ordinary slaves were to be found in the Ottoman Empire: he gave examples of Christians captured by the Ottomans in recent wars being sold there as slaves. But he was also aware that Muhammad had 'proposed liberty for all who followed him', which meant that Muslims did not—at least, officially did not—enslave Muslims.[28] (Indeed, in the *Methodus* he wrote that the Christian emancipation of slaves took place merely as an imitation of the emancipation by Muhammad and his followers.[29]) As for the Christian subjects of the Sultan who were seized in the *devşirme*, Bodin explicitly denied, as we have seen, that their experience resembled ordinary slavery: 'as concerning the Turkes Pretorian souldiors, and those youths which are taken from the Christians as tribute, and are called tribute children, I neuer accounted them for slaues, seeing that they are enrolled in the princes familie, and that they alone enioy the great offices, honours, priesthoods, authoritie and honour; which nobilitie extendeth also vnto their [grandsons].'[30] And if this was true of people who had been formally enslaved (as the *devşirme* intake had), the slave-like status that applied—according to Bodin— to all the subjects of the Sultan was very much a formal and theoretical condition, having, in practice, little in common with actual slavery.

Where the Sultan's lordship over property was concerned, the facts, as Bodin understood them, offered more obvious support for the 'seigneurial' theory. In the *Methodus* he reported, on the strength of information given to him by two French statesmen and diplomats, that in the Ottoman Empire 'all lands, with the exception of only a few', were entrusted as feudal

28. Bodin, *Six livres*, p. 64 (*Six Bookes*, p. 44F–G) (Muhammad); Bodin, *Colloquium of the Seven*, p. 231 ('he summoned those in servitude to freedom and proposed liberty for all who followed him and his teaching') (*Colloquium heptaplomeres*, pp. 176–7: 'servitia ad pileum vocavit, libertate proposita iis omnibus, qui se suamque disciplinam sequerentur').
29. Bodin, *Methodus*, p. 343. Cf. also *Six livres*, p. 58; *Six Bookes*, p. 39D–E.
30. Above, p. 154.

holdings ('timars') to knights ('timariots'). 'When a timariot dies, the
military office is arbitrarily awarded by grace of the prince, as once fiefs and
benefices used to be given.' This system of strict military feudalism, together
with the 'Praetorian legions' paid from the state treasury, rendered the
Ottoman state 'invincible'.[31] In the *République* he returned to this theme,
writing that the timariots 'hold all their possessions in fealtie of the Prince,
as it were during pleasure, renewing their letters patents from ten yeares to
ten yeares: neither when they dye can they leaue their children heires of
their possessions, but of their moueables onely'. But in the Latin version he
added a qualification showing that he understood that the system was rather
less strict in practice: 'except by the gift of the prince they keepe the possession of their fathers lands, as they doe of his goods'.[32] In another discussion
of the timar system in the *République* he noted that it had been imposed
only in areas conquered by the Ottomans 'by the law of armes'; so the 'auntient subiects' of the Ottoman heartland had not been affected by it.[33] In any
case, the great majority of the Sultan's subjects were not timariots; and while
Bodin supposed that they could not own land outright in those territories
where the timar system operated, he also stated that the Sultan took only
ten per cent of the non-timariots' wealth when they died.[34] So it seems that,
once again, the notion of a Sultan enjoying absolute ownership of both the
persons and the property of his subjects did not match the reality of the
Ottoman system as Bodin saw it: if the ownership existed in theory, it was
not exercised, or exercised only very partially, in practice. This disparity was
clearly sensed by Bodin himself, by the time he wrote the Latin version of
his political treatise: there, after the phrase 'The Emperour of the Turkes
styleth himself *Sultan*, that is to say Lord ... for that he is lord of their persons
and goods', he added the phrase: 'whom for all that he gouerneth much
more courteously and freely, then doth a good housholder his seruants'.[35]

---

31. Bodin, *Method*, p. 262 (*Methodus*, pp. 413–14: 'omnia praedia, paucissimis admodum exceptis',
    'mortuo Timariota, Principis beneficio tribuitur militia ex casu, vt olim feuda seu beneficia
    dari consueuerant', 'Praetorianae ... legiones', 'inuictam').
32. Bodin, *Six Bookes*, p. 201D (*Six livres*, p. 275: 'ne tiennent leur timar que par souffrance, & faut
    que leur bail soit renouuelé de dix en dix ans: & s'ils meurent, les heritiers n'emportent que
    les meubles'; *De republica*, p. 191: 'nisi Principis beneficio paternorum praediorum ac veluti
    bonorum, possessionem accipiant').
33. Bodin, *Six Bookes*, p. 656H (*Six livres*, p. 866: 'par droit de guerre', 'les subiects anciens').
34. Bodin, *Six Bookes*, p. 65A ('the Grand Signior ... is heire ... to his other subiects for the tenth';
    Six livres, p. 94: 'le grand Seigneur est heritier ... des autres subiects pour la disme').
35. Bodin, *Six Bookes*, p. 201C–D (*Six livres*, pp. 274–5: 'le Roy des Turcs est appellé le grand
    Seigneur ... pour estre aucunement seigneur des personnes & des biens'; *De republica*, p. 190:
    'quos tamen multò humaniùs ac liberius, quàm bonus paterfamilias seruos moderatur').

Bodin's praise of various aspects of the Ottoman state has already been noted. But it should be emphasized, in addition, that there was one fundamental criterion on which he clearly regarded seigneurial rule as better or more effective than royal rule: that of the stability and durability of the regime or state. Given the practical concerns of this 'politique' theorist, who set a high value on civil peace and declared that even the worst tyranny was preferable to anarchy, this must have been, for him, an important consideration.[36] As he put it when introducing the subject of seigneurial monarchy, 'The Lordly Monarchies haue bene both great and of long continuance...the Lordly Monarchie is more durable than the royall.' The reason he gave for this was 'for that it is more maiesticall'. Only when he went on to explicate this point did a note of moral criticism creep into the argument: he wrote that such a regime endured because each subject, having been reduced to the status of a slave, 'becommeth humble, abiect, and hauing as they say a base and seruile hart'.[37]

However, elsewhere in his writings Bodin suggested that servility was a vice against which Muslims were to some extent protected or fortified by their religion. Commenting acerbically in the *Methodus* on Paolo Giovio (who had accused the French of worshipping their kings), he exclaimed: 'all his life he did not blush to kiss more than servilely the feet of his master [*sc.* the Pope]. Not only the kings of the Persians and of the Turks, but even the most haughty caliphs of the Arabs always abhorred that kind of worship.'[38] In the *Colloquium* the Muslim convert Octavius likewise states, of the Islamic peoples, that 'no nation is any farther removed from the suspicion of idolatry'.[39] So, while Muslim subjects of 'lordly' rule might well be cowed, for all practical purposes, by the power and majesty of the monarch, they would not make the mistake of engaging in the sort of self-abasement towards their ruler that was appropriate only towards God. And there is another way in which Bodin believed that 'lordly' rule was attempered by

36. Bodin, *Six Bookes*, p. 539D ('the greatest tyranny is nothing so miserable as an Anarchie'; *Six livres*, p. 655: 'la plus forte tyrannie n'est pas si miserable que l'anarchie').
37. Bodin, *Six Bookes*, p. 204G–I (*Six livres*, pp. 278–9: 'laissant la liberté naturelle, & la proprieté des biens à chacun', 'les Monarchies seigneuriales ont esté grandes, & fort durables...Et la raison pourquoy la Monarchie seigneuriale est plus durable que les autres, est pour autant qu'elle est plus auguste', 'deuient humble, lasche, &, comme l'on dit, ayant le coeur seruil').
38. Bodin, *Method*, p. 258 (*Methodus*, p. 406: 'toto vitae decursu, domini sui pedes plusquam seruiliter osculari non erubuit: quod adorationis genus, non modò Persarum aut Turcarum reges, sed etiam superbissimi Caliphae Arabum semper abhorruerint').
39. Bodin, *Colloquium of the Seven*, p. 219 (*Colloquium heptaplomeres*, p. 167: 'nulla gens ab idololatriae suspicione longius absit').

Islam, at least in the case of the Ottoman Empire: in the *Methodus* he wrote
that 'The man who is mufti, or chief priest, is indeed regarded as interpreter
of the divine law to this extent, that no one may introduce legislation which
violates religion.'[40] In the Latin version of the *République* he declared that
'the Turkish and Arabian princes...honour and obserue their Mufties, or
high Bishops, with the greatest honour and respect possibly to bee giuen
vnto them, still referring vnto them the greatest and most doubtful questions
of their law, to be by them decided.'[41] While the suggestion that irreligious
law-making was prohibited to the Sultan may have been quietly dropped in
the latter work, the claim that religion operated as a source of norms external
to the Sultan was clearly maintained.

It seems, then, that if 'lordly' monarchy was to be thought of as occupying
a spectrum, the rule of the Ottoman Sultans was placed by Bodin not at
the extreme end of that spectrum but rather towards the end that came
closest to 'royal' monarchy. The vice of servility was moderated; some check
or control was supplied by superior (or, at least, independent) norms; and
besides, as we have seen, the whole system of rule worked not to crush the
people into an undifferentiated mass, but to elevate and reward those of
them who displayed virtue. Indeed, at one point in his argument Bodin
came close to suggesting that the Sultan's rule shared one of the essential
characteristics of 'royal' monarchy. When he presented his famous distinction between the nature of the sovereign and the nature of the government,
he wrote that a monarchical sovereign might have a popular government if
he distributed offices and honours indifferently among the people; 'But if
the prince shall giue all commaund, honours, and offices, vnto the nobilitie
onely, or to the rich, or to the valiant, or to the vertuous onely, it shall be a
royall Monarchie, and that simple and pure, but yet tempered in maner of
an Aristocracie.'[42] Since Bodin had already praised the Sultan for awarding

---

40. Bodin, *Method*, pp. 211–12 (*Methodus*, p. 326: 'Nam qui Mofti, seu Pontifex maximus est,
    diuinae quidem legis interpres habetur, eatenus ne quis in legibus humanis à religione aberrare
    possit').
41. Bodin, *Six Bookes*, p. 393D (*De republica*, pp. 353–4: 'Diximus antea Turcarum & Arabum princi-
    pes in singulis imperijs etiamnum Mophtas pontifices maximos praecipuis honoribus colere &
    obseruare, & eorum quae in iure maxima sunt, maximéque ambigua summam ad illos deferre').
42. Bodin, *Six Bookes*, p. 199E (combining *Six livres*, p. 272: 'la Monarchie sera gouuernee
    Aristocratiquement quand le Prince ne donne les estats & benefices qu'aux nobles, ou bien
    aux plus vertueux seulement, ou aux plus riches', and *De republica*, p. 189: 'si verò Princeps
    imperia, honores, magistratus patriciis, vel diuitibus, vel fortibus, vel studiosis tantùm impertiat,
    regis potestas erit, & quidem simplex ac pura, sed Aristocratica ratione temperata' (where
    'studiosis' apparently means those zealous in the ruler's service)).

high office on the basis of 'vertue and noble acts', this comment could easily have been taken to imply that the Ottoman system combined essential features of both lordly and royal rule.

Similarly, if the 'royal' monarchy of north-western Europe, as portrayed by Bodin in the *République*, were placed on its own spectrum, it would be situated somewhere towards the 'lordly' end. Bodin described the origins and development of the feudal system in north-western Europe as a kind of penumbral version of lordly rule. When 'Northern' people such as the Goths, Lombards, Franks, and Saxons had 'tasted the maners and customs of the Hunnes' (an Asiatic people who did practise lordly rule), 'they began to make themselues Lords, not of the persons, but of all the lands of them whom they had vanquished'; the feudal estates which they gained in this way 'for this cause are called Seigneuries, or Lordships; to show that the shadow of the auncient lordly Monarchie as yet remayneth, although greatly diminished.'[43] So Western feudalism was just a shadowy version of Ottoman-style seigneurialism. Perhaps, indeed, those two spectrums should be seen as sections of one larger continuum, with a central area in which the distance between a feudally based royal monarchy on the one hand and a well-managed and Islam-fortified version of lordly rule on the other, was not so very great—in which case, the task of deciding which was better might not be so simple after all.

Bodin's remark about 'Northern people' supplies a clue as to how this issue might have been resolved in his mind. For it brings us to a major feature of his political theory, as set out in both the *Methodus* and the *République*: his climatic (or, more strictly speaking, zonal) theory of human nature. Different parts of the world were subject not only to different effects of temperature and atmosphere, but also to different astrological influences. These factors, while not absolutely determining human characteristics, had a large influence upon them: so people with different qualities and ten-dencies, both physical and mental, would be found in different zones of the habitable earth.[44] Bodin divided that territory into three zones. In the North, people were naturally warlike; they were good at seizing territory but not good at holding it, since they lacked wisdom. In the South, people

43. Bodin, *Six Bookes*, p. 202I (*Six livres*, p. 276: 'eurent gousté la coustume des Hongres...ils se commencèrent à se porter seigneurs, non des personnes, ains de toutes les terres des vaincus...qui pour ceste cause sont appellés seigneuriaux, pour montrer que l'ombre des Monarchies seigneuriales est demeuree, & toutesfois beaucoup diminuee').
44. See Tooley, 'Bodin and the Medieval Theory'.

were contemplative, and could be spiritual or indeed fanatical; they had a talent for religion and philosophy, but were bad at practical organization. And in the Middle zone the people had characteristics between those two extremes, with more of a talent for the practicalities of human life.

> The people therfore of the middle regions haue more force than they of the South, & lesse pollicie [*sc.* cunning]: and more wit than they of the North, & lesse force; and are more fit to commaund and gouerne Commonweales, and more iust in their actions. And if we looke well into the histories of all nations, we shall find, That euen as great armies and mighty powers haue come out of the North; euen so the [occult sciences,] Philosophie, the Mathematikes, and other contemplatiue sciences, are come out of the South; and the politike sciences, lawes, and the studie thereof, the grace of well speaking and discoursing, haue had their beginnings in the middle regions.[45]

As Bodin went on to explain in the *République*, the principles of government of the three zones were force (for the North), equity and justice (for the Middle), and religion (for the South).[46] And the virtues naturally possessed by the three types of people were as follows: mechanical skill, and force to execute (in the North), ethical wisdom (in the Middle), and philosophical wisdom (in the South). From which it followed that each had a role to play in what Bodin called 'the vniuersall Commonweale of this world': the southerners were made to instruct others in 'occult sciences' and religion; the northerners were made 'for labour and manuall artes'; and those of the Middle zone were designed by God 'to negotiat, traffique, iudge, plead, command, establish Commonweales; and to make lawes and ordinances for other nations'.[47]

While Bodin's views were not completely deterministic, he did argue that these characteristics must be taken into account when designing appropriate

45. Bodin, *Six Bookes*, p. 550G (*Six livres*, p. 671: 'Donques les peuples des regions moyennes ont plus de force que ceux de Midy, & moins de ruses: & plus d'esprit que ceux de Septentrion, & moins de force, & sont plus propres à commander & gouuerner les Republiques, & plus iustes en leurs actions. Et si bien on prend garde aux histoires de tous les peuples, on trouuera que tout ainsi que les grandes armees & puissances sont venues de Septentrion: aussi les sciences occultes, la Philosophie, la Mathematique, & autres sciences contemplatiues sont venues du peuple Meridional: & les sciences politiques, les loix, la Iurisprudence, la grace de bien dire, & de bien discourir, ont pris leur commencement & origine aux regions metoyennes').

46. Bodin, *Six Bookes*, p. 559B (*Six livres*, p. 686). In the *Methodus* the principle for the Middle zone was described as 'law and legal decision': *Method*, p. 115 (*Methodus*, p. 167: 'legibus, ac iudiciis').

47. Bodin, *Six Bookes*, p. 561C (*Six livres*, p. 690: 'la Republique vniuerselle de ce monde', 'des sciences les plus occultes', 'au labeur & aux arts mechaniques', 'pour negocier, traffiquer, iuger, haranguer, commander, establir les Republiques, composer loix & ordonnances pour les autres peuples').

forms of rule for different populations: a system suitable to the people of
Spain could not simply be imposed, for example, on the people of the
Netherlands. The Northerners, 'being fierce and warlike, trusting in their
force and strength, desire popular Estates, or at the least electiue Monarchies;
neither can they easily endure to be commaunded imperiously'. The
Southerners (and people of the East, who have a natural affinity with them)
were better suited to living under lordly rule; 'But the people of Europe
more couragious, and better souldiers then the people of Africke or Asia,
could neuer endure the lordly Monarques.'[48] This was not in any full sense
a revival of the doctrine of 'natural slavery'; it pursued, rather, Melanchthon's
suggestion that different treatments were appropriate in different regions of
the world. As Bodin's comments on the origins of European feudalism
showed, however, while the Northerners might have been inclined to resist
lordly rule, they were at the same time apt to impose it, as their warlike pro-
pensities often put them in the position of successful conquerors. Hence,
perhaps, the shadowy, half-and-half nature of seigneurial power in those
parts of Europe where the Northerners had played a significant role.

This whole pattern of argument supplies a way of explaining why, in
Bodin's opinion, a country such as France (a Middle-zone territory, strongly
touched by Northern influences) had been and should continue to be a
'royal' monarchy. For any individual country, located in a particular zone,
the theory would suggest an appropriate form of government—something
to be commended not in absolute terms, but because it was relatively most
suited to the nature of that particular population. This does not mean, it
should be noted, that Bodin was necessarily committed to simple relativism.
It does seem that (as some commentators have suggested) he regarded the
people of the Middle zone as possessing superior qualities; in which case it
might be true to say that the perfect Middle-zone state—which would have
to be a royal monarchy—was the 'best' state of all.[49] The point is merely that
the 'best' model might not be applicable to human kind more generally.

But what of the Ottoman Empire, a polity that encompassed many countries and peoples? It may not have covered all three zones equally; it largely

48. Bodin, *Six Bookes*, pp. 202H (*Six livres*, p. 276: 'mais les peuples d'Europe plus hautains &
guerriers que les peuples d'Asie & d'Afrique, n'ont iamais peu souffrir des Monarches
seigneuriaux'), 563C–D (*Six livres*, p. 694: 'fiers & guerriers, se fians en la force de leurs corps,
veulent les estats populaires: ou du moins les monarchies electiues: & ne peuuent aisement
souffrir qu'on leur commande par brauerie').

49. See, for example, J. W. Allen, *History*, pp. 431–8.

lacked territory in the North. But, on the other hand, Bodin constantly emphasized that the Turks were themselves a Northern people, who had originally moved southwards thanks to their successes in war against their southern neighbours. (Here his views were influenced by two things: the common identification of the Turks with Scythians, and his attentive reading of the Armenian historian Hayton or Hetoum, who, as we have seen, located the origin of the Turks in Turkestan.)[50] Gradually, what emerges from his portrayal of the Ottoman Empire is a picture of a polity which—unlike, perhaps, any other polity in recorded history—is structured in such a way as to create a successful combination of the virtues and abilities of people from all three zones. The Turks themselves, as people from the North, are suited to fighting and labour; they have taken their religion, Islam, from the South, relying on 'priests' and philosophers imbued with Arabic culture; and for the practical tasks of state administration they have selected, through the *devşirme*, talented people (mainly Greeks, Slavs, and Albanians) from their Middle-zone territories. One might almost describe this as an optimal combination of the qualities of all three zones; but it should be emphasized that this is an optimum which works on a very different basis from that of the 'best' state (i.e. the perfect royal monarchy). The 'best' state is too good for most people, as it requires the best subjects; whereas this model can encompass all of humanity, including both the belligerent Northerners and the timid and/or fanatical people of the South.

It is true, of course, that the theoretical fit here is not a perfect one. Law, as applied by the muftis, is drawn from the religious culture of the South, not from traditions of the people of the Middle zone (it may be relevant that, as we have seen, the legal system was the one area in which Bodin did not echo the positive appraisals found in the recent literature); and Bodin must also have been aware that the *devşirme* supplied Janissaries as well as administrators. It is also true that Bodin nowhere made this connection explicitly between the division of tasks in the Ottoman state and his tri-zonal scheme of human aptitudes. But that scheme was so fundamental to his thinking that he must surely have given some thought to the idea of a state in which the three elements were optimally combined; and, when he did so, he could hardly have failed to notice the resemblance with the Ottoman Empire. For in many ways, the Ottoman system of government and society, as described by Bodin, could be seen as satisfying the

50. See above, pp. 19–24.

general principles of harmony in multiplicity, 'concordia discors', which had for him a cosmological, as well as a political, significance. As he put it in the *Methodus*:

> If we refer all things to nature...it becomes plain that this world...consists of unequal parts and mutually discordant elements and contrary motions of the spheres, so that if the harmony through dissimilarity is taken away, the whole will be ruined. In the same way the best republic, if it imitates nature, which it must do, is held together stable and unshaken by those commanding and obeying, servants ['servis'] and lords, powerful and needy, good and wicked, strong and weak, as if by the mixed association of unlike minds. As on the lyre and in song itself the skilled ears cannot endure that sameness of harmony which is called unison; on the contrary, a pleasing harmony is produced by dissimilar notes, deep and high.[51]

This grand vision of potential strength and world-historical role of the Ottoman Empire takes us a long way away from the mainstream development of the theory of despotism in sixteenth-century Europe; for Jean Bodin was as untypical as he was original. It is true that the recent descriptive literature, which he had studied so carefully, had moderated some of the more extreme claims that had previously been made about the oppressive nature of Ottoman rule. On the question of the inheritance of property, for example, Djurdjević wrote that the terms of testaments were observed (in such matters as charitable bequests), and that the sons of timariots normally succeeded to their fathers' timars on the same conditions; Bassano recorded only that the estates of Christians who died intestate and without heirs reverted to the Sultan; Geuffroy wrote that the Sultan took one-third of each estate, or the whole in the case of a senior pasha; and Postel discussed the laws of succession without mentioning any reversion to the Sultan at all.[52] While these accounts differed, none of them supported the view that the Sultan owned or inherited all property. Nevertheless, the general

---

51. Bodin, *Method*, p. 268 (*Methodus*, pp. 423–4: 'nam si ad naturam, quae rerum Princeps est, omnia reuocemus, perspicuum sit mundum hinc...ex inaequalibus partibus, & maximè sibi repugnantibus elementis, orbiúmque agitationibus contrariis ita sibi constare, vt sublata illa congruenti discordia interitus sit: non aliter optima Respublica, si naturam imitetur, id quod necesse est, imperantibus ac subditis, seruis ac dominis, potentibus & egenis, probis & improbis, robustis ac imbecillis; quasi temperata repugnantium inter se animorum societate, stabilis & inconcussa retinetur. & quemadmodum in fidibus & cantu ipso concentum aequalem, quem vnisonum vocant, aures eruditae ferre non possunt: contrà verò dissimillimis inter se vocibus, tum grauibus tum acutis, moderatione quadam inter se confusis harmonia concors efficitur').
52. Djurdjević, *De turcarum moribus*, sigs. C1v (testaments), C3v (timariots); Bassano, *I costumi*, fo. 51r; Geuffroy, *Briefve description*, sig. f2v; Postel, *De orbis terrae concordia*, p. 238. The source of Bodin's idea that the Sultan took one-tenth is not apparent.

assumption that Ottoman subjects lived under slave-like conditions was and remained active and influential, keeping that and other misunderstandings alive; as the philosopher Girolamo Cardano wrote about the inhabitants of the Ottoman Empire in 1562, 'they are all slaves, and no power or wealth passes to their descendants.'[53]

One source of the slavery theory's continuing vitality was the 'relazioni' composed by Venetian envoys and 'baili' (resident representatives) on their return from Istanbul.[54] That such a theory should draw any support from these documents is on the face of it surprising, as the baili, at least, became well acquainted with the realities of Ottoman life, and filled their reports with generally reliable factual detail. But hostility towards the Ottomans was always a major current in Venetian public opinion; there were three Venetian–Ottoman wars in the sixteenth century (1499–1503, 1537–40, 1570–3), the third of which was hugely damaging and created a lasting legacy of resentment. What is more, when the Venetians defended their normally close trading relationship with the Sultan against Western critics who accused them of collaboration driven only by greed, the prime justification they gave for avoiding unnecessary wars with him was that large numbers of Christians lived in the vulnerable Venetian territories in the Balkans (especially in Dalmatia); since a major defeat could lead to these populations being absorbed into the Ottoman Empire, it suited Venetian purposes to portray that as a terrible fate, from which they must protect their subjects by all means possible.[55] So it is understandable that general comments on Ottoman 'tyranny', and statements which described conditions in the Ottoman Empire as slavish, did surface from time to time in these official reports. Nevertheless, with almost all of the references to slavery, a closer reading shows either that the phrase applied only to the Sultan's officials and Janissaries or that, if it was about the whole population, it was making a rhetorical comparison with slavery, and not putting forward the kind of factual claim that would give solid support to the theory of despotic rule.

The earliest surviving relazione to provide such comments is so untypical that it must be set aside as an outlier. Written in 1534 not by a resident bailo but by an official who had made only a brief visit to Istanbul to defuse a

53. Cardano, 'Neronis encomium', p. 153 ('serui enim sunt omnes: nec potentia uel opes ad descendentes perueniunt').
54. On these see above, p. 136, n. 16.
55. For an example (the citing of Dalmatia by Paolo Paruta as a reason for not joining the Habsburg–Ottoman war in 1593) see De Leva, ed., La legazione, ii, p. 191.

diplomatic crisis, it airily described all the Sultan's subject populations as 'his slaves, placed under his arbitrary will, and all so abandoned and broken down that none of them has any strength or energy'. (For good measure, it also asserted that the Janissaries had much worse discipline than Christian armies, and that Süleyman the Magnificent, then at the height of his power, was a very unimpressive figure, negligent and lacking in 'virtù'.)[56] A relazione of 1550, by the bailo Alvise Renier, did say that 'His Majesty [the Sultan] enjoys great obedience from his people, as all of them, from the great ones to the lowest, are his slaves'; such a statement, if taken out of context, would be very striking, but the surrounding passage makes clear that Renier had in mind the Sultan's officials and Janissaries only. (The same applies to the phrase 'all of them being slaves' in a relazione of 1558.)[57] A relazione written in 1553 by the bailo Bernardo Navigero used the term 'servitude' in a much more general way: 'all of them [sc. the Sultan's subjects] having been born in poverty, and in such servitude that not only have they not tasted the fruits of freedom, but they have not even heard its name'. But the passage in which this remark was made expressed as much an appreciation of the Sultan's statecraft as a denunciation of his oppressive rule: the order in his Empire was

> maintained with a high reputation, and kept among his subjects more by fear than by love, which I think is a better and easier way to keep them obedient; because, all of them having been born in poverty, and in such servitude that not only have they not tasted the fruits of freedom, but they have not even heard its name, one might fear that if they were ruled in any other way they might sometimes, as an ignorant people, raise some revolts.[58]

Another comment from a bailo's relazione of 1557 was similarly general: 'The other [sc. non-Muslim-born] subjects...who are not called slaves, although they could be considered to be slaves de facto, live under conditions of very strict obedience'.[59]

---

56. Albèri, ed., *Relazioni*, ser. 3, i, pp. 6 ('sono schiavi di lui e posti ad arbitrio suo, e tutti derelitti e distrutti sì che non è in alcuno nè forza nè vigore'), 8–10 (Janissaries, Süleyman).

57. Pedani, ed., *Relazioni*, pp. 78 ('Ha Sua Maestà obedientia grande della sua gente per esser tutti dal grando al minimo suoi schiavi'), 123 ('sendo loro tutti schiavi').

58. Albèri, ed., *Relazioni*, ser. 3, i, p. 154 ('ordine mantenuto con molta riputazione, e conservato presso li suoi sudditi più presto col timore che coll'amore, come mezzo, per mia opinione, migliore e più facile a tenerli nell'obbedienza; perchè essendo nati tutti in povertà ed in servitù tale, che non solo non hanno gustato il frutto della libertà, ma né anco udito il nome di quella, sarebbe da temersi che altrimenti governati non facessero coll'occasione, come gente ignorante, alcuna sollevazione').

59. Ibid., ser. 3, iii, p. 131 ('Li altri sudditi...che non sono chiamati sotto nome di schiavi, se ben dalli effetti possono esser tenuti per tali...vivono sotto una strettissima obbedienza').

After the traumatic experience of the Venetian–Ottoman War of 1570–3 (which saw the Ottoman conquest of Cyprus), the mood of the relazioni darkened. During that conflict, for the first time, Venice had tried to encourage uprisings by Christian subjects of the Sultan; for those who hoped for a future military defeat of the Ottoman Empire, such revolts became an important part of their strategic plans (or rather, strategic fantasies), and this was also a reason for painting a more sombre picture of Ottoman conditions. The bailo Marcantonio Barbaro, who had been held in Istanbul under strict house arrest and in fear for his life during the war, wrote on his return in 1573: 'all the Sultan's territories are so tyrannized, and the country is so destroyed, and the territories held in such misery and desperation, that it would be extremely dangerous for the Ottoman sultans to depend on them.' He went on to describe all of the subjects as slaves (using the phrases 'all of them being slaves' ('essendo tutti schiavi') and 'the said people all being slaves' ('essendo la detta gente . . . tutti schiavi')—the frequency with which such phrases recur in late-sixteenth-century texts suggests the strong subliminal influence of chapter IV of Il principe, with its ambiguous 'sendoli tutti stiavi'). Yet his analysis could not reduce everything to a matter of immiseration and fear; he also commented that the Ottoman system had 'a very advantageous way of maintaining and expanding a state, which is perhaps practised more among the Ottomans than in any other place, namely, the hope of rewards and the fear of punishments, since they are all ruled by a lord from whom alone property, life, and honours depend, just as all creatures take their strength from the sun.'[60]

Nine years later, in 1582, the relazione of the ambassador Giacomo Soranzo referred in passing to the Sultan as the 'despotic lord' ('dispotico padrone') of the Ottoman Empire; this was the first use of the term 'despotic' in these documents, and the only one until the 1630s.[61] In 1585 another bailo described

---

60. Ibid., ser. 3, i, pp. 307 ('Tutte le provincie del Signor-Turco sono talmente tiranneggiate, e così distrutti i paesi, e tenute in tanta viltà e disperazione, che sarebbe pericolosissimo agli Ottomani imperatori valersi di loro'), 327–8 ('essendo tutti schiavi', 'un mezzo utilissimo per la conservazione ed aumento di uno stato (e questo è forse più fra Turchi che in ogni altro luogo), ed è la speranza del premio e il timor della pena, essendo tutti retti da un signore dal quale solamente dispendono la facoltà, la vita, e gli onori, siccome dal sole prendono vigore tutte le cose create', 'essendo la detta gente dal primo all'ultimo tutti schiavi'). On the ambiguous phrase from Machiavelli see above, p. 166. Barbaro's relazione later enjoyed a wide readership, being printed in Comino Ventura's popular compilation Tesoro politico, fos. 78v–93v.

61. Albèri, ed., Relazioni, ser. 3, i, p. 439 (for the date and authorship of this relazione, printed as anonymous by Albèri, see Pedani, 'Elenco', p. 34). The next use was in 1634: see Valensi, Venise, p. 99.

the Ottoman political system as 'the government or republic of slaves'; but this, once again, referred to the officials who were doing the governing, not the general population.[62] Five years after that, the bailo Lorenzo Bernardo wrote very generally that 'the Turks are almost all slaves by origin', describing them as 'slaves of a single lord from whom property, life, and honours depend'—a phrase borrowed from Barbaro's text of 1573. In a later report (of 1592) Bernardo borrowed from himself, changing 'by origin' to 'by nature', and thus appearing to invoke the Aristotelian theory of natural slavery: 'being all of them slaves by nature, and slaves of a single lord'.[63] But this was more a rhetorical dismissal than a commitment to a worked-out theory. Overall, these Venetian relazioni, some of which circulated quite widely, contributed to a sense that life under Ottoman rule was generally comparable to slavery, without providing any specific details that would justify the proper use of that term.

What finally crystallized the theory of Ottoman despotism—as a thoroughly negative phenomenon, not the more or less positive one described by Bodin—was the anti-Ottoman project of the Catholic 'reason of state' theorists in the 1580s and 1590s. Their hostility to the Ottoman Empire was as intense as that of the pro-Habsburg humanist writers of the 1520s and 1530s, and could be just as rhetorically expressed. In his *De regia sapientia* (1583), for example, Botero insisted that since the Sultan's rule rested on fear, it could not last for long:

> What indeed could be judged to be less durable than that empire, which is founded on the loyalty of foreigners, and administered on the advice of renegades? Where slaves rule? Where force takes the place of law; where right and equity are located in the sword? Where greed takes precedence over judgments, and avarice rules over equity? Where no wife is certain, there is no love towards children, and no charity to neighbours?[64]

This was wild rhetoric, and had the argument stayed at such a level it could have carried little weight with those who had read the recent descriptions

---

62. Albèri, ed., *Relazioni*, ser. 3, iii, p. 267 ('il dominio o la repubblica de' schiavi').

63. Pedani, ed., *Relazioni*, pp. 350–1 ('Li Turchi per origine sono quasi tutti schiavi', 'schiavi d'un sol Signore dal quale solo depende la facoltà, la vita e l'honore'; the borrowing is confirmed by the passage that follows, which matches that in Barbaro's text); Albèri, ed., *Relazioni*, ser. 3, ii, p. 369 ('essendo tutti per natura schiavi, e schiavi di un solo signore').

64. Botero, *De regia sapientia*, p. 112 ('Quid verò minus durabile iudicari possit, eo Imperio, quod exterorum hominum fide nititur, perfugarum consilijs administratur? vbi serui dominantur? vbi vis est pro lege; ius, & aequum situm est in gladio? vbi iudicijs cupiditas praeest; aequitati auaritia dominatur? vbi nulla est certa vxor, nullus erga liberos amor, nulla caritas erga propinquos?').

of Ottoman life, with their evidence of effective justice, active charity, and so on. But Botero's friend René de Lucinge found a way of dealing with those descriptions—not by dismissing or denying them, but by incorporating them in his own theory, in a reinterpreted form.

On every key point, Lucinge was able to revalorize the description, switching the value from positive to negative. On the widely admired meritocracy of the Ottoman system, for example, he wrote that 'If they want to rise to obtain some rank and dignity, they have to beg for it from the goodness and will of their sovereign prince'; so this was not so much meritocracy as abject dependence, on the part of people who had been subjected to a miserable levelling. (Commenting on the lack of a hereditary nobility, Lucinge also emphasized the Sultan's elimination, by death or blinding, of such people in newly conquered territories, as well as the murder of members of the Ottoman dynasty to secure the throne.)[65] The much-praised public order that reigned in Ottoman territory was a sign of deep oppression: it was caused by disarming the subjects and keeping them under a kind of permanent military occupation, with garrisons of Janissaries throughout the Empire. Remarkably, Lucinge described the provision of peace, tranquillity, justice, and prosperity as a cynical tactic aimed at keeping the people subdued and contented; the Sultan 'maintains great peace and tranquillity throughout his state, and takes care that justice is delivered even-handedly, and that they have an abundance of provisions, and of all the other commodities that normally put the people's anger to sleep.' As for religious toleration: Lucinge did not address this topic directly, but he did comment that the Sultan cleverly sustained the schismatic Orthodox Church to stop his Christian subjects from joining forces with the Catholic powers.[66] Overall, the Sultan was master of the 'persons, properties, goods, houses, and possessions of his subjects', and they in turn 'all describe themselves as slaves of their ruler'.[67]

This text marked a real turning point: the negativization of the new paradigm. Order and discipline now became terror and servility; the sobriety

---

65. Lucinge, *De la naissance*, pp. 172 ('s'ils veulent parvenir et se hausser en quelque grade et dignité, il faut qu'ils le mendient de la bonté et vouloir de leur prince souverain'), 191 (nobility, dynasty).

66. Ibid., pp. 177, 180 (disarming), 181 ('Il maintient une grande paix et tranquillité par tout son estat, prend garde que la justice soit esgallement distribuee, qu'ils ayent abondance de vivres, et de toutes autres commoditez coustumieres d'endormir la fureur'), 184 (garrisons), 193 (Orthodox Church).

67. Ibid., p. 172 ('des personnes, des facultez, des biens, des maisons et possessions de ses vassaux', 'se disent tous esclaves de leur prince').

and lack of unnecessary luxury of ordinary life became a fear of confiscation; justice became a mere trick; and so on. For the first time, a writer had sketched something recognizable as a system of (negative) despotism—even if that term itself was not used by him. This was a system of rule which had its own peculiar features, and which, thanks to its extraordinary concentration of power in the hands of the ruler, and its reduction of the subjects to extreme dependence, looked as if it might enjoy considerable stability, or even permanency. (Lucinge's intention may have been to demonstrate that it must collapse, but in the last part of his book, on the 'chute des estats', the fall of states, he had some difficulty in showing how or why that would happen.)

Once Lucinge had changed the description in this way, it was easy for Giovanni Botero, in his popular geographical work, the *Relationi universali* (1591–2), to summarize it, adding the final touch—the word 'despotic':

> The rule of the Ottomans is completely despotic ('despotico'): for the Sultan is the owner of everything contained in his dominion, in such a way that the inhabitants call themselves his slaves, rather than subjects; and no one is owner of himself, nor of the house where he lives, nor of the land he cultivates... and there is no individual so great that he is sure of his own life, or of the position he occupies, except by the grace of the Sultan. And he maintains himself in this rule, of such an absolute kind, by means of two things: taking away all weapons from his subjects, and entrusting everything to renegades, who are taken in their childhood as a tithe from his territories.[68]

Botero was a keen student of the Venetian relazioni, so it is likely that his use of the word 'despotico' was derived from the report of 1582 by Giacomo Soranzo. (Having been a lecturer in Jesuit colleges, Botero would also have been familiar with the Aristotelian origin of the term.) But the most influential thing about his account was not the word itself, but the idea of a distinctive system of rule, differing from ordinary tyranny and having at least an appearance of stability and good order—a system based on the quasi-slavery of the whole population, the Sultan's ultimate ownership of all

---

68. Botero, *Relationi*, fo. 223r ('Il gouerno de gli Ottomani è affatto despotico: perche il Gran Turco è in tal modo padrone d'ogni cosa compresa entro i confini del suo dominio, che gli habitanti si chiamano suoi schiaui, non che sudditi: e niuno è padrone di se stesso, non che della casa: oue egli habita, ò del terreno, ch'egli coltiua... e non è nissuno personaggio cosi grande, che sia sicuro della uita sua, non che dello stato, nel quale egli si troua, se non per la gratia del gran Signore. Egli poi si mantiene in questo dominio così assoluto con due mezi, cioè co'l torre affatto l'arme a i sudditi suoi, e co'l metter ogni cosa in mano di renegati, tolti per uia di decima da gli stati suoi nella loro fanciullezza').

property, the elimination of hereditary nobility and independent social rank, and the effective control of force. While some writers on reason of state continued, as we have seen, to identify particular devices of Ottoman government as worthy of imitation, the generally positive image of the new paradigm, which Bodin had absorbed into his own account of 'lordly' rule, had finally been overcome and overturned. Now, insofar as Ottoman rule had its own special nature, it was based on a cunningly constructed monopoly of power, combined with a psychology of fear.

TEN

Analyses of Ottoman strength and weakness

In 1591 the German historian Johannes Leunclavius (Johann Löwenklau) published his *Historiae musulmanae Turcorum, de monumentis ipsorum exscriptae, libri XVIII.* This was a major contribution to Western knowledge of Ottoman history, as it was based on two manuscript versions of Ottoman Turkish chronicles (one of them translated by a dragoman in Istanbul, Murad Bey— formerly Balázs Somlyai, a Hungarian captive who had converted to Islam).[1] Leunclavius was a scholar, but he was also an activist in the anti-Ottoman cause, and he began his work with a dedicatory epistle addressed to the Electors of the Holy Roman Empire, urging them to take up arms against the Sultan. Relations between the Habsburgs and the Ottomans were at a dismally low point, thanks to the raiding activities of the *beylerbeyi* (regional governor) of Bosnia; these were on such a scale that the outbreak of the 'Long' Habsburg–Ottoman war of 1593–1606 is dated by Hungarian historians to 1591. The length of that war, and the fact that its final outcome involved little territorial change from the situation at its start, indicate that the geostrategic balance of forces in Central Europe was by then more or less equal. Arguably, therefore, it was this conflict, not the 'Great' war of 1683–99, that marked the end of the process—which had begun in the fourteenth century—of major territorial expansion by the Ottomans in continental Europe. While this war demonstrated that the Sultan could still call on huge military resources, it also showed up some weaknesses in the Ottoman military-administrative machine that had not been apparent in previous conflicts. So it may seem appropriate that Leunclavius should have

---

1. On the manuscripts see Ménage, *Neshri's History*, pp. 31–2, and Kreutel, ed. and tr., *Der fromme Sultan*, p. 182; on Murad Bey see Krstić, 'Of Translation', pp. 136–9.

included, in his dedicatory epistle, both a list of 22 factors that counted in favour of the Ottomans ('Pro Turcis') and a list of 27 that pointed the other way ('Contra Turcos').[2]

The pro-Ottoman factors make up a rather disparate assortment. The first two are the religious unity of the Ottomans, and the freedom of religion they grant to Christians. Then come their general political prudence, which is very sophisticated ('not at all barbarous'), and the skill and experience of the viziers. The next points are that they record their internal history and learn from it; that they do the same with the history of their foreign relations; and that their other studies are related to practice, not scholastic matters. They have a monarchy; it is hereditary, not elective; they are zealous for the public good more than the private; they practise military virtue; their justice is rigorous; it enjoys 'Laconismus', the virtue of brevity; and the subjects' conduct can earn either rewards, including high office; or punishments. The state is endowed with great strength in terms of population, treasure, and weapons; the government enjoys strong authority, with a severe 'form of rule'; the Ottomans practise many tricks (in which they exceed all other barbarians in 'all kinds of fraud, perfidy, and injustice'); they are well prepared for war; they have many soldiers; they have good military discipline; and their army consists of their own subjects, not foreign mercenaries.[3]

This analysis by Leunclavius, which incorporated various components of the 'new paradigm', had a wide influence. It was repeated, for example, by the popular French writer Louis Guyon in his *Diverses leçons* (1617), and formed the starting point for a list of no fewer than 50 such factors published by the Lutheran pastor Johannes Praetorius in 1664.[4] But it was not the first attempt to enumerate the causes of Ottoman success. Several of the authors whose works helped to form the new paradigm had drawn attention to particular factors. Paolo Giovio's analysis of Ottoman military superiority had singled out obedience, religious fatalism, and austerity (or, in a later version of the argument, obedience, austerity, and huge numbers). Pierre Belon's equivalent list consisted of martial valour, huge numbers— made possible, as he explained, by their austerity, which reduced the need

2. Leunclavius, *Historiae musulmanae*, pp. 4–10.
3. Ibid., pp. 4–6 ('minime barbara', 'forma imperij', 'omni genere doli, perfidiae, iniustitiae').
4. Guyon, *Diverses leçons*, iii, pp. 570–1 (material appearing for the first time in the 3rd edn., 1617); [Praetorius,] *Arcana*, pp. 5–7. Praetorius's real name was Hans Schulz. This book was published anonymously, but is identifiable by a reference to one of his other works, *Catastrophe muhammetica*, as written by him: p. 33.

for supplies of food—and the use of subjects, not mercenaries, as soldiers.[5] And Postel had specified 'sobriety, patience, obedience, wealth, large forces, speed of action, and having all parts of one's country well inhabited'; as we have seen, this enumeration was expanded by Louis Le Roy into 'sobriety, patience, obedience, concord, diligence, order, valour, abundance of men, horses, and weapons, and . . . the use of good military and political discipline'.[6] Occasionally the Venetian relazioni also attempted this sort of analysis. In 1590, for instance, Lorenzo Bernardo generalized as follows: 'Whoever studies this empire carefully will find that it has had, from its beginning, four great foundation stones, building on which, it has been able to rise to such heights and such success: . . . religion, discipline, and obedience, from which there quickly developed the fourth foundation stone, which is strength and power.'[7]

That comment by Bernardo, like Le Roy's listing, had implications that went beyond the strictly military, even if its primary focus was on Ottoman success in warfare. Scipione Ammirato's 'Oration' to Sixtus V of 1585, part of which has been quoted above, concentrated more closely on military matters, specifying

> the marvellous obedience which they show to their ruler, their modest diet, the rarity of fights and quarrels among them, their belief that in dying for their king they die in the service of God, their certain hope of rewards, the absence of gambling among them, the fact that they have regard to no kind of nobility other than that of virtue, the fact that they know few ways of life other than that of warfare, and finally the fact that the art of war constitutes the beginning, the middle, and the end of all their honour, all their wealth, and all their well-being.[8]

And René de Lucinge's analysis was also military, though with a more strategic emphasis. He listed seventeen factors—to each of which he devoted a

5. Above, p. 64 (Giovio); Belon, *Voyage*, pp. 477–9.
6. Above, p. 152.
7. Pedani, ed., *Relazioni*, p. 349 ('Quest'Imperio, chi ben lo considera, troverà che nel suo principio ha havuti quattro gran fondamenti, sopra li quali fondandosi ha potuto ascendere a tanta altezza e felicità . . . la religione, la disciplina, e l'obedienza; dalli quali poi in breve tempo è nato il quarto fondamento, che è la forza e la potenza').
8. Above, p. 182; Ammirato, *Orazioni*, pp. 6–7 ('l'vbbidienza marauigliosa, che essi portano al lor Principe, la sobrietà del mangiare, le poche gare, e contese, che sono in fra di loro; la credenza che hanno, che morendo in seruigio del lor Rè muoiano per seruigio d'Iddio; la speranza certa de premi, il non esser fra loro giuochi, il non hauer riguardo ad altra nobilità, che a quella della virtù, il saper pochi altri mestieri, che quel della guerra, & finalmente l'arte militare esser principio, mezzo, & fine d'ogni loro honore, d'ogni loro ricchezza, d'ogni lor bene').

chapter in the first part of his book—that had ensured the success of the (generically described) Ottoman Sultan:

> He has devoted himself to war above all; he has always made offensive war; he has cared little for fortresses; he has trained his soldiers to be courageous and hardy; he has kept his large and powerful armies under discipline and military control; he has made no use of forces other than his own; he has mingled tricks and deceptions with strength; he has used excellent officers; his conquests have not jumped ahead to non-contiguous territories; he has not wasted his energies on unimportant targets; he has made use of his opportunities; he has swiftly carried out his plans; he has gone to war in person; splendidly equipped; in the appropriate season for campaigning; without dividing his forces; and he has not fought for long against one enemy.[9]

Reducing politico-military practice to techniques, maxims, and principles was a familiar style of analysis, aimed in almost every case at providing models for Western rulers and commanders to copy; the only exception on Lucinge's list was the reference to tricks and deceptions—which, in the relevant chapter, he utterly rejected. Similarly, the historian Richard Knolles, in the preface to his *Generall Historie of the Turkes* (1603), ran through the standard list of causes of Ottoman military success (the 'rare vnitie and agreement amongst them'; 'their courage'; 'frugalities and temperatnesse in their diet'; 'their strait obseruing of their auntient militarie discipline'; 'their cheerfull and almost incredible obedience vnto their princes and Sultans', and so on), concluding that these were all 'commendable and lawfull meanes', before adding two immoral principles from which Ottoman statecraft had also benefited: breaking the law of nations (abandoning alliances when it was advantageous to do so), and breaking the law of nature (the main example being the practice of fratricide by an incoming sultan, to eliminate threats to his rule).[10] And these were not the only points on which the Ottomans might be found to derive advantages from practices that were not

---

9. Lucinge, *De la naissance*, p. 42 ('Il s'est premierement du tout adonné à la guerre. Il a tousjours fait guerre offensive. Il s'est peu soucié des forteresses. Il a dressé ses soldats valeureux et hardiz. Il a contenu en discipline et police militaire ses grandes et puissantes armees. Il n'a fait d'estat d'autres forces que des siennes. Il a meslé, avec la puissance, les ruses et les tromperies. Il s'est servy de capitaines excellents. Il n'a fait aucun sault en ses entreprises [the translation expands here, in the light of the argument of the relevant chapter]. Il ne s'est amusé à choses de peu d'importance. Il s'est prevalu des occasions. Il a executé promptement ses desseings. Il est allé en personne à la guerre. Avec un brave equipage. En saisons convenables. Il n'a divisé ses forces. Et n'a continué longuement la guerre contre un seul').
10. Knolles, *Generall Historie*, sigs. A4v–A5r. On fratricide see Vatin and Veinstein, *Le Sérail ébranlé*, pp. 150–60.

to be imitated. Some writers also included, in their analysis of Ottoman success, aspects of Islamic belief and practice that could only be reprobated by Christian readers. Giovio's reference to fatalism—which allegedly caused Ottoman soldiers to act fearlessly in battle, in the belief that the time and manner of their death was entirely foreordained, whatever they might do— was one example of that; and there were other, more detailed attempts to analyse particular points of Islamic practice in functional terms as politico-military devices (as we shall see in chapter 12).

Western writers in the Machiavellian tradition developed a way of dealing with these effective but objectionable practices. In the late sixteenth and early seventeenth centuries many of them cultivated a special interest in the works of Tacitus; they admired his cool analysis of power politics and, in particular, his focus on the tricks and devices by means of which canny rulers controlled their subjects—both by keeping them in awe and by giving them the 'simulacra' of freedom. In this way the stratagems of the Machiavellian prince were identified with a set of 'arcana imperii', secrets of rule.[11] These could be expressed in discrete maxims which lent themselves to list-making. Some writers found useful lessons for modern rulers to copy, but others were concerned to expose political fraud and deception. The German jurist Arnoldus Clapmarius (Klapmeier) straddled that divide, developing the positive theory of reason of state that he found in the writings of Scipione Ammirato (who himself wrote a commentary on Tacitus), but also drawing attention to the methods of tyrannical regimes. In his influential work *De arcanis rerumpublicarum libri sex* (1605) Clapmarius gave a very negative account of the 'arcana' of Ottoman rule:

> The Ottomans also have their secret maxims of empire and rule, such as: violent government; persuading the common people, by means of great fear and the greatest superstitions, to agitate for war plans rather than peaceful ones; never ceasing to engage in warfare; not going away from Istanbul for any light reason; keeping their sons and the heirs to the Empire so strictly confined, to stop them from breaking free and making revolutions; allowing great shows of power to the pashas and viziers, even bestowing honours on their relatives; and keeping the common people occupied with either commerce or military affairs.[12]

11. See Toffanin, *Machiavelli*; De Mattei, *Il problema*; Behnen, '"Arcana"'; Donaldson, *Machiavelli*, pp. 111–40.
12. Clapmarius, *De arcanis*, p. 287 ('Turcae habent occulta sua consilia imperij ac dominationis, ut sunt, violenta gubernatio; magno metu maximisque superstitionibus indu[c]ere plebem, consilia agitare non tam pacis, quam belli; nunquam à bello cessare; non facilè deserere Constantinopolim; filios atque Imperij heredes ita arcte in custodia tenere, ne erumpant, & res

One other cynical device was added to the list by the Tacitist and satirical writer Traiano Boccalini, in his highly popular, fanciful, but sharp-edged miscellany on historical and political matters, the *Ragguagli di Parnaso* (1612–15). It was from the Ottomans, he wrote, that the 'modern opinion' had arisen that the best way to rule people was to keep them ignorant. Boccalini was drawing here on a long tradition of Western commentary on the Ottoman Empire that portrayed it as hostile to education and culture; the origins of this lay partly in the complaints of the early humanists about the destruction of books and libraries, and partly in a tradition of Christian anti-Muslim polemic which accused Muhammad of forbidding the teaching of critical thinking for fear that it would undermine his religion. Boccalini himself voiced a version of the latter argument in an imaginary dialogue between Jean Bodin and the (personified) Ottoman Empire: the Empire explained that it had 'exterminated all sciences, and all fine literature, so that my subjects may live in the simplicity which is absolutely required by my religion'.[13] Boccalini was not the first to make this point about the nature of Ottoman rule; the French traveller Jean Palerne, whose description of the Empire, based on his experiences there in 1582–3, was published posthumously in 1606, had included it in his own list of the four things 'that enable the Ottoman Emperors to live in peace, and to maintain their Empire for a long time':

> The first is that they kill the sons of the ruling family, which is the most effective way of forestalling divisions and factions; and they do the same to their pashas, when they have acquired great riches. This is something only tyrants do. The second point is: indescribable obedience. The third is the order that the Sultan ensures in his army. And if you want to add a fourth reason, you could say that the ignorance in which they are brought up, without much reading, can greatly contribute [to the stability of the Sultan's rule]. For when the people are ignorant, they lack the means to understand that they are wronged.[14]

novas moliantur; magna simulacra Bassis Visieris indulgere, etiam affinitatibus ornare; plebem vel mercatura, vel rebus bellicis occupatam tenere'). On Clapmarius's debt to Ammirato see Donaldson, *Machiavelli*, pp. 129–36.

13. Boccalini, *Ragguagli* I.64, i, p. 224 ('esterminate tutte le scienze e tutte le buone lettere, che acciò i miei sudditi vivino in quella semplicitá, della quale la mia Religione ha somma necessitá'), III.93, iii, p. 269 ('moderna opinione'). On Boccalini's attitude to Ottoman rule, condemning it morally but admitting its effectiveness, see Sterpos, 'Boccalini tacitista', p. 262, and D'Ascia, 'L'impero macchiavellico', pp. 130–1.

14. Palerne, *D'Alexandrie*, p. 263 ('par lesquels les Empereurs Turcs peuvent régner en paix, & maintenir longuement leur Empire', 'Le premier est, qu'ils tuent les enfants de Brutus [Palerne explains this expression on p. 256]...qu'est le plus expédient pour couper chemin aux divisions & partialités. & en font autant à leurs Bachats, lors qu'ils ont acquis beaucoup de moyens.

This idea would keep its currency for a long time. In 1640 the Spanish diplomat and littérateur Diego de Saavedra Fajardo confidently asserted that 'ignorance is the main foundation of the Ottoman Empire.' And as late as 1709 the young writer Aaron Hill, who had travelled in the Levant and spent time in Istanbul, produced a rather old-fashioned list of the 'maxims' of '*Turkish* Policy', of which the fourth was:'Learning is of all things the most dangerous to an Arbitrary Monarchy.' In his view, the Ottoman authorities feared that education would make the people 'throw off (with their Ignorance) the dull Stupidity of their slavish Ancestors', after which 'they would soon perceive the Felicity of other Nations in a Glorious Liberty.'[15]

A way of analysing the strength of Ottoman rule that was based at least partly on identifying the deceptive trickery of morally debased sultans, and partly on practices such as fratricide which matched the worst forms of intrigue described by writers such as Tacitus and Suetonius, could be connected rather easily with a view of the Ottoman Empire as a corrupted state that already carried the seeds of its own destruction. There was, in other words, some possible overlap here with the other exercise conducted increasingly by Western writers in this period: analysing the nature and causes of Ottoman weakness.

This practice also had a long history. From the early humanist writers onwards, people had searched for cracks in the edifice of Ottoman power, often going far beyond what the empirical evidence would justify— asserting, for example, that Ottoman troops must be weak because they were 'Asiatic', or that all Christian subjects of the Sultan would rise up at the slightest opportunity. In the second half of the sixteenth century, however, the writers of the Venetian relazioni had developed some lines of argument which, although influenced by their underlying political animus, were at least partly based on direct observation. In 1560 the bailo Marino Cavalli discussed both the strength and the weakness of the Empire. Having insisted that the Ottomans were for the time being genuinely powerful and 'not, as some Christians believe, straw men', he went on to sketch three things that

Chose qui n'appartient qu'aux tyrans. L'obeissance indicible pour le second poinct. Et pour le troisiesme l'ordre qu'il observe en la milice. Et qui voudroit adjouster une quatriesme raison, on pourra dire, que l'ignorance, en laquelle ils sont nourris, sans avoir cognoissance de beaucoup de lettres, y peut beaucoup ayder. Car le peuple estant ignorant n'a pas de moyen de cognoistre si on luy faict tort').

15. Saavedra Fajardo, *Idea*, p. 497 ('La ignorancia es el principal fundamento del Imperio del Turco'); Hill, *Full and Just Account*, p. 6.

might ruin them: internal division, leading to civil war; corruption, 'if they were to continue in their current practice of avarice, luxury, and the corrupt conduct and government of the state'; and a strong Persian king. The idea of corruption included not only improper financial influences, but also the degeneration of traditional institutions: thus in 1573 Marcantonio Barbaro referred to the *devşirme* system and the formation of the Janissaries, where 'with corruption and scandal, they are bringing in, through favouritism, the sons of Muslims.'[16] Some of the writers thought that one major external shock—a significant defeat by the Shah of Persia, for instance—might be enough to destroy the Empire, as the general population was so discontented. Giovanni Correr made that point in a striking way in 1578: 'The most fitting thing to which I could compare the Ottoman Empire is a clock, in which the force of one wheel alone drives many other wheels; if that wheel loses its cogs, or is broken in some other way, all the others are equally prevented from moving'—the one essential wheel here being military force and military success.[17] But most of these Venetian officials concentrated on internal weaknesses. In 1590 Lorenzo Bernardo, a tenacious critic, went through his three primary 'foundation stones' of Ottoman rule—religion, obedience, and discipline—describing how each was being eroded. On the last of these, fitting the Ottoman case into a much more general schema, he commented:

> Now that, after the conquest of so many kingdoms, this Sultan and the great men of this government have taken into their hands so many riches, this nation too has been unable to avoid the corruption which such great riches and comforts bring with them. For nothing does more to wither the glory which comes from feats of arms than luxury and fine pleasures, as experience has shown in the case of many empires, especially the Assyrian, the Persian, and the Roman.[18]

16. Albèri, ed., *Relazioni*, ser. 3, i, pp. 280–1 ('Non sono, come alcuni cristiani credono, uomini di paglia', 'se continuassero, come fanno, nell'avarizia, nelle delicatezze, e nel corrotto vivere e governo dello stato'), 317 ('con corruttela e scandalo, si vanno introducendo con favore figliuoli di Turchi').

17. Pedani, ed., *Relazioni*, p. 237 ('Né certo saprei assimigliar l'imperio turchesco a nessuna cosa più propriamente che ad un horologio, nel quale una rotta sola con la sua violenza ne fa caminar molte, ma se quella si sdenta, o guasta in altro modo, tutte l'altre restano parimente impedite').

18. Ibid., p. 352 ('Hora che quel Signore e tutti i grandi di quella Porta con l'occasione di tanti regni debellati ha convertito in sé tante ricchezze, non ha potuto fugire anco quella natione la corruttione che sogliono portar seco tante ricchezze e commodità, essendo che niun altra cosa mortifica magiormente quella gloria che s'acquista coll'armi quanto il lusso e le delizie, sì come per esperienza si è veduto in molti imperii, e specialmente in quello d'Assiria, in quello di Persia e nell'Imperio Romano').

And two years later he repeated this analysis (using the terms religion, obedience, and parsimony), stressing the general discontent of the population: the ordinary people resented the Ottoman officials, who squeezed them for money to recoup the bribes they paid to stay in office, and there was universal hatred of the Sultan as a 'Sardanapalus, brought up in the seraglio among buffoons, dwarfs, and mutes'. The rot had started, he observed, under Selim II (r. 1566–74), who was the first sultan to think that 'the true happiness of a king or an emperor consists not in military tasks and actions of valour and glory, but in inaction ["ozio"] and rest'—a comment which shows how far Machiavellian assumptions had entered even the minds of peace-loving Venetians. Repeating Cavalli's analysis of 32 years earlier (in a notable display of intertextuality), he concluded that three things might bring the Ottoman Empire to an end: internal division; the loss of the Sultan's reputation, thanks to avarice, luxury, and other forms of corruption; and defeat by an external power.[19]

There was thus quite a wide range of factors to choose from. Moral corruption, venality, and the decay of traditional institutions were things complained about by Ottoman writers too, especially during the half-century from 1580 to 1630; Western observers in Istanbul who had dealings with local people may have picked up some of their ideas from the Ottomans themselves.[20] Of the threats to the Empire considered by the Venetians, division in the form of an outright civil war between claimants to the throne—of the sort that had convulsed it in the early years of the fifteenth century—was perhaps the least likely; but division caused by revolt from below would have seemed a serious possibility when the so-called Celali rebellions took over parts of Anatolia in the period 1596–1610.[21] One other possible threat, not highlighted by the Venetian writers, had already been mentioned in the Western literature: as early as 1550 Jacques Gassot had written that when a sultan died, his successor was chosen, in effect, by 'the favour of the Janissaries'. Nicolay's book had given a more detailed account of the outrageous behaviour of the Janissary corps on the death of their ruler: they would pillage the Christian and Jewish merchants who lived in

19. Albèri, ed., *Relazioni*, ser. 3, ii, pp. 372 (resentment), 373 ('Sardanapalo allevato nelli serragli fra buffoni, nani e muti'), 374 ('la vera felicità di un re e di un imperatore non consista nelle fatiche militari e nelle operazioni di valore e gloria, ma nell'ozio e quiete'), 377–8 (three things).
20. On the Ottoman 'decline' literature see Howard, 'Ottoman Historiography'; Sariyannis, 'Ottoman Critics'.
21. See Griswold, *Great Anatolian Rebellion*; White, *Climate of Rebellion*.

Istanbul, Edirne, Salonica, and elsewhere, and then swear loyalty to the new sultan only on condition that he pardoned these crimes and allowed them to keep their loot. This, Nicolay commented, was 'the real exemplary sign of the coming ruin of this great eastern Empire', as it matched so closely the behaviour of the Praetorian legions of ancient Rome, who acquired a taste for 'ruling over their masters'.[22] (Very likely, Machiavelli's observation on the need of the Ottoman sultans to please their soldiers more than their people was not far from his mind.) Nicolay's argument was picked up by René de Lucinge when he came to write the chapter in his treatise (book 3, chapter 12) on the internal causes that might undermine the Ottoman Empire. First, he suggested, the death of a sultan without heirs could prompt large-scale conflict between rival pashas. Secondly, if the soldiers found that 'they were dealing with a ruler devoted to leisure and luxury', or whom they thought to be cowardly and unmartial, 'they would turn their weapons against him.' The third cause would be rivalry between a sultan's sons after his death; the fourth, 'the daring and rash conduct of the Janissaries, who might undertake and carry out what was done in the past by the Praetorian troops of the Romans'; and the fifth, 'the ambition or despair of the country's grandees, or of the government ministers'.[23]

So when Johannes Leunclavius came to list his 27 factors 'contra Turcos', he had plenty of material. The list is nevertheless a somewhat rambling and repetitive one, of uneven quality, consisting partly of standard criticisms, and attesting mainly to his desire to animate his dedicatees (the Electors) to go to war. He begins with religion: Islam is divided into sects; Christians outnumber Muslims in the Ottoman Empire; some Muslims believe that Islam will end after 1,000 years (an anniversary that was just approaching); and Muhammad himself, on his deathbed, promised that it would. Then come the general political points: the viziers have declined in virtue; the recent increase in their number will cause instability; Janissaries and spahis have contempt for them; there are factions among the viziers; the Sultan is weak-minded; and he is in thrall to women as well as men. And then an assortment of generalities: the Ottomans are 'Machiavelliani', who violate promises and

22. Gassot, *Le Discours du voyage*, fo. 21r ('la faueur des Gennissaires'); Nicolay, *Dans l'empire*, pp. 157 ('présage exemplaire de la prochaine ruine de ce grand Empire oriental'), 158 ('seigneurier leur maître').
23. Lucinge, *De la naissance*, pp. 245 (death), 246 ('avoyent affaire à un prince adonné à l'oysiveté, à la luxure', 'ils tourneroient leurs armes contre luy'), 248 (rivalry), 249 ('l'audace et temerité des Janissaires, lesquels pourroient entreprendre et executer ce que firent autrefois les bandes pretoriennes des Romains'), 250 ('l'ambition ou desespoir des grands du pays, ou des ministres').

treaties; the asylum they give to foreigners is deceptive; they lack modesty and chastity; they are cruel; their 'majesty' is just a cover for savagery; 'they regard both their subjects, and their clients or vassals, and their allies, as slaves, hardly distinguishing between them'; they are perfidious towards their allies; and contemptuous towards God; all their officials are greedy and venal; the sultan receives no proper advice, because 'among them there is no freedom to express one's opinions'; they are complacent about their own power; over-bold; and immensely greedy; they impose heavy taxes and dues; so in response there is widespread hatred of the Sultan; and of his officials; and there are many reasons for hatred.[24]

Reading this sort of critical analysis, and similar (though less elaborate) accounts written during the following few decades, one is struck by how quickly opinion was veering away from the pure concept of despotism so recently developed by Lucinge and Botero. What Lucinge had cleverly constructed was a theory which absorbed the essential features of the new paradigm: the subjects, though filled with fear when confronted by their ruler's extreme power, could at the same time show a sheep-like contentment with their lot, as they benefited from the order, justice, and relative prosperity which the sultan deceptively bestowed upon them. Lucinge's short list of factors that might break up the Empire consisted either of cases where the Sultan died without a clear heir, or of high-level conflicts generated by his ministers, or of cases involving hostile actions by soldiers. (The first of those scenarios, however, would surely be aimed not at overthrowing the Empire but rather at replacing an unmartial despot with a martial one; only the Praetorian scenario, by its corrosive effects on the other institutions and practices of the Empire, might undermine Ottoman power altogether in the long run.) Otherwise, his account suggested that the system, though oppressive and evil, worked very effectively. No sooner had this theoretical construction been assembled, however, than it began to seem unconvincing as a matter of fact. It is true that elements of the new paradigm lingered on for quite some time; the popular French historical writer Michel Baudier, for example, who was 'royal historiographer' under Louis XIII, devoted part of his *Histoire generale de la religion des Turcs* (1625) to a glowing account of Ottoman alms-giving and public philanthropy, concluding that 'a monarchy

---

24. Leunclavius, *Historiae musulmanae*, pp. 6–10 (pp. 8: 'Machiavelliani'; 9: '& subditos suos, & clientes siue vasallos...& foederatos, nullo prope discrimine, pro mancipiis habeant', 'maiestas'; 10: 'Libertas apud ipsos, sententiis dicendis, nulla').

can hardly fail to flourish, when each person cares more about the public good than about the private.'[25] But increasingly the Western descriptive literature of the late sixteenth and early seventeenth centuries was turning away from the positive aspects of civic life and looking instead at structural problems, or problems with potentially structural effects: moral corruption at the top of the system; venality (caused by such corruption) leading to financial oppression, as officials tried to recoup their bribes; oppression causing the general population to live not just in fear but in precarious poverty, and to hate the regime; the regime therefore becoming even more dependent on its control of armed force; and the soldiers then exploiting this dependence in a politically and socially harmful way. Against such a background, conflict caused by a power struggle among pashas and grandees—rather an off-chance in Lucinge's account—would become a more credible scenario.

Many writers concentrated on the apparent erosion of the Ottoman military ethos. George Sandys, in his frequently reprinted travelogue, *A Relation of a Journey begun An: Dom: 1610* (1615), observed that the standards of the Janissaries, who served the Sultan like 'the *Pretorian* cohorts with the *Romans*', were much decayed; many of them were married, and they had begun to admit 'naturall Turkes', i.e. boys born to Muslim families, not Christian ones. The sultans were nowadays 'vnwarlicke', and the soldiers generally were 'corrupted with ease and liberty, drowned in prohibited wine, enfeebled with the continuall conuerse of women, and generally lapsed from their former austerity of life.'[26] But Sandys was just a traveller, picking up points made to him by Westerners who had spent longer *in situ* (as well as repeating points already made by other writers). One of the most penetrating critical accounts of conditions within the Ottoman Empire was written by François Savary de Brèves, who had spent roughly 20 years in Istanbul, fourteen of them (1591–1605) as French Ambassador. In a short 'Discours' published between 1614 and 1620, he urged the Christian powers to attack the Ottoman Empire and gave his reasons for thinking that it could easily be overcome. The soldiers were less valiant than they used to be, 'because of the venality which has crept in among them'. The whole court and structure of government had become venal too: 'everything is sold there

25. Baudier, *Histoire generale*, pp. 90–126 (p. 126: 'il est presque impossible qu'une Monarchie ne soit florissante, en laquelle vn chascun a plus de soin du bien public, que du particulier'). On Baudier, who never visited Ottoman territory but published three books on the Ottoman Empire and Islam, derived from textual sources, see Uomini, *Cultures historiques*, pp. 191–225.
26. Sandys, *Relation*, pp. 49–50.

and given to the highest bidder, even the most menial and petty positions. Bear in mind that those who get these posts hold them for only one or two years, and, having paid a high price for them, they commit intolerable extortions on the people.' The best timar estates were so valuable that everyone at court lobbied to obtain them ('the pashas, the eunuchs, the mutes, the dwarfs, and even the women'); the result was that they no longer had resident timariots to govern the local people, and they raised fewer soldiers in wartime. And the Janissary system had also been corrupted, with Muslims paying to get their own children into the *devşirme* in the hope that they would rise to high office. As adult Janissaries, these native Muslims would revisit their families in the provinces and hear their complaints about the 'tyrannical oppression' which they received; they would then return to Istanbul, determined to avenge their parents, and would demand the execution of senior pashas—something that did not happen in the old days, as the ex-Christian Janissaries were taught to hate their families, and to be ultra-loyal to the Sultan. This constituted 'a definite sign of the decline of this monarchy'.[27] Such an opinion about the decline of the Janissary system was shared by seventeenth-century Ottomans too. In 1675 a retired Janissary officer, Seyyid Ali, son of Mehmed Efendi, would write a treatise on this subject, confirming Savary de Brèves's remarks about Muslims bribing the recruitment sergeants to take their sons, and about the alienation of ex-Christian Janissaries from their original communities; 'the discipline which was so necessary [in the recruitment process] has been abolished, and that is the reason why the Sultan is badly served, and the state perishes.'[28]

Savary de Brèves's analysis was echoed by the young Louis Deshayes, who travelled with his father, the baron de Courmenin, on a mission to the Holy Land in 1621. He did praise some aspects of the Ottoman system (public philanthropy, meritocracy, well-ordered army), even commenting at one point that 'there is no monarchy with better order, or where things are

27. Savary de Brèves, 'Discours abregé des asseurez moyens d'aneantir & ruiner la Monarchie des Princes Ottomans', in his *Relation*, separate pagination, pp. 16 ('à cause de la venalité qui s'est glissée parmy eux', 'tout y est vendu & donné au plus offrant, voire mesmes iusques aux offices les plus vils & petits. Il faut considerer que ceux qui en sont pourueus ne les possedent qu'vn ou deux ans, & les ayant cherement acheptez, ils font des concussions insupportables sur le peuple'), 18 (timars, 'les Bassas, les Eunuques, les muets, les nains, & mesmes les femmes'), 24 (Muslim parents), 25 ('l'oppression tyrannique'), 26 ('vne marque asseurée de la decadence de cette Monarchie'). The 'Discours' was first printed without place or date of publication; the Bibliothèque nationale de France catalogue assigns it to 1614–20.
28. Bibliothèque Inguimbertine, Carpentras, MS 268, Seyyid Ali, 'Traité de l'Institution des Regles et Disciplines des Janissaires', tr. J.-B. de Fiennes, pp. 15 (alienation), 17 ('cette discipline si necessaire est abolie et c'est ce qui est cause que le Prince est mal serui et que l'Etat périt'), 28 (bribery).

better regulated than among them'—though it seems likely that his knowledge of these positive aspects came mainly from the standard sixteenth-
century literature. Nevertheless, he observed, 'this state has not been free of
the corruption which creeps into the best-maintained monarchies.' He then
repeated all the points Savary de Brèves had made about corrupt officials
practising extortion, the sale of timars at court, and the ill-effect of recruit-
ing Muslims in the *devşirme*, and concluded: 'the Sultan, who was previously
the most absolute of all rulers on earth, depends nowadays entirely on his
army, which deprives him of his rule and puts him to death as it wills.' The
best that could happen for this state was therefore that in future 'he who
gives the greatest amount to the army will be Sultan.' But the imperial
income was simply insufficient, as the soldiers' pay was too high; so 'necessarily, a different kind of government must follow this one.'[29]

When Deshayes wrote those words in 1624, recent events had lent
strength to such negative views. After the death of Ahmed I in 1617, palace
factions had secured the succession of his younger brother Mustafa instead
of his eldest son, Osman. (The practice of fratricide had been suspended
when Ahmed came to the throne in 1603, with brothers being secluded in
the palace instead; the reason for this was that the elimination by Ahmed's
father, Mehmed III, of nineteen brothers on his own succession had led to
fears that the entire dynasty might become extinct.) In 1618 other factions
deposed Mustafa and put the young Osman in his place; but the latter
became unpopular after the failure of his campaign against Poland in 1620–1.
His apparent wish to reform or even replace the Janissary corps provoked an
uprising by the Janissaries in 1622, when first they demanded the execution of
several leading ministers, and then they deposed and murdered the Sultan
himself. (Hence Deshayes's comment about the army putting the sultan to
death as it wills.) Mustafa returned to the throne, but his ineffectual rule, at
a time of large-scale revolt in Anatolia, led to his deposition—again, at the
insistence of the Janissaries, and of a new Grand Vizier appointed at their
request—less than sixteen months later.[30]

29. [Deshayes,] *Voiage*, pp. 235 (philanthropy), 251 ('il n'y a point de Monarchie où il y ayt vn plus
    grand ordre, ny où toutes choses soie[n]t mieux reglées que parmy eux'), 251–3 (meritocracy),
    266 ('cét Estat n'a pas esté exempt de la corruption qui se glisse dans les Monarchies les mieux
    policées'), 270 ('le *Grand Seigneur*, qui estoit autrefois le plus absolu de tous les Princes de la
    terre, dépend auiourd'huy entierement de sa milice, qui luy oste l'Empire, & le fait mourir
    selon sa volonté', 'celuy qui donnera le plus à la milice sera Empereur', 'il faudra par necessité
    qu'il s'ensuiue vn autre sorte de gouuernement').
30. See Shaw, *History*, pp. 190–4; Vatin and Veinstein, *Le Sérail ébranlé*, pp. 218–43; Piterberg, *Ottoman
    Tragedy*, pp. 10–28; Tezcan, *Second Ottoman Empire*, pp. 108–75.

Events such as these attracted much attention in the West. In England three separate news pamphlets were devoted to the murder of Osman. One of them was a substantial narrative by the English Ambassador in Istanbul, Sir Thomas Roe; his verdict on Osman was that 'he had one vice that resisted all hope of prosperity, which was extreme auarice, and he fell into the latter times and decrepit age, *vbi vires luxu corrumpebantur, contra veterem disciplinam*'—'where the armed forces were corrupted by luxury, in contravention of the old discipline', one of several quotations from Tacitus with which Roe larded his account.[31] In the small Dutch city of Gorinchem, a play about the death of Osman was printed in the following year, 1623.[32] But West Europeans had other, more pressing issues to think about, as the war which began in Bohemia in 1618 gradually spread into other parts of the Holy Roman Empire, drawing in several external powers and lasting until 1648. The Ottoman Empire recovered some of its strength under its new Sultan, Murad IV (1623–40); its main strategic interests at this time lay in its conflict with Persia over Mesopotamia, which is the essential reason why its interaction with Western Europe's Thirty Years' War was very slight. The only Ottoman attacks on Christian powers in this period were a campaign against Poland in 1633 and the invasion of Crete in 1645 (initiating a long-drawn-out struggle against Venice that would end in Ottoman victory only in 1669). A major anti-Habsburg campaign in 1663–4 was halted at the Battle of St Gotthard and quickly abandoned, though on terms quite favourable to the Ottomans; thereafter the Habsburgs would wait for eighteen years before the next significant conflict.[33] So it was not until after the breaking of the Siege of Vienna in 1683 that any large-scale land war against the Ottoman Empire could involve the invasion of that Empire's territory, and thereby begin to test on the ground the claims, made by so many Western writers, that it was a corrupted, unstable, and generally declining power.[34]

Throughout the century, those claims had continued to be made. Three examples may suffice here. In 1625 Giovanni Battista Montalbani, who had

---

31. Anon., *A True Relation*; Anon., *The Strangling*; Roe, *A True and Faithfull Relation*, sigs. B4v–C1r (citing Tacitus, *Historiae* II.69, on the brief reign of Vitellius).

32. Brouwer, ed., *Sultan Osman*. The playwright was a local notary, Abraham Kemp.

33. For a summary account of all these events see Shaw, *History*, pp. 194–215.

34. I must leave aside here the question of whether or to what extent the Empire was really in 'decline'—something assumed by Shaw, but contested by more recent Ottoman historians. For a balanced revisionist account, in which the Empire is seen as modernizing rather than simply declining, see Tezcan, *Second Ottoman Empire*.

served in the Moldavian army during the rebellion of the Voivod of Moldavia against the Ottomans in 1620, published an account of the Ottoman Empire, *De moribus Turcarum commentarius*. It was reprinted five years later in *Turcici imperii status*, the Ottoman volume in the popular Elzevir series of so-called 'republics' (geographico-political descriptions of countries, printed in a pocket-sized duodecimo format), which enjoyed a broad European readership.[35] From the outset, Montalbani structured his work on a comparison between the present state and prospects of the Ottoman Empire, and the history of the decline of the Roman Empire. When he contemplated the Ottoman realm and government, Montalbani wrote,

> I seemed to see those things which are related by writers about the Roman Empire: everything entrusted to the will of one man; huge military forces; savage peace; blood-thirsty wars; unbearable extortions against the subjects; and almost the same raging vices as those which, if you merely change the name, caused that empire to grow in this huge expanse of territory, and which, if similar circumstances apply, indicate that it may collapse, and for the same reason. The Sultan is judge and lord over all things, enjoying ease that matches his power; it is difficult to catch sight of him; he leaves his palace seldom, and in great state; hence his vices remain hidden, and the reverence felt for him, from a distance, is all the greater, and there is private terror at the thought of the sudden execution of his decrees.[36]

In 1666 Paul Rycaut, who had gone to Istanbul in 1660 to serve as private secretary to the English Ambassador and had acquired a good knowledge of Turkish, published what would become an influential book, *The Present State of the Ottoman Empire*. His underlying thesis was that the whole structure of the Ottoman Empire rested on a military basis, and that its expansionary success had arisen from this, in the period when the military foundations were well maintained. But now, as he explained, the army had become 'degenerate, soft, and effeminate'; the Janissaries were marrying; the timar system was in decline (not because of the accumulation of estates by

---

35. Further printings were in Rome (1636) and Leiden (1634, 1643, 1654). On Montalbani, who later worked as an unofficial Spanish diplomatic agent in Istanbul, see Pippidi, *Visions*, pp. 185, 248 (n. 105).

36. Montalbani, *De moribus*, pp. 3–4 ('Videre videbar ea, quae de Romanorum Imperio Scriptores prodidere, cuncta scilicet vnius arbitrio permissa, vires immensas…pacem saeuam, cruentia bella, intolerandas in subditos extorsiones, atq[ue] eadem penitùs debacchantia vitia, quibus diuerto tantùm nomine non minùs in hanc vastitatem excreuisse Imperium istud, quàm (si congrua adsint) eodem & casu ruere posse demonstrent. Omnium vnus arbiter, & dominus est Imperator potestati par otium habens, visu difficilis, egressuq[ue] iuxta rarus, & grauis, vndè vitiorum latebrae, ac maior tanquam ex longinquo reuerentia, & ob praecipites mandatorum executiones arcanus terror').

court favourites, but thanks to the creeping in of a hereditary principle); and the problem of Janissary revolts had led to a deliberate policy 'to diminish the strength of this Militia by the destruction of the veterane Souldiers, and ruine of their reputation'. Conjuring up—by means of a negative statement—an earlier golden age of Ottoman statehood, he wrote: 'In brief there are no reliques of ancient justice, or generosity, or discreet Government, or Obedience to it, of Courtesie or Concord, of Valour or Counsel'.[37]

Finally, in 1682, just before the outbreak of the 'Great' war, the French Capuchin Michel Febvre (who had spent eighteen years in Ottoman territory, and was fluent in Turkish, Kurdish, Armenian, and Arabic) published an account which emphasized internal corruption and military weakness, and ended by calling for the Christian conquest of the entire Empire. His concluding list of the ten causes of Ottoman strength was given not in order to account for success and expansion, but merely to explain why, despite its many failings, the Empire still somehow managed to survive: lack of unity among Christian powers; severity of punishments; frequent changes of pashas; impoverishment of the people; new conquests; attacking only one enemy at a time; promise-breaking; population growth, thanks primarily to slavery; the absoluteness of the Sultan's power; and the fact that the sultans ruined any existing nobility and advanced only those whose ruin could be accomplished without risk.[38] As he had explained in his preface to the reader, he had resolved to write this book because of 'the desire I felt to communicate— for the good of Christianity—the truth about the powerlessness and feebleness of the Sultan, by showing the ruinous state and disorders of his empire, so that the peoples of Europe, being better informed about it, should lose the grand idea of him which they have had until now, and should rouse their spirits to conquer his territory—something much easier than may be imagined, so long as the Christian rulers are united'.[39]

37. Rycaut, *Present State*, pp. 170 ('degenerate...', 'In brief...'), 171 (marrying), 182 (timars), 199 ('to diminish...'). The 1st edn., of 1666, was almost entirely destroyed by the Fire of London; I quote from the 1668 edn. On Rycaut see Anderson, *English Consul*.

38. Febvre, *Theatre*, pp. 550–3. Cf. also the account of Ottoman corruption and military weakness in his earlier *Specchio*, pp. 80–97. There is some uncertainty about 'Febvre's' identity (or identities); the earlier work names him as Justinien de Neuvy-sur-Loire (title page, and sigs. A4v–A5r), but other sources ascribe the later work to Jean-Baptiste de Saint-Aignan (see Bibliothèque des Capucins, Paris, MS 49, p. 35, and Clemente da Terzorio, 'Il vero autore').

39. Febvre, *Theatre*, sig. A4v ('le desir que j'avois de faire connoistre (pour le bien du Christianisme) la verité touchant l'impuissance & la foiblesse du Turc, en faisant voir la ruine & les desordres de son Empire, afin que les peuples d'Europe en estant mieux informez, perdent cette grande idée qu'ils ont eu de luy jusqu'à present, & s'animent à la conqueste de son païs plus facile qu'on ne se la peut imaginer, supposée l'union des Princes Chrestiens').

ELEVEN

Justifications of warfare, and plans for war and peace

From the late sixteenth century to the late seventeenth, Western writers continued to advocate offensive war against the Ottoman Empire. Some—typically, legal and political theorists, or at least those with legal training—did pause to consider what sort of principle would justify an attack on that state, though many simply took both the desirability and the rightness of such a project for granted. It has long been commonplace to say that, where the theory was concerned, this period saw a steady shift from religious to secular justifications; but on the one hand the basic change had already happened, and on the other hand some 'secular' theorists continued to attribute, to a certain extent, a special importance to religion.

The essential shift had occurred in the mid-thirteenth century, when Innocent IV had established that no infidel rulers could justifiably be attacked simply because they were infidels.[1] In the sixteenth century, neo-scholastic writers such as the Spanish theologian and jurist Francisco de Vitoria and his pupil Diego de Covarrubias had reaffirmed and elaborated that basic position. In his *Relectio de Indis*, a set of lectures given in Salamanca in 1539 and printed in Lyon in 1557, Vitoria argued that war against non-Christian rulers could not be justified by the mere fact that they adhered to a false religion: 'being an infidel does not prevent anyone from exercising valid rule.'[2] However, if those rulers—he was writing about native rulers in the New World, though his argument was a general one—prevented the Spanish from exercising basic rights under both natural law and the law of nations, such as the right to trade with them or to travel peacefully through

1. See above, p. 9.
2. Vitoria, *Relectio*, p. 20 ('Infidelitas non est impedimentum quominus aliquis sit verus dominus'); cf. Covarrubias, *Opera*, i, fo. 243r, arguing that there can be no just war against infidels as such.

their territory, that would be a *casus belli*. The same applied (also as an application of natural law) if they refused to allow the Spanish to preach the Gospel to them, though Vitoria was insistent that a refusal to convert to Christianity did not qualify: 'if the barbarians permit the Christians to preach the Gospel, freely and without any obstacles, whether they accept the faith or even if they do not, it is not licit to declare war on them for that reason or otherwise to occupy their territory.'[3] The other major category of legitimate reasons for warfare involved gross breaches of natural law committed by the infidel government against its own people:'tyranny' or 'tyrannical laws', inflicting such enormities as human sacrifice or cannibalism. In these cases 'the rulers of Spain can forbid the barbarians to follow all such wicked customs and rites, since they can protect the innocent from unjust death.'[4] This category of wicked practice was not closely defined, but the impression was given that only the deliberate taking of human life for evil purposes would begin to qualify.

With few exceptions, the legal and political theorists of the late sixteenth and seventeenth centuries followed this fundamental pattern of argument. Neither the mere fact that another state followed a different religion nor the positive desire to convert its people to Christianity would justify going to war against it; some more secular reason was needed. But there was room for disagreement, both about the precise nature of the secular justification and about the way in which religion could still play a supplementary role in the story.

The most influential discussion of these issues in the late sixteenth century was the treatise *De iure belli* (1598) by the Protestant Italian jurist, Professor of Civil Law at Oxford, and enthusiast for anti-Ottoman warfare, Alberico Gentili. (Its treatment of the question of alliances with infidel powers has already been discussed, above.[5]) On most of the underlying issues he adhered to mainstream positions. So, for example, in an early study of the law of embassies he argued that there was nothing inherently invalid about government by infidels, and that it was therefore right to exchange ambassadors

3. Vitoria, *Relectio*, pp. 80–1 (commerce), 89 ('Si barbari permittant christianos libere et sine impedimento praedicare Evangelium, sive illi recipiant fidem sive non, non licet hac ratione intentare illis bellum nec alias occupare terras illorum').
4. Ibid., p. 93 ('tyrannidem', 'leges tyrannicas', 'possunt hispani principes prohibere barbaros ab omni nefaria consuetudine et ritu, quia possunt defendere innocentes a morte iniusta').
5. See above, pp. 125–30. What follows here is drawn partly from Malcolm, 'Alberico Gentili'. More generally, see the other essays in Kinsbury and Straumann, *Roman Foundations*, and the classic biographical monograph by Panizza, *Alberico Gentili*.

with Muslim rulers; religious difference, in itself, did not justify war.[6] The
clarity with which he distinguished between offences against God (such as
idolatry) and offences against fellow human beings has led to his being
hailed as a 'secularizing' thinker. In his discussion of 'virtuous' reasons for
going to war against another state, he did include wars aimed at putting a
stop to gross breaches of the laws of nature, 'for these are sins against the
nature of the human race'; here he referred specifically to Vitoria.[7] However,
although Gentili was fiercely hostile to the Ottoman Empire, and although
he did criticize the behaviour of the Turks as belligerents, he did not argue
that the Ottomans' treatment of their own subjects was so contrary to
natural law as to warrant an attack on them by external powers. Far from it;
at one point in *De legationibus* he ridiculed those who denounced the Sultan
as a tyrant and an unjust ruler.[8]

Gentili's main justification for offensive war against the Ottomans was
that it was necessary for the sake of pre-emptive self-defence. This, in his
argument, was merely an application of the general principle of self-defence,
which was a basic rule of justice. But here a significant difference did open
up between him and the theological mainstream. For although self-defence
had become, especially in the hands of writers such as Vitoria, an essential
element of natural law theories about the justification of war, the theologians
remained much more cautious about the conditions under which preventive action might be justified: they required the war-wager to have firm evidence that an injury was planned and impending. Gentili did not ignore this
problem; early on in his chapter on pre-emptive defence he agreed that 'a
just cause of fear is required; suspicion is not enough', and thereafter he
wrestled with the difficulty of forming any general rule that would distinguish between a just fear and an unjust one. At the end of the chapter he
admitted that the criteria were still rather obscure, and that the mere power
of a foreign state, or the fact that its territories had grown larger, would not
necessarily count as just causes of going to war against it.[9]

6. A. Gentili, *De legationibus* II.11, pp. 98–9.
7. A. Gentili, *De iure belli* I.25, p. 198 ('Sunt enim haec peccata contra naturam humani generis').
8. A. Gentili, *De legationibus* II.7, p. 82. The likely influence on him here was Bodin.
9. A. Gentili, *De iure belli* I.14, pp. 99 ('Iusta caussa metus requiritur: suspicio non est satis'), 106–7.
    On the distinctiveness of Gentili's theory see Piirimäe, 'Alberico Gentili's Doctrine'. However,
    while it was unusual among jurists, it was in tune with the writings of some reason of state
    theorists, including Botero, who argued that a pre-emptive defensive war was permanently
    justified: *Della ragion*, p. 311 ('he who wants to fight a war cannot excuse his failure to do so by
    saying that there is no public enemy... it is an enemy who aims permanently at the oppression
    of Christianity... we have the Sultan at our gates and on our flanks' ('chi vuol guerreggiare non

Nevertheless, for all these lingering uncertainties, this was the fundamental argument on which Gentili based his call to arms against the Ottoman Empire. That the English state was threatened in any direct way by Ottoman expansion would have been hard to maintain, though; and so he added an observation which in some ways weakened his case, while attempting to render it more general: 'It is indeed true that the Sultan does not cause injury to many states, and neither does the King of Spain; nor is either of them capable of doing so. But they do to some; and he who causes injury to one, threatens to do so to more.'[10] In an earlier chapter (I.12), Gentili had offered a much stronger version of the pre-emptive argument. Rejecting the idea that war against the Ottomans was either a war for the sake of religion or a war dictated by 'nature', he had written: 'But there is war with the Ottomans—because they act as our enemies, and lie in wait for us, and threaten us, and always seize our possessions by means of every form of perfidy of which they are capable. Thus there is always a just cause of war against the Ottomans.' No, he admitted, they should not be attacked when they were quiescent, promoting peace, and 'making no preparations against us'. But, exclaimed Gentili, when do the Ottomans behave like that?— adding the phrase for which he has become most famous, 'Silete theologi in munere alieno' ('Theologians, be silent in other people's affairs'—or, more colloquially, 'Theologians, mind your own business').[11] This famous remark, sometimes adduced by modern writers as evidence of a decisive move towards making international law or politics autonomous vis-à-vis theology, was thus uttered specifically in connection with his argument about pre-emptive war: the theologians whose advice he rejected were those whose criteria for justified pre-emption were much stricter than Gentili's, and who thought that any non-belligerent state that was not actually and ascertainably preparing an attack must be treated as if it were peaceful. In this context, the phrase does not really bear all the significance that later interpreters of Gentili have tried to give it; 'in munere alieno' here does not mean the whole business of political theory or just war theory, but refers rather to the

si può scusare di non aver nemico publico...e un nimico tale, che non pensa mai d'altro che dell'oppressione della Christianità...Noi abbiamo il Turco alla porta, l'abbiamo a i fianchi')).

10. A. Gentili, *De iure belli* I.14, p. 103 ('Non quidem facit multis Turca iniuriam, & nec Hispanus: neque id ille potest, aut iste: sed quibusdam facit. atque vni qui faciat, is plurimis minitatur').

11. Ibid. I.12, p. 92 ('Sed est cum Turcis bellum: quia illi ferunt se nobis hostes, & nobis insidiantur, nobis imminent, nostra rapiunt per omnem perfidiam, quum possunt, semper. Sic iusta semper caussa belli aduersus Turcas...non inferendum bellum quiescentibus, pacem colentibus, in nos nihil molientibus: non. Sed quando sic agunt Turcae? Silete theologi in munere alieno').

sort of political knowledge—about the true nature of Ottoman behaviour and Ottoman policy—which, once properly taken into account, would show up the inadequacy of one particular set of claims that the theologians made.

The difference between this sweeping declaration in *De iure belli* I.12 and the more modest argument in I.14 that if the Ottomans injured one state they might do it to others raises, however, a different point, which may situate Gentili somewhere a little closer to a 'theological' position. In that more modest argument, Gentili considered the Ottomans merely from the point of view of England, a distant and rather obviously unthreatened state. But in I.12, when he discussed something resembling a natural enmity between 'us' and the Ottomans, the point of view he adopted was that of Christendom; in the only previous passage mentioning the 'Turks' in that chapter, he had discussed the treatment of a 'Turk' who entered 'our' territory, and a Christian who entered theirs.[12] It seems that the categories of 'Christian' and 'infidel' (or, in this case, 'Turk', which was also used to mean 'Muslim') still had some significance for Gentili's political and legal theory—as his treatment of the question of alliances with infidels has already suggested. So, whilst the underlying structure of his argument was secular, concerned with pre-emptive defence, it did acquire a kind of theological tincture, as he related the idea of self-defence to a 'self' constituted by the shared Christianity of the West European states.

Francis Bacon followed in Gentili's footsteps, while strengthening a little the religious colouring of the argument. In a memorandum of 1624 urging warfare against Spain, he divided legitimate pre-emptive war into two categories, secular and religious: 'I shall make it plain that wars preventive upon just fears are true defensives...and again, that wars defensive for religion...are most just; though offensive wars for religion are seldom to be approved.' His comments on secular pre-emptive war followed Gentili's line particularly closely: 'in deliberations of war against the Turk...Christian princes and states have always a sufficient ground of invasive war against the enemy; not for cause of religion, but upon a just fear; forasmuch as it is a fundamental law in the Turkish empire that they may (without any other provocation) make war upon Christendom for the propagation of their law.'[13] As for pre-emptive warfare in defence of religion: here Bacon had

---

12. Ibid. I.12, p. 90 ('si qui Turca ad nos peruenisset...& contra, si Christianus ad illos peruenisset').

13. Bacon, 'Considerations', pp. 470 ('I shall...'), 475 ('in deliberations...'). On Bacon's moderating of Gentili's argument see Piirimäe, 'Alberico Gentili's Doctrine', pp. 199–200.

some difficulty in devising a specifically religious argument, resorting first to sheer assertion ('no man will doubt that a defensive war against a foreigner for religion is lawful'), and then to a comparison which seemed to put the religious case back within a secular template ('No man, I say, will doubt [that] if the Pope or King of Spain would demand of us to forsake our religion upon pain of a war, it were as unjust a demand as the Persians made to the Grecians of land and water'). But at least the impression was given that a war against a potential invader who had a hostile religious agenda—such as the Spanish, who 'would plant the Popes law by arms, as the Ottomans do the law of Mahomet'—was as justified as any normal pre-emptive war, only more so. Indeed, since Bacon's argument for a 'secular' pre-emptive war against the Ottomans rested on the idea that their perpetual hostility towards Christendom flowed from their own doctrine of holy war, which he understood to involve forcing Christians to become Muslims, the two arguments were hard to tell apart in practice. In this way a certain amount of religious content was installed within the framework of a primarily secular theory.[14]

In his influential work *De iure belli ac pacis libri tres* (1625), the Dutch theorist Hugo Grotius reacted against what he thought to be the excessively vague nature of Gentili's 'just fear' doctrine: 'some people have taught that it is justified under the law of nations to take up arms to curb a power which is growing, and which, if it becomes too great, could cause us harm; but this is not at all acceptable.'[15] Grotius's basic assumption was that a just war was a punitive action to redress a wrong—and that that wrong must be clearly ascertainable. A war of self-defence against unjustified aggression would obviously qualify as just, as would a defensive war undertaken when 'the crime [of aggression] was begun but not yet accomplished' (when, for instance, the enemy's army was known to be approaching, but had not

14. Bacon, 'Considerations', pp. 481 ('no man will...'), 482 ('No man, I...', 'would plant...'). Johnson, *Ideology*, pp. 85–94, argues that in effect there would be little difference between Bacon's pre-emptive defensive war for religion and a traditional Christian 'holy war'; nevertheless, the main emphasis was on a secular 'just fear' theory, with the religious case a subset of it. I leave aside Bacon's 'Advertisement touching an Holy War' (1622), an unfinished dialogue in which, as it stands, no speaker's view is definitely assignable to Bacon himself. The fullest statement is given by someone listed at the outset as 'a Romish Catholic Zelant' (pp. 28–36), who extends Vitoria's argument, saying that war is lawful against the Ottoman Empire because of its systematic violations of the laws of nature. (This is taken to be Bacon's view in Patrick, 'Hawk versus Dove'.)

15. Grotius, *De iure belli* II.i.17, vol. i, p. 224 ('Illud vero minime ferendum est, quod quidam tradiderunt, jure gentium arma recte sumi ad imminuendam potentiam crescentem, quae nimium aucta nocere posset').

yet arrived at the frontier). A breach of natural law by a foreign state that impinged directly on one's own state—such as denying peaceful transit through its territory, or denying commerce—would also be a relevant crime. And so, importantly, would certain breaches of natural law committed by a foreign state against its own subjects: 'sins which are serious, and which offend nature or human society'. Perhaps because he was following here the well-beaten path of Vitoria and others, Grotius did not enter into much detail about what would qualify as such sins. Briefly, he mentioned as examples ancient tyrants such as Busiris, Phalaris, and Diomedes of Thrace, who had committed 'manifest wrongs'. (Busiris, a mythical king of Egypt, had sacrificed visitors to his gods; Phalaris, tyrant of Sicily, was said to have practised cannibalism; the mythical Diomedes of Thrace had fed visitors to his man-eating horses.) Expanding slightly on this point, Grotius also commended certain Roman emperors who 'took up arms against the Persians, or threatened to do so, if they did not protect their Christian subjects from religious persecution'.[16]

Yet at the same time he warned against wars of liberation. The defence of freedom, 'whether of individuals or of states—that is, self-government—does not establish a right to go to war, as if freedom belonged to everyone, naturally and at all times'. Grotius was no less steeped in Roman law than Bodin, and therefore no less happy to accept the idea that slavery was a proper legal category; so 'those who have been reduced in a legitimate way to servitude, whether personal or civil, must accept their condition.'[17] On the other hand he rejected, like most early modern theorists, Aristotle's concept of natural slavery; even if it were factually correct to say that some people would benefit from being controlled and directed by others, he argued, that would not give others the right to impose themselves on them. Similarly, 'the Greeks were wrong to speak of the barbarians as if they were somehow their natural enemies, just because they had different customs, and perhaps also because they seemed less intelligent.'[18] Although Grotius

16. Ibid. II.i.16, vol. i, p. 224 ('delictum coeptum jam, sed non consummatum'), II.ii.13, vol. i, pp. 243–7 (transit, trade), II.xxii.10(2), vol. ii, p. 386 ('peccata gravia et naturam aut societatem humanam impugnantia'), II.xxv.8(2), vol. ii, p. 440 ('manifesta...injuria', 'Persas...arma coeperunt, aut capere minati sunt, nisi vim a Christianis religionis nomine arcerent').
17. Ibid. II.xxii.11, vol. ii, pp. 386–7 ('sive singulorum sive civitatum, id est, αὐτονομία, quasi naturaliter, et semper quibusvis competat, jus bello praestare potest', 'qui legitima causa in servitutem sive personalem sive civilem devenerunt, contenti sua conditione esse debent').
18. Ibid. II.xxii.10, vol. ii, p. 386 ('Male... Graeci Barbaros ob morum diversitatem, forte et quod ingenio cedere viderentur, hostes sibi quasi naturaliter dicebant'), II.xxii.12, vol. ii, p. 387 (against natural slavery). Grotius's argument against natural slavery thus went one step beyond

did not write directly about the legitimacy of an offensive war against the Ottoman Empire, therefore, it is clear that he was setting the bar quite high: gross outrages against the population, including religious persecution, would qualify, but general conditions of 'servitude' would not.

Perhaps the most purely secular theory about these matters propounded in the seventeenth century was that of Thomas Hobbes. In his late work *A Dialogue between a Philosopher and a Student, of the Common Laws of England* (written some time between 1669 and 1673) he gave 'Necessity' and 'Security' as the two basic justifications for going to war. The former covered not only self-defence, but also some special circumstances that might call for offensive warfare: the example he gave was that of the Children of Israel invading the land of the Canaanites, because of 'the right of nature, which they had to preserve their lives, being unable otherwise to subsist'. The latter was, in itself, as open-ended a principle as anything envisaged by Gentili: security was a solid justification for 'invading those whom they have just cause to fear'.[19] But 'just cause' had to rest on some factual basis. And even where it did properly exist, the benefit of strengthening 'security' had to be balanced against the risks and disbenefits of war itself. Since, in Hobbes's overall scheme, the ultimate aim was inherently defensive, the optimum strategy would be not belligerence but deterrence—by joining a strong alliance, for example. Throughout his writings, Hobbes argued against the idea that any prestige should attach to foreign victories and conquests as such. In *The Elements of Law* (1640) he criticized 'such commonwealths, or such monarchs, as affect war for itself, that is to say, out of ambition, or of vain-glory', and in *Leviathan* (1651) he included in his list of the 'diseases' of a state 'the insatiable appetite, or *Bulimia*, of enlarging Dominion; with the incurable *Wounds* thereby many times received from the enemy'.[20] So although Hobbes's theory might have justified a pre-emptive war against the Ottoman Empire by a power (such as the Holy Roman Empire, or Venice) that felt strategic-ally threatened by it, he would have advised a very cautious assessment of the likely balance of advantages and disadvantages; and much of the rhetoric of honour and glory that commonly accompanied calls for such warfare

the denial of it, on empirical grounds, by Suárez: 'hitherto, in my opinion, no such barbarous peoples have ever been found' (*Selections*, i, p. 482: 'hactenus... vt existimo, tam barbarae gentes inuentae non sunt').

19. Hobbes, *Writings on Common Law*, pp. 135–6.
20. Hobbes, *Elements* II.ix.9, p. 184; Hobbes, *Leviathan*, ch. 29, ii, p. 518. On Hobbes's theory see Malcolm, *Aspects*, pp. 432–56.

would have seemed to him not just empty, but positively pernicious. As for going to war for the sake of propagating Christianity, or recovering the Holy Places: such considerations were ruled out altogether.

Yet, in the century roughly corresponding to Hobbes's lifetime, from the 1580s to the 1680s, there were many people who regarded religion as providing a solid justification for war. Among Catholic writers on this topic the main concern was with Protestantism, and it is true that different principles applied to the treatment of heresy within Christendom, as opposed to infidelity outside it. But sometimes the arguments were generalized to the point of embracing non-Christians too. Cardinal William Allen, writing in 1584 (four years before the Spanish campaign to conquer England, of which he was an active supporter), declared that 'Ther is no warre in the world so iust and honorable be it ciuil or forraine, as that which is waged...for the true, ancient, Catholique, Romane religion.' He cited Deuteronomy 13, where 'expresse charge was giuen to slea al false Prophets, and who so euer should auert the people from the true worship of God', and followed this with a whole series of Old Testament examples of the killing of unbelievers. Then he supplied multiple examples of the use of force to protect Christians in the early centuries of Christianity.[21] He continued: 'Yea the quarel of Religion and defence of innocencie is so iust, that heathen Princes, not at al subiect to the Churches lawes and discipline, may in that case by the Christians armes be resisted, and might laufullie haue bene repressed in times of the Pagans and first great persecutions, when they vexed and oppressed the faithful.' Only then, restrained at last by the orthodox theological position, did he qualify his argument: 'but not otherwise (as most men thinke) if they would not annoy the Christians, nor violentlie hinder or seeke to extirpate the true faith and cours of the Gospel.'[22]

Some Catholic theologians who adhered to the standard Vitorian tradition did make room for directly religious justifications within the overall framework of the argument. Thus Francisco Suárez, having repeated Vitoria's general points about the non-coercion of infidels and the requirement (under the law of nations) that infidel states permit Christians to preach the

---

21. W. Allen, *True Defence*, pp. 103 ('There is...'), 104–5 (Old Testament; p. 104: 'expresse charge...'), 105–7 (early centuries).

22. Ibid., p. 107. He added: 'Though S. Thomas seemeth also to say, that anie heathen king may be laufullie depriued of his superioritie ouer Christians'; this was a misrepresentation of Thomas Aquinas's argument (in *Summa theologiae* IIa IIae, qu. 10, art. 10, p. 539), which said that it was forbidden for unbelievers to acquire dominion over believers, but that such dominion, when already existing, could not be taken away on the grounds of their unbelief.

Gospel, added the claim that if the infidels uttered blasphemies, whether in contempt of the Church or to insult the Christian religion, 'then from that moment there arises a right to wage a just war.'[23] This line of argument would make it easy to go to war against a Muslim power, since any straightforward statement of the Muslim view of Jesus—that he was a holy man, but only a man, not the Son of God—would necessarily count as blasphemous from a Christian point of view.

For those who were actively campaigning for a war against the Ottomans, there were more familiar arguments available, going back all the way to the Crusades. Several of the Catholic reason of state theorists were happy to adopt them. In an oration addressed to Pope Clement VIII, for example, Scipione Ammirato wrote that if Christendom was not moved to take military action against the Sultan by the thought of the threat he posed, or by any calculation of 'human interest', it should nevertheless be inspired by the desire 'to free Christ's sepulchre from the hands of the infidels'. An anonymous 'discourse' of 1585, later printed in the *Tesoro politico*, made a similar appeal, calling for a league of Christian princes to liberate the Holy Sepulchre.[24] And René de Lucinge pleaded with the rich princes of Europe to fund a war against the Sultan: 'all the money should be used for spreading the name of Jesus Christ, freeing the Holy Places, which are tyrannized by these barbarians... and avenging the insults and blasphemies which this tyrant and his people have committed against God's glory, His holy name, and His Church.'[25]

To present-day eyes, such language may seem to have been peculiarly rhetorical, quite unconnected with the real motives for early modern warfare. Yet there were real plans for crusades, or crusade-like enterprises, in the late sixteenth and early seventeenth centuries. From the moment the 'Long' Habsburg–Ottoman war began in 1593, Pope Clement VIII worked tirelessly, using crusading language, to persuade other Catholic powers to come

23. Suárez, *Selections*, i, pp. 476 (preaching Gospel), 482 ('tunc iam inde oritur titulus iusti belli'). Suárez was developing Aquinas's argument here; but whereas Aquinas had been concerned with blasphemy as a form of active oppression of Christian subjects by an infidel ruler (*Summa theologiae*, IIa IIae, qu. 10, art. 8, resp., p. 538), Suárez's formulation was significantly more open-ended.
24. Ammirato, *Orazioni*, p. 104 ('humano interesse', 'di liberare il sepolcro di Cristo dalle mano degli infedeli'); Ventura, ed., *Tesoro politico*, fo. 100v.
25. Lucinge, *De la naissance*, p. 234 ('C'est donc à l'amplification du nom de Jesus-Christ qu'il faut employer le total, et à la delivrance des lieux sacrez, que ces barbares tyrannisent... et faire vengeance des injures et blasphemes que ce tyran et les siens ont commis contre la gloire de Dieu, son sainct nom et son Eglise').

to the aid of the Austrian Habsburgs in what he hoped would be a grand campaign to defeat the Sultan and liberate all his Christian subjects.[26] In 1607, only a year after the end of that war, it was Henri IV, the ex-Protestant King of France, who instructed his Ambassador in Istanbul to travel to Rome in order to discuss plans for a new crusade.[27] His underlying motive may have been to divert the military power of Spain (his main strategic opponent) towards a new target; yet there were many people, in Rome and elsewhere, who saw such a crusading war as admirable and desirable in itself. One of these was Charles de Gonzague (Carlo Gonzaga), duc de Nevers, whose interest in the subject was piqued by the fact that he was descended, through his grandmother, from the Palaeologus dynasty of Byzantine emperors. In 1608–9 a delegation from the Mani peninsula in southern Greece came to see him, asking him to help organize a revolt against the Ottomans in the Peloponnese. That and subsequent plans proved abortive, but Nevers remained a zealot for anti-Ottoman warfare, and in later years he collaborated with another such enthusiast, Richelieu's 'éminence grise', the Capuchin friar known as Père Joseph (François Leclerc du Tremblay). The years 1616–18 saw a flurry of activity: Père Joseph visited Pope Paul V in Rome to discuss plans for a grand coalition to fight the Ottomans; Paul authorized him to promote the idea among a number of Christian rulers; both Père Joseph and the duc de Nevers spent time lobbying for it in Madrid; and the friar also wrote a long Latin poem, entitled *Turcias*, to encourage support for it.[28]

During these years they also founded a new order of chivalry, the 'Milice Chrétienne' or Christian Militia, to which they recruited rulers, princes, and aristocrats in France, Italy, Spain, the German lands, Hungary, and Poland. Its central aim was the recovery of the Holy Places. The two subsequent popes, Gregory XV and Urban VIII, were strongly pro-crusade, and in 1625 Urban formally consecrated the order. But by then France's relations with the Papacy had been severely strained by a military conflict in the Valtelline, and the Thirty Years' War was well under way, rendering all such grand anti-Ottoman plans completely unrealistic.[29] It is easy to agree

---

26. See Bartl, ' "Marciare verso Costantinopoli" '; Niederkorn, *Die europäischen Mächte*, pp. 70–102.

27. Vaumas, *L'Éveil missionnaire*, p. 89.

28. Djuvara, *Cent projets*, pp. 185–98; Dedouvres, *Le Père Joseph*, i, pp. 356–98; Papadopoulos, *Hē kinēsē*, pp. 26–53, 97–111, 141–7; on the poem see Braun, *Ancilla Calliopeae*, pp. 237–59.

29. See Göllner, 'La Milice Chrétienne'; Dedouvres, *Le Père Joseph*, i, pp. 417–26; Papadopoulos, *Hē kinēsē*, pp. 148–96; Humbert, 'Charles de Nevers et la Milice'. The Valtelline was a small region commanding a strategic route between Lombardy and Switzerland.

that the chances of schemes of this kind actually bringing about a major campaign would have been slim even in a time of intra-European peace. Yet this was not mere play-acting, and the idea of a pan-European aristocratic order was not drawn from the realms of sheer fantasy; the Knights of Malta, who continued to attack Ottoman shipping throughout this period, were an order of just that kind.

Nor was the notion of a crusade so far removed from the thinking of ordinary Europeans. A study of a collection of more than 50 French pamphlets on Ottoman and Persian affairs, mostly from the period 1600–30, has found that thirteen were on the subject of holy war against the Sultan, and that the idea of a crusade, 'always in accordance with medieval patterns of thought', was a secondary theme in the majority of the others.[30] There was some conscious revival of crusading ideas—or, at least, of the idea of a religious duty to fight for Christendom as a whole against the Ottomans— during the Cretan War in the middle part of the century, and again at the time of the Ottoman campaign against Habsburg territory in 1663–4. In 1670 one of the victors at the Battle of St Gotthard, the Habsburg field marshal Count Raimondo of Montecuccoli, wrote a memorandum urging the Emperor Leopold to embark on a new crusade to 'liberate Christ's Sepulchre'.[31] Sixteen years later, when the French soldier-turned-Levantine-consul-turned-priest Jean Coppin addressed his own appeal to the rulers of Christendom, he began by invoking the glorious memory of the First Crusade, and then commented: 'if I proposed a similar expedition, I do not doubt that people would regard my scheme as chimerical, and that the Devil, that enemy of the glory of Jesus Christ, would use all his tricks to make people think it unrealistic and impossible.' Yet he went on to offer primarily religious motives for an anti-Ottoman war (above all, the liberation of the Sultan's Christian subjects), while also suggesting that it might indeed accomplish the recovery of the Holy Land prophesied long ago by Isaiah.[32]

One of the strangest proposals for anti-Ottoman warfare in the latter part of the seventeenth century was composed by the philosopher Gottfried Wilhelm Leibniz in 1671–2. This text, known as his 'Consilium aegyptiacum'

30. Billacois, 'Le Turc' (p. 238: 'toujours...selon des schèmes médiévaux').
31. Aretin, 'Die Türkenkriege', pp. 22–3 (Cretan War, 1663–4 campaign); Wagner, *Das Türkenjahr*, p. 494 ('liberare il sepolcro di Cristo').
32. Coppin, *Le Bouclier*, pp. 3 ('Si je proposois une expedition semblable, je ne doute pas que l'on ne traitât mon proiet de chimerique, & que le démon ennemi de la gloire de Jesus-Christ n'employât tous ses artifices pour le faire regarder comme hors d'apparence & impossible'), 4 (Isaiah).

or 'Egyptian plan', was distinctive not only because of its proposed target, the Ottoman territory of Egypt, but also because of the heightened religious rhetoric on which so much of its argumentation depended. It was addressed to Louis XIV, who was thought to be planning a large-scale attack on the Netherlands; Leibniz's aim was to divert him from that by proposing a much more attractive conquest in a distant corner of the Mediterranean. (There was a risk that a Franco-Dutch war would spread to the northwestern territories of the Holy Roman Empire, or, at the least, cause serious disruption to trade; such consequences would affect the Elector of Mainz, for whom the 25-year-old philosopher had recently begun to work.) Leibniz began with surprising directness, informing Louis that the conquest of Egypt would give him real, not chimerical, power—not 'universal monarchy' (which was the chimerical variety) but the 'overall direction' of Europe—and that trying to conquer Christian European peoples was 'not only wicked, but foolish'. Whereas if he took Egypt, the Germans and Poles would then attack and vanquish the Sultan, and the 'better part' of the Ottoman Empire would be awarded to France, which would then have its own empire stretching from the Atlantic coast of North Africa to Egypt, plus the Red Sea down to the Persian Gulf. From there Louis could advance to expel the Portuguese from the Indies, and the 'rule of the world' would be shared between Louis and the Habsburgs, controlling east and west respectively.[33]

This line of argument was at least concerned with power calculations, albeit wildly optimistic ones. But other parts of Leibniz's text had a much more exalted religious colouring. In the introductory section he was quick to invoke the expedition to Egypt by Saint Louis (King Louis IX, whose unsuccessful campaign against the Ayyubid Sultan there in the mid-thirteenth century is also known as the Seventh Crusade). Later on, when summarizing the justice of the cause, he wrote: 'First, there is the Sultan, who is invaded; Palestine, which is liberated—and, moreover, more territory beyond Palestine; the Church, which is served; and God, who will reward you with the success you desire.' He continued: 'what is at stake in considering this scheme is the salvation of a large part of the human race'; the conquest of Egypt would allow Christianity to spread beyond Ottoman

---

33. Leibniz, 'Justa dissertatio' [= the main draft of the 'Consilium aegyptiacum'], pp. 273 ('Monarchiam Vniuersalem', 'Directionem Generalem', 'non impia tantum, sed et inepta'), 278 ('pars melior'), 279 ('imperium Orbis').

territory to Japan, China, and Australia. 'Turn your mind towards every part of the world', he urged the French King, 'and tell me, if you can, if there is anything easy to do that is greater than this; anything great that is more holy than this; and anything at all that is more universal.'[34] The whole text was an exercise in deliberative rhetoric on a grand scale, and Leibniz was of course eager to deploy every possible argument that might sway hearts as well as minds. But he was not just a scholar in his study composing a rhetorical showpiece; he travelled to Paris in order to present this proposal to French ministers, and must have believed that arguments in favour of holy war would be accepted by them with some degree of seriousness.

Leibniz's scheme was also unusual in that it was aimed essentially at one European power. (He did mention in passing the possibility of a wider 'anti-Ottoman alliance', but that was not at all central to his argument.[35]) Most other grand schemes envisaged a much broader collaboration. That some kind of unity, or at least coordination, between Christian states was a condition of successful warfare against the Ottomans had long been a commonplace—from the earliest descriptions of the fall of Constantinople as a divine punishment for Christian disunity, to the oft-repeated observation that the Sultan took care to attack West European states individually and not collectively. But in the early seventeenth century such calls for Christian unity sometimes took a more specific form, sketching possible systems of international organization. These have attracted, naturally enough, much attention from historians seeking to trace the ancestry of more recent international projects.[36] It is hard to speak of a tradition here, as most of those who constructed such schemes appear to have had no knowledge of their predecessors; the earliest worked-out plan of this kind, put forward by the King of Bohemia, George Podiebrad (Jiří z Poděbrad), in 1462–3 and involving a formal league with a permanent assembly at which delegates would vote on policy-making, was not mentioned by any of the later devisers of these plans. It would be even more misleading to speak of a continuous tradition of international idealism, as in several cases underlying political motives are not hard to discern—including the case of George Podiebrad, whose scheme, ostensibly

34. Ibid., pp. 268 (Saint Louis), 378 ('Primum Turca est, qvi invaditur, Palaestina qvae liberatur, licet extra Palaestinam, Ecclesia cui inservitur, Deus qvi remunerabit successu optato'), 379 ('Pendet ab hac deliberatione magnae generis humani partis salus', 'Verte animum in omnes partes, et dic, si potes, aliqvid inter facilia maius, inter magna sanctius; inter omnia universalius').
35. Ibid., p. 369 ('foedus AntiTurcicum').
36. See for example ter Meulen, Der Gedanke; Saitta, Dalla res publica.

aimed at ensuring Christian unity for the sake of anti-Ottoman warfare, had the unavowed purpose of curbing the authority of both the Habsburgs and the Pope.[37] Nevertheless, these projects do illustrate the way in which the conflict between Western Christendom and the Ottoman Empire could act as a stimulus to some quite original thinking about the possible restructuring of Western Christendom itself.

One such scheme was put forward in Rome some time between 1605 and 1621—perhaps in connection with the discussions that took place there with the duc de Nevers and Père Joseph. Its author was a senior cardinal, Ottavio Pallavicino, and the surviving manuscript was submitted by him to the Pope; but the plan's ambitions were so exorbitant that it is not surprising that it seems to have left no further trace in the historical record. In order to bring about a successful anti-Ottoman crusade, Pallavicino proposed forming an alliance of all major European states, including Protestant England and Orthodox Muscovy; each would send delegates to a special assembly, where the campaign plans—involving armies attacking on seven different fronts simultaneously, plus a coordinated assault by the Shah of Persia—would be agreed. Once the Sultan was fully defeated, the allied powers were to set up a new 'Christian republic' in the conquered territories, which would be governed by a 'senate' of their representatives, meeting in Istanbul. It would have Latin as its official language, and would permit freedom of conscience to all its subjects; over time the Muslims would convert to Catholicism, but they would do so only as a result of persuasion, and of the good examples of Christian piety which they were able to observe.[38] The Erasmian flavour of that final suggestion, and the surprising inclusion of heretical and schismatic states, may not have been the only reasons why this plan was taken no further.

What became the most famous of these schemes may also have had its origins in the second decade of the century. Before Richelieu's rise to power, his nearest equivalent in French political history had been Maximilien de Béthune, duc de Sully, who served as a key adviser and administrator under Henri IV. When that king was assassinated in 1610 the duc de Sully was removed from power, and settled into a lengthy retirement, during which he compiled memoirs of his royal service. These accounts were not just

37. On Podiebrad's scheme see Housley, *Crusading*, pp. 56–8; for the text see Kejř, ed., 'Tractatus pacis'.
38. See Pásztor, 'La repubblica cristiana'; Eliav-Feldon, 'Grand Designs', pp. 62–4.

burnished in retrospect, as most political memoirs are; Sully resorted to outright invention—even the forging of documents—in order to improve the record. At various points he referred to the general geopolitical strategy of Henri IV, which was aimed at constructing a new network of alliances that would curb Habsburg power in Europe. But then he began to fabricate an elaborate scheme for a new European system, calling it the 'Grand Dessein' ('Grand Design') and attributing it to Henri IV personally.[39] It envisaged gathering the main European powers (six hereditary monarchies, six elective ones, and three republics) in a single quasi-state; as the Preface to Sully's *Mémoires* put it, the idea was 'to put together a European Christendom of fifteen states, with such adjustments and refinements that one could make out of them what would be called a Most Christian Republic, permanently at peace with itself.'[40] There would be six regional assemblies, and one general one which would exercise supreme power. Internally all the member states would enjoy freedom of trade, and externally their forces would be combined to drive the Ottomans out of Europe. The Tsar would not be included, but would be offered an associated role, on condition that he also contributed his army; if he refused, he too would be treated like the Sultan.[41]

This was a fantastic scheme, going far beyond any plans that can be attributed, on the strength of other evidence, to Henri IV himself. The one authentic element was the anti-Habsburg animus behind it, as it stipulated that that dynasty must give up the Holy Roman Empire and all territory outside Spain on the mainland of Europe.[42] Another of Henri's advisers, Théodore-Agrippa d'Aubigné, would write long after Henri's death that he had entertained grand plans to drive the Habsburgs out of Italy, and/or to conquer Spain; with audible scepticism he summarized Henri's ambition as being 'to make [himself] an Emperor of Christendom, whose threat of force would halt the Ottomans; to reconstitute Italy, subdue Spain, reconquer Europe, and make the world tremble'.[43] There the effect on the Ottomans

39. Ogg, ed., *Sully's Grand Design*, pp. 8–9 (compiling, falsification).
40. Béthune, *Mémoires*, Preface ('De composer la Chrestienté d'Europe de quinze Dominations & ce auec de tels temperamens & assaisonnemens que l'on en pûst former vne Republique nommée Tres-Chrestienne, tousiours pacifique en elle mesme').
41. Ogg, ed., *Sully's Grand Design*. See also ter Meulen, *Der Gedanke*, pp. 160–8; Saitta, *Dalla res publica*, pp. 43–57.
42. Ogg, ed., *Sully's Grand Design*, p. 35 (Habsburgs).
43. D'Aubigné, *Histoire*, iii, p. 544 ('pour faire un Empereur des Chrestiens, qui de sa menace arresteroit les Turcs; pour Refformer l'Italie, dompter l'Espagne, reconquerir l'Europe, & faire

was just something to be mentioned in passing. Sully's scheme, stimulated perhaps by the interest shown in anti-Ottoman warfare by Père Joseph and (for a while) Richelieu, presented it as a much more central purpose. But his scheme also involved making Henri not a European emperor but just a component of a larger sovereign entity—a prospect which the French King would never have entertained, even as the price of permanently confining the Habsburgs to an equal status.

Two other schemes from the early seventeenth century deserve brief mention, though neither seems to have had any influence on opinion more generally. In one of the 'discorsi' he wrote in prison (probably in 1606–7, on the basis of an earlier draft of 1594), Tommaso Campanella proposed that all the Catholic rulers of Europe should form a 'senate' in Rome, with the Pope as its head, to decide 'all matters of state'. Anti-Ottoman warfare was not a major consideration here, although Campanella would certainly have been aware that, since the 1570s, that had been the main issue on which the popes had tried to exercise such a superior coordinating role. This text circulated in numerous later manuscript copies, but it is hard to find any echo of this particular plan in the works of subsequent writers.[44]

The other text is very different in character, conducting a much broader argument and arriving at a truly original conclusion. Almost nothing is known about its author, Émeric Crucé, except that he was said to have been a member of a monastic order and a teacher at one of the colleges in Paris.[45] His *Le Nouveau Cynée ou discours d'état représentant les occasions et moyens d'établir une paix générale et liberté du commerce par tout le monde* was published in two editions there, in 1623 and 1624; both are very rare today. The main purpose of this work was to solve the problem of intra-European religious conflict. Crucé combined the pragmatism of the *politique* tradition, which had learned the bitter lessons of the French Wars of Religion, with a view of the true nature of religion that focused on internal belief and the worship of the heart, relegating ceremonies to a much lower level of importance. Yes, he admitted, it would of course be better if there were only one religion, as religious passions do divide people; but where a different religion is well established, wise rulers let it be. The French kings took a long time to

trembler l'Vnivers'). Kükelhaus associates d'Aubigné's account with Sully's scheme (*Der Ursprung*, pp. 59–64), but the two seem fundamentally different.

44. Campanella, *Discorsi politici*, p. 35 ('tutte le cose di stato'). On the dating and the MSS see Firpo, *Bibliografia*, item 28.

45. For the very few biographical details that are known, see Saitta, 'Un riformatore', pp. 183–4.

discover that it was easier to maintain two religions in peace than to enforce one by war. Indeed, 'we see that the Ottomans live peacefully, even though they allow the practice of religions that are contrary to Islam.'[46]

Cruce's proposal, therefore, was to accept the status quo of religious difference in Europe, and stabilize the situation by gathering all countries in a single peaceful structure, to be strengthened by freedom of commerce. A permanent assembly of ambassadors would be set up in Venice, mainly for the purpose of settling any disputes. What made Cruce's plan truly exceptional, however, was his idea that the Sultan should also be invited to take part. At the assembly the Pope would preside, for reasons of historic dignity (and the veneration of so many Catholic countries), but the second place of honour would go to the Sultan; he would be followed by the Holy Roman Emperor, then the King of France in fourth place, and then the King of Spain.[47] Cruce explained that the Sultan had ceased to fight wars of expansion against Europe, and—here he clearly had in mind the murder of Osman II in 1622—that his powers had been greatly diminished: 'his aim is little more than to defend himself, and he has been reduced to the last extremity by his own subjects, who must indeed make him think more of preserving himself than of undertaking a new conquest.' The Christian powers did not keep their wartime gains, while the Ottomans stood firm, so this would be a good time for a peace agreement; and that would make Christian rulers more likely to make peace with other Christians, as well as promoting the chances of peace between the Ottomans and the Persians, thus leading in the direction of 'universal peace'. Some rulers might object that they had lost territories to the Sultan which were rightfully theirs; but 'monarchies derive immediately from God, and are established by his providence alone.'[48] With this heady mixture of pragmatism, idealism, providentialism, and sheer illogical assertion (in the form of the argument about Christian–Ottoman peace leading to further pacifications, when past experience strongly suggested that the suspension of that threat of war freed up forces for belligerence against other targets), Cruce thus put together an intriguing picture of a highly unlikely future.

46. Cruce, *Le Nouveau Cynée*, pp. 5 (edns.), 82–5 (religion, ceremonies, wise rulers), 87 ('nous voyons que les Turcs vivent paisiblement, bien qu'ils permettent l'exercice des Religions contraires à la Mahométane').
47. Ibid., pp. 88–90.
48. Ibid., pp. 66 ('Il n'a quasi que se défendre & a été réduit à des extrémités par ses propres sujets, qui lui doivent bien faire penser à sa conservation plutôt qu'à une nouvelle conquête', 'paix universelle'), 67 ('les Monarchies... viennent immédiatement de Dieu & sont établies par sa seule providence').

Of all these schemes, only Sully's became widely known. Its direct influence has sometimes been claimed on the famous *Projet pour rendre la paix perpétuelle en Europe* (1713) of Charles Irénée Castel, the Abbé de Saint-Pierre, which proposed a treaty of union and a 'perpetual congress' of eighteen European sovereign states; but that was a much more carefully worked-out plan for a kind of European constitution, with the Ottoman issue almost completely sidelined. (The abbé's only general comment on the Ottomans, Tatars, and 'Barbary' North Africans was that they should not be included in the congress, but that the union, once established, should seek to make treaties of peace and commerce with them; if they refused, it should go to war in order to force them to give guarantees of peace, and to promise the protection of their Christian subjects.)[49] A slightly later project, attributed to Cardinal Giulio Alberoni in the 1730s, reversed that pattern, briefly discussing a perpetual assembly of Christian powers that would meet in Regensburg, but concentrating much more heavily on the plan to raise a pan-European force, conquer the entire Ottoman Empire, and share out all its territories. A significant part of the text was lavished on the partition plan, which proceeded in increasingly implausible detail: England would be given Crete and Smyrna, Holland would have Rhodes and Aleppo, Denmark would get the Duchy of Holstein-Gottorp (whose Duke would become Emperor of Constantinople and ruler of all Ottoman territories in Asia and Africa), the King of Sicily would be given Tuscany, and so on, and so on. While one historian has called this work a plagiarism of Sully's, it is hard to see more than a generic resemblance, and difficult, indeed, to know how seriously the semi-retired Cardinal (if he was the author) intended it to be taken.[50]

All of the plans mentioned thus far were by Catholic authors, except for Sully's, which was written by a Huguenot but attributed by him to a Catholic king. It is understandable that Protestants were much less likely to call for setting up pan-European congresses and forming international armies, as the dominant powers of most of continental Europe were Catholic.

49. Castel, *Projet*, original pagination, i, pp. vii ('Congrez perpetuel'), 283 (Ottomans, Tatars, etc.). Miriam Eliav-Feldon has commented that Sully's scheme has 'nothing to do' with this project ('Grand Designs', p. 66).

50. Alberoni, *Scheme*, pp. 36–45 (partition details), 65–6 (congress); Ogg, ed., *Sully's Grand Design*, p. 10 (plagiarism). One possible influence on this text may have been Coppin's *Le Bouclier d'Europe*, which offered (pp. 136–40) its own, rather more rational, partition plan: the Pope would get Jerusalem; France Egypt; the Emperor Hungary and Serbia; Venice Epirus, Albania, and Bosnia; the Peloponnese would be shared between all powers; 'Barbary' between Spain, France, Portugal, and Holland; and England, which already held Tangier, would be given more of the nearby coastal territory, plus Thessaly.

The most prominent exception was the Quaker William Penn, who in 1693 proposed a European assembly as a mechanism for settling disputes and thereby ending intra-European wars. Penn was such a convinced pacifist that he showed no interest whatsoever in turning the combined forces of these united European states against the Ottoman Empire. He thought it sufficient that the peaceful conjoining of these states would have an over-whelming deterrent effect on the Sultan:

> Another Advantage is, *The Great security it will be to Christians against the Inroads of the Turk, in their most prosperous fortune.* For it had been impossible for the *Port[e]* to have prevailed so often, and so far upon *Christendom,* but by the care-lessness or wilful connivence, if not aide, of some *Christian Princes.* And for the same reason why no *Christian Monarch* will adventure to oppose or break such an Union, the *Grand-Seignior* will find himself obliged to concur for the secur-ity of what he holds in *Europe*: Where, with all his strength, he would feel it an over-match for him.[51]

(In this case, at least, the influence of Sully's writings is clear: at the end of his pamphlet Penn acknowledged that 'something of the nature of our expedient' had been planned by Henri IV.[52])

However, there is one earlier example of a similar pattern of thought—though without the formal apparatus of an assembly or a confederation—appealing to a Protestant ruler. King James VI of Scotland and I of England was both a committed Protestant who devoted much intellectual energy to theological or theologico-political disputes and a religious and political irenicist. In 1589, long before he acceded to the English throne, he proposed the formation of a Christian league, beginning with an alliance of Scotland, Denmark, and the German Protestant states, and then embracing England, France, and Spain; its aim would be to bring about the 'common peace of Christendom'. Perhaps not coincidentally, it was in that same year that he also composed a poem celebrating the defeat of the 'circumsised Turband Turkes' by the 'baptiz'd race' at the Battle of Lepanto eighteen years earlier.[53] At the end of the next decade he was making tentative efforts to form an alliance between moderate Protestant and Catholic powers, apparently with a view to facilitating military action against the Ottomans, and was even conducting delicate negotiations with the Pope. The main purpose here was no doubt to mollify the Catholic authorities in order to ease his succession

---

51. Penn, *Essay*, pp. 33–4.   52. Ibid., p. 41.
53. James VI, *Poems*, i, p. 202; Baumer, 'England, the Turk', pp. 43–4.

to Elizabeth, but the intra-Christian irenicism was genuine, and within a short time of his entry into England in 1603 James and his ministers were talking quite openly about organizing a new Ecumenical Council of the Church.[54] Years later, the Venetian Ambassador in London was assured by 'a personage who knows the King's mind' that when he came to the English throne 'he had a great desire to form a league of Christian Princes against the Turk, and would have done his share by paying ten thousand foot if everyone else had done his duty.'[55]

So there can be nothing too surprising about the grand prospects briefly sketched in the set of additional instructions given to Sir John Digby in 1617, when he was sent by King James to Madrid to negotiate with Philip III over the marriage of Prince Charles to the Infanta. The words of this document were penned by Francis Bacon, but the ambitious ideas were surely those of his sovereign master. Digby was to commend the marital alliance on the grounds 'that it may be a beginning... of a holy war against the Turk, whereunto the events of time doth invite Christian kings, in respect of the great corruption and relaxation of discipline of war in that empire; and much more in respect of the utter ruin and enervation of the Grand Signor's navy'. And at the same time he was to explain 'that by the same conjunction there will be erected a tribunal or praetorian power to decide the controversies which may arise amongst the princes and estates of Christendom without effusion of Christian blood; for so much as any estate of Christendom will hardly recede from that which the two kings shall mediate or determine'.[56] This second point prefigured what would later become one of the most important purposes of the 'Spanish Match': persuading Spain to lend its authority to a political intervention in the war between the Austrian Habsburgs and James's son-in-law, the Elector Palatine, with a view to restoring the latter to the peaceful possession of his original domains. But when these instructions were written, that conflict—the genesis of the Thirty Years' War—had not yet begun. So what this document represents is, in part at least, just the general set of ideas, present in some Protestant minds as well as Catholic ones, that associated the promotion of

54. Baumer, 'England, the Turk', pp. 44–5 (alliance); Patterson, *King James*, pp. 34–9 (Council). Patterson's study charts James's many irenicist plans and interests throughout his English reign.
55. *Calendar of State Papers, Venice*, xii, *1610–1613*, no. 585, 19 July 1612.
56. Bacon, 'A Remembrance', pp. 158 ('that it may...'), 158–9 ('that by...'). The three points about the Ottomans (corruption, indiscipline, decline of navy) may have been drawn from Sandys, *Relation*, pp. 50–1 (where Sandys described the Sultan's navy as so reduced as to be 'contemptible').

anti-Ottoman warfare with the setting up of some sort of political structure in Western Europe to guarantee the 'common peace of Christendom'.

Within a few years of its outbreak, however, the Thirty Years' War raised the issue of the relationship between Christian states and the Ottoman Empire in a very different way. When the Elector Palatine's army was decisively defeated at the Battle of the White Mountain outside Prague in November 1620, his personal baggage train fell into the hands of the Habsburgs. This included a large collection of documents and correspondence, the so-called 'chancery' of his strategic adviser, Christian of Anhalt-Bernburg. Within a few months the Habsburgs began to publish a selection of the most incriminating pieces, first in German and then, for a Europewide readership, in Latin translation; the main purpose was to scandalize European opinion by revealing the extent to which the Elector's advisers, in association with the Transylvanian leader Gábor Bethlen, had been willing to encourage an Ottoman invasion of Habsburg territory.[57]

In the propaganda war that followed, many familiar issues were raked over: standard arguments about the legitimacy of alliances with infidels, comparisons between the Sultan and the Pope or between Islam and Roman Catholicism, and so on. On the Habsburg side, this was an opportunity not only to draw the concept of 'Calvinoturcism' out of the doctrinal realm and into the arena of politics, but also to engage in heightened polemics about the evils of Ottoman rule. One of the first pamphleteers to make use of the 'Anhalt chancery', the French Jesuit Étienne Moquot, gave a characterization of the Ottoman system which began with the statements, '(1) all people, from the Grand Vizier down to the lowest hewer of wood, are slaves—they, and their children, and their possessions; (2) the Ottomans eliminate all princes and nobles who are unaccustomed to servitude'; such was the system to which the Elector, in his devotion to 'Calvinoturcism', had wished to consign the inhabitants of Habsburg Hungary.[58] Responding to this, one apologist for Gábor Bethlen declared that while the Pope and the Sultan were both Antichrists, the Sultan was the lesser of those two evils: the former was a persecutor of Christians, whereas the latter 'allows maintenance and

---

57. On this and the subsequent publication of 'chancery' documents from both sides see Koser, *Die Kanzleienstreit*. On the diplomatic initiatives of the Elector and Bohemia towards Istanbul see Polišensky, 'Bohemia', pp. 106–7; Mout, 'Calvinoturcisme', pp. 589–90.

58. Moquot, *Secreta secretorum*, p. 28 ('1. Omnes a supremo Vieziro [*sic*], ad infimum lignatorem, mancipia sunt, & ipsi, & liberi, & fortunae. 2. Omnes Principes, nobiles, servituti inassuetos, è medio tollunt').

tranquillity to the Church even where he exercises full authority and dominion'. As for using Ottoman forces to fight against Christians: 'the war was not undertaken against Christians *qua* Christians, even though they are that kind of Christians [*sc.* Catholics]—rather, against men who are trouble-makers and disturbers of the peace.' (Besides, he added, Catholic princes made use of Cossacks, who were just as bad as Turks, and altogether 'without religion'.)[59]

A fuller reply to Moquot was published by the Elector Palatine's chief adviser, the jurist Ludwig Camerarius, in 1625. On the question of alliances with non-Christians he was able to push back by pointing to the Catholic polemicist Kaspar Schoppe, who in a recent book had advised the Emperor that he was permitted to ally himself with Muslims, Jews, and pagans, but not with heretics; and besides, Camerarius observed, there were many Christian rulers in the past who had made treaties with the Ottomans. Responding to Moquot's characterization of sultanic rule, he agreed that all Ottoman subjects were physically 'under the absolute power of the Sultan'; but their souls were not. 'The Sultan allows everyone to live in accordance with his own religion, and he even favours Christian Orthodox monks with daily supplies, as Bodin, drawing on writers on Ottoman affairs, has observed.' And while it was true that the Ottomans eliminated nobility in the traditional sense, Bodin had also commented that only the Ottomans had true nobility, judged on the basis of virtue, not birth. As for the *devşirme*, of which Moquot had also complained: it was certainly an oppressive practice, but the Jesuits also took boys from their parents, and 'indeed, in this sort of matter they far exceed the Ottomans.'[60] This last claim would become a popular debating point among Protestant polemicists. In 1628 an anonymous German writer, offering a hostile commentary on two 'discourses' by Campanella in favour of the Papacy and Spain, observed that at least the *devşirme* took only one or two boys from each family, whereas the Jesuits— whose imposition of sharp discipline and blind obedience was just like that of the Janissaries—took them all. The main question addressed by this writer

---

59. Plosarius, *Oratio*, pp. 29 (two Antichrists), 30 ('qui etiam ubi plenum exercet jus ac dominium, Ecclesiae hospitium ac tranquillitatem concedit', 'non adversus Christianos est bellum susceptum, quatenus sunt Christiani; quanquam quales Christiani. Sed adversus homines molestos inquietos'), 35 ('sine religione').

60. L. Camerarius, *Mysterium iniquitatis*, pp. 34 (Schoppe), 57 (treaties with Ottomans), 138 ('sub absolutâ Regis Turcici potestate', 'Turcarum Rex suo quemque ritu vivere patitur, atque adeò Calogerontas Christianos quotidianis largitionibus fouet, ut Bodinus obseruauit ex Rerum Turcicarum scriptoribus'), 139 ('Imò in hoc genere Turcas longè superant').

was: 'is it better to live under the Spanish Inquisition and papal-imperial persecution than under the Sultan?' Campanella—who, it was gleefully observed, had himself suffered terribly under the Inquisition—answered 'yes', while this author answered 'no'. The old slogan 'Rather Turkish than Popish' was thus openly avowed. And once again, the key argument was about religious toleration. Citing a comment made to the Lutheran scholar Michael Neander by a Greek Orthodox priest from Corinth, 'Pay the Sultan his dues, and believe what and how you like', the author asked: was this not the same as Jesus's own injunction: 'Render unto Caesar the things that are Caesar's ...'?[61]

Since the logic of the situation did clearly imply that the pro-Palatine forces would benefit from Ottoman intervention, some Protestants looked for more providentialist justifications of such help. In 1622 the Lutheran preacher Samuel Martinius claimed to have obtained a 'Rosicrucian prophecy' which foretold that the Kings of England and Sweden would come to the Elector's aid, and that 'the Sultan will free Hungary from its misery.' Later in the 1620s Christoph Kotter, a tanner from the small Silesian town of Sprottau (modern Szprotawa), issued a number of prophecies, foretelling the fall of the Habsburgs, the restoration of the Elector Palatine to the throne of Bohemia, and the conversion of the 'Turks' (Ottoman Muslims); these were passed on to the Elector himself by the Czech theologian and educationalist Comenius (Jan Komenský).[62] In the early 1640s a Moravian, Mikuláš Drabík, who had been one of Comenius's school-fellows, began making similar claims to divine revelation. In 1643, for example, God told him that the Prince of Transylvania should prepare for war against 'Babylon' (the Habsburgs), declaring: 'Let him call for help from the Turk, the Tatar, Moscow, or Poland; and he will see that none of them will refuse it.' In 1650—two years after the Treaty of Westphalia, which ended the war and, to the despair of local Protestants, left the kingdom of Bohemia in Habsburg hands—Drabík returned to this theme, but added an important new element. God now informed him that the peoples of the East, 'those servants of mine', were preparing for a war against the Habsburgs: 'For many of the Turks will recognize that the cause of this war is the fact that the worship of me has been defiled by idolaters throughout these kingdoms; they will

---

61. Anon., *Compendium*, sigs. C2r ('Ob es unter deren Spanischen *inquistion* und Bäpst-Keyserlichen *persecution* besser, als unter den Türcken seye?'), G3v ('Ehe Türckisch als Bäpstisch'), H3r ('Gieb dem Türcken was ihm gebühret, und glaube was, und wie du wilt'), I4r (Jesuits).

62. Blekastad, *Comenius*, p. 117 ('der Türke wird Ungarn aus der Not befreien'), 123–5 (Kotter); Mout, 'Calvinoturcisme', p. 593 (Kotter's prophecy).

take up the teaching of the Gospel, and on their foreheads they will accept this sign of mine: JESUS OF NAZARETH, KING OF THE JEWS.'[63] In this way Drabík's prophecies tapped into two well-established lines of apocalyptic thought: the Joachimite idea that the destruction of a corrupt Western Empire would be accomplished by means of powerful forces—probably Muslim ones—from the East, and the general assumption (based on biblical texts such as Ps. 22: 27, 'All the ends of the world shall remember and turn unto the Lord') that the conversion of not only the Jews but also the heathen would be one of the signs that ushered in the Last Days.

These and other such revelations were later published by Comenius in Amsterdam, and thus reached a Europe-wide audience. (In his memorandum addressed to Louis XIV in 1671–2, Leibniz would refer to 'those foolish but grandiloquent prophets Kotter and Drabík', while giving as an additional reason for attacking the Ottoman Empire the fact that hardline Calvinists in Holland would share Drabík's pro-Ottoman sentiments.)[64] They also had a significant effect on Comenius himself, spurring him in the late 1650s to try to organize a translation of the Bible into Turkish in order to speed up the process of converting the 'Turks' to Christianity.[65] Not long thereafter, the Ottoman campaign against Habsburg Hungary and Austria in 1663–4 gave new interest to Drabík's predictions. In 1664 a Swiss disciple of Comenius, Johann Jakob Redinger, was so inspired by Drabík's words that he travelled to the Ottoman campaign headquarters in Hungary and had two interviews with the Grand Vizier, whom he tried to convert to Christianity. (Fourteen years later, the German poet and visionary Quirinus Kuhlmann would also go to Istanbul, inspired by similar prophecies, in order to convert the Sultan.) It is significant that, before he set off for Ottoman territory, Redinger had visited Fontainebleau and Paris, where he had left copies of Drabík's prophecies for Louis XIV and had discussed the matter with the Archbishop of Paris, Louis's confessor and former tutor; and

---

63. Comenius, ed., *Lux in tenebris*, part 3, pp. 9 ('Advocet auxilio Turcam, vel Tartarum, vel Moscum, vel etiam Polonorum: & videbit neminem horum refragaturum esse'), 51 ('illi servi mei…Multi enim Turcarum agnoscent causam belli hujus, esse Cultum meum, ab Idolatris per haec Regna contaminatum, suscipientque doctrinam Evangelii, & frontibus suis admittent signum meum hoc: JESUS NAZARENUS REX JUDAEORUM'). On Drabík see Blekastad, *Comenius*, pp. 616–27.

64. Leibniz, 'Justa dissertatio', p. 373 ('Inepti illi sed grandiloqvi prophetae, Cotterus, et…Drabitius'). Comenius issued three different edns.: *Lux in tenebris* (1657), the expanded *Lux e tenebris* (1665), and a further expansion of that in 1667. The work contained prophecies by Drabík, Kotter, and a Bohemian woman, Kristina Poniatowska.

65. See Malcolm, 'Comenius, Boyle'; Malcolm, 'Comenius, the Conversion'.

he would return to Paris on a similar errand, at Comenius's request, bearing the second edition of the work in 1666.[66] This turn towards the French King was once again in accordance with the logic of anti-Habsburg geopolitics. Hermann Conring, for example, an eminent Lutheran scholar and a much cooler head than Comenius, issued a compilation of anti-Ottoman works in 1664 with a dedicatory epistle to the French ambassador in which, while praising Louis for the support he had given to the Holy Roman Emperor, he urged him to seize the opportunity to conquer Istanbul and make himself master of the Ottoman Empire.[67] The most extreme position, for those who were caught up in the prophetic excitement, would have been to say that an attack on the Habsburgs by the Ottomans should be coordinated with French military action against the Holy Roman Emperor in a kind of divinely ordained pincer action, with the final suppression of Habsburg 'Babylon' then coinciding with the conversion of the Muslims to the true faith. Even Comenius seems to have drawn back, at least in public, from promoting such a plan; in the address to Louis XIV which he added to his expanded edition of the prophecies in 1667, he merely called on him to summon a General Council of the Church to settle all the differences within Christianity, and assured him that he would become greater than Cyrus, Alexander, or Augustus.[68] And when another Comenian, the Huguenot merchant Pierre de Cardonnel, wrote his own prophetic poem in 1667 and sent it to Louis XIV, he concentrated just on the future victory of the French King over the Ottoman Empire, which itself would lead to the conversion of all the Muslim territories to Christianity.[69]

For mainstream Protestant millenarianism, scenarios involving helpful military interventions by the 'Turks' and their peaceful conversion were an unnecessary elaboration; it was sufficient to descry their absolute defeat and downfall. During the early seventeenth century a distinctive strain of Calvinist millenarianism had developed, thanks to the writings of three men: Thomas Brightman (whose seminal work *A Revelation of the Revelation* was published in Amsterdam in 1615), Joseph Mede, and Johann Heinrich

66. Schaller, 'Johann Jakob Redinger', pp. 148, 153–6; Schader, *Johann Jakob Redinger*, pp. 21–3; Dietze, *Quirinus Kuhlmann*, pp. 153–8.
67. Conring, *De bello*, sigs. (:)4v–2(:)2v.
68. Comenius, ed., *Lux e tenebris*, 2nd edn., p. 19 (Council), 24 (Cyrus).
69. Bibliothèque nationale de France, MS f. fr. 12,499, fos. 38r–47v. On Cardonnel see Malcolm, *Aspects*, pp. 259–316 (esp. pp. 302–7 on the poem).

Alsted.[70] These authors differed on various points, but shared the general view that the sequence of events predicted in Revelation would include the restoration of the Jews to Palestine and their conversion to Christianity: the lost tribes of Israel would assemble, cross the Euphrates (Rev. 16: 12), convert to the true faith, and fight under Christ in the battle of Armageddon. Against whom would they fight? The obvious candidate was the dominant and godless power in that part of the world: the Ottoman Empire. According to Brightman, the 'beleeving Iewes' would fight the Ottomans at Armageddon; according to Mede, the reference to the Euphrates was itself a symbolic reference to the Ottoman empire and its soldiers, 'which shall be the onely obstacle to those new enemies from the East, and on that part the only defence of the Beast'.[71] And when would those events happen? Brightman put the final fulfilment of the prophecies of Revelation in the years 1690–6, but calculated that the Turks would start to 'totter' forty years before that, when they began to be challenged by the converted Jews. Following Brightman, a general consensus arose that the first significant indications of the conversion of the Jews and the fatal weakening of the Ottoman Empire would appear in 1650, or by 1656 at the latest.[72] A similar conclusion was reached by studying the vision of Daniel, with its horned beast sprouting a new 'little horn' (identified by Justus Jonas, Melanchthon, and Luther with Muhammad, as we have seen). Here it was a simple matter to run Islam and the Ottomans together: as Brightman put it, 'that *little Horn* is the *Turke*'.[73] His follower Ephraim Huit likewise argued in 1644 that 'the little horne intends [*sc.* means] the Turkish state'; taking the traditional date of 1300 for the rise of that state, and interpreting the cryptic phrase (Dan. 7: 25) 'until a time and times and the dividing of time' to mean 350 years (one century plus two, plus a half), he too felt able to conclude that the Turkish dominion over the Jews would begin to fail in 1650.[74] Such teachings exerted a significant cultural influence in England during the religious and political upheavals of the 1640s; the country was of course too far removed from the Ottoman Empire, and too embroiled in its own political crisis, for this to

---

70. See Clouse, 'Johann Heinrich Alsted'; Toon, ed., *Puritans*; Ball, *A Great Expectation*; Hotson, *Paradise Postponed*.
71. Brightman, *Revelation*, p. 831; Mede, *Key*, 2nd pagination, p. 119. See also Cogley, 'Fall of the Ottoman Empire'.
72. Brightman, *Revelation*, pp. 324, 831; Capp, *Fifth Monarchy Men*, p. 28; Ball, *Great Expectation*, p. 145; Katz, *Philo-Semitism*, pp. 98–9.
73. Brightman, *Revelation*, p. 689.
74. Huit, *The Whole Prophecie*, pp. 187 (quotation), 210–12.

have any practical effect in terms of foreign policy, but the desire to speed up the divine plan, where the conversion of the Jews was concerned, may have contributed to the decision in the mid-1650s to readmit them to England.

Early modern millenarianism was essentially a Protestant phenomenon. Yet Catholics did believe in prophecy, both biblical and post-biblical (as we have seen in the case of Campanella), and did also seek to interpret the Book of Revelation, albeit without invoking a thousand-year reign of Christ on Earth. One example of a late seventeenth-century Catholic text devoted to prophecies about the fall of the Ottoman Empire may be given here. In early 1684, after the decisive defeat of the Ottoman army at the gates of Vienna in the previous year, and with the Emperor's forces poised for the invasion of Ottoman territory, the Dominican theologian Nicolas Arnoux published a book entitled *Presagio dell'imminente rovina, e caduta dell'imperio ottomano*. Every relevant prophecy and prognostication from every possible source was put to work, starting with the Ottoman prediction, as reported by Djurdjević, about the Sultan conquering the 'red apple', holding it for twelve years, and then being driven out by the Christians. (Ingeniously, Arnoux suggested that this referred to the Polish fortress-town of Kamianets-Podilskyi (now in the Ukraine), which had been taken by the Ottomans twelve years earlier; it was, he pointed out, in a region famous for its apples.) As for the Book of Revelation: it had predicted the fall of Constantinople, i.e. Istanbul (Rev. 14: 8, 'Babylon is fallen, is fallen, that great city'); the Scarlet Woman was also a representation of Istanbul; the Beast was the Ottoman monarchy; the ten horns were ten other kings (Algiers, Tunis, etc.) who allied themselves with the Sultan; and the 'four beasts that fell down and worshipped God' (Rev. 19: 4) were the four patriarchs of the Eastern Church, who would submit to the primacy of Rome. The whole of Revelation 17, describing the victory of the Lamb over the Beast and its allies, the ten kings, was thus a prophecy of the capture of Istanbul by the Holy League (the alliance, formed by the Pope in early 1684, of the Holy Roman Empire, the Papal States, Poland, and Venice).[75] This was not the work of a writer on the eccentric fringe. Arnoux was a lecturer in metaphysics at the University of Padua, and his book was printed at the newly established press of the Paduan seminary under the auspices of the influential Cardinal Gregorio Barbarigo, who was busily converting the seminary into a training centre, with tuition

75. Arnoux, *Presagio*, pp. 6–8 (red apple), 72–91 (exegesis of Revelation).

in Arabic, Turkish, and Persian, for missionary priests to preach the Catholic faith in infidel lands. Barbarigo was passionately following the progress of the Imperial troops, and predicting that Mass would soon be celebrated again in the Hagia Sophia in Istanbul; and he was also in touch with Marco d'Aviano, the charismatic Capuchin preacher who was urging the Austrians to fight a holy war.[76] Here, in the final decades of the seventeenth century, we can still find that the justification of warfare, and even the choice of military target, could be derived not just from general religious considerations, but from the very word of God.

76. Gios, ed., *Lettere*, p. 75 (Mass). On Barbarigo see Billanovich and Gios, eds., *Gregorio Barbarigo*; on the seminary press see Bellini, *Storia* (mentioning another edn. or issue of Arnoux's book in 1686: p. 302); on the link with d'Aviano see Pobladura, 'De amicitia'.

TWELVE

Islam as a political religion

While Islam retained an apocalyptic significance in some people's minds, it was commonly viewed as very much a human phenomenon. These two approaches were not mutually exclusive: human machinations could be guided by the Devil, whose own activities were ultimately subsumed under God's cosmic plan. But, for reasons which have been sketched already, the general tendency of early modern Christian authors looking in any detail at the origins and nature of Islam was to analyse it in secular terms, both psychological and political: it appealed to human nature in certain ways, it was designed to modify human behaviour, and, in so doing, it served the ulterior purposes of its founder and his successors.[1] As we have also seen, Machiavellian ideas about the power of religion to condition obedience, and about the need for 'legislators' to harness that power, if necessary by a tactic of religious imposture, had been commonly applied to the case of Muhammad; and Counter-Reformation writers, while denouncing Machiavelli for his criticism of Christianity (which might even have implied that Islam was a better religion), nevertheless accepted and developed his idea that religion gave essential support to secular rule.[2] One or two particular tenets of Islam that allegedly strengthened the Ottoman state have been mentioned already. But a fuller account is needed, in order to show some of the ways in which early modern interpretations of the nature of Islam were interwoven with those of the nature of Ottoman power.

The medieval view of Islam as essentially a religion of 'the sword' was extremely long-lasting. While it sought its original confirmation in some passages in the Koran, and in the history of the early Arab conquests, including that of Spain, it was naturally taken by most post-medieval writers as applying to the Ottoman wars of expansion too. Some did try to make a

1. See above, pp. 31–5.   2. See above, pp. 172–6.

distinction between religious and secular motives. In the fifteenth century, for example, Andrea Biglia wrote that the Arab conquests had been partly for religious purposes and partly for political and strategic ones, and in the sixteenth Theodore Bibliander observed that the Ottomans made war for two different reasons, religion and dominion.[3] Quite untypically, Louis Le Roy argued that religion was merely a pretext: 'all the wars that are waged nowadays by the Ottomans in order to extend their empire are put under the cover of religion, either when they attack the Christians, whom they accuse of being infidels, or when they attack the Persians, whom they judge to be heretics.' And Giovanni Tommaso Minadoi, in his account of the Ottoman–Persian war which began in 1578, did point out that it was motivated 'not by religious zeal, but simply by Murad's greed in wishing to conquer a kingdom'.[4] But the general view of the great majority of writers on the Ottomans was that Islam played an important role. Bibliander said that their wars against non-Muslim powers were dictated by Islam, which 'orders them to propagate their religion by force of arms'.[5] George of Hungary commented that one of the great strengths of Islam was 'the extreme eagerness which the people have to defend and propagate this sect—such that when the call goes out to gather the army, they rush together and assemble so promptly and quickly that you would think they were invited to a wedding, not to a war'.[6] In the early seventeenth century the writer known as Domenico Hierosolimitano, a rabbi who had served as a physician to Murad III before converting to Catholicism in 1593, composed an account of life in Istanbul which would prove an influential text, as it would be heavily plagiarized by the French historian Michel Baudier; his account of the 'commandments' of Islam—artificially numbered as ten, in order to fit Jewish and Christian preconceptions—specified *kâfirler döğüşü*, fighting against unbelievers, as the seventh commandment, which also included the provision that anyone who died while waging such a war would count as a martyr.[7] (As we have seen, Scipione Ammirato had

3. Meserve, *Empires of Islam*, p. 176 (Biglia); Bibliander, *Ad socios consultatio*, sig. h8r.
4. Le Roy, *Des troubles*, p. 13 ('Toutes les guerres qu'entreprennent maintenant les Turcs, pour eslargir leur Empire, sont couuertes de la religion: ou en venant contre les Chrestiens, qu'ils cuident mescreans: ou en allant contre les Perses, qu'ils iugent heretiques'); Minadoi, *Historia*, p. 24 ('non zelo di religione…ma la sola cupidità d'Amurat di soggiogare un regno').
5. Bibliander, *Ad socios consultatio*, sig. h8v ('iubet armis religione[m] propagare').
6. George of Hungary, *Tractatus*, p. 236 ('feruor maximus, quem habent ad illius secte defensionem et propugnationem. Unde quando fit commotio ad congregandum exercitum, cum tanta promptitudine et celeritate concurrunt et conueniunt, ut crederes non ad bellum, sed ad nuptias inuitari').
7. Domenico Hierosolimitano, *Domenico's Istanbul*, p. 51.

expressed the view, common in Western culture, that this divine sanction extended to any war conducted by the Sultan, referring to 'their belief that in dying for their king they die in the service of God'. According to Louis Deshayes, Muhammad had decreed that a Muslim would go straight to Paradise if he died in the service of his temporal ruler.[8])

That Islam imposed a duty of holy war on all its followers was mostly taken for granted; Francis Bacon's formulation, already quoted, was that 'it is a fundamental law in the Turkish empire that they may (without any other provocation) make war upon Christendom for the propagation of their law.'[9] But the word *jihad* was not in use in the West, and there was no accurate information about the Muslim teaching on this subject until 1708, when the Dutch scholar Adriaen Reland published a detailed account, based on an Islamic treatise. Here he explained the origin of the doctrine in the Koran and the hadiths, citing, for example, the second Sura of the Koran for the belief that those who die in a war for religion go straight to Paradise (and adding that Catholic canon law had contained, since the time of Leo IV, a very similar provision). Every Muslim was bound to join in a defensive war if the invader was an infidel; there was no such general duty to engage in offensive fighting, but men must obey their imam or ruler if called up, and the ruler was obliged to attack infidels at least once a year, manpower and supplies permitting. It was wrong to kill infidels before efforts had been made to convert them, though this applied only in cases where the infidels had never heard of Muhammad or Islam; and it was always wrong to kill women, children, or old men. Truce-breaking was also forbidden; it was permissible to make truces with infidels, but not treaties of perpetual peace.[10] After the publication of Reland's dissertation it was at least possible for Western readers with a serious interest in these matters to acquire this degree of understanding; until then, the much more general idea held sway of Islam as a militaristic religion, imposing an obligation of violence.

Whether the violence was ultimately for the sake of religion (to increase the number of Muslims by whatever means), or whether the religion had been endowed with such combative qualities for the sake of extending temporal rule, should still have been an open question at the theoretical

---

8. Above, p. 231 (Ammirato); Deshayes, *Voiage*, p. 248.   9. See above, p. 250.

10. Reland, 'De jure militari', pp. 6–7 (Koran, Leo IV, defensive war), 9–10 (offensive war, annual duty), 20–1 (efforts to convert), 22–3 (women, etc., truce-breaking), 50 (perpetual peace). Reland did not identify the treatise he used, beyond saying (p. 4) that it set out the principles accepted by Persian and Mughal jurists. On Reland see Hamilton, 'From "a Closet at Utrecht"'.

level, even for those who assumed that the sultans were acting on sincere religious beliefs when they went to war; for this question was primarily about the original intentions of Muhammad. As we shall see, differing answers would eventually be given to it. But until at least the mid-seventeenth century, the long Christian tradition of anti-Muslim polemics, relentlessly focusing on Muhammad's ambition and cunning, more or less dictated the answer: Islam was a religion devised for the sake of temporal power. As Fulke Greville put it, writing in the 1620s:

> Now when the policies of great Estates,
> Doe *Mars* professe, Religion then to *warre*
> It selfe must fashion, and indure such rates,
> As to the ends of Conquest proper are;
>
> [...]
>
> Such the Religion is of *Mahomet,*
> His doctrine, onely *warre,* and hazard teaching,
> His Discipline, not how to vse, but get,
> His Court, a campe, the Law of Sword his Preaching.[11]

The general assumption, therefore, was that particular aspects of Islamic belief and practice had been devised in order to facilitate military success and political rule. An unusually thorough statement of this view was set out by the Venetian envoy Giacomo Soranzo in the relazione which he wrote on his return from Istanbul in 1582. He listed ten features which, he said, demonstrated that Islam was 'instituted for the sake of expanding that empire': the practice of frequent washing, which made people hardier; the belief that faith must be defended by the sword; the religious duty to war against infidels; the ban on surrendering any land on which a mosque had been built; the prohibition of wine (for the sake of military discipline); the forbidding of pork (which was harmful to man, because of its 'moistness or fattiness'); the belief in fate; the practice of polygamy; the rule that a man could take as many slave-girls as he wished; and the fact that Muslim men were allowed to take wives of other religions, and that the children they had by them would be equally legitimate—'by which methods they increase the production of children, and swell their armies'.[12]

---

11. Greville, *Certain Workes*, p. 73 ('A Treatie of Warres', stanzas 16–17); 'rates' here means costs, in a figurative sense; 'hazard' means physical danger.
12. Albèri, ed., *Relazioni*, ser. 3, i, pp. 457–8 ('sia instituta ad aumento di quell'impero', 'umidità o pinguedine', 'per le quali vie aumentano la generazione, e ingrossano gli eserciti').

To the modern eye, only a minority of these beliefs and practices would have any direct connection with warfare or empire-building. The principles of *jihad* would of course be relevant, and so would the requirement not to give up any land on which a mosque had been built. (This was indeed a stipulation of Islamic law, and had been put forward by the Ottomans as one of the various justifications for their ultimatum to Venice in 1570 to surrender the island of Cyprus. It was mentioned in the *relazione* of the Venetian bailo who spent the years 1570–3 under house arrest in Istanbul, and became much more widely known when that text was published in the *Tesoro politico* in 1602.)[13] The theory that Islamic 'fatalism' endowed Muslim soldiers with reckless courage had a long history in the West. Paolo Giovio gave this (as we have seen) as one of the fundamental causes of Ottoman military success; the historian Michel Baudier emphasized that it was the basis of the Ottoman soldiers' valour in battle; the traveller Jean Thévenot, who spent time in Istanbul, the Levant, and Egypt in the late 1650s, likewise wrote that it was the main reason for their courage: 'for they firmly believe that if they are to die today, they will die just the same, whether they are at home or in the army; and if their day has not yet come, 100,000 men would not be able to take their life away, because it says in the Koran that a person cannot die before his time.' The German-born Oriental scholar Levinus Warner, who was resident in Istanbul from 1645 and Dutch representative there from 1655, wrote very similarly in 1664 about the soldiers in the campaign against Austria: 'their belief in fate makes them so fearless that they rush intrepidly into all kinds of danger.'[14]

Other aspects of Islam were less easily related to empire-building. Where the ban on drinking alcohol was concerned, Christian commentators on Islam had to wrestle with the fact that prohibiting such a common and pleasurable activity was not obviously a way for Muhammad, or any subsequent Muslim ruler, to expand the ranks of his followers. As has already been noted, Pius II was reduced to arguing that wine was harmful in hot countries; several

---

13. Ibid., ser. 3, i, p. 326 (relazione of Marcantonio Barbaro, 1573); Ventura, ed., *Tesoro politico*, fo. 89r. For the Ottoman claim see Charrière, *Négociations*, iv, p. 759(n.); Barbero, *La Bataille*, p. 77. The reference may have been to a brief period of Arab domination of Cyprus in the mid-seventh century, or possibly to the Mamluk subjugation of Cyprus in 1424–6.
14. Above, p. 64 (Giovio); Baudier, *Histoire generale*, p. 163; Thévenot, *L'Empire*, p. 197 ('car ils croient fermement que s'ils ont à mourir aujourd'hui, ils mourront aussi bien dans leur chambre qu'à l'armée; et que si leur jour n'est pas arrivé, cent mille hommes ne leur sauraient ôter la vie, parce qu'il est dit dans l'Alcoran que l'homme ne peut mourir avant son heure'); Bodleian Library, Oxford, MS Rawl. D 399, fo. 267r, Warner to States General, 5 Jan. 1664 ('Adhuc illos reddit interritos persuasio fati . . . intrepidi ruunt in quaevis pericula').

later writers, such as the Dominican Angelo Pientini and the Dutch scholar Hugo Grotius, rejected this line of argument, insisting that wine in moderation must be beneficial, as it was a gift of God and its use was permitted by Jesus.[15] For some commentators, at least, the strangeness of this Muslim prohibition was such that only a strong ulterior purpose could explain it. The natural link to make was with the marvellous peace and order that had so impressed those Western Europeans who had visited Ottoman army camps; hence Giacomo Soranzo's inclusion of the ban on wine in his ten-point list. Discussing this issue—alongside the similar ban on gambling—the Arabic scholar Lodovico Marracci wrote in 1698 that it was absurd to try to forbid something which 'had been universal practice almost from the beginning of the world', and argued that the real reason must have been to make people fitter for war.[16] One might have expected a similar explanation to be given for the fasting month of Ramadan, but this was not commonly included in the list of practices introduced by Muhammad for military purposes. As for Soranzo's inclusion of washing, a subject on which many Western observers wrote, often conflating the ritual ablutions of Islam with the general practice of using hamams: this too was unusual, as most authors supposed that Muslims performed these actions in the foolish belief that they would thereby wash away their sins.[17] But one writer who did emphasize this point was Scipione Gentili, who, immediately after explaining that Muhammad's prohibition of alcohol was for the sake of military effectiveness, added:

> The unusual and almost unbelievable cleanliness of the Turks, and the care they take over their bodies, were also ordered by the law of Muhammad, so that they would be immune from those diseases which are spread by contagion and by the quantity of people gathered together in army camps, and so that they might turn out fitter for the travails and exercises of war. In this way, under the appearance of a simulated religion, he strengthened military virtue and discipline.[18]

---

15. Above, p. 35 (Pius II); Malvezzi, *L'Islamismo*, p. 146 (Pientini); Grotius, *De veritate* VI.8, p. 287.
16. Marracci, *Prodromus*, part 4 (separately paginated), pp. 37–8 ('ab Orbe prope condito omnibus in usu fuisset').
17. See e.g. Heers and de Heyer, eds., *Itinéraire*, p. 72; Schiltberger, *Reisen*, p. 144; Palerne, *D'Alexandrie*, p. 277; Heberer, *Aegyptiaca servitus*, p. 392; Febvre, *Specchio*, p. 5.
18. S. Gentili, *Orationes*, p. 33 ('singularis, ac propè incredibilis illa Turcarum mundities, curatióque corporis, lege etiam imperata Mahumetis est: ideò, ut & à morbis iis, qui ex confertâ in castra multitudine ac contagione vulgantur, immunes, & ad belli labores atque exercitationes paratiores evaderent. Ita specie religionis assimulatae militarem virtutem disciplinamque firmavit').

Polygamy had always received a special emphasis in Christian anti-Muslim polemical works, which treated it as a sign of Muhammad's pandering to sensual human motives. An author such as the humanist scholar (and student of Arabic) Nicolaus Clenardus could confidently write in 1539 that polygamy and the promise of sexual pleasure in Paradise were essential features of Islam.[19] Some mid-sixteenth-century writers did point out that the great majority of Muslim men in the Ottoman Empire had only one wife each, and in the early seventeenth century Louis Deshayes explained that they were much too poor to take on extra wives; but the topic retained a certain fascination for Western readers nonetheless.[20] The idea that Muhammad had a general policy of increasing the population may possibly have taken its origin from the claim, made by George of Hungary and repeated by Christophe Richer, that the duty to get married was a fundamental 'commandment' of Islam.[21] (This way of putting it may have been too peremptory, but there was a clear basis for this view in the Koran, 24: 32.) Why polygamy should have made any significant contribution to population growth—given that the most relevant statistic would surely have been not the number of wives per man but the number of children per woman—was never clearly explained; but the desire to fit the precepts and practices of Islam into a framework of politico-military expansionism seems to have enabled some writers to take this point for granted. The traveller Henry Blount (who, as we shall see, had a Machiavellian view of Islam which was both strong and positive) was happy to write in 1636 that it was one of the 'politick acts of the *Alcoran*' to permit polygamy, 'to make a numerous People, which is the foundation of all great *Empires*'.[22] Even Paul Rycaut, with a much longer experience of conditions in the Ottoman Empire, could write thirty years later that Muhammad's main reason for allowing polygamy, apart from 'the satisfaction of his own carnal and effeminate inclination' and the appeal of this measure to his 'Disciples', was 'the encrease of his people... knowing that the greatness of Empires and Princes consists

19. Clenardus, *Peregrinationum epistolae*, fos. 21v–22r (letter to J. Latomus, from Granada, 12 July 1539). On his Arabic studies, which included a stay in Fez, see Olbrecht, 'Rond Niklaas Cleynaerts' Reis'.
20. Geuffroy, *Briefve description*, sig. f1r; Postel, *De la république*, p. 5; Deshayes, *Voiage*, p. 170.
21. George of Hungary, *Tractatus*, p. 258; Richer, *Des coustumes*, p. 21.
22. Blount, *Voyage*, p. 82.

more in the numbers or multitudes of their people, than the compass or
large extent of their dominions'.[23]

Another element of the Ottoman system remarked on by many Western
writers, and which one might expect to have been commonly put on the
list of Islamic practices that had an ulterior political purpose, was its
toleration of Christianity and Judaism. Yet the picture here is a rather
confusing one, with little general argumentation of that kind, and no dominant view of the principles on which the toleration was based. As we have
seen, the positive highlighting of Ottoman religious toleration in the
sixteenth century was largely a by-product of Christian intra-confessional
polemics. It was easy to put a positive, shame-praising gloss on the Ottoman
practice, when comparing it with either the Inquisition or various Protestant
policies (Luther's campaign against the monasteries, Queen Elizabeth's anti-
Catholic penal laws, and so on), without even trying to explain the reasons
for Ottoman toleration. Those who did make the attempt were more likely
to have recourse to a separation between temporal and religious concerns,
attributing the Ottoman policy to the secular ruler's desire for peace and
security. Pierre Belon's version of this has already been cited: 'That is what
has always sustained the great power of the Sultan: for if he conquers a
country, it is sufficient for him that he be obeyed, and so long as he receives
the tribute payment, he does not concern himself with people's souls.'[24]
Such an approach was of course congenial to the French 'politique' theorists
of the latter part of the sixteenth century, who were happy to use the
Ottoman example as a positive model when urging toleration on their
rulers—writers such as Innocent Gentillet, François Baudouin, and (as we
have seen) Jean Bodin.[25] And it was also commended by that rarity among
sixteenth-century writers, Sébastien Châteillon (Castellio), an author who
argued that toleration was a real good in itself: as he put it, 'the Sultan well
defends those Christians and Jews who are his subjects against the violence
that might be done to them, and he does so not because of their religion,
which he despises, but because they are his subjects.'[26]

23. Rycaut, *Present State*, p. 153; 'effeminate' here has the general sense of 'voluptuous'.
24. Above, p. 148.
25. See Lecler, *Toleration*, ii, p. 104 (Gentillet); Pippidi, *Visions*, pp. 96–7 (Baudouin); above,
    pp. 154–5 (Bodin).
26. Châteillon, *Conseil*, p. 91 ('Le Turc maintient bien les Chrestiens & Iuifs ses subietzs co[n]tre la
    uiolence qui leur pourroit estre faite, & les maintient non a cause de leur religion, laquelle il a
    en dedain, mais a cause qu'ilz sont ses subiectzs').

Given the insistence of post-Tridentine Counter-Reformation theorists
on the need to bring temporal and spiritual authority into close alignment, it
is not surprising to find that—with the exception of politique Catholics—
most of those who drew attention to the beneficial effect of Ottoman
toleration were on the Protestant side. On this point, while the shame-
praising by Catholics functioned only in relative terms, that by Protestants
could incorporate at least an element of absolute approval.[27] But militantly
anti-Ottoman Protestants did find ways of explaining the Ottoman policy
that reduced its approvability to zero. François de La Noue, a Huguenot
advocate of a new crusade, was happy to commend intra-Christian irenicism as a means towards forming a united front against the Sultan; but when
he turned to the actual practice of toleration by the Ottomans he dismissed
it as 'just like the way in which we allow cattle and sheep to live in our
fields, for the sake of the advantage which we draw from them'.[28] (A Venetian
relazione of 1596 would make a similar point, explaining that the Sultan's
toleration policy was driven by two purposes: avoiding the risk of depopulating his territories, and raising extra taxation from the Churches.[29]) And
Hugo Grotius's comment on the Ottoman policy was merely to say that
when this Muslim power had conquered non-Muslim territories in order
to impose Islam at the point of the sword, it absurdly contradicted itself by
permitting the people to practise their own religion.[30]

One particular way of justifying religious toleration was occasionally
attributed to the Ottomans. It seems first to have surfaced in an essay, published in 1591 and frequently reprinted thereafter, by the German Protestant
scholar Philipp Camerarius. On the general issue of toleration, Camerarius
began by saying that temporal rulers who maintained order and meted out
justice without any regard to religion were not troubled by religiously
motivated revolts, in the way that those who imposed one particular version of religion were. He added that the Ottomans understood this well.

---

27. For a striking example see the comments by Lutheran pastor Salomon Schweigger (who
    served as chaplain to the Imperial Ambassador in Istanbul between 1578 and 1581) on the fact
    that the Sultan was more tolerant of Protestantism than most Christian rulers: *Ein newe
    Reyssbeschreibung*, p. 69.
28. La Noue, *Discours*, pp. 81–8, 474 (intra-Christian), 459 ('tout ainsi que nous souffrons viure en
    nos campagnes les boeufs & les moutons, pour l'vtilité que nous en tirons'). La Noue may have
    been influenced by the use of the term 'cattle' ('pecudes') by humanist writers (see above,
    pp. 207–8); he is less likely to have known that the Arabic and Turkish term for the tax-paying
    subjects of the Sultan, 'ra'aya' or 'reaya', derived from a word for 'flock'.
29. Relazione of Leonardo Donà, in Seneca, *Il doge*, pp. 314–15.
30. Grotius, *De veritate* VI.7, p. 286.

And then he told a story (for which, rather suspiciously in an otherwise well-referenced work, he gave no source) about Sultan Süleyman the Magnificent. At one point, he said, the Mufti and other senior officials had visited the Sultan in his palace and urged him to expel or forcibly convert his non-Muslim subjects. Süleyman told them to look through a window at his garden, where many different flowers were growing together, and said:

> Just as that decorative variety of herbs and flowers not only does no harm, but marvellously refreshes the eyes and the senses, so too the diversity of faiths and religions in my empire is an advantage to me, not a liability, so long as they live in peace and obey my commands in other political matters. Therefore it is better to let them continue to follow their religions in their own way, as my ancestors permitted them to do, rather than provoke uprisings and see my state ruined. That would be just as if I were to pull up all my flowers except those of one single colour; and then what would I be doing except depriving my garden or meadow of its own natural grace and beauty, instead of improving it?[31]

Here, while the basis of the argument seemed to be simply the point about maintaining temporal peace, there was an intriguing suggestion—conveyed through the aesthetic metaphor—that variety in itself was of positive value. The point was echoed, though not developed, by other writers. Christoph Harant, for example, inserted this passage (in his own German translation) into his description of the coexistence of different confessions in Jerusalem, in the account he wrote of his pilgrimage to the Holy Land in 1598.[32] A similar view was expressed by Richard Knolles in his history of the Ottoman Empire. Discussing the policy of Tamerlane (Timur Leng), a Muslim ruler who had tolerated all varieties of religion except idolatry and atheism, he described him as 'disliking of no man for his religion whatsoeuer ... Being himself of opinion, That God ... as he had created in the world sundrie kinds of people, much differing both in nature, manners, and condition ... so was he also contented to be of them diuersly serued'.[33] And the anonymous German defender of 'Calvinoturcism', in his

---

31. P. Camerarius, *Operae horarum*, I.58, pp. 261 (general issue, Ottomans), 262 ('Quemadmodum ista varietas distincta herbarum & floru[m] non solum nihil obest, sed mirifice oculos & sensus recreat, ita in imperio meo diuersa fides, & religio potius vsui qua[m] oneri mihi est, si modo pacate viuunt, & in aliis rebus politicis mandatis meis parent. Praestat igitur eos diutius, sicut maiores mei permiserunt, ita more suo religiones suas sequi, quam turbas excitari, & imperium meum deformari. Non secus ac si flosculos vnicoloros tantum relinquerem, & reliquos euellerem. Quid facerem enim aliud, quam vt hortum vel pratu[m] sua natiua elegantia & decore, potius spoliarem, quam ornarem?').

32. Harant, *Der christliche Ulysses*, p. 433.   33. Knolles, *Generall Historie*, p. 211.

critical commentary on Campanella published in 1628, invoked the same metaphor as Camerarius when explaining why the Ottomans had welcomed 800,000 Jews expelled from Spain: 'the Sultan simply wants to increase his empire, which he thinks of as like a pleasant garden, more beautified by the differently coloured flowers of several religions than by one on its own.'[34]

Overall, therefore, while explanations of the Ottoman policy of religious toleration typically concentrated on the temporal benefits to the ruler, they also tended to assume that the policy was the creation of successive sultans, not one of those devices for extending or enforcing temporal dominion that had been built into Islam itself by its original deviser. (Significantly, in Camerarius's story it was the Grand Mufti, speaking apparently on behalf of Islam, who had demanded an end to toleration.) It is hard to find examples of Western writers attributing the policy to Muhammad; but occasionally the claim was made. One striking expression of that view was given by the Venetian nobleman Nicolò Contarini, in the manuscript history of Venice which he composed during the 1620s (before his rather brief tenure as Doge in 1630–1). Islam, he explained, had been concocted for temporal purposes by Muhammad and his three assistants and advisers, Ali, Omar, and Abu Bakr. Of all four he wrote:

These new legislators, who were more cunning than all others when it came to gathering as many people as possible from all places and of all kinds, constructed the cleverest device that could ever be put together, as follows: they said that even though God designated the law preached by Muhammad as the best one, nevertheless He likes to be worshipped through various different religions, not despising any of them, and for that reason no religion should be rejected, so long as it recognizes the Muslim ruler as its lord, and pays the *haraç* or poll tax imposed on it.[35]

---

34. Anon., *Compendium*, sig. K2r ('der Türcke nur sein Reich erweitern wil, welches er einen lustigen Garten gleich zu sein vermeinet, welcher von unterschiedenen Farben Blumen der mancherley Religionen besser, als von einerley geziert wurde').

35. British Library, London, MS King's 151, Contarini, 'Historie venete', book 2, fos. 164r (Muhammad and assistants), 164v–165r ('li nuoui legislatori sopra tutti gli altri astutissimi per raccogliere da ogni luogo ogni sorte di persone, quanti più si potesse, innalzarono sopra di essa una machinazione la più artificiosa, che potesse esser costrutta, et è: che Dio, sebbene uolle, che la Legge insegnata da Maometto fosse la migliore, nondimeno hà caro di esser adorato con uarie religioni, nè sdegna alcuna, e perciò che niuna deue esser rifiutata, purchè riconosca il Rè Maomettano per superiore, e le sia pagato il Carazzo, cioè il censo capitale decretatole'). On this text (of which four MS copies are known) see Cozzi, *Il doge*, pp. 199–217.

The most likely basis for this view was the commonly held idea that anyone who led a virtuous life could, according to the basic tenets of Islam, be saved in his or her own faith. This idea—derived ultimately from the Koran, 2: 62—was persistent in much Western anti-Muslim literature, from medieval writers, Torquemada, and Pius II onwards; Tommaso Campanella, for example, vehemently denounced it as one of the chief 'lies' of the Koran.[36] (Scholars of Islam such as Adriaen Reland would eventually dismiss it as a misunderstanding, but there is evidence that many Muslims did hold this view. Seventeenth-century Jesuits engaged in the conversion of Muslims, such as Tirso González de Santalla and Emmanuele Sanz, found that this belief was a real obstacle to their work; in 1699 a Bosnian slave in Malta, hauled before the Inquisition because she had renounced her conversion to Christianity and returned to Islam, testified that 'in my country I heard people say that those who live well will be saved, and those who live badly will be damned.'[37])

Only one Western writer seems to have connected this idea—or, at least, a version of it—with the practice of religious toleration in a way that involved attributing to Muhammad not Machiavellian cunning but rather a genuine theological insight. Jean Bodin's comments on toleration embraced both the politique view that persecution was to be avoided because it would lead to civil unrest, and the traditional Christian idea that religious belief cannot be produced by coercion. But in his manuscript dialogue work, the *Colloquium*, he also went further, introducing a principle which he identified particularly with the teachings of Islam. As Senamus (the speaker commonly identified as a 'sceptical naturalist') puts it: 'If all people could be persuaded, as the Muslims, Octavius, and I are, that all the prayers of all people which come from a pure mind are pleasing to God, or surely are not displeasing, it would be possible to live everywhere in the world in the same harmony as those who live under the emperor of the Ottomans or Persians.'[38] Senamus echoes here a statement of fundamental principle made a few

36. Kedar, *Crusade and Mission*, p. 172 (medieval); Adeva Martín, 'Juan de Torquemada', p. 202; Pius II, *Epistola*, p. 32; Campanella, *Legazioni*, p. 61.
37. Reland, *De religione mohammedica*, pp. 96–105; González de Santalla, *Manuductio*, 2nd pagination, pp. 32–4; Sanz, *Breve trattato*, pp. 38–41; Mdina, Cathedral Archives, Archive of the Inquisition, MS Processi, 95A, case 5, Anna Maria (Fatima) (1698–9), fos. 160r–189v, at fo. 173v ('nel mio paese sentiuo dire chi uiue bene si salua, e chi uiue male si danna').
38. Bodin, *Colloquium of the Seven*, p. 467 (emended); *Colloquium heptaplomeres*, p. 355 ('Si omnibus id persuaderi posset, quod Ismaëlitis, quod mihi, quod Octavio, scilicet omnia omnium vota, quae a pura mente proficiscuntur, Deo grata vel certe non ingrata esse, ubique terrarum eadem concordia vivi posset, qua vivitur sub imperatore Turcarum vel Persarum').

pages earlier by the convert to Islam, Octavius: 'The prayer of the multitude is efficacious if it has besought eternal God with a sincere mind.'[39] This was a principle which Bodin himself endorsed—and, at the same time, associated with the Ottomans—in his discussion of religious toleration in the Latin version of the *République*. In that discussion he not only emphasized that coerced worship could not be pleasing to God; he also gave the example of the toleration of different religions by the Sultan, comparing his policy to that of Augustus and concluding: 'For why the people of auncient time were persuaded, as were the Turks, all sorts of religions which proceed from a pure mind, to be acceptable vnto the gods.'[40]

Here as elsewhere, however, Bodin was an exception. Generally, there was a kind of cognitive dissonance at work on this issue: one part of the literature took it for granted that this surprisingly complaisant belief in the salvation of all people of good will was a standard component of Muslim faith, rooted in the text of the Koran, while another part insisted that Muslims were especially devoted to imposing their faith on non-Muslims by violence and coercion. But most writers chose to represent Ottoman religious toleration as a policy developed by the sultans in their capacity as temporal rulers, not as something planned by Muhammad and dictated by Islam; just too much, it seems, had been invested in the notion that Islam was an intrinsically coercive religion. No real attempt was made to solve this puzzle until 1666, when Paul Rycaut offered an explanation. The toleration of other faiths, he wrote, was a 'policy' adopted by Muhammad during the first phase of the preaching of Islam. (Here Rycaut quoted at length from the so-called 'Testament' of Muhammad, a forged Arabic text, eloquently proclaiming tolerance and protection for Christians, which had been found in the monastery of Mount Carmel, sent back to France by a missionary, and printed, in Arabic and Latin translation, in 1630.) Only when his own temporal rule was fully secured, Rycaut argued, did Muhammad change his tune and demand the propagation of Islam by the sword.[41]

39. Bodin, *Colloquium of the Seven*, p. 464 (emended); *Colloquium heptaplomeres*, p. 353 ('Multitudinis quidem rogatio efficax est, si mente sincera Deum aeternum appellaverit').
40. Bodin, *Six Bookes*, p. 538F (*De republica*, p. 484: 'Idem enim veteres populi quod Turcae...persuasum habuerunt, omnes omnium religiones, quae à pura mente proficiscantur, diis immortalibus gratas esse').
41. Rycaut, *Present State*, pp. 99–102; Sionita, ed. and tr., *Testamentum*. On the *Testamentum*, which was recognized as a forgery by Grotius and Voetius, but taken as genuine by other scholars, see Bayle, *Dictionaire*, iii, p. 1,859, note AA. Johannes Praetorius, who gave a German translation of the whole text in 1664, regarded it as genuine but said that the Ottoman sultans systematically broke it, as they thought that promise-keeping 'befits merchants, not princes' (*Catastrophe*, sig.

As the standard approach to the issue of Ottoman religious toleration shows, early modern writers were able to distinguish between the dictates of Islam and the secular policies of the Ottoman state. Indeed, there was some significant debate about the relative power of the two—a debate which could involve shadow-boxing with Protestant–Catholic arguments about the power of the Papacy, intra-Catholic ones about Gallicanism, and intra-Protestant ones about Erastianism. Much depended on how Western observers interpreted the status and the authority of the Grand Mufti. In the sixteenth century it was common to assess these very highly; as we have seen, Bodin emphasized that the sultans 'honour and obserue their Mufties, or high Bishops, with the greatest honour and respect possibly to bee giuen vnto them'.[42] Edward Barton, the English Ambassador in Istanbul, reported in 1590 that the Mufti was 'elected by the gran sig^r: [sc. Sultan] for the ancienst, and of the best lyfe, amongst all the cheife doctors of theire lawe; wch sayed Mufty is of such authority thatt none, no nott the gran sig^r: will gainsay his sentence'; in the following decade the Venetian bailo Ottavio Bon similarly observed that the Mufti always prevailed over the Sultan.[43] It was on the basis of such reports that the anti-Protestant polemicist William Rainolds portrayed the Ottoman system as better than the English one, as it more closely resembled the relationship between a pious Catholic sovereign and the Pope. However, as we have also seen, Rainolds distinguished between this current system and the one originally intended by Muhammad, in which the temporal ruler also held all spiritual authority in his own hands—an arrangement which he denounced as similar to that of the Elizabethan Church of England.[44]

During the seventeenth century, Western estimates of the authority of the Mufti became more qualified. As part of his systematically negative portrayal of the Ottoman state, George Sandys wrote that the Sultan could take action against the lives and properties of his subjects 'by no other rule then that of his will; although sometime for forme he vseth the assent of the neuer gain-saying *Mufti*'.[45] Louis Deshayes gave a more balanced account, saying that the Mufti was greatly honoured by the Sultan, who wanted his subjects to

---

Oo3v: 'komme den Kauffleuten und nicht den Fürsten zu'). Lancelot Addison gave an English translation, but pronounced the text spurious (*Life of Mahumed*, pp. 104–12, 116).

42. Above, p. 216. As this example illustrates, most Western writers used ill-fitting Christian categories (such as bishop or pope) to describe what was in fact a senior legal authority.

43. The National Archives, Kew, SP 97/2, fo. 6or (Barton to Burghley); Bon, *Sultan's Seraglio*, p. 131.

44. See above, pp. 98–9, and Rainolds, *Calvino-Turcismus*, pp. 315–16.

45. Sandys, *Relation*, p. 47.

believe that he (the Sultan) derived his authority from God and Muhammad. Before making a decision about war or peace, the Sultan would send to the Mufti for his opinion, 'to find out if he can do it in accordance with the law, so that he may seem just and religious, and so that he can, by these religious means, make his subjects amenable to what he wants'; this description put the emphasis on keeping up religious appearances, with the implication that the Mufti was more a facilitator than a decisive arbiter of sultanic policy.[46] A similar account (influenced, as it seems, by Deshayes) was given by Paul Rycaut: 'In matters of State the *Sultan* demands his opinion...either to appear the more just and religious, or to incline the people more willingly to obedience.' But he went on: 'And the Grand Signior, though he himself is above the Law, and is the Oracle and Fountain of Justice, yet it is seldome that he proceeds so irregularly to contemn that Authority wherein their Religion hath placed an ultimate power of decision in all their controversies.' Nevertheless, he noted that the Mufti could be dismissed and executed, if the Sultan so decreed.[47] Some other writers, as we shall see, not only accepted that the Mufti was the Sultan's creature, but welcomed that as a sign of a properly Erastian system in which religion was fully under temporal control. In so doing, they narrowed the divide between the Ottoman system and the one originally set up by Muhammad, in which, as they saw it, temporal power was primary and all spiritual authority was also held, as a necessary adjunct to temporal power, by the temporal ruler.

What is striking about the development of this argument in the first half of the seventeenth century is the degree to which the Machiavellian analysis of Islam could be made to yield a positive valuation of that religion. Previously we have seen how some of the underlying Machiavellian assumptions—about the dependence of temporal rule on the religious beliefs of the ruled, and even about the instrumental effectiveness of 'pious frauds' by pagan legislators—were taken up by Counter-Reformation 'reason of state' theorists. But their view of Islam was always, and indeed could not have failed to be, essentially negative. Christianity was perfect and true, and therefore gave the best possible support to the temporal state, whereas the provisions of Islam were necessarily defective. There was, in other words, a mismatch between the ingenuity, or even, in purely temporal and instrumental terms, the wisdom, of Muhammad in bamboozling the population with his claims of divine

---

46. Deshayes, *Voiage*, p. 218 ('pour sçauoir s'il peut faire la chose selon la loy, afin de paroistre iuste & Religieux, & de disposer ses sujets par ce moyen de Religion à ce qu'il desire').
47. Rycaut, *Present State*, pp. 6 (dismissed), 106 (quotations), 107 (dismissed).

revelation, and the inadequacy or foolishness of many of the actual precepts of his new religion. However, the kind of analysis conducted by writers such as Giacomo Soranzo suggested a very different view. The particular precepts of Islam were subtly devised to aid military efficiency and empire-building; the cleverness of the imposture and the cleverness of the contents of the religion were thus one and the same. This way of looking at it made possible an appreciation of Islam which was both Machiavellian and admiring.

The first large-scale statement of this position was, admittedly, ambivalent in the extreme. When Traiano Boccalini put together his political assessment of Islam he was writing as a satirist, opposed both to Islam in particular and to the deception of the people by powerful rulers in general. Yet his account (clearly drawing on Soranzo's comments, which he must have known from their publication in the *Tesoro politico*) was systematic and, from the point of view of mere temporal effectiveness, quite compelling. In one of Boccalini's imaginary dialogues on Mount Parnassus, chaired by the god Apollo, the Emperor Maximilian I expounds his theory that the introduction of Islam was 'entirely a matter of policy, of bare ambition, and mere interest in ruling'. The ban on wine was a shrewd device to improve military efficiency (Maximilian ruefully admits that he has 'suffered much worse trouble from the drunkenness of my German soldiers than from the weapons of my enemies'); polygamy was designed to increase the population, and, combined with a law of equal inheritance, prevented the accumulation of wealth, thereby obliging men to serve in the army to earn a salary; the doctrine of fate rendered soldiers fearless ('what more politically canny and diabolical precept could an ambitious legislator make in order to reach the point, after a short time, of ruling the whole world?'); sultans were forbidden to surrender land where there had been a mosque, and were not allowed to commemorate their own names by building a mosque unless they had conquered a new kingdom; and 'the most important political law' consisted of Muhammad's warning that those who disobeyed their ruler would not go to Heaven.[48] Boccalini also adds an original satirical point, if only to show more clearly which side he is on. Muhammad's most politically canny precept was his refusal to let women pray in mosques: true religion would have preached the principles of a good life applicable to all, but Muhammad was concerned

---

48. Boccalini, *Ragguagli* II.68, ii, pp. 238 ('tutta è politica, nuda ambizione, semplice interesse di regnare'), 239–40 ('travagli molto maggiori ricevei dall ubriachezza de' miei soldati alemanni che dale armi de' miei nemici', polygamy, 'Qual piú politico e diabolico precetto da un ambizioso legislatore, per arrivare in tempo brieve a dominar l'universo tutto?'), 240–1 (mosques, 'principalissima legge politica').

only with men, as women are 'not suited to setting up states, and not good at acquiring or maintaining them'. Overall, however, the effectiveness of this politico-religious system is not challenged; Apollo's judgment is that Maximilian's analysis was entirely correct, and he adds as an afterthought the further point that Muhammad cleverly forbade any disputing about Islam, ordering people to defend it with force instead.[49]

This sort of analysis, itself prompted by a Venetian relazione, had its entirely non-satirical counterparts in other Venetian accounts of the early seventeenth century. Nicolò Contarini took this approach, not only praising Muhammad's policy of religious toleration as an ingenious tactic for extending his rule, but also extolling the ban on alcohol as a highly political device, which he compared to the decrees of Lycurgus. Contarini's attitude was openly and unashamedly Machiavellian. At the beginning of his section on Islam and the Ottoman Empire, he announced that the success of all states depends on two things, 'laws, and arms', and explained that the term 'laws' included religions. Leaving aside the true Christian religion, he wrote, he would speak of 'those religions that were invented by wise men for the simple purpose of keeping the people dutiful, and thereby establishing and expanding states'.[50] Contarini's views chimed perfectly with those of the returning bailo Giorgio Giustinian, whose relazione of 1627 declared:

> The false prophet Muhammad was truly a great architect when it came to building a monarchy: since he knew very well how powerful respect for religion is in the minds of men, he constructed his out of the Mosaic and Christian religions, and out of the pagan religion too, in order to entice everyone to adopt it, making a mixture of them which was useful not only for religious purposes, but also for political ones.

Pursuing this argument, he continued, predictably enough: 'It was for the same purpose, monarchy, that in his law [sc. religion] Muhammad directed everything towards warfare'.[51]

49. Ibid., ii, pp. 241 ('non atte a sollevar gli Stati, non buone per acquistarli e mantenerli'), 242 (Apollo).
50. British Library, London, MS King's 151, fos. 163v ('le Leggi, e l'Armi'), 164r ('quelle ... che furono dalli homini sagaci inuentate, per semplice scopo di tener in Officio gli popoli, e p[er] mezzo di esse stabilire et aggrandire gli Stati'), 174r (alcohol, Lycurgus).
51. Pedani, ed., Relazioni, pp. 541–2 ('Fu veramente Mahometto pseudo proffetta grand'architetto per fabricar una monarchia, poiché sapendo egli molto bene quanta forza habbia negl'animi degl'huomini il rispetto della religione, compose la sua della mosaica, christiana e pagana ancora, per allietar ciascuno ad abbracciarla, facendo un misto che servisse non solo per la religione, ma per la politica ancora', 'All'istesso fine della monarchia indrizzò Mehemet con la sua legge tutte le cose alla guerra'). The point about the mixture of religions was made in similar terms by Contarini: British Library, London, MS King's 151, fo. 165r.

Machiavellianism of this kind was not an exclusively Italian phenomenon. In May 1634 the lawyer and gentleman-scholar Henry Blount, then aged 31, set off from Venice on an eleven-month-long tour of the Levant. His purpose, as he explained in the book he published two years later, was to study the Turks, 'who are the only moderne people, great in action, and whose Empire hath suddenly invaded the World and fixt it selfe such firme foundations as no other ever did'. What he wanted to know was 'whether to an unpartiall conceit, the *Turkish* way appeare absolutely barbarous, as we are given to understand, or rather an other kinde of civilitie, different from ours, but no lesse pretending'.[52] Part of his account was devoted to the institutions of the Ottoman state; here he expanded on his sense of what it was to be an 'unpartiall' observer, insisting that he would not 'censure them by any rule, but that of more, or less *sufficiency* to their aime, which I suppose to be the *Empires* advancement'. Even in this section, the functional role of Islam was noted. The volunteer cavalry units were the best fighting force in the Ottoman army, because they were motivated by the desire to go straight to the sensual Paradise promised by Muhammad; 'so *effectuall* an *Instrument* of State i[s] *Superstition*, and such deepe *Impressions* does it make, when fitted to the *passions* of the *Subject*; and that usefull in those whom neither reason, nor honour could possesse.'[53]

Blount opened his main discussion of Islam with a rather formulaic disclaimer. 'Now followes their *Religion*, wherein I noted only the *Politicke* Institutions thereof; these observations moving only in that *Sphere*, cannot jarre with a higher, though the motion seeme contrary.' Muhammad had understood that hope and fear were the springs of human action, and that hopes and fears of rewards and punishments in the afterlife were the strongest motives of all. He designed his Paradise accordingly: 'for hee finding the *Sword* to be the foundation of *Empires*, and that to manage the Sword, the rude and sensuall are more vigorous, then wits softned in a mild *rationall* way of *civilitie*, did first frame his *institutions* to a rude insolent sensuality.' That his sensual Paradise was a mere invention did not matter; it was a device 'whereby, their *hopes* and *feares* though false, prevailes [*sic*] as strongly as if true, and serve the *State* as effectually, because *Opinion* which moves all our *Actions*, is governed by the *Apparency* of things'.[54] In his positive assessment

---

52. Blount, *Voyage*, p. 2; 'pretending' here means 'having a claim on our attention'. On Blount's life see Maclean, *Rise*, pp. 117–22.
53. Blount, *Voyage*, pp. 61–2 ('censure them...'), 68 ('so *effectuall*...').
54. Ibid., pp. 77 ('Now followes...'), 78 ('for hee...', 'whereby, their...').

of the strength and coherence of the Ottoman system of government, Blount did not attempt to tie everything to the precepts of Islam. Rather, he looked for the successful application of the motives of hope and fear—a general phenomenon of which Islam was merely a subset. Observing, for example, that Ottoman justice was 'more *Severe, Speedy*, and *Arbitrary*' than that of any other states, he said that this was necessary because the population was 'made up of severall People different in *Bloud, Sect*, and *Interesse*, one from another, nor linkt in affection, or any common engagement toward the publique good, other then what meere terror puts upon them.' The system was, he approvingly noted, more 'effectuall' in deterring rebellion than that of ancient Rome.[55]

To call Blount's general approach 'Machiavellian' is not to say that it was simply derived from a reading of Machiavelli's texts. It reflected, rather, a Machiavellian tradition which had gone some way beyond the original views of that author, especially where the treatment of the common people was concerned. Whereas Machiavelli himself aimed at the inculcation of political virtue in the citizenry, this tradition saw the subjects as incurably ignorant and foolish; Machiavelli had allowed pious fraud as a kind of 'quick fix' by legislators who had to impose their will on a newly gathered, uncivilized group of people, but this tradition was prepared to accept a deceptive religion as a permanent method of control. One of the key figures in the development of this tradition was the philosopher Girolamo Cardano, whose treatise *De sapientia* was published in 1544. Cardano distinguished between three levels of wisdom: the highest was concerned with divine truths; the next, 'natural' wisdom, allowed people to access objective truths, such as ethical principles, when they had freed themselves of the passions; and the lowest, 'human' wisdom, involved knowing how best to deal with those ordinary human beings whom the passions still held in their grip. (Typical methods would include dissimulation, simulation, and eloquence.)[56]

This scheme was developed further by Pierre Charron in his *De la sagesse* (1602): his approach incorporated neo-Stoicism for the truly wise, Montaignian scepticism and relativism when considering the behaviour of ordinary people and the customs to which they adhered, and Machiavellian cunning when dealing with them. The underlying assumption was that the common people were fickle and gullible—too fickle, because they were

55. Ibid., pp. 89–90.
56. See Procacci, *Studi*, pp. 77–106, emphasizing Cardano's debt to Machiavelli.

driven this way and that by their short-term desires and fears, to act in themselves as a stable support for rule, but sufficiently gullible that a clever legislator could find ways to manage them. This way of thinking could easily incorporate Tacitean ideas about how the people could be fobbed off with 'simulacra' of freedom and power. But the most powerful device of social and political control would always be religion, as it harnessed the greatest fear of all, fear of supernatural power and eternal punishment. (One other factor that could restrain the common people was the force of custom, to which they were surprisingly submissive; like religious belief, custom could be obviously irrational and foolish in the eyes of the wise, yet it might still have a strong functional value.) This whole pattern of thought was potentially radical in intellectual terms, as it allowed the critical thinking of a wise elite—communicating among themselves, at least—to dismantle all kinds of commonly accepted beliefs and practices. Yet at the same time it was, as a political position, not only non-radical but conservative and potentially absolutist in its desire to shore up the power of the state over the unruly multitude.[57]

One of the leading proponents of this view was the Parisian scholar, bibliophile, and graduate of the University of Padua (where a tradition of naturalistic Aristotelianism had continued long after Pomponazzi's death) Gabriel Naudé. In one of the opening chapters of his first major work, published in 1625 when he was 25 years old, *Apologie pour tous les grands personnages qui ont esté faussement soupçonnez de magie*, he gave a classic statement of the Machiavellian defence of religious imposture by the founders of states.

> All the most subtle and cunning legislators, being well aware that the best way to acquire and retain authority over their people was to persuade them that they themselves were simply being used by some supreme Deity who wished to favour them with its help and take them under its protection, have very appropriately made use of those feigned deities, those imaginary conversations, those bogus apparitions, and, in a word, that magic of the ancients, in order to soften the appearance of their ambition and set the initial design of their rule on a more secure foundation.[58]

57. On this whole pattern of thought, which is associated particularly with the *libertins érudits* of the early and mid-seventeenth century, see Pintard, *Le Libertinage*, pp. 539–64; Battista, *Alle origini* (esp. on Charron); Castrucci, *Ordine*; Charles-Daubert, 'Le "Libertinage"'; Taranto, *Pirronismo*, pp. 17–129.

58. Naudé, *Apologie*, pp. 49–50 ('tous les plus fins & rusez Legislateurs n'ignorant pas que le plus suffisant moyen pour s'acquerir authorité envers leur peuples, & se maintenir en icelle, estoit de leur persuader qu'ils n'estoient que l'organe de quelque Deité supreme qui les vouloit

A standard list of examples followed, including Zamolxis, Charondas, Lycurgus, Numa Pompilius, and Muhammad, who claimed that the Angel Gabriel 'often came to whisper in his ear in the form of a pigeon'. And in a later chapter Naudé returned to this theme, insisting that such deception was 'useful and salutary for the people who were made to believe in it'.[59]

Within seven or eight years of publishing that book, Naudé wrote another work in which the same topic was handled at greater length. This treatise, which remained for some time in manuscript, was at first entitled 'De veris rerumpublicarum arcanis' or 'Arcana imperiorum'; when a version of it was eventually published (with the probably fictitious imprint 'Rome, 1639'—it is more likely to have been printed in the Netherlands some time between 1642 and Naudé's death in 1653), it bore the title *Considerations politiques sur les coups d'estat*.[60] What Naudé meant by 'coups d'état' was something quite different from the modern sense of the phrase. He defined them as 'bold and extraordinary actions which rulers are obliged to carry out in difficult and rather desperate circumstances, contrary to ordinary right, and not even preserving any principle of order or appearance of justice, jeopardizing private interest for the sake of public good'. These, he explained, were like those 'maxims' of reason of state that justified what would otherwise be immoral or illegal actions, except that whereas maxims could be understood and even avowed as regular rules of conduct, 'coups d'état' were by their nature either unexpected or secret.[61] His concern was thus with what Clapmarius had called the 'arcana' or secrets of rule—or rather, with that special category of 'arcana' that dealt with the handling of irregular or extreme situations.

Foremost among such special situations were the moments at which a clever legislator founded a state, or began to impose his rule. 'If we consider the starting points of all monarchies', Naudé wrote, 'we shall always find that

favoriser de son assistance & recevoir en sa protection, se sont servis fort à propos de ces Deitez feintes, de ces colloques supposez, de ces apparitions mensongeres, & en un mot de cette Magie des anciens, pour mieux palier leur ambition & fonder plus assurément le premier dessein de leurs Empires').

59. Ibid., pp. 50 ('lequel luy venoit souvent chucheter à l'aureille sous la forme d'un pigeon'), 258 ('utile & salutaire à ceux mesmes à qui ils la faisojent accroire').

60. See Pintard, *Le Libertinage*, pp. 614–15 (early titles); Donaldson, *Machiavelli*, pp. 160–5 (printing history). On this text see Donaldson, pp. 141–85; Cavaillé, 'Gabriel Naudé'; Schmeisser, ' "Mohammed" ', pp. 88–93.

61. Naudé, *Considerations*, pp. 65–6 (p. 65: 'des actions hardies & extraordinaires, que les Princes sont contraints d'executer aux affaires difficiles & comme desesperées, contre le droit commun, sans garder mesme aucun ordre ny forme de iustice, hazardant l'interest du particulier, pour le bien du public', pp. 65–6: maxims).

they began with some of these fictions and frauds, making religion and miracles march at the vanguard of a long procession of barbarous and cruel actions.'[62] The reason for this was to be found in the irrational nature of the common people—a subject on which Naudé waxed indignantly eloquent. What he called 'the vulgar mob, the crowd, the dregs of the people' were worse than animals because, although they were endowed with reason, they made no use of it. Only two things could keep them under control: 'the rigour of extreme physical punishments established by ancient legislators, and fear of the gods and of their thunderbolts'.[63] So, when he turned to the case of Muhammad, Naudé was happy to make use of all the standard Christian accusations of religious imposture (the trained pigeon, the writing of the Koran with the help of the monk Sergius, the voice of the man concealed in a well, and so on). For him, these were not so much accusations as creditable accounts of masterly ingenuity. The story that Muhammad had employed an astrologer to circulate predictions of a great religious transformation showed that he had a canny understanding of popular psychology; and if he hit on the idea of claiming to receive ecstatic visions as a way of explaining his epileptic fits, this was just a sign of his talent for brilliant improvisation. These, Naudé wrote with open admiration, were the tactics adopted by Muhammad 'when establishing not only his religion, but an empire which is today the most powerful in the world'.[64]

This was a bold work, by an author who was not afraid of causing offence; not every Catholic writer of this period would have been content to describe the St Bartholomew's Day Massacre as 'very just, and very remarkable'.[65] Yet although shocking in some ways, Naudé's text was much less challenging and critically stimulating—in the sense of raising critical arguments against the author's own society and religion—than another great seventeenth-century work on this topic in the Machiavellian tradition: Francis Osborne's *Politicall Reflections upon the Government of the Turks*,

---

62. Ibid., pp. 84–5 ('si nous considerons quels ont esté les commencemens de toutes les Monarchies nous trouuerons tousiours qu'elles ont commencé par quelques-vnes de ces Inuentions & supercheries, en faisant marcher la Religion & les miracles en teste d'vne longue suite de barbaries & de cruautez').

63. Ibid., pp. 153 ('le vulgaire ramassé, la tourbe & lie populaire'), 158 ('la rigueur des supplices establis par les anciens legislateurs... & la crainte des Dieux & de leur foudre').

64. Ibid., pp. 91–2 ('à l'establissement non moins de sa Religion, que d'vn Empire lequel est auiourd'huy le plus puissant du monde', epilepsy, pigeon, Koran, etc.), 164–5 (astrologer), 182 (improvisation).

65. Ibid. p. 110 ('tres-iuste, & tres-remarquable'). Naudé's only criticism of it (p. 109) was that it had not been carried out thoroughly enough, with the elimination of all Protestants.

published in London in 1656.[66] Francis Osborne was not, on the face of it, the most likely person to give a positive assessment of any aspect of sultanic rule or Ottoman culture. Unlike Henry Blount, he had never set foot in the Levant. A supporter of the parliamentarian side in the English Civil War, Osborne had strongly republican views; in a pamphlet written to persuade people to obey the new regime three years after the execution of Charles I, he argued that monarchy was inevitably subject to moral corruption, and cited the Ottoman sultans' murder of their sons as a particularly repugnant example of that.[67] Two things, however, made him take a positive interest in the Ottoman system. One was his unashamed Machiavellianism: in the same volume as his *Politicall Reflections* he also published 'A Discourse upon Nicholas Machiavell', praising his works as 'so full of Truth, Learning and Experience'. ('Why is he blamed', Osborne asked, 'for setting downe the most *generall Rules*, and such as all Statesmen make use of, either to benefit themselves, or hurt others?')[68] The other was his strong sense of the danger posed to stable rule by theological zeal and religious discord. As he put it in what would become his most famous work, *Advice to a Son*: 'A *Multitude* inflamed under a *religious* pretence, are at first as unsafely opposed, as joyned with ... Zeale, like the Rod of *Moses*, devouring all for Diabolicall, that dares but appear before it in the same shape: the inconsiderate Rabble, with the Swine in the Gospell, being more furiously agitated by the discontented Spirits of others, then their owne.' On this point he would have agreed whole-heartedly with Thomas Hobbes, whose 'great acquaintance' he was.[69]

The problem of how to contain religion within a stable political structure exercised many minds in Interregnum England. Francis Osborne believed that Muhammad and, following him, the Ottoman sultans had solved it; indeed, they had gone further, making religion a mighty bulwark of temporal rule. As he explained in his Epistle to the Reader, the aim of his *Politicall Reflections* was to take 'some choice *Observations* out of the Turkish *Arcana*, which ... may not unpossibly minde those at the Helm of *Expedients* more proper for *Unity*, than have yet been employed among *Christians*'. The underlying problem was the lack of obedience to 'God's Viceregents', and interference by religion 'in things purely belonging to the Magistrate'.[70] In

---

66. I use the general title of the volume; the first part has its own title, *The Turkish Policy: Or, Observations upon the Government of the Turks*.

67. Osborne, *Perswasive*, p. 33. 68. Osborne, *Politicall Observations*, pp. 129, 145.

69. Osborne, *Advice*, pp. 92–3; Aubrey, *'Brief Lives'*, i, p. 370 ('great acquaintance').

70. Osborne, *Politicall Reflections*, sigs. A2v–A3r. The verb 'minde' here has the sense 'remind', 'put in mind'.

the main body of the work he set out his case in a deliberately provocative way, and thereby created one of the most remarkable texts on Islam and the Ottoman Empire of this entire period.

Osborne begins by praising 'the prudent *Deportment of Mahumet*', and commenting that the reason why due credit has not been given is simply that the Muslims have not written their history properly: 'the main *difference*,' he observes, 'between *Alexander, Caesar*, and *Mahumet*, consists in a *Feather*, or the *Quill* of a *Goose*.'[71] A brisk and unabashed summary of the standard Christian stories follows: Muhammad's fraudulent claim to speak with an angel, the pretence of 'holy *Extasies*' as a cover for epilepsy, the devising of a 'Law' to appeal to 'humane Sensuality', and so on. His followers were stirred up to 'the intended *Worke of the Lord*, which was to spoile others, and enrich themselves'.[72] Muhammad borrowed from both Judaism and Christianity, honouring Moses to please the Jews and honouring Jesus to please the Christians, while cleverly plotting the subjugation of both. His banning of images was 'out of a deep Reason of State': image worship provides too easy a target for seditious reformers 'to foment a change, by discovering to the people *absurdities* in their *Worship*, which is better prevented in one directed, as his is, to the onely invisible and omnipotent *Creator*'. Thanks to Muhammad's foresight in such matters, there is no real schism in Islam; even the difference between (Sunni) Turks and (Shiite) Persians is about genealogy, not essential doctrine.[73] Every aspect of Islam was devised in accordance with a wise political programme: 'the Turks Sabbath', for instance, was a political device, as 'these *weekly meetings*, doe much civilize a Nation', and wine was banned for no fewer than five reasons (including military discipline, 'The *Transparency of Drunkennesse*' and the fact that 'Wine effeminates'). Muhammad also understood that '*Austerity* and *Reverence* in externall Worship . . . cannot be denied to have a huge operation upon *Obedience* to the *civill Magistrate*'. Overall, 'No *Law* is more intent upon the *Honour* and *Profit of Monarchy*, then the Turks.'[74]

Christian rulers, at first, exercised power just as absolute as the Sultan's, but over time their subjects found ways of moderating it by means of 'Money, Importunity, or Armes'—'which we doe not finde this Nation [*sc.* the Turks] ever went about: Servitude, by use, becoming a second nature'. However, Osborne's general argument implies that it is not mere 'use', the force of habit or the passage of time, that has preserved the power of the

---

71. Ibid., p. 2.   72. Ibid., pp. 4–6.
73. Ibid., pp. 6–8.   74. Ibid., pp. 8–10, 27 (wine).

Sultan, but rather the principles of Islam. These he summarizes as: 'The *Honour* of *God*, *Obedience* to their *Prince*, *Mutuall Love*, *Resolution* in *Warre*, with an invincible *Patience* in bearing all terrestriall wants'. Islam keeps people both obedient and honest, and 'This proves, *A false Religion doth contribute more to safety, then Atheisme*, or a stupid neglect of all Worship; and that *a Clergy is of excellent concernment*, provided they keep close in their Doctrine, to *Reason of State*.'[75] On the place of the Mufti in Muhammad's scheme, Osborne is not entirely consistent. At one point he commends, in passing, the fact that Muhammad forbade anyone to interpret the Koran except the Mufti; but later he explains that it was Muhammad's successors who set up this figure, in order 'to have withal a favourable Vmpire of a seeming more indifferent & sanctified allay'. The fact that the Sultan honours his Mufti with great reverence in public is 'true *Reason of State*'; but it is also commendable that if the Mufti goes against the Sultan he is executed. The Sultan's position is thus much better than that of Roman Catholic kings, insofar as 'the *Mufty* his *Pope*, no lesse then *Meca* his *Rome* are within the reach of his power.'[76]

Conscious of the long Western tradition of accusing Islam, and the Ottomans, of aggression, cruelty, and barbarity, Osborne is quick to turn the tables on the critics. He insists that nothing as evil as the St Bartholomew's Day Massacre was ever perpetrated by either Muhammad or any of his followers. Yes, it is true that their 'Law' justifies enlarging their empire; but if you berate them for this, they will ask in return how the King of Spain got Portugal, Naples, Milan, and Sicily—to say nothing of the 'Ocean' of blood shed in the New World, 'upon no more serious occasion, then Gold, and the Conversion of the people into slaves to dig it.'[77] Those who criticize Islam as 'subservient to worldly *Policy*' do not have far to look in order to 'finde other *Courts* standing in as profane a posture, especially that of *Rome*'. The resort of the sultans to '*Clandestine Deaths*' in order to preserve their rule is compared favourably with the carnage of civil wars in Christendom; Osborne notes that an assassin '*may be cheaper employed, then an Army*, and with lesse prejudice to *the good of the Generality*'. Even the murder by the Sultan of his sons or brothers, which Osborne had reprobated only four years earlier, is glossed here with the comment that the royal and princely

75. Ibid., pp. 11 ('Money...', 'which we...'), 15 ('The *Honour* ...'), 19 ('This proves...').
76. Ibid., pp. 13 (forbade), 29–30 ('to have...' (where 'allay' means 'character', 'nature'), 'true *Reason*...'), 31 ('the *Mufty*...'), 32–3 (executed).
77. Ibid., pp. 17–18.

houses of Italy and France have done the same—though this servant of the English Republic does add in passing that '*Republicks have not such impulsive causes to shed innocent blood, as Kings.*'[78]

As Osborne makes no attempt to distinguish between the secular policies of the Ottoman state and the principles of Islam, his account develops seamlessly into a celebration of several of those positive features of the Ottoman system that had been highlighted by the 'new paradigm'. He commends Ottoman punishments as swift and effective. He strongly approves of the meritocratic principle, which, he says, governs the distribution of all honours and government offices, and he goes out of his way to denounce the non-meritocratic nature of Western society. Where property ownership is concerned, he takes the most extreme interpretation available and puts it in a positive light: 'The *Emperour's* being here *Administrator to all dead mens Estates*, forceth their *Children* to be solicitous after *trades.*' This he describes as a 'laudable custome', praising the emphasis on practical pursuits in Ottoman life; 'Neither have they such a confluence of *Idle men, Lawyers* and *Scholars*, which among us make up a third of the people, and are, for the most part, Contrivers and Fomenters of all the distractions found in *Church* and *State.*'[79] These tendencies also lead to more frugality, less luxury, and no horse races or hunting. At this point, adopting a more brazenly 'free-thinking' tone than elsewhere in the work, he adds to the evidence of frugality and rationality the fact that they waste no money on 'amorous Entertainments: Their *plurality* of *Women* quenching with more security in regard of *Health*, and lesse *charge*, the thirst of *Change* ordinarily attending the tedious cohabitation with *one*'.[80]

Osborne does not use the word 'despotism'; he is happy to accept that the Sultan's power is absolute and unchallengeable, but although he employs the general term 'servitude' he neither directly describes the subjects as slaves nor suggests that the Sultan acts on mere whim. While the Sultan 'appears ever before his people like the Sun', he does not use arbitrary power, but hands over all grievances to his ministers (whom, in an emergency, he can sacrifice to the anger of the people). It is a principle of Ottoman—and Islamic—rule, according to Osborne, that civil obedience is sheer 'Patience',

---

78. Ibid., pp. 21 ('subservient to...', 'finde other...'), 34 ('*Clandestine Deaths*...', 'may be...'), 38–9 (sons or brothers, '*Republicks have*...').
79. Ibid., pp. 42–3 (punishments), 46–7 (meritocracy, 'The *Emperour's*...', 'laudable custome', 'Neither have...').
80. Ibid., p. 48 (frugality, 'amorous Entertainments...').

i.e. submission to power. Significantly, for one who had lived through the English constitutional debates of the 1640s and had written in favour of accepting the authority of the new regime *de facto*, he adds that there is 'no *Instrument* appearing of any mutuall *Compact* betwixt *Him* [*sc.* the Sultan] and the *People*'.[81] In the final analysis, Ottoman rule is sustained by three principles, all of which Osborne attributes ultimately to Muhammad's devising. First there is the clever apparent division of power between temporal and spiritual; the common people regard the authority of the Mufti as more 'sanctified', not realizing that he is merely 'a weather-cock pointing onely that way which the breath of *Policy* blowes'. Secondly, there is the reduction to 'an impartiall *Parity*' of the entire population, who are all equal 'in relation to everything but *Desert*... Thus are the Rich humbled into Thraldome out of *Feare*, and the rest out of *Hope*.' And finally there is a remarkable degree of 'Fortitude' in the service of the state, encouraged both by the prospect of gaining high office and by the incentive of 'the *joyes of Heaven*'.[82]

At one level, there is an element of *jeu d'esprit*, or indeed of *épater les bourgeois*, about this work. There were many aspects of Ottoman rule that Francis Osborne could not seriously have expected to be imitated by an English government, even—or, in some ways, especially—one that had attained power through civil war and regicide. Nor was it practical politics to promote any change by telling readers that if they adopted it, they would become more like Muslims. Only seven years earlier, the mere discovery that an English translation of the Koran was being printed in London had led to a panicky demand by the House of Commons to have it investigated, and much opportunistically hostile comment by royalist propagandists when the translation actually appeared.[83] Osborne's use of the Islamic and/ or Ottoman model goes far beyond the methods of conventional shame-praising. It is, rather, an exercise in a kind of Machiavellian analysis which challenges the reader: 'once you accept the premises of this way of looking at politics and religion, you will not be able to deny the advantages, in those terms, of the Ottoman system, and this will force you to think in a new way about the disadvantages of your own.'

Nowhere, it seems, did this exercise matter more to Francis Osborne than where the relationship between religion and political stability was concerned. He insisted that 'the first intent of *Religion*' was 'to set a bar against

81. Ibid., pp. 54 ('Patience', 'no *Instrument*...'), 102–3 ('appeares ever...', grievances).
82. Ibid., pp. 54–6.   83. See Malcolm, 'The 1649 English Translation', pp. 261–6.

strife ... This brought *Government* into use among such as had felt the heavy experiment of *Anarchy*, to avoid which nothing contributes more then *Vnity* in *Religion*, and where that cannot be compassed without much strife, a *Liberty* to professe what opinions men please, provided they be not repugnant to the generall welfare.' Islam itself, in contrast with Christianity, did not develop internal disunity, because Muhammad 'tempered' his religion with 'moderation'; unlike the Roman Catholics, the Muslim clergy did not perplex people's consciences with 'uselesse terrours or hard questions'.[84] But the Muslim solution to the problem of religion and order went further than that: as the example of the Ottoman Empire showed, the toleration of 'severall Religions' was a much better policy than any attempt to enforce uniformity.[85] Here, at least, was a lesson from the Levant that could resonate in Cromwellian England.

84. Osborne, *Politicall Reflections*, pp. 71–3.   85. Ibid., p. 77.

THIRTEEN

Critical and radical uses of Islam I
Vanini to Toland

Francis Osborne's work offers an example of an early modern writer using Islam (as he understood it) to probe and criticize the nature of his own society. There were many ways of doing this: some expressed criticism only insofar as they applied familiar, accepted standards; some could be critical in a more subversive way, but by more or less unintended implication; and in some cases the intention was deliberately radical and challenging.

At its simplest, the criticism of Western practice was nothing more than shame-praising, aimed at reinforcing values which Christian readers would fully accept in theory, even if they failed to live up to them in practice. The main example of this consisted of praise for the piety and devotion of ordinary Muslims. These qualities were commented on, as we have seen, by writers from Riccoldo da Monte Croce and George of Hungary onwards. The theme remained a fairly constant one; Busbecq wrote admiringly about the great 'ceremony and attention' of Muslims at prayer, and Postel exclaimed that 'anyone who witnessed their modesty, silence, and reverence in their *mescid*s or prayer meetings should be very ashamed to see that our own churches serve as places for chatting, wandering around, doing business, and creating a den of thieves.' Given that travellers also commonly reported that non-Muslims were not allowed to attend prayers inside a mosque, we may wonder how far this sort of comment represented first-hand experience.[1]

---

1. Above, p. 36 (Riccoldo, George of Hungary); Busbecq, *Life and Letters*, i, p. 303; Postel, *De la république*, p. 54 ('qui verroit la modestie, silence & reuerence qu'ils ont en leurs Mesgeda ou d'oraison [*sic*], deuroit auoir grand'honte de voir que les eglises de deça seruent de causer, pourmener, & marchandiser, & faire spelonque de Larrons'). *Mescid* is a word for mosque

But in some cases it was possible for an outside observer to see men at prayer in the mosque's courtyard; and besides, there was other evidence of Muslim devotion in Ottoman society. Seventeenth-century writers, whether Catholic or Protestant, continued to make the same point. Jean Thévenot wrote that 'you never see them chatting or joking in their mosques, where they always behave with great respect, and the certainly teach us a lesson where devotion is concerned.' Even the Anglican chaplain Thomas Smith, who had almost nothing good to say about the Ottomans, felt obliged to admit in 1678 that there was 'a great semblance of Devotion in their Churches', and went on to describe evening prayers during Ramadan at the Yeni Cami in Istanbul (attended by more than 2,000 people), where, 'Lifting up the Antiport, and advancing a little forward, I could not perceive the least noise; no coughing or spitting, no disorderly running up and down, no gazing one upon another, no entertainments of discourse, nothing of irreverence or heedlesness.'[2]

More complex kinds of criticism could arise from those intra-confessional arguments where, as we have seen, Catholics accused Protestants of resembling Muslims, and vice versa. An interesting example of this was given by the Bohemian nobleman Václav Budovec z Budova, who spent the years 1577–81 in Istanbul as chancellor to the Imperial Ambassador, and later published both a refutation of the Koran (*Antialkorán*, 1614) and a theological text directed against Muslims and Socinians (*Circulus horologi*, 1616).[3] In the latter work special attention was paid to the discussions which Budovec had had in Istanbul with converts from Christianity to Islam, the majority of whom had originally been Catholics; he described them as 'quite a few people, mostly Italian, who had an extremely good knowledge of philosophical writings, and were not ignorant of the Word of God either'.[4] Budovec, who was a member of the Protestant Unity of Brethren—and who would later play a role in precipitating the Thirty Years' War by helping to choose the

---

(from Arabic 'masjid', from which 'mosque' is ultimately derived). Aaron Hill commented in 1709 that the Ottomans 'severely . . . Guard their Publick Mosques from *Christian* Observation', and that a non-Muslim found at one of their services would be forced to convert: *Full and Just Account*, p. 47.

2. Thévenot, *L'Empire*, p. 138 ('On ne les voit jamais causer ni badiner dans leurs mosquées, où ils sont toujours en grand respect, et assurément ils nous font la leçon pour la dévotion'); Smith, *Remarks*, pp. 54–5.

3. On Budovec see Rataj, *České země*, pp. 129–35; Lisy-Wagner, *Islam*, pp. 75–80, 94–9.

4. Budovec, *Circulus horologi*, p. 173 ('complures, & praecipuè Italos homines in philosophicis scriptis versatissimos, & verbi Dei quoque non ignaros').

Elector Palatine as King of Bohemia—gave an account of these renegades' arguments that indicated none too subtly why it was that Roman Catholics might turn into Muslims. They told him that the Catholic Church defended itself against Protestantism on five points: Scripture derives its authority from that of the Roman Church; the truth of Catholic doctrine is supported by a greater number of teachers; within the Roman Church there is unanimity about dogma, unlike the mutual disagreement among the heretics; similarly, there is obedience to one head of the Church, unlike the situation among the Protestants; and there is only one source of authority, while among the heretics there are as many opinions as people.' "So", they say, "if these principles held by Christians serve as valid proofs of the Christian religion, why may they not be put forward by Muslims, much more convincingly than by Christians, to prove the Muslim religion against the Christians?" '[5] And Budovec then adds two more of their arguments: the 'Christians' (*sc.* Catholics) say that the Pope can issue dispensations relieving people of obligations that are stated in the Gospels, but no one can dispense from those of the Koran; and ' "your Pope gives orders to the Emperor and to kings, fomenting disputes between them and insinuating himself into the business of temporal government, whereas the *Padişah* [*sc.* Sultan], our emperor, alone gives orders to everyone, including the Mufti himself." '[6]

Budovec also described a discussion he had had with an Italian priest at a monastery in Galata (the town across the Golden Horn from Istanbul proper) in 1579, in which he had told the priest that if he thought the truth of Scripture depended on the Church, it meant that he believed only in human authority. With barely concealed satisfaction, he then related the story of how that priest, one year later, had stood up in the pulpit and announced his conversion to Islam.[7] To a Protestant it was obvious that the authority of the Bible was to be ascertained from the very nature of the Bible itself. Yet on this very point Budovec quoted, in his preface to the book, a rather fundamental objection made by the renegades in his debates with them: when he persuaded them to admit that they had never seen such 'absurd fables' as the stories contained in the Koran, 'they said: "yes, that is

5. Ibid., p. 173 (five points, 'Haec ergo, inquiunt...axiomata Christianorum si ad probandam religionem Christianam valent, cur non aequè à Turcis, imò longè melius quam à Christianis ad probandam religionem Mahumetanam, Christianis obiici possunt').
6. Ibid., p. 174 (dispensation, 'Vester Pontifex imperat Imperatori & regibus, alit lites inter eos, immiscet sese politico regimini...At Badescha, id est, Imperator noster solus imperat omnibus, & ipsi Mufty').
7. Ibid., pp. 179 (authority of Scripture), 183 (conversion).

true, but the Christians also follow fables, and all religions were instituted for the sake of political order." [8] Budovec seems to have felt no need to answer that objection here, as he felt that is was so self-evidently wicked and false; but some readers might still have been troubled by it.

Budovec's anti-Catholic line of argument was extended by the Swiss scholar of Arabic Johann Heinrich Hottinger in his *Historia orientalis* (1651). While discussing the success of what he called the 'Muslim empire' (meaning not just the Ottoman Empire, but all territories under Muslim rule), Hottinger seized on a classic list of 'signs' or 'marks' of the true Church put forward by the great Catholic controversialist Roberto Bellarmino. Each of these, Hottinger pointed out, could just as well be made to serve an argument in support of Islam. [9] Bellarmino's first sign was the name 'Catholic', which showed that the Roman Church was universal; Hottinger said that Islam also referred to Muslims using the universal term 'the faithful'. The second was the antiquity of the Roman Catholic Church; but Islam also laid claim to a tradition that began with Adam. [10] Bellarmino's third sign was the long, uninterrupted duration of the Church; however, many Catholic doctrines had been established only at the Council of Trent, whereas Islam had remained unchanged for a thousand years. His fourth was the fact that the membership of the Roman Church extended to a great variety of peoples; yet that was exceeded by Islam. [11] Fifthly, there was the succession of bishops; but this had been matched by the succession of caliphs, until the establishment of the Ottoman sultans, who, being occupied with public affairs, appointed 'Pontifices' (muftis) instead. The sixth sign was 'the glory of miracles'; but claims about miracles were also made by Muslims. [12]

The seventh of these signs was the holiness or saintliness ('sanctitas') of the lives led by the early teachers and leaders of the Church. Hottinger's response on this point took up 34 pages. He began by observing that if such holiness was internal it was invisible, and if it was external it might well be deceptive. Muslims certainly exhibited plenty of external holiness, and there were many Islamic texts—quoted here at length—commending the virtues

---

8. Ibid., sig. *3v ('absurdas fabulas', 'Verum aiebant, christianos quoque sequi fabulas: & religiones omnes politici ordinis causa institutas esse').

9. Hottinger, *Historia*, 1st edn., pp. 274 ('Imperium Muslimicum'), 275; on Hottinger see Loop, *Johann Heinrich Hottinger*. Bellarmino's list of 'notae' is in his 'Prima controversia generalis, de conciliis et ecclesia militante', book 4, chs. 4–18 (*Disputationes*, ii, pp. 219–85); he gives 15, of which Hottinger selects 1–5, 10–11, and 13–15.

10. Hottinger, *Historia*, 1st edn., pp. 275 ('fideles'), 278 (antiquity).

11. Ibid., pp. 279 (duration, variety).   12. Ibid., pp. 284 (succession), 291 (miracles).

of humility, modesty, contempt of the world, hope, alms-giving, justice, generosity, self-reliance, constancy, and honouring one's parents. The Golden Rule was well established in the proverbs of the Arabs, and they had much literature condemning vice.[13] Bellarmino's eighth 'sign' was that even the enemies of the Roman Church felt obliged to attest to its merits: he gave examples from heretics, Jews, and also Muslims (citing praise of Jesus in the Koran, and the Mamluk Sultan's respectful treatment of St Francis). Hottinger responded that the Muslims claimed similar attestations from Christians and Jews.[14] And the last two signs were providentialist ones. Those who opposed the true Church—including Luther, Zwingli, and Calvin— had come to bad ends; and the Church, on the other hand, had enjoyed 'temporal success' (the most recent examples offered by Bellarmino being military victories by Catholic forces in the French Wars of Religion and the Dutch Revolt). Not surprisingly, Hottinger had no difficulty in turning these arguments around to vindicate Islam.[15] One thing is quite clear: this Swiss Calvinist, whose own pronouncements on Islam were as denunciatory as those of any medieval cleric, had not the slightest intention of either promoting that religion, or weakening the faith of his readers in the truth of Christianity. And yet some Christians, including non-Catholics, might well have been made uneasy by the implications of some of these arguments; providentialist thinking, for instance, was certainly not the exclusive preserve of Catholics. In this way, an argument set up to target just one kind of Christianity might have some unintentionally negative effects on the authority of the Christian faith more generally.

The greatest threat to Christianity came, however, not from showing that arguments used to defend it (or some version of it) might just as well be used to defend other religions, but rather from showing that arguments used to attack other religions might just as easily be turned against Christianity itself. The concept of 'imposture' here played a central role. In itself, it did not depend on the example of Muhammad and Islam; Christian writers had wrestled from an early stage with the problem of false prophets and pagan miracle-workers. But the large body of medieval and post-medieval polemics against Islam had turned the story of Muhammad into the most prominent

13. Ibid., pp. 303–4 (internal, external), 315–28 (Islamic texts), 329 (Golden Rule), 329–34 (vice).
14. Ibid., p. 337; Bellarmino, *Disputationes*, ii, pp. 280–1.
15. Hottinger, *Historia*, 1st edn., p. 338; Bellarmino, *Disputationes*, ii, pp. 282–5 (p. 284: 'Felicitas temporalis'; p. 285: victories).

and, as it seemed, best documented case of religious imposture known to Western culture—a template into which other cases could be fitted.

An essential factor here was the development of the Machiavellian theory of religions as political devices, and therefore also of the *invention* of religions for political purposes. In principle, at least, there was nothing necessarily offensive to Christianity about this. On the face of it, what the theory offered to explain was the origin of various non-Christian religions or cults; the inclusion of Moses in Machiavelli's own listing of legislators or state-founders sailed much closer to the wind, but it was always possible to maintain that Moses had done under divine instruction the kind of thing that others had done out of their own human intelligence—and there was no suggestion that Jesus Christ might also be included in the list. However, as this theory developed in the sixteenth century, it also interacted with the larger range of philosophical ideas that is usually characterized as Renaissance naturalism. Natural explanations were put forward for apparently supernatural phenomena such as miracles or prophecies; and it became painfully clear—to some, perhaps, exhilaratingly clear—that such explanations could be offered even for the phenomena described in the Old and New Testaments. One writer who absorbed this whole body of thought was the Italian philosopher and ex-friar Lucilio (or, as he styled himself, Giulio Cesare) Vanini, who studied at Padua in 1608–12 and developed a particular veneration for the works of Pomponazzi. In 1616, three years before he was executed for blasphemy and atheism in Toulouse, Vanini published a set of dialogues which represented in effect a *summa* of this naturalistic tradition; entitled *De admirandis naturae arcanis*, it was concerned mainly with natural history, but its fourth and final book was on the subject of pagan religions. Here he set out the view, which he attributed to ancient philosophers, that the only true 'law' or religion was the law 'of nature itself, which is God', and that all other religions were created not by evil demons (which, as true philosophy taught, did not exist) but by rulers in order to manage their subjects. The rulers were abetted by professional priests who, 'for the sake of grasping after honour and gold', confirmed the fraud. And they did so not by performing miracles but by promulgating 'a Scripture, the original of which is nowhere to be found', which told stories of miracles and issued promises of rewards in a future life.[16]

---

16. Vanini, *Opere*, ii, p. 276 ('Natura, quae Deus est', 'ob honoris et auri aucupium', 'Scriptura, cuius nec originale ullibi adinvenitur').

The whole configuration of Vanini's argument here was clearly designed to take in Christianity as an example of a fraudulent religion. In the next passage, he returned to a more traditionally Machiavellian theme: wise men in the ancient world understood that religion was just a means to an end, 'the maintaining and extending of empire, which cannot be done without some religious pretext; for eternal rewards were promised to those who died for the state, just as happens among the Ottomans today.'[17] But the dialogue resumes with his interlocutor asking why there were so many stories of miracles and prodigies in ancient religion. Vanini responds: 'Ask Lucian. He will tell you in reply that all these things were nothing other than the impostures of priests. But I, in order not to seem to duck the question, shall show that all those things can be reduced to natural causes.'[18] In a later chapter, on miraculous cures, he discusses the story (told by Tacitus and Suetonius) of the Emperor Vespasian healing a blind man by rubbing saliva in his eye. This was a potentially fraught example, as it so closely matched the account in Mark 8: 22–5 of Jesus using his saliva to cure a blind man at Bethsaida. Vanini gives various possible explanations of a medical or psychological kind, but in the end he declares that the whole episode was a fraud, involving a man paid by Vespasian to pretend to be blind; Vespasian wanted to acquire a reputation of being blessed by the gods with supernatural power, because he had learned from the example of Numa Pompilius that 'temporal rule is maintained and extended by religion.' Immediately after this, Vanini offers the example of Muhammad persuading his friend and supporter to descend into a well or pit in order to utter a supernatural-sounding proclamation that Muhammad was the prophet of God.[19]

Vanini's work thus represented what might be called the third type of application of the Machiavellian theory. The first, as we have seen, was its limited acceptance by Catholic writers of the Counter-Reformation

17. Ibid., ii, p. 276 ('imperii conservatio et ampliatio, quae nonnisi aliquo religionis praetextu haberi potest; pro republica enim morientibus praemia aeterna promittebantur, ut nunc apud Turcas').
18. Ibid., ii, p. 277 ('Lucianum interroga. Ipse tibi responsum dabit haec omnia nihil aliud quam sacerdotum imposturas fuisse. Ego vero, ne respondendi onus subterfugere videar, ad naturales causas illa omnia reducam'). The 2nd-century Greek satirical writer Lucian of Samosata commented on religious imposture in several of his works, especially in his history of 'Alexander, the False Prophet'; he was also regarded as an anti-Christian writer, because of his dismissive comments on Christians (whom he described as easily imposed on by charlatans) in 'The Passing of Peregrinus'. But many humanists and reformers appreciated his sceptical attitude to superstitions, oracles, claims of miraculous cures, etc.: see Mayer, *Lucien de Samosate*, pp. 22–30.
19. Vanini, *Opere*, ii, pp. 326–8 (explanations), 329 (fraud, 'religione dominia conservari et augeri', Muhammad).

(beginning with Postel), who were willing to cite Numa Pompilius and other examples to illustrate the basic principle that temporal rule needs the support of religion; for them, the argument was rendered safe by their confident assertion that Christianity offered the most effective support of all. The second, adopted by bold spirits such as Naudé and Osborne, regarded the 'invention' of Islam by Muhammad as a positive achievement: not a moral outrage but a display of great political wisdom. From such a perspective, the notion of imposture hardly carried a negative charge at all. But in this third kind of approach, a writer such as Vanini marshalled the more traditional—indeed, medieval—accusations of fraud and moral turpitude that had always belonged to the depiction of Muhammad's 'imposture', and applied them, by clear implication, not only to other religions but to Christianity itself.

That this approach itself contained more than one possible line of argument was made clear by a later anti-Christian text, the *Theophrastus redivivus*—a lengthy, anonymous treatise, written probably in France in the late 1650s, which remained in manuscript until the twentieth century.[20] The author of this work had not only read Vanini, but was also deeply influenced by Pomponazzi and Cardano. The account given here of the origins of religion operated, accordingly, at two different levels. At the purely human level, it put forward a strong version of the 'imposture' theory. All legislators were 'deceivers and simulators, and the religion by means of which they lead their peoples is nothing other than a trick and a fiction, designed to be useful for their rule'; Moses was driven by 'avarice and an insatiable thirst for gold'; Jesus was accused by wise men of 'impostures', and the underlying cause of Christianity was 'just the same as that of the others, namely, the desire to possess a kingdom and the lust for rule'; so by the time Muhammad began his work, all he had to do was 'follow in the footsteps of all the other founders of religions, and build his authority on their impostures'.[21] Yet at the same time the arguments of Pomponazzi and Cardano suggested a very different explanation. At special moments in the history of the world, astrological forces came together in new ways to cause great changes. These

---

20. On this work (dated 1659 in the surviving manuscripts) see Gregory, *Theophrastus redivivus*; Gengoux, ed., *Entre la Renaissance*.

21. Anon., *Theophrastus*, ii, pp. 357 ('deceptores ac simulatores religionemque qua populos trahunt nihil esse quam astutiam et commentum ad dominatus utilitatem'), 443 ('avaritia et auri sitis inexplebilis'), 457 ('imposturae'), 511 ('profecto non diversa ab aliis est...scilicet, ad regni cupiditatem et dominatus libidinem'), 515 ('in omnibus aliorum legislatorum vestigia sequeretur et imposturis iisdem authoritatem suam stabiliret').

could give rise to exceptional individuals who founded new religions; and those individuals might perform actions which seemed to involve supernatural powers, but were in fact natural, though so untypical of the normal course of nature as to appear miraculous to any observers.[22] The author described the human explanation as secondary, and the astrological one as primary; most of the discussion in this text of the actual invention and imposition of religions was conducted, however, at the human level.[23] Some variation of argument was also possible at that level. The specific teachings of Christianity were, this author noted, morally better than those of the other religions—something attributable to the more benign astrological conditions of its origins. The teachings of Islam were singled out for praise on a different basis: Muhammad issued 'many extremely good laws for the benefit of society', as he knew that 'a lawgiver needed to establish his rule not only by means of arms and religion but also using civil laws and works of charity and piety.'[24] But that was only a brief nod in the direction of the Naudéan positive view (and the residue of the new paradigm which it contained). The fact remained that Muhammad had 'cultivated the art of ruling no less than Moses and all the others like him, and had equally made use of frauds, tricks, and crimes, under the cover of religion'; in a text directed primarily at the discrediting of all religion, those frauds and tricks—including all the familiar stories of the pigeon, the bull, the man in the well, and so on—still had real work to do in the argument.[25]

One special factor also contributed to the tendency, among radical thinkers, to treat Christianity and Judaism as on a par with the 'imposture' of Islam. Since the thirteenth century, a slogan or saying, 'the three impostors'— referring to Moses, Jesus, and Muhammad—had undergone a shadowy circulation in Europe. In 1239 Pope Gregory IX had accused the Holy Roman Emperor, Frederick II, of uttering the gross blasphemy that 'the whole world had been deceived by three swindlers, namely Jesus Christ, Moses, and Muhammad.' (The saying had in fact originated in Islamic culture; the first known instances of it were in Arabic texts of the eleventh century,

22. Ibid., ii, pp. 398–410, esp. 406, 409. The author also tries (pp. 410–12) to assimilate Bodin's zonal theory to this kind of explanation of religions.
23. Ibid., ii, pp. 398 (secondary, primary).
24. Ibid., ii, pp. 404, 460 (Christianity and astrological influence), 521 ('Plurimas...optimas leges ad societatis utilitatem', 'ad principatum stabilendum non solum armis et religione sed etiam legibus civilibus et charitatis pietatisque operibus legislatori opus esse').
25. Ibid., ii, pp. 519–20 (pigeon, bull, well), 521 ('regnandi artem non minus calluisse, quam Mosem et caeteros illi similes, fraudesque, dolos et scelera aeque adhibuisse, religionis specie').

relating the claims of the Qarmati, a rebellious philosophico-religious sect.)[26] The phrase percolated down to the Renaissance period, and in the mid-sixteenth century Guillaume Postel spread the idea that there was a blasphemous treatise on this subject; in 1563 he alleged that Calvinists had printed it, and variants on this claim—often giving the title of the work as 'De tribus impostoribus' ('On the Three Impostors'), sometimes referring only to a manuscript text—soon began to crop up in anti-Protestant writings by Catholic polemicists.[27] From the early seventeenth century onwards various people claimed to have seen copies of this treatise, or to have met or heard of others who had seen it; and there were many wild surmises about the identity of the author, with even Postel himself, and Campanella, among the suspects. Some people with strong intellectual appetites and deep pockets, such as Queen Christina of Sweden, instructed agents to search for it, but the work was nowhere to be found.[28] Only in the final decades of the century was the problem of the non-existence of this tantalizing text solved at last, by enterprising authors who sat down and wrote it.

One version was composed in Latin by a German scholar, Johann Joachim Müller, in 1688 (possibly on the basis of a shorter text which he had written previously). It became one of the most widely circulated 'clandestine' works of the late seventeenth and eighteenth centuries; 95 manuscript copies are known today, with another five having existed until the Second World War, and the text would also receive several printings, of which the first clearly datable one was in 1753.[29] Müller set out the anti-Christian and generally anti-religious version of the Machiavellian argument, declaring that all the founders of new religions depended on 'frauds', and putting a special emphasis on the 'interest' not only of the founders but also of the priests whose comfortable livings the religion subsequently guaranteed.[30] Much of

26. Huillard-Bréholles, *Historia diplomatica*, p. 339 ('a tribus baratoribus...scilicet Christo Jesu, Moyse et Mahometo, totum mundum fuisse deceptum'). On the Arabic origin see Massignon, 'La Légende'; Niewöhner, *Veritas*, pp. 233–7. On the early history of this idea see Gruber, 'Ungodly Paths'.

27. See Mothu, 'Guillaume Postel'.

28. See Presser, *Das Buch*, pp. 41–91 (surmises); Minois, *Le Traité*, pp. 84–109 (surmises); Åkerman, 'John Adler Salvius' *Questions*', pp. 407–14 (Christina).

29. Benítez, *La Face cachée*, pp. 29–30 (95, 5); Schröder, 'Einleitung', pp. 36–8 (printings), 40–66 (Müller's authorship). The early manuscript history indicates a division of the text into two parts. Germana Ernst has suggested that the first part was independent and much earlier ('Introduzione', pp. 18–19), but such a dating is contradicted by that part's evident debt to the Latin edition of Hobbes's *Leviathan* (1668). Sergio Landucci has suggested, more plausibly, that the first part was written by Müller some time before 1688 ('Il punto', pp. 1,053–4).

30. J. J. Müller, *De imposturis*, pp. 109 ('interesse', priests), 117 ('fraudes').

the second part of the treatise was structured as a comparison between Moses and Muhammad. In both cases, Müller observed, there were texts, written by those men or their followers, which portrayed them as acting under divine instruction.

> Among us Christians Muhammad is regarded as having been, without any doubt, an impostor. Yet on what grounds? Not from his own testimony, or that of his friends, but rather from that of his enemies. Among Muslims, on the contrary, he is regarded as a most holy prophet. And on what grounds? From attestations partly by him and partly by his friends. Those who regard Moses as either an impostor or a holy teacher proceed in the same way. So there is just as much reason for raising or dismissing the accusation of imposture against Muhammad as there is against the others, even though, contrary to the dictates of justice, the others are still regarded as holy men, and he is regarded as a scoundrel.[31]

The general thrust of Müller's argument was to claim that all three were in fact impostors. But his cultural starting point ('Among us Christians') led him to adopt a method of argument that involved taking some of the standard accusations against Muhammad and showing that similar charges could be made against Moses and Jesus; as a consequence, the argument seemed in places to take on a relatively defensive tone where Muhammad was concerned. If Muhammad allowed polygamy, so too did Moses; if the Koran appeared to describe a physical Paradise, so too did the New Testament. (In support of the idea that such passages in the Koran should be read allegorically, Müller adduced the Old Testament's thoroughly sensual Song of Songs: if rigorous literalism was to be applied to the Koran, it should also be applied to 'the writings of Moses and the others'. Here, apparently, the requirement of equal treatment took priority over the need to prove gross fraudulence.) Whilst some things in the Koran were indeed absurd fables, just the same could be said of the Book of Genesis. Overall, the comparison between Moses and Muhammad kept up its theoretical equivalence, but the

---

31. Ibid., pp. 126–7 ('indubie Mahumethes apud nostrates pro impostore habetur. Sed unde? Non ex proprio, non ex amicorum, sed inimicorum testimonio. E contrario apud Mahumetanos pro sanctissimo propheta. Sed unde? Ex propria partim, partim amicorum attestationibus. Qui Mosen vel pro impostore vel pro sancto doctore habent, eodem modo procedunt. Atque adeo aequalis ratio adest tam quoad accusationem quam declinationem imposturae in Mahumethe atque in reliquis, etsi nihilominus hi pro sanctis, ille pro nebulone contra justitiae debitum haberentur').

main concentration was on the crimes and deceptions of the former, to the relative exculpation, as it might sometimes seem, of the latter.[32]

The other major attempt to compose a 'treatise of the three impostors', this time in French, had a more complex history. The earliest and shortest version, entitled 'L'Esprit de Monsieur de Spinosa', was probably written in the 1680s; by 1704, or possibly 1700, an altered version of this text was being presented as the long sought-after treatise on the three impostors; and in the second decade of the eighteenth century two main versions emerged, a short one in six chapters entitled 'Le Fameux Livre des trois imposteurs', and a long one in 21, which was printed as *La Vie et l'esprit de Mr Benoît de Spinosa*. (A further variant, based on the earlier six-chapter text, was printed as *Traité des trois imposteurs* in 1768 and frequently reprinted thereafter.) This text, in its various versions, became the most popular of all the clandestine works in manuscript circulation, with a total of at least 169 copies recorded today.[33] Its general approach was similar to that of the Latin treatise, but it concentrated more heavily on discrediting Jesus Christ, who had been somewhat marginalized by the lengthy Moses–Muhammad comparison in that other work. In all versions but one of the French text the treatment of Muhammad was quite crude, presenting the story of the man in the well as the main example of his trickery; only in the 'Fameux Livre' was a more detailed and more political account of his life supplied, in which he was given the extra motive of seeking to recover a position of tribal authority that had belonged to his grandfather. In this account, Muhammad's initial imposture was supplemented by his more straightforward strategy of making his followers impose Islam on others by military violence. The result was that he died 'having entirely fulfilled his great plan, as much by means of his hypocrisy and impostures as by his military exploits, which raised him to the dignity of a sovereign—a status which he left to his successors, so well entrenched that after enduring for 600 years it shows no sign yet of being about to falter'.[34] In achieving his goal within his own lifetime, as every

---

32. Ibid., pp. 128 (allegorical reading, polygamy), 129 (New Testament (citing Matt. 26: 29), 'contra Mosis et aliorum scripta'), 135–6 (fables, Genesis).

33. See Charles-Daubert, 'Introduction', esp. pp. 5–7, 102–6, 449–55; Benítez, 'Une histoire', p. 54 (169 copies).

34. Anon., *Le 'Traité'*, pp. 604 (grandfather), 605 (strategy, 'après avoir entierement executé son grand projet tant par son hypocrisie & ses impostures, que par ses Exploits militaires qui l'eleverent a la dignité Souveraine, qu'il a laissée à des Successeurs, si bien affermie, qu depuis six cens ans qu'elle dure il n'y a pas d'apparence qu'elle soit encore sur le point d'etre ebran-lée'). The use of '600 years' here was perhaps a device to suggest a medieval provenance for the treatise; the other versions give the figure of 1,000.

version of the text agreed, Muhammad was much more successful than Jesus Christ; on the same count, as all but one version agreed, he was also more successful than Moses.[35]

Comparing Muhammad to Moses was always a simpler task than comparing either of them to Jesus; for the first two had acquired earthly as well as spiritual power, whereas the third, far from seeking temporal rule, had explicitly declared (John 18: 36): 'My kingdom is not of this world.' The authors of these various works dealt with this problem in different ways. The simplest line of argument, followed by the writer of the French treatise, was to say that Jesus had sought temporal power like the others, but, as a prophet unarmed, had miserably failed: 'since he lacked forces, it was impossible that his plan should succeed; as he had neither money nor an army, it was inevitable that he would perish.'[36] A later eighteenth-century work in this tradition, entitled *La Fausseté des miracles*, portrayed Jesus as internalizing that failure in the very nature of his 'law': knowing that the people to whom he preached were fixed irredeemably under the heel of the Romans, he taught a miserable religion of poverty and self-abnegation.[37]

The problem was finessed by Johann Joachim Müller, who, whenever he needed to provide the Christian counterpart to the worldly ambition of Moses and Muhammad, turned instead to developments that took place after the life of Christ. Muhammad had promised the world to his followers, 'and the Christians from time to time prophesy the massacre of their enemies and the subjugation of the enemies of the Church—a subjugation which has indeed been considerable, since the time when the Christians became rulers of states'.[38] The author of the *Theophrastus redivivus* similarly diverted attention to the period after Christ. As he explained, the growth of Christianity after the death of Jesus reached a point where 'the rulers themselves, and the powerful and wise men' decided to declare their allegiance to it too. 'For to such men, any religion is good if they see that it pleases the

35. Ibid., pp. 513, 605 (not including Moses), 678, 742.

36. Ibid., p. 734 ('dénué de forces comme il étoit, il étoit impossible que son dessein réussît... n'ayant ni argent ni armée, il ne pouvoit manquer de périr').

37. Anon., *La Fausseté*, p. 9. This text, which falsely claimed to be a translation of parts of the *Theophrastus redivivus*, was put together in the period 1761–75, but was based primarily on two manuscript treatises (on miracles and oracles) from the early decades of the century: see Bianchi, 'Impostura'.

38. J. J. Müller, *De imposturis*, p. 102 ('Et Christiani passim de strage suorum inimicorum et subjugatione hostium ecclesiae vaticinantur, quae sane non exigua fuit, ex quo Christiani ad rerum publicarum gubernacula sederunt'); cf. p. 109, on the rulers of Italy, especially the Pope, deriving power and revenues from the credulity of their Christian subjects.

people; they do not think it matters of what kind it is, so long as the people in their credulity are seduced by it, and, following that religion's dictates, serve their rulers and obey their laws.' Returning later to this point, he emphasized that the 'lust for rule' was to be found not in Jesus himself but in his 'successors and vicars' (sc. the popes), who had tried to exercise power even over kings and emperors.[39] But how had Christianity expanded so successfully in the first place, when it was quite unsupported by temporal power? Here the author of the French treatise supplied the answer: a clever and ambitious young man, St Paul, had practised his own mini-imposture, by claiming to have received direct instruction from God on the road to Damascus. He had then turned Christianity into a universal religion, preaching a doctrine of eternal rewards and punishments, and finding ways of dealing with the objections of those Gentiles who—like the well-educated Paul, but unlike the ignorant peasants and fishermen who were the disciples of Christ—had some philosophical training.[40]

This author did not quite say that Paul invented the theory of the divinity of Jesus, and hence also the dogma of the Trinity; on his account, the disciples had begun to claim that Jesus was the son of God soon after his death (in desperation, after the dashing of their hopes to enjoy positions of power under his temporal leadership), but had lacked the intellectual sophistication to turn this into a convincing doctrine. Nevertheless, it is possible to sense here a connection with the argument, developed by Unitarian Christians in the early modern period, which presented the doctrine of the divinity of Jesus as a corruption of the original Christian religion. Of course there was a large gulf between the mentality of sincere, theistic, Christ-honouring Unitarians and that of any of the 'three impostors' treatises, which expressed a belief either in no God at all, or in a Deistic or Epicurean God without any special interventions or revelations. But the radical argument which put Moses, Jesus, and Muhammad in a single category did suggest a reduction of the second of those religious founders to the same level as the other two—that is, it suggested that the 'imposture' of Jesus consisted of persuading people that he was a man sent by God, not that he was God himself. And if belief in Christ had begun on that basis, it became a matter

---

39. Anon., *Theophrastus*, ii, pp. 457–8 ('principes et potentes viri, sapientesque huic sese addixerunt. Eis enim religio placet quam populis placere vident; nihil referre arbitrantur qualis illa sit, modo populus credulitate seducatur, religioneque obstrictus principibus serviat ac legibus pareat'), 511 ('dominatus libidinem', 'successoribus et vicariis'), 512 (kings, emperors).
40. Anon., *Le 'Traité'*, p. 740.

for historical explanation to say how and when the nature of that belief had subsequently changed.

This was an issue on which Christian anti-Trinitarian thinkers had already been at work. Mostly, they made use of the discoveries and arguments of textual and historical scholars in the field of patristic studies—such as the Jesuit Denis Petau—whose own theological views were orthodox, but whose work gave inadvertent support to the idea that Trinitarianism was inauthentic because it was not fully formulated until some centuries after the death of Christ. (This serves as an example of the much larger process in this period whereby ideas which we identify as 'radical' were generated in the first place not by radicalism but by the unexpected implications of orthodox-minded scholarship.)[41] Connecting this early Church history in any way to the story of Muhammad was not an obvious tactic for anti-Trinitarians to use, not least because it was a standard propaganda ploy of their opponents to liken Unitarianism to Islam. Only at the beginning of the modern anti-Trinitarian tradition had there been a serious attempt to draw on the evidence of Islam itself. In 1553 Miguel Servet (Servetus) had quoted from the Koran to suggest that Muhammad had preserved an authentic, non-Trinitarian belief about the nature of Jesus. Indeed, it was the introduction of Trinitarianism that had caused not only the doctrinal fragmentation of Christianity into rival Churches, but also the development of Islam itself: Muhammad 'departed from Christianity because of that corrupt doctrine of the Trinitarians'. Servet's work was vigorously suppressed, but his argument on this point lived on in the writings of two of the founders of the Unitarian tradition in Transylvania, Giorgio Biandrata and Ferenc Dávid.[42] A century after Servet, a little more support—of an entirely inadvertent kind—was given to this line of argument by Johann Heinrich Hottinger, who presented a scholarly account of the early Muslim hostility to Christian Trinitarianism, citing Arabic sources which referred to a saving remnant of Christians who did believe in the 'unity' (in the Muslim sense) of God. Hottinger also related a story, which he had found in an anti-Jewish

---

41. On Petau see Hofmann, *Theologie*, esp. pp. 234–5; for a classic case of an anti-Trinitarian writer using his work see Sandius, *Nucleus*. On the larger process see Levitin, *Ancient Wisdom* (which also discusses Petau's influence, pp. 455–541, *passim*).

42. Servet, *Restitution du Christianisme*, i, pp. 175 (Muhammad's belief about Jesus), 177 ('Ob prauam illam trinitariorum doctrinam desciuit à christianismo'); Hughes, 'In the Footsteps' (Biandrata, Dávid). On Servet's use of the Koran see Hughes, 'Servetus', and Loop, *Johann Heinrich Hottinger*, pp. 208–9. In the 1590s the citation of the Koran by Transylvanian ministers was defended by Fausto Sozzini: see Klein, 'Muslimischer Antitrinitarismus', p. 51.

and anti-Christian treatise by the thirteenth-century writer known as Ahmed ibn Edris (Shihab al-Din al-Qarafi), of how St Paul had divided Christianity by teaching differing accounts of the doctrine of the Trinity to three different followers.[43]

Hottinger's work acted as a stimulant to one of the most original treatments of the origins of Islam to be written in early modern Europe: the treatise by Henry Stubbe entitled 'An Account of the Rise [or: "the Original"] and Progress of Mahometanism'. This was composed in the early 1670s and had some circulation in manuscript, but would remain unprinted until the twentieth century. Stubbe benefited not only from Hottinger's work, but also from that of other scholars such as Thomas Erpenius and Edward Pococke, who had published editions and translations of several medieval Arabic histories of the Eastern Churches or the early phase of Islam.[44] But although Henry Stubbe had a scholarly formation—he began his career as a brilliant student of classics at Oxford, and spent some years during the Interregnum as deputy Keeper of the Bodleian Library there— he was not himself a scholar of Arabic; it was his own religious and political concerns that drove his interest in this relatively recondite field. In the 1650s he occupied an ideological position broadly similar to that of Francis Osborne: tolerationist, and also Erastian in the sense that he wanted all power over the practice of religion to be placed the hands of the civil sovereign. On this last point he also drew support from the political theory of Thomas Hobbes, whose friendship he cultivated, and whose treatise *Leviathan* he began to translate into Latin in 1656. Since his main protectors in the Interregnum were Puritans such as Sir Henry Vane and Dr John Owen, this connection with Hobbes (who was increasingly criticized for impiety from the mid-1650s onwards) was a serious liability; but Stubbe had not only a taste but a talent for adopting unpopular positions. Even after the Restoration, when he kept his head down on religious matters and practised as a physician, he continued to polemicize in print on a range of other issues.[45]

43. See Hottinger, *Historia orientalis*, p. 350, and the discussion in Loop, *Johann Heinrich Hottinger*, pp. 139–40 (ibn Edris), 209–16 (early Islam and Christianity). On the Muslim anti-Pauline tradition see Van Koningsveld, 'Islamic Image'.
44. On the three most important, al-Makin (translated by Erpenius) and ibn al-Batriq and Abu al-Faraj (translated by Pococke), see Matar, *Henry Stubbe*, pp. 21–9. Stubbe's sources are given in the marginal notes to two manuscripts of sections of his work (British Library, London, MSS Sloane 1709, fos. 94r–115v, and Sloane 1786, fos. 181r–189r); apart from those three editions, the most important are Selden and Hottinger. See also Champion, '"I remember"'.
45. On Stubbe see Holt, *Seventeenth-Century Defender*; Jacob, *Henry Stubbe*. For his connection with Hobbes see Hobbes, *Correspondence*, i, *passim*, and ii, pp. 899–902.

In his treatment of the story of Muhammad, Stubbe followed, to a significant extent, the positive Machiavellian line developed by writers such as Gabriel Naudé: the prophet of Islam was a man of extraordinary abilities, a wise legislator—indeed, 'the wisest legislator that ever was'—and a very canny politician. 'He daily spread abroad relations of his discourses with God and his conferences with the angel Gabriel and used such a sagacity in discovering all plots and counsels held against him that his followers believed God almighty did reveal all to him.'[46] Yet at the same time Stubbe's account has quite a different flavour from that of Naudé or even Osborne; and the easiest way to express the difference is to say that Stubbe supplies a version of the Machiavellian interpretation that has been realigned in the direction of Hobbes.

At first sight, this would not seem to involve any great alteration, as the account of heathen religions in chapter 12 of *Leviathan* includes a classic statement of the Machiavellian view. Discussing superstitious beliefs introduced by the 'authors of the Religion of the Gentiles, partly upon pretended Experience, partly upon pretended Revelation', Hobbes comments: 'So easie are men to be drawn to believe any thing, from such men as have gotten credit with them, and can with gentlenesse, and dexterity, take hold of their fear, and ignorance.' He goes on to explain that 'the first Founders, and Legislators of Common-wealths amongst the Gentiles, whose ends were only to keep the people in obedience, and peace' had always claimed some kind of divine warrant for their religious precepts; his examples were Numa Pompilius, the founders of the Inca Empire, and Muhammad, who, 'to set up his new Religion, pretended to have conferences with the Holy Ghost, in forme of a Dove'.[47] Hobbes certainly had no doubt that human beings were easily imposed upon. However, unlike Naudé, he did not think that such religious imposture was desirable or even necessary in the long term. Quite the contrary, for two reasons: religion based on absurd claims was bound to unravel eventually, so could not be a stable basis of temporal rule; and, in the meantime, people whose heads were filled with superstitious beliefs would be easy prey for religious demagoguery and priestcraft—again, to the detriment of the sovereign ruler. The only way to ensure long-term stability was to teach the people the true, rational grounds of civil obligation, as set out in Hobbes's own philosophy.

46. Stubbe, 'Originall', pp. 129 ('He daily ...'), 192 ('the wisest ...').
47. Hobbes, *Leviathan*, ii, pp. 174–8.

Against this background, the possibility of anyone finding a way to praise, on Hobbesian grounds, a founder of a religion such as Muhammad (as portrayed in the Machiavellian tradition) must seem slight indeed. Yet Henry Stubbe did manage to square this circle. On his account, Muhammad was much more a rational reformer of religion than an inventor of it. To borrow a Hobbesian metaphor, Muhammad did not take the blank sheet of people's minds and scribble it over with superstitions; rather, he found a set of badly scribbled-over minds and left them much clearer, with reasonable doctrines and just a practical minimum of religious observances. Thus was Hobbesian rationalism combined with the Machiavellian notion of the religious legislator and clever inculcator of beliefs.

Stubbe's account involved, in fact, a major reinterpretation of the history of early Christianity in relation to the origins of Islam. Drawing above all on the scholarly work of John Selden, he argued that Christianity began as a form of Messianic Judaism; even after the death and alleged resurrection of Jesus, the belief was that he would come again as Messiah to rule a temporal kingdom on Earth. Jews who became Christians continued to observe the Mosaic Law, while Gentile converts were allowed (in keeping with earlier Jewish rules about proselytes) to confine themselves to the seven basic commandments of the 'sons of Noah', as handed down by Jewish tradition.[48] None of the early Christians believed that Jesus was divine, or that God was triune—claims that would have seemed blasphemous to all Jews, including the Christian ones. But gradually the character of Christianity changed and deteriorated. St Paul introduced many pagan rites and superstitions in order to pander to Gentile tastes. (Stubbe's treatment of Paul is notably hostile, and he repeats, from Hottinger, the story of his deceptive behaviour given by Ahmed ibn Edris.) The Jewish observances were dropped, for prudential reasons, after the crushing of the last great Jewish revolt against Roman rule in AD 132–6; the last remnants of Jewish Christianity then became isolated and persecuted sects known as Ebionites or Nazarenes. The Emperor Constantine built up the Church hierarchy for his own political purposes, to the point where prelates acquired 'a kind of princely dignity.' And doctrine was corrupted by 'subtle distinctions of essence and person, consubstantiation, eternal generation', and so on, with the generally

---

48. Stubbe, 'Originall', pp. 77 (Messianism), 78, 87 (Noachid commandments), 88 ('Christianity itself was but a reformation of Judaism (as Mr. Selden more than once inculcates)'). On the Noachid commandments see Novak, *Image*; Toomer, *John Selden*, ii, pp. 502–10, 694–6.

ignorant and uncouth Trinitarians triumphing over the more learned and sensible Arians.[49] By the time of the Emperor Heraclius, in the first half of the seventh century, 'Christianity was then degenerated into such a kind of paganism as wanted nothing but the ancient sacrifices and professed polytheism, and, even as to the latter, there wanted not some who did make three gods of the Trinity.'[50]

Such, then, was the background to the birth of Islam. The persecuted Jewish Christians had retreated into the remoter parts of Arabia; Muhammad was familiar with other varieties of Christianity too, and with Judaisim and pagan religion, but he himself 'was a convert to the religion of the Judaizing Christians and did form his religion as far as possible in resemblance of theirs'. He understood that true Christianity consisted in living a holy life; yet for most adherents to mainstream Christianity at that time, their religion was a matter of external ceremonies and 'zealous adherence to the party they owned'. So the only way for Muhammad to restore the true nature of Christianity was to found a new faith which, on the face of it, seemed 'directly opposite to the Christian religion'.[51] The basic doctrine of that new faith is presented by Stubbe as a pure and almost philosophical theology: God is one, eternal, and omnipotent, his providence directs all things, and so on. Fundamentally, this is a rational religion; Stubbe draws here on a tradition of Christian criticism of Islam—expressed, as we have seen, by Melanchthon— which had depicted it as a faith carefully designed to cause no offence to natural reason. Discussing Muhammad's prohibition of divinatory practices, he even declares that 'This great prophet would not suffer his Musulmen to employ anything but reason in their debates.'[52] Yet at the same time he notes that some pagan rites were retained (such as the 'stoning of the Devil' during the Hajj), insofar as 'It was the policy of the prophet not to . . . affright the Arabians into a rebellion or irreligion by making a total change in the substance and ceremonies of their devotion', and he also explains the imposition of some apparently irrational practices as tests of obedience.[53]

Where many of the best-known Muslim beliefs and observances are concerned, Stubbe follows a very positive version of the Machiavellian line,

49. Stubbe, 'Originall', pp. 80 (seemed blasphemous), 82 (Nazarenes, Ebionites), 89 ('subtle distinctions . . .'), 90–1 (Paul, revolt, Ebionites), 94 (Constantine), 96–102 (Trinitarians, Arians), 191 (Ahmed ibn Edris).
50. Ibid., p. 102.
51. Ibid., pp. 186–7 (holy life, 'zealous adherence . . .', 'directly opposite . . .'), 190 ('was a . . .').
52. Ibid., pp. 199–200 (basic doctrine), 206 ('This great . . .'); above, p. 39 (Melanchthon).
53. Stubbe, 'Originall', pp. 171 ('It was . . .'), 201 (tests).

while also, in some cases, fitting them into a Jewish or Christian context. Thus the Islamic doctrine of predestination (which was 'the general tenet of the Jews and primitive Christians') did indeed confer a huge military advantage; and 'it was an observation of O. Cromwell's that the best fighters were of this opinion and he gave no encouragement to such preachers as taught the contrary.' Ramadan and the Hajj instilled physical fortitude, and were thus of value because Muhammad 'designed a military empire to the support whereof valiant and hardy soldiers were necessary'. The duty to give alms was also 'political in its original', as it made for a more equal society and prevented people from growing 'effeminate through luxury or mutinous by means of their riches'.[54] Polygamy and the use of concubines were customs of the Jews, possibly also of the early Christians, and certainly of the Judaizing ones; and of course such practices were 'exceedingly subservient to the multiplying of subjects which is the sinew of empire and therefore prudential'. There was political wisdom too in the ban on translating the Koran, since 'unity of language, religion, and customs conduceth very much to the strength and peace of a monarchy.' As for the duty to make war against infidels: this ensured not only a permanent expansion of empire, but also peace at home, as it directed outwards those potentially rivalrous energies that would otherwise cause civil wars and rebellions. Yet the purpose of fighting the non-Muslims was not to convert them; 'the Mahometans did propagate their empire, but not their religion, by force of arms', and Christians were allowed to live in peace as their subjects. Thus, Stubbe observes, the Orthodox Greeks live better now under the Sultan than they did under their previous Christian rulers, and indeed 'it is more the interest of the princes and nobles than of the people at present which keeps all Europe from submitting to the Turks.' In conclusion, Stubbe exclaims that 'It were an endless task to descant upon the particular motives upon which depends the excellence of his [sc. Muhammad's] laws', and then adds, tantalizingly: 'What a discourse might be made upon his uniting the civil and ecclesiastical powers in one sovereign'.[55]

That Muhammad's own rule (once established) over his people was absolute was not denied by Stubbe. The term 'despotic' did not feature in his

54. Ibid., pp. 197 ('designed a . . .'), 198 ('political', 'effeminate through . . .'), 200 ('the general . . .', 'it was . . .'),
55. Ibid., pp. 179 ('the Mahometans . . .', 'it is . . .') 182 (duty to make war), 201 ('unity of . . .'), 202–3 (polygamy, concubines; p. 203: 'exceedingly subservient . . .'), 207 ('It were . . .').

account, but he did make a distinction between this kind of rule and tyranny, drawing on the Machiavellian notion of 'the prophet armed':

> such was their reverence to their commander that one would have thought they had been slaves all, & could not retain a bold spirit under so imperious a general: but there is a difference betwixt the ordinary effects of tyrannical power, & where a prophet commands. [T]he dexterity of Mahomet was able to reconcile the greatest contradictions & manifested...that the prudent may be absolute without tyranny, without regret of the most valiant, & without enfeebling their spirits; that the arts of government consisted not in the shews but in the use of authority: & the true use thereof is to insinuate into mens reason not impose upon it, or insult over it.[56]

Overall, therefore, Henry Stubbe's portrait of the founder of Islam was of an extraordinarily gifted and perceptive man, whose wisdom could be discerned at both the theological and the political level. Stubbe had no difficulty in brushing aside the traditional Christian accusations—the pigeon, the bull with the Koran on its horns, the epileptic fits, and so on. 'With such stories as these have the Christians represented him to be the vilest impostor in the world and transformed the wisest legislator that ever was into a simple cheat.' The charge that he promoted sensuality was quite false; his laws were no more sensualist than those of Lycurgus. The idea that the Koran was incoherent and absurd was based essentially on a failure to recognize its nature as poetry—and besides, 'I have often reflected upon the exceptions made by the Christians against the Alcoran and find them to be no other than what may be argued with the same strength against our Bible.'[57] But was it not an inescapable fact that Muhammad had practised deception? Stubbe had no doubt that Muhammad's claim to converse with the Angel Gabriel was a fiction. There is just one point in his entire account where he does call Muhammad, at least by implication, an impostor: describing the upstart preacher Musaylima ibn Habib, who claimed a spiritual partnership with him, Stubbe writes that the reason why 'the sage Mahomet despised this new imposture' may have been that 'he thought the same cheat was not to be acted twice with success in so short a time'. The whole nature of Stubbe's account, however, implies that the cheat committed by Muhammad

56. British Library, London, MS Sloane 1709, fo. 102r. (I quote here from this early copy of one section of the text, as this passage is corrupted in the text given in the printed edition.) 'Regret' here means 'protest' or 'complaint'.

57. Stubbe, 'Originall', pp. 191–2 (pigeon, etc., 'With such...'), 203 (sensuality, Lycurgus), 208–9 (Koran, 'I have...').

was the most commendable of pious frauds, serving not only earthly purposes but spiritual ones too. How one is to distinguish between those two types of purpose is, however, another question. Discussing a particular issue such as Muhammad's prohibition of games of chance, Stubbe can write: 'Whether it were his great prudence or care for the worship of the true God, I shall not determine.'[58] An essential ambiguity thus remains in Stubbe's argument, reflecting the idea that this temporal legislator was also motivated, at a deep level, by genuine religious concerns.

Little is known about the circulation of Stubbe's treatise in manuscript, but there is evidence that it had an influence not only on 'free-thinkers' such as Charles Blount (who plagiarized it in print) but also, directly or indirectly, on sincere Unitarian theologians. In 1690, for example, Arthur Bury could write that Muhammad had professed the articles of the Christian faith, 'and declared himself not an Apostate, but Reformer; pretending to purify it from the Corruptions wherewith it had been defiled'. Stephen Nye, in the following year, wrote that the most ancient version of Christianity was that of the Unitarian '*Nazarens*', and insisted that

> *Mahomet* is affirmed by divers Historians, to have had no other Design in pre-tending himself to be a Prophet, but to restore the Belief of *the Vnity of GOD*, which at that time was extirpated among the Eastern Christians . . . They will have it, that *Mahomet* meant not his Religion should be esteemed a new Religion, but only the Restitution of the true intent of the Christian Religion.[59]

But espousing such arguments was a risky strategy, given that it had long been the favourite tactic of anti-Unitarian writers to associate denial of the Trinity with Islam; as the conservative-minded clergyman Charles Leslie wrote in 1708, 'I think, That our *English Vnitarians* can in no Propriety be call'd *Christians*; that they are more *Mahometans* than *Christians*.'[60]

It was left to a radical free-thinker, John Toland, in his *Nazarenus: Or, Jewish, Gentile and Mahometan Christianity* (1718), to carry Stubbe's argument some steps further. Toland too was a man of great intellectual energies who

---

58. Ibid., pp. 167 ('the sage . . .'), 206 ('Whether it . . .').

59. Jacob, *Henry Stubbe*, p. 140 (Blount); Bury, *Naked Gospel*, sig. A3v; Nye, *Letter of Resolution*, pp. 11 ('*Nazarens*'), 18.

60. Leslie, *Socinian Controversy*, part 6 (separately paginated), p. xxv ('I think . . .'). Leslie gleefully gave details of an attempt by a group of Unitarians to share their theological views with the Moroccan Ambassador to England in 1682 (pp. iii–xiii); on this episode see Mulsow, '"New Socinians"', pp. 57–61.

stood some way outside the scholarly establishment and displayed a special gift for polemics and trouble-making.[61] Although evidence of direct borrowing from Stubbe is lacking, the whole nature of Toland's argument—his use of the distinction between Jewish and Gentile converts to early Christianity, and his claim that 'the Mahometans may not improperly be reckon'd and call'd a sort or sect of Christians, as Christianity was at first esteem'd a branch of Judaism'—was Stubbian through and through.[62] Toland went beyond Stubbe in several ways. He offered to solve some basic problems of Christian doctrine, reconciling the 'Old Law' and the 'New', and explaining that Protestant–Catholic controversies about the value of 'works' were based on an elementary failure to understand that the 'works' discussed in the New Testament were the Mosaic observances that were binding on only some Christians. He put forward a novel piece of evidence, a recently discovered Muslim 'Gospel', identified by him as a version of the lost Gospel of Barnabas, in which one could see 'the ancient Ebionite or Nazaren system, as to the making of JESUS a mere man'. (This text was in fact a seventeenth-century forgery, written probably by a convert to Islam under the influence of some Morisco writings, for the purpose of reinforcing the faith of other converts.)[63] And, on the strength of the basically 'Christian' nature of Islam, Toland presented an argument for the religious toleration of Muslims, who 'might with as much reason and safety be tolerated at London and Amsterdam as the Christians of every kind are so at Constantinople and thro-out Turkey'. Toleration within Christianity—or, to be precise, the comprehension of different beliefs and practices within a single Christian Church—was also one of his aims: the early Christians had practised 'Union without Uniformity', knowing that 'true religion is inward life and spirit.' For in practical terms, Toland's most important purpose was to use Islam as a device for criticizing priestly power. As he explained, Islam was closer to Christianity as it had at first been instituted—'the original, uncorrupted, easy, intelligible Institution; but not the fabulous systems, lucrative inventions,

61. See Sullivan, *John Toland*; Champion, *Republican Learning*.
62. Toland, *Nazarenus*, pp. 4–5 ('the Mahometans...'). Toland's argument was associated with Stubbe's work by one early critic, Thomas Mangey: *Remarks*, p. 43.
63. Toland, *Nazarenus*, pp. viii (Old and New Laws, works), 5 ('might with...'), 14–17 (Gospel; pp. 16–17: 'the ancient...'), 62–3 (works). For an edition and analysis of the 'Gospel of Barnabas' see Cirillo and Frémaux, eds., *Évangile*. On its sources and nature see also Bernabé Pons, *El evangelio*; Wiegers, 'Muhammed as the Messiah'; Van Koningsveld, 'Islamic Image', pp. 216–21.

burthensome superstitions, and unintelligible jargon early substituted to it.'[64] The phrase 'lucrative inventions' struck a key note in his argument, indicating some of the all-too-human motives that had led to the growth of Christian priestcraft. For centuries, Western writers had portrayed Islam as a religion to be explained in terms of human motivation, and their own faith and Church as divine. Toland's radical historicizing of both religions reversed that pattern in a truly shocking way.

64. Toland, *Nazarenus*, pp. v ('Union without...', 'true religion...'), 5 ('might with...'), 70 ('the original...').

FOURTEEN

Critical and radical uses
of Islam II

Bayle to Voltaire

The positive revaluation of Muhammad, whether openly available in Osborne's work or circulating more clandestinely in Stubbe's, provoked an orthodox response. Lancelot Addison's *The First State of Mahumedism*, published in 1678 and reissued in the following year as *The Life and Death of Mahumed*, may have claimed to have dispensed with 'many ridiculous but usual stories', yet it happily reasserted some of the standard medieval accusations: the prophet of Islam was 'insatiably given to Venery', he attracted followers by indulging them in 'all manner of Carnal and filthy enjoyments', and so on.[1] Addison, an Anglican divine who had suffered for his anti-Puritanism during the 1650s, had intra-Christian scores to settle; not only did he make a predictable comparison between Islamic and Roman Catholic credulity, but also, more centrally in this work, he waged an argument against the English Puritan tradition. At one point he likened Muhammad to Cromwell, saying of the former that 'he so well managed his ambition and injustice, under the cloak of Religion, as never any have yet proved his Equal: the nearest and most exact Transcript of this great Impostor, was the late Usurper.' And in his dedicatory epistle he expressed the hope that the book would 'awaken all Christian Magistrates into a timely suppression of *False Teachers* ...lest (like *Mahumed*) they second *Heresie* with *Force*, and propagate *Enthusiasm* with *Conquest*'.[2]

1. Addison, *Life of Mahumed*, sig. A2v ('many ridiculous...'), pp. 26 ('insatiably given...'), 119 ('all manner...'). On Addison see Bulman, *Anglican Enlightenment*, esp. pp. 87–9 on the report to the publisher by Thomas Smith, requesting that he remove 'stories' viewed as ridiculous by serious Muslims.
2. Addison, *Life of Mahumed*, sig. A2r–v ('awaken all...'), pp. 15 (Catholic comparison), 35 ('he so...'). Bulman suggests that the '*False Teachers*' he had in mind were Titus Oates and Israel

In England, such use of the term 'enthusiasm' was itself an inheritance from anti-Puritan writers of the 1650s and 1660s, who had sought to deflate any claims to act by direct instruction or illumination from God. Those who made such claims, it was argued, were most likely to be suffering from the delusions of an overheated imagination, a condition with natural causes, not supernatural ones; the condition might involve an impressive heightening of certain abilities, such as eloquence, but it was natural nonetheless. This argument required a clear theoretical separation between enthusiasm and imposture. As Meric Casaubon put it in his *A Treatise concerning Enthusiasme, as it is an Effect of Nature: but is Mistaken by Many for either Divine Inspiration, or Diabolical Possession* (1654), enthusiasm involved 'an opinion of divine Inspiration' which was sincere, though mistaken; it was thus quite different from the sort of claim that was 'counterfeit, and simulatory, for politick ends'. He was happy to allow such simulation as 'one of the main crafts and mysteries of government, which the best of heathens sometimes (as well as the worst, more frequently) ... have been glad to use'; but his concern was with those who, 'upon some grounds of nature, producing some extraordinary, though not supernaturall effects', had 'really, not hypocritically, and yet falsely, and erroniously' believed themselves to be inspired.[3] With some hesitation, Casaubon put forward a claim 'which perchance hath not yet been said, or thought upon' where the founder of Islam was concerned: 'We are commonly told that *Mahomet* did assume to himself divine authority by feigned Enthusiasmes. By false, we are sure enough ... but whether feigned, I make some question; and whether himself, and those about him, that helped to promote his phrensies, were not at first really beguiled themselves, before they began to seduce others.'[4] This was a naturalistic explanation of a rather different kind from the astrological one floated by Cardano and taken up by the writer of the *Theophrastus redivivus*; that theory had supported the idea that a religious founder such as Muhammad was raised above the normal run of humanity by his exceptional powers and talents, whereas this was designed to portray such a person (and Casaubon's main target, the religious 'enthusiasts' of his own time) as suffering from a mental illness. It is easy to see how the deflationary implications of this appealed to a writer such as Lancelot Addison, who was content to talk about Muhammad's 'Lunacy'

Tonge, whose hysterical campaign against the 'Popish Plot' had just begun in the autumn of 1678 (*Anglican Enlightenment*, pp. 232–3).

3. Casaubon, *Treatise*, pp. 3–4.   4. Ibid., p. 11.

and to quote a description of the Koran as 'the ragings of a Man in a Fever, or the Enthusiasmes of a Drunkard'.[5] Yet at the same time Addison seems to have been curiously unaware of, or unconcerned by, the obvious contradiction between this approach, which dominated his portrayal of Muhammad, and his occasional invocations of the standard view of him as a cunning and calculating impostor.

Humphrey Prideaux, an Anglican priest and scholar of Hebrew, showed more awareness of this problem when he published the next major account of the life of Muhammad, *The True Nature of Imposture fully Display'd in the Life of Mahomet*, in 1697. His own interpretation stuck firmly to the traditional view of the prophet of Islam as a perpetrator of deliberate fraud: the desire for political power was always the main motive. So, when Muhammad had considered the divisions and disputes of the Christians, and the disagreements between them and the Jews, he had concluded that 'nothing would be more likely to gain a Party firm to him for the compassing of his Ambitious Ends, than the making of a New *Religion*.' Prideaux was willing to accept that Muhammad had unusual natural gifts: he had 'a very piercing and sagacious Wit', and was 'thoroughly versed in all the Arts, whereby to insinuate into the favour of Men, and wheedle them to serve his purposes'.[6] But that was not the same as 'enthusiasm'. In a separate essay added to this text, Prideaux discussed the different possible degrees of deception and self-deception; significantly, this essay was entitled 'A Discourse for the Vindicating of Christianity from the Charge of Imposture', which shows how far the radical anti-Christian argument had penetrated public debate. Real imposture, Prideaux argued, must have a 'carnal' interest as its purpose, and a wicked person as its author; it must contain falsities, be propagated by fraud, and depend on force in order to become fully established.[7] Meeting the possible objection that fraud and falsehood could be used 'to establish commendable designs', as in the examples of Minos and Numa Pompilius, Prideaux explained that when a good person uses such deception for a good end, this is no more than a 'pious fraud' (so long as the end is not the intrinsically wicked one of setting up a false religion, which, according to Prideaux, neither Minos nor Numa was attempting). The other possibility involved

---

5. Addison, *Life of Mahumed*, pp. 33 ('Lunacy'), 52–3 ('the ragings...', quoting the Huguenot theologian Moïse Amyrault).

6. Prideaux, *True Nature*, 1st pagination, pp. 12 ('nothing would...'), 136 ('a very...', 'thoroughly versed...').

7. Ibid., 2nd pagination, p. 7.

genuine self-deception, when a person was 'an *Impostor* by *Enthusiasm*'. Here Prideaux simply declared that whereas enthusiasm did lead people into strange adaptations and distortions of existing religions, it could not propel them so far as to set up a new one; this argument protected Jesus from such an accusation—and, by the same token, Muhammad too.[8] Prideaux's book was widely read, both in England, where it went through eight editions in 26 years, and on the Continent, where translations into French and Dutch appeared in 1698. The credit that was given to it derived on the one hand from the fact that Prideaux had dispensed with some of the more foolish anecdotes of the medieval anti-Muslim tradition, and on the other hand from the way in which he managed to preserve a very traditional—indeed, essentially medieval—interpretation of Muhammad as a mere impostor.

Authors such as Addison and Prideaux had some genuine interest in the nature of Islam (having spent seven years in Tangier, the former had experienced Muslim society at first hand); but their motives in writing related more to issues that affected their own society and religion. Addison was waging an argument against Christian 'enthusiasts', as we have seen; and Prideaux's emphasis on the danger of intra-Christian divisions and disputes signalled a concern that English Christianity, divided between Anglicans and Dissenters, might similarly fall prey to the modern equivalent of Islam—Socinianism, Deism, or Quakerism.[9] Another influential author, whose comments on Muhammad were also published for the first time in 1697, also fits this pattern: the French Protestant Pierre Bayle. In the article 'Mahomet' in his *Dictionaire historique et critique* he wrestled with the question of whether the prophet had been an 'enthusiast' or a cunning impostor. Whilst he granted that there were some plausible arguments for the former view (for instance, the rhapsodic and apparently disordered nature of the Koran), he concluded that Muhammad acted in a calculating way; here he referred to passages in al-Makin, as cited by Hottinger, on the prophet's suave manner and skill in gaining followers.[10]

Bayle's account of that skill took him in a very different direction from the traditional arguments of Christian polemics against Islam. As he had

---

8. Ibid., 2nd pagination, pp. 64 ('to establish...', 'an *Impostor*...'), 65 ('pious fraud'), 66–7 (exculpating Numa), 77 (could not make new religion).

9. Ibid., 1st pagination, pp. x–xii.

10. Bayle, *Dictionaire*, iii, p. 1,853. This article remained almost unchanged after the 1st edn., with only the addition of some references to recent works such as the French translation of Prideaux's book.

already observed in his *Pensées diverses*, people always want their religion to embody high moral standards, even though they themselves fail to live up to those standards in practice. Muhammad, far from offering an easy religion that pandered to human sensuality, had retained the moral teachings of the Gospel, and added new burdens—new to Christians, at least—to the list of religious duties: circumcision, the prohibitions of pork and wine, fasting, ablutions, frequent prayers, and pilgrimage. Bayle also pointed out that, logically, people cannot have converted to Islam simply because they were attracted by the promise of a sensual Paradise, since they would have accepted such a promise as valid only if they already believed Muhammad to be a genuine prophet. But while his personal skill and charisma had established his initial following, the large-scale expansion of Islam had a different explanation: 'the main reason for his successes was undoubtedly his policy of using armed force towards those who did not voluntarily submit to his religion, to oblige them to do so.' This, for Bayle, was the central point, and the one of most topical relevance; as he said, Louis XIV's dragoons, when forcing French Protestants to accept Catholicism after the Revocation of the Edict of Nantes, could just as easily have compelled them to become Muslims.[11]

Beyond that essential point about the misuse of violence for religious purposes, Bayle's article explored a variety of ways in which Islam could be used to put critical pressure on Christian claims and Christian practices. The severer duties of Islam made it a more demanding religion, he noted, than that practised by several monastic orders. The argument that the wide extent of Christianity was proof of divine favour could just as well be applied to Islam (here he cited Hottinger's arguments against Cardinal Bellarmino); and the argument that Christian orthodoxy does need to be enforced by the temporal power was a similar hostage to fortune (here the target was his Calvinist opponent Jurieu). As for the complacent claim that the inferiority of Islam was demonstrated by immoral practices in the Muslim world: some travellers' reports commented on the charity and honesty of the Turks, and other observers noted the immorality of Catholics, so the only safe conclusion was that 'Christians and infidels have no reason to reproach each other, and if there is some difference between the ways in

---

11. Ibid., pp. 1,853 (duties), 1,854 (Paradise, 'La principale cause de ses progrès fut sans doute le parti qu'il prit de contraindre par les armes à se soumettre à sa Religion ceux qui ne le faisoient pas volontairement', dragoons); Bayle, *Pensées diverses*, pp. 121–2.

which they behave immorally, it is caused more by the difference in climate than by the difference in religion.'[12] But the main point to which Bayle returned was the use of coercive power. On the issue of religious toleration, both Islam and Christianity had diverged from their official doctrines, yet they had done so in diametrically opposite ways: 'The Muslims, according to the principles of their religion, are under an obligation to use violence to destroy other religions, but nevertheless they have tolerated them for several centuries. The Christians were ordered only to preach and teach, but nevertheless from time immemorial they have used fire and the sword to exterminate those who are not of their religion.'[13]

A thinker such as Bayle could make use of Islam for such critical purposes not only because moral shame-praising was still an effective exercise, but also because he believed that true faith—true Christian faith—was neither to be located in (or validated by) externalities nor to be propagated by temporal means. Such points could all be made while broadly adhering to the traditional view of Muhammad as an impostor. But a more radical opinion, first expressed by Stubbe, taken up by Unitarians such as Nye, and then developed further by Toland, was that Muhammad had not so much invented a new religion as restored an older and truer one; the criticism here, in its fullest form, was not just of Christianity as currently established, but of almost every aspect of Christianity except its basic theism. On this interpretation it was possible to treat the prophet of Islam as both a man of extraordinary natural abilities (including political skills), and an 'enthusiast' in the sense that he was passionately committed to his cause for genuine religious reasons. Only in a very subsidiary way would he still be seen as an 'impostor', in the sense that some of his claims, such as the accounts of conversations with the Angel Gabriel, were pious frauds carried out for the best reasons. Such was the portrayal given in a major work of the early eighteenth century, Henri de Boulainvilliers's La Vie de Mahomed, composed in 1718–21 and published posthumously in London in 1730. Boulainvilliers had been deeply influenced by Spinoza, whose Ethics he had translated into French,

12. Bayle, Dictionaire, iii, pp. 1,853 (monastic orders), 1,854–5 (Jurieu, Bellarmino), 1,856 ('les Chrestiens & les Infidelles n'ont rien à se reprocher; & que s'il y a quelque différence entre leurs mauvais moeurs, c'est plutôt la diversité de climat qui en est la cause, que la diversité de Religion').

13. Ibid., iii, p. 1,859 ('Les Mahométans, selon les principes de leur foi, sont obligez d'employer la violence pour ruiner les autres Religions; & néanmoins ils les tolérent depuis plusieurs siecles. Les Chrétiens n'ont reçu ordre que de prêcher & d'instruire; & néanmoins de tems immémorial ils exterminent par le fer & par le feu ceux qui ne sont point de leur Religion').

and a kind of philosophical naturalism—from which all supernatural phenomena, apart from the existence of God, were entirely excluded—lay at the foundations of his thinking.[14] But there were other influences too, including the Naudéan view of Muhammad as a wise legislator, and the Unitarian or Deist interpretation of the history of the Church, in which the original truth had been obscured both by doctrinal inventions such as the Trinity and by priestly corruption.

Again and again, Boulainvilliers rejected emphatically the idea that Muhammad was a mere impostor. The standard Christian portrayal of him as an ignorant, petty cheat, who depended on the monk Sergius when cobbling together his artificial new faith, was absurd. Islam was 'the fruit of a long and powerful meditation on the nature of things, and on the compatibility of the objects of religion with reason'.[15] Muhammad was a genuine prophet, not in the sense that he predicted the future, but insofar as he expressed divine truths: what he did was to restore an ancient religion based on natural theology and the natural moral law.[16] He possessed 'extraordinary talents for reasoning, eloquence, and composition'; using those skills, he was able to 'intoxicate people with the same enthusiasm that was at work in him'. The term 'enthusiasm' here thus indicated only the intensity of his commitment to the cause he preached, given that not only was the theology rational, but also the specific rules that he laid down had sensible rationales of their own. (Boulainvilliers offered some familiar explanations, though without going through the whole list: circumcision and the ban on pork were for health reasons, and polygamy was for population growth.)[17] As he put it in the draft materials for an unpublished final section of the work, the fact that Muhammad was fanatical did not prove imposture, as the imagination can be violently aroused by truth as well as by lies; yet, at the same time, such 'enthusiasm' must rule out the idea of a cold, calculating cheat.[18]

14. On his Spinozism see Brogi, *Il cerchio dell'universo*, pp. 137–214, and Israel, *Radical Enlightenment*, pp. 565–74; on his *Vie de Mahomed* see Venturino, 'Un prophète'. Occasional references to Christian revelation (e.g. *Vie de Mahomed*, p. 247) seem to be mere window-dressing.

15. Boulainvilliers, *Vie de Mahomed*, p. 226 ('une longue & forte méditation sur la nature des choses… & sur la compatibilité des objets de la Religion avec la Raison'); cf., against the traditional criticisms, pp. 94, 165–7, 178–9, 247–8.

16. Ibid., pp. 31 (restored natural religion), 119 (natural law) 187 (prophet, restoring ancient truths), 253–5 (morality, natural theology, prophet).

17. Ibid., pp. 133 ('enyvrer les hommes du même enthousiasme qui agissoit en lui'), 148–9 (circumcision, pork), 154 (polygamy), 255 ('des talens extraordinaires pour le raisonnement, l'éloquence & la composition').

18. Boulainvilliers, *Vita di Maometto*, p. 223 (edited and translated by Diego Venturino from the notes in the Bibliothèque municipale, Angoulême).

Boulainvilliers deftly turned the tables on organized Christianity where the concept of imposture was concerned. Muhammad 'regarded the bishops and priests, and all the secular clergy, as a political organization dedicated to making use of religion to serve their own passions of greed, avarice, ostentation, and domination, having found the secret of how to persuade people that the blind obedience which they demanded from them was inseparable from that obedience which is due to God'.[19] The idea that Muhammad was motivated at least partly by a desire to liberate people from oppression was a remarkable reversal of standard Christian arguments; and Boulainvilliers was happy to extend this principle from the religious realm to the secular one too, declaring that the prophet was moved by 'the compassion he felt for so many unfortunate people subjected to the caprice of wicked rulers and their ministers'.[20] At one point in his account, he even suggested that Muhammad's whole project was primarily political. Having observed the decay and imminent collapse of the Persian and Byzantine empires, the Prophet had considered ways of 'reuniting the Arab nation, and then using it to destroy both empires'; and it was with that purpose in mind that he chose religion as his modus operandi, knowing that the Arabs had a natural inclination towards it, and that, 'if prudently managed, it could be brought to the point of enthusiasm, or fanaticism.'[21] Other passages, however, emphasizing Muhammad's devotion to religious truth, make any monocausal explanation unviable. As in the case of Stubbe—whose work Boulainvilliers is very unlikely to have known, but whose ideas may have trickled down to him in indirect ways—there is an unresolved tension here between the political and theological arguments. Neither author, it seems, would have wished to give a logically streamlined account, if doing so would have reduced the range of ways in which they could use Muhammad and Islam to criticize aspects of their own religion and society.

Boulainvilliers's book was recognized as a radical and rather dangerous work. Jean Gagnier, a French orientalist who had moved to England and

19. Boulainvilliers, *Vie de Mahomed*, pp. 207–8 ('regardoit…les Evêques, les Prêtres, & tout le Clergé séculier…comme un assemblage politique d'hommes réunis à ce point cy; de faire servir la Religion à leurs passions, convoitise, avarice, faste, domination; & qui avoient trouvé le secret de persuader aux Peuples, que l'obeïssance aveugle qu'ils en exigoient est inséparable de celle qui est düe à Dieu').

20. Ibid., p. 227 ('la compassion qu'il avoit pour tant de malhûreux, soumis au caprice de méchans Princes & de leurs Ministres').

21. Ibid., p. 221 ('de réunir la Nation Arabe, & de l'employer ensuite à la destruction de l'un & de l'autre Empire', 'prudemment ménagée, pouvoit être portée jusqu'à l'entousiasme, ou au fanatisme').

converted to Anglicanism, becoming Professor of Arabic at Oxford in 1724, was quick to denounce it. In the Preface to his own *Vie de Mahomet*, published two years after Boulainvilliers's, he declared himself horrified by the latter's claim that Muhammad had fulfilled a divine design by spreading the doctrine of the unity of God; Marracci and Prideaux had spoiled their accounts by making false accusations against Muhammad, but Boulainvilliers had committed the opposite fault, praising him excessively.[22] Yet the reason why Gagnier went out of his way to oppose Boulainvilliers would have become clear to those who read his own *Vie de Mahomet*. Since he had drawn almost exclusively on Muslim sources (especially the life of the Prophet by the fourteenth-century Syrian writer Abu'l Fida, which he had edited and translated in 1723), Gagnier's account was filled with positive statements and appraisals: 'As for the natural qualities of the Apostle of God, and for his mental perfections, the Prophet surpassed all the rest of humanity in wit and intelligence', and so on.[23] A new generation of Western Arabic scholars was exploring a wide range of Islamic textual sources, and it was inevitable that their findings would seem relatively pro-Muslim, as they sought to correct several centuries' worth of ill-informed European writing. In 1705 the Dutch scholar Adriaen Reland, whose account of the laws of *jihad* has already been mentioned, published an influential work, *De religione mohammedica*, containing not only a translation of a Muslim summary of Islamic faith, but also a long essay by Reland debunking common misrepresentations of Islam.[24] And twelve years later Simon Ockley, Professor of Arabic at Cambridge, who was no admirer of Muhammad (he referred to him as 'the great Impostor'), decried 'The Folly of the *Westerlings*, in despising the Wisdom of the *Eastern* Nations, and looking upon them as Brutes and Barbarians', insisting that the Arabs and other Easterners were superior in 'the Fear of God, the Regulation of our Appetites, prudent Oeconomy, Decency and Sobriety of Behaviour'.[25]

22. Gagnier, *Vie de Mahomet*, i, pp. xv–xvii (unity), xlii (excessive praise). On Gagnier see Franklin, 'Gagnier, John'.
23. Gagnier, *Vie de Mahomet*, ii, pp. 317–18 ('Quand aux qualités naturelles de l'Apôtre de Dieu, & aux perfections de son ame, le Prophéte surpassoit en Esprit & en Intelligence tout le reste des hommes'); Abu'l-Fida, *De vita Mohammedis*.
24. Reland's book was translated into English (1712), German (1716), Dutch (1718), and French (1721). On Reland and *jihad* see above, p. 277.
25. Ockley, p. 1 ('the great...'); Ockley, *Sentences of Ali*, sigs. A3v ('The Folly...'), A4r ('the Fear...'). On Ockley see Holt, 'Ockley'.

It is thanks to the effects of the new scholarship of writers such as Reland and Gagnier that the next major account of Muhammad, George Sale's 'Preliminary Discourse' to his English translation of the Koran (1734) seems to belong to a different world from Prideaux's book, published just 37 years earlier. Sale had worked for the Society for the Promotion of Christian Knowledge, readying an Arabic translation of the New Testament for the press, and sincerely desired to convert Muslims to Christianity; but this aim itself was offered by him as a reason for treating Muhammad and the Koran with 'common decency', since wilfully hostile reproaches would only be counterproductive. And as he pointed out, it was necessary to understand the doctrinal rationale of Islam, because 'they are greatly deceived who imagine it to have been propagated by the sword alone.'[26]

Overall, Sale's account reads like a somewhat diluted version of Boulainvilliers's; and he does refer unashamedly to the French writer's work in his notes when discussing such matters as the 'ambition of the clergy' and the corruption of doctrine in the Roman Church before Muhammad.[27] Harping on one of Boulainvilliers's main themes, he writes that Muhammad 'formed the scheme of establishing a new religion, or, as he expressed it, of replanting the only true and ancient one'. He continues:

> Whether this was the effect of enthusiasm, or only a design to raise himself to the supreme government of his country, I will not pretend to determine. The latter is the general opinion of *Christian* writers, who agree that ambition, and the desire of satisfying his sensuality were the motives of his undertaking. It may be so; yet his first views perhaps were not so interested. His original design of bringing the pagan *Arabs* to the knowledge of the true GOD, was certainly noble, and highly to be commended.[28]

In the early stage of Muhammad's career, 'the whole success of his enter-prize . . . must be attributed to persuasion only, and not to compulsion.' Sale is content to attribute such forbearance simply to Muhammad's lack of power at that time; for the Prophet did know that 'innovators, when they depend solely on their own strength, and can compel, seldom run any risque; from whence, the politician observes, it follows, that all the armed prophets have succeeded, and the unarmed ones have failed'—the

26. Sale, *Koran*, pp. iii ('they are . . . '), v ('common decency'). On Sale see Vrolijk, 'Sale'; on his translation of the Koran see Elmarsafy, *Enlightenment Qur'an*, pp. 37–63.
27. Sale, *Koran*, p. 33.
28. Ibid., p. 38; 'interested' here has the sense of 'self-interested'.

'politician' being identified in a footnote as Machiavelli.[29] Adopting a cool and delicately satirical tone, Sale comments that 'The method of converting by the sword, gives no very favourable idea of the faith which is so propagated, and is disallowed by every body in those of another religion, tho' the same persons are willing to admit of it for the advancement of their own.' The fact that Islam had subsequently made use of the sword for its propagation showed that it was 'no other than a human invention'; Christianity had spread without compulsion during its first three centuries, which demonstrated that it was divine, but thereafter 'this proof seems to fail, *Christianity* being then established and *Paganism* abolished by public authority.' (As another footnote made clear, this point was drawn from Bayle.)[30] The implications of this ironic style of argument were potentially quite subversive; even a respectable, mainstream writer such as Sale was now deploying the early history of Islam as a way of demoting or invalidating a large part—though not quite all—of the history of the Christian Church.

It would be wrong to suggest that this kind of interpretation of the story of Muhammad became the new orthodoxy, however; for the old one was still well entrenched. In England, Prideaux's book continued to be regularly reprinted. In France, the much-admired work by Jean-Antoine Guer, *Moeurs et usages des Turcs* (1747), reproduced the standard line: Muhammad was a wicked deceiver who, with seeming zeal, 'made profitable use of religion, but did so by disfiguring and corrupting it'. Guer happily cited sixteenth-century authorities for his account of the Ottoman Empire (a territory in which he himself had never set foot); he was aware of the scholarship of Reland and other recent Arabists, but dismissed them as 'the panegyrists and admirers of Muhammad and of the Koran, who are usually Protestants, or perhaps worse than Protestants'.[31] That characterization had an element of truth in it, partly because the academic study of Arabic, being closely associated with biblical scholarship, had begun to flourish to a differential degree in Protestant northern Europe. And while Boulainvilliers did have views that were, by ordinary Catholic standards, so heterodox as to count as 'worse than Protestant', there was certainly a spectrum of overlapping agreement on various points that would connect him with a writer such as Sale.

29. Ibid., pp. 48 ('the whole . . .'), 49 ('innovators, when . . .', footnote).
30. Ibid., p. 49 ('The method . . .', footnote).
31. Guer, *Moeurs et usages*, i, pp. xxiv (16th-century authors), 148–9 ('se servit utilement de la Religion, mais en la défigurant, en la corrompant'), 335 ('Les Panégyristes & les Admirateurs de Mahomet & de l'Alcoran, gens ordinairement Protestans, ou pis peut-être que Protestans').

Such was the background to the writings on Islam of Voltaire, who drew from this early-eighteenth-century literature while developing his own distinctive patterns of argument. Although he was an attentive reader of Boulainvilliers, he did not base his interpretation on a fixed attribution of 'rational religion' to Muhammad; his view on that point changed over time, having been influenced at the outset by the major reference work of the oriental scholar Barthélemy d'Herbelot, who argued that Islam and Deism were quite different things.[32] And unlike Sale (whose work he knew and valued), Voltaire did not indulge in the criticism of Christianity as a mere by-product of the study of Islam; for him it was the primary purpose.[33] His presentation of Muhammad thus varied, according to which polemical points he was most concerned to make. In his play Le Fanatisme, ou Mahomet le prophète, first performed in 1741 but suppressed by the authorities in Paris in the following year, his target was religious fanaticism and hypocrisy as such; the stronger the caricature of Muhammad, the more satisfying the play was to undiscerning Christians, but the more subversive its implications— about any person who gained authority over others by claiming to be sent by God—for those who could read between the lines.[34] On the other hand, in an essay on Muhammad and the Koran, first published as a supplement to the play in 1748 and later incorporated in the article 'Alcoran' in his Dictionnaire philosophique, Voltaire defended the Prophet from the 'stupidities' uttered against him by 'monks' (i.e. Christian theologians). Muhammad had introduced good laws—the examples Voltaire gave were the prohibition of usury and the requirement to give alms—and had taught a simple faith in one God, which was true so far as it went and greatly preferable to the idolatry of the time. 'It would have been very difficult for such a simple and wise religion, taught by someone who was always victorious, not to conquer part of the world. Indeed, the Muslims made as many converts by persuasion as they did by the use of the sword.'[35] However, he criticized Muhammad for two things:'trickery and murder'. His account of the former

32. D'Herbelot, Bibliothèque orientale, pp. 295–7; on this point see Gunny, Images, pp. 47–8. On d'Herbelot see below, p. 416, n. 7.
33. On Voltaire's use of Sale see Gunny, Images, pp. 143–5; Elmarsafy, Enlightenment Qur'an, pp. 84–95.
34. See Pomeau, La Religion, pp. 148–52; Gunny, Images, pp. 135–8; Neaimi, L'Islam, pp. 238–44; Todd,'Introduction', pp. 7–32.
35. Voltaire, 'De l'Alcoran', pp. 335–6 ('moines', 'sottises', 'Il était bien difficile, qu'une religion si simple et si sage enseignée par un homme toujours victorieux ne subjuguât pas une partie de la terre. En effet, les musulmans ont fait autant de prosélytes par la parole que par l'épée').

put Muhammad back in the traditional 'impostor' category, thereby enabling Voltaire to make a more general point about religion: the common people have a hunger for the supernatural, and while 'wise people speak against it secretly, the people force them to be silent'. As for murder: Muhammad deliberately instilled a spirit of 'enthusiasm' in the Arabs, who were in any case a population of brigands; and 'there is nothing more terrible than a people which, having nothing to lose, is at the same time motivated to fight both by the desire for plunder, and by religion.'[36]

This was a presentation of Islam that faced both ways—each of which carried some negative implications for Christianity. The standard Christian criticisms of Islam were hypocritical, and in some respects it was more 'simple and wise' than Christianity itself; but on the other hand the early history of Islam exemplified the irrationalism that disfigures all organized religion, Christianity included. Voltaire developed this interpretation further in his *Essai sur les moeurs*, a long account of the history of civilization which was intended as a counterblast to Bossuet's providentialist Christian view of world history. In this work, the line taken by Voltaire drew closer to that of Boulainvilliers. Muhammad was not an ignorant man; he was an enthusiast, who 'in the end imposed, by means of necessary tricks, a doctrine which he believed to be good'. Muhammad had restored a simple faith in both the unity of God and rewards in a future life, and many of the other observances of Islam, such as circumcision, fasting, and pilgrimage, were just continuations of existing practices. It was by persuasion rather than force that this simple and austere religion was spread.[37] True, the Koran contained 'incoherent declamations', though it did also have some passages that seemed sublime. But here Voltaire could not resist the opportunity for a sideswipe at the Bible: yes, the Koran was full of contradictions, anachronisms, and elementary errors about physics, but so too are the sacred books of all false religions. In his later writings, however, Voltaire came closer to the 'Deistic' interpretation of Islam, in which whatever might have seemed irrational in the Koran was simply overlooked: writing in 1767, he described Islam as 'more

---

36. Ibid., pp. 334 ('Les sages contredisent en secret, et le peuple les fait taire'), 338 ('la fourberie et le meurtre'), 339 ('enthousiasme', 'Rien n'est plus terrible qu'un peuple, qui n'ayant rien à perdre combat à la fois par esprit de rapine et de religion').
37. Voltaire, *Essai*, i, pp. 257 ('appuya enfin, par des fourberies nécessaires, une doctrine qu'il croyait bonne'), 272–3 (simple faith, observances), 275 (simple, austere, spread by persuasion). See also Badir, *Voltaire*, pp. 164–7.

reasonable than Christianity', and declared that 'it was simple theism, the natural religion, and therefore the only true one.'[38]

For a writer such as Voltaire, Islam provided a critically useful counterpart to Christianity. It was a parallel religion, a familiar enemy, traditionally and easily denigrated; but some of the criticisms levelled against it were such that, if suitably expressed, they could rebound on Christian practices, and some of the things for which Christians praised their own faith might turn out to be more praiseworthy in the Muslim case. What these critical manoeuvres required was a decentring of Christianity, taking an external view of it in the same way that one might look at other religions. One of the most effective ways of doing so involved the literary device of the fictive observer; and it is surely not a coincidence that the vogue for works by fictitious Muslims flourished in just this period, from the 1680s to the 1740s. The topics dealt with in these works ranged well beyond religion, of course, taking in many aspects of social and political life in Western Europe; generally, they reflected the relativizing perception that had been expressed by Henry Blount when he visited the Ottoman Empire in order to find out 'whether to an unpartiall conceit, the *Turkish* may appear absolutely barbarous, as we are given to understand, or rather an other kinde of civilitie, different from ours, but no lesse pretending'.[39] But the 'Muslim' aspect of these works was always their leading characteristic, giving extra piquancy to the criticisms they made of Western society, and making possible some daring arguments—implicit or explicit—about Christianity itself.

The main founder of this tradition was a little-known Genoese exile in Paris, Giovanni Paolo Marana, whose *L'esploratore turco* was published there in 1684; the original Italian edition seems hardly to have circulated, but a French translation, *L'Espion turc*, quickly became a major publishing success. Marana produced at least one more volume, but the English version, *The Turkish Spy*, was so popular that an unknown English author produced further instalments, and these in turn were translated into French and frequently reprinted.[40] What this work purported to present was a translation

38. Voltaire, *Essai*, i, pp. 271–2 ('déclamations incohérentes', sublime, contradictions etc.); Voltaire, *Textes sur l'Orient*, p. 227 ('plus sensé que le christianisme', 'C'était le simple théisme, la religion naturelle, et par conséquent la seule véritable') (from the supplementary ch. 35 added to his *Examen important de Milord Bolingbroke*).

39. Above, p. 292.

40. On Marana see Roscioni, *Sulle traccie* (esp. pp. 185–201 on the first publications). For a brief account of the edns. see Van Roosbroeck, *Persian Letters*, pp. 42–5, noting 22 English edns. by 1734.

from Arabic of a series of letters sent to various people in the Ottoman Empire from Paris, by a man called Mehmet who had lived there continuously since 1638. The conceit made possible a range of approaches and themes, including social observation, philosophical disquisition, and commentary on past political events. With its clever, obliquely satirical criticisms of Western society and its novelistic characterization of the fictional letter-writer, it enjoyed a success, and a spate of imitations, similar to those achieved by that earlier free-wheeling politico-satirical invention, Boccalini's *Ragguagli di Parnasso*.

The best-known work in this new genre was Montesquieu's *Lettres persanes* of 1721, but there were others before and after that: Jean Frédéric Bernard's *Réflexions morales* (1711), Joseph Bonnet's pamphlet *Lettre écrite à Musala* (1716), Germain-François Poullain de Saint-Foix's *Lettres d'une Turque à Paris* and *Lettres de Nedim Coggia* (1732; later issued as *Lettres turques*), and Claude Godard d'Aucour's *Mémoires turcs* (1742). There were other texts which, although not quite in the same genre, adopted the fiction of a Muslim author: Anthony Collins's *Letter from an Arabian Physician* (*c.*1706), translated as *Lettre d'un médecin arabe* in 1713; a lengthy anonymous essay entitled 'A Defence of Mahomet: A Paradox', in the form of a letter from 'Abdulla Mahumed Omar' (1720); the treatises *A Comical and True Account of the Modern Canibals's Religion, by Osmin, a True Believer* (1734) and *La Religion muhammedane, comparée à la paienne de l'Indostan, par Ali-Ebn-Oman, Moslem* (1737), by the anti-Catholic free-thinker Alberto Radicati, conte di Passerano; and Voltaire's mischievous 'Projet secret présenté à l'Empereur Ottoman Mustapha III par Ali ben Abdallah, pacha du Caire' of 1748. In a related vein, there were also imaginary voyages in which significant roles were given to Muslim characters, such as Claude Gilbert's *Calejava* (1700) and the popular work by Simon Tyssot de Patot, *Voyages et avantures de Jacques Massé* (1710).[41]

These texts displayed a variety of different approaches, some less subtle than others. Bonnet's pamphlet engaged in simple shame-praising, commenting on the wine-bibbing French 'dervishes' and the Parisian 'muftis' with their large revenues.[42] Some entered more directly into the Christian–Muslim debate. The 'Defence of Mahomet' argued resourcefully—in ways that suggest that its author had read Stubbe's work—against the hostile

41. On the French imaginary voyages and epistolary satires see Dufrenoy, *L'Orient romanesque*, i, pp. 145–91.
42. Bonnet, *Lettre*, pp. 2–3.

account of Muhammad given by Prideaux. The *Letter from an Arabian Physician* presented, in a similarly open way, Bayle's argument about the misuse of coercion by Christians and the relative tolerance of the Muslims.[43] Radicati's *Comical and True Account* ridiculed Roman Catholicism (and, with it, much basic Christian doctrine) through the eyes of a pious young Muslim who had been forced to convert when captured by Christians; his *La Religion muhammedane* used Hinduism as a stand-in for Christianity, to enable the fictional Muslim letter-writer to argue that Muhammad's imposture was a permissible pious fraud, comparable to that of any other founder of a faith who added some claims about special revelation to the basic truths of a philosophical religion. Voltaire's 'Projet secret' was a text written ostensibly from Cairo to Istanbul, so did not involve direct commentary on Western mores, but its recommendation that the Sultan should gradually dismantle Islam was transparently aimed at Christianity: the reasons given for wanting to abolish the Muslim faith included not only the fact that it filled people's minds with absurd fears, but also the 'considerable sums spent on maintaining an infinite number of holy layabouts', and one of the ways of discrediting it was to involve making a collection of all the 'fables' in the Koran and the Bible, so that 'everyone may be able to see that our religion is almost as ridiculous as the Christian one.'[44]

If one general theme emerges from many (though not all) of these texts, it is that the essential nature of all religions is or should be the same, combining basic theistic beliefs with high moral standards, and that the more contingent aspects of a faith, such as its particular claims to revelation or its special ceremonies, constitute a kind of superstructure, of little or no intrinsic importance. This attitude is expressed repeatedly in the *Espion turc*, where the writer declares that Muslims and Christians worship the same God, although their religions are mutually opposed, and expects one of his correspondents, a chief dervish, to agree that 'a man can have a happy life after death, whatever religion he may have belonged to, so long as he acted well.'[45] Even Montesquieu, no admirer of Islam—he is one of the few

---

43. Collins, *Letter*, pp. 7–8, targets Jurieu on this point in a manner very reminiscent of Bayle. I follow here the now standard attribution of this text to Collins; it has previously been attributed to Toland (see Carabelli, *Tolandiana*, pp. 167–8), but lacks his originality. See also Minuti, *Orientalismo*, pp. 214–17.

44. Voltaire, 'Projet secret', pp. 110 (fears, 'sommes considérables que coute l'entretien d'un nombre infini de fainéans sacrés'), 111–12 ('chacun puisse appercevoir, que notre Religion est à peu près aussi ridicule que la Chrêtienne').

45. Marana, *L'Espion du Grand Seigneur*, pp. 38 (one God), 52 ('l'homme puisse estre heureux après la mort de quelque Religion qu'il ait pû estre, s'il a vêcu en homme de bien').

authors in this genre to compare Christians and Muslims to the advantage of the former, saying that Christendom is at last becoming less intolerant, and describing the Koran as consisting, unlike genuine sacred books, of human ideas in divine language and not the other way round—follows this rational and moralizing approach. In a crucial passage in Letter 46 of the *Lettres persanes*, one of the two main characters, Usbek, writes that 'whatever religion one lives by, its prime observances always consist of obeying the laws, loving one's fellow-humans, and honouring one's parents.' He goes on to express his perplexity at the problem of how to know which ceremonies to use in worshipping God, given that so many religions differ about these.[46] But the answer is implicit in his whole presentation of the issue: if 'obeying the laws' is part of one's religious duties, even though the contents of those laws will vary from one society to another, the same will surely apply to obeying the ceremonial precepts of one's religion. A similar defence, at the doctrinal level, is mounted in Poullain de Saint Foix's *Lettres turques*, where one of the main characters, Fatima, passionately rejects the idea that those who belong to the 'wrong' religion will be damned. Her brothers had died 'while defending their fatherland and their religion; they never wronged anyone, and they worshipped only one God'. It was natural, she explained, that 'we are attached to a religion by the prejudices of our childhood, and by the authority of our parents, who died in it'; the teachings of that religion 'have grown in the fibres of our brains'.[47] Thus, while our attachment to our particular religion has merely contingent origins, it would be artificial and unnecessarily unsettling to try to detach ourselves from it.

What we see here is only one step away from the line of argument, drawing originally on the writings of Cardano and Charron, that was developed by some of the 'libertins érudits' of the first half of the seventeenth century. Wise people will understand that many of the special claims made by religion are bogus, and that much custom and ceremonial—in the social and political realm as well as the religious—varies contingently from one society to another, and is thus of no intrinsic worth; but they will also appreciate the importance of stability and order, and will respect the functional or

46. Montesquieu, *Lettres persanes*, no. 46, pp. 84 ('dans quelque religion qu'on vive, l'observation des lois, l'amour pour les hommes, la piété envers les parents, sont toujours les premiers actes de religion'), 85 (ceremonies), no. 60, p. 93 (intolerance), no. 97, p. 113 (Koran).
47. Poullain de Saint Foix, *Lettres turques*, pp. 49 ('en défendant leur Patrie & leur Religion: ils n'ont jamais fait tort à personne: ils n'ont adoré qu'un seul Dieu'), 50 ('préjugés de l'enfance, & l'autorité de nos Parens qui y sont morts, nous attachent à une Religion dont les idées se sont accrues avec les fibres de notre cerveau').

instrumental value of all those doctrines, ceremonies, and traditions that help to bind their own society together. This combination of attitudes, intellectually radical and externally conservative, permeates several of these texts. In Claude Gilbert's novel the *Histoire de Calejava* the two main characters, a Huguenot and a Muslim, debate their religious disagreements at length before turning to a wise elder of Calejava (the mysterious, distant land to which they have travelled) for advice on how they should live when they return to their own societies. 'Whatever the laws may be,' he replies, 'you must follow them, at least externally, otherwise civil society would be destroyed'; for laws are like the rules of a game, where each must accept what the others have already agreed.[48] In Tyssot de Patot's novel the eponymous hero, Jacques Massé, has a long discussion with a French convert to Islam in Algiers. When he upbraids him for his apostasy, the convert replies that 'having closely examined all the different religions that he had come across, he had found nothing in any of them that could satisfy a reasonable person; therefore he saw no reason why a wise man should not conform, at least externally, to the dominant religion of the country where he lived.' (Not all religions were equally unsatisfactory, however: he went on to say that Christianity was 'a hundred times more absurd and ridiculous' than Islam.)[49]

One final example may be given here: an anonymous eighteenth-century text entitled 'Dialogue entre un François et un Algerien sur leurs religions'. A noble Frenchman, Montane, enslaved in Algiers, debates with a Muslim, Muley, who encourages him to convert. Muley declares that the principle of all religions is to worship an omnipotent God, and that this must be done by behaving morally. 'Everywhere the basic morality is the same: evil is prohibited and good is preached in Istanbul just as in Rome.' Therefore, it makes sense to adapt to whichever religion is the prevailing one, and 'I would regard someone as mad and pig-headed if he sacrificed his life, pointlessly, to the precepts of one particular religion.' Man was created to worship God, and that can be done in any religion; 'all that is required of you is a form of worship with ceremonies that differ a little from yours,

---

48. Gilbert, *Histoire*, pp. 79 ('Quelles que soient ces Loix...il les faut suivre, du moins exterieurement, ou l'on ruineroit la société civile'), 80 (game).

49. Tyssot de Patot, *Voyages*, pp. 457 ('après avoir bien examiné toutes les différentes Religions qui étoient venuës à sa connoissance, il n'avoit rien trouvé dans aucune qui pût satisfaire une personne raisonnable; & qu'ainsi il ne voyoit rien qui dût empêcher un homme sage, de se conformer, pour le moins extérieurement, à la Religion dominante du Païs où il demeure'), 458 ('cent fois plus absurde & impertinente').

being merely different shades of the same colour.'[50] Any author could have
made these points in the abstract, without bringing in Islam or any other
specific religion. And yet, as we have seen, there was a whole pattern of
available argument that encouraged the use of Islam in particular. The
various traditional anti-Islamic accusations of fanaticism, sensuality, and
coercion by 'the sword' had been dismantled to such an extent that it was
now possible to appeal to the fictional figure of the wise Muslim in order
to teach rational principles to unreasonable and intolerant Christians.

50. Bibliothèque Mazarine, Paris, MS 1194, pp. 3 ('c'est partout le même fond de morale, on
    defend le mal, et on exhorte au bien à Constantinople comme à Rome'), 5–6 ('je regarderois
    comme un fou et comme un obstiné celui qui sacrifieroit infructueusement sa vie aux
    preceptes d'une religion particuliere'), 7 ('on exige seulement de vous un hommage dont les
    ceremonies different un peu des vôtres, et ne sont que comme des nuances de la même
    couleur').

FIFTEEN

Despotism II
Seventeenth-century theories

In the late 1590s the courtier and littérateur Edmund Tilney, who had served as Queen Elizabeth's Master of the Revels, wrote a long treatise surveying the different 'Regimentts and Pollicies' of all the states of Europe. His section on the 'Turkish Gouermentt' began as follows:

> This turkishe Empire is so absolute, that ye Princes pleasure serueth in place of lawe and his worde in steade of Judgment, who raigneth as sole lorde so rigorouslie ouer his subiects, y^t he placeth and displaceth, chaungeth & deposeth as it pleaseth himselfe, wthout all daunger or envie, yea he causeth ye Greateste of them to be strangled vpon ye least suspition or discontentm^t, not sparinge his owne children & kinsmen, cheeflie seruinge himselfe in his principall affaires both of warre and peace, & in matters of Gouerment by abiured Slaues y^t haue renounced their faith, who easilie may be aduanced w^{t}out daunger to ye Prince, and as lightly be abased w^{t}out envie or tumulte of ye people.[1]

The description of Ottoman rule here—rigorous, arbitrary, capable of summary executions, and cunning in its use of administrators who, unlike the noblemen of Western European societies, could be raised up and cast down without political repercussions—was broadly in line with that given by Lucinge and Botero. But there were some differences. Tilney did not seek to describe all the subjects as slaves or slave-like, clearly stating at the outset that it was only the administrators who were slaves; and Botero's heavy stress on the Sultan's ownership of all property was absent from Tilney's account. So too was the term 'despotic'. Tilney's opening phrase described the Ottoman Empire as 'absolute' instead.

---

1. Folger Shakespeare Library, Washington DC, MS V. b. 182, fo. 349v. On Tilney and the composition of this treatise see Streitberger's 'Introduction' to his partial edition (containing only the English, Scottish, and Irish sections): Tilney, *Topographical Descriptions*, pp. i–xxxix.

The concept of 'absolute' rule would play a significant role in both English and French political thinking in the seventeenth century. The meaning of the term was never precisely fixed, but generally it lay within the range of meanings of the Latin 'absolutus', from the verb 'absolvo', meaning either to release or unbind, or to perfect or finish. An absolute monarch was not a monarch who enjoyed total effective power over everything, but rather one whose authority was not bound by any superior human authority, whether within the state or outside it; and in that sense the ruler would have perfect authority, authority that could be taken no further. Several seventeenth-century monarchs regarded themselves as 'absolute' rulers, including James I of England, to whom in 1603 Tilney dedicated a fair copy of his treatise.[2] In 1665 King Frederik III of Denmark promulgated an absolutist constitutional law, declaring that for his subjects he was 'the highest authority here on earth, the highest arbiter of all matters both ecclesiastical and worldly', and that he had 'the highest and most unlimited law-making power'.[3] And Louis XIV, most famously, had a similar idea of his own monarchical status; even if he never quite said 'L'état, c'est moi', he did write in his private *Mémoires* that 'kings are born to possess everything and to command everyone.'[4]

The positive view of despotic rule, developed by Jean Bodin, had presented it as a third category: it differed from both the tyrannical and the 'royal' varieties of monarchy, as it combined the former's extreme and arbitrary power with the latter's basic legitimacy and acceptance by the subjects. The negative view, developed by Lucinge and Botero, also gave it third-category status, since although it displayed some of the features of sheer tyranny, it had its own coherence as a system, and cleverly tricked the subjects into acquiescence. But with the growth of the concept of 'absolute' rule from the end of the sixteenth century onwards, it became harder to tell whether such a special third category was needed. Might it not be simpler to categorize the Sultan as just an extreme example of an absolute monarch?

---

2. Tilney, *Topographical Descriptions*, pp. xxxvii, 7–8 (dedication).

3. Fabricius, *Kongeloven*, p. 313 ('det øverste Hoved her paa Jorden, øverste Dommer i alle baade kirkelige og verdslige Sager og hævet over alle menneskelige Love', 'den øverste og mest ubundne lovgivende Magt').

4. Thireau, *Les Idées politiques*, p. 71 ('Les rois sont nés pour posséder tout et commander à tout'). As Thireau shows, however, Louis did not actually believe that he owned the property of all his subjects (pp. 88–9), even if he did think he had the right to tax them without their consent (pp. 72–4).

348 USEFUL ENEMIES

At the end of his description of the Ottoman Empire in 1636, Henry Blount concluded that the Sultan

> hath not the inconvenience of Tyrants, which is to secure themselves against their People by Strangers . . . neither hath he the uncertaintie of a civill Prince, who much subsists on fickle Popular love; for he raignes by force; and his *Turkes* are a number able to make it good; wherefore he seemes as absolute as a Tyrant, as happy as a King; and more establisht then either.[5]

The form of the argument may have been broadly Bodinian, bringing together aspects of tyranny on the one hand and royal (or, in Blount's phrase, 'civill') monarchy on the other; but the word 'absolute', associated here with tyranny, was one that many writers of the period could happily apply to a monarchy that was considered to be neither tyrannical nor despotic. When Michel de Marolles ran through the classic Bodinian taxonomy in 1657, he listed tyrannical rulers, such as usurpers; seigneurial ones, such as the Sultan and the Mughal Emperor (who held their people in servitude, but 'under certain laws, nevertheless, which they keep inviolably'); and 'royal' ones, who observed divine, natural, and human laws. But he went on to explain that the types of royal rule could themselves be put into different categories, and one of these was the 'absolute' variety—as exemplified by the King of France.[6]

So wherein might the difference lie between a despot and a thoroughly absolute monarch? The easiest answer would have been that, in the Bodinian schema, the subjects of the despot were all slaves; as Marolles pointed out, no Christian European state had ever rested on such a basis.[7] But the factual basis of this claim, in the Ottoman case, was known by many to be shaky; Botero himself, when setting out the negative version of the despotism theory, had written only that the Sultan was owner of everything 'in such a way that the inhabitants *call themselves* [italics added] his slaves'.[8] Botero's argument suggested instead that the primary emphasis should be on the ownership of property. Here, as we have seen, even the standard sixteenth-century accounts of the Ottoman Empire heavily qualified the idea that the Sultan was sole proprietor or sole inheritor; nevertheless, this idea did enjoy continued currency all through the seventeenth century. If correct, it would certainly supply an important distinction between the 'absolute' rule of the Danish or French kings and that of the sultans in Istanbul. Another aspect of

---

5. Blount, *Voyage*, p. 122.   6. Marolles, *Suitte des memoires*, p. 107.
7. Ibid., p. 104.   8. See above, p. 227.

Ottoman rule that was given some theoretical importance (as we shall see) in the seventeenth and eighteenth centuries was the lack of a hereditary nobility; the idea that the nobles should have a constitutional role, as a counterbalance to the monarch, developed particularly strongly in France, where some saw it as a key factor distinguishing acceptable or at least tolerable absolute rule from unacceptable despotism. But the most important and most problematic questions that arose in any comparison between those two forms of rule concerned the authority to make laws. If the absolute monarch could govern by decree, and could unmake any existing laws at will, would not all these apparent differences between absolutism and despotism crumble away? What solidity could the laws of private property and inheritance have, if they were always capable of being repealed at will? What status, ultimately, could the nobility possess, if its rights and privileges could be undone by fiat? How would the position of any subject differ from that of a slave of the king, dependent, in the final analysis, on his will and his will alone? Some writers, pursuing anti-absolutist arguments—or even anti-monarchical ones—were happy to conclude that it would not differ at all.

Comparing a Christian king to an Ottoman sultan in order to portray him as oppressive was a familiar polemical tactic. In 1576, for example, a pamphlet by an anonymous Huguenot, *La France-Turquie*, had accused the French King of taking advice from someone who, allegedly, had lived for many years in the Ottoman Empire, and had urged him to imitate the sultans in suppressing the nobility and ruthlessly enforcing the state religion.[9] But in the mid-seventeenth century, during the violence and constitutional crises of the Parisian 'Fronde' and the English Civil War, the comparison took on a greater role. It was used not just to stigmatize unusual, tyrannical measures, but to argue against certain powers which, in the eyes of defenders of the monarchy, were entirely right and proper. Thus in 1649 the great orator of the Parisian Parlement, Omer Talon, attacking the use of royal edicts, and of taxes not approved by the Parlement, exclaimed:'This despotic and sovereign government would be fine among the Scythians... but in France, which has always been the best governed country in the world, the people have always relied on the fact that they were born free, and lived as

---

9. Anon., *La France-Turquie*, pp. 1–13. The argument about religion (a surprising reversal of standard comments on Ottoman toleration) was that the Ottomans tolerated other faiths only in newly conquered territories. On this text see Lestringant, *La Monarchie*, p. 52; for a similar charge in a pamphlet of 1589 see Göllner, *Turcica*, iii, p. 277, n. 130.

true Frenchmen; nevertheless, they see themselves treated as slaves.'[10] Talon's speech was widely circulated in print; its influence can be seen in the texts of other pamphlets, such as the anonymous *Lettre d'avis à Messieurs du Parlement de Paris* (1649), which argued against the claim that the crown could impose taxation without consent:

> France has never been a despotic government, except perhaps in the last 30 years, when we have been at the mercy of ministers, and exposed to their tyranny. France is a pure royal monarchy, where the ruler is obliged to conform to the laws of God, and where his people, in obeying his laws, retain their natural liberty and the ownership of their property; whereas despotic monarchy governs the subjects as the head of a household governs his slaves. Such is the government of the Sultan, who for that reason is called the 'Grand Seigneur' ['Great Lord']; he can order his pashas, without injustice, to render their own heads, as he acquired his rule by military means, and has always retained the power of a conqueror, who, by the law of nations, has the power to treat those he has vanquished as his slaves. But France is not a conquered land.[11]

One ultra-royalist response to this pamphlet did contend (on biblical grounds) that all kings had total power over their subjects; but that was an extreme and untypical position. Most supporters of the French monarchy were convinced that its powers did differ significantly from that of a despot, as they were limited by divine law, reason, and justice—the last of these including the rights of private property ownership.[12]

In England, however, the negative argument from Ottoman 'despotism' was employed in a more far-reaching way. Henry Parker's *The Case of Shipmony briefly Discoursed* (1640) used it to argue against any taxation—even 'ship

---

10. Talon, *Harangue*, pp. 4–5 (edicts, taxes), 6 ('Ce gouuernement despotique & souuerain seroit bon parmy les Scithes...Mais en la France qui a tousiours esté le Pays le mieux policé du monde, les peuples ont tousiours fait estat d'estre nais libres, & de viure comme veritables François; Cependant ils se voyent traittez comme des esclaues').

11. Anon., *Lettre d'avis*, p. 21 ('Iamais la France n'a esté un gouuernement despotique, si ce n'est depuis 30. ans que nous auons esté soûmis à la misericorde des Ministres, & exposez à leur tyrannie...la France est vne pure Monarchie Royale, ou le Prince est obligé de se conformer aux loix de Dieu, & où son peuple obeïssant aux siennes demeure dans sa liberté naturelle, & dans la proprieté de ses biens: au lieu que la Despotique gouuerne les subjets comme vn pere de famille ses esclaues. Tel est le gouuernement du Turc, qui pour cela s'appelle le Grand Seigneur, qui peu sans iniustice mander à ses Bassa de luy apporter leurs testes, s'estant fait Maistre par la voye des armes, & aiant tousiours retenu le pouuoir de Conquerant, qui donne suiuant le droict des Gens la puissance de traitter en Esclaues ceux qu'on subiuge. La France n'est pas vne terre de conqueste'). On Talon's influence and the use of 'despotism' in these pamphlets see Carrier, *Le Labyrinthe*, pp. 174–5.

12. See Doolin, *Fronde*, 84–98 (general royalist views), 99–100 (ultra-royalist, referring to the *Véritable censure de la Lettre d'avis*).

money', which had a historic basis and had been upheld by the courts—that could be imposed by the King at his sole discretion. 'There is no Tyranny', he wrote, 'more abhorred than that which hath a controlling power over all Law, and knowes no bounds but its owne will: if this be not the utmost of Tyranny, the Turks are noe more servile than we are: and if this be Tyranny, this invention of ship-money makes us as servile as the Turks.'[13] Two years later he put forward the corollary of this argument, which was that there were occasions on which it was right to disobey the king's command. The immediate context of his discussion was the refusal of the Governor of Hull (a city containing an important military depôt) to open the city gates to Charles I—the act which, more than any other, precipitated the actual outbreak of the Civil War. Parker declared:

> Those men therefore that maintain, That all Kings are in all things and commands... to be obeyed, as being like Gods, unlimitable... are sordid flatterers. And those which allow no limits but directive only, And those no other but divine and naturall; And so make all Princes as vast in power as the Turk, (for He is subject to the directive force of God, and natures Laws;)... are almost as stupid as the former.[14]

Parker was one of a number of writers on the Parliamentarian side who were developing the position that monarchy must be constrained, in all its actions, by human laws, as interpreted by a judiciary that was fully independent of the monarch; only in this way could the use of arbitrary power be eliminated. A basic assumption shared by several of these writers was that it was being subject to another person's will that constituted the essence of slavery. Uncompromisingly, they developed the view that it would not be enough for a king to forbear from misusing arbitrary powers; if he did have such powers under the constitution, the mere fact that he possessed them was sufficient to qualify his rule as despotism, a constitution of slavery.[15] This meant that there would be no difference in principle between such a West European monarchy and Ottoman rule, even if the ways in which the European king chose to use his power gave rise to a large difference in practice.

Whilst such a theory reduced the role of a legitimate king to that of an executive officer acting on behalf of the people in a fundamentally democratic constitution, it did not remove the possibility of kingship as

---

13. Parker, *Case of Shipmony*, p. 22.   14. Parker, *Observations*, p. 44.
15. For the classic discussion of this argument see Skinner, *Liberty*, esp. pp. 38–41, 68–71.

such. But after the execution of Charles I in 1649 and the declaration of an English commonwealth or republic, some of these writers were keen to eliminate monarchy altogether. John Milton argued that to be subject to a king was 'slavery' or 'thraldom', since kingship would always seek to exercise arbitrary powers.[16] The republican theorist and propagandist Marchamont Nedham, nursing secret fears about the quasi-monarchical rule of Oliver Cromwell, argued in 1656 for vigilance against the 'Interest of Monarchy', which had an uncanny ability to reinsert itself into what seemed to be a non-monarchical regime. For Nedham, there was no fundamental differ- ence between monarchy, 'absolute Monarchy', and 'Monarchick Tyranny'. 'The Interest of absolute Monarchy', he explained, was 'an unlimited, uncontrolable, unaccountable station of Power and Authority in the hands of a particular person, who governs onely according to the Dictates of his own Will and Pleasure.'[17] Whilst some of the examples Nedham gave did come from the Ottomans, he did not need to invoke any special model of 'despotism'; following the logic of that 'interest of monarchy', all kings would naturally seek to develop the powers that would ultimately reduce their subjects to slave-like status. One characteristic move was the setting up of a salaried army at the monarch's personal disposal, instead of a citizens' militia: hence the Praetorian guard of the Roman emperors, imitated, as Nedham explained, by the Ottoman Sultan, Grand Duke Cosimo of Tuscany, the Tsar of Russia, the Tatar Khan, and the King of France. And another was the gathering of not only the power of the executive, but also that of the legislature, into the monarch's own hands. 'What made the Grand Seignior [sc. the Sultan] absolute of old, but his ingrossing both these Powers? and of late the Kings of Spain and France?'[18]

The same year, 1656, saw the publication of James Harrington's Oceana. Its purpose was to advocate a republican constitution of Harrington's own devising, based on the 'ancient prudence' of Greece, Rome, and early Israel. The most important principle was that people should be ruled by laws, not by individual, passionate human beings: 'the liberty of a commonwealth consisteth in the empire of her laws, the absence whereof would betray her unto the lusts of tyrants.' There was thus a strong moral impulse behind Harrington's writings, a desire to save people from what he elsewhere called

---

16. Skinner, 'John Milton', pp. 299–305.
17. Nedham, Excellencie, pp. 79 ('The Interest...'), 82 ('Interest of Monarchy', 'Monarchick Tyranny').
18. Ibid., pp. 92 (Praetorian guards), 112 ('What made...').

'slavery, beggary and Turkism'.[19] Yet he was at the same time a political scientist, with a master hypothesis: political power could function effectively only as a reflection of the power that was generated by, and embodied in, land-ownership. And this meant that he looked at the Ottoman Empire not as a mere tyrannical distortion of proper rule, but as a system of 'absolute' monarchy that was fully functional on its own terms. 'If one man be sole landlord of a territory, or overbalance the people, for example, three parts in four, he is grand signor, for so the Turk is called from his property; and his empire is absolute monarchy.' Harrington was even prepared to say that, among types of monarchy, the Ottoman system was 'the most perfect that ever was', since it was a 'pure' monarchy, without being diluted in any way (as the Roman one was, by its 'mixture of the senate and the people'). This was due not so much to the wisdom of Muhammad, as some had supposed, as to the different character of Eastern peoples, who had hardly ever experienced anything other than slavery.[20]

Even when looked at only in functional terms, however, each variety of monarchy had its own 'dangerous flaw'. All monarchies must depend either on their own soldiers or on forces raised by their nobility; the Ottomans were a prime example of the former type, and this brought with it the inevitable problem that 'the janissaries have frequent interest and perpetual power to raise sedition.'[21] (However, as he noted elsewhere, since the Janissaries were not foreigners and represented no 'national interest', their revolts, while possibly fatal to individual sultans, would not alter the Ottoman system as such.) As for the monarchies that rested on nobilities: there the flaw was that it was often in the interest of the nobles to engage in rebellion and civil war. Harrington's division of monarchies into army-supported and nobility-supported reflected, of course, the contrast drawn by Machiavelli—whom Harrington cited admiringly—between the Ottoman Empire and France in chapter IV of *Il principe*. The former type was described by Harrington as 'absolute monarchy', hard for a foreign enemy to conquer but easy to hold if conquered; the latter was 'aristocratical monarchy', easy to conquer but hard to hold. Confining the use of the term 'absolute' to systems that had eliminated the nobility was idiosyncratic usage, but the overall implication of Harrington's argument was in line with that of many other republican

19. Harrington, *Oceana*, pp. 170 ('the liberty...'); Harrington, *Prerogative*, p. 400 ('slavery, beggary...').
20. Harrington, *Oceana*, pp. 163 ('If one...'), 189 ('the most...', 'mixture of...', different character).
21. Ibid., p. 179 ('dangerous flaw', 'the janissaries...').

writers: the purest form of kingship, in which the monarch had the greatest
scope for arbitrary rule, was the one commonly described as despotic,
entailing 'slavery, beggary and Turkism'.[22]

It was not only in England that republicans found it useful to take the
Ottoman sultans as exemplifying the essential nature of kingly rule. In the
United Provinces, the widely read treatise by the brothers Johan and Pieter
de la Court, *Consideratien van staat, ofte polityke weeg-schaal* (1661), devoted
nearly 30 pages to the evils of Ottoman rule, beginning with the observation that monarchy leads not to a 'godly perfect government', but rather to
bestial behaviour, with a debauched king indulging his personal lusts.[23]
Selecting from, and sometimes embellishing upon, the range of negative
phenomena to be found in the standard literature, they described the dynastic
fratricide, the killing of local nobilities in conquered lands, the forbidding
not only of printing books but also, they claimed, of reading them ('which
might give rise to revolts'), the pashas submitting obediently to execution,
the Sultan cooped up in his harem, isolated from the people, the rule by
corrupt officials, and so on.[24] 'No one in that country', they concluded,
'lives well, or possesses his property and life securely, except only the Sultan,
to whom all labour, property, blood, life, and beloved children must be
offered up, as if to a god.' But they emphasized that the root cause was to be
located not in Islam, nor in the peculiarly Asiatic nature of the Turks, but
simply in 'the malicious nature of human beings'; such a system could have
developed anywhere, and if it had done so in Christendom it would have
been even worse.[25] (Without this proviso, of course, the argument might
lose its admonitory effect in a European context.)

Among the attentive readers of this book was Benedictus (Baruch) de
Spinoza; he had a copy in his library, and singled it out for praise as an 'extremely
shrewd' work in his own *Tractatus politicus* (published posthumously in 1677).[26]
In that text he went so far as to concede that the Ottoman Empire was, in

22. Harrington, *Prerogative*, pp. 441 (Machiavellian distinction), 446 (Janissary revolts).
23. De la Court and de la Court, *Consideratien*, p. 139 ('Goddelicke perfecte regeering'). On the
    authorship and complex history of this work, which developed through several editions, see
    Malcolm, *Aspects*, p. 43, n. 61. On the de la Courts see van Thijn, 'Pieter de la Court', and van
    Gelder, *Getemperde vrijheid*, pp. 250–5.
24. De la Court and de la Court, *Consideratien*, pp. 147 (fratricide), 148 (nobility, books, 'waar door
    oproer zoude konnen werden gevoed'), 160 (pashas), 161 (Sultan), 178 (corruption).
25. Ibid., pp. 178 ('niemand in dat Lant wel vaard, ofte zijn goed en leven in zekerheid bezit, *als de
    Keiser allen, wien alle het zweet, goed, bloed, leven, en lieve Kinderen, als aan een God, moeten werden
    opgeoffert*'), 184 ('de boosaardigheid der menschen').
26. Freudenthal, *Die Lebensgeschichte*, p. 161 (library); Spinoza, *Tractatus politicus* VIII.31, p. 332
    ('prudentissimus').

its way, an outstandingly successful example of a monarchy: 'no rule has lasted as long, without any notable change, as that of the Ottomans.' However, this stasis was not true peace, but rather 'slavery, barbarity, and desolation', and nothing could be more miserable. If democratic citizens were sources of disorder, so too were children in a family; yet that did not mean that it would be better for fathers to treat their children as slaves. Spinoza concluded: 'Thus it promotes slavery, not peace, to hand over all power to one person; for peace consists not in the absence of war, but in the union or agreement of minds.'[27]

Such arguments, connecting Ottoman 'despotism' (whether so labelled or not) with monarchy in general, came from only one part of the political spectrum, of course—committed republicans, who made up a small minority in most places (and perhaps not even a majority in the Dutch Republic, where support for the House of Orange was strong and persistent). But if their opponents, the defenders of monarchy or even of monarchical absolutism, ever paused to consider the Ottoman linkage, their natural response would have been to seek to widen the difference between sultanic rule and normal kingship, thereby offering an even more negative picture of the Ottoman case. So there was little reason for people on either side of this dispute to defend the nature of Ottoman rule. A few writers, engaged more in general description than in any discussion of political theory, did strike a positive note. Henry Blount, as we have seen, said that the Sultan was 'as absolute as a Tyrant, as happy as a King; and more establisht then either'.[28] Francis Osborne—who, only four years before he wrote about Islam and the Ottomans, had been one of the republican authors denouncing monarchy as such—praised various aspects of Ottoman rule, while sticking, at the basic analytic level, to the concepts of 'absolute' power and 'servitude': 'Neither were many *Christian Princes* less *absolute* at first, then he [*sc.* the Sultan], till their Subjects by Money, Importunity, or Armes had moderated their power, which we doe not finde this Nation [*sc.* the Turks] ever went about: Servitude, by use, becoming a second nature.'[29] A more straightforwardly positive assessment was given by the German 'cameralist' writer

27. Spinoza, *Tractatus politicus* VI.4, p. 298 ('nullum imperium tamdiu absque ullâ notabili mutatione stetit, quàm Turcarum', 'servitium, barbaries & solitudo', 'Servitutis igitur, non pacis, interest, omnem potestatem ad unum transferre: nam pax...non in belli privatione, sed in animorum unione, sive concordia consistit').

28. Above, n. 5.

29. Osborne, *Politicall Reflections*, p. 11; and see above, pp. 297–302. For his earlier denunciation see Osborne, *Perswasive*, esp. pp. 17, 23.

(and physician, and alchemist) Johann Joachim Becher, in a book first published in 1678. Discussing the best places in the world for establishing prosperous colonies, he recommended sending people to Ottoman Hungary: 'nothing would be better than to set up colonies among the Turks; for they have no civil wars, they protect their subjects, keep their promises, allow all people to enjoy their own religion and liberty, and have an excellent, fertile land; so it is very good to live among them, paying low taxes.'[30] But that was just a passing comment—refreshingly different in tone from the standard view, but hardly amounting to a theoretical reflection on the distinctive nature of the Ottoman monarchy.

Among the political theorists of this period, on the other hand, one stands out both for the depth of his own theoretical investigations and for his relatively positive account of 'despotic' government: Thomas Hobbes. In *The Elements of Law* (1640) and *De cive* (1642) he used the word 'despotical' ('despoticus' in Latin) to refer—in accordance with the original Greek meaning—to the kind of rule exercised by a master of a household over his slaves, noting as he did so that individuals could acquire such slave status by being defeated in war. In *Leviathan* (1651) he extended this to include rule over an entire 'Conquered Nation'; his argument was that the vanquished enter into a contractual arrangement ('either in expresse words, or by other sufficient signes of the Will') with the victor, under which they promise obedience in return for the preservation of their lives and their physical safety.[31] This contract, between each person and the sovereign, was different from the one which, in Hobbes's initial statement of his political theory, was responsible for setting up a sovereign; that other kind involved a web of mutual agreements between the people, each contracting with each of the others, to accept a sovereign as a third party. There were thus two kinds of sovereign, by 'acquisition' and by 'institution'. But it was fundamental to Hobbes's argument that the nature of the sovereignty—its essential rights and powers—was identical in both cases.[32]

---

30. Becher, *Psychosophia*, p. 173 ('wäre noch nirgends besser / als unter den Türcken / Colonien auffzurichten / dann sie führen unter sich keine Kriege / beschützen ihre Unterthanen / halten was sie versprechen / lassen einen jeden bey seiner *Religion* und Freyheit / haben ein herrliches fruchtbares Land / und ist sehr wol unter ihnen zu leben / unter kleiner Contribution'). On Becher see P. Smith, *Business of Alchemy* (noting his involvement in a colonizing project: pp. 141–72); on the 'cameralist' tradition, which theorized about the management of the economy by princely rulers, see Dittrich, *Die deutschen Kameralisten*.
31. Hobbes, *Elements* II.3.2, p. 128; Hobbes, *De cive* V.2, p. 135; Hobbes, *Leviathan*, ii, pp. 312–14.
32. Hobbes, *Leviathan*, ii, p. 314 (identical, 'absolute').

It might therefore be said that Hobbes resembled the hardline republicans in thinking that there was no essential difference between 'despotical' monarchy and any other kind of monarchy. James Harrington played on this point when he made a little anti-Hobbesian jibe in his dialogue *Valerius and Publicola: Or, The True Form of a Popular Commonwealth* (1659):

> PUBLICOLA: There are royalists who derive the original right of monarchy from the consent of the people.
>
> VALERIUS: There are so.
>
> PUBLICOLA: And these hold the king to be nothing else but the representor of the people and their power.
>
> VALERIUS: As the Turk.
>
> PUBLICOLA: Yes, as the Turk.[33]

However, Hobbes's political theory was not about monarchy in particular (even though he did believe that it was better, for some practical reasons, than other forms of rule). It was a theory about the origins, nature, and rights of sovereignty as such. Sovereignty was the same in a monarchical state, an aristocratic one, or a democracy: in each case, the sovereign person or body would have just the same powers as a 'despotical' monarch, and would be 'the representor of the people and their power'. And just as the sovereignty was the same, so too was the essential freedom enjoyed by the subject vis-à-vis the state. As Hobbes put it: 'There is written on the Turrets of the city of *Lucca* in great characters at this day, the word *LIBERTAS*; yet no man can thence inferre, that a particular man has more Libertie, or Immunitie from the service of the Commonwealth there, than in Constantinople.'[34]

At a deep theoretical level, Hobbes did indeed argue that the rights of the sovereign trumped such things as the property rights of the subjects, or the status rights of the nobility: those things could be changed by law, and all human law depended on the authority of the sovereign—whatever form that sovereign might take. But this did not mean that his theory advocated or defended the sort of practical arrangements that his contemporaries associated with despotic rule. Even within the monarchical subset of sovereigns, he was happy for the nobility to exist, for parliaments to be called by monarchs, for customary laws to operate, and so on, so long as it was understood that the authority of all these flowed ultimately from the sovereign. And in

---

33. Harrington, *Valerius*, p. 785.   34. Hobbes, *Leviathan*, ii, p. 332.

one important way his theory actually ran contrary to the standard notion of despotic government: he insisted that the sovereign acts always in a 'public' way, above all through law. This did not mean that rulers could not make ad hoc or ad hominem edicts (he gave the examples of King David ordering the fatal deployment of Uriah the Hittite, and the Athenian people—a democratic sovereign—banishing individuals by ostracism); but it did mean that a pre-existent framework of law must always be in place, to make such edicts valid acts of sovereign power. Sheer human will was not enough.[35]

While it can hardly be a coincidence that the two most positive accounts of Islam as a 'political' religion penned in seventeenth-century England were written by friends of Hobbes (Francis Osborne and Henry Stubbe), the Hobbesian element in their argumentation was mostly confined to his ideas about religion and priestcraft. But one of his closest friends and intellectual disciples in France, the natural philosopher and physician Samuel Sorbière, did draw on Hobbesian political principles when he wrote a remarkably pro-Ottoman essay contrasting the nature of sultanic rule with conditions in the states of Western Europe.[36] Delivered initially as a 'discourse' to a group of friends in 1656 and published by one of them, Michel de Marolles, in the following year, it was entitled 'A sceptical discourse: is it not the case that human malice, which comes from our corrupted nature, increases under less absolute government, because of the faults of society?'; but in the list of contents of that book it was called, rather startlingly but quite accurately, 'A sceptical discourse in favour of animals and of despotic government'.[37]

Sorbière's argument placed all human societies on a spectrum, with primitive savages at one end and Oriental or Muslim absolute monarchy—he did not actually use the term 'despotism', but that was clearly what he meant—at the other. While the human and physical conditions differed greatly between those two extremes, there was an important similarity. Savages live, like animals, in a 'state of nature', and follow the laws of nature. 'Hunger, thirst, and harmful weather are all that they fear'; within

35. On all these points see Malcolm, 'Thomas Hobbes'.
36. See Hobbes, *Correspondence*, *passim* (Sorbière's relationship with Hobbes), and ii, pp. 893–9 (his biography); on his political thought see Gouverneur, *Prudence*, pp. 187–208.
37. Sorbière, *Discours*, p. 83 ('Discours sceptique . . . Si la malice des hommes, qui vient de la nature corrompue, n'est point augmentée en l'état du gouvernement moins absolu, par les défauts de la société?'); Marolles, *Suitte*, p. 2 ('Discours sceptique, en faueur des Bestes & du Gouuernement Despotique').

those simple limits they enjoy genuine happiness, just as animals do. And at the opposite extreme:

> In the East, absolute rule has almost the same effect, or at least it seems that the people there live less wretchedly than they do in Europe, where sovereignty is qualified, and where we pride ourselves on having a better political system and more freedom than the people we call barbarians. The sovereign law of the ruler goes uncontested in Constantinople, Isfahan, and Agra; all the subjects think they are highly honoured to be called the slaves of their king, and never excuse themselves from obedience to him. And this total dependence of their life and fortune does not make them more wretched. On the contrary: they are better protected from some disadvantages that trouble us; they have less to fear from the offensive behaviour of private individuals; they are all immediately under the protection of their sovereign. There are no gentlemen there to play the petty king; the Emperor's head is the only one whose whims they have to suffer.[38]

This type of rule creates 'public tranquillity'. In Western Europe, on the other hand, people live in a very unsatisfactory situation, somewhere in the middle of the spectrum: 'I suspect that all our misery and foolishness comes from the fact that in our European civil societies we live neither completely under political rule, nor as mere subjects of nature.'[39] (The phrase translated here as 'under political rule', 'sous l'état de l'Empire', harks back to the word 'imperium', as used generically in Hobbes's *De cive*—the major text of which Sorbière himself arranged the first commercial publication—for the political condition, as opposed to the natural one; and a Hobbesian would know that the absoluteness of sovereignty was intrinsic to the political condition.) As Sorbière explains, the problem is that we fondly imagine that there should be 'counterweights' to sovereign authority, such as estates of the realm; here he adheres closely to Hobbes's argument against the idea

38. Sorbière, *Discours*, p. 85 ('La faim, la soif, les injures de l'air sont tout ce qu'ils craignent', 'En Orient l'Empire absolu fait presque le même effet, ou du moins il semble que les peuples y vivent moins malheureux qu'en Europe, où la souveraineté est tempérée et où nous nous piquons de meilleure politique et de plus de liberté que les peuples que nous nommons barbares...La souveraine loi du prince est sans réplique à Constantinople, à Ispahan et à Agra; tous les sujets s'estiment fort honorés du titre d'esclaves de leur roi et ne se dispensent jamais de son obéissance...Et cette entière dépendance de leur vie et de leur fortune ne les rend pas plus malheureux. Au contraire, ils en sont mieux à couvert de quelques incommodités qui nous travaillent, ils en ont moins à craindre les insultes des personnes privées, ils sont tous immédiatement sous la protection de leur souverain. Il n'y a point là de gentilhomme qui fasse du roitelet et l'empereur est la seule tête du caprice de laquelle il y ait à souffrir').

39. Ibid., pp. 84 ('je doute si tout notre malheur et notre sottise ne vient pas de ce que nous ne vivons dans nos sociétés civiles de l'Europe, ni tout à fait sous l'état de l'Empire, ni rendus à celui de la nature'), 85 ('tranquillité publique').

that sovereignty can be parcelled out in a 'mixed' constitution.[40] Referring to the upheavals of the Fronde, Sorbière exclaims: 'This so-called freedom of the Estates, what has it been good for, except to tear the kingdom apart? And what effect does it have, except that people live neither in freedom nor in submission, and that as they attack the sovereign power, in return the sovereign power attacks them and mistreats them?'[41]

This 'discourse' is a highly unusual work; but even though Pierre Bayle, who was no stranger to paradox and counter-intuitive argument, was bemused by it, the sincerity of the basic argument should not be doubted.[42] Three things are striking about Sorbière's approach here. One is his ruthless utilitarianism: discussing the fratricides and blindings that went on in the Sultan's palace, he calls them wise measures which, by inflicting harm on a few, save all the rest from the greater evil of civil war. Exactly the same view was expressed by Francis Osborne, who defended such palace murders by observing that '*a Physitian* [*sc.* administering poison]... *may be cheaper employed, then an Army*, and with lesse prejudice to *the good of the Generality*.' And the same logic was applied by Hobbes in his later work *Behemoth*, where he suggested that if Charles I had simply killed up to one thousand seditious Presbyterian ministers, he might have prevented the Civil War in which nearly 100,000 people had died.[43] Also noteworthy, and Hobbesian, is Sorbière's emphasis on the need for sovereign power to protect the ordinary subject from oppression by others within the state; this did express a genuine and principled reason for wanting sovereign authority to be absolute.[44]

But the third remarkable feature of Sorbière's argument seems to have been peculiar to him. By comparing the condition of the subjects of despotic or absolute rule to that of savages and animals in the natural world, he implied that the ways in which the sovereign's power impinged on the former somehow had the quality of natural effects—sheer conditions of existence, like the wind and the rain. And in doing so he offered, in an

40. Ibid., p. 86 ('contrepoids'); Hobbes, *De cive*, p. 87 (section heading: 'imperii'); Hobbes, *Leviathan*, ii, pp. 420, 512 (mixed monarchy).
41. Sorbière, *Discours*, p. 86 ('Cette prétendue liberté des États, à quoi a-t-elle servi qu'à déchirer le royaume, et que fait-elle autre chose si ce n'est que les peuples ne vivent ni libres, ni soumis et que comme ils attaquent la souveraineté, réciproquement la souveraineté les attaque et les maltraite').
42. Bayle, *Réponse*, chs. 64–5, pp. 620–7.
43. Sorbière, *Discours*, pp. 85–6 (fratricides argument); Osborne, *Politicall Reflections*, p. 34; Hobbes, *Behemoth*, p. 231.
44. On this theme see Malcolm, 'Thomas Hobbes', pp. 121–5.

unspoken but strangely suggestive way, an answer to the very problem that troubled the extreme anti-monarchical writers of the time. Even though, as he put it, the subjects of a despot called themselves his slaves, and even though they had to suffer his 'whims', it was somehow the case that being under such absolute sovereignty was less like being under the will of a particular individual and more like being subject to a natural phenomenon—perhaps because the power and scope of the Sultan's commands were on such a grand scale that they did not need to concern themselves with this or that individual subject. This was Sorbière's ultimate paradox. Despotism—commonly depicted as the most extreme form of arbitrary rule—could actually free people from subjection to the will of another, or at least to the will of another comparable human being. 'Total dependence' was liberating. In a certain sense this was a very Hobbesian position; for in Hobbes's theory, subjection to the sovereign, in the sovereign's capacity as bearer of the 'artificial' personhood of the state, was not like subjection to the will of an ordinary individual. But it was almost perversely paradoxical of Sorbière to choose, of all examples, Eastern despots—rulers who were always depicted as operating from mere private will—in order to make that point.

Sorbière's vision of an Ottoman Empire in which the Sultan protected all his subjects from any improper interference on the part of local lords or governors was, to put it mildly, an idealized one. His discourse is an extreme example of the general tendency of European writers to develop their arguments on these matters for intra-European purposes, picking and choosing those particular aspects of the Ottoman case that suited them and ignoring other evidence. Yet, as the seventeenth century progressed, the number of available descriptions of life in the Ottoman Empire—and of other 'despotic' regimes, such as Persia and Mughal India—continued to grow. None of the authors of these descriptions was free of theoretical preconceptions, of course, and the balance between *parti pris* theorizing and genuine attempts to understand empirical evidence varied from writer to writer.[45]

One of the most influential authors of this kind was the philosopher and physician François Bernier, who left France in 1656 to spend two years in Ottoman Egypt, and then nearly a decade in the Mughal Empire, before returning to France (via Persia and Istanbul) in 1669. Extracts from his letters from India were published in Paris in 1660, and after his return he produced several publications discussing Mughal history, politics, and culture;

---

45. For a study emphasizing the empirical element see Rubiés, 'Oriental Despotism'.

several of these were quickly translated into English, Dutch, German, and Italian.[46] Bernier came from very much the same mental world as Sorbière (both had been pupils and friends of the philosopher Pierre Gassendi); but their views on the nature of Eastern despotism were diametrically opposed. In a long letter about India written to Louis XIV's chief minister, Colbert, Bernier argued that the conditions there were miserable, and the economy much weaker than it should have been, for one fundamental reason: the fact that 'all land in the kingdom belongs to the King.' Much of that land was distributed to military-feudal tenants under a type of tenure called *jagir*, and the rest consisted of royal estates, managed by tax farmers who paid for their positions, just as the local governors did. All of them squeezed the population for as much money as they could obtain, and because there were no local nobles or parlements to restrain them, they acted with brutal impunity. Consequently, ordinary people, knowing that any sign of prosperity would merely attract the attention of these harpies, had no incentive to improve the land or repair buildings. Bernier extended this analysis to both the Ottoman Empire and the Persian kingdom, adding only the mild qualification that in Persia the Shah was less likely to sell government offices and more inclined to let them pass from father to son, which meant that 'the people there are subject to less maltreatment than in the Ottoman Empire.'[47] He concluded with a passionate exclamation:

> These three countries, the Ottoman Empire, Persia, and Hindustan, having abolished, where land and possessions are concerned, private ownership, which is the basis of everything that is fine and good in the world, must sooner or later suffer as necessary consequences the same ill-effects: tyranny, ruin, and desolation. So may it please God that our European monarchs never become sole proprietors of all their subjects' estates. They would soon discover that they were kings of deserts and wastelands, of beggars and barbarians.[48]

It does seem very likely that Bernier's argument here was partly driven by intra-European—indeed, intra-French—concerns: for it was one of

46. See Tinguely, 'Introduction', pp. 11–23 (p. 22: translations).
47. Bernier, *Un libertin*, pp. 219–26 (p. 219: 'toutes les terres du royaume étant en propre au roi'; p. 226: 'les peuples y sont moins maltraités qu'en Turquie').
48. Ibid., pp. 226–7 ('Ces trois États, Turquie, Perse et l'Hindoustan, comme ils ont tous ôté ce mien et ce tien à l'égard des fonds de terre et de la propriété des possessions, qui est le fondement de tout ce qu'il y a de beau et de bon dans le monde...il faut de nécessité que tôt ou tard ils tombent dans les mêmes inconvénients qui en sont des suites nécessaires, dans la tyrannie, dans la ruine et dans la désolation. À Dieu ne plaise donc que nos monarques d'Europe fussent ainsi propriétaires de toutes les terres que possèdent leurs sujets...Ils se trouveraient bientôt des rois de déserts et de solitudes, de gueux et de barbares').

Colbert's long-term aims to bring back into the 'domaine royal' of the French crown many of the lands that had been sold or given away in the earlier part of the century. Yet Bernier was also reporting the reality as he had experienced it. Several other Europeans who visited the Mughal court had given similar accounts of the *jagir* system.[49] And where the Ottoman Empire was concerned, the notion that all property belonged to the Sultan was so well established that it did not quickly succumb to evidence to the contrary. Bernier's analysis, although hastened on its way by his own ideological concerns, was at the same time a genuine attempt to seek out the structural problem that lay behind the facts as he saw them. It is important to understand that his apparently *a priori* desire to teach a European lesson and his apparently empirical attempt to study an Oriental phenomenon and reduce it to its underlying cause were not pulling in opposite directions: the presupposition of both was that certain ways of doing things, carried out by any human beings in any part of the world, would always have certain consequences. A different (and more shallow) observer might have noted the rapacity of the local governors and blamed it on some specially Oriental characteristic, but then the possibility of drawing a lesson that could be applied to France would have evaporated. Writers such as Bernier are sometimes portrayed as engaged in an 'orientalist' project, constructing an alien and intrinsically inferior 'other'. That is precisely not what he was doing. Weighing both 'them' and 'us' in the same scales, he assumed that they were made of just the same substance as we are. Recapitulating the argument about property in his *Abregé de la philosophie de Gassendi*, Bernier wrote that 'I have sometimes defined a Turk as an animal born for the destruction of everything that is fine and good in the world, even the human race.' But he immediately went on: 'Not that Turks, in real life, are not, in many cases, quite good-natured; but because their false politics, ignorance, or negligence has the effect of removing and abolishing private ownership, from which there follows public sloth, the abandonment of agriculture, tyranny, and the depopulation of provinces.'[50]

---

49. For other accounts, by Francisco Pelsaert, William Hawkins, and Sir Thomas Roe, see Rubiés, 'Oriental Despotism', pp. 144–7.
50. Bernier, *Abregé*, viii, pp. 320–1 ('Aussi ay-je quelquefois defini un Turc, un Animal né pour la destruction de tout ce qu'il y a de beau & de bon au Monde, jusqu'au genre humain mesme: Non que les vrays Turcs ne soient souvent d'un assez bon naturel, mais parce que leur fausse Politique, ignorance, ou negligence va à oster, & à exterminer ce Mien & ce Tien, d'où suivent, comme je viens de marquer, la Paresse des peuples, l'abandon de l'Agriculture, la Tyrannie, & le Depeuplement des Provinces').

This analysis had its own logic, and was based on some direct observation, at least in the Mughal case. Where Persia was concerned, other travellers, such as Jean-Baptiste Tavernier, also reported that most land was owned by the Shah.[51] But in the case of the Ottoman Empire, the claim that all property belonged to the Sultan was a large exaggeration. In Anatolia and the European provinces, arable, pastoral, and forest lands were indeed *miri*, state-owned, if they did not belong to a *vakıf* or religious foundation, but other types of land, including orchards and vineyards, could be privately owned. So too could all kinds of moveable goods, as well as buildings in towns, and village houses, together with the small plots of land attached to them; and a peasant farming on *miri* land had, so long as he fulfilled his duties, a legal right to pass on the tenancy to his sons.[52] The idea that the Sultan inherited all property had long been disputed in the Western literature, as we have seen, and knowledgeable writers in the seventeenth century continued to reject it: Savary de Brèves's book, published in 1628, noted that the Sultan inherited only from his soldiers and salaried employees, being sole heir only if they died without children, and that property left to a *vakıf* was normally beyond his reach. Paul Rycaut, writing in 1666, confined himself to the observation that the Sultan 'makes seisure of the Estates of all *Pashaws* that die, who having Children, such part is bestowed on them for their maintenance as the Grand Signior shall think fit and requisite'.[53]

It may well be true that, even if the Sultan had no legal right to the property of all his subjects, it would have been very difficult for any of them to obtain legal redress if he had chosen to act by confiscation. This might have seemed sufficient to justify the traditional claim, at least in the mind of an armchair historian such as Claude Vanel, who asserted: 'The Ottoman government is completely despotic; the Sultan is absolute master of the life and the goods of his subjects.'[54] But in the eyes of some observers, the fact that actual practice was less extreme and more law-abiding than that did make a significant difference. In 1675 Sir John Finch, the English Ambassador in Istanbul, was happy to describe the Ottoman

51. Tavernier, *Voyages*, p. 250.
52. See Gibb and Bowen, *Islamic Society*, i, pp. 236–40; İnalcık, *Ottoman Empire*, pp. 109–10.
53. Above, p. 221; Savary de Brèves, *Relation*, p. 10; Rycaut, *Present State*, p. 71.
54. Vanel, *Abregé*, i, sig. A6r ('Le Gouvernement des Turcs est entierement Despotique, le Grand-Seigneur est Maître absolue de la vie & des biens de ses sujets').

system (in a letter to his sister, Lady Conway) as absolute but not—where property rights were concerned—as despotic:

> The Governm^r: here is absolute, depending upon ye will of ye Gran Signor; but the People enjoy their Meum and Tuum [*sc*. private ownership] without His invading their rights; For though the Gran Signor does usually seize all the Estate of any officer that is grown Rich by manadging the Gran Signors mony, as the Trea[sure]r, the Pashas, & ye Customers [*sc*. customs officials], yet if any Merch^t: dyes extremely rich the Gran Signor leaves ye Estate untouch'd to ye Heirs, as happened since my Arrivall where a Turkish Merchant dy'd Here worth 150^{mll} sterl. [*sc*. £150,000] & yet though the Officers seis'd ye Estate for ye Gran Signor He freed it all, because the Man had never manag'd his Mony. And thus there are severall Bei's or Lords who enjoy Great Estates in Land wch descend from father to sonne & have done so for many Generations. The People are all free, and unlesse in time of warr pay no Taxes nor Tributes.[55]

If the standard view of Ottoman despotism was questionable where the issue of property was concerned, it was perhaps more easily defended, at the factual level, on the issue of the absence of a hereditary nobility. That the crushing or eliminating of the noble class was an essential aspect of despotic rule was a point much harped on when European polemical writers conjured up the spectre of despotism. Louis Machon, writing during the 'Fronde des Princes', declared that 'not all monarchies are despotic, only the Ottoman one; all the others that we have today are qualified by a kind of aristocracy which supports and preserves them'; the author of the satirical attack on Louis XIV *Het France Turckye* (1673) advised the French King to imitate the Ottomans and reduce the nobility to a total and abject dependence on him.[56] Some writers on the Ottoman Empire did give weight to this argument. Paul Rycaut quoted approvingly from Francis Bacon's essay 'Of Nobility', 'A Monarchy where there is no Nobility at all, is ever pure and absolute Tyranny, as that of the *Turks*; for Nobility attempers Sovereignty' (though Rycaut did note that in some provinces—Gaza, Kurdistan, and several *sancak*s in Syria—the pashas had obtained hereditary rights to govern).[57]

---

55. British Library, London, MS Add. 23, 215, fo. 85v (Finch to Lady Conway, from Pera, 8/18 Feb. 1675).

56. Machon, *Les Véritables Maximes du gouvernement de la France* cited in Carrier, *Le Labyrinthe*, p. 177 ('Les monarchies ne sont pas toutes despotiques, il n'y a que celle du Turc: toutes les autres que nous avons aujourd'hui sont tempérées par une espèce d'aristocratie qui les maintient et qui les conserve'); Anon., *Het France Turckye*, p. 25.

57. Rycaut, *Present State*, pp. 69 (Bacon), 70 (pashas). A *sancak* was a military-administrative district.

The significance of this theme became more uncertain, however, when writers turned to the government of Persia, which was also generally agreed to be despotic. Early accounts had suggested that it did have a noble class; Botero, for instance, praised the Persians for respecting nobility, and said that this made them better than the Ottomans, though he still described the Shah, the Sultan, and other Muslim rulers as 'all tyrants'. A report of 1608 by a Carmelite friar, sent as a papal envoy to Shah Abbas, confirmed that a nobility did exist, but said that the Shah had killed most of the old nobles and 'put in their stead low-bred persons whom he has aggrandized'.[58] Jean-Baptiste Tavernier's account of the 'orders' of society in Persia made no mention of noblemen, merely observing that governmental positions were normally hereditary; and Sir John Chardin (the Huguenot jewel merchant Jean Chardin, whose account of his travels in Persia in the 1670s was very widely read) declared that 'there is no Title of Nobility, and therefore little Authority annexed to the Birth'—while puzzlingly adding, in the next sentence, that commerce enjoyed social respect 'because the Noblemen profess it'.[59]

What mostly concerned those who described the reality of Ottoman life was not so much the lack of a noble element in the Ottoman constitution, as the effects on ordinary life of a system in which outsiders came to provinces for short periods to govern them. As we have seen, François Bernier complained—in total opposition to Sorbière's rosy view—that it was the absence of an established local nobility that enabled these officials to oppress a defenceless population. In many accounts of conditions in the Ottoman Empire it was the tyrannizing of the local governors rather than the despotism of the Sultan that received the main emphasis, even if it was easily assumed that the former flowed naturally from the latter. A report on the French Jesuit mission to Syria in 1654–5 commented that 'Ottoman rule has reached the point of such extreme tyranny on the part of the administrators of the cities and provinces that this is one of the reasons why we hope that the Empire is nearing its end'; Jean Coppin, the former French consul in Egypt, wrote in 1686 that the pasha of Cairo governed 'in a despotic way, that is, since his wishes take the place of rules and laws, he can imprison people, take their goods, and have them killed, without needing any authorization

58. Botero, *Relationi*, fos. [205v] ('tutti...tiranni'), 206r (praise); Chick, ed., *Chronicle*, p. 159.
59. Tavernier, *Voyages*, p. 229; Chardin, *Travels*, p. 279.

other than the order he gives'.[60] But it was not obvious that the fundamental problem here was either the absence of a local nobility or the lack of private property. It would have been simpler to describe it as a failure to enforce justice over local officials; and it was certainly possible to imagine a despotic regime in which, while specific sultanic decisions could be made in an absolute and arbitrary way, the general conditions of rule did include the strict enforcement of justice, to the benefit of ordinary subjects. That, indeed, was the picture that had been presented by René de Lucinge when he first formulated the idea of a system of 'despotic' government.

As we have seen, it was not long after that first formulation that European writers began to look at Ottoman despotism not as a powerful and coherent system but as a rather ramshackle type of government in which corruption and venality performed their own negative dynamic, interacting with the violence and collective self-interest of the salaried soldiers.[61] This view continued to develop throughout the seventeenth century, and there were many who regarded the day-to-day oppressions experienced in the Ottoman Empire not so much as essential features of Ottoman-style absolute rule, but rather as deformations and corruptions of it. Rycaut harked back to a golden age of Ottoman government—the age, presumably, of Süleyman the Magnificent—characterized by justice and obedience; what his whole account showed was that even if the present-day sultans had possessed the moral qualities of a Süleyman, they would not have had the power to enforce such a system. So while writers routinely continued to describe the sultans as enjoying the untrammelled authority of despots, they increasingly commented on the real limitations to their power. Claude Vanel may have begun by declaring that the Ottoman ruler was 'the absolute master of the life and the goods of his subject', but he swiftly went on to say: 'notwithstanding all this unlimited power, the life and freedom of the Sultan depend on the whim of his soldiers. Since they fell away from the virtue of their ancestors, they have given themselves the power to depose, imprison, and even execute their Sultan.' (He added that 'they follow some formality in

60. Bibliothèque nationale de France, Paris, MS Moreau 842, report by Nicolas Poirresson, fo. 44v ('l'extremité de la tyrannie ou est venu auiourdhuy le gouuernement des Turcs par ceux qui sont dans les villes et dans les prouinces pour les administrer est vn des motifs de nostre esperance que l'Empire aproche de sa fin'); Coppin, *Le Bouclier*, p. 232 ('d'une manière despotique, c'est à dire que ses volontez tenant lieu de regle & de loix il peut emprisonner, il peut prendre les biens et faire mourir sans avoir besoin d'aucun jugement que l'ordre qu'il en donne').
61. Above, pp. 239–42.

the matter, asking the Mufti for a fatwa or declaration of approval', but also explained that they would kill the Mufti if he failed to supply it.)[62]

Similarly, the traveller Jean Dumont, writing from Smyrna in 1691, described the Ottoman Empire as 'absolutely entirely *Despotic*; that is, a Supream and Arbitrary Power is lodg'd in the Person of the Emperor, whose *Will* is the only *Law* by which he rules'. However, 'the *Turks* of late have render'd their Slavery more tolerable; for tho' they have made no Alteration in the Constitution of the Government, their Practices are very different from what they were heretofore.' The Grand Vizier had a degree of power almost equal to that of the Sultan, and the pashas who governed the provinces were a law unto themselves, using all kinds of oppression to grow rich.

> The *Sultan* is forc'd to dissemble his Knowledge of these Disorders, for want of Power to suppress 'em: for every *Bassa* [*sc.* pasha] maintains some standing Forces at his own Charge... Whereas the *Sultan*, who for the most part wants Money to pay his Army, and perhaps does not shew himself twice in his Life to the Soldiers, is so far from being Master of 'em, that he is almost always constrained to submit to their Authority. This is the fatal Source of all those Seditions that have so often shaken, and will at last overturn the Empire. For how can we suppose that Subjects will either love or fear a lazy Prince, that contents himself with a Chimerical Show of Grandeur and Power, and seems rather to be a *Mock-King* in a *Farce* than a *Ruler* of *Kingdoms*?[63]

Six years later, Pierre Bayle's verdict was very much along the same lines. In the article 'Osman' in his *Dictionaire* he noted that no nation on earth spoke more devotedly of its rulers than the Turks. 'They make absolutely no mention of any original contract between people and king, and no investigation whatsoever of whether the right to rule comes from the people, nor of the extent to which it can be transferred. According to them, the best form of government is a monarchy with despotic power.' They even believed that subjects who died in the service of the Sultan would go straight to Paradise. And yet 'if we look at history, we shall not find any monarchs whose authority is more fragile than that of the Ottoman Sultans. People are not content just with revolting against them, dethroning them, and strangling them before bringing the revolt to an end; they have calm and

---

62. Above, pp. 244–5 (Rycaut); Vanel, *Abregé*, i, sig. a7r ('avec toute cette puissance sans bornes, la vie & la liberté du Grand Seigneur dépend du caprice de ses milices. Elles se sont attribuez le pouvoir de déposer, d'emprisonner même de faire mourir leur Sultan: depuis qu'ils ont dégeneré de la vertu de leurs Ancêtres', 'elles y observent neanmois quelque formalité & demandent un Festa [*sic*] ou acte d'approbation au Mufti').

63. Dumont, *New Voyage*, pp. 232–4.

serious debates about what to do with them; they gather votes, and condemn them to perpetual imprisonment.' That, Bayle observed, was what had happened to Mustafa I, and also, most recently, to Mehmed IV.[64]

This view of the fragility of sultanic power was becoming well established. Three years after Bayle's book appeared, the botanist Joseph Pitton de Tournefort was sent by Louis XIV on a two-year mission to the Levant, with instructions that he should send reports back not only on plants and natural history, but also on religion, commerce, and the way of life. When a version of these was printed posthumously in 1717 it became a publishing success, with several further editions in France and Holland, and an English translation. In his letter on the Ottoman system of government Pitton de Tournefort did not use the word 'despotic', but described the Sultan as an 'absolute master' who owned all fiefs and enjoyed power over life and death; however, he also noted that the Janissaries and spahis counterbalanced his power, deposing and killing their ruler more easily than the Roman soldiers ever did, and that this was 'a brake on the sultans which prevents tyranny'.[65]

The final development of this interpretation was given by Luigi Ferdinando Marsigli, in his posthumously published *Stato militare dell'Imperio Ottomano* (1732). An intellectual from a Bolognese patrician family, Marsigli spent one year in Istanbul as a young man (1679–80), indulging his scientific and antiquarian interests and learning some Turkish. His own later career in Habsburg military service also brought him into contact with the Ottoman world, both when he was a prisoner of war in Ottoman Hungary and Bosnia (1683–4) and when he led the Habsburg border commission mapping the Habsburg–Ottoman border after the Treaty of Karlowitz (1699).[66] Marsigli's *Stato militare* was a knowledgeable work, containing much first-hand observation and a mass of details and statistics about revenues and military forces,

64. Bayle, *Dictionaire*, iii, p. 2,132 ('ils ne parlent point de contract original entre les Peuples & les Rois; ils n'éxaminent point si le droit de commander émane du Peuple, ni jusqu'où on le communique. A leur dire, la meilleure forme de Gouvernement est le pouvoir despotique du Monarque', 'si nous consultons l'Histoire, nous trouverons qu'il n'y a point de Monarques, dont l'autorité soit plus fragile que celle des Empereurs Ottomans. On ne se contente pas de se mutiner contre eux, de les déthrôner, de les étrangler, avant que la sédition finisse; on se sert aussi d'autres moiens: on les dépose fort bien par des procédures juridiques; on délibere tranquillement & gravement sur leur destinée; on recueille les suffrages, & on les condamne à un prison perpetuel'). This article was unchanged from the 1st edn.
65. Pitton de Tournefort, *Relation*, i, sig. a9r–v (mission), pp. 268 ('maître absolu', power), 270 ('un frein pour les Sultans qui empêche la Tyrannie').
66. See Stoye, *Marsigli's Europe*, esp. pp. 17–20 (1679–80), 20–1 (1683–4), 176–215 (boundary commission). On Marsigli see also Gherardi, *Potere e costituzione*, esp. pp. 435–42 on the *Stato militare*.

so its analysis of the political system also carried much weight; and that analysis ran counter to the old image of despotic power in a quite radical way.

'In all our history books', Marsigli wrote, 'we hear exalted accounts of the sovereignty which the Sultan exercises so despotically. But how far are they from the truth?' Perhaps that picture had been an accurate one in the time of Süleyman the Magnificent, but it was quite false now. For the Sultan's guard was entitled to imprison or kill him, and to give the throne to another member of his family; such a deposition would be formally correct if the palace guard was backed by the 'Ulama' (ulema, Muslim scholars), which gave legal authority to its actions. Such, he noted, had been the fate of Mehmed IV in 1687. How this change had come about was not properly explained; at the end of the book Marsigli commented rather casually that the Ottoman people had regarded all the sultans after Süleyman as either tyrannical or too devoted to their wives and concubines, and had therefore put them under the power of the soldiery.[67] The result was a system of rule in which the Sultan's authority had been eviscerated. At the very least, Marsigli wrote, one would expect a monarch to have the power to declare war or peace; but under Mehmed IV it was in effect the Grand Vizier who made those decisions, partly by feeding the Sultan false information about Habsburg actions, and partly by getting the Mufti—his creature—to decree that Mehmed had no right to delay going to war. What this showed, Marsigli noted (using surprisingly constitutional language as he did so), was that the Sultan would never make war or peace 'without the consent of both Estates, the judicial one and the military one'.[68]

The appearance of sultanic authority, and the reality, were now far apart. 'Behold the miserable sovereignty of the Sultan!'—someone who was highly exalted, but only in superficial ways, involving, for example, the taboo on looking him in the face, and the duty to kiss the ground at his feet. Appearance and reality also diverged in the case of the regional governors, who likewise enjoyed immense deference, dressed splendidly, and were surrounded by servants; in fact they were obliged to spend lavishly on gifts to the viziers in Istanbul, but were not allowed to touch the public revenues in

---

67. Marsigli, *Stato militare*, 1st pagination, p. 28 ('In tutte le nostre Storie sentiamo esaltare la Sovranità, che cosi dispoticamente praticasi dal *Sultano*. Ma quanto si scostano elle dal vero?'), 2nd pagination, p. 199 (where the word 'Effeminati' means not 'effeminate' in the modern sense, but rendered woman-like by too much involvement with women).

68. Ibid., 1st pagination, pp. 28–9 (war and peace, 'senza il consenso d'ambi gli Stati, Giuridico e Militare').

order to do so. The decisions and sentences they issued in their provinces were often ignored by the Janissaries, and others appealed over their heads to Istanbul. From all of these details, Marsigli drew the general conclusion that this was a system in which real power was exerted, over the apparent rulers, by the subjects. In what was surely the most surprising of all analyses of Ottoman despotism in this period, he delivered his final verdict: 'From these premises we see that this government deserves to be called a monarchy-cum-aristocracy—or rather, a democracy.'[69]

69. Ibid., 1st pagination, pp. 29 ('Ecco la misera Sovranità del *Sultano*', pashas), 30–1 (decisions ignored, conclusion, 'Da queste premesse vediamo se questo Impero meriti il nome di Monarchia, e Aristocrazia; o piu tosto di Democrazia'). Marsigli's judgement would be echoed, perhaps unconsciously, by the reformist intellectual Namık Kemal, who wrote in 1868: 'the Ottoman Empire was governed by the will of the community in a sort of constitutionalism . . . The janissaries were the armed consultative assembly of the people' (cited in Yaycioglu, *Partners of the Empire*, p. 231).

SIXTEEN

Despotism III
Montesquieu

By the early decades of the eighteenth century, those West Europeans who wrote directly about the nature of Ottoman government were giving, typically, a very qualified account of the Sultan's 'despotic' power. If one studied only this kind of descriptive writing, one would expect the concept of despotism itself to have entered into a steady decline, becoming less and less potent or relevant in the eyes of Western readers. The need for West Europeans to analyse the nature of sultanic rule, which had felt so pressing in the sixteenth century and, to some extent, the seventeenth, also seemed to fade with the waning of the Ottoman military threat against the West European heartlands; and under the Treaty of Karlowitz in 1699 the Sultan accepted, for the first time, the loss of significant amounts of his own territory. (The Ottoman Empire was not a spent force militarily, however. It fought successfully against both Russia in 1710–11 and Venice in 1714–18, and in the period 1735–9 it took on both Russia and Austria, losing to the former but making significant gains against the latter.) And yet the mid-eighteenth century saw a huge efflorescence in the use of the notion of despotism, which seemed for a while to become a fundamental category of political analysis. This was thanks to one person and one book: Charles-Louis de Secondat, baron de La Brède et de Montesquieu, and his *De l'esprit des lois* of 1748.

Montesquieu's revival of the term was not, in fact, either sudden or unprecedented. For the concept of despotism had become more commonly applied, rather than less, in writings on intra-European—above all, French—political affairs in the late seventeenth and early eighteenth centuries. The reason for this was the increasingly imperious absolutism of Louis XIV; 'despotism' was a term employed either by respectful critics and advisers, who used it in contradistinction to the kind of moderated absolutism they recommended, or by hostile polemicists, damning the excesses that had already been committed. One particularly inflammatory text, which reached a wide audience, was printed in 1689: *Les Soupirs de la France esclave, qui aspire après la liberté.* The anonymous author (who has been plausibly identified as Michel Levassor, an Oratorian priest who later became a Protestant and moved to Rotterdam) surveyed every aspect of Louis's rule and declared it no less 'despotic' than that of the Sultan, the Shah of Persia, or the Mughal Emperor. The French nobility had been crushed and abased, and the common people were subject to arbitrary taxation by a monarch who 'thinks that all things are his own property'.[1] In all countries except France and those under 'Muslim rulers' the ordinary laws acted as 'protectors of honest people'; but 'in France today, there are no laws any more, other than the sovereign will of the ruler.' Religious life was similarly afflicted: Louis had made himself 'Mufti' of the Church, and the Revocation of the Edict of Nantes (with its subsequent mass expulsion of French Protestants) was also an act of 'despotic and arbitrary power'. Even Louis's foreign wars were the wars of a despot, conducted for reasons of personal interest and not for the good of the state. Overall, the power exercised by the King of France was 'just as despotic as that of the Sultan'.[2]

Among the more moderate critics and advisers, the Oriental model was sometimes used as an illustration of tyrannical misgovernment. When Claude Fleury, in a treatise written during the 1690s for the education of Louis's grandson the duc de Bourgogne, warned against confusing the King's universal public lordship with universal property-ownership, he explained that such confusion characterized Muslims, Turks, and Mughals.[3] Other such writers, who were royalist—indeed, absolutist—but deplored the actual tendency of Louis's rule, included the theologian François Fénelon, who was appointed tutor to the duc de Bourgogne. In several of his writings he used the term 'despotisme' to describe direct personal government untrammelled by the traditional constitutional role of the nobility; and this theme was

---

1. Levassor, *Les Soupirs*, pp. 11 (nobility), 19 ('le Prince regarde tout comme luy appartenant en propre'). On Levassor see Haase, *Einführung*, pp. 112–13; on the *Soupirs* see Koebner, 'Despot', pp. 297–300; on other, similar polemical works see Stelling-Michaud, 'Le Mythe', pp. 333–4.

2. Levassor, *Les Soupirs*, pp. 5 ('Mufti'), 29 ('tout aussi Despotique que celle du Grand Seigneur'), 33 ('Pouvoir Despotique & Arbitraire'), 40 ('Princes Mahometans', 'Protectrices des honnêtes Gens', 'Aujourd'huy en France, il n'y a plus de Loix que la Souveraine volonté du Prince'), 43 (wars).

3. Ellis, *Boulainvilliers*, p. 38.

taken up by another figure in the circle around Louis's grandson, the courtier and memoirist Louis de Rouvroy, duc de Saint-Simon.[4]

While the concept of despotism covered both the denial of the property rights of ordinary subjects and the elimination of the political rights of the nobility, these two concerns could be differently aligned, as opinions clashed over the history and political significance of feudalism in France. The survival of 'allodial' lands (ancient freeholds which had never been part of the feudal system) made it possible for some writers to posit an earlier age, subsequently corrupted by feudal lords, in which an absolute—but not despotic—monarch had ruled over a mass of independent freeholders. Defenders of the nobility, on the other hand, tended to accept that their estates had originally been fiefs distributed by the king, while insisting that reliance on noble advisors and governors had always been an essential part of kingship.[5] But a more radical defence of the nobility was put forward by Henri de Boulainvilliers: in his view, the Franks who had conquered Roman Gaul had reduced the local population to serfdom, developing a society governed by a Frankish aristocracy long before monarchy was introduced. Unlike Fénelon and Saint-Simon, whose defence of the nobility went hand-in-hand with advocating a certain kind of absolute monarchy, Boulainvilliers was much more inclined to see any assertion of monarchical power as incipient despotism. When the duc d'Orléans took over as regent in 1715, he succeeded, according to Boulainvilliers, to 'a despotic and brutal reign'. In a later work the comparison was specifically made with oriental despots: the maxims of government followed by recent French kings were like 'those of the Chinese or Tatar monarchies'.[6]

It is on the face of it surprising that the author of such passages should also have written in praise of Muhammad, who gained such thoroughly monarchical power over his people. Certainly, the main focus of Boulainvilliers's *Vie de Mahomed* was on religious issues rather than political ones. But his broader political concerns do help to explain some features of that book. Boulainvilliers emphasized there that the Arabs had enjoyed a free society like that of the early Israelites, featuring 'the exclusion of any king, or absolute ruler capable of suppressing the liberty of other men; and the paternal

4. Ibid., pp. 58–61, 97–100 (circle, Saint-Simon); Sée, 'Les Idées politiques', esp. pp. 552–6 (Fénelon); von der Heydte, 'Die Stellung Fénelons', p. 311 (Fénelon).
5. Ellis, *Boulainvilliers*, pp. 31–51.
6. Gargallo, *Boulainvilliers*, pp. 39 ('un regne despotique, brutal'), 58 ('celles de la Monarchie Chinoise ou Tartare'); cf. Ellis, *Boulainvilliers*, pp. 164–5, 192–3.

power of heads of family who governed independently of one another'. He also suggested, as we have seen, that Muhammad's conquests had been wars of liberation inspired by 'the compassion he felt for so many unfortunate people subjected to the caprice of wicked rulers and their ministers'. As for the severity of Muslim kings and emperors: here he argued, with particular ingenuity, that Islam demanded blind obedience only to God, which left people free in principle to rebel against mere human overlords, and that Muslim rulers clamped down all the harder on their subjects because they were aware of that fact.[7]

When Montesquieu turned to Boulainvilliers's theory about the origins of the French nobility in De l'esprit des lois, he was quick to point out that its central claim, about the noble Franks reducing the Roman Gauls to servitude, was historically false. But he did so more in sorrow than in anger, commenting that 'as his work is written without any art, and he speaks in it with the simplicity, frankness, and ingenuousness of the ancient nobility, from which he came, everyone can form a judgment on both the fine things he says, and the errors into which he falls.'[8] In the same chapter Montesquieu also criticized, much less sympathetically, the abbé Jean-Baptiste Dubos, who had published a major refutation of Boulainvilliers's thesis in 1734. In Dubos's view the powers of the French monarchy derived from the ones exercised by the Emperors over the later Roman Empire; and he did not hesitate to call those powers 'like those of a despot'.[9] It is not surprising that Montesquieu, who maintained and developed the argument that the constitutional role of the nobility was essential to the French system of monarchy, was deeply hostile to this view. Elsewhere in De l'esprit des lois he criticized Dubos severely, dismissing his basic idea that the French kings, far from entering Gaul as conquerors, had been summoned there by the inhabitants to take the place of the Roman Emperors. 'It is easy to see', he concluded, 'that the abbé Dubos's entire system falls apart from the bottom upwards, and that whenever he draws some consequence from his principle that the Gauls were not conquered by the Franks, that consequence can always

7. Boulainvilliers, La Vie de Mohamed, pp. 30 ('Exclusion de Roi , ou de Chefs absolus, capables de soumettre la liberté des autres hommes; Pouvoir paternel des Chefs de famille, qui se gouvernoient indépendamment les uns des autres'), 45 (Muslim rulers); above, p. 334 ('the compassion...').
8. Montesquieu, De l'esprit XXX.10, p. 758 ('comme son ouvrage est écrit sans aucun art, et qu'il y parle avec cette simplicité, cette franchise et cette ingénuité de l'ancienne noblesse dont il était sorti, tout le monde est capable de juger et des belles choses qu'il dit, et des erreurs dans lesquelles il tombe').
9. Dubos, Histoire critique, iii, p. 532 ('comme Despotique').

be denied.'[10] Montesquieu also rejected the extreme royalist account of the Frankish invasion, under which the whole of Gaul had been divided into fiefs by the Frankish king. If that were true, he wrote, 'the king, who would have been able continually to dispose of the fiefs, that is to say, of the sole form of property, would have had a power as arbitrary as that of the Sultan in the Ottoman Empire—a claim that overturns all history.' Rather, the Franks—who, being Germanic barbarians, were a pastoral people—had merely taken the lands they needed, acting with moderation and leaving most of the territory to its existing proprietors. Only by later, incremental processes had feudal servitude spread more widely. The vassal Frankish lords, meanwhile, had remained loyal to a monarchy which valued their services, and which was naturally adapted to a freedom-loving people.[11]

The necessary connection between monarchy and nobility lay at the heart of Montesquieu's theory, and his account of despotism was, in the first place, concerned with the destruction or the absence of that linkage. As he put it in the second book of *De l'esprit des lois*:

> Intermediate, subordinate, and dependent powers constitute the nature of monarchical government— that is, of a government where one sole person rules by fundamental laws. These fundamental laws necessarily presuppose the existence of intermediate channels through which power flows; for if there is nothing in the state other than the momentary and capricious will of one sole person, nothing can be fixed, and neither, consequently, can any fundamental law. The most natural subordinate and intermediate power is that of the nobility. In some way nobility enters into the essential nature of monarchy, for the fundamental maxim of monarchy is 'no monarchy, no nobility; no nobility, no monarchy'—in which case there is a despot.[12]

10. Montesquieu, *De l'esprit* XXX.12, p. 760 (severe criticism), XXX.24, p. 771 ('il est aisé de voir que tout le système de M. l'abbé Dubos croule de fond en comble; et toutes les fois qu'il tirera quelque conséquence de ce principe, que les Gaules n'ont pas été conquises par les Francs…on pourra toujours la lui nier').

11. Ibid. XXX.5, p. 757 ('le roi, qui aurait disposé continuellement des fiefs, c'est-à-dire de l'unique propriété, aurait eu une puissance aussi arbitraire que celle du sultan l'est en Turquie: ce qui renverse toute l'histoire'), XXX.6–12, pp. 757–61.

12. Ibid. II.4, p. 535 ('Les pouvoirs intermédiaires, subordonnés et dépendants, constituent la nature du gouvernement monarchique, c'est-à-dire de celui où un seul gouverne par des lois fondamentales…Ces lois fondamentales supposent nécessairement des canaux moyens par où coule la puissance: car, s'il n'y a dans l'État que la volonté momentanée et capricieuse d'un seul, rien ne peut être fixe, et par conséquent aucune loi fondamentale. Le pouvoir intermédiaire subordonné le plus naturel est celui de la noblesse. Elle entre en quelque façon dans l'essence de la monarchie, dont la maxime fondamentale est: *point de monarque, point de noblesse; point de noblesse, point de monarque*. Mais on a un despote'). Montesquieu added the terms 'subordinate' and 'dependent' here at a late stage, to avoid giving offence to the King: see Shackleton, *Montesquieu*, p. 279.

The difference between monarchy and despotism was primarily a structural one. The nobility was the most important 'subordinate power', but Montesquieu also included the clergy, the judiciary in the parlements, town councils, and other corporate bodies; and it was thanks to all these powers and institutions dependent on the constitution that monarchy enjoyed its tremendous stability.[13] His opinion seems to have changed here from the one he previously expressed in his *Lettres persanes*, where one of his characters described European monarchy as an unstable thing, which 'always degenerates into despotism or into a republic'. But Montesquieu's own view of the royal government of Louis XIV was almost as critical as Fénelon's, regarding it not as an actual despotism but as a monarchy corrupted by despotic tendencies. He did not give a precise account of where those tendencies came from (beyond his general observation that 'every man who has power is led to abuse it'), though his remarks about an earlier phase of French absolutism suggested that unscrupulous and power-hungry ministers might be to blame: on Richelieu he commented that 'even if this man did not have despotism in his heart, he had it in his head.'[14]

Montesquieu thus stood in the broad tradition of Fénelon, Saint-Simon, and Boulainvilliers, conducting an intra-French argument about the constitutional role of the nobility and using the concept of despotism as a theoretical—or rhetorical—counterweight. If that was all he had done, the discussion of his theory of despotism could end at this point. But his treatise *De l'esprit des lois* was not just about France; it was a hugely ambitious attempt to set out a general theory of law and government, applicable to human beings everywhere. In some ways the theory went further than that, seeking to develop a science of mankind that was not only political but also social and psychological. Montesquieu had read very widely in the recent literature by travellers, mariners, merchants, and missionaries, and was able to incorporate information about a range of societies that had been little known to Europeans a century before (one of them being China, which greatly puzzled Western observers by appearing to combine 'despotic' rule with generally civilized and tranquil conditions of life).

---

13. Montesquieu, *De l'esprit* II.4, pp. 535–6 (clergy, towns, *parlements*), V.10, p. 550 (corporate bodies, *parlements*), V.11, p. 550 (stability).
14. Montesquieu, *Lettres persanes*, no. 102, p. 115 ('dégénère toujours en despotisme ou en république'); Weil, 'Montesquieu', p. 197 (corrupted); Montesquieu, *De l'esprit* V.10, p. 550 ('Quand cet homme n'aurait pas eu le despotisme dans le coeur, il l'aurait eu dans la tête'), XI.4, p. 586 ('tout homme qui a du pouvoir est porté à en abuser').

And even though it would be wrong to describe his whole approach as empirical, he clearly took interest and pride in being able to draw into his theory a wide range of concrete examples and facts from history, geography, and the natural sciences.[15]

Despotism was, for Montesquieu, one of the three basic types of government, the others being monarchy and a republic. In a republican system all the people or some of the people rule; in a monarchy, one person rules, but in accordance with fixed laws and a constitution; and in a despotism one person rules merely at will. This classification diverged from the traditional scheme of rule by the many, the few, or the one. In effect, Montesquieu was putting forward one primary distinction, between what might be called constitutional and non-constitutional systems, and one secondary distinction, between two types of constitutional government—for republics depended, like monarchies, on their constitutions, and rule by the many or the few would not be possible without some such framework. (However, he did note that if, as had happened in some of the aristocratic republics of Italy, the constitution placed all the key powers, legislative, executive, and judicial, in the hands of the same body of people, that republican government would become significantly like a despotism. This view also allowed him to accommodate the opinions of recent writers on the 'Barbary' states of North Africa, which classified them as despotic military-aristocratic republics.)[16] Like Bodin, Montesquieu thought of despotism as a distinct system of rule, but in effect he was reverting to the more traditional view of those who contrasted monarchy with tyranny and had nothing positive to say about the latter—though in his case the traditional criteria for distinguishing between them, such as the consent of the ruled or whether the rule was in the interests of the ruled or the ruler, fell away.[17] And since he did not attend to those criteria, his grounds for positing despotism as a fundamental category were thoroughly non-Bodinian. The simplest reason

15. On Montesquieu's reading see Dodds, *Les Récits*, and Shackleton, *Montesquieu*, pp. 229–35, 411–18; on his sources concerning the Ottoman Empire and Muslim world see Vernière, 'Montesquieu', pp. 177–8; on French interest in China see Pinot, *La Chine*; on Montesquieu's non-empiricism see Waddicor, *Montesquieu*, pp. 22–33.

16. Montesquieu, *De l'esprit* II.1–5, pp. 532–6 (three types), XI.6, pp. 586–7 (aristocratic republics; cf. also his comments on Poland, an aristocratic republic where the common people were the 'slaves' ('esclaves') of their rulers: II.3, p. 535); Montesquieu, *Pensées*, pp. 372, no. 940 (comparing Algiers to Genoa), 553, no. 772 (Algiers a military aristocracy). Among his likely sources were Laugier de Tassy, *Histoire*, p. 78 (Algiers a despotic noble republic), and d'Arvieux, *Mémoires*, iv, pp. 49–50 (Tunis a military republic), v, p. 249 (Algiers a military republic).

17. See Rahe, *Montesquieu*, p. 66.

why it existed was that forming a viable constitution was hard work, both intellectually and morally, whereas despotism would happen by itself if the passions were given free rein; in that way one might even say that it was a more fundamental category than the other two.[18] But there were other, more specific, reasons for the existence of despotic states; indeed, as Montesquieu's theory tried to prove, in some countries despotism was actually the most suitable form of government.

Famously, Montesquieu assigned to each of the three categories of government a particular 'principle', which animated its subjects and characterized their relationship to the state. For a republic the principle was virtue (not moral virtue in general, but the special 'political' virtue that made people subordinate their own interests to that of the country as a whole); for a monarchy, honour; and for a despotism, fear.[19] Once again despotism stood apart from the others: its principle was just a blind passion, whereas those of the other two, though described as passions by Montesquieu because they motivated human action, incorporated beliefs about values. By distinguishing honour from virtue, he was able to protect his vision of a monarchy-cum-hereditary-nobility from some of the criticisms traditionally aimed at it by classical republicanism. And by distinguishing honour and virtue on the one hand from fear on the other, Montesquieu suggested that while the subjects of monarchs and republics live like human beings, those who are under despotic rule are treated like animals, or even like physical objects. 'In despotic states the nature of the government requires extreme obedience; and the will of the ruler, once known, must have its effect as infallibly as that of one ball thrown against another. All that is reserved for human beings there is instinct, obedience, and chastisement, just as it is for animals.'[20]

Nevertheless, these 'principles', although given great prominence at the outset, do surprisingly little explanatory work in the rest of the treatise. The main interest of Montesquieu's theorizing lies not in these, but in the complex set of interrelated and overlapping causes and conditions which he tries to analyse in relation to different forms of government and laws. Some of these factors are physical, such as a country's climate, the size of its territory, and the fertility of its soil. Some are cultural, such as religion and

---

18. Montesquieu, *De l'esprit* V.14, p. 553 (constitution, passions).
19. Ibid. III, pp. 536–40.
20. Ibid. III.10, p. 539 ('Dans les États despotiques la nature du gouvernement demande une obéissance extrême; et la volonté du prince, une fois connue, doit avoir aussi infailliblement son effet qu'une boule jetée contre une autre doit avoir le sien…Le partage des hommes, comme des bêtes, y est l'instinct, l'obéissance, le châtiment').

the mores ('moeurs', i.e. customary ways of behaving) of a society, or its particular history—for example, the way in which it has been subjected to military conquest. Any one of these, in a specific case, may seem to have a determining role, but Montesquieu does not supply any method for assessing their relative weights, so the possibility of a genuine 'science of mankind' emerging from these observations remains very remote. Moreover, causation works in more than one direction here: while the system of rule has an effect on the nature of the subjects from above, and physical conditions influence them from below, human mores can also have effects both on the people who abide by them and on the nature and actions of their government.

All of which means that Montesquieu's account of despotism can seem heavily overdetermined. The physical cause to which he seems to give most weight is climate, conceived of primarily in terms of the effect of temperature on the human body. In very hot countries, people will become passive, lacking all curiosity, enterprise, and courage; this makes them well adapted to servitude.[21] In such a climate, Montesquieu also assures us, women must be kept in 'dependence' because they mature sexually at an age when they are not yet entirely rational; what is more, as they quickly lose their beauty it is reasonable that men should take further wives, polygamously. A hot climate therefore requires a kind of 'rule over women' that would not be compatible with the mores of a republic, and that is one reason why those places that naturally tend towards despotic government also tend to place women in a position of domestic servitude. In cold climates, on the other hand, women have more responsibility and autonomy because they are already fully rational when they become marriageable, and the men are—for climatic reasons—frequently drunk.[22] The crudity of Montesquieu's argumentation on such points is quite striking. In De l'esprit des lois he can happily assert that 'the cowardice of the peoples who live in hot climates has almost always turned them into slaves, and the courage of the peoples who live in cold climates has kept them free'; in an earlier work, the Réflexions sur la monarchie universelle en Europe (1734), he declared that it was almost impossible for the Ottomans to conquer northern Europe, because soldiers from the south could not tolerate its low temperatures.[23]

21. Ibid. XIV.2, p. 614 (lack of curiosity, servitude), XVII.2, p. 630 (lack of courage).
22. Ibid. XVI.2, p. 625 (lower age, 'dépendance'), XVI.9, p. 627 ('L'empire sur les femmes'); Montesquieu, Pensées, p. 343, no. 757 (cold climates).
23. Montesquieu, De l'esprit XVII.2, p. 630 ('la lâcheté des peuples des climats chauds les ait presque toujours rendus esclaves, et que le courage des peuples des climats froids les ait maintenus libres'); Montesquieu, Réflexions, pp. 92–3.

Although climatic explanations of human culture and politics had a long history, going back to Aristotle and Hippocrates, few early modern writers on the Ottoman or Middle Eastern lands had theorized seriously in such terms since Bodin; Sir John Chardin did assert at one point that 'The Climate of each People is always, as I believe, the principal Effect on the Inclinations and Customs of the Men', but that was just a passing remark. Marsigli also commented briefly on the influence of the climate, though his observation that Istanbul varied between great heat and great cold (he had experienced snow and hail there in February) would not have given Montesquieu's theory much support.[24] Several writers, on the other hand, had put forward obvious objections to the climatic approach. When Nicolas Du Loir, who was in Istanbul in the period 1639–41, commented on the good moral qualities of ordinary Turks, he wrote: 'they are good by nature, and you mustn't say that the climate makes them so, since the Greeks are born in the same country, with such different tendencies that they have retained only the bad qualities of their ancestors, namely trickery, perfidiousness, and vanity.' And Joseph Pitton de Tournefort, whose work Montesquieu did study carefully, also pointed out that Greeks and Turks had very different 'humeurs', which must be attributed to the differences in their upbringing, as the climate they lived under was the same.[25] But Montesquieu's urge to systematize, wielding large-scale causal factors, would not have been thwarted by such arguments—not least because he could invoke counter-vailing influences (such as the differing religions of Greeks and Turks) if and when he wanted.

Another cause of despotism to which Montesquieu attributed real importance was the size of the country, something dictated by primary geographical conditions. As he put it in his *Réflexions*, Asia had always had great empires of a kind that could not exist in Europe, because it consisted of huge plains, divided by rivers which were less impassable because of evaporation in the hot climate. And 'a great empire necessarily presupposes despotic authority in the ruler', because unless the fear of severe punishment guaranteed

24. Chardin, *Travels*, p. 193 (where 'on' is an emendation of 'of'); Marsigli, *Stato militare*, 1st pagination, pp. 31–2. One possible influence on Montesquieu was the climatic theory presented by the abbé Dubos in his *Réflections critiques sur la poésie et la peinture*: see Gargallo, *Boulainvilliers*, pp. 71–2, 85.

25. Du Loir, *Voyages*, p. 166 ('Naturellement ils sont bons, et il ne faut pas dire que le climat les rende tels, puis que les Grecs naissent dans le mesme pays, avec des inclinations si différentes, qu'ils n'ont retenu de leurs ancestres que les mauvaises qualitez; à sçavoir, la fourberie, la perfidie et la vanité'); Pitton de Tournefort, *Relation*, ii, p. 377.

that all orders were carried out immediately and unquestioningly, local governors would become negligent, and subject peoples in the provinces would seek to break away. 'So power must always be despotic in Asia, because if the servitude there was not extreme, the territory would immediately become divided in a way that the nature of the country [sc. its lack of natural divisions] could not allow.'[26] In De l'esprit des lois Montesquieu added a further consideration. 'An immense conquest presupposes despotism. For at such a time the army, spread out in the provinces, is not enough. The ruler must always have around him a particularly loyal corps, ready to pounce on any part of the empire that might become unstable'—hence the Janissary corps, directly salaried by the Sultan.[27] This emphasis on the size of the territory was also quite distinctive. Machiavelli had commented, as we have seen, on the 'inactive' nature of large Asian empires, contrasting it unfavourably with the state of affairs in Europe, divided into many kingdoms and republics, but his suggestion was merely that this made the empires weaker militarily.[28] One oft-repeated argument (which seems to have originated in a Venetian relazione of 1573, and was taken up by Louis Deshayes, Paul Rycaut, and Aaron Hill) was that in these huge states it was impossible for criminals to flee quickly to a foreign jurisdiction, with the result that rebellions, or crimes such as murder, were much rarer there; but this implied that less severity was needed on the part of the ruler in such countries, not more. Only a brief comment by Rycaut at the beginning of his book ('the large territories and remote parts of the Empire require speedy preventions, without processes of law, or formal indictment') seems to have prefigured Montesquieu's argument here, though Rycaut himself did not have any kind of geographical determinism in mind.[29]

   In fact there had been curiously little general theorizing about the origins or causes of despotism on the part of those writers who had used the

26. Montesquieu, Réflexions, pp. 82 ('Un grand Empire suppose nécessairement une autorité despotique'), 83 ('La puissance doit donc être toujours despotique en Asie, car si la servitude n'y était pas extrême, il se ferait d'abord un partage que la nature du pays ne peut pas souffrir'). Cf. similar remarks in Montesquieu, De l'esprit VIII.19, pp. 575–6, XVII.6, p. 632.

27. Montesquieu, De l'esprit X.16, p. 585 ('Lorsque la conquête est immense, elle suppose le despotisme. Pour lors l'armée répandue dans les provinces ne suffit pas. Il faut qu'il y ait toujours autour du prince un corps particulièrement affidé, toujours prêt à fondre sur la partie de l'empire qui pourrait s'ébranler').

28. Above, pp. 163–4.

29. Albèri, ed., Relazioni, ser. 3, i, p. 328 (Marcantonio Barbaro, 1573); Deshayes, Voiage, p. 249; Rycaut, Present State, pp. 3 (brief comment), 68 (rebels, criminals unable to flee); Hill, Full and Just Account, p. 5.

concept in the seventeenth and early eighteenth centuries. Paul Rycaut did offer a basic explanation of the character of Ottoman rule: 'The *Turks* had the original of their Civil Government founded in the time of war: for when they first came out of *Scythia*...it is to be supposed, that they had no Laws but what were Arbitrary and Martial...The whole condition of this people was but a continued state of war; wherefore it is not strange, if their laws are severe, and in most things arbitrary; that the Emperor should be absolute and above law'.[30] The same point was made by Pitton de Tournefort, and would later be taken up by the economist Anne-Robert-Jacques Turgot, who, writing two or three years after the publication of Montesquieu's *De l'esprit des lois*, put a special emphasis on it: 'when *military government* is the only bond of the state, the government is despotic in its essential principle.'[31] But Montesquieu did not pursue the idea that despotic government originated from martial law—perhaps because history showed too many examples of conquests by military powers that had not had this political effect in the longer term. Similar considerations may explain why it was that, although the linkage between despotism and the denial of private property was a commonplace, no writer simply argued that the former was caused by the latter; some rulers, on conquering a territory, might decide to keep all its land as their own, but others might not, and the difference between them would presumably depend on one or more prior factors.

Another possible explanation of the nature of despotic rule was that it was a reflection or expression of religious beliefs. As we have seen, elements of a 'political' interpretation of Islam had been current in Western culture for a long time: the idea that certain Islamic practices were instituted by Muhammad in order to increase the population or improve the army; the emphasis on holy war, with its promises of instant passage to Paradise to those who died fighting it; and so on. Yet these in themselves did not amount to an argument that the despotic nature of the Sultan's rule was derived from, or caused by, Islam. In the late seventeenth and early eighteenth centuries some writers did put more stress on the idea that Islam required blind obedience to the ruler. Samuel Schelwig, in his inaugural lecture in Gdańsk, *De philosophia turcica* (1686), said that Muslims had a doctrine of total obedience. Four years later the diplomat and essayist William Temple

---

30. Rycaut, *Present State*, p. 3.
31. Pitton de Tournefort, *Relation*, ii, p. 268; Turgot, 'Plan du premier discours', p. 292 ('Lorsque le *gouvernement militaire* est le seul lien de l'État...ce gouvernement est despotique dans son principe').

attributed to the Sultan's Muslim subjects a strong doctrine of divine right; because of their belief in the 'Divine Designation of the Ottoman Line to reign among them', he explained, they 'held Obedience to be given in all things to the Will of their Ottoman Prince as to the Will of God... This gives such an abandoned Submission to all the frequent and cruel Executions among them by the Emperors Command, tho' upon the meer Turns of his own Humour.' Aaron Hill similarly described obedience to the Sultan's will as a religious duty.[32] In 1734 this idea received significant support from an unusually authoritative source, the *History of the Growth and Decay of the Othman Empire* by Dimitrie Cantemir. The author, a former Voivod of Moldavia who had passed into exile in Russia after a failed revolt, was fluent in Turkish, having received a high-level education in Istanbul; another treatise he wrote, on Islam, was one of the most knowledgeable works on that subject written by a non-Muslim in the early modern period.[33] According to Cantemir, 'The Emperor's Orders, of whatever kind, are received by the *Turks* as coming from the Hand of God, and to disobey them is reckon'd the highest Impiety'; that was why a vizier would meekly submit to execution, as any resistance would call in doubt his piety as a Muslim. (He also wrote that 'the *Turks* allow that their Emperor may kill every day fourteen of his Subjects with impunity and without impeachment of Tyranny, because (say they) He does many things by divine impulse'—a claim that would be repeated verbatim in the article 'Sultan' in the *Encyclopédie*.)[34]

Despite the long Western tradition of vilifying Muhammad himself as a tyrannical autocrat, this linkage between Muslim beliefs and despotic rule never turned into a general theory that Islam was the cause of despotism. The most obvious reason for this is that several non-Muslim countries were also seen as being under despotic rule. Although Montesquieu was happy to say that 'moderate government is better suited to the Christian religion, and despotic government to the Muslim one', he could not simply derive despotism from Islam while identifying as despotic a whole range of non-Muslim regimes, including the later Roman Empire, China, Japan, Mexico, Peru, and

32. Schelwig, *De philosophia*, p. 31; Temple, *Miscellanea*, pp. 261–2; Hill, *Full and Just Account*, p. 8. On this theme see also above, pp. 276–7.
33. On Cantemir see Panaitescu, *Dimitrie Cantemir*; Lemny, *Les Cantemir*, pp. 29–173. The treatise on Islam was written in Latin but published in Russian translation in 1722, and therefore had little or no influence on Western readers: see Cândea, 'Introducere', pp. vii–xiv (noting that Cantemir planned a longer work, 'De muhammedana religione, deque politico musulmanae gentis regimine', of which only the first half, the treatise on Islam, survives). The *History* was a translation of a Latin manuscript text, 'De incrementis', which had circulated more widely.
34. Cantemir, *History*, pp. 71(n.) ('the *Turks*...'), 121(n.) ('The Emperor's...'); Anon., 'Sultan'.

also Russia, a Christian state.[35] His views about the relationship between religion and despotism are, in any case, quite hard to reduce to general principles. Usually he treats religion as a preexisting and powerful social phenomenon, on which a despotic regime may or may not supervene—so powerful, in fact, that in the case of Ethiopia, where both the climate and the size of the country made it a ripe candidate for despotic rule, the presence of Christianity kept despotism at bay. (He also gives an example, from Chardin, of religious observance being the one thing that can make a Persian willing to disobey the Shah.)[36] In despotic states, where there are no fundamental laws, religion and mores take their place, thus carrying more weight and—in the case of religion—receiving greater veneration; a despot who tried to change the dominant religion would thereby run a greater risk of being overthrown than if he performed any acts of tyranny, however monstrous.[37] At this point in his argument Montesquieu almost seems to be siding with those observers who, discussing the role of the Mufti or the influence of the *ulema*, argued that the despotic power of the Sultan was thereby limited and ameliorated. If so, it may be in order to counter that impression that he argues that in normal cases religion itself operates primarily by means of fear. Discussing the brutally fierce punishments laid down by the civil laws in Japan, he says that these are needed because the Japanese religion—unusually and defectively—does not say anything about Heaven or Hell. And in a chapter on despotic countries (including Russia) he writes: 'In these states religion has more influence than anywhere else; it is a fear added to fear. In Muslim empires it is partly from religion that people derive the astonishing respect which they have for their ruler.' Later in the same chapter, however, he observes that the tenure of power by a despot in a Muslim country may be more precarious because of the nature of the subjects' beliefs. The despot will know that a successful usurper would be obeyed just as devotedly, because Islam 'sees victory or success as a judgment of God, so that no one is sovereign *de jure*—only *de facto*'.[38]

---

35. Montesquieu, *De l'esprit* VI.13, pp. 561–2 (Japan), VIII.21, pp. 576–7 (China), XIII.6, pp. 608–9 (Russia), XVII.2, p. 630 (Mexico, Peru), XXIV.3, pp. 698 ('Que le gouvernement modéré convient mieux à la religion chrétienne et le gouvernement despotique à la mahométane'), 699 (Roman Empire).
36. Ibid. III.10, pp. 539–40 (Persian), XXIV.3, p. 699 (Ethiopia).
37. Ibid. II.4, p. 536 (more weight), XXV.11, p. 708 (greater risk; note that the same claim is made about a despot trying to change mores: XIX.12, p. 643).
38. Ibid. V.14, pp. 551 ('Dans ces États, la religion a plus d'influence que dans aucun autre; elle est une crainte ajoutée à la crainte. Dans les empires mahométans, c'est de la religion que les peuples tirent en partie le respect étonnant qu'ils ont pour leur prince'), 552 ('regarde la

Overall, Montesquieu seems to relate religion to climate in a way that suggests that it will in most cases cohere with other climate-related aspects of human life, including the form of government, but without implying a strict point-by-point correlation. One effect of this approach is to downgrade the significance of the Machiavellian religious legislator: the traditional naturalistic account of the rationale for Muhammad's specific precepts dissolves into a larger naturalism here. Thus Montesquieu's comment on the prohibition of wine in Islam is that alcohol is bad for the human body in hot climates, and that for this reason ancient Carthaginians also banned wine, and Arabs were drinking only water long before Muhammad; no special political wisdom was needed on Muhammad's part, therefore. And in some cases it seems that religion just acts as a reinforcing mechanism for a tendency which has its own climatic (or other natural) causes. 'Laziness of the soul gives rise to the dogma of Muslim predestination, and the dogma of predestination gives rise to laziness of the soul.'[39]

While there is much that is arbitrary or selective about Montesquieu's use of particular points to construct and confirm his theory, one of the most interesting things about his account is the care he takes to show that certain ways of behaving, associated with the method of government, are also reflected and expressed at different levels of life among the governed. Despite his occasional examples of religion or mores clashing with government, the model here is not that of a given society, as a simple unit, being mechanically harmed or benefited by an extraneous system of rule. Rather, in Montesquieu's vision the values or disvalues embodied in that system also percolate into the texture of social and personal life, giving a kind of organic character to everything contained within the state. Previous writers had of course made some connections between the nature of the Ottoman regime and the attitudes of those who lived under it. For example, where early writers such as Pierre Belon and George Sandys had commented merely that people did not construct grand houses there because the Ottoman system did not recognize the hereditary principle, Paul Rycaut said that it was because of the fear of being expropriated that they neglected their lands and did not build anything to last long. (Thomas Smith likewise observed that the pashas were 'afraid to build rich and great Palaces' because that

victoire ou le succès comme un jugement de Dieu; de sorte que personne n'y est souverain de droit, mais seulement de fait'), XXIV.14, p. 701 (Japan).

39. Ibid. XIV.10, p. 616 (alcohol), XXIV.14, p. 701 ('De la paresse de l'âme, naît le dogme de la prédestination mahométane; et du dogme de la prédestination naît la paresse de l'âme').

might 'draw the envy and ill-will of the Emperor upon them'.)[40] But it was Montesquieu who combined Rycaut's account—which he cited—with other details to build up a pattern of precariousness at every level: the common people were more at risk from the depredations of the pashas because the pashas themselves had no security, and the Sultan himself was under threat from both his army and the other members of his own family. This was an example of the way in which fear characterized the whole system of life within a despotic state.[41]

The most prominent example of this approach in Montesquieu's work is his account of the condition of women under despotism. This was a topic to which he devoted particular attention. As we have seen, he viewed both polygamy and 'rule over women' as natural consequences of a hot climate. Some previous writers had defended polygamy on the grounds that it was authorized by natural law (Henry Stubbe) or by Judaism (George Sale), and Francis Osborne had made the more pragmatic point that it reduced the use of prostitutes, and thus also the incidence of venereal disease.[42] But Montesquieu did not show any interest in those arguments, nor in the claim, repeated by authors such as Blount, Rycaut, and Boulainvilliers, that polygamy was a political device designed to boost population growth.[43] In the *Lettres persanes* he argued that it actually reduced the birth rate overall, partly because husbands were rendered feeble and infertile by having to perform sexually so often, and partly because so many men were turned into eunuchs in order to act as guards in the harems. (These were fanciful arguments, not least because of the fact—attested by Louis Deshayes almost a century earlier—that the great majority of Muslims had only one wife. However, one observer did note in 1724 that the ownership of female slaves and concubines was a cause of a relatively low birth rate in Tunis, as a master of many such slaves would not wish to support as many children; and this judgement would be echoed by the English diplomat Henry Grenville on his return from Istanbul in 1765.)[44]

40. Belon, *Voyage*, p. 404; Sandys, *Relation*, p. 36; Rycaut, *Present State*, p. 78; T. Smith, *Remarks*, p. 290.
41. Montesquieu, *De l'esprit* V.14, pp. 551–3; on this theme see Felice, 'Dispotismo', pp. 210–14. Again, Montesquieu thus assimilated the point made by recent writers such as Marsigli that the Sultan's rule was precarious, without accepting their argument that this made it less despotic.
42. Stubbe, 'Originall', p. 201; Sale, 'Preliminary Discourse', pp. 40–1; Osborne, *Politicall Reflections*, p. 48.
43. Blount, *Voyage*, p. 82; Rycaut, *Present State*, p. 153; Boulainvilliers, *Vie de Mahomed*, pp. 154–5.
44. Montesquieu, *Lettres persanes*, no. 114, pp. 122–3; Deshayes, *Voiage*, p. 170; Peyssonel, *Voyage*, pp. 82–3 (Tunis); Grenville, *Observations*, p. 71.

Montesquieu's climatic theory was much closer to that of Bodin, who had contrasted chaste northerners with lascivious southerners, and it chimed with the facile assumptions of several early European visitors to the Ottoman Empire, who wrote that the Ottoman women were such wanton creatures that they needed to be carefully guarded.[45] Some writers had given these arrangements their broad approval: the geographer Boemus, for instance, praised the strict decorum governing Ottoman marital relations (the 'gravitas' of the husband, the 'reverentia' of the wife). Pierre Belon gave an appreciative description of peaceful households—including polygamous ones—where the women were content merely to look after their children, leaving all other decision-making to the master of the house, and Postel explained that 'both in Italy and in the Ottoman Empire, where confining and monitoring wives and young women are concerned, they have the same custom, which does not seem too bad to me.' Lancelot Addison had praised the Moroccan women for devoting themselves to 'thrifty huswifry', commenting that 'this prevents that custom of *expensive gossippings*, with which in some Nations so many wives are debauched, and husbands *beggar'd*'.[46] But other accounts had sharply criticized the treatment of women in Muslim society. Postel himself, in his earlier, more anti-Islamic work, had inveighed against it: 'no one who has not seen it can believe how tyrannically and imperiously the women—half the human race—are treated.' Thomas Smith wrote that women were obliged to live 'an idle and melancholick kind of life at home'; and a description of conditions in Morocco by a former captive, published by Simon Ockley in 1713, observed that

> their Confinement would be unsupportable, but that the Custom of the Place, and the Manner of their Education, make it familiar and easie. For they see no other; and they are taught nothing by their Parents but to Wash and Scour Houses, to Bake a little Bread, and to serve their Husbands, &c. who treat them like Handmaids rather than Wives: For they are never taught to believe any Equality between Husband and Wife.[47]

45. Bodin, *Six Bookes*, p. 557; Merle, *Le Miroir ottoman*, p. 193 (wanton); Bon, *Sultan's Seraglio*, p. 144 (wanton).

46. Boemus, *Omnium gentium mores*, p. 125; Belon, *Voyage*, p. 476; Postel, *De la république*, p. 7 ('& en Italie & en Turquie, quant a garder & regarder les femmes & jeunes filles, ont vne mesme coustume, qui ne me semble trop mauuaise'); Addison, *West Barbary*, p. 114.

47. Postel, *De orbis terrae concordia*, p. 235 ('Nullus qui illa non uiderit, potest credere, quàm tyrannicè & imperiosè foeminae, dimidia naturae pars, tractentur'); T. Smith, *Remarks*, p. 191; Anon., *Account of South-West Barbary*, p. 35.

It was hardly to be expected that anything like an accurate Western account of female life in these societies could be given until West European women gained opportunities to speak to their Ottoman counterparts. One of Lady Mary Wortley Montagu's letters from Istanbul (which circulated from 1718, and was published posthumously in 1763) ridiculed those male travel-writers who 'lament the miserable confinement of the Turkish Ladys, who are (perhaps) freer than any Ladys in the universe, and are the only Women in the world that lead a life of unintterupted pleasure, exempt from cares'; but her ideas were inevitably conditioned by the high social status of the Ottoman women she knew.[48] No such account from inside the women's quarters was available to Montesquieu when he wrote. However, he may have known Deshayes's book, which claimed that just as men could divorce their wives, so women could divorce their husbands, and he certainly did know the work by Pitton de Tournefort, which offered a more detailed account of these matters: marriage was a civil contract which a wife could terminate if the man turned out to be impotent, was 'addicted to unnatural pleasures', failed to have sex with her from Tuesdays to Fridays, or generally refused to feed or clothe her adequately.[49] Such a description did suggest that Muslim women enjoyed at least a degree of freedom that was denied to their European Christian counterparts; yet although Montesquieu was strongly in favour of divorce, he discussed the matter only in general terms, passing over the evidence of its actual practice in the Ottoman world, and commenting that the justifications for it were fewer in the case of a polygamous marriage.[50] For what interested him was the possibility of constructing a sociopolitical account of the Ottoman household in which the worst features of despotism were reflected by, and transmitted through, the most basic institutions of private life.

According to Montesquieu, the strict subordination of women within the household in the Ottoman Empire and similar countries is not just something induced by the climate; it is also an expression of the political values of despotism. 'Female servitude is very much in conformity with the spirit of despotic government, which likes to abuse everything. That is why one has always seen, in Asia, domestic servitude and despotic government

48. Wortley Montagu, *Complete Letters*, i, p. 406 (and cf. i, pp. 327–30).

49. Deshayes, *Voiage*, p. 243; Pitton de Tournefort, *Relation*, ii, p. 263 ('addonné aux plaisirs contre nature').

50. Montesquieu, *Lettres persanes*, no. 116, pp. 123–4 (favouring divorce); Montesquieu, *De l'esprit* XVI.15, pp. 628–9 (general discussion).

marching in step. In a government where tranquillity is required above all else, and where extreme subordination is called peace, wives must be enclosed; their intrigues would be fatal to their husbands.'[51] An idea of how destructive those 'intrigues' could be is given in the final pages of the *Lettres persanes*, where letters from the harem of one of the main characters reveal a catastrophic collapse of trust and order—fatal, not to the absent husband, but to at least one of the women involved. In *De l'esprit des lois* Montesquieu paints a much less lurid picture of Ottoman conditions, saying that thanks to the strict enclosure of women there (and in other Asian despotisms) the women possess 'admirable' mores.[52] But according to the general account he gives, the nature of family life there is still tainted, all the way through, with despotism. Thanks to the lack of what later theorists would call the institutions of civil society, each household is 'a separate empire', a small island of despotism in its own right. In despotic states women 'must be held in a condition of extreme slavery' because 'each man follows the spirit of the government, and brings into his home what he sees established elsewhere.' Since the laws in a despotic state are so strict, imposing severe and instant punishments, men feel the need for similar severity in the home, as they fear that to grant any liberty at all to their womenfolk would lead to riotous disorder.[53] And there is another way in which domestic conditions reflect, albeit less consciously, the nature of despotic rule. Montesquieu repeatedly emphasizes the theme of enclosure and separation: the women are separated from other men by the enclosure of the household, and it is recommended that within it the individual women should also be isolated. This seems to be a reflection both of the situation of a despotic state, which tends to reduce its contact with neighbouring countries, often deliberately depopulating its border areas for strategic defensive purposes, and also of the despot's own position, 'shut in' within his palace and isolated from his subjects.[54]

51. Montesquieu, *De l'esprit* XVI.9, p. 627 ('la servitude des femmes est très conforme au génie du gouvernement despotique, qui aime à abuser de tout. Aussi a-t-on vu, dans tous les temps, en Asie, marcher d'un pas égal la servitude domestique et le gouvernement despotique. Dans un gouvernement où l'on demande surtout la tranquilleté, et où la subordination extrême s'appelle la paix, il faut enfermer les femmes; leurs intrigues seraient fatales au mari').
52. Ibid. XVI.10, p. 627 ('admirables', enclosure, isolation of women).
53. Ibid. IV.3, p. 541 ('un empire séparé'), VII.9, p. 568 ('doivent être extrêmement esclaves. Chacun suit l'esprit du gouvernement, et porte chez soi ce qu'il voit établi ailleurs', fear of disorder).
54. Ibid. V.14, pp. 551–2 (ruler isolated, 'enfermé', country isolated), XVI.10, p. 627 (enclosure of women). Montesquieu comments only indirectly on the deliberate depopulation of border zones, but this was a familiar topic, discussed by many writers (e.g. della Valle, *Pilgrim*, pp. 122, 146; Rycaut, *Present State*, p. 68; Chardin, *Travels*, pp. 125, 132; Guer, *Moeurs*, ii, pp. 366–8).

Montesquieu's method of building up his argument in such cases is almost an intuitive one, sensing connections and adding weight to one point by adducing an analogy with another. At its best, this style of exposition can be very suggestive. But it depends at the same time on passing over any counter-evidence as quietly as possible; his silence on the ability of wives to initiate divorce in Islamic law is one relatively small example of that, and his refusal to consider the practice of religious toleration in the Ottoman Empire, Persia, and the Mughal Empire is a large and blatant one.[55] And while Montesquieu's approach is sometimes subtle and oblique, he is also capable of expressing his argument in extreme, hyperbolic terms, which have caused real difficulties to his readers. More than once, for example, he declares that despotism functions without laws. 'In despotic states there is no law at all: the judge himself is his own rule'; and since, according to Montesquieu, each official under a despot acts as a mini-despot himself, this means that everything is done out of pure 'caprice', the only basis—apart from fear—of the despot's own decision-making.[56] Here he paints a picture so extreme that it seems incompatible with any functioning system of government. It is also hardly compatible with his own references to laws in despotic states—for instance, the civil laws which, he says, have to be severe in Japan (a fierce despotism) to compensate for the lack of Japanese religious sanctions—or with his statements about the conscientious *kadis* of the Ottoman system, where 'in doubtful cases, the judges consult the ministers of religion'.[57] At one level of the argument, what Montesquieu conjures up is a wilful, passionate, and blindly ignorant despot shut up in his palace, issuing random commands through a chain of officials who otherwise occupy themselves by giving equally arbitrary commands of their own: a state of affairs so dysfunctional that it could not possibly last. And yet, when he talks about how systems of government become corrupted and decline, he says that a monarchy and a republic, when corrupted, will change into one of the other forms, but that 'the principle of despotic government is unceasingly self-corrupting, since it is corrupt by its nature.'[58]

---

55. Montesquieu did write in favour of religious toleration, though without referring to its existence in 'despotic' states: see Minuti, *Orientalismo*, pp. 331–402.

56. Montesquieu, *De l'esprit* III.8 p. 539 (caprice), V.16, pp. 553–4 (officials as mini-despots), VI.3, p. 557 ('Dans les États despotiques, il n'y a point de loi: le juge est lui-même sa règle'); cf. also XIX.12, p. 643.

57. Ibid. XII.29, p. 607 ('dans les cas douteux, les juges consultent les ministres de la religion'), XXIV.14, p. 701 (Japan).

58. Ibid. VIII.10, p. 573 ('Le principe du gouvernement despotique se corrompt sans cesse, parce qu'il est corrompu par sa nature').

In contrast with his extreme general statements, there are many passages in Montesquieu's work that offer a much more qualified picture of actual despotisms. In passing, he mentions that only in the most oppressive cases does the despot declare himself the sole landowner and sole heir: generally, the Ottoman Sultan levies an inheritance tax of only 3%. Some despotic states have customary laws that counteract the ruler's power: Persian law permits people to leave the country whenever they want to, and this 'puts a stop to, or moderates, the persecutions by pashas and tax-collectors'.[59] In Russia the reforms of Peter the Great are gradually moving the country away from despotism, towards monarchy.[60] In China 'the first legislators were obliged to make very good laws, and the government was often obliged to follow them'; indeed, here Montesquieu seems to contradict one of his basic categorizations—that republics and monarchies are moderate forms of government, and despotisms are tyrannical—when he writes that it was necessary for the Chinese Emperor to have 'more the legitimate power of a monarch than the tyrannical power of a despot', and that 'power was moderated there, as it was previously in Egypt.'[61] Yet still he insists that China is a despotism, based on the principle of fear—though elsewhere he has explained that a despotism can exist without fear, in that case having an 'imperfect' government.[62]

Montesquieu writes that 'particular circumstances, perhaps unique ones, may bring it about that the government of China is not as corrupt as it should be'; and this brings us close to the heart of his theory of despotism.[63] The 'particular circumstances' which counteract despotism are at the same time the things that preserve it. Reducing everything to the despot's will would produce total instability and self-destruction. One might say that Montesquieu's theory of despotism breaks the concept down into two countervailing yet complementary elements, the 'despot' and the '-ism', since the factors that work against the pure, arbitrary will of the despot are the ones that make it possible for that will to be executed through a *system*

---

59. Ibid. V.14, p. 552 (3%), XII.30, p. 607 ('arrête ou modère les persécutions des bachas et des exacteurs'; this information about Persia was drawn from Chardin, *Travels*, p. 130).

60. Montesquieu, *De l'esprit* V.14, p. 552, XIII.6, pp. 608–9, XIX.15, p. 644.

61. Ibid. XVIII.6, p. 634 ('plutôt le pouvoir légitime d'un monarque que la puissance tyrannique d'un despote', 'que le pouvoir y fût modéré, comme il l'était autrefois en Égypte', 'les législateurs furent obligés de faire de très bonnes lois, et le gouvernement fut souvent obligé de les suivre').

62. Ibid. III.11, p. 540 ('imparfait'), VIII.21, pp. 576–7 (based on fear).

63. Ibid.VIII.21, p. 576 ('Des circonstances particulières, et peut-être uniques, peuvent faire que le gouvernement de la Chine ne soit pas aussi corrompu qu'il devrait l'être').

of rule. As he puts it in his chapter on the corruption of the principle of despotic government, a despotism will destroy itself by the dynamic of its own principle, fear, 'when the self-corruption of that principle is not at all prevented by some contingent causes. So it sustains itself only when circumstances, drawn from the climate, from religion, from the situation or the spirit of the people, force it to follow some order and to accept some rule.'[64] In an earlier work, the *Considérations sur les causes de la grandeur des Romains et de leur décadence* (published in 1734), Montesquieu had offered a much more rudimentary version of this argument, observing that a purely despotic power had never existed and never could exist, as there was always some limit to it: the examples he gave were of popular revolts against new taxes in Istanbul, and religious opposition to any order to ignore the precepts of Islam in Persia.[65] Had he stuck to that observation, he would have moved little beyond the mainstream view of Ottoman power which had emerged in the late seventeenth and early eighteenth centuries, portraying it merely as a despotism which had been weakened and limited. The originality of his treatment of this subject in *De l'esprit des lois* lay not only in his extracting and isolating the 'pure' nature of despotism, but also in his attempt to show that the factors which limited and opposed despotism were at the same time the very ones that strengthened it and kept it alive.

For all its omissions and its exaggerations, therefore, this was a resourceful theory, and it is not surprising that aspects of it were taken up by several other writers. Elements of Montesquieu's account were included in the article 'Turquie', written by Louis de Jaucourt for the *Encyclopédie*: 'In order for a despotic state to avoid total perdition, the greed of the ruler must at least be moderated by some custom. Thus in the Ottoman Empire the ruler normally contents himself with taking 3% of the estates of ordinary people', and so on.[66] A much more substantial debt to Montesquieu is visible in one

---

64. Ibid.VIII.10, p. 573 ('lorsque quelques causes accidentelles n'empêchent point son principe de se corrompre. Il ne se maintient donc que quand des circonstances tirées du climat, de la religion, de la situation ou du génie du peuple, le forcent à suivre quelque ordre et à souffrir quelque règle'). Cf. his draft of this passage in a notebook, saying that these factors have an effect on despotism like that of force on a wild animal, subduing it but not taming it: Montesquieu, *L'Atelier*, p. 73.

65. Montesquieu, *Considérations* XXII, p. 483.

66. Jaucourt, 'Turquie', p. 759 ('Pour que tout ne soit pas perdu dans un état despotique, il faut au-moins que l'avidité du prince soit modérée par quelque coutume. Ainsi, en *Turquie*, le prince se contente ordinairement de prendre trois pour cent sur les successions des gens du peuple'). On Jaucourt, a disciple of Locke and Montesquieu who wanted a limited monarchy in France with special powers for the nobility, see Kafker and Kafker, *Encyclopedists*, pp. 175–80.

of the major works of Enlightenment politico-historical theory, Adam Ferguson's *Essay on the History of Civil Society* (1767). Here Ferguson devotes many pages to expounding Montesquieu's theory, emphasizing that despots lie in reality on a spectrum of greater or lesser power, and also pointing out the resemblance, and easy transition, between despotism and radical democracy. He tones down the role of the climate, acknowledging its influence only in extreme cases, and he says very little about religion. Ferguson's main concern is to fit despotism into an overarching historical account, in which the key development is the corruption of the people, their loss of virtue; this is caused in the first place by a shift towards military government (which may happen merely because geographical expansion prompts the use of military rule in distant provinces), and then by the moral incapacities of a ruler endowed with too much power. His description of conditions in the 'seraglio', where 'Caprice and passion are the rules of government', strikes a familiar note. But at the end of his book Ferguson goes beyond Montesquieu, suggesting the mechanism whereby despotic regimes such as the Ottoman one will collapse and a virtuous society will be reborn. Referring rather airily to evidence from 'many parts of the East' where people have fled their villages, he observes that when people take to the hills as bandits they regain 'personal confidence and vigour', and society begins to improve: 'When human nature appears in the utmost state of corruption, it has actually begun to reform.'[67]

Montesquieu's influence is clearly visible even in the cases of writers who offered a differing explanatory scheme. In his major treatise *De l'esprit* (1758), the philosopher Claude Adrien Helvétius dispensed entirely with the role of the climate, and reduced all human behaviour to the effect of passions concerned with pleasure or pain. His master idea was that the same passions, modified by different forms of government, could produce different vices and virtues; the role of the good legislator was to direct people's passions towards 'the general interest'. This was a very top-down theory, in which despotism was simply the most flagrant example of how a bad ruler—himself motivated by the desire for pleasure—could corrupt and destroy the moral life of the population. Helvétius paid much more attention to ancient history than to modern conditions, but he did refer to

---

67. Ferguson, *Essay*, pp. 100–10 (expounding Montesquieu; pp. 109–10: spectrum, democracy), 165–85 (climate), 418–23 (military rule, corruption), 424–5 (seraglio, 'Caprice and...'), 428–9 ('many parts...', 'personal confidence...', 'When human...').

enslaved peoples ruled by pleasure-loving sultans who were kept in ignorance by manipulative viziers, and his overall view of life in the 'Orient' was that it was 'similar to the picture given by Milton of the empire of Chaos'—a view fully in keeping with Montesquieu's extreme account of despotism in its pure form.[68]

The economist Turgot, as we have seen, also had a simpler theory of the origin of despotism than Montesquieu, making military rule after extensive conquests the essential cause. (Climatic factors were, for him as for Helvétius, insignificant.) Discussing the nature of those conquests, he was able to answer a question which dogged Montesquieu's theory: how was it that the barbarian invasions of Western Europe had led to freedom and moderate government, while the equivalent conquests by the Turks and other such peoples in Asia had led to slavery and despotism? Turgot's reply was that the Germanic barbarians were themselves free, so that their conquests were 'in the name of the people, not in that of the king'. Moreover, in Asia 'the conquered peoples were already accustomed to despotism, because the first conquests, prior to the period in which mores could have been formed, had been huge and rapid.'[69] Like Montesquieu, Turgot placed great emphasis on the role of social mores; unlike him, he saw these as largely the products of top-down processes of conditioning and education. In despotic states, education is used to destroy the people's spirit: 'Fear and veneration take over the imagination. The sovereign, surrounded by intimidating obscurity, seems to govern from the heart of a storm-cloud, whose lighting-bolts dazzle and whose thunderclaps inspire terror.' Despotic rule changes the mores of the people, forbidding social relations between the sexes and halting all change and progress. 'Despotism perpetuates ignorance, and ignorance perpetuates despotism. What is more, this despotic authority becomes a matter of custom, and custom corroborates its abuses.' And all these things are rendered worse by Islam: 'we do not find in the history of China or Japan these excesses of self-abasement of the Muslim peoples.'[70] Here again, though the

68. Helvétius, *De l'esprit* III.16, pp. 49–59 (master idea, 'l'intérêt général'), III.17–18, pp. 61–73 (p. 61: desire for pleasure; p. 62: 'assez semblable à la peinture que Milton fait de l'empire du Chaos', pp. 64, 71–3: viziers, sultan ignorant).
69. Turgot, 'Plan', p. 293 ('au nom du peuple, et non pas à celui du roi', 'où les peuples conquis se trouvaient d'avance accoutumés au despotisme, parce que les premières conquêtes, antérieures au temps où les moeurs auraient pu se former, avaient été vastes et rapides'). See also the discussion in Laurens, *Les Origines*, pp. 48–52.
70. Turgot, 'Plan', pp. 294 ('La crainte et le respect s'emparent de l'imagination. Le souverain, environné d'une obscurité formidable, semble gouverner du sein d'un nuage orageux, dont les éclairs éblouissent et les tonnerres inspirent la terreur', 'Le despotisme perpétue l'ignorance et

general scheme of explanation is differently configured, we see the strong imprint of Montesquieu's description.

A much more speculative account, taking the argument in a much less Montesquieuian direction, was given by the philosopher Nicolas-Antoine Boulanger, whose *Recherches sur l'origine du despotisme oriental* was published in 1761, two years after his death. Boulanger constructed an elaborate history of religion and government from the dawn of human societies, in which the essential theme was the emergence first of theocracy, and then of priestcraft and idolatry. In Eastern countries, the priests paved the way for despotism by requiring blind trust and 'voluntary slavery', and by introducing the idea of rule by divine right; despotism itself was a kind of 'pagan theocracy'.[71] While this primary causal explanation was quite different from Montesquieu's, several elements of Boulanger's account showed the influence of the earlier writer: the climate, for example, had contributed to the growth of despotism in Asia, where people were naturally submissive, whereas Europeans had thrown off despotism when they felt 'the privileges of their nature, and the force of their climates'.[72] Boulanger declared that 'idolatry and despotism both had fear and terror as their principle and their foundation', and his portrait of life under an Asiatic despot could have come straight from Montesquieu's darkest pages: 'it is in these miserable regions that one sees human beings bereft of will, kissing their chains, with no secure possessions and no property-ownership, worshipping their tyrant, with no knowledge of mankind or of reason, and with no virtue other than fear; it is there that human beings bless, with religious feeble-mindedness, the ferocious caprice which often deprives them of their lives.' Certainly Boulanger himself felt that his account was compatible with Montesquieu's. In a brief appendix to his treatise, he paid him the somewhat back-handed compliment of saying that Montesquieu had written with admirable wisdom about despotic governments despite his utter unawareness of their true origins: he 'began where I have just ended'.[73]

---

l'ignorance perpétue le despotisme. Il y a plus: cette autorité despotique devient usage, et l'usage confirme les abus'), 297 ('On ne trouve, ni dans l'histoire de la Chine et du Japon, ces excès d'abaissement des peuples mahométans').

71. Boulanger, *Recherches*, pp. 137–63 (theocracy), 172–87 (priestcraft), 192–3 (idolatry), 239 (blind trust, 'esclavage volontaire', divine right), 400 ('Théocratie Payenne'). On Boulanger see Minerbi Belgrado, *Paura e ignoranza*, pp. 51–102; Cristani, 'Teocrazia'.

72. Boulanger, *Recherches*, pp. 376–7 (Asian climate), 405 (Europe, 'les privilèges de leur nature, & la force de leurs climats').

73. Ibid., pp. 2–3 ('C'est dans ces tristes régions que l'on voit l'homme sans volonté, baiser ses chaînes; sans fortune assurée & sans proprieté, adorer son Tyran; sans aucune connoissance de

For many other writers, however, it was precisely the extreme, negative portrayal by Montesquieu of conditions in the Ottoman Empire that rendered his whole theory unreliable. 'I feel it is my duty', wrote Voltaire, 'to counter here a prejudice: the idea that the Ottoman government is an absurd government, described as "despotic"; that all the people are the Sultan's slaves, that they have no property, and that their life and their goods belong to their master.' (These particular details were not specific to Montesquieu, of course; Voltaire was also contesting a longer tradition here.) Neither the Greeks nor the Turks themselves were slaves, he insisted, and the Ottomans did have laws of inheritance—such laws were even specified in the Koran. Voltaire also emphasized that the sultans showed more toleration of other religions than did the rulers of Christendom. And while it was true that the Ottoman system of government was unlike any European model, nevertheless 'one must not imagine that it is an arbitrary government in all matters.' There were certainly some terrible abuses, but they fell most heavily on the governing class; indeed, the lack of legal and constitutional checks meant that not only the subjects were more vulnerable, but also the Sultan himself, who had almost no institutional protection against conspiracy and revolution.[74] Voltaire's main authority here was Marsigli, who, as we have seen, had dismissed the idea that the Sultans were real despots; as Voltaire put it, they enjoyed 'only the external appearance of despotism', sometimes resorting to the 'fury of arbitrary power', but only when others—Janissaries, or the leaders of the political and military establishment, or the common people—allowed it. Yes, pashas were sometimes executed, just as the officials of French kings had been in the past, but 'no Christian ruler was ever despotic, and neither is the Sultan.'[75]

In a four-volume *Histoire de l'empire ottoman* Voltaire's nephew, the abbé Mignot, broadly echoed this judgment. There were real limits *de facto* on the

l'homme & de la raison, n'avoir d'autre vertu que la crainte... c'est là que les hommes... bénissent avec une religieuse imbécillité le caprice féroce qui souvent les prive de la vie'), 364–5 ('L'idolatrie & le Despotisme eurent donc l'un & l'autre la crainte & la terreur pour principe & pour fondement'), 428 ('a commencé où je viens de finir').

74. Voltaire, *Essai*, i, pp. 822 (toleration), 832 ('Je crois devoir ici combattre un préjugé: que le gouvernement turc est un gouvernement absurde qu'on appelle *despotique*; que les peuples sont tous esclaves du sultan, qu'ils n'ont rien en propre, que leur vie et leurs biens appartiennent à leur maître', Greeks, Turks, inheritance), 833–4 ('il ne faut pas imaginer que ce soit un gouvernement arbitraire en tout', abuses, lack of checks).

75. Ibid., i, p. 835 ('Aucun prince chrétien n'etait despotique, et le Grand Seigneur ne l'est pas davantage', 'n'ont donc que le dehors du despotisme', 'fureur du pouvoir arbitraire'). The point about the Janissaries was repeated (with other criticisms) in one of Voltaire's last works, his *Commentaire sur l'Esprit des lois de Montesquieu* (here p. 338).

power of the Sultan, even though it was not regulated *de jure*. 'If one defines despotism as unlimited power, the Ottoman sultans are not despotic, and there are no despots anywhere on earth. Yet if one defines it as unregulated power, no monarch is more despotic than the Ottoman sovereign.'[76] But the nephew, like the uncle, was only an armchair historian. A more powerful rejection of Montesquieu's thesis came from Sir James Porter, who, having spent sixteen years as British Ambassador in Istanbul, published his *Observations on the Religion, Law, Government, and Manners of the Turks* in 1768. (A French translation appeared in the following year.) Having begun with some scathing remarks about all those authors whose accounts were 'evidently collected from the idle report and absurd tradition of the ignorant vulgar', Porter insisted that the Ottoman system of government had been 'injuriously misrepresented'. Their empire was 'solidly founded on the basis of religion, combined with law'. Far from being ruled by sheer caprice, 'the Turks have laws to secure property and regulate commerce; they have others to punish crimes and restrain vice. It is not their laws, but the corrupt administration of them...that is the opprobrium of the Turkish empire.' The property of the *vakıfs* (religious foundations) was always respected; the Mufti exercised genuine authority, and his refusal to authorize a policy could act as a real restraint. As for private ownership, Porter told the story of an old woman who refused to give up her house for an important rebuilding scheme in Istanbul in 1755; when the Sultan was asked why he did not simply confiscate it, he replied 'it cannot be done, it is her property.'[77] Porter's book would later be attacked by an author styling himself 'Elias Habesci', who claimed to be a Greek who had worked as secretary to a Grand Vizier; he insisted that the whole Ottoman realm was 'an empire of slaves', that the Sultan was 'universal heir', and so on. This work may have had some influence on public debate, but painstaking modern scholarship has identified the pseudonymous author as an adventurer and fantasist, from Naples, who had spent little time in the Ottoman Empire.[78] While various

76. Mignot, *Histoire*, i, p. 97(n.) ('si l'on définit le despotisme une puissance sans bornes, les Empereurs Ottomans ne sont pas despotiques, & il n'y en a point sur la terre. Mais si on le définit une puissance sans regle, aucun Monarque n'est plus despotique que le Souverain des Turcs'). Mignot disagreed with Marsigli's suggestion that there was a quasi-democratic constitution giving Janissaries the right to overthrow the Sultan: iv, p. 453.
77. Porter, *Observations*, i, pp. 2 ('evidently collected...'), 81 ('injuriously misrepresented'), 83–4 ('solidly founded...','the Turks...'), 86–9 (*vakıfs*), 104–5 (Mufti), 105–7 (woman,'it cannot...').
78. 'Habesci', *Present State*, p. 258 ('empire of...'); see also Çırakman, *From the 'Terror of the World'*, pp. 137–41. For the identification (as Alexander or Antonio Ghika) see Pippidi, *Byzantins*, pp. 267–88.

writers continued to debate the degree to which sultanic power was or was not limited in practice, there was general agreement that Montesquieu's account of a system based purely on caprice and fear was simply unviable. Known facts disproved it.[79]

The most remarkable response to Montesquieu came, however, from someone who had no special claim to be an expert on Ottoman affairs. After a brilliant career as a student at the Sorbonne, Simon-Nicolas-Henri Linguet became a provincial mathematics teacher before training as a lawyer.[80] He was a natural contrarian with egalitarian sympathies: one of his first publications was *Le Fanatisme des philosophes* (1764), an attack on the French 'philosophes', whom he accused of ingratiating themselves with oppressive rulers. In 1767 he published an ambitious treatise on law and government, the *Théorie des loix civiles, ou principes fondamentaux de la société*, in which he argued that government was inherently conflictual: it had begun with the rule of masters over slaves, when groups of hunters had conquered groups of pastoral people, and the unpalatable truth about all systems of society was that almost everyone lived in quasi-servitude, subject to the power of another, which was exercised for the good of the power-holder. What stabilized society was property rights; but these included the rights of the father over his children, which meant that everyone began life under a kind of subjection.[81] As Linguet developed his theory, he became convinced that the best protection of people's property rights was supplied by a paternalistic absolute monarch, who guaranteed the freedom of each owner to govern his own little property realm without interference from others; the most unstable and unsatisfactory system, on the other hand, was the sort of multilayered feudal structure in which each social layer had the power to interfere with the ones below it. In the *Théorie* he included a chapter defending the Ottoman Empire and other Asian states from the charge of despotism, saying that there had never been a country in which the ordinary people were more fortunate and better looked after: 'the ruler and his ministers care about nothing except the security of the people, feeling that their own security depends on it.'[82] And in a supplementary work, published in

79. On the general turn against Montesquieu's concept of despotism see Osterhammel, *Die Entzauberung*, pp. 289–308.
80. On Linguet see Levy, *Ideas and Careers*.
81. Linguet, *Théorie*, i, pp. 288–301 (hunters, pastors), ii, pp. 49–75 (property rights, fathers), 509–21 (all in quasi-servitude).
82. Ibid., ii, pp. 205–22 (Asian states; p. 214: 'Le Prince & ses Ministres veillent uniquement à sa securité, dont ils sentent que la leur dépend').

1771, he returned to this point. The best governments were the ones in which the ruler had an interest in supplying order and equity to the people—an interest generated by the fact that such rulers would fall if they failed to do so. But, Linguet explained,

> this has never been done except in the wise, enlightened monarchies of Asia. It is there, and there alone, that the slightest change in the time-honoured ways of doing things, the slightest abuse against the lowliest citizen, had consequences for the head of state himself. It is there that the sultans and the shahs are tied to the pursuit of the public good by thinking about their own good, and the viziers are kept from the temptation to become oppressors by fear of a punishment which is always visible and never far away. It is there that one finds, under the appearance of a dreary solemnity and a gloomy dullness, contented peoples, nations given over to pure and sweet contentment, people whose days are passed in the most happy peace, and who never cease to bless, unanimously, the admirable government to which they owe this fortunate tranquillity.[83]

It seems to have been the scandalized reaction of many readers to these passages that prompted Linguet to devote, four years later, a full-length treatise to the subject of the so-called despotic states of Asia: *Du plus heureux gouvernement, ou parallele des constitutions politiques de l'Asie avec celles de l'Europe*. This was one of the most uncompromising rejections of Montesquieu's theory ever to be published. Linguet began with a direct attack on the author of *De l'esprit des lois*: his claim that oriental governments were 'unregulated and without law' was not only absurd, as no such government could exist, but also disproven by known facts, since 'throughout Asia the Koran and its rulings are a chain which even the most domineering sultans, shahs, and Mughal emperors dare not break.'[84] On one factual point after another, Linguet convicted Montesquieu of distorting the truth to fit his theory. It was not the case that the Sultan owned all property, or inherited the estates of all officials. That successful people showed little interest in

---

83. Linguet, *Réponse*, pp. 247–8 (interest), 248–9 ('Or c'est ce qu'on n'a jamais fait que dans les monarchies sages, éclairées, de *l'Asie*. C'est là, & là seulement, que la moindre altération dans les formalités consacrées, le moindre abus contre le dernier des citoyens, auoit des conséquences pour la tête même de l'état. C'est là que les *sultans*, les *sophis* sont enchaînés au bien publique par la considération du leur, & que les *visirs* sont préservés de la tentation de devenir oppresseurs, par la crainte d'un châtiment toujours visible & toujours prochain. C'est là que, sous l'apparence d'une gravité triste & d'une morne pesanteur, on trouve des peuples satisfaits, des nations livrées à une joie pure & douce, des hommes dont les jours s'écoulent dans la paix la plus heureuse, & qui ne cessent de benir d'une voix unanime l'administration admirable à laquelle ils sont redevables de ce calme fortuné').

84. Linguet, *Du plus heureux gouvernement*, i, pp. xxiii (scandalized reaction), 7 ('sans regle & sans loi'), 8–9 ('Dans toute l'Asie l'alcoran & ses décisions sont une chaîne que les Sultans, les Sophis, les Mogols les plus impérieux n'osent briser').

building up landed estates in the Ottoman Empire was due not to fear of
arbitrary seizure, but rather to the fact that in Asia such estates did not
confer titles, rank, or distinction—a difference between Asian and European
societies which reflected well on the Asians. It was not true that every official under the Sultan was himself endowed with despotic power; on the
contrary, the Sultan retained all authority, unlike European kings who gave
their subordinates offices that could not be rescinded, and privileges that
enabled them to resist royal power. Montesquieu contradicted himself when
he asserted that despotisms had no fundamental laws and then said that a
fundamental law dictated appointing a vizier; and he did so again when he
claimed that such states had no permanent records or depositories of law
and then explained that religion and custom performed that function.
Customs functioned everywhere as fundamental laws, so these so-called
despotic states had them too—'or at least some laws, prior to the will of the
ruler, and independent of him'.[85]

More shocking than these factual or logical errors, however, was the attitude Montesquieu expressed when discussing the way in which uprisings in
Istanbul led simply to the replacement of one individual ruler by another, a
revolution without a civil war: he seemed to think that the European alternative, frequent civil wars without revolutions, was preferable. It was astonishing, Linguet exclaimed, that such an 'enlightened' thinker could take
such a view of civil war, the worst evil of all.[86] What caused such terrible
internal conflicts to happen in Europe was precisely the distribution of
authority, so highly recommended by Montesquieu, among intermediate
powers and institutions, including, above all, the nobility. Only in this part
of the world, Linguet argued, had such a dysfunctional system—'these ideas
of a scale of powers, all reacting one against another, all claiming preroga-
tives inherent in their nature, all authorized to call themselves independent
of the sovereign'—developed. 'These phantoms, which, I admit, can easily
be dressed up to look imposing, have become the real enemies of the people,
and the guarantees of its slavery.'[87] Conditions were much better in the

85. Ibid., i, pp. 87–8 (all property), 89 (estates of officials), 95 (landed estates), ii, 26–7 (officials
    endowed with power), 54 (contradictions), 55 ('ou au moins des loix quelconques, antérieures
    à la volonté du prince, & indépendantes de lui').
86. Ibid., ii, p. 21 (revolution, 'éclairé').
87. Ibid., ii, p. 23 ('ces idées d'une échelle de pouvoirs tous réagissants les uns contre les autres,
    tous prétendants à des prérogatives inhérentes à leur nature, tous autorisés à se dire indépendants
    du souverain', 'Ces fantômes qu'il est facile, je l'avoue, de revêtir d'une apparence imposante,
    sont devenus les véritables ennemis du peuple, & les cautions de son esclavage').

Ottoman Empire, where the sudden and violent dismissals of ministers showed how severely the Sultan punished any abuses of power; whereas 'among us, justice is often nothing more than the instrument of violence used by the grandees'.[88]

In the course of setting out these criticisms and claims, Linguet expounded his own general political theory. All government, wherever it is, consists in two things: commanding and obeying. If each form of government had its own principle (as Montesquieu supposed), there would be hundreds of different principles animating hundreds of variant forms; but in reality all governments perform the same function, by the same fundamental means. We can never escape the basic division of society into those who are ruled and those who do the ruling—the latter being naturally inclined to exploit their powers over the former for their own advantage. But while that problem cannot be altogether removed, it can be mitigated by a system which 'establishes the greatest possible balance between the two groups', giving the ruled majority as much freedom as possible, and holding the ruling minority to account by making them fear punishment for abusing their powers. According to Linguet, that was to be achieved not by multiplying governmental mechanisms, but merely by the simplicity and speed of punishments administered by an overriding authority. And the way to make that authority exercise such corrective justice was to make it fear, in turn, that popular dissatisfaction would lead almost immediately to its own ejection from power. Checks and balances were not the answer here; indeed, they might protect the ruler from such risks, and reduce his ability to right wrongs with due speed and severity.[89]

The one aspect of Montesquieu's account that Linguet seems to have been happy to accept was his portrayal of Asian (male) householders as absolute rulers of their own families. 'In Asia', Linguet wrote, 'there is more freedom than in any other country in the world. All those men who are not slaves enjoy, each within his own family, a despotic power. Thus they are the most free of all human beings.'[90] This chimed with Linguet's own assumption that the family was the natural starting point for all commander–obeyer

---

88. Ibid., i, pp. 28–9 ('la justice n'est souvent parmi nous que l'instrument de la violence des grands').

89. Ibid., i, pp. 11–12 (all government, commanding and obeying), ii, pp. 8 ('établisse le plus grand équilibre possible entre les deux classes'), 9–10 (higher authority).

90. Ibid. ii, pp. 15–16 ('qu'en Asie il y a plus de liberté qu'en aucun autre pays du monde. Tous les hommes qui ne sont pas esclaves jouissent, chacun dans leur famille, d'un pouvoir despotique. Ils sont donc les plus libres de tous les êtres humains').

relationships. It might seem that, on this account, Asian women were the most unfree human beings of all; but Linguet devoted a whole chapter to arguing that they were generally in a better condition than their European counterparts. The number of women kept in the harems of the rich was very small. Women 'of the middle class', on the other hand, were happy and free; their husbands could not afford the expense of locking them up, so these marriages depended on mutual trust. Indeed, Linguet commented, 'I am persuaded that there are more prisoners enclosed in our convents than in the harems.' And the nuns' fate is worse: 'the women in the harems do at least have one man to share between them all, and a little is better than nothing.' But if that remark created an impression of flippancy, the mood was quickly dispelled by a diatribe, extending over many pages, eloquently complaining about how badly women were treated in Europe. At the lower levels of society they were worked hard and mercilessly; at the upper ones, marriage made a woman humiliatingly dependent on husband without the possibility (available in Asia) of divorce; and those women who did not marry were isolated and weak.[91] A woman's predicament in the so-called despotic states of the East was usually much better than that.

Overall, Linguet was happy to argue that conditions of life were more pleasant in those countries; in doing so, he restored much of the picture of Ottoman society that had been put together in the 'new paradigm', while adding to it an even more optimistic gloss of his own. Generally all ways of doing things in Asia were 'redolent of simplicity, goodness, and humanity'; Western writers had been wrong to focus on sinister events in the sultans' seraglios, which were utterly untypical of society at large. The ordinary mores of the people were more 'gentle' than those in Europe: they were philanthropic and immensely hospitable, for example, to travellers and strangers. The administration of justice was much better there, with speedy processes unencumbered by the work of professional advocates; the taxation system was superior, with mild customs duties and no private monopolies of goods such as salt and tobacco. The Ottoman army was better administered too: Janissaries were well fed and clothed, unlike European soldiers, who sometimes died of neglect.[92] And in one other respect these countries

---

91. Ibid., ii, pp. 60–2 (harems, 'de l'état médiocre', 'Je suis persuadé que nos couvents renferment encore plus de prisonnieres que les harems', 'celles-là ont du moins un homme à partager entre elles toutes, & un peu vaut mieux que rien'), 63–70 (diatribe).
92. Ibid., i, pp. 98 ('respire la simplicité, la bonté, l'humanité'), 106 (customs, no monopolies), 116–17 (Janissaries), 139 (mores, 'doux'), 142–4 (hospitality).

were superior to those of Christian Europe: while religious principles exerted real moral force on the consciences of the Sultan and his officials, these were societies in which religion functioned without a clergy. The idea that despotism and superstitious priestcraft went hand in hand in these parts of the world was thus quite false. Where pagans had solved the problem of conflicts between religious and temporal power by uniting the two power structures, 'the Muslims have done even better', for 'every kind of ecclesiastical hierarchy is unknown to them; the Mufti, whom we regard as he head of their religion, is in reality only the head of their legal system.'[93] Here the picture given by the new paradigm was extended to include the kind of positive view of Muslim 'church–state' relations that was developed by Machiavellians such as Francis Osborne and Hobbesians such as Henry Stubbe. There is no evidence that Linguet knew their work, nor even that he had read the discourse by Sorbière which his own work so strongly resembled in its general argument. But frequent references to *De cive*— some respectful, some dissenting—in his *Théorie des loix civiles* do show that he had made a careful study of Hobbes's political theory. (Among the spines of books with imaginary titles painted as a *trompe l'oeil* in Turgot's library was 'Hobbes, *Leviathan,* Illustrated with a New Commentary by S.-N.-H. Linguet'.)[94]

These arguments against Montesquieu, although buttressed by citations of Tavernier, Chardin, and other travellers, were essentially those of a theorist—and one with strong and specific political points to make about Europe in general and France in particular. The final rejection of Montesquieu's theory of despotism was brought about, on the other hand, by a scholar with a direct and deep knowledge of conditions in a so-called despotic empire. Abraham-Hyacinthe Anquetil-Duperron, who had been only sixteen years old when Montesquieu's work was published, went to India in 1755 and spent six years there. He learned Hindi, Sanskrit, and Persian, and acquired a well-deserved reputation as a textual scholar; his translation of the *Zend-Avesta* (1771) was a landmark in Western studies of

---

93. Ibid., ii, pp. 114–15 (superstition, no clergy, 'Toute espece d'hiérarchie ecclésiastique leur est inconnue. Le muphti, que nous regardons comme le chef de leur religion, ne l'est réellement que de leur jurisprudence').

94. Levy, *Ideas and Careers*, p. 112 ('*Hobb. Leviathan* novo Comment. illustratum a S.N.H. Linguet'). Eugenio di Rienzo suggests that Linguet had read Sorbière ('Per una storia', p. 327), but specific evidence for this is lacking.

Zoroastrianism. His refutation of Montesquieu was published in 1778, under a lengthy title which usefully summarized his argument:

> *The Legislation of the East: A Work in which, by Demonstrating what the Fundamental Principles of Government are in the Ottoman Empire, Persia, and Hindustan, it is Proved (i) That the Way in which People have hitherto Represented the Despotism which is Said to be Absolute in these Three States, can only Give an Absolutely False Idea of it; (ii) That in the Ottoman Empire, Persia, and Hindustan there is a Written Code of Laws, which Oblige the Ruler as well as the Subjects; and (iii) That in these Three States, Private Individuals have Property in Mobile and Immobile Goods, which they Enjoy Freely.*[95]

Although Anquetil-Duperron had a detailed knowledge of textual sources (including ones in the Arabic language, which he had studied before he went to India), he had not lived in Persia or the Ottoman Empire, so his understanding of actual conditions in those states was largely dependent on the writings of travellers and diplomats. Drawing both on these sources and on his knowledge of the Islamic legal tradition, he had no difficulty in showing that Montesquieu's claim about the absence of law in those societies was unsustainable, just as it was in the Mughal case. Such a description might apply to an abuse of power by a particular ruler, but as an analysis of the whole system of rule it was 'absolutely false'. Even when great misrule existed, it did not have all the devastating consequences alleged by Montesquieu: misgovernment would sooner or later be checked by popular rebellion, and, all the while, many laws would remain in effect. The idea that 'despotism' made people give up cultivating the soil was absurd; Anquetil-Duperron had travelled widely in the territories that were or had been under Mughal rule, and had seen productive agriculture wherever he went. As for the role of Islam: he criticized Rycaut for making exaggerated claims about how it placed the Sultan above the law, and he dismissed Boulanger's whole politico-religious thesis as depending on 'absolute falsehoods'.[96] He was happy to quote Sir James Porter's anecdote about the old woman who

---

95. Anquetil-Duperron, *Législation orientale, ouvrage dans lequel, en montrant quels sont en Turquie, en Perse et dans l'Indoustan, les principes fondamentaux du gouvernement, on prouve, I. Que la manière dont jusqu'ici on a représenté le DESPOTISME, qui passe pour être absolu dans ces trois ETATS, ne peut qu'en donner une idée absolument fausse. II. Qu'en TURQUIE, en PERSE & dans l'INDOUSTAN, il y a un Code de Loix écrites, qui obligent le Prince ainsi que les sujets. III. Que dans ces trois ETATS, les particuliers ont des PROPRIÉTÉS en biens meubles & immeubles, dont ils jouissent librement.*

96. Ibid., pp. 2 ('absolument fausse'), 4 (misrule, rebellion), 8 (cultivating land), 9 (Boulanger, 'des choses absolument fausses'), 46–7 (Rycaut).

refused to give up her house to the Sultan, and supplied other evidence from Persia to make the same point. Gleefully, Anquetil-Duperron cited a passage from a French summary of William Blackstone (the great English constitutional lawyer), in which it was stated that if the King of England required a person's property for some essential purpose relating to the public good, he could compulsorily purchase it, so long as full compensation was given to the property-owner. 'In the Ottoman Empire', he concluded, 'the Sultan finds this absolutely impossible to do. Thus property is more highly respected there than it is in England.'[97]

On an intellectual level, Anquetil-Duperron's reason for writing this book can easily be stated: he wished to correct an influential error, and was in possession of enough relevant knowledge to make that correction a compelling one. On an ideological level, he has sometimes been associated with a 'royalist' current of thought which sought to justify renewed relations between France and the Ottoman Empire. However, he had good reason to send the manuscript of his *Législation orientale* to Holland for printing, as some of its contents led to its being regarded as a subversive text in France; and eleven years later he would welcome the advent of the French Revolution, believing (if only at first) that it would lead to some long-overdue reforms of abuses.[98] So far as Anquetil-Duperron's political motives for writing the book were concerned, they were clearly set out in the dedicatory epistle which, unusually and very strikingly, was addressed to the people of Hindustan. With great indignation he described the economic harm and the disruption to their way of life which they were suffering under their new European masters—something far worse than all that they had experienced under the earlier Muslim conquerors. Whilst their current oppressors were the British, who had supplanted the French in north India, this line of criticism, which referred in general terms to Europeans, clearly applied also to the French.[99] The concept of Asiatic despotism had become, in Anquetil-Duperron's view, a convenient pretext for Western interference in these parts of the world, and it was his moral duty to show what a falsehood it was.

---

97. Ibid., pp. 123–4 (Porter), 210–11 (Blackstone, 'En Turquie le Sultan trouve la chose absolument impossible. La propriété y est donc plus respectée qu'elle ne l'est en Angleterre').
98. Kaiser, 'Evil Empire?', pp. 17–20 (royalist); Baghdiantz McCabe, *Orientalism*, pp. 284–6 (royalist); Schwab, *Vie d'Anquetil-Duperron*, pp. 109 (subversive), 114 (Revolution).
99. Anquetil-Duperron, *Législation orientale*, pp. i–ii.

Many previous writers had sought to apply the same standards to both East and West, and had been prepared to make comparative judgments in favour of the former, for domestic 'shame-praising' purposes. Some writers, such as Henry Blount, had also challenged the common Western assumption that if Easterners had different ways of doing things, there must be something less civilized about them. But in the Preface to Anquetil-Duperron's work a new note was struck: he felt an urgent desire to correct such prejudices, not just to contribute to the moral improvement of the West, but to stop it from causing real detriment to the people of the East. For the age of West European imperial power over Muslim populations had now—only recently—begun. In closing an intellectual chapter where the old theory of 'oriental despotism' was concerned, he was also helping to open a new one, in which some of the cultural assumptions of Western imperial and colonial power would be contested on principled grounds. Let Anquetil-Duperron have the final words.

> What do people mean by 'barbarian peoples'? Inhuman peoples, among whom the poor man is crushed by the weight of injustice, and the rich criminal is honoured? In that case, what a lot of barbarians there are in the world! But those are the real barbarians, and not the people who speak, dress, and, in a word, live differently from us. For all our knowledge, our sophisticated behaviour, our 'civilization', if the Ancient Greeks were to reappear, they would treat us as barbarians. Would they be right? Well then, let us stop using these partisan terms. Let us believe that every people, even if it differs from us, can have a real value, and reasonable laws, customs, and opinions.[100]

---

100. Ibid., p. v ('Qu'entend-on par *peuples barbares*? Des peuples inhumains, chez qui le pauvre succombe sous le poids de l'injustice, chez qui le riche criminel soit en honneur? Alors que de barbares sur la terre! Voilà pourtant les vrais Barbares, & non ceux qui parlent, s'habillent, en un mot qui vivent autrement que nous. Avec toutes nos connoissances, nôtre politesse, nôtre *civilisation*, si les anciens Grecs reparoissoient, ils nous traiteroient de Barbares. Auroient-ils raison? Défaisons nous donc de ces mots de parti. Croyons que tout peuple peut, même en différant de nous, avoir une valeur réelle, des Loix, des Usages, des opinions raisonnables').

Conclusion

The choice of an end-point for this book—the publication of Montesquieu's *De l'esprit des lois*, and the debate it engendered—is rather more arbitrary than the selection of its starting point. Discussion of Islam, of the Ottoman Empire, and of the nature of rule in other Muslim territories continued uninterruptedly, of course, throughout the latter part of the eighteenth century, and Western understanding of Islam in particular grew significantly during the nineteenth. But it is not unreasonable to take Montesquieu's theory of despotism as marking the end of an era. While his thinking was original in many ways, his view of Ottoman and 'Asiatic' rule functioned as a kind of *summa* of earlier ideas and assumptions, going back to the moment in the late sixteenth century when René de Lucinge and Giovanni Botero crystallized the concept of despotism as a peculiar, systematic, and wholly negative phenomenon.

On some points the sources of Montesquieu's theory went back further than that. The fundamental contrast between a monarchy that relied on the advice and cooperation of a hereditary nobility and one that ruled only through officials who could be raised up and cast down at will had structured much Western thinking about the Ottoman Empire ever since the publication of Machiavelli's *Il principe* in 1532. Similarly, Montesquieu's observation (seized on by Linguet) that the former kind of monarchy was vulnerable to civil wars, and the latter to revolutions, was little more than a modified version of Machiavelli's statement that external aggressors would find it easy to gain supporters in a European kingdom, because of rivalries among its noblemen, whereas if they succeeded in the more difficult task of defeating the Sultan they would be able to take over and continue his system of undisputed rule. And, more generally, the idea that the lack of a hereditary nobility in the Ottoman Empire was an example of brutal oppression, not a positive sign of meritocracy, had a long history of its own: it had played a role in the Habsburgs' propaganda within the Holy Roman Empire in the sixteenth century, as they sought to galvanize the German nobility into contributing money and men to their anti-Ottoman wars.

Equally, in Linguet's hostile response to Montesquieu we can see elements of what I have called the new paradigm, a picture which had been assembled out of the accounts written by sixteenth-century observers (plus one fifteenth-century one, George of Hungary). Straightforwardly positive presentations of this paradigm were, admittedly, a rarity by the eighteenth century. The negativization of its key components, as carried out by the early theorists of despotism, had been quite effective; insofar as those components still featured in the analyses of eighteenth-century writers, they were more likely to be presented as parts of a cunning system of control, not as signs of beneficent rule. (Thus Aaron Hill, for instance, said that the delivery of speedy justice was a 'maxim' of Ottoman policy, on the grounds that 'a tedious Legality is far more dangerous than a swift Injustice'; rapid sentencing and punishment engendered fear and awe in the population.[1]) Yet even with this negative coloration, the list of key aspects of Ottoman government and public life remained largely unchanging, with a history going back to the earliest accounts by Western travellers and captives. To some degree this descriptive and analytic inertia reflected some simple realities: it had been true in the sixteenth century, for example, that Ottoman court cases were more speedy and less procedurally complicated than their West European equivalents, and it was still true in the eighteenth. But to a large extent what we see in the works of Western writers over this period is a consequence of long-term intertextuality.

The stock of known facts—or rather, of claims accepted as true—about the Ottoman Empire was passed on with little alteration from one text to another. And the more general the claim, the more immune it seems to have been to mere empirical disproof. So, as we have seen, generalizing statements about the Sultan's ownership of all property, about his status as universal heir to all his subjects, and about their status as his slaves, continued to be repeated even when solid evidence had accumulated to disprove them. Of course the main reason why these beliefs remained so persistent was that they were used to support some larger theoretical claims which, for other ideological reasons, writers were keen to make. But those claims were not made in a vacuum. The whole enterprise of formulating what were often

1. Hill, *Full and Just Account*, p. 6.

essentially intra-Western arguments in terms of what went on in an Eastern state depended on there being a corpus of apparently authoritative descriptions and analyses of the latter.

Over time, the descriptive literature did incorporate new knowledge, and the analytic approaches were adjusted accordingly. During the seventeenth century there was a growing appreciation of the practical limitations on sultanic power: the role of the Janissaries and spahis in making or breaking their rulers at critical moments, the influence of the *ulema*, and so on. The theory of Ottoman despotism was not undone by these observations (even if some influential writers, such as Marsigli, were led to doubt its value); rather, it was adapted to embrace a more problematic and dysfunctional kind of system, in place of the finely tuned engine of oppression that the original framers of the theory had had in mind. But new information about the fragility of sultanic rule was not fed into a neutral system of Western thinking that processed all incoming data; it was seized on, rather, by writers who were interested parties keen to find signs of impending collapse, or at least to fit the current state of the Ottoman Empire into a template of corruption and decay supplied by the late history of the Roman one. At the same time, other information was coming in during the seventeenth century about a different Muslim 'despotic' state, Persia, and some of it clashed with the standard interpretations of the Ottoman system: Persia seemed to have a nobility, or at least to respect the hereditary principle; according to Chardin, the peasants there lived better than in many parts of Western Europe; and the use of torture by the judicial authorities was much rarer.[2] But those who theorized about Eastern despotism largely ignored this evidence.

Where Islam was concerned, the power of long-lasting intertextuality was even greater, for obvious reasons. While any observant Western traveller could learn many things at first hand about the nature and effects of Ottoman government, very few had either the linguistic capacity or the social opportunity to engage in religious discussions with imams, *hoca*s, and dervishes. (The exceptions were some of the Catholic missionaries of the seventeenth and eighteenth centuries, especially in Persia, where such religious debates were tolerated; but what they learned thereby tended to be put into manuscript reports to their superiors, rather than books published for general readers.) The degree to which armchair writers in Western Europe relied on a standard body of Christian texts about Islam—some of them

2. See Osterhammel, *Die Entzauberung*, pp. 281–2.

medieval, and most of them polemical—is very striking. As a consequence, many of the grosser Christian inventions about Muhammad and Islam remained current in the general literature for an extraordinarily long time: the pigeon, the man in the well, the instruction by Sergius, and so on. Nor was it only the armchair authors who were guilty here: as late as 1632 the Scottish traveller William Lithgow confidently asserted that Muhammad's body was entombed in Mecca in an iron coffin, suspended in mid-air between two powerful magnets—'as I have been informed of sundry Turkes who saw it'.[3]

Gradually, from Postel onwards, study of the Koran and of other texts in Arabic had begun to unpick many of the false claims that had traditionally been made about Islamic practices and beliefs. By the final decades of the seventeenth century, knowledgeable polemicists against Islam such as Lodovico Marracci, Lancelot Addison, and Humphrey Prideaux did feel obliged to dissociate themselves from at least some of the ridiculous fictions which had featured so largely in earlier anti-Muslim writings. During that century, editions and translations of medieval Arab historians contributed new information about Muhammad and the early development of Islam; as we have seen, this was put to use by writers such as Stubbe when constructing an account that diverged radically from the traditional one. And yet, for all the increases in real understanding of Islam made by scholars such as Pococke and Reland, it would be an exaggeration to say that the changes in the political interpretation of Islam described in this book were brought about primarily by gains in objective knowledge about the origins or contents of that faith. Stubbe's basic ideas about the nature of religion, its political role, and the correct relationship between it and temporal power were ideas he had arrived at on other grounds. It was because he already held those opinions that he found the early history of Islam—as enhanced by recent scholarship—of interest, realizing that it could be used as grist to his mill.

It would be simplistic to say that there was a steady reduction in Western hostility to Islam because—and insofar as—Western writers gradually knew more about it. Marracci, Addison, and Prideaux did not become more favourable to Islam when they dispensed with some of the medieval anti-Muslim legends. They merely wanted to disembarrass their case of foolish claims which, being false, could only be counter-productive in the long run;

---

3. Lithgow, *Totall Discourse*, p. 133. As this example shows, invoking eyewitness authority did not always signal the onward march of empirical knowledge.

the basic Christian theological reasons for opposing Islam remained just the same, and they were keen to advance them. (Western scholarship certainly did make real advances in the study of Islam in this period, and it need not be doubted that people such as Pococke and Reland pursued their studies for scholarly, not polemical, reasons. But this book has been about the history of various forms of political and politico-religious argument, not about the history of scholarship as such.) Also potentially misleading is the tendency of some modern writers to pick out comments in praise of Muhammad, or of Islam, by writers such as Stubbe, Toland, and Boulainvilliers, and to describe those authors as 'Islamophile'. What is misleading here is not the fact of drawing attention to their positive statements about Muhammad and Islam, which are indeed remarkable, but the implication that some general disposition of 'Islamophilia' caused the making of those statements. Rather, what some choose to call Islamophilia was the *consequence* of positions the authors had adopted, and polemical strategies they were pursuing, in mostly intra-European controversies.

Much the same can be said about the general tendency to identify 'Turcophile' elements in Western writings on the Ottoman Empire. Some of the appreciative comments made by the writers who contributed to the new paradigm could be classified as embodying a kind of empirical Turcophilia—admiration, that is, for things which they saw done well in the Ottoman system. Jean Bodin, the person who took the new paradigm and built it up into a larger positive theory about Ottoman rule, might not unreasonably be described in that way as a Turcophile thinker. But almost all the other writers on political and social matters who made positive remarks about Ottoman ways of doing things were engaged in some kind of shame-praising activity vis-à-vis their own society. To say this is not to diminish the importance of such comments. The relatively free practice of Christianity and Judaism within the Ottoman Empire, for instance, was an important weapon in the hands of polemicists in intra-Christian debates on religious toleration. The Ottoman model played a significant rhetorical role here; shame-praising could be quite a powerful tactic. But it was primarily a move in an intra-Western argument.

If we step back from the signs of alleged Islamophilia and Turcophilia, it should not be difficult to see that there were long-running, continuous traditions of direct hostility to both Islam and the Ottoman Empire. These underwent no systematic transformation; but there were variations over time, in accordance with changes in the ways in which Western Christianity, and Western Christendom, felt threatened by their Islamic and Ottoman counterparts. The polemical anti-Muslim theological tradition was rooted in places and periods that had experienced threat or competition: the Byzantine Empire, the Crusader states, and Spain. In the early modern period hostile feelings of that traditional kind remained active in Spain, both before and after the expulsion of the Moriscos, and some people in Christian countries bordering the Mediterranean did worry about the conversion of Christian captives in North Africa and elsewhere in the Ottoman Empire. A new type of concern arose, from the mid-sixteenth century onwards, about anti-Trinitarianism, to which Islam seemed uncomfortably close. These general grounds for concern do not relate directly to the political arguments explored in this book, but they help to explain why an anti-Muslim *odium theologicum* remained an active force in Western culture during this period.

It should not surprise us that the status of the Ottomans as 'infidels' continued to have real significance in Western thinking about relations with them. Christian theology was an essential part of the mental framework within which people thought about society, law, and government. Although the basic principle of the legitimacy of temporal rule by non-Christians had been established in the thirteenth century, ruling out the idea that they should be warred against merely because they were infidels, there were nevertheless some important aspects of interstate relations where this religious distinction could be seen as relevant—for example, where the sale of military matériel to the infidels was concerned, or the formation of alliances with them. Even those who defended such alliances would typically invoke precedents from the Old Testament, to show that sacred history itself condoned them.

As we have seen, ideas about the continuing sacred history in which people lived, and especially about its impending conclusion, also shaped attitudes towards the Ottomans. For unlike the infidels of, say, China or Japan, these were infidels whose special role in world events seemed to have been prophesied in the Book of Daniel and in Revelation; and the fact that the Holy Land itself was under Muslim (and, after 1516, Ottoman) rule contributed an extra significance. From the mid-fifteenth century to the late seventeenth, crusading rhetoric about the recovery of the Holy Places was combined with prophetic fervour, not just in the popular pamphlet literature, but in treatises written by intellectuals and addressed to rulers. Modern historiography tends to play down the significance of this phenomenon

from the latter part of the sixteenth century onwards, as it does not fit standard
assumptions about the steady onset of secularization. It would be more
accurate to say that while some new, secularizing currents of thought grew
up alongside it, this current—often expressing Pseudo-Methodian or
Joachimite views that had been part of Western culture for centuries—
continued on its way with very little change. Until at least the end of the
seventeenth century it was an active element in the religious and political
culture of many Western European societies, flaring up each time there was
an anti-Ottoman war.

And such wars were frequent. One or more Christian powers fought
against the Ottomans at some time in every quarter-century between 1450
and 1750. On the secular side of the argument, when it comes to explaining
why there was a long-running tradition of direct hostility to the Ottoman
Empire, this point is elementary; one has only to look at the flow of anti-
Ottoman publications, which surged during every period of conflict. (This
too was a stimulus to intertextuality as, at the outbreak of a new war, pub-
lishers would rush to reissue the anti-Ottoman texts printed in the previous
one.) In the early part of this period, many of the works that were published
about and against the Ottomans were either penned at the request of popes
and other rulers, or produced by writers keen to ingratiate themselves by
providing justifications of war and exhortations to it. These conditions had
some effect on the nature and quality of the work produced. In the second
quarter of the sixteenth century, for example, powerful rhetorical exercises
were issued by humanist intellectuals such as Vives and Agricola, who had
little knowledge of Ottoman realities and were eager to give the most exaggerated accounts of the misery of life under Ottoman rule. Writers who
were equipped with more knowledge might still bend the facts to suit their
exhortatory purposes, either building up the Ottoman threat to energize
defence against it or toning it down to encourage offensive warfare. But one
of the overall changes in this period was that, starting perhaps with Pierre
Belon in the mid-sixteenth century, there were gradually more and more
writers who were free of such essentially rhetorical agendas; the point is not
that pure objectivity suddenly broke in, but that ways of writing developed
which were not geared primarily to the support of a political or military
project. The authors producing these works may have been admirers of the
Ottoman system (such as Henry Blount) or critics of it (such as Paul Rycaut),
but they wrote for a general book-buying public that wanted to understand
conditions in the world beyond their own countries, not for rulers who

sought encouragement for warfare or subjects who had to be cajoled into it. This point raises some larger issues of cultural history, which, unfortunately, lie beyond the scope of this book.

That some Western writing about the Ottomans was strongly moulded by hostile prejudice is quite clear. Few authors wrote purely *a priori*, however; the descriptive details that were used to corroborate their arguments had to be drawn from available materials, not just invented out of thin air, and there was a real appetite in Western culture for new information about these Eastern enemies and neighbours. And there is another, more important, reason why we should not regard Western writers on the Ottoman and Islamic world as merely indulging their prejudices to construct an artificial hate-object on the page. As this book has repeatedly stressed, many of them had ulterior critical purposes relating to their own societies; it is a very blinkered view that supposes that their only aim was to engage in some kind of intellectual hostility against, or superior dismissal of, the East.

In recent decades much of the literature on these matters has been written under the influence of Edward Said's *Orientalism: Western Conceptions of the Orient* (1978), which described 'Orientalism' (taken as a broad cultural category, in which the products of Western scholarship on Islam and the Asiatic world feature prominently, but not exclusively) as 'a kind of Western projection onto and will to govern over the Orient'.[4] This is unfortunate, as Said's thesis is hardly applicable to the early modern period at all. The subject matter of his book belonged almost entirely to the nineteenth and twentieth centuries, when Western powers such as Britain and France did 'govern over' large parts of the Orient. But even if one were to accept his argument that Western Oriental scholarship was essentially an instrument of imperial power at that time, it is very difficult to see how this could be applied to the sixteenth and seventeenth centuries, when no major territory in 'the East' was under Western European rule, and the Ottomans themselves were the imperial power in a large part of Europe.[5]

Said's only extended discussion of an early modern text concerns Barthélemy d'Herbelot's *Bibliothèque orientale* (1697), an encyclopaedic reference work with short entries on a huge range of people, places, and topics from the Islamic world and the Orient more generally. Here d'Herbelot is

---

4. Said, *Orientalism*, p. 95.

5. I must leave aside here the question of whether Said's argument is valid for the 19th and 20th centuries. For strong arguments to the contrary see R. Irwin, *For Lust of Knowing*, pp. 277–99; Varisco, *Reading Orientalism*; cf. also Marchand, *German Orientalism*, pp. xviii–xix.

accused of imposing 'a disciplinary order'; his work displays 'a triumphant technique for taking the immense fecundity of the Orient and making it systematically, even alphabetically, knowable by Western laymen'. Of the entry for Muhammad, Said writes: 'The dangers of free-wheeling heresy are removed when it is transformed into ideologically explicit matter for an alphabetical item. Mohammed no longer roams the Eastern world as a threatening, immoral debauchee: he sits quietly on his (admittedly prominent) portion of the Orientalist stage.'[6] Here the claim about imperial political power has dwindled into an argument about 'power' of such an abstract or metaphorical kind—the power that a writer exercises over Muhammad when placing an entry for him under 'M'—that it loses all real force. And it is unfortunate that Said had not studied d'Herbelot's work sufficiently closely to see the deep impress made on that scholar by compilations and reference works written by Muslim authors, above all the great bibliographical encyclopaedia of Katib Çelebi. Indeed, d'Herbelot not only followed Katib Çelebi's own principle of strict alphabetical order, but relied almost exclusively on 'Oriental' sources, eschewing Western ones, and even using the categorizations that came to him from his mostly Islamic materials.[7] That d'Herbelot, a pious Catholic, disapproved of Islam is as clear as it is unsurprising. But the fact that he spent years of his life immersing himself in Arabic, Persian, and Turkish texts in order to convey a new world of information to Western readers is itself remarkable, and cannot be adequately characterized by portraying him as simply engaged in a malign exercise in disciplinary 'control' over a suspect 'other'.

If Said's approach fails in the one early modern case to which he himself applied it, it can only be even more of a failure where the huge range of early modern writings on Islam and the Ottoman Empire are concerned. The reality here is altogether too multiform, too various and dynamic, to be confined by Said's own narrow and prescriptive 'disciplinary order'. Some of the works that have been discussed in this book were deeply prejudiced, and others testified to a genuine search for knowledge. But it is not sufficient

---

6. Said, *Orientalism*, pp. 65 ('a triumphant...'), 66 ('The dangers...', 'a disciplinary...').
7. There is, for example, no entry for 'Foi' or 'Religion', but there is one for the Arabic term 'Din'; none for 'Dieu', but one for 'Allah'; none for 'Diable', but one for 'Scheithan' (d'Herbelot, *Bibliothèque orientale*, pp. 99–101, 295–6, 785). On d'Herbelot see Dew, *Orientalism*, pp. 41–80; on the work and its arrangement see Bevilacqua, 'How to Organise the Orient'; on its sources see Laurens, *Aux sources*, esp. pp. 49–61; for a reliable appraisal of its treatment of Muhammad and Islam, see Gunny, *Images*, pp. 45–54. On Katib Çelebi see Hagen, *Ein osmanischer Geograph*, pp. 7–78 (esp. p. 49 on the work used by d'Herbelot).

just to place them on a simple scale of ignorance and knowledge, or prejudice and open-mindedness. Again and again, what they show is active—even, creative—engagement with their Islamic or Ottoman subject matter as part of a larger pursuit of religious and political arguments within their own culture. The Eastern material was not there to be beaten down, as Said imagined, into conformity with complacent Western attitudes; often it was used to shake things up, to provoke, to shame, to galvanize. Such uses have featured in many of the chapters of this book. Sometimes the point at issue was just a practical one: for example, the superiority of Ottoman military discipline, emphasized by writers such as Paolo Giovio in the hope that Christian armies would take note and learn to match it. But in other cases the use made of the Eastern example was radically at odds with the norms of Western life: for instance, Samuel Sorbière's praise of a 'despotic' system in which ordinary people were freed from an oppressive and conflictual hereditary nobility, or the glowing portrayals, by Stubbe and Boulainvilliers, of Muhammad as an exemplary religious leader.

To study the history of Western ideas about Islam and the Ottoman Empire in this period may help us to understand some of the origins, or at least the development, of Western prejudices that have had long subsequent histories. But it should also show us something else: that early modern Europeans viewed the government and religion of their powerful Eastern neighbours with a whole gamut of attitudes, from fear and fierce disapproval to fascination, admiration, and envy. For many Western thinkers, the Ottoman Empire and Islam played an important part in their own mental world, not as mere 'others' to be put in their subordinate place, nor simply as threats to be conceptually isolated and neutralized, but as active ingredients to be worked into their theories. Western political thought, in this period, was in the West and for the West, but never exclusively about the West. The East was not only too important to be ignored; it was too interesting—and, most of all, too useful.

List of Manuscripts

CARPENTRAS

Bibliothèque Inguimbertine

268: Seyyid Ali, son of Mehmed Efendi, 'Traité de l'Institution des Regles et Disciplines des Janissaires', tr. J.-B. de Fiennes.

1777: F. Savary de Brèves, untitled memorandum on the importance of the Franco-Ottoman alliance.

FLORENCE

Biblioteca Nazionale Centrale

II. II. 140 (formerly Magl. XXIV. 134): F. Pigafetta, treatise (1593).

KEW

The National Archives

SP 97/2: E. Barton, report to Lord Burghley.

LONDON

British Library

Add. 23,215: Sir John Finch to Lady Conway (1675).

King's 151: N. Contarini, 'Historie venete et altre a loro annesse libri otto' (1620s).

Sloane 1709: H. Stubbe, 'An Account of the Rise and Progress of Mahometanism' (fragment).

Sloane 1786: H. Stubbe, 'An Account of the Rise and Progress of Mahometanism' (fragment).

MDINA, MALTA

Cathedral Archives

Archive of the Inquisition, Processi, 95A, case 5: case of Anna Maria (Fatima) (1698–9).

MILAN

Biblioteca Ambrosiana

P 145 sup., item 4: G. Moleti ['Moleto'], 'Discorso che il Re Catolico sia il maggior Principe del Mondo'.

R 125 sup.: F. Pigafetta, treatise (1593).

NAPLES

Archivio Storico Diocesano di Napoli

Sant'Ufficio 89.1075: case of Anastasia of Paramythia (1598).

OXFORD

Bodleian Library

D'Orville 607: A. Gentili, 'De papatu romano Antichristo assertiones ex uerbo Dei et SS. Patribus'.

Rawl. D 399: L. Warner, report to States General (1664).

Rawl. D 618: extracts from F. Gondola [Gundulić], 'relazione' (1574).

Tanner 7: W. Harborne, papers.

PARIS

Bibliothèque des Capucins

49: 'Histoire de la mission des Capucins d'Alep'.

Bibliothèque Mazarine

1194: 'Dialogue entre un François et un Algerien sur leurs religions'.

Bibliothèque nationale de France

f. fr. 12,499: P. de Cardonnel, 'Predictions remarquables de l'etablissement de l'Empire françois par... Louis XIV'.

Moreau 842: N. Poirresson, report on the French Jesuit mission to Syria (1655).

Bibliothèque Sainte-Geneviève

3086: Racauld, 'Apologie po[r] l'alliance du treschrestien roy de france auec l'empereur du Leuant'.

3366: G. Nani, 'Relatione dell'Ambasceria straordinaria alla Corte di Francia'.

VATICAN CITY

Biblioteca Apostolica Vaticana

Cod. Urb. Lat. 1492: G. Frachetta, 'Discorso de modi, che si possono tenere al presente per guerreggiare contra il Turco per terra'; 'Se l'Imperatore debba attendere alla pace col Turco o proseguir la guerra'; 'Discorso del modo di regolar la guerra d'Ungheria l'anno 1596'.

VIENNA

Haus-, Hof- und Staatsarchiv
Türkei I, Karton 36: A. de Alegretti, letter to Rudolf II.

WASHINGTON, DC

Folger Shakespeare Library
V. b. 182: E. Tilney, 'The Descriptions Regimentts and Pollicies... of Italy and France, Germanie, Spaine, England, & Scotland, &c' (c.1598–1600).

ZURICH

Zentralbibliothek
Car. I. 92: T. Bibliander, theological works.
Car. I. 93: T. Bibliander, theological works.

Bibliography

This bibliography is confined to listing works cited in the text and notes of this book. Anonymous works are listed under 'Anon.' The alphabetical order is English.

Abu'l-Fida ['Abu'l-Feda'], I., *De vita, et rebus gestis Mohammedis, moslemicae religionis auctoris, et imperii saracenici fundatoris*, ed. and tr. J. Gagnier (Oxford, 1723).

Adams, R. P., *The Better Part of Valor: More, Erasmus, Colet, and Vives on Humanism, War, and Peace, 1469–1535* (Seattle, WA, 1962).

Addison, L., *West Barbary: Or, A Short Narrative of the Revolutions of the Kingdoms of Fez and Morocco, with an Account of the Present Customs, Sacred, Civil, and Domestick* (Oxford, 1671).

——, *The Life of Mahumed, the Author of the Turkish Religion* (London, 1679).

Adeva Martín, I., 'Juan de Torquemada y su Tractatus contra principales errores perfidi Machometi et turcorum sive sarracenorum (1459)', *Anuario de historia de la Iglesia*, 16 (2007), pp. 195–208.

Agricola, G., *Oratio de bello adversus Turcam suscipiendo, ad Ferdinandum Ungariae Boemiaeque regem, & principes Germaniae* (Basel, 1538).

Ajello, A., *La croce e la spada: i Francescani e l'Islam nel duecento* (Naples, 1999).

Akbari, S. C., *Idols in the East: European Representations of Islam and the Orient, 1100–1450* (Ithaca, NY, 2009).

Åkerman, S., 'Johan Adler Salvius' *Questions to Baruch de Castro concerning* De tribus impostoribus', in S. Berti, F. Charles-Daubert, and R. H. Popkin, eds., *Heterodoxy, Spinozism, and Free Thought in Early-Eighteenth-Century Europe: Studies on the Traité des trois imposteurs* (Dordrecht, 1996), pp. 397–423.

Aksulu, N. M., *Bartholomäus Georgevićs Türkenschrift 'De Turcarum ritu et caeremoniis' (1544) und ihre beide deutschen Übersetzungen von 1545* (Stuttgart, 2005).

Albèri, E., ed., *Relazioni degli ambasciatori veneti al Senato durante il secolo decimosesto*, ser. 3, *Relazioni dagli Stati Ottomani*, 3 vols. (Florence, 1840–55).

Alberoni, G., *Cardinal Alberoni's Scheme for reducing the Turkish Empire to the Obedience of Christian Princes: And for a Partition of the Conquests*, tr. anon. (London, 1736).

Alexander, P. J., *The Byzantine Apocalyptic Tradition*, ed. D. deF. Abrahamse (Berkeley, CA, 1985).

Allen, J. W., *A History of Political Thought in the Sixteenth Century* (London, 1928).

Allen, W., *A True, Sincere and Modest Defence of English Catholiques that Suffer for their Faith both at Home and Abrode* (n.p., n.d. [Rouen, 1584]).

Álvarez Gómez, M., *Über die Bedingungen des Friedens im Glauben bei Johannes von Segovia und Nikolaus von Kues* (Trier, 2003).

Alverny, M.-T. d', 'Deux traductions latines du Coran au Moyen Âge', *Archives d'histoire doctrinale et littéraire du Moyen Âge*, 22–3 (1947–8), pp. 69–131.

—— 'La Connaissance de l'Islam en Occident du IXe au milieu du XIIe siècle', in Centro Italiano di Studi sull'Alto Medioevo, *L'Occidente e l'Islam nell'alto medioevo*, 2 vols. (Spoleto, 1965), ii, pp. 577–602.

Amabile, L., *Fra Tommaso Campanella: la sua congiura, i suoi processi e la sua pazzia*, 3 vols. (Naples, 1882–7).

Ammirato, S., *Orazioni del sig. Scipione Ammirato, a diversi principi, intorno i preparamenti, che s'avrebbono a farsi contra la potenza del Turco* (Florence, 1598).

Ancona, A. d', *La leggenda di Maometto in Occidente*, ed. A. Borruso (Rome, 1994).

Anderson, S. P., *An English Consul in Turkey: Paul Rycaut at Smyrna, 1667–1678* (Oxford, 1989).

Annius of Viterbo ['Annius Viterbensis', G. Nanni], *Glosa super Apocalipsim de statu ecclesie ab anno salutis praesenti scilicet Mcccclxxxi usque ad finem mundi. et de preclaro & gloriosissimo triumpho christianorum in Turcos & Maumethos* (Gouda, c.1481–2).

Anon., *La France-Turquie, c'est à dire, conseils et moyens tenus par les ennemis de la couronne de France, pour réduire le royaume en tel estat que la tyrannie turquesque* (Orléans, 1576).

——, *The Strangling and Death of the Great Turke, and his Two Sons, with the Strange Preservation and Deliverance of his Uncle Mustapha from Perishing in Prison* (London, 1622).

——, *A True Relation of the Murther of Osman the Great Turke, and Five of his Principal Bashawes, and of the Election and Coronation of Mustapha his Unckle in his Stead* (London, 1622).

——, *Compendium librorum politicorum de papanâ & hispanicâ monarchiâ: Zwey Discurs Bruder Thomas Campanellen, von des Bapsts, und Spaniers vermeinter rechtmessiger Gewalt, und deroselbigen mit dem Römischen und Türckischen Keyser Vergleichunge* (n.p., 1628).

——, *Lettre d'avis à Messieurs du Parlement de Paris, escrite par un provincial* (Paris, 1649).

——, *Tisch-Reden, eines türckishen fürnehmen Bassa zu Constantinopel, mit einem teutschen Connestabel, christlicher Religion, das jetzige türckische Kriegswesen betreffend* (n.p., 1663).

—— ['A. C. de Metre'], *Het France Turckye, toegestellt door Ariante en Polidor de groote Staetsmannen* (Rotterdam, 1673).

——, *An Account of South-West Barbary: Containing what is most Remarkable in the Territories of the King of Fez and Morocco. Written by a Person who had been a Slave there a Considerable Time; and published from his Authentick Manuscript*, ed. S. Ockley (London, 1713).

——, *Lettre d'un médecin arabe* ('London', 1713), printed with [A. Collins,] *Discours sur la liberté de penser* ('London', 1714).

——, 'A Defence of Mahomet: A Paradox', in [T. Killigrew, ed.,] *Miscellanea aurea: Or, the Golden Medley* (London, 1720), pp. 165–88.

——, 'Sultan', in D. Diderot and J. le Rond d'Alembert, eds., *L'Encyclopédie ou Dictionnaire raisonné des sciences, des arts et des métiers*, 28 vols. (Paris, 1751–72), xvi, p. 655.

————, *La Fausseté des miracles des deux testamens, prouvée par le parallele avec de semblables prodiges operés dans diverses sectes* ('London' [Amsterdam?], 1775).

————, *Theophrastus redivivus*, ed. G. Canziani and G. Paganini, 2 vols. (Florence, 1982).

————, *Le 'Traité des trois imposteurs' et 'L'Esprit de Spinosa': philosophie clandestine entre 1678 et 1768*, ed. F. Charles-Daubert (Oxford, 1999).

Arblaster, P., *Antwerp & the World: Richard Verstegan and the International Culture of Catholic Reformation* (Leuven, 2004).

Aretin, K. O. von, 'Die Türkenkriege als Traditionselement des katholischen Europa', in W. Barner and E. Müller-Luckner, eds., *Tradition, Norm, Innovation: soziales und literarisches Traditionsverhalten in der Frühzeit der deutschen Aufklärung* (Munich, 1989), pp. 19–29.

Ariosto, A., *Itinerarium (1476–1479)*, ed. F. Uliana (Alessandria, 2007).

Aristotle, *Politicorum libri octo cum vetusta translatione Guilelmi de Moerbeka*, ed. F. Susemihl (Leipzig, 1872).

————, *Politics*, ed. and tr. H. Rackham, revd. edn. (Cambridge, MA, 1944).

Arnoux ['Arnu'], N., *Presagio dell'imminente rovina, e caduta dell'imperio ottomano, delle future vittorie, e prosperi successi della christianità. Cavata da diverse profetie, oracoli, vaticinij, e pronostici antichi, e moderni* (Padua, 1684).

Arredondo y Alvarado, G. de, *Castillo inexpugnable defensorio de la fee… y exortación para yr contra el turco: y le vencer: y anichilar la seta de mahoma* (Burgos, 1528).

Arrighi, D., *Écritures de l'ambassade: les* Lettres turques *d'Ogier Ghiselin de Busbecq* (Paris, 2011).

Arvieux, L. d', *Memoires du chevalier d'Arvieux, envoyé extraordinaire du Roy à la Porte, Consul d'Alep, d'Alger, de Tripoli, & d'autres echelles du Levant*, 7 vols. (Paris, 1735).

Asher, R. E., *National Myths in Renaissance France: Francus, Samothes and the Druids* (Edinburgh, 1993).

Aubigné, T.-A. d', *L'Histoire universelle du sieur d'Aubigné*, 3 vols. (Maillé, 1616–20).

Aubrey, J., *'Brief Lives', chiefly of Contemporaries, Set down by John Aubrey, between the Years 1669 & 1696*, ed. A. Clark, 2 vols. (Oxford, 1898).

Aulinger, R., 'Kundschafterberichte über den Aufmarsch der Türken am Balkan 1532: Meldungen an den Reichstag', *Mitteilungen des Österreichischen Staatsarchivs*, 34 (1981), pp. 147–73.

Avenel, D. L. M., ed., *Lettres, instructions diplomatiques et papiers d'état du Cardinal de Richelieu*, 8 vols. (Paris, 1853–77).

Babinger, F., 'Introduzione', in L. Bassano, *Costumi et i modi particolari della vita de' Turchi*, ed. F. Babinger (Munich, 1963), pp. v–xi.

————, 'Lorenzo de' Medici e la corte ottomana', *Archivio storico italiano*, 121 (1963), pp. 305–61.

————, 'Maometto il Conquistatore e gli umanisti d'Italia', in A. Pertusi, ed., *Venezia e l'Oriente fra tardo medioevo e rinascimento* (Florence, 1966), pp. 433–49.

————, 'Pio II e l'oriente maomettano', in D. Maffei, ed., *Enea Silvio Piccolomini, Papa Pio II: atti del convegno per il quinto centenario della morte* (Siena, 1968), pp. 1–13.

————, *Mehmed the Conqueror and His Time*, tr. R. Manheim, ed. W. C. Hickman (Princeton, NJ, 1978).

Bacon, F., 'An Advertisement touching an Holy War', in F. Bacon, *The Works*, ed. J. Spedding, R. L. Ellis, and D. D. Heath, 14 vols. (London, 1868–1901), vii, pp. 117–36.

——, 'Certain Observations Made upon a Libel Published this Present Year, 1592', in F. Bacon, *The Works*, ed. J. Spedding, R. L. Ellis, and D. D. Heath, 14 vols. (London, 1868–1901), viii [= *The Letters and the Life*, i], pp. 144–208.

——, 'A Remembrance Additional to the Instructions of Sir John Digby', in F. Bacon, *The Works*, ed. J. Spedding, R. L. Ellis, and D. D. Heath, 14 vols. (London, 1868–1901), xiii [= *The Letters and the Life*, vi], pp. 158–9.

——, 'Considerations touching a War with Spain', in F. Bacon, *The Works*, ed. J. Spedding, R. L. Ellis, and D. D. Heath, 14 vols. (London, 1868–1901), xiv [= *The Letters and the Life*, vii], pp. 469–505.

Badir, M. G., *Voltaire et l'Islam* (Oxford, 1974).

Baghdiantz McCabe, I., *Orientalism in Early Modern France: Eurasian Trade, Exoticism, and the Ancien Régime* (Oxford, 2008).

Balázs, M., *Early Transylvanian Antitrinitarianism (1566–1571): From Servet to Palaeologus* (Baden-Baden, 1996).

Baldini, A. E., 'Botero et Lucinge: les racines de la *Raison d'État*', in Y. C. Zarka, ed., *Raison et déraison d'état: théoriciens et théories de la raison d'état aux XVIᵉ et XVIIᵉ siècles* (Paris, 1994), pp. 67–99.

——, 'L'Antimachiavélisme en Italie au début de la littérature de la raison d'État', in A. Dierkens, ed., *L'Antimachiavélisme, de la Renaissance aux Lumières*, Problèmes d'histoire des religions, 8 (Brussels, 1997), pp. 15–30.

Ball, B. W., *A Great Expectation: Eschatological Thought in English Protestantism to 1660* (Leiden, 1975).

Balsamo, J., '"Une parfaite intelligence de la raison d'estat": le *Trésor politique*, René de Lucinge et les Turcs (1588–1608)', in P. Desan and G. Dotoli, eds., *D'un siècle à l'autre: littérature et société de 1590 à 1610* (Paris, 2001), pp. 297–321.

Barbero, A., *La Bataille des trois empires: Lépante, 1571*, tr. P. Farazzi and M. Valensi (Paris, 2012).

Barbuto, G. M., *Il principe e l'Anticristo: gesuiti e ideologie politiche* (Naples, 1994).

Bartl, P., '"Marciare verso Costantinopoli"—zur Türkenpolitik Klemens' VIII.', *Saeculum*, 20 (1969), pp. 44–56.

Bassano, L., *Costumi et i modi particolari della vita de' Turchi*, ed. F. Babinger (Munich, 1963).

Bataillon, M., *Le Docteur Laguna auteur du Voyage en Turquie* (Paris, 1958).

——, 'Mythe et connaissance de la Turquie en occident au milieu du XVIᵉ siècle', in A. Pertusi, ed., *Venezia e l'oriente fra tardo medioevo e rinascimento* (Florence, 1966), pp. 451–70.

Battista, A. M., *Alle origini del pensiero politico libertino: Montaigne e Charron* (Milan, 1966).

Baudier, M., *Histoire generale de la religion des Turcs* (Paris, 1625).

Baumer, F. L., 'England, the Turk, and the Common Corps of Christendom', *American Historical Review*, 50 (1944), pp. 26–48.

Bayle, P., *Dictionaire historique et critique*, 3rd edn., 4 vols. (Rotterdam, 1720).

——, *Pensées diverses… à l'occasion d'une comète*, in his *Oeuvres diverses*, 4 vols. (The Hague, 1727–31), iii, pp. 1–417.

——, *Réponse aux questions d'un provincial*, in his *Oeuvres diverses*, 4 vols. (The Hague, 1727–31), iii, pp. 500–1084.

Becher, J. J., *Psychosophia, oder Seelen-Weissheit*, 2nd edn. (Frankfurt am Main, n.d. [1683]).

Behnen, M., '"Arcana—haec sunt ratio status." Ragion di stato und Staatsräson: Probleme und Perspektiven (1589–1651)', *Zeitschrift für historische Forschung*, 14 (1987), pp. 129–95.

Bellarmino ['Bellarminus'], R., *Disputationes de controversiis christianae fidei, adversus huius temporis haereticos*, 4 vols. (Lyon, 1610).

[Bellay, G. du,] *Double d'une lettre envoyee a ung Alemant touchant les differens qui sont entre le Roy treschrestien & L'empereur, & les motifz de la Guerre presente* (Lyon, 1536).

Bellini, G., *Storia della tipografia del Seminario di Padova, 1684–1938* (Padua, 1938).

Belon, P., *Voyage au Levant (1553): les observations de Pierre Belon du Mans de plusieurs singularités & chose mémorables, trouvées en Grèce, Turquie, Judée, Égypte, Arabie & autres pays étranges*, ed. A. Merle (Paris, 2001).

Benítez, M., *La Face cachée des Lumières: recherches sur les manuscrits philosophiques clandestins de l'âge classique* (Paris, 1996).

——, 'Une histoire interminable: origine et développement du *Traité des trois imposteurs*', in S. Berti, F. Charles-Daubert, and R. H. Popkin, eds., *Heterodoxy, Spinozism, and Free Thought in Early-Eighteenth-Century Europe: Studies on the Traité des trois imposteurs* (Dordrecht, 1996), pp. 53–74.

Benzoni, G., 'Scipione Cicala', *Dizionario biografico degli italiani* (Rome, 1960–), xxv, pp. 320–40.

——, 'A proposito della fonte prediletta di Ranke, ossia delle relazioni degli ambasciatori veneziani', *Studi veneziani*, 16 (1988), pp. 245–57.

Bérenger, J., 'La Collaboration militaire franco-ottomane à l'époque de la Renaissance', *Revue internationale d'histoire militaire*, 68 (1987), pp. 51–66.

Berger de Xivrey, [J.,] ed., *Recueil des lettres missives de Henri IV*, 7 vols. (Paris, 1843–58).

Bernabé Pons, L. F., *El evangelio de San Bernabé: un evangelio Islámico español* (Alicante, 1995).

Bernard, J. F., *Réflexions morales, satiriques et comiques sur les moeurs de notre siècle*, in G. L. van Roosbroeck, *Persian Letters before Montesquieu* (New York, 1932), pp. 85–147.

Bernier, F., *Abregé de la philosophie de Gassendi*, 8 vols. (Lyon, 1678).

——, *Un libertin dans l'Inde Moghole: les voyages de François Bernier (1656–1669)*, ed. F. Tinguely (Paris, 2008).

Berriot, F., 'Jean Bodin et l'Islam', in *Jean Bodin: actes du Colloque Interdisciplinaire d'Angers, 24 au 27 mai 1984* (Angers, 1985), pp. 171–82.

Béthune, M. de, duc de Sully, *Mémoires des sages et royales oeconomies d'estat, domestiques, politiques et militaires de Henry le Grand* ('Amsterdam' [Angers: Château de Sully], 1638).

Bevilacqua, A., 'How to Organise the Orient: d'Herbelot and the *Bibliothèque orientale*', *Journal of the Warburg and Courtauld Institutes*, 79 (2016), pp. 213–61.

Bezzola, G. A., *Die Mongolen in abendländischer Sicht (1220–1270): ein Beitrag zur Frage der Völkerbegegnungen* (Bern, 1974).

Bianchi, L., 'Impostura religiosa e critica storica: *La Fausseté des miracles des deux testamens*', in G. Canziani, ed., *Filosofia e religione nella letteratura clandestina, secoli XVII e XVIII* (Milan, 1994), pp. 237–66.

Bibliander, T., *Ad nominis christiani socios consultatio, quanam ratione Turcarum dira potentia repelli possit ac debeat a populo christiano* (Basel, 1542).

——, *A Godly Consultation unto the Brethren and Companyons of the Christian Religion*, tr. anon. (n.p., n.d.).

——, 'Apologia pro editione Alcorani', in T. Bibliander, ed., *Machumetis Sarracenorum principis vita ac doctrina omnis, quae & Ismahelitarum lex, & Alcoranum dicitur*, 3 vols. (Basel, 1543), i, sigs. α3v–β6r.

Bilici, F., 'Les Relations franco-ottomanes au XVIIᵉ siècle: réalisme politique et idéologie de croisade', in G. Veinstein et al., *Turcs et turqueries (XVIᵉ–XVIIIᵉ siècles)* (Paris, 2009), pp. 37–61.

——, *XIV. Louis ve İstanbul'u fetih tasarısı. Louis XIV et son projet de conquête d'Istanbul* (Ankara, 2004).

Billacois, F., 'Le Turc: image mentale et mythe politique dans la France du début du XVIIᵐᵉ siècle', *Revue de psychologie des peuples*, 21 (1966), pp. 233–46.

Billanovich, L., and P. Gios, eds., *Gregorio Barbarigo, patrizio veneto, vescovo e cardinale nella tarda Controriforma (1625–1697)*, 2 vols. (Padua, 1999).

Binder, L., *Grundlagen und Formen der Toleranz in Siebenbürgen bis zur Mitte des 17. Jahrhunderts* (Vienna, 1976).

Binder, P., 'Transylvanian Saxons as Turkish Clerks: Marcus Scherer and Marcus Benkner', *Revue des études sud-est européennes*, 12 (1974), pp. 397–401.

Biondo, F., *Scritti inediti e rari*, ed. B. Nogara (Rome, 1927).

Bireley, R., *The Counter-Reformation Prince: Anti-Machiavellianism and Catholic Statecraft in Early Modern Europe* (Chapel Hill, NC, 1990).

Birnbaum, M. D., 'Attila's Renaissance in the Fifteenth and Sixteenth Centuries', in F. H. Bäuml and M. D. Birnbaum, eds., *Attila: The Man and His Image* (Budapest, 1993), pp. 82–96.

Bisaha, N., *Creating East and West: Renaissance Humanists and the Ottoman Turks* (Philadelphia, 2004).

Bitossi, B., 'Genova e i turchi. Note sui rapporti tra genovesi e ottomani fra medioevo ed età moderna', in F. Meier, ed., *Italien und das Osmanische Reich* (Herne, 2010), pp. 87–117.

Black, R., *Benedetto Accolti and the Florentine Renaissance* (Cambridge, UK, 1985).

Blekastad, M., *Comenius: Versuch eines Umrisses von Leben, Werk und Schicksal des Jan Amos Komenský* (Oslo, 1969).

Blount, H., *A Voyage into the Levant* (London, 1636).

Blythe, J. M., *The Worldview and Thought of Tolomeo Fiadoni (Ptolemy of Lucca)* (Turnhout, 2009).

Bobzin, H., *Der Koran im Zeitalter der Reformation: Studien zur Frühgeschichte der Arabistik und Islamkunde in Europa* (Beirut, 1995).

——, 'Islamkundliche Quellen in Jean Bodins *Heptaplomeres*', in G. Gawlick and F. Niewöhner, eds., *Jean Bodins Colloquium Heptaplomeres* (Wiesbaden, 1996), pp. 41–57.

Boccalini, T., *Ragguagli di Parnaso e Pietra del paragone politico*, ed. G. Rua and L. Firpo, 3 vols. (Bari, 1910–48).

Bock, G., *Thomas Campanella: politisches Interesse und philosophische Spekulation* (Tübingen, 1974).

Bodin, J., *Methodus ad facilem historiarum cognitionem* (Paris, 1572).

——, *De la démonomanie des sorciers* (Paris, 1580).

——, *Les Six Livres de la république* (Paris, 1583; photo-reproduction, Aalen, 1977).

——, *De republica libri sex* (Paris, 1586).

——, *Colloquium heptaplomeres de rerum sublimium arcanis abditis*, ed. L. Noack (Schwerin, 1857).

——, *Method for the Easy Comprehension of History*, tr. B. Reynolds (New York, 1945).

——, *The Six Bookes of a Commonweale*, tr. R. Knolles, ed. K. D. McRae (Cambridge, MA, 1962).

——, *Colloquium of the Seven about the Secrets of the Sublime*, tr. M. L. Kuntz (Princeton, NJ, 1975).

Boemus, J., *Omnium gentium mores, leges & ritus ex multis clarissimis rerum scriptoribus* (Lyon, 1536).

Bohnstedt, J. W., *The Infidel Scourge of God: The Turkish Menace as Seen by German Pamphleteers of the Reformation Era*, Transactions of the American Philosophical Society, n.s., 58, part 9 (Philadelphia, 1968).

Bon, O., *The Sultan's Seraglio: An Intimate Portrait of Life at the Ottoman Court*, tr. J. Withers, ed. G. Goodwin (London, 1996).

Bonazzoli, V., 'Ebrei italiani, portoghesi, levantini sulla piazza commerciale di Ancona intorno alla metà del Cinquecento', in G. Cozzi, ed., *Gli Ebrei a Venezia, secoli XIV–XVIII* (Milan, 1987), pp. 727–70.

[Bonnet, J.,] *Lettre écrite à Musala, homme de loi à Hispaham, sur les moeurs et la religion des François, & sur la querelle entre les Jésuites & les Jansenistes* (n.p., n.d. [Paris, 1716]).

Bonora, E., *Ricerche su Francesco Sansovino, imprenditore, librario e letterato* (Venice, 1994).

Borsa, G., 'Die Buchdrucker des XV. und XVI. Jahrhunderts in Ungarn', *Bibliothek und Wissenschaft*, 2 (1965), pp. 1–33.

Bosbach, F., *Monarchia universalis: storia di un concetto cardine della politica europea (secoli XVI–XVIII)*, tr. C. De Marchi (Milan, 1998).

——, '*Imperium Turcorum* oder *Christianorum Monarchia*—die Osmanen in der heilgeschichtlichen Deutung Mercurino Gattinaras', in M. Kurz et al., eds., *Das Osmanische Reich und die Habsburgermonarchie* (Vienna, 2005), pp. 167–80.

Botero, G., *De regia sapientia libri tres* (Milan, 1583).

——, *Relationi universali*, 2nd edn. (Vicenza, 1595).

——, *Della ragion di stato*, ed. C. Morandi (Bologna, 1930).

Boulainvilliers, H., comte de, *La Vie de Mahomed* (London, 1730).

——, *Vita di Maometto*, ed. and tr. D. Venturino (Palermo, 1992).

Boulanger, N.-A., *Recherches sur l'origine du despotisme oriental*, ed. P. Sadrin (Paris, 1988).

Bouwsma, W. J., *Concordia mundi: The Career and Thought of Guillaume Postel, 1510–1581* (Cambridge, MA, 1957).

Braun, L., *Ancilla Calliopeae: ein Repertorium der neulateinischen Epik Frankreichs (1500–1700)* (Leiden, 2007).

Brenz ('Brentius'), J., *Wie sich Prediger und Leyen halten sollen, so der Türck das Teutsch land uberfallen würde, Christliche und notturfftige unterricht* (Wittenberg, 1531).

Brerewood, E., *Enquiries touching the Diversity of Languages, and Religions through the Cheife Parts of the World* (London, 1614).

Brèves, S. de: *see* Savary de Brèves.

Breydenbach, B. von, *Peregrinatio in terram sanctam: eine Pilgerreise ins Heilige Land, frühneuhochdeutscher Text und Übersetzung*, ed. I. Mozer (Berlin, 2010).

Brightman, T., *The Revelation of St John Illustrated*, 4th edn. (London, 1644).

Brogi, S., *Il cerchio dell'universo: libertinismo, spinozismo e filosofia della natura in Boulainvilliers* (Florence, 1993).

Brotton, J., *This Orient Isle: Elizabethan England and the Islamic World* (London, 2016).

Brouwer, C. G., ed., *Sultan Osman (1623) & Bedroge bedriegers (1646): turkse tragedies van Kemp en Kroes* (Amsterdam, 1994).

Brundage, J. A., 'Holy War and the Medieval Lawyers', in T. P. Murphy, ed., *The Holy War* (Columbus, OH, 1976), pp. 99–140.

Budovec z Budova, V. ['W. Budowez'], *Antialkorán, to jest: mocní a nepřemožení důvodové toho, že Alkorán Turecký z ďábla pošel a to původem ariánů, s vědomým proti Duchu Sv. rouháním* (Prague, 1614).

——, *Circulus horologi lunaris et solaris, hoc est, brevissima synopsis, historica, typica et mystica* (Hanau, 1616).

Bull, H., *The Anarchical Society: A Study of Order in World Politics* (London, 1977).

Bullinger, H., *Der Türgg. Von anfang und ursprung desz Türggischen Gloubens, der Türggen, ouch jrer Königen und Keyseren, und wie fürträffenlich vil landen unnd lüthen, sy inner 266 jaren, yngenommen, und der Christenheit abtrungen habind* (n.p. [Zurich], 1567).

——, 'Brève et pieuse institution de la religion chrétienne écrite aux ministres des églises de Christ et autres serviteurs de Dieu dispersés en Hongrie', tr. M. Makay and M. Reulos, in J. Allier, ed., *Divers aspects de la Réforme aux XVIᵉ et XVIIᵉ siècles: études et documents*, supplement to *Bulletin de la société de l'histoire du protestantisme français*, July–Sept. 1975 (Paris, 1975), pp. 239–86.

Bulman, W. J., *Anglican Enlightenment: Orientalism, Religion and Politics in England and its Empire, 1648–1715* (Cambridge, UK, 2015).

Bundy, D. D., 'Hetᶜum's La Flor des Estoires de la terre d'Orient: A Study in Medieval Armenian Historiography and Propaganda', *Revue des études arméniennes*, n.s., 20 (1986–7), pp. 223–35.

Bunes Ibarra, M. A. de, *La imagen de los musulmanes y del Norte de África en la España de los siglos XVI y XVII: los caracteres de una hostilidad* (Madrid, 1989).

Burchill, C. J., *The Heidelberg Antitrinitarians* (Baden-Baden, 1989).

Burman, T., *Reading the Qur'ān in Latin Christendom, 1140–1560* (Philadelphia, 2007).

Bury, A., *The Naked Gospel* (n.p., 1690).

Busbecq, O. G. de ['A. G. Busbequius'], 'Exclamatio, sive de acie contra Turcam instruenda consilium', in his *Itinera constantinopolitanum et amasianum* (Antwerp, 1581), pp. 113–67.

Bussi, E., 'La condizione giuridica dei musulmani nel diritto canonico', *Rivista di storia del diritto italiano*, 8 (1935), pp. 459–94.

Cabanelas Rodríguez, D., *Juan de Segovia y el problema islámico* (Madrid, 1952).

Calendar of State Papers Relating to English Affairs in the Archives of Venice, v, *1534–1554*, ed. R. Brown (London, 1873).

Calendar of State Papers Relating to English Affairs in the Archives of Venice, xii, *1610–1613*, ed. H. F. Brown (London, 1905).

Calvin, J., *Institutes of the Christian Religion*, tr. H. Beveridge, 2 vols. (London, 1953).

Camerarius, L. ['J. Justinus'], *Mysterium iniquitatis, sive secreta secretorum turco-papistica secreta, contra libellum famosum, sub titulo secreta calvino-turcica ... editum* (n.p. ['Justinopolis'], 1625).

Camerarius, P., *Operae horarum subcisivarum, sive meditationes historicae*, 3 vols. (Frankfurt am Main, 1602–9).

Campanella, T., *Atheismus triumphatus, seu reductio ad religionem per scientiarum veritates* (Rome, 1631).

——, *Disputationum in quatuor partes suae philosophiae realis libri quatuor* (Paris, 1637).

——, *Discorsi politici ai principi d'Italia*, ed. P. Garzilli (Naples, 1848).

——, *Lettere*, ed. V. Spampanato (Bari, 1927).

——, *Quod reminiscentur et convertentur ad Dominum universi fines terrae*, ed. R. Amerio, 3 vols. (Padua, Florence, 1939–60).

——, *La città del sole: testo italiano e testo latino*, ed. N. Bobbio (Turin, 1941).

——, *La prima e la seconda resurrezione. Inediti: Theologicorum libri XXVII–XXVIII*, ed. and tr. R. Amerio (Rome, 1955).

——, *Legazioni ai maomettani*, ed. R. Amerio (Florence, 1960) [= vol. 3 (book 4) of *Quod reminiscentur*).

——, *De antichristo. Inediti: Theologicarum liber XXVI*, ed. and tr. R. Amerio (Rome, 1965).

——, *Metafisica*, ed. G. di Napoli, 3 vols. (Bologna, 1967).

——, *Articuli prophetales*, ed. G. Ernst (Florence, 1976).

——, *La città del sole: dialogo poetico. The City of the Sun: A Poetical Dialogue*, ed. and tr. D. J. Donno (Berkeley, CA, 1981).

——, *Monarchie d'Espagne et Monarchie de France*, ed. G. Ernst, tr. N. Fabry and S. Waldbaum (Paris, 1997).

——, *Lettere, 1595–1638, non comprese nell'edizione di Vincenzio Spampanato*, ed. G. Ernst (Pisa, 2000).

Cândea, V., 'Introducere', in D. Cantemir, *Sistemul sau întocmirea religiei muhammedane*, ed. and tr. V. Cândea (Bucharest, 1977).

Cantemir, D., *History of the Growth and Decay of the Othman Empire*, tr. N. Tindal (London, 1734).

Cantimori, D., 'Note su alcuni aspetti della propaganda religiosa nell'Europa del Cinquecento', in G. Berthoud et al., *Aspects de la propagande religieuse* (Geneva, 1957), pp. 340–52.

Capaccio, G. C., *Il forastiero: dialogi* (Naples, 1634).

Capp, B. S., *The Fifth Monarchy Men: A Study in Seventeenth-Century English Millenarianism* (London, 1972).

Carabelli, G., *Tolandiana: materiali bibliografici per lo studio dell'opera e della fortuna di John Toland (1670–1722)* (Florence, 1975).

Cardano, G., 'Neronis encomium', in his *Somniorum Synesiorum, omnis generis insomnia* (Basel, 1562), pp. 138–231.

——, *De sapientia libri quinque*, ed. M. Bracali (Florence, 2008).

Cargill Thompson, W. D. J., *The Political Thought of Martin Luther*, ed. P. Broadhead (Brighton, 1984).

Carretto, G. E., 'Bessarione e il Turco', in G. Fiaccadori, ed., *Bessarione e l'umanesimo* (Naples, 1994), pp. 261–74.

Carrier, H., *Le Labyrinthe de l'état: essai sur le débat politique en France au temps de la Fronde (1648–1653)* (Paris, 2004).

Carter, C. H., *The Secret Diplomacy of the Habsburgs, 1598–1625* (New York, 1964).

Casaubon, M., *A Treatise concerning Enthusiasme, as it is an Effect of Nature: but is Mistaken by Many for either Divine Inspiration, or Diabolical Possession* (1654 ['1655']).

Castel, C. I., abbé de Saint-Pierre, *Projet pour rendre la paix perpétuelle en Europe*, ed. S. Goyard-Fabre (Paris, 1981).

Castrucci, E., *Ordine convenzionale e pensiero decisionista: saggio sui presupposti intellettuali dello stato moderno nel seicento francese* (Milan, 1981).

Caye, P., 'Campanella critique de Machiavel. La politique: de la non-philosophie à la métaphysique', *Bruniana & campanelliana: ricerche filosofiche e materiali storico-testuali*, 6 (2002), pp. 333–51.

Céard, J., 'L'Image de l'Europe dans la littérature cosmographique de la Renaissance', in F. Autrand, N. Cazauran, and S. Follet, eds., *La Conscience européenne au XVe et au XVIe siècle* (Paris, 1982), pp. 49–63.

Champion, J. A. I., *Republican Learning: John Toland and the Crisis of Christian Culture, 1696–1722* (Manchester, 2003).

——, '"I remember a Mahometan Story of Ahmed Ben Edris": Freethinking Uses of Islam from Stubbe to Toland', *Al-Qantara*, 31 (2010), pp. 443–80.

Chardin, Sir John, *Travels in Persia*, ed. Sir Percy Sykes (London, 1927).

Charles-Daubert, F., 'Le "Libertinage érudit" et le problème du conservatisme politique', in H. Méchoulan, ed., *L'État baroque: regards sur la pensée politique de la France du premier XVIIe siècle* (Paris, 1985), pp. 179–202.

——, 'Introduction', and 'Choix des textes et principes d'édition', in *Le 'Traité des trois imposteurs' et 'L'Esprit de Spinosa': philosophie clandestine entre 1678 et 1768*, ed. F. Charles-Daubert (Oxford, 1999), pp. 1–455.

Charrière, E., ed., *Négociations de la France dans le Levant*, 4 vols. (Paris, 1848–60).

Châteillon [Castellio], S., *Conseil à la France désolée, auquel est monstré la cause de la guerre présente, & le remede qui y pourroit estre mis; & principalement est auisé si on doit forcer les consciences* (n.p., 1562).

[Chick, H., ed.,] *A Chronicle of the Carmelites in Persia and the Papal Missions of the XVIIth and XVIIIth Centuries*, 2 vols. (London, 1939).

Çırakman, A., *From the 'Terror of the World' to the 'Sick Man of Europe': European Images of Ottoman Empire and Society from the Sixteenth Century to the Nineteenth* (New York, 2002).

Cirillo, L., and M. Frémaux, eds., *Évangile de Barnabé* (Paris, 1977).

Clapmarius [Klapmeier], A., *De arcanis rerumpublicarum libri sex* (Bremen, 1605).

Clemen, O., 'Schriften und Lebensausgang des Eisenacher Franziskaners Johann Hilten', *Zeitschrift für Kirchengeschichte*, 47 (n.s., 10) (1928), pp. 402–12.

Clemente da Terzorio, 'Il vero autore dell' "Teatro della Turchia" e "Stato presente della Turchi"', *Collectanea franciscana*, 3 (1933), pp. 384–95.

Clenardus [Cleynaerts], N., *Peregrinationum ac de rebus machometicis epistolae elegantissimae* (Leuven, 1550).

Clouse, R. G., 'Johann Heinrich Alsted and English Millennialism', *Harvard Theological Review*, 62 (1969), pp. 189–207.

Coccio, M. ['Coccius Sabellicus'], *Opera omnia* (Basel, 1560).

Cochlaeus [Drobneck], J., *Dialogus de bello contra Turcas, in antilogias Lutheri* (Leipzig, 1529).

Cogley, R. W., 'The Fall of the Ottoman Empire and the Restoration of Israel in the "Judeo-centric" Strand of Puritan Millenarianism', *Church History*, 72 (2003), pp. 304–32.

Colish, M. L., 'Juan Luis Vives on the Turks', *Medievalia et humanistica: Studies in Medieval and Renaissance Culture*, n.s., 35 (2009), pp. 1–14.

[Collins, A.,] *Letter from an Arabian Physician to a Famous Professor in the University of Hall in Saxony, concerning Mahomet's Taking up Arms, his Marrying of Many Wives, his Keeping of Concubines, and his Paradise* (n.p., n.d. [London, *c.*1706]).

——, *Lettre d'un médecin arabe* ('London', 1713), printed with [A. Collins,] *Discours sur la liberté de penser* ('London', 1714).

Colombo, E., 'Jesuits and Islam in Seventeenth-Century Europe: War, Preaching and Conversions', in B. Heyberger et al., eds., *L'Islam visto da Occidente: cultura e religione del Seicento europeo di fronte all'Islam* (Genoa, 2009), pp. 315–40.

Comenius [Komenský], J. A., ed., *Lux in tenebris* (n.p. [Amsterdam], 1657).

——, ed., *Lux e tenebris, novis radiis aucta* (Leiden, 1665; 2nd, enlarged edn. '1665' [1667]).

——, 'Clamores Eliae', in J. A. Comenius, *Opera omnia*, xxiii, ed. J. Otáhalová-Popelová and J. Nováková (Prague, 1992).

Connell, C. W., 'Western Views of the Origin of the "Tatars": An Example of the Influence of Myth in the Second Half of the Thirteenth Century', *Journal of Medieval and Renaissance Studies*, 3 (1973), pp. 115–37.

Conring, H., *De bello contra Turcas prudenter gerendo* (Helmstedt, 1664).

Coppin, J., *Le Bouclier de l'Europe, ou la guerre sainte, contenant des avis politiques & chrétiens, qui peuvent servir de lumière aux rois & aux souverains de la Chrêtienté, pour garantir leurs estats des incursions des Turcs, & reprendre ceux qu'ils ont usurpé sur eux* (Lyon, 1686).

Corsi Prosperi, A., 'Sulle fonti del *Viaje de Turquía*', *Critica storica*, 14 (1977), pp. 66–90.

Court, J. de la, and P. de la Court, *Consideratien van staat, ofte polityke weeg-schaal* (Amsterdam, 1661).

Covarrubias ['Covarruvias'], D. de, *Opera omnia* 2 vols. (Frankfurt am Main, 1583).

Cozzi, G., *Il doge Nicolò Contarini: ricerche sul patriziato veneziano agli inizi del seicento* (Venice, 1958).

Crahay, R.,'L'Utopie religieuse de Campanella', in M. Thiry, ed., *Hommages à Marie Delcourt* (Brussels, 1970), pp. 374–91.

Crijević Tuberon ['Tubero'], L., *Commentariorum de temporibus suis libri XI*, in J. G. Schwandtner, ed., *Scriptores rerum hungaricarum veteres, ac genuini*, 3 vols. (Vienna, 1746–8), ii, pp. 111–381.

Cristani, G., 'Teocrazia e dispotismo in Nicolas-Antoine Boulanger', in D. Felice, ed., *Dispotismo: genesi e sviluppi di un concetto filosofico-politico*, 2 vols. (Naples, 2001), i, pp. 257–80.

Croce, B., *Materialismo storico ed economia marxistica*, 5th edn. (Bari, 1927).

Crucé, É., *Le Nouveau Cynée, ou discours d'état représentant les occasions et moyens d'établir une paix générale et liberté du commerce par tout le monde*, ed. A. Fenet and A. Guillaume (Rennes, 2004).

Čvrljak, K., *Filozofija u enciklopedizmu Pavla Skalića* (Zagreb, 2004).

Daiber,T.,'Sarmatismus: Identitätsdiskurse der Frühen Neuzeit', in M. Długosz and P. O. Scholz, eds., *Sarmatismus versus Orientalismus in Mitteleuropa: Sarmatyzm versus orientalizm w Europie Środkowej* (Berlin, 2013), pp. 31–66.

Damian, I. M., 'From the "Italic League" to the "Italic Crusade": Crusading under Renaissance Popes Nicholas V and Pius II', in I. M. Damian et al., eds., *Italy and Europe's Eastern Border (1204–1669)* (Frankfurt, 2012), pp. 79–94.

Dandelet,T. J., *The Renaissance of Empire in Early Modern Europe* (Cambridge, UK, 2014).

Danes, P., *Apologie pour le Roy, contre les calomnies des Imperiaulx* (Paris, 1551).

Daniel, N., *Islam and the West: The Making of an Image* (Edinburgh, 1960).

——, *Heroes and Saracens: An Interpretation of the Chansons de Geste* (Edinburgh, 1984).

Darricau, R., 'Mazarin et l'Empire Ottoman: l'expédition de Candie (1660)', *Revue d'histoire diplomatique*, 74 (1960), pp. 335–55.

D'Ascia, L.,'L'impero macchiavellico. L'immagine della Turchia nei trattatisti italiani del Cinquecento e del primo Seicento', in F. Meier, ed., *Italien und das Osmanische Reich* (Herne, 2010), pp. 119–40.

Davis, N. Z., *Trickster Travels: A Sixteenth-Century Muslim between Worlds* (New York, 2006).

Decianus,T., *Responsorum*, 5 vols. (Venice, 1602).

Dedouvres, L., *Le Père Joseph de Paris, capucin: l'éminence grise*, 2 vols. (Paris, 1932).

Delumeau,J.,'Un ponte fra oriente e occidente:Ancona nel Cinquecento', *Quaderni storici*, 13 (1970), pp. 26–47.

De Mattei, R., 'Fonti, essenza e fortuna della "Città del sole"', *Rivista internazionale di filosofia del diritto*, 18 (1938), pp. 405–39.

——, *Il pensiero politico di Scipione Ammirato* (Milan, 1963).

——, 'Il mito della Monarchia Universale nel pensiero politico italiano del Seicento', *Rivista di studi politici internazionali*, 32 (1965), pp. 530–50.

——, *Il problema della 'ragion di stato' nell'età della Controriforma* (Milan, 1979).

Deny, J., 'Les Pseudo-prophéties concernant les Turcs au XVIe siècle', *Revue des études islamiques*, 10 (1936), pp. 201–20.

[Deshayes, L.,] *Voiage de Levant fait par le commandement du Roy en l'année 1621 par le Sr D. C.* (Paris, 1624).

Desplat, J. J., *La Boëtie, le magistrat aux nombreux mystères* (Le Bugue, 1992).

Dew, N., *Orientalism in Louis XIV's France* (Oxford, 2009).

Díaz Tanco, V., *Libro intitulado Palinodia, de la nephanda y fiera nacion de los Turcos* (Orense, 1547).

Dietze, W., *Quirinus Kuhlmann, Ketzer und Poet: Versuch einer monographischen Darstellung von Leben und Werk* (Berlin, 1963).

Diez del Corral, L., 'La città utopistica di Campanella: da Bisanzio alle Indie', in A. Pertusi, ed., *Venezia e l'oriente fra tardo medioevo e rinascimento* (Florence, 1966), pp. 309–22.

Dimmock, M., '"Captive to the Turke": Responses to the Anglo-Ottoman Capitulations of 1580', in M. Birchwood and M. Dimmock, eds. *Cultural Encounters between East and West, 1453–1699* (Newcastle-upon-Tyne, 2005), pp. 43–63.

Di Napoli, G., 'L'Eresia e i processi campanelliani', in N. Badaloni et al., *Tommaso Campanella (1568–1639): miscellanea di studi nel 4° centenario della sua nascita* (Naples, 1969), pp. 169–258.

Di Rienzo, E., 'Per una storia del concetto di dispotismo nel '700 francese: il manoscritto inedito dell'Abbé Morellet, "Sur le Despotisme légal et contre M. De la Riviere"', in V. Dini and D. Taranto, eds., *Individualismo, assolutismo, democrazia* (Naples, 1992), pp. 321–8.

Dittrich, E., *Die deutschen und österreichischen Kameralisten* (Darmstadt, 1974).

Djurdjević ['Georgievich'], B., *De Turcarum ritu et caeremoniis* (Antwerp, 1544).

—— ['Georgievits'], *Exhortatio contra Turcas* (Antwerp, 1545).

—— ['Georgievits'], *Prognoma, sive praesagium mehemetanorum* (Antwerp, 1545).

—— ['Georgewitz'], *Pro fide christiana cum turca disputationis habitae et mysterio sanctae Trinitatis in Alchorano invento... brevis descriptio* (Kraków, 1548).

Djuvara, T. G., *Cent projets de partage de la Turquie (1281–1913)* (Paris, 1914).

Dodds, M., *Les Récits de voyage, sources de L'Esprit des lois de Montesquieu* (Paris, 1929).

Domenico Hierosolimitano, *Domenico's Istanbul*, tr. M. J. L. Austin, ed. G. Lewis (Warminster, 2001).

Donado da Lezze: *see* Lezze, D. da.

Donaldson, P. S., *Machiavelli and Mystery of State* (Cambridge, UK, 1988).

Doolin, P. R., *The Fronde* (Cambridge, MA, 1935).

Dorez, L., ed., *Itinéraire de Jérome Maurand d'Antibes à Constantinople (1544)* (Paris, 1901).

Dubos, J.-B., *Histoire critique de l'établissement de la monarchie françoise dans les Gaules*, 3 vols. (Amsterdam, 1734).

Dufrenoy, M.-L., *L'Orient romanesque en France, 1704–1789: étude d'histoire et de critique littéraires*, 2 vols. (Montreal, 1946).

Dujčev, I., 'La Conquête turque et la prise de Constantinople dans la littérature slave contemporaine', *Byzantinoslavica*, 14 (1953), pp. 14–54; 16 (1955), pp. 318–29; 17 (1956), pp. 276–340.

Du Loir, N., *Les Voyages du Sieur Du Loir* (Paris, 1654).

Dumont, J. ['the Sieur du Mont'], *A New Voyage to the Levant*, tr. anon. (London, 1696).

Duparc, P., ed., *Recueil des instructions données aux ambassadeurs et ministres de France depuis les traités de Westphalie jusqu'à la révolution française*, xxix, *Turquie* (Paris, 1969).

Eck, J., *Sperandam esse in brevi victoriam adversus Turcam* (Vienna, 1532).

Ehmann, J., *Luther, Türken und Islam: eine Untersuchung zum Türken- und Islambild Martin Luthers (1515–1546)* (Heidelberg, 2008).

Eliav-Feldon, M., 'Grand Designs: The Peace Plans of the Late Renaissance', *Vivarium*, 27 (1989), no. 1, pp. 51–76.

Elmarsafy, Z., *The Enlightenment Qur'an: The Politics of Translation and the Construction of Islam* (Oxford, 2009).

Erasmus, D., *Adagiorum chiliades quatuor, centuriaeque totidem. Quibus etiam quinta additur imperfecta* (Venice, 1520).

——, *The 'Adages' of Erasmus*, tr. M. M. Phillips (Cambridge, UK, 1964).

——, *Utilissima consultatio de bello Turcis inferendo*, ed. A. G. Weiler, in J. H. Waszink et al., eds., *Opera omnia Desiderii Erasmi roterodami* (Amsterdam, 1969–), ser. 5, vol. 3 (Amsterdam, 1986), pp. 1–82.

Ernst, G., 'L'alba colomba scaccia i corbi neri: profezia e riforma in Campanella', in R. Rusconi, ed., *Storia e figure dell'Apocalisse fra '500 e '600* (Rome, 1996), pp. 107–25.

——, 'Introduzione', in Anon. [J. J. Müller], *I tre impostori: Mosè, Gesù, Maometto*, ed. G. Ernst, tr. L. Alfinito, 2nd edn. (Calabritto, 2006), pp. 5–27.

——, *Tommaso Campanella: The Book and the Body of Nature*, tr. D. L. Marshall (Dordrecht, 2010).

Esprinchard, J., *Histoire des Ottomans, ou empereurs des Turcs, iusques à Mahomet III*, 2nd edn. (Paris, 1609).

Etényi, N. G., I. Horn, and P. Szabó, *Koronás fejedelem: Bocskai István és kora* (Alapítva-Budapest, 1988).

Evert-Kappesova, H., 'La Tiare ou le turban', *Byzantinoslavica*, 14 (1953), pp. 245–57.

Fabri, F., *Evagatorium in Terrae Sanctae, Arabiae et Egypti peregrinationem*, ed. K. ['C.'] D. Hassler, 3 vols. (Stuttgart, 1843–9).

Fagniez, G., *Le Père Joseph et Richelieu (1577–1638)*, 2 vols. (Paris, 1894).

Fava, D., 'La fortuna del pronostico di Giovanni Lichtenberger in Italia nel Quattrocento e nel Cinquecento', *Gutenberg-Jahrbuch*, 5 (1930), pp. 126–48.

Febvre, M., *Specchio o vero descrizione della Turchia*, 2nd edn. (Florence, 1674).

——, *Theatre de la Turquie* (Paris, 1682).

Felice, D., 'Dispotismo e libertà nell'*Esprit des lois* de Montesquieu', in D. Felice, ed., *Dispotismo: genesi e sviluppi di un concetto filosofico-politico*, 2 vols. (Naples, 2001), i, pp. 189–255.

Fermo, S. da: *see* Serafino da Fermo.

Finlay, R., 'Al servizio del Sultano: Venezia, i Turchi e il mondo cristiano, 1523–1538', in M. Tafuri, ed., *'Renovatio urbis': Venezia nell'età di Andrea Gritti (1523–1538)* (Rome, 1984), pp. 78–118.

Firpo, L., *Bibliografia degli scritti di Tommaso Campanella* (Turin, 1940).

——, 'Una autoapologia di Campanella', *Rivista di filosofia*, n.s., 2 (= 32) (1941), pp. 96–110.

——, 'Appunti campanelliani XXII: un opere che Campanella non scrisse: Il "Discorso sui Paesi Bassi"', *Giornale critico della filosofia italiana*, 31 (1952), pp. 331–43.

——, 'Tommaso Campanella', *Dizionario biografico degli italiani* (Rome, 1960–) xvii, pp. 372–401.

——, 'Appunti campanelliani', *Giornale critico della filosofia italiana*, 41 (1962), pp. 364–404.

——, 'La città ideale di Campanella e il culto del Sole', in L. de Rosa, ed., *Ricerche storiche ed economiche in memoria di Corrado Barbagallo*, 3 vols. (Naples, 1970), pp. 377–89.

——, *Il supplizio di Tommaso Campanella: narrazioni, documenti verbali delle torture* (Rome, n.d. [1985]).

——, 'Introduzione' to T. Campanella, *La città del sole*, ed. L. Firpo, revd. G. Ernst and L. S. Firpo (Bari, 1997).

Fischer-Galaţi, S., *Ottoman Imperialism and German Protestantism, 1521–1555* (Cambridge, MA, 1959).

Flacius [Vlačić], M., et al., *Ecclesiastica historia, integram ecclesiae Christi ideam . . . secundum singulas centurias, perspicuo ordine complectens*, 8 vols. (Basel, 1560–74).

Fodor, P., 'The View of the Turk in Hungary: The Apocalyptic Tradition and the Legend of the Red Apple in Ottoman–Hungarian Context', in B. Lellouch and S. Yerasimos, eds., *Les Traditions apocalyptiques au tournant de la chute de Constantinople* (Paris, 1999), pp. 99–131.

Fonseca, C. D., ed., *Otranto 1480: atti del convegno internazionale per il V. centenario della caduta di Otranto*, 2 vols. (Galatina, 1986).

Forster, C. T., and F. H. B. Daniell, *The Life and Letters of Ogier Ghiselin de Busbecq*, 2 vols. (London, 1881).

Frachetta, G., *Il prencipe* (Venice, 1599).

Frajese, V., *Profezia e machiavellismo: il giovane Campanella* (Rome, 2002).

Fraknói, W., *Melanchthons Beziehungen zu Ungarn*, tr. A. Dux (Budapest, 1874).

Francisco, A. S., *Martin Luther and Islam: A Study in Sixteenth-Century Polemics and Apologetics* (Leiden, 2007).

François I, King of France, attrib., *Oratio de sententia Christianissimi Regis, scripta ad serenissimos, reverendissimos, illustrissimos, excellentissimos, magnificos, spectabiles viros, universósque sacri Imperii ordines Spirae conventum agentes* (Paris, 1544).

Franklin, M. J., 'Gagnier, John (*c.*1670–1740), Orientalist', *Oxford Dictionary of National Biography* (http://www.oxforddnb.com).

Freudenthal, J., *Die Lebensgeschichte Spinoza's in Quellenschriften, Urkunden und nichtamtlichen Nachrichten* (Leipzig, 1899).

Fruytiers, I., *Corte beschrijvinghe van de strenghe belegheringhe . . . der stadt Leyden* (Delft, 1577).

Füssel, S., 'Die Funktionalisierung der "Türkenfurcht" in der Propaganda Kaiser Maximilians I.', in F. Fuchs, ed., *Osmanische Expansion und europäischer Humanismus* (Wiesbaden, 2005), pp. 9–30.

Gaeta, F., 'Sulla "Lettera a Maometto" di Pio II', *Bulletino dell'Istituto Storico Italiano per il Medio Evo e archivio Muratoriano*, 77 (1965), pp. 127–227.

Gagnier, J., *La Vie de Mahomet; traduite et compilée de l'Alcoran, des traditions authentiques de la Sonna, et des meilleurs auteurs arabes*, 2 vols. (Amsterdam, 1732).

Ganz-Blättler, U., *Andacht und Abenteuer: Berichte europäischer Jerusalem- und Santiago-Pilger (1320–1520)* (Tübingen, 1990).

Gargallo, G., *Boulainvilliers e la storiografia dell'illuminismo francese* (Naples, 1954).

Garnier, É., *L'Alliance impie: François 1er et Soliman le Magnifique contre Charles Quint (1529–1547)* (Paris, 2008).

Gassot, J., *Le Discours du voyage de Venise à Constantinople, contenant la querele du grand Seigneur contre le Sophi* (Paris, 1550).

Gelder, H. A. E. van, *Getemperde vrijheid* (Groningen, 1972).

Gengoux, N., ed., *Entre la Renaissance et les Lumières, le* Theophrastus redivivus *(1659)* (Paris, 2014).

Gentili ['Gentilis'], A., *De legationibus libri tres* (Hanau, 1594; photo-reproduction, New York, 1924).

——, *Disputationum duae: I. De actoribus & spectatoribus fabularum non notandis; II. De abusu mendacii* (Hanau, 1599).

——, *De iure belli libri III* (Hanau, 1612).

——, *The Wars of the Romans: A Critical Edition and Translation of De armis romanis*, tr. D. Lupher, ed. B. Kingsbury and B. Straumann (Oxford, 2010).

Gentili ['Gentilis'], S., *Orationes rectorales: I. Pro C. Caesare; II. De re militari romana et turcica: III. De lege regia* (Nuremberg, 1600).

George of Hungary ['Georgius de Hungaria'], *Tractatus de moribus, condicionibus et nequicia Turcorum*, ed. R. Klockow (Vienna, 1993).

George-Tvrtković, R., *A Christian Pilgrim in Medieval Iraq: Riccoldo da Montecroce's Encounter with Islam* (Turnhout, 2012).

Georgewitz: *see* Djurdjević.

Geuffroy, A., *Briefve description de la court du Grant Turc et ung sommaire du regne des Othmans* (Paris, 1543).

Gherardi, R., *Potere e costituzione a Vienna fra Sei e Settecento: il 'buon ordine' di Luigi Ferdinando Marsili* (Bologna, 1980).

Ghiselin de Busbecq: *see* Busbecq.

Gibb, H. A. R., and H. Bowen, *Islamic Society and the West: A Study of the Impact of Western Civilisation on Moslem Culture in the Near East*, 2 vols. (London, 1950–7).

Gilbert, C., *Histoire de Calejava ou de l'isle des hommes raisonnables*, ed. M. S. Rivière (Exeter, 1990).

Gilles, H., 'Législation et doctrine canonique sur les Sarrasins', in E. Privat, ed., *Islam et chrétiens du Midi (XIIᵉ–XIVᵉ s.)* (Toulouse, 1983), pp. 195–213.

Giombi, S., 'La cristianità dell'Umanesimo e del Rinascimento di fronte al Turco', in G. Ruggieri, ed., *I nemici della cristianità* (Bologna, 1997), pp. 163–203.

Gios, P., ed., *Lettere di Gregorio Barbarigo a Cosimo III de' Medici (1680–1697)* (Padua, 2003).

Giovio, P., 'Consiglio di Monsignor Giovio intorno al modo di far l'impresa contra infideli', in P. Giovio, *La seconda parte dell'istorie del suo tempo . . . con un supplimento,* tr. L. Domenichi (Venice, 1560), 2nd pagination (*Supplimento di Girolamo Ruscelli nell'istorie di monsignor Giovio*), pp. 89–100.

——, *Opera quotquot extant omnia*, 5 vols. (Basel, 1575–8).

——, *Commentario de le cose de'Turchi*, ed. L. Michelacci (Bologna, 2005).

Godard d'Aucour, C., *Mémoires turcs, avec l'histoire galante de leur séjour en France* (Paris, 1743).

Gökbilgin, M. T., 'Ciğala-zâde', *Islâm ansiklopedisi*, 13 vols. (Istanbul, 1940–86), iii, pp. 161–4.

Göllner, C., 'La Milice Chrétienne, un instrument de croisade au XVIIe siècle', *Mélanges de l'École Roumaine en France*, 13 (1935–6), pp. 59–118.

—— *Turcica*, 3 vols. (Bucharest, 1961–78).

Gomez-Géraud, M.-C., *Le Crépuscule du Grand Voyage: les récits des pèlerins à Jérusalem (1458–1612)* (Paris, 1999).

——, and S. Yérasimos, 'Introduction', in N. de Nicolay, *Dans l'empire de Soliman le Magnifique*, ed. M.-C. Gomez-Géraud and S. Yérasimos (Paris, 1989), pp. 9–40.

González de Santalla, T., *Manuductio ad conversionem mahumetanorum, in duas partes divisa. In prima veritas religionis christianae catholicae romanae manifestis argumentis demonstratur. In secunda falsitas mahumetanae sectae convincitur* (Dillingen, 1689).

Gouverneur, S., *Prudence et subversion libertines: la critique de la raison d'état chez François de La Mothe le Vayer, Gabriel Naudé et Samuel Sorbière* (Paris, 2005).

Graf, T., *The Sultan's Renegades: Christian-European Converts to Islam and the Making of the Ottoman Elite, 1575–1610* (Oxford, 2017).

Gragger, R., 'Türkisch-ungarische Kulturbeziehungen', in F. Babinger et al., eds., *Literaturdenkmäler aus Ungarns Türkenzeit* (Berlin, 1927), pp. 1–32.

Gregory, T., *Theophrastus redivivus: erudizione e ateismo nel seicento* (Naples, 1979).

Grenville, H., *Observations sur l'état actuel de l'Empire Ottoman*, ed. A. S. Ehrenkreutz (Ann Arbor, MI, 1965).

Greville, F., *Certain Learned and Elegant Workes* (London, 1633).

Griswold, W. J., *The Great Anatolian Rebellion, 1000–1020 / 1591–1611* (Berlin, 1983).

Groot, A. H. de, *The Ottoman Empire and the Dutch Republic: A History of the Earliest Diplomatic Relations, 1610–1630* (Leiden, 1978).

Groote, E. von, ed., *Die Pilgerfahrt des Ritters Arnold von Harff* (Cologne, 1860).

Grotius, H., *De veritate religionis christianae*, ed. J. Leclerc ['Clericus'] (Amsterdam, 1709).

——, *De iure belli ac pacis* ['*De jure belli et pacis*'], ed. W. Whewell, 3 vols. (Cambridge, UK, 1853).

Gruber, T., 'Ungodly Paths: A History of the Idea of the Three Impostors (Moses, Jesus, Mohammad) until 1300', Oxford University DPhil dissertation (2016).

Gualdo Rosa, L., I. Nuovo, and D. Defilippis, eds., *Gli umanisti e la guerra otrantina: testi dei secoli XV e XVI* (Bari, 1982).

Guer, J.-A., *Moeurs et usages des Turcs, leur religion, leur gouvernement civil, militaire et politique, avec un abregé de l'histoire ottomane*, 2 vols. (Paris, 1747).

Guignard, F. E., comte de Saint-Priest, *Mémoires sur l'ambassade de France en Turquie et sur le commerce des français dans le Levant*, ed. C. Schefer (Paris, 1877).

Gundersheimer, W. L., *The Life and Works of Louis Le Roy* (Geneva, 1966).

Gunny, A., *Images of Islam in Eighteenth-Century Writings* (London, 1996).

Gussmann, W., 'Reipublicae christianopolitanae descriptio: eine Erinnerung an Johann Valentin Andreae zu seinem dreihundertsten Geburtstag', *Zeitschrift für kirchliche Wissenschaft und kirchliches Leben*, 7 (1886), pp. 326–33, 380–92, 434–42, 465–72, 531–48.

Guyon, L., *Les Diverses Leçons de Loys Guyon*, 3rd edn., 3 vols. (Lyon, 1617).

Haase, E., *Einführung in die Literatur des Refuge: der Beitrag der französischen Protestanten zur Entwicklung analytischer Denkformen am Ende des 17. Jahrhunderts* (Berlin, 1959).

'Habesci, E.' [A. Ghika], *The Present State of the Ottoman Empire* (London, 1784).

Hagen, G., *Ein osmanischer Geograph bei der Arbeit, Entstehung und Gedankenwelt von Kātib Čelebis Ğiinānnümā* (Berlin, 2003).

Hamilton, A., 'From "a Closet at Utrecht": Adriaan Reland and Islam', *Nederlands archief voor kerkgeschiedenis*, 78 (1998), pp. 243–50.

Hammer-Purgstall, J. von, *Geschichte des osmanischen Reiches*, 10 vols. (Budapest, 1827–35).

Hankins, J., 'Renaissance Crusaders: Humanist Crusade Literature in the Age of Mehmet II', *Dumbarton Oaks Papers*, 49 (1995), pp. 111–207.

Haran, A. Y., *Le Lys et le globe: messianisme dynastique et rêve impérial en France à l'aube des temps modernes* (Seyssel, 2000).

Harant, C., *Der christliche Ulysses, oder weit-versuchte Cavallier fürgestellt in der denckwürdigen Bereisung so wol dess Heiligen Lands als vieler andrer morgenländischer Provinzen, Landschaften und berühmter Städte* (Nuremberg, 1678).

Harrington, J., *The Commonwealth of Oceana*, in J. Harrington, *The Political Works*, ed. J. G. A. Pocock (Cambridge, UK, 1977), pp. 155–359.

——, *The Prerogative of Popular Government*, in J. Harrington, *The Political Works*, ed. J. G. A. Pocock (Cambridge, UK, 1977), pp. 389–566.

——, *Valerius and Publicola: Or, The True Form of a Popular Commonwealth Extracted e puris naturalibus*, in J. Harrington, *The Political Works*, ed. J. G. A. Pocock (Cambridge, UK, 1977), pp. 781–806.

Havas, L., and S. Kiss, 'Die Geschichtskonzeption Antonio Bonfinis', in J. Helmrath, U. Muhlack, and G. Walther, eds., *Diffusion des Humanismus: Studien zur nationalen Geschichtsschreibung europäischer Humanisten* (Göttingen, 2002), pp. 281–308.

Headley, J. M., 'The Habsburg World Empire and the Revival of Ghibellinism', *Medieval and Renaissance Studies*, 7 (1978), pp. 93–127.

——, '"Ehe Türkisch als Bäpstisch": Lutheran Reflections on the Problem of Empire, 1623–8', *Central European History*, 20 (1987), pp. 3–28.

——, *Tommaso Campanella and the Transformation of the World* (Princeton, NJ, 1997).

——, 'The Reception of Campanella's *Monarchia di Spagna* in Spain and the Empire', in J.-L. Fournel et al., *Tommaso Campanella e l'attesa del secolo aureo* (Florence, 1998), pp. 89–105.

Heath, M. J., 'Renaissance Scholars and the Origins of the Turks', *Bibliothèque d'humanisme et renaissance*, 41 (1979), pp. 453–71.

Heberer, M., *Aegyptiaca servitus, das ist, Warhafte Beschreibung einer dreyjährigen Dienstbarkeit, so in Alexandrien in Egypten ihren Anfang, vnd zu Constantinopel ihr Endschafft genommen* (Heidelberg, n.d. [1610?]).

Heers, J., and G. de Heyer, eds., *Itinéraire d'Anselme Adorno en Terre Sainte (1470–1471)* (Paris, 1978).

Helmrath, J., 'Pius II. und die Türken', in B. Guthmüller and W. Kühlmann, eds., *Europa und die Türken in der Renaissance* (Tübingen, 2000), pp. 79–137.

Helvétius, C. A., *De l'esprit*, 2nd edn., 2 vols. (Paris, 1758).

Herbelot, B. d', *Bibliothèque orientale, ou dictionaire universel, contenant tout ce qui regarde la connoissance des peuples de l'Orient* (Paris, 1697).

Hess, A. C., 'The Moriscos: An Ottoman Fifth Column in Sixteenth-Century Spain', *American Historical Review*, 74 (1968), 1–25.

Heydte, F. A. Freiherr von der, 'Die Stellung Fénelons in der Geschichte der Staatstheorien' in J. Kraus and J. Calvet, eds., *Fénelon: Persönlichkeit und Werk* (Baden-Baden, 1953), pp. 307–17.

Hill, A., *A Full and Just Account of the Present State of the Ottoman Empire in All its Branches: With the Government, and Policy, Religion, Customs, and Way of Living of the Turks, in General* (London, 1709).

Hobbes, T., *The Elements of Law*, ed. F. Tönnies (London, 1889).

——, *De cive: The Latin Version*, ed. H. Warrender (Oxford, 1983).

——, *The Correspondence*, ed. N. Malcolm, 2 vols. (Oxford, 1994).

——, *Writings on Common Law and Hereditary Right: A Dialogue between a Philosopher and a Student, of the Common Laws of England*, ed. A. Cromartie, and *Questions Relative to Hereditary Right*, ed. Q. Skinner (Oxford, 2005).

——, *Behemoth or the Long Parliament*, ed. P. Seaward (Oxford, 2010).

——, *Leviathan*, ed. N. Malcolm, 3 vols. (Oxford, 2012).

Hochedlinger, M., 'Die französisch-osmanische "Freundschaft", 1525–1792: Element antihabsburgischer Politik, Gleichgewichtsinstrument, Prestigeunternehmung—Aufriss eines Problems', *Mitteilungen des Instituts für Österreichische Geschichtsforschung*, 102 (1994), pp. 108–64.

Höfert, A., *Den Feind beschreiben: 'Türkengefahr' und europäisches Wissen über das Osmanische Reich, 1450–1600* (Frankfurt am Main, 2003).

Hofmann, M., *Theologie, Dogma und Dogmenentwicklung im theologischen Werk Denis Petau's* (Frankfurt am Main, 1976).

Holt, P. M., *A Seventeenth-Century Defender of Islam: Henry Stubbe (1632–76) and His Book* (London, 1972).

——, 'Ockley, Simon (*bap.* 1679, *d.* 1720), Orientalist', *Oxford Dictionary of National Biography* (http://www.oxforddnb.com).

Hottinger, J. H., *Historia orientalis*, 1st edn. (Zurich, 1651).

——, *Historia orientalis*, 2nd edn. (Zurich, 1660).

Hotson, H., *Paradise Postponed: Johann Heinrich Alsted and the Birth of Calvinist Millenarianism* (Dordrecht, 2000).

Housley, N., *The Later Crusades: From Lyons to Alcazar, 1274–1580* (Oxford, 1992).

——, *Crusading and the Ottoman Threat, 1453–1505* (Oxford, 2012).

Howard, D. A., 'Ottoman Historiography and the Literature of "Decline" of the Sixteenth and Seventeenth Centuries', *Journal of Asian History*, 22 (1988), pp. 52–77.

Hoyland, R. G., *Seeing Islam as Others Saw It: A Survey and Evaluation of Christian, Jewish and Zoroastrian Writings on Early Islam* (Princeton, NJ, 1997).

Hughes, P., 'Servetus and the Quran', *Journal of Unitarian Universalist History*, 30 (2005), pp. 55–70.

——, 'In the Footsteps of Servetus: Biandrata, Dávid, and the Quran', *Journal of Unitarian Universalist History*, 31 (2006–7), pp. 57–63.

Huillard-Bréholles, J.-L.-A., *Historia diplomatica Friderici Secundi, sive constitutiones, privilegia, mandata, instrumenta quae supersunt istius imperatoris et filiorum ejus*, vol. v, part 1 (Paris, 1857).

Huit, E., *The Whole Prophecie of Daniel explained* (London, 1644).

Hultsch, P., *Der Orient in der deutschen Barockliteratur* (Lengerich, 1936).

Humbert, J., 'Charles de Nevers et la Milice Chrétienne, 1598–1625', *Revue internationale d'histoire militaire*, 68 (1987), pp. 85–109.

Huppert, G., *The Style of Paris: Renaissance Origins of the French Enlightenment* (Bloomington, IN, 1999).

İnalcık, H., *The Ottoman Empire: The Classical Age, 1300–1600* (London, 1973).

Irwin, R., *For Lust of Knowing: The Orientalists and their Enemies* (London, 2006).

Irwin, T. H., 'Splendid Vices? Augustine for and against Pagan Virtues', *Medieval Philosophy and Theology*, 8 (1999), pp. 105–27.

Isom-Verhaaren, C., *Allies with the Infidel: The Ottoman and French Alliance in the Sixteenth Century* (London, 2011).

Israel, J. I., *Radical Enlightenment: Philosophy and the Making of Modernity, 1650–1750* (Oxford, 2001).

Jacob, J. R., *Henry Stubbe, Radical Protestantism and the Early Enlightenment* (Cambridge, UK, 1982).

James VI, King of Scotland, *The Poems*, ed. J. Craigie, 2 vols. (= The Scottish Text Society, ser. 3, xxii, xxvi) (Edinburgh, 1955–8).

Jankovics, J., 'The Image of the Turks in Hungarian Renaissance Literature', in B. Guthmüller and W. Kühlmann, eds., *Europa und die Türken in der Renaissance* (Tübingen, 2000), pp. 267–73.

Jaroszewska, T., 'À la découverte de l'Europe de l'Est: *Tractatus de duabus Sarmatiis, Asiana et Europiana*, de Mathias de Miechow (1517)', in E. Berriot-Salvadore, ed., *Les Représentations de l'autre du moyen âge au XVIIe siècle* (Saint-Étienne, 1995), pp. 17–30.

Jaucourt, L. de, 'Turquie', in D. Diderot and J. le Rond d'Alembert, eds., *L'Encyclopédie ou Dictionnaire raisonné des sciences, des arts et des métiers*, 28 vols. (Paris, 1751–72), xvi, pp. 755–9.

Jembrih, A., *Hrvatski filološki zapisi* (Zagreb, 1997).

Jesu, T. à: see Thomas à Jesu

Joachim of Fiore, *Liber de concordia Noui ac Veteris Testamenti*, ed. E. R. Daniel, Transactions of the American Philosophical Society, 73, part 8 (Philadelphia, 1983).

——, *Sull'apocalisse* [*Enchiridion super apocalypsim*], ed. and tr. A. Tagliapietra (Milan, 1994).

Johannesson, K., *The Renaissance of the Goths in Sixteenth-Century Sweden: Johannes and Olaus Magnus as Politicians and Historians*, tr. J. Larson (Berkeley, CA, 1991).

Johnson, J. T., *Ideology, Reason, and the Limitations of Law: Religious and Secular Concepts, 1200–1740* (Princeton, NJ, 1975).

Jonas, J., *Das siebend Capitel Danielis, von des Türcken Gottes lesterung und schrecklicher mörderey, mit unterricht Justi Jonae* (Wittenberg, 1530).

Jug, S., 'Turški napadi na Kranjsko in Primorsko do prve tretjine 16. stoletja', *Glasnik muzejskega društva za Slovenijo*, 24 (1943), pp. 1–61.

Kafker, F. A., and S. L. Kafker, *The Encyclopedists as Individuals: A Biographical Dictionary of the Authors of the* Encyclopédie (Oxford, 1988).

Kaiser, T., 'The Evil Empire? The Debate on Turkish Despotism in Eighteenth-Century French Political Culture', *Journal of Modern History*, 72 (2000), pp. 6–34.

Katz, D. S., *Philo-Semitism and the Readmission of the Jews to England, 1603–1655* (Oxford, 1982).

Kaufmann, T., '1600—Deutungen der Jahrhundertwende im deutschen Luthertum', in Manfred Jakubowski-Tiessen et al., eds., *Jahrhundertwenden: Endzeit- und Zukunftsvorstellungen vom 15. bis zum 20. Jahrhundert* (Göttingen, 1999), pp. 73–128.

Kedar, B. Z., *Crusade and Mission: European Approaches toward the Muslims* (Princeton, NJ, 1984).

Kejř, J., ed., 'Tractatus pacis toti christianitati fiendae', in F. Kavka, V. Outrata, and J. Polišenský, eds., *The Universal Peace Organization of King George of Bohemia: A Fifteenth-Century Plan for World Peace, 1462/1464* (Prague, 1964).

Kersken, N., 'Geschichtsbild und Adelsrepublik: zur Sarmatentheorie in der polnischen Geschichtsschreibung der frühen Neuzeit', *Jahrbücher für Geschichte Osteuropas*, 52 (2004), pp. 235–60.

Khoury, A.-T., *Polémique byzantine contre l'Islam (VIIIᵉ–XIIIᵉ s.)*, 2nd edn. (Leiden, 1972).

Kingsbury, B., and B. Straumann, eds., *The Roman Foundations of the Law of Nations: Alberico Gentili and the Justice of Empire* (Oxford, 2010).

Kiss, F. G., 'Political Rhetorics in the Anti-Ottoman Literature: Martinus Thyrnavinus: To the Dignitaries of the Hungarian Kingdom', in N. Spannenberger, Sz. Varga, and R. Pech, eds., *Ein Raum im Wandel: die osmanisch-habsburgische Grenzregion vom 16. bis zum 18. Jahrhundert* (Stuttgart, 2014), pp. 141–57.

Kissling, H.-J., 'Die Türkenfrage als europäisches Problem', *Südostdeutsches Archiv*, 7 (1964), pp. 39–57.

——, 'Militärisch-politische Problematiken zur Türkenfrage im 15. Jahrhundert', *Bohemia: Jahrbuch des Collegium Carolinum*, 5 (1964), pp. 108–36.

——, *Sultan Bayezid's II. Beziehungen zu Markgraf Francesco II. von Gonzaga* (Munich, 1965).

Klein, D., 'Muslimischer Antitrinitarismus im lutherischen Rostock: Zacharias Grapius der Jüngere und die *Epistola theologica* des Ahmad ibn 'Abdallah', in D. Klein and B. Platow, eds., *Wahrnehmung des Islam zwischen Reformation und Aufklärung* (Munich, 2008), pp. 41–60.

Klockow, R., 'Einleitung', in George of Hungary ['Georgius de Hungaria'], *Tractatus de moribus, condicionibus et nequicia Turcorum*, ed. R. Klockow (Vienna, 1993), pp. 11–142.

Knolles, R., *The Generall Historie of the Turks from the First Beginning of That Nation to the Rise of the Ottoman Familie*, 2nd edn. (London, 1610).

444

Koebner, R., 'Despot and Despotism: Vicissitudes of a Political Term', *Journal of the Warburg and Courtauld Institutes*, 14 (1951), pp. 275–302.

Köhbach, M., 'Caesar oder imperator? Zur Titulatur der römischen Kaiser durch die Osmanen nach dem Vertrag von Zsitvatorok (1606)', *Wiener Zeitschrift für die Kunde des Morgenlandes*, 82 (1992), pp. 223–34.

Kohler, A., *Ferdinand I. 1503–1564: Fürst, König und Kaiser* (Munich, 2003).

Köhler, M., *Melanchthon und der Islam: ein Beitrag zur Klärung des Verhältnisses zwischen Christentum und Fremdreligionen in der Reformationszeit* (Leipzig, 1938).

Kołodziejczyk, D., *Ottoman–Polish Diplomatic Relations (15th–18th Century): An Annotated Edition of 'Ahdnames and Other Documents* (Leiden, 2000).

Komatsu, G., 'Die Türkei und das europäische Staatensystem in 16. Jahrhundert: Untersuchungen zu Theorie und Praxis des frühneuzeitlichen Völkerrechts', in C. Roll, B. Braun, and H. Stratenwerth, eds., *Recht und Reich im Zeitalter der Reformation: Festschrift für Horst Rabe*, 2nd edn. (Frankfurt am Main, 1997), pp. 121–44.

Koningsveld, P. S. van, 'The Islamic Image of Paul and the Origin of the Gospel of Barnabas', *Jerusalem Studies in Arabic and Islam*, 20 (1996), pp. 200–21.

Koser, R., *Die Kanzleienstreit: ein Beitrag zur Quellenkunde der Geschichte des dreissigjährigen Krieges* (Halle, 1874).

Kreutel, R. F., ed. and tr., *Der fromme Sultan Bayezid: die Geschichte seiner Herrschaft (1481–1512) nach den altosmanischen Chroniken des Oruç und des Anonymus Hanivaldanus* (Graz, 1978).

Kritzeck, J., *Peter the Venerable and Islam* (Princeton, NJ, 1964).

Krstić, T., 'Of Translation and Empire: Sixteenth-Century Ottoman Imperial Interpreters as Renaissance Go-Betweens', in C. Woodhead, ed., *The Ottoman World* (Abingdon, 2012), pp. 130–42.

Krueger, P., et al., eds., *Corpus iuris civilis*, 3 vols. (Berlin, 1911–12).

Kükelhaus, T., *Der Ursprung des Planes vom ewigen Frieden in den Memoiren des Herzogs von Sully* (Berlin, 1893).

Kuntz, M. L., *Guillaume Postel and the Restitution of All Things: His Life and Thought* (The Hague, 1981).

Kürkçüoğlu, Ö., 'The Adoption and Use of Permanent Diplomacy', in A. N. Yurdusev, ed., *Ottoman Diplomacy: Conventional or Unconventional?* (Basingstoke, 2004), pp. 131–50.

Kurze, D., *Johannes Lichtenberger († 1503): eine Studie zur Geschichte der Prophetie und Astrologie* (Lübeck, 1960).

La Boétie ['Boétie'], E. de, *De la servitude volontaire ou le contr'un*, ed. N. Gontabert, with: La Boétie, *Mémoire touchant l'édit de janvier 1562*, ed. A. Prassoloff (Paris, 1993).

Laguna, A., *Europa heautentimorumene, es decir, que míseramente a sí misma se atormenta y lamenta su propia desgracia*, ed. and tr. M. Á. González Manjarrés (Valladolid, 2001).

Landucci, S., 'Il punto sul "De tribus impostoribus"', *Rivista storica italiana*, 112 (2000), pp. 1036–71.

La Noue, F. de, *Discours politiques et militaires . . . nouvellement recueillis & mis en lumiere* (Basel, 1587).

Laugier de Tassy, J. P., *Histoire du royaume d'Alger, avec l'état présent de son gouvernement, de ses forces de terre & de mer, de ses revenus, police, justice, politique & commerce* (Amsterdam, 1725).

Laurens, H., *Aux sources de l'orientalisme: la Bibliothèque orientale de Barthélemi d'Herbelot* (Paris, 1978).

——, *Les Origines intellectuelles de l'expédition d'Égypte: l'orientalisme islamisant en France (1698–1798)* (Istanbul, 1987).

Lecler, J., *Toleration and the Reformation*, tr. T. L. Westow, 2 vols. (New York, 1960).

Lefaivre, A., *Les Magyars pendant la domination ottomane en Hongrie (1526–1722)*, 2 vols. (Paris, 1902).

Le Guay, G., *Alliances du Roy avec le Turc, et autres: iustifiés contre les calomnies des Espagnols & de leurs partisans* (Paris, 1625).

Leibniz, G. W., *Sämtliche Schriften und Briefe*, ed. Deutsche Akademie der Wissenschaften zu Berlin (Darmstadt, Berlin, 1923–).

——, 'Justa dissertatio', in *Sämtliche Schriften und Briefe*, ed. Deutsche Akademie der Wissenschaften zu Berlin (Darmstadt, Berlin, 1923–), Reihe 4, i, pp. 267–382.

Lemmens, L., 'De sancto Francisco Christum praedicante coram sultano Aegypti', *Archivum franciscanum historicum*, 19 (1926), pp. 559–78.

Lemny, S., *Les Cantemir: l'aventure européenne d'une famille princière au XVIIᵉ siècle* (n.p. [Paris], 2009).

Lerner, R. E., *The Powers of Prophecy: The Cedar of Lebanon Vision from the Mongol Onslaught to the Dawn of the Enlightenment* (Ithaca, NY, 2008).

Le Roy, L., *Oratio ad invictissimos potentissimósque principes Henricum II. Franc. & Philippum Hispan. Reges, de pace & concordia nuper inter eas inita, & bello religionis Christianae hostibus inferendo* (Paris, 1559).

——, *Des troubles et differents advenans entre les hommes par la diversité des religions* (Paris, 1567).

——, *Les Politiques d'Aristote, esquelles est monstree la science de gouverner le genre humain en toutes especes d'estats publics* (Paris, 1568).

——, *De la vicissitude ou variété des choses en l'univers, et concurrence des armes et des lettres par les premières et plus illustres nations du monde* (Paris, 1576).

Lestringant, F., 'Guillaume Postel et "l'obsession turque"', in J.-C. Margolin, ed., *Guillaume Postel, 1581–1981* (Paris, 1985), pp. 265–98.

——, 'La Monarchie française au miroir ottoman: le portrait de Soliman le Magnifique, de Charles IX à Henri III', in G. Veinstein, ed., *Soliman le Magnifique et son temps* (Paris, 1992), pp. 51–68.

Letts, M., ed., *Mandeville's Travels: Texts and Translations*, 2 vols. (London, 1953).

Leunclavius [Löwenklau], J., *Historiae musulmanae Turcorum de monumentis ipsorum exscriptae libri xviii* (Frankfurt am Main, 1591).

Leva, G. de, ed., *La legazione di Roma di Paolo Paruta (1592–1595)*, 3 vols. (Venice, 1887).

[Levassor, M.,] *Les Soupirs de la France esclave, qui aspire après la liberté* (n.p., 1689).

Levitin, D., *Ancient Wisdom in the Age of the New Science: Histories of Philosophy in England, c.1640–1700* (Cambridge, UK, 2015).

Levy, D. G., *The Ideas and Careers of Simon-Nicolas-Henri Linguet: A Study in Eighteenth-Century French Politics* (Urbana, IL, 1980).

Lezze, D. da, *Historia turchesca (1300–1514)*, ed. I. Ursu (Bucharest, 1909).

Linguet, S.-N.-H., *Le Fanatisme des philosophes* (Abbeville, 1764).

——, *Théorie des loix civiles, ou principes fondamentaux de la société*, 2 vols. ('London', 1767).

——, *Réponse aux docteurs modernes, ou apologie pour l'auteur de la théorie des loix, et des lettres sur cette théorie* (n.p., 1771).

——, *Du plus heureux gouvernement, ou parallele des constitutions politiques de l'Asie avec celles de l'Europe*, 2 vols. ('London', 1774).

Lipsius, J., *De militia romana libri quinque, commentarius ad Polybium* (Antwerp, 1596).

Lisy-Wagner, L., *Islam, Christianity and the Making of Czech Identity, 1453–1683* (Farnham, 2013).

Lithgow, W., *The Totall Discourse of the Rare Adventures & Painefull Peregrinations of Long Nineteene Yeares Travayles from Scotland to the most Famous Kingdomes in Europe, Asia and Affrica* (Glasgow, 1906).

Lloyd, H. A., *Jean Bodin, 'This Pre-eminent Man of France': An Intellectual Biography* (Oxford, 2017).

Loop, J., *Johann Heinrich Hottinger: Arabic and Islamic Studies in the Seventeenth Century* (Oxford, 2013).

Lucinge, R. de, *Dell'origine, conservazione, et decadenza de gli stati*, tr. G. Naselli, with *Un discorso del S. Conte Horatio Malaguzzi sopra i cinque potentati maggiori del mondo* (Ferrara, 1590).

——, *De la naissance, durée et chute des estats*, ed. M. J. Heath (Geneva, 1984).

Lukes, T. J., 'To Bamboozle with Goodness: The Political Advantages of Christianity in the Thought of Machiavelli', *Renaissance and Reformation*, n.s., 8 (1984), pp. 266–77.

Luther, M., *Resolutiones disputationum de indulgentiarum virtute*, in his *Werke*, i (Weimar, 1883), pp. 525–628.

——, *Assertio omnium articulorum M. Lutheri per bullam Leonis X. novissimam damnatorum*, in his *Werke*, vii (Weimar, 1897), pp. 94–151.

——, *Unterricht der Visitatorn an die Pfarhern ym Kurfurstenthum zu Sachssen*, in his *Werke*, xxvi (Weimar, 1909), pp. 195–240.

——, *Vom Kriege widder die Türcken*, in his *Werke*, xxx, part 2 (Weimar, 1909), pp. 107–48.

——, *Eine Heerpredigt widder den Türcken*, in his *Werke*, xxx, part 2 (Weimar, 1909), pp. 160–97.

——, 'Vorwort' to *Libellus de ritu et moribus Turcorum*, in his *Werke*, xxx, part 2 (Weimar, 1909), pp. 198–208.

Lutz, H., *Ragione di stato und christliche Staatsethik im 16. Jahrhundert* (Münster in Westfalen, 1961).

Machiavelli, N., *Libro della arte della guerra* (Florence, 1521).

——, *Il principe*, in N. Machiavelli, *Opere*, ed. M. Bonfantini (Milan, 1954), pp. 1–86.

——, *Istorie fiorentine*, in N. Machiavelli, *Opere*, ed. M. Bonfantini (Milan, 1954), pp. 561–980.

——, *Opere letterarie*, ed. A. Borlenghi (Naples, 1969).

——, *Opere*, ed. F. Gaeta (Turin, 1984).

——, *Discorsi sopra la prima deca di Tito Livio*, ed. F. Bausi, in E. Malato et al., eds., *Edizione nazionale delle opere di Niccolò Machiavelli*, section 1, vol. 2, tomes i–ii (Rome, 2001).

MacKay, P. A., 'The Content and Authorship of the *Historia Turchesca*', in S. Atasoy, ed., *İstanbul Üniversitesi 550. yıl, Uluslararası Bizans ve Osmanlı Sempozyumu (XV. yüzyıl)* (Istanbul, 2004), pp. 213–223.

Maclean, G., *The Rise of Oriental Travel: English Visitors to the Ottoman Empire, 1580–1720* (Basingstoke, 2004).

Malcolm, N., *Aspects of Hobbes* (Oxford, 2002).

——, 'The Crescent and the City of the Sun: Islam and the Renaissance Utopia of Tommaso Campanella', *Proceedings of the British Academy*, 125 (2003), 41–67.

——, 'Jean Bodin and the Authorship of the *Colloquium heptaplomeres*', *Journal of the Warburg and Courtauld Institutes*, 69 (2006), pp. 95–150.

——, 'Comenius, Boyle, Oldenburg, and the Translation of the Bible into Turkish', *Church History and Religious Culture*, 87 (2007), pp. 327–62.

——, 'Comenius, the Conversion of the Turks, and the Muslim–Christian Debate on the Corruption of Scripture', *Church History and Religious Culture*, 87 (2007), pp. 477–508.

——, *Reason of State, Propaganda, and the Thirty Years' War: An Unknown Translation by Thomas Hobbes* (Oxford, 2007).

——, 'Alberico Gentili and the Ottomans', in B. Kingsbury and B. Straumann, eds., *The Roman Foundations of the Law of Nations: Alberico Gentili and the Justice of Empire* (Oxford, 2010), pp. 127–45.

——, 'The 1649 English Translation of the Koran: Its Origins and Significance', *Journal of the Warburg and Courtauld Institutes*, 75 (2012), pp. 261–95.

——, 'Positive Views of Islam and of Ottoman Rule in the Sixteenth Century: The Case of Jean Bodin', in A. Contadini and C. Norton, eds., *The Renaissance and the Ottoman World* (Farnham, 2013), pp. 197–217.

——, *Agents of Empire: Knights, Corsairs, Jesuits and Spies in the Sixteenth-Century Mediterranean World* (London, 2015).

——, 'Thomas Hobbes: Liberal Illiberal', *Journal of the British Academy*, 4 (2016), pp. 113–36.

Mallett, M. E., and J. R. Hale, *The Military Organization of a Renaissance State* (Cambridge, UK, 1984).

Malvezzi, A., *L'Islamismo e la cultura europea* (Florence, 1956).

Mangey, T., *Remarks upon Nazarenus, wherein the Falsity of Mr Toland's Mahometan Gospel, and his Misrepresentation of Mahometan Sentiments in Respect of Christianity, are Set Forth* (London, 1718).

Marana, G. P., *L'Espion du Grand Seigneur, et ses relations secretes envoyées au Divan de Constantinople; & découvertes à Paris, pendant le Regne, de Louis le Grand* ('Amsterdam', 1684).

Marchand, S. L., *German Orientalism in the Age of Empire: Religion, Race, and Scholarship* (Cambridge, UK, 2009).

Marenbon, J., *Pagans and Philosophers: The Problem of Paganism from Augustine to Leibniz* (Princeton, NJ, 2015).

Margolin, J.-C., 'Erasme et la güerre contre les Turcs', *Il pensiero politico*, 13 (1980), pp. 3–38.

———, 'Conscience européenne et réaction à la menace turque d'après le "De dissidiis Europae et bello turcico" de Vivès (1526)', in A. Beck, ed., *Juan Luis Vives: Arbeitsgespräch in der Herzog August Bibliothek Wolfenbüttel vom 6. bis 8. November 1980* (Hamburg, 1981), pp. 107–40.

———, ed., *Guillaume Postel, 1581–1981* (Paris, 1985).

Marolles, M. de, *Suitte des memoires de Michel de Marolles, abbé de Villeloin* (Paris, 1657).

Maróth, M., 'The Library of Sultan Bayazit II', in É. M. Jeremiás, ed., *Irano-Turkic Cultural Contacts in the 11th–17th Centuries* (Piliscsaba, 2003), pp. 111–32.

Marracci, L., *Prodromus ad refutationem Alcorani* (Padua, 1698).

Marsigli, L. F., *Stato militare dell'Imperio Ottomano, incremento e decremento del medesimo: L'État militaire de l'Empire Ottoman, ses progrès et sa décadence* (The Hague, 1732).

Mas, A., *Les Turcs dans la littérature espagnole du siècle d'or*, 2 vols. (Paris, 1967).

Massignon, L., 'La Légende "De tribus impostoribus" et ses origines islamiques', *Revue de l'histoire des religions*, 82 (1920), pp. 74–8.

Matanic, A., 'L'idea e l'attività per la crociata anti-turca del papa Pio II (1458–64)', *Studi francescani*, 61 (1964), pp. 382–94.

Matar, N., *Henry Stubbe and the Beginnings of Islam: The Originall & Progress of Mahometanism* (New York, 2014).

Mayer, C.-A., *Lucien de Samosate et la Renaissance française* (Geneva, 1984).

Mede, J., *The Key of the Revelation* (London, 1643).

Melanchthon, P., *Commentarii in aliquot politicos libros Aristotelis*, in *Corpus reformatorum*, 101 vols. (Halle, 1834–1959), xvi, cols. 416–51.

———, *Epistolae, iudicia, consilia, testimonia aliorumque ad eum epistolae quae in Corpore Reformatorum desiderantur*, ed. H. E. Bindseil (Halle, 1874).

Ménage, V. L., *Neshri's History of the Ottomans: The Sources and Development of the Text* (London, 1964).

Menavino, G. A., *I cinque libri della legge, religione, et vita de' Turchi: et della corte, & d'alcune guerre del Gran Turco* (Venice, 1548).

Mérigoux, J.-M., 'L'Ouvrage d'un frère prêcheur florentin en Orient à la fin du XIIIᵉ siècle', in E. Panella, ed., *Fede e controversia nel '300 e '500* (Pistoia, 1986) [= *Memorie domenicane*, n.s., 17 (1986)], pp. 1–144.

Merle, A., 'Introduction', in P. Belon, *Voyage au Levant (1553): les observations de Pierre Belon du Mans de plusieurs singularités & chose mémorables, trouvées en Grèce, Turquie, Judée, Égypte, Arabie & autres pays étranges*, ed. A. Merle (Paris, 2001), pp. 7–48.

———, *Le Miroir ottoman: une image politique des hommes dans la littérature géographique espagnole et française (XVIᵉ–XVIIᵉ siècles)* (Paris, 2003).

Mertens, D., 'Europäischer Friede und Türkenkrieg im Spätmittelalter', in H. Duchhardt, ed., *Zwischenstaatliche Friedenswahrung in Mittelalter und Früher Neuzeit* (Cologne, 1991), pp. 45–90.

———, ' "Europa, id est patria, domus propria, sedes nostra ...": zu Funktionen und Überlieferung lateinischer Türkenreden im 15. Jahrhundert', in F.-R. Erkens, ed., *Europa und die osmanische Expansion im ausgehenden Mittelalter* (Berlin, 1997), pp. 39–57.

Meserve, M., *Empires of Islam in Renaissance Historical Thought* (Cambridge, MA, 2008).

Meulen, J. ter, *Der Gedanke der internationalen Organisation in seiner Entwicklung 1300–1800*, 2 vols. (The Hague, 1917–29).

Meulen, R. van der, 'Liever turksch dan paapsch', *Tidschrift voor nederlandsche taal- en letterkunde*, 53 (1934), pp. 117–23.

Meuthen, E., 'Der Fall von Konstantinopel und der lateinische Westen', *Historische Zeitschrift*, 237 (1983), pp. 1–35.

Mignot, V., *Histoire de l'empire ottoman, depuis son origine jusqu'à la paix de Belgrade en 1740*, 4 vols. (Paris, 1771).

Minadoi, G. T., *Historia della guerra fra Turchi, et Persiani, descritta in quattro libri* (Turin, 1588).

Minerbi Belgrado, A., *Paura e ignoranza: studio sulla teoria della religione in d'Holbach* (Florence, 1983).

Minois, G., *Le Traité des trois imposteurs: histoire d'un livre blasphématoire qui n'existait pas* (Paris, 2009).

Minuti, R., *Orientalismo e idee di tolleranza nella cultura francese del primo '700* (Florence, 2006).

Möhring, H., *Der Weltkaiser der Endzeit: Entstehung, Wandel und Wirkung einer tausendjährigen Weissagung* (Stuttgart, 2000).

Molen, G. H. J. van der, *Alberico Gentili and the Development of International Law: His Life, Work and Times* (Amsterdam, 1937).

Monfasani, J., *George of Trebizond: A Biography, and a Study of his Rhetoric and Logic* (Leiden, 1976).

Montaigne, M. de, *Les Essais*, ed. P. Villey, 3 vols. (Paris, 1930).

Montalbani, G. B. ['J. B. Montalbanus'], *De moribus Turcarum commentarius* (Rome, 1625).

——, et al., *Turcici imperii status* (Leiden, 1630).

Montesquieu, C.-L. de Secondat, baron de La Brède et de, *Lettres persanes*, in Montesquieu, *Oeuvres complètes*, ed. D. Oster (Paris, 1964), pp. 61–151.

——, *Considérations sur les causes de la grandeur des Romains et de leur décadence*, in Montesquieu, *Oeuvres complètes*, ed. D. Oster (Paris, 1964), pp. 435–85.

——, *De l'esprit des lois*, in Montesquieu, *Oeuvres complètes*, ed. D. Oster (Paris, 1964), pp. 528–795.

——, *Pensées; Le Spicilège*, ed. L. Desgraves (Paris: 1991).

——, *Réflexions sur la monarchie universelle en Europe*, ed. M. Porret (Geneva, 2000).

——, *L'Atelier de Montesquieu: manuscrits inédits de La Brède*, ed. C. Volpilhac-Auger and C. Bustarret (Naples, 2001).

Moquot, É. ['T. Cogamandolus'], *Secreta secretorum: calvino-turcica secreta eorundemque apocalypsis* (n.p., 1621).

Mornay, P. de, *De la vérité de la religion chrestienne: contre les athées, Epicuriens, payens, Juifs, Mahumedistes, & autres infidèles* (Antwerp, 1581).

Mothu, A., 'Guillaume Postel, le *Traité des trois imposteurs* et les athées de Caen', *La Lettre clandestine*, 17 (2009), pp. 195–204.

Motika, R., 'Adam Neuser, ein Heidelberger Theologe im Osmanischen Reich', in S. Prätor and C. K. Neumann, eds., *Frauen, Bilder und Gelehrte: Studien zu Gesellschaft und Künsten im Osmanischen Reich*, 2 vols. (Istanbul, 2002), ii, pp. 523–38.

Mout, M. E. H. N., 'Calvinoturcisme in de zeventiende eeuw: Comenius, Leidse orientalisten en de Turkse bijbel', *Tijdschrift voor geschiedenis*, 91 (1978), pp. 576–607.

——, 'Turken in het nieuws. Beeldvorming en publieke opinie in de zestiende eeuwse Nederlanden', *Tijdschrift voor geschiedenis*, 97 (1984), pp. 362–81.

[Müller, J. J.,] *De imposturis religionum (De tribus impostoribus), Von den Betrügereyen der Religionen*, ed. W. Schröder (Stuttgart, 1999).

Müller, R. C., *Franken im Osten: Art, Umfang, Struktur und Dynamik der Migration aus dem lateinischen Westen in das Osmanische Reich des 15./16. Jahrhunderts auf der Grundlage von Reiseberichten* (Leipzig, 2005).

——, *Prosopographie der Reisenden und Migranten ins Osmanische Reich (1396–1611) (Berichterstatter aus dem Heiligen Römischen Reich, ausser burgundische Gebiete und Reichsromania)*, 10 vols. (Leipzig, 2006).

Mulsow, M., 'The "New Socinians": Intertextuality and Cultural Exchange in Late Socinianism', in M. Mulsow and J. Rohls, eds., *Socinianism and Arminianism: Antitrinitarians, Calvinists and Cultural Exchange in Seventeenth-Century Europe* (Leiden, 2005), pp. 49–78.

——, 'Fluchträume und Konversionsräume zwischen Heidelberg und Istanbul: der Fall Adam Neuser', in M. Mulsow, ed., *Kriminelle—Freidenker—Alchemisten* (Cologne, 2014), pp. 33–60.

Mureşan, D. I., 'La Croisade en projets: plans présentés au Grand Quartier Général de la croisade, le Collège des cardinaux', in J. Paviot, ed., *Les Projets de croisade: géostratégie et diplomatie européenne du XIVᵉ au XVIIᵉ siècle* (Toulouse, 2014), pp. 247–86.

Musculus, A., *Beider Antichrist, des Constantinopolitanischen, und Römischen, einstimmig und gleichförmig Leer, Glauben, und Religion, wieder Christum den Son dess lebendigen Gottes* (Frankfurt an der Oder, 1557).

Naff, T., 'The Ottoman Empire and the European State System', in H. Bull and A. Watson, eds., *The Expansion of International Society* (Oxford, 1984), pp. 143–69.

Nardi, B., *Studi su Pietro Pomponazzi* (Florence, 1965).

Naudé, G., *Considerations politiques sur les coups d'estat* ('Rome, 1639'; photoreproduction, ed. F. Charles-Daubert, Hildesheim, 1993).

——, *Apologie pour tous les grands personnages qui ont esté faussement soupçonnez de magie*, 2nd edn. (The Hague, 1653).

Neaimi, S., *L'Islam au siècle des Lumières: image de la civilisation islamique chez les philosophes français du XVIIIᵉ siècle* (Paris, 2003).

Nedham, M., *The Excellencie of a Free-State: Or, The Right Constitution of a Commonwealth*, ed. B. Worden (Indianapolis, IN, 2011).

Neuber, W., 'Grade der Fremdheit: Alteritätskonstruktion und *experientia*-Argumentation in deutschen Turcica der Renaissance', in B. Guthmüller and W. Kühlmann, eds., *Europa und die Türken in der Renaissance* (Tübingen, 2000), pp. 249–65.

Neumann, W., 'Die Türkeneinfälle nach Kärnten (Wahrheit und Dichtung in der Kärntner Geschichtsschreibung von Jakob Unrest bis zur Gegenwart)', *Südost-Forschungen*, 14 (1955), pp. 84–109.

Niccoli, O., *Prophecy and People in Renaissance Italy*, tr. L. G. Cochrane (Princeton, NJ, 1990).

Nicholas of Cusa, *De pace fidei and Cribratio Alkorani*, ed. and tr. J. Hopkins (Minneapolis, MN, 1990).

Nicolay, N. de, *Dans l'empire de Soliman le Magnifique*, ed. M.-C. Gomez-Géraud and S. Yérasimos (Paris, 1989).

Niederkorn, J. P., *Die europäischen Mächte und der 'Lange Türkenkrieg' Kaiser Rudolfs II (1593–1606)* (Vienna, 1993).

Niedźwiedź, J., 'Orientalizm', in A. Borowski, *Słownik sarmatyzmu: idee, pojęcia, symbole* (Kraków, 2001), pp. 127–30.

Niewöhner, F., *Veritas sive varietas: Lessings Toleranzparabel und das Buch Von den drei Betrügern* (Heidelberg, 1988).

Novak, D., *The Image of the Non-Jew in Judaism: An Historical and Constructive Study of the Noahide Laws* (Lewiston, NY, 1983).

[Nye, S.,] *A Letter of Resolution concerning the Doctrines of the Trinity and the Incarnation* (n.p., n.d. [1691]).

Nyitrai, I., 'The Third Period of the Ottoman–Safavid Conflict: Struggle of Political Ideologies (1555–1578)', in É. M. Jeremiás, ed., *Irano-Turkic Cultural Contacts in the 11th–17th Centuries* (Piliscsaba, 2003), pp. 161–75.

Ockley, S., *The Conquest of Syria, Persia, and Aegypt, by the Saracens: Containing the Lives of Abubeker, Omar and Othman, the Immediate Successors of Mahomet* (London, 1708).

Ogg, D., ed., *Sully's Grand Design of Henry IV*, Grotius Society Publications, no. 2 (London, 1921).

Okál, M., 'La Vie et l'oeuvre de Sigismond Gélous Torda', *Zborník Filozofickej Fakulty Univerzity Komenského: graecolatina et orientalia*, 6, for 1974 (1975), pp. 105–55.

Olbrecht, F. M., 'Rond Niklaas Cleynaerts' reis naar Marokko en zijn verblijf te Fes', in H. de Vocht et al., *Nicolaus Clenardus* (Antwerp, 1942), pp. 22–51.

Olearius, J., *Türckenfall, und seiner Grossmächtigen Tyrannischen Grausamkeit entgegen gesetzter unüberwindlicher Wiederstand, zu Erweckung warer Busse, kindliches Vertrauens, Hertzerquickenden Trosts, und unablässigen Gebets aus Gottes Wort gezeiget* (Leipzig, 1664).

Olivieri, A., *Immaginario e gerarchie sociali nella cultura del '500* (Verona, 1986).

Osborne, F. [Anon.], *A Perswasive to a Mutuall Compliance under the Present Government* (London, 1652).

——, *Advice to a Son: Or, Directions for Your Better Conduct through the Various and Most Important Encounters of This Life* (London, '1656' [1655]).

——, *Politicall Reflections upon the Government of the Turks; Nicholas Machiavel; The King of Sweden's Descent into Germany* . . . (London, 1656).

Osiander, A., *Unterricht und vermanung, wie man wider den Türcken peten und streyten soll* (n. p. [Nuremberg], 1542).

Osterhammel, J., *Die Entzauberung Asiens: Europa und die asiatischen Reiche im 18. Jahrhundert* (Munich, 1998).

Őze, S., *Apocalypticism in Early Reformation Hungary (1526–1566)* (Budapest, 2015).

Paganini, G., ' "*Legislatores*" et "*impostores*": le *Théophrastus redivivus* et la thèse de l'imposture des religions au milieu du XVIIe siècle', in D. Foucault and J.-P. Cavaillé, eds., *Sources antiques de l'irréligion moderne: le relais italien, XVe–XVIIe siècles* (Toulouse, 2001), pp. 181–218.

Palerne, J., *D'Alexandrie à Istanbul: pérégrinations dans l'Empire ottoman, 1581–1583*, ed. Y. Bernard (Paris, 1991).

Panaitescu, P. P., *Dimitrie Cantemir: viaţa şi opera* (Bucharest, 1958).

Panizza, D., *Alberico Gentili, giurista ideologo nell'Inghilterra elisabettiana* (Padua, 1981).

Pannier, J., 'Calvin et les Turcs', *Revue historique*, 180 (1937), pp. 267–86.

Papadopoulos, S. I., *Hē kinēsē tou douka tou Never Karolou Gonzaga yia tēn apeleutherōsē tōn valkanikōn laōn (1603–1625)* (Salonica, 1966).

Papp, S., 'Bocskai István török politikája a felkelés előestéjén', *Hadtörténelmi közlemé-nyek*, 117 (2004), pp. 1,198–1,211.

Parker, H., *The Case of Shipmony briefly Discoursed, according to the Grounds of Law, Policie, and Conscience* (n.p. [London], 1640).

——, *Observations upon some of His Majesties Late Answers and Expresses* (n.p., n.d. [London, 1642]).

Paruta, P., *Discorsi politici . . . ne i quali si considerano diversi fatti illustri, e memorabili di principi, e di republiche antiche, e moderne* (Venice, 1599).

Pásztor, E., 'La repubblica cristiana di Ottavio Pallavicino', *Rivista di studi politici internazionali*, 18 (1951), pp. 67–84.

Patrick, J. M., 'Hawk versus Dove: Francis Bacon's Advocacy of a Holy War by James I against the Turks', *Studies in the Literary Imagination*, 4 (1971), pp. 159–71.

Patrinelis, C. G., 'Mehmed II and His Presumed Knowledge of Greek and Latin', *Viator*, 2 (1971), pp. 349–54.

Paul of Burgos [Pablo de Santa Maria, 'Paulus a Sancta Maria'], *Scrutinium scriptur-arum* (Paris, c.1520).

Paudice, A., *Between Several Worlds: The Life and Writings of Elia Capsali. The Historical Works of a 16th-Century Cretan Rabbi* (Munich, 2010).

Paviot, J., *Les Ducs de Bourgogne, la croisade et l'Orient (fin XIVe siècle–XVe siècle* (Paris, 2003).

Pedani, M. P., *In nome del Gran Signore: inviati ottomani a Venezia dalla caduta di Costantinopoli alla guerra di Candia*, Deputazione di storia patria per le Venezie, Miscellanea di studi e memorie, xxx (Venice, 1994).

—— ['Pedani Fabris'] and A. Bombaci, *I 'documenti turchi' dell'Archivio di Stato di Venezia* (Rome, 1994).

—— ['Pedani-Fabris'], ed., *Relazioni di ambasciatori veneti al Senato*, xiv: *Costantinopoli: relazioni inedite (1512–1789)* (Padua, 1996).

——, *Dalla frontiera al confine*, Quaderni di Studi Arabi, Studi e testi, v (Venice, 2002).

——, 'Elenco degli inviati diplomatici veneziani presso i sovrani ottomani', *Electronic Journal of Oriental Studies*, 5 (2002), no. 4, pp. 1–54 (accessible at https://iris.unive.it/retrieve/handle/10278/14216/17947/044_ejos_elenco%20inviati.pdf).

Penn, W., *An Essay towards the Present and Future Peace of Europe by the Establishment of an European Dyet, Parliament, or Estates* (London, 1693).

Pertusi, A., 'I primi studi in Occidente sull'origine e la potenza dei Turchi', *Studi veneziani*, 12 (1970), pp. 465–552.

——, 'Giovanni Battista Egnazio (Cipelli) e Ludovico Tuberone (Crijeva) tra i primi storici occidentali del popolo turco', in V. Branca, ed., *Venezia e Ungheria nel Rinascimento* (Florence, 1973), pp. 479–87.

——, *La caduta di Costantinopoli*, 2 vols. (Milan, 1976).

——, *Testi inediti e poco noti sulla caduta di Costantinopoli* (Bologna, 1983).

——, *Bizanzio e i Turchi nella cultura del Rinascimento e del Barrocco*, ed. C. M. Mazzucchi (Milan, 2004).

Péter, K., 'Das skythische Selbstbewusstsein des ungarischen Adels', in V. Zimány, ed., *La Pologne et la Hongrie aux XVIᵉ–XVIIIᵉ siècles* (Budapest, 1981), pp. 121–33.

Petry, Y., *Gender, Kabbalah and the Reformation: The Mystical Theology of Guillaume Postel (1510–1581)* (Leiden, 2004).

Peyssonel, J.-A., *Voyage dans les régences de Tunis et d'Alger*, ed. L. Valensi (Paris, 2001).

Pfeffermann, H., *Die Zusammenarbeit der Renaissancepäpste mit den Türken* (Winterthur, 1946).

Pfister, R., 'Reformation, Türken und Islam', *Zwingliana*, 10 (1956), pp. 345–75.

Piccolomini, E. S.: *see* Pius II.

Piirimäe, P., 'Alberico Gentili's Doctrine of Defensive War and its Impact on Seventeenth-Century Views', in B. Kingsbury and B. Straumann, eds., *The Roman Foundations of the Law of Nations: Alberico Gentili and the Justice of Empire* (Oxford, 2010), pp. 187–209.

Pinot, V., *La Chine et la formation de l'esprit philosophique en France (1640–1740)* (Paris, 1932).

Pintard, R., *Le Libertinage érudit dans la première moitié du XVIIᵉ siècle* (Paris, 1943).

Pippidi, A., *Byzantins, Ottomans, Roumains: le Sud-Est européen entre l'héritage impérial et les influences occidentales* (Paris, 2006).

——, *Visions of the Ottoman World in Renaissance Europe* (London, 2013).

Pirnát, A., *Die Ideologie der Siebenbürger Antitrinitarier in dem 1570er Jahren*, tr. E. Roth (Budapest, 1961).

Piterberg, G., *An Ottoman Tragedy: History and Historiography at Play* (Berkeley, CA, 2003).

Pitton de Tournefort, J., *Relation d'un voyage du Levant, fait par ordre du Roy*, 3 vols. (Lyon, 1717).

Pius II, 'Cum bellum hodie', in *Chroniques relatives à l'histoire de la Belgique sous la domination des ducs de Bourgogne: chroniques des religieux des Dunes, Jean Brandon, Gilles de Roye, Adrien de But*, ed. K. de Lettenhove (Brussels, 1870), pp. 398–414.

—— ['A. S. Piccolomini'], *Epistola ad Mahomatem II*, ed. and tr. A. R. Baca (New York, 1990).

——, *Commentaries*, ed. M. Meserve and M. Simonetta, tr. F. A. Gragg (Cambridge, MA, 2004–).

Plosarius, D., *Oratio apologetica pro serenissimo Gabriele Bethleno: in qua partim aliae calumniae in ipsum conjectae solidè confutantur: partim etiam ostenditur, culpari non posse, quod auxilio Turcico in his bellis utatur* (Bratislava ['Poszony'], 1624).

Pobladura, M. de ['a'], 'De amicitia S. Gregorii Barbadici cum servo Dei Marco ab Aviano, O.F.M.C.A.P.', *Collectanea franciscana*, 31 (1961), pp. 61–79.

Polišensky, J. V., 'Bohemia, the Turk and the Christian Commonwealth', *Byzantino-slavica*, 14 (1953), pp. 82–108.

Pomponazzi, P., *Abhandlung über die Unsterblichkeit der Seele*, ed. and tr. B. Mojsisch (Hamburg, 1990).

Porter, Sir James, *Observations on the Religion, Law, Government, and Manners of the Turks*, 2 vols. (London, 1768).

Postel, G., *Alcorani seu legis Mahometi et Evangelistarum concordiae liber, in quo de calamitatibus orbi Christiano imminentibus tractatur* (Paris, 1543).

——, *De orbis terrae concordia libri quatuor* (Basel, 1544).

——, *L'Histoire memorable des expeditions depuys le deluge faictes par les Gauloys ou Francoys depuis la France iusques en Asie, ou en Thrace & en l'orientale partie de l'Europe, & des commodités ou incommodités des divers chemins pour y parvenir & retourner*, with *Apologie de la Gaule contre les malevoles escripvains qui d'icelle ont mal ou negligentement escript* and *Les tresanciens droictz du peuple Gallique, & de ses princes* (Paris, 1552).

——, *Histoire et consideration de l'origine, loy, et coustume des Tartares, Persiens, Arabes, Turcs, & tous autres Ismaelites ou Muhamediques, dits par nous Mahometains, ou Sarrazins* (Poitiers, 1560).

——, *De la république des Turcs: & là ou l'occasion s'offrera, des moeurs & loy de tous Muhamedistes* (Poitiers, 1560).

——, *La Tierce Partie des orientales histoires, ou est exposée la condition, puissance, & revenu de l'Empire Turquesque* (Poitiers, 1560).

——, *Cosmographicae disciplinae compendium, in suum finem, hoc est ad divinae providentiae certissimam demonstrationem conductum* (Basel, 1561).

[Poullain de Saint Foix, G.-F.,] *Lettres turques* ('Cologne', 1744).

Poumarède, G., *Pour en finir avec la Croisade: mythes et réalités de la lutte contre les Turcs aux XVIe et XVIIe siècles* (Paris, 2004).

[Praetorius, J.,] *Arcana reipublicae turcicae detecta. Das ist: funfftzig Türckische Regimentsgeheimnisse, worauff solch Reich, als auff so viel Seulen bisshero sich gestützet, und wie selbige durch Göttliche Hülffe und Christlicher Prudenz zu stürtzen seyn. Aus vielfältigen Autoribus geoffenbahret* (n.p. [Leipzig?], 1664).

——, *Catastrophe muhammetica, oder das endliche Valet, und schändliche Nativität des gantzen, und nunmehr vergänglichen Türckischen Reichs, aus ziemlich vielen, so wohl geistlichen Prophezeyhungen, als weltlichen Weissagungen . . . entdecket* (Leipzig, 1664).

Presser, J., *Das Buch De tribus impostoribus, von den drei Betrügern* (Amsterdam, 1926).

Price Zimmermann, T. C., *Paolo Giovio: The Historian and the Crisis of Sixteenth-Century Italy* (Princeton, NJ, 1995).

Prideaux, H., *The True Nature of Imposture fully Display'd in the Life of Mahomet*, 2nd edn. (London, 1697).

Procacci, G., *Studi sulla fortuna di Machiavelli* (Rome, 1965).

Prosperi, A., 'Un'Europa dal volto umano: aspetti della propaganda asburgica del '500', *Critica storica*, 27 (1991), no. 2, pp. 335–52.

Pseudo-Methodius, *Apocalypse*, with *An Alexandrian World Chronicle*, ed. and tr. B. Garstad (Cambridge, MA, 2012).

Ptolemy of Lucca [Tolomeo Fiadoni], *On the Government of Rulers: De regimine principum*, tr. J. M. Blythe (Philadelphia, 1997).

Pujeau, E., '*Conseils pour l'entreprise contre les Infidèles* ou le *modus operandi* de la croisade au XVIe siècle', in J. Paviot, ed., *Les Projets de croisade: géostratégie et diplomatie européenne du XIVe au XVIIe siècle* (Toulouse, 2014), pp. 287–314.

——, *L'Europe et les Turcs: la croisade de l'humaniste Paolo Giovio* (Toulouse, 2015).

Quaglioni, D., *Politica e diritto nel Trecento italiano: il 'De Tyranno' di Bartolo da Sassoferrato (1314–1357)* (Florence, 1983).

Queller, D. E., 'The Development of Ambassadorial Relazioni', in J. R. Hale, ed., *Renaissance Venice* (1973), pp. 174–96.

Raby, J., 'Mehmed the Conqueror as a Patron of the Arts', *Oxford Art Journal*, 5 (1982), pp. 3–8.

[Radicati di Passerano, A.,] *A Comical and True Account of the Modern Canibals's* [sic] *Religion, by Osmin, a True Believer* (1734).

——, *La Religion muhammedane, comparée à la paienne de l'Indostan, par Ali-Ebn-Oman, Moslem: épitre à Cinkniu, bramin de Visapour. Traduite de l'Arabe* ('London', 1737), printed with his *Sermon, prêché dans la grande assemblée des Quakers de Londres par le fameux frère E. Elwall, dit l'inspiré. Traduit de l'anglois* ('London', 1737).

Rahe, P., *Montesquieu and the Logic of Liberty* (New Haven, CT, 2009).

Rainolds, W., *Calvino-Turcismus, id est Calvinisticae perfidiae, cum mahumetana collatio, et dilucida utriusque sectae confutatio* (Antwerp, 1597).

Rataj, T., *České země ve stínu půlměsíce: obraz Turka v raně novověké literatuře z Českých zemí* (Dolní Břežany, 2002).

Reddig, W. F., *Reise zum Erzfeind der Christenheit: der Humanist Hans Dernschwam in der Türkei (1553–1555)* (Pfaffenweiler, 1990).

Reeves, M., *The Influence of Prophecy in the Later Middle Ages: A Study in Joachimism* (Oxford, 1969).

Reinink, G. J., 'Der edessenische "Pseudo-Methodius"', *Byzantinische Zeitschrift*, 83 (1990), pp. 31–45.

Reland, A. ['H.'], *De religione mohammedica libri duo* (Utrecht, 1705).

——, 'De jure militari mohammedanorum contra christianos bellum gerentium', in his *Dissertationes miscellaneae*, 3 vols. (Utrecht, 1706–8), iii, pp. 1–53.

Rescius [Reszka], S., *De atheismis et phalarismis Evangelicorum libri duo* (Naples, 1596).

Revelli, P., 'Un trattato geografico-politico di Giuseppe Moleti: "Discorso che il re cattolico sia il maggior principe del mondo" (1580–81)', *Aevum*, 1 (1927), pp. 417–54.

Rezar, V., 'Dubrovački humanistički historiograf Ludovik Crijević Tuberon', *Anali Dubrovnik*, 37 (1999), pp. 47–94.

Ricci, G., *Appello al Turco: i confini infranti del Rinascimento* (Rome, 2011).

Riccoldo da Monte Croce ['Ricoldus de Montecrucis'], *Confutatio Alcorani*, with M. Luther, *Verlegung des Alcoran*, ed. J. Ehmann (Würzburg, 1999).

Richer ['Richerius'], C., *De rebus Turcarum* (Paris, 1540).

——, *Des coustumes et manieres de vivre des Turcs* (Paris, 1540).

Roe, Sir Thomas, *A True and Faithfull Relation . . . of what hath lately happened in Constantinople, concerning the Death of Sultan Osman* (London, 1622).

Roggema, B., *The Legend of Sergius Bahira: Eastern Christian Apologetics and Apocalyptic in Response to Islam* (Leiden, 2009).

Romano, G., 'Filippo Maria Visconti e i Turchi', *Archivio storico lombardo*, vol. 7, year 17 (1890), pp. 585–618.

Roosbroeck, G. L. van, *Persian Letters before Montesquieu* (New York, 1932).

Roscioni, G. C., *Sulle traccie dell' 'Esploratore turco'* (Milan, 1992).

Ross, E., *Picturing Experience in the Early Printed Book: Breydenbach's Peregrinatio from Venice to Jerusalem* (University Park, PA, 2014).

Rother, C., *Siebenbürgen und der Buchdruck im 16. Jahrhundert* (Wiesbaden, 2002).

Rubiés, J.-P., 'Oriental Despotism and European Orientalism: Botero to Montesquieu', *Journal of Early Modern History*, 9 (2005), pp. 109–80.

Runciman, Sir Steven, 'Teucri and Turci', in S. A. Hanna, ed., *Medieval and Middle Eastern Studies in Honor of Aziz Suryal Atiya* (Leiden, 1972), pp. 344–8.

Rupel, M., *Primus Truber: Leben und Werk des slowenischen Reformators* (Munich, 1965).

Rycaut, P., *The Present State of the Ottoman Empire*, 2nd edn. (London, 1668).

Saavedra Fajardo, D. de, *Idea de un principe político-cristiano* (Milan, 1642).

Said, E. W., *Orientalism: Western Conceptions of the Orient*, 2nd edn. (London, 1995).

Saint-Pierre, abbé de: *see* Castel, C. I.

Saitta, A., *Dalla res publica christiana agli Stati Uniti di Europa: sviluppo dell'idea pacifista in Francia nei secoli XVII–XIX* (Rome, 1948).

——, 'Un riformatore pacifista contemporaneo del Richelieu: E. Crucé', *Rivista storica italiana*, 63 (1951), pp. 180–215.

Salazar, J. de, *Política española*, ed. M. Herrero Garcia (Madrid, 1945).

Sale, G., *The Koran, Commonly Called the Alcoran of Mohammed, Translated into English . . . To which is Prefixed a Preliminary Discourse* (London, 1734).

Salinero, F. G., ed., *Viaje de Turquía (La odisea de Pedro de Urdemalas)* (Madrid, 1980).

Sandius, C., *Nucleus historiae ecclesiasticae* ('Cosmopolis' [Amsterdam], 1668).

Sandys, G., *A Relation of a Journey begun An: Dom: 1610* (London, 1615).

Sanz, E., *Breve trattato nel quale con ragioni dimostrative si convincono manifestamente i Turchi, senza che in guisa veruna possano negarlo, esser falsa la legge di Maometto, e vera solamente quella di Cristo* (Catania, 1691).

Sanz Santacruz, V., 'Juan de Segovia y Nicolás de Cusa frente al Islam: su comprensión intelectualista de la fe cristiana', *Anuario de historia de la Iglesia*, 16 (2007), pp. 181–94.

Sariyannis, M., 'Ottoman Critics of Society and State, Fifteenth to Early Eighteenth Centuries: Toward a Corpus for the Study of Ottoman Political Thought', *Archivum ottomanicum*, 26 (2009), pp. 127–50.

Savary de Brèves, F., *Relation des voyages de Monsieur de Breves, tant en Grèce, Terresaincte et Aegypte, qu'aux royaumes de Tunis & Alger* (Paris, 1628).

Schader, B., *Johann Jakob Redinger (1619–1688), Sprachwissenschaftler und Pädagoge im Gefolge des Comenius* (Zurich, 1985).

Schaller, K., 'Johann Jakob Redinger in seinem Verhältnis zu Johann Amos Comenius', in M. Bircher, W. Sparn, and E. Weyrauch, eds., *Schweizerisch-deutsch Beziehungen im konfessionellen Zeitalter: Beiträge zur Kulturgeschichte 1580–1650* (Wiesbaden, 1984), pp. 139–66.

Schelwig ['Schelguigius'], S., *De philosophia turcica, oratio inauguralis* (Gdańsk, n.d. [1686]).

Schiltberger, J., *Reisen in Europa, Asia und Afrika von 1394 bis 1427*, ed. K. F. Neumann (Munich, 1859).

Schlüsselburg, K. ['C.'], *Theologiae calvinistarum libri tres* (Frankfurt am Main, 1594).

Schmeisser, M., '"Mohammed, der Erzbetrüger": negative Darstellungen des Propheten in den religionskritischen Produktionen des Libertinismus und der Radikalaufklärung', in D. Klein and B. Platow, eds., *Wahrnehmung des Islam zwischen Reformation und Aufklärung* (Munich, 2008), pp. 77–108.

Schröder, W., 'Einleitung', in [J. J. Müller] *De imposturis religionum (De tribus impostoribus), Von den Betrügereyen der Religionen*, ed. W. Schröder (Stuttgart, 1999), pp. 7–77.

Schulze, W., *Reich und Türkengefahr im späten 16. Jahrhundert* (Munich, 1978).

Schwab, R., *Vie d'Anquetil-Duperron* (Paris, 1934).

Schweigger, S., *Ein newe Reyssbeschreibung auss Teutschland nach Constantinopel und Jerusalem*, ed. R. Neck (Graz, 1964).

Schwoebel, R., *The Shadow of the Crescent: The Renaissance Image of the Turk (1453–1517)* (Nieuwkoop, 1967).

Scuccimarra, L., *I confini del mondo: storia del cosmopolitismo dall'Antichità al Settecento* (Bologna, 2006).

Secret, F., 'La Tradition du "de omni scibili" à la renaissance: l'oeuvre de Paul Scaliger', *Convivium*, n.s., 23 (1955), pp. 492–7.

——, *Postel revisité: nouvelles recherches sur Guillaume Postel et son milieu* (Paris, 1998).

Sée, H., 'Les Idées politiques de Fénelon', *Revue d'histoire moderne et contemporaine*, 1 (1899), pp. 545–65.

Segesvary, V., *L'Islam et la Réforme: étude sur l'attitude des Réformateurs zurichois envers l'Islam (1510–1550)* (Geneva, 1977).

Seneca, F., *Il Doge Leonardo Donà: la sua vita e la sua preparazione politica prima del dogado* (Padua, 1959).

Sepúlveda, J. G. de, *Ad Carolum V. Imperatorem invictissimum ut facta cum omnibus Christianis pace bellum suscipiat in Turcas Io. Genesii Sepulvedae cordubensis cohortatio* (n.p., n.d.).

——, *Gonsalus seu de appetenda gloria dialogus*, ed. J. J. Valverde Abril, in J. G. de Sepúlveda, *Obras completas*, vi, ed. J. M. Pérez-Prendes Muñoz-Arraco et al. (Pozoblanco, 2001), pp. 211–49.

——, *De conuenientia militaris disciplinae cum christiana religione dialogus, qui inscribitur Democrates*, ed. V. Lavenia (Macerata, 2015).

Serafino da Fermo, *Breve dichiaratione sopra l'apocalipse de Gioanni, doue si proua esser uenuto il precursore de Antichristo* (Venice, 1541).

Servet [Servetus], M., *Restitution du Christianisme [Christianismi restitutio]*, ed. R.-M. Bénin, 2 vols. (Paris, 2011).

Setton, K. M., *The Papacy and the Levant (1204–1571)*, 4 vols. (Philadelphia, 1976–84).

Sextus Empiricus, *Adversus mathematicos: hoc est, adversus eos qui profitentur disciplinas, opus eruditissimum*, ed. and tr. G. Hervet (Antwerp, 1569).

Shackleton, R., *Montesquieu: A Critical Biography* (Oxford, 1961).

Shaw, S. J., *History of the Ottoman Empire and Modern Turkey*, i: *Empire of the Gazis: The Rise and Decline of the Ottoman Empire, 1280–1808* (Cambridge, UK, 1976).

Sheehan, M., *The Balance of Power: History and Theory* (London, 1995).

Sieber-Lehmann, C., 'Der türkische Sultan Mehmed II. und Karl der Kühne, der "Türk im Occident" ', in F.-R. Erkens, ed., *Europa und die osmanische Expansion im ausgehenden Mittelalter* (Berlin, 1997), pp. 13–38.

Sionita, G., ed. and tr., *Testamentum et pactiones initae inter Mohamedem et christianae fidei cultores* (Paris, 1630).

Skalić ['Scalichius'], P., *Miscellaneorum de rerum caussis, et successibus . . . libri septem* (Cologne, 1570).

Skilliter, S. A., *William Harborne and the Trade with Turkey, 1578–1582: A Documentary Study of the First Anglo-Ottoman Relations* (London, 1977).

Skinner, Q., *Liberty before Liberalism* (Cambridge, UK, 1998).

——, 'John Milton and the Politics of Slavery', in Q. Skinner, *Visions of Politics*, 3 vols. (Cambridge, UK, 2002), ii, pp. 286–307.

Smith, M., 'Introduction', in E. de La Boëtie, *De la servitude volontaire ou contr'un*, ed. M. Smith (Geneva, 1987), pp. 7–32.

Smith, P. H., *The Business of Alchemy: Science and Culture in the Holy Roman Empire* (Princeton, NJ, 1994).

Smith, T., *Remarks upon the Manners, Religion and Government of the Turks* (London, 1678).

Sorbière, S., *Discours sceptiques*, ed. S. Gouverneur (Paris, 2002).

Soto, D. de, *De iustitia et iure libri decem* (Salamanca, 1573).

Southern, R. W., *Western Views of Islam in the Middle Ages*, 2nd edn. (Cambridge, MA, 1978).

Spandounes, T., *On the Origin of the Ottoman Emperors*, ed. and tr. D. M. Nicol (Cambridge, UK, 1997).

Spini, G., *Ricerca dei libertini: la teoria dell'impostura delle religioni nel seicento italiano*, 2nd edn. (Florence, 1983).

Spinoza, B. de, *Tractatus politicus*, in B. de Spinoza, *Opera*, ed. C. Gebhardt, 5 vols. (Heidelberg, 1925), iii, pp. 269–360.

Srodecki, P., '*Validissima semper Christianitatis propugnacula*: zur Entstehung der Bollwerksrhetorik in Polen und Ungarn im Spätmittelalter und in der Frühen Neuzeit', in M. Długosz and P. O. Scholz, eds., *Sarmatismus versus Orientalismus in Mitteleuropa: Sarmatyzm versus orientalizm w Europie Środkowej* (Berlin, 2013), pp. 131–68.

Stagl, J., 'Die Apodemik oder "Reisekunst" als Methodik der Sozialforschung vom Humanismus bis zur Aufklärung', in M. Rassem and J. Stagl, eds., *Statistik und Staatsbeschreibung in der Neuzeit, vornehmlich im 16.–18 Jahrhundert* (Paderborn, 1980), pp. 131–202.

Stelling-Michaud, S., 'Le Mythe du despotisme oriental', *Schweizer Beiträge zur allgemeinen Geschichte*, 18/19 (1960/1), pp. 328–46.

Sterpos, M., 'Boccalini tacitista di fronte al Machiavelli', *Studi secenteschi*, 12 (1971), pp. 255–83.

Stoye, J., *Marsigli's Europe, 1680–1730: The Life and Times of Luigi Ferdinando Marsigli, Soldier and Virtuoso* (New Haven, CT, 1994).

Strémooukhoff, D., 'Moscow the Third Rome: Sources of the Doctrine', *Speculum*, 28 (1953), pp. 84–101.

Stubbe, H., 'The Originall & Progress of Mahometanism', in N. Matar, ed., *Henry Stubbe and the Beginnings of Islam: The Originall & Progress of Mahometanism* (New York, 2014), pp. 65–257.

Sturmberger, H., *Georg Erasmus Tschernembl: Religion, Libertät und Widerstand. Ein Beitrag zur Geschichte der Gegenreformation und des Landes ob der Enns* (Graz, 1953).

Suárez, F., *Selections from Three Works of Francisco Suárez, S.J.*, ed. J. B. Scott, 2 vols. (Oxford, 1944).

Sullivan, R. E., *John Toland and the Deist Controversy: A Study in Adaptations* (Cambridge, MA, 1982).

Sully, duc de: *see* Béthune, M. de.

Sutcliffe, M. ['M. S.'], *De turco-papismo: hoc est, de Turcarum et Papistarum adversus Christi ecclesiam & fidem coniuratione, eorumque in religione & moribus consensione & similitudine* ('London' [Hanau], 1604).

Talon, O., *Harangue faite au Roy par Monsieur Talon son Advocat General au Parlement de Paris* (Paris, 1649).

Taranto, D. *Pirronismo ed assolutismo nella Francia del '600: studi sul pensiero politico dello scetticismo da Montaigne a Bayle (1580–1697)* (Milan, 1994).

Tateo, F., 'L'ideologia umanistica e il simbolo "immane" di Otranto', in C. D. Fonseca, ed., *Otranto 1480: atti del convegno internazionale per il V. centenario della caduta di Otranto*, 2 vols. (Galatina, 1986), i, pp. 151–223.

Tavernier, J.-B., *Voyages en Perse*, ed. V. Monteuil (n.p. [Paris], 1964).

Temple, Sir William, *Miscellanea: The Second Part, in Four Essays* (London, 1690).

Tenison, T., *Of Idolatry: A Discourse, in which is Endeavoured a Declaration of its Distinction from Superstition* (London, 1678).

Terbe, L., 'Egy európai szállóige életrajza (Magyarország a kereszténység védőbástyája)', *Egyetemes philologiai közlöny*, 60 (1936), pp. 297–350.

Terzorio, C. da: *see* Clemente da Terzorio.

Tezcan, B., *The Second Ottoman Empire: Political and Social Transformation in the Early Modern World* (Cambridge, UK, 2010).

Thévenot, J., *L'Empire du Grand Turc vu par un sujet de Louis XIV*, ed. F. Billacois (Paris, 1965).

Thevet, A., *Cosmographie de Levant* (Lyon, 1554).

Thijn, T. van, 'Pieter de la Court: zijn leven en zijn economische denkbeelden', *Tijdschrift voor geschiedenis*, 69 (1956), pp. 304–70.

Thireau, J.-L., *Les Idées politiques de Louis XIV* (Paris, 1973).

Thomas à Jesu [D. Sánchez d'Avila], *De procuranda salute omnium gentium, schismaticorum, haereticorum, Iudaeorum, Sarracenorum, caeterorumq[ue] infidelium libri XIII* (Antwerp, 1613).

Thomas Aquinas, St, *Summa theologiae*, in *S. Thomae Aquinatis opera omnia*, ed. R. Busi, 7 vols. (Stuttgart, 1980), ii, pp. 184–926.

Thomas of Pavia ['Tuscus'], 'Gesta imperatorum et pontificum', ed. E. Ehrenfeuchter, in *Monumenta Germaniae historica*, Scriptorum, xxii (Hanover, 1872), pp. 483–528.

Thuasne, L., *Djem-Sultan, fils de Mohammed II, frère de Bayezid II (1459–1495), d'après les documents originaux en grande partie inédits: étude de la question d'Orient à la fin du XVᵉ siècle* (Paris, 1892).

Thumser, M., 'Türkenfrage und öffentliche Meinung: zeitgenössische Zeugnisse nach dem Fall von Konstantinopel (1453)', in F.-R. Erkens, ed., *Europa und die osmanische Expansion im ausgehenden Mittelalter* (Berlin, 1997), pp. 59–78.

Tilney ['Tyllney'], E., *Topographical Descriptions, Regiments, and Policies, Books VI, VII, VIII*, ed. W. R. Streitberger (New York, 1991).

Tinguely, F., *L'Écriture du Levant à la Renaissance: enquête sur les voyageurs français dans l'empire de Soliman le Magnifique* (Geneva, 2000).

——, 'Introduction' to F. Bernier, *Un libertin dans l'Inde Moghole: les voyages de François Bernier (1656–1669)*, ed. F. Tinguely (Paris, 2008), pp. 7–34.

Todd, C., 'Introduction' to Voltaire, *Le Fanatisme, ou Mahomet le prophète*, in Voltaire, *Les Oeuvres complètes*, ed. N. Cronk et al., vol. 20B (Oxford, 2003), pp. 7–139.

Toffanin, G., *Machiavelli e il 'tacitismo'* (Padua, 1921).

Tolan, J. V., *Saracens: Islam in the Medieval European Imagination* (New York, 2002).

Toland, J., *Nazarenus*, ed. J. Champion (Oxford, 1999).

Tomassetti, L. ['A'.], et al., eds., *Bullarum diplomatum et privilegiorum sanctorum romanorum pontificum taurinensis editio*, 24 vols. (Turin, 1857–72).

Tomljenović, I., 'Dubrovčanin Ivan Stojković (1390/95–1443), borac za jedinstvo Zapada i zbližavanje s Istokom', *Croatica christiana periodica: časopis Instituta za Crkvenu Povijest Katoličkog Bogoslovnog Fakulteta u Zagrebu*, 6 (1982), no. 9, pp. 1–12.

Tommasino, P. M., 'Discussioni di confine sul dogma della Trinità: l'uso della *basmala* in Bartholomaeus Georgevits (Transilvania, 1547) e nel monaco 'Enbaqom (Etiopia, 1540)', *Islamochristiana*, 35 (2009), pp. 101–39.

Tongas, G., *L'Ambassadeur Louis Deshayes de Cormenin (1600–1632): les relations de la France avec l'Empire Ottoman, le Danemark, la Suède, la Perse et la Russie* (Paris, 1937).

Tooley, M. J., 'Bodin and the Medieval Theory of Climate', *Speculum*, 28 (1953), pp. 64–83.

Toomer, G. J., *John Selden: A Life in Scholarship*, 2 vols. (Oxford, 2009).

Toon, P., ed., *Puritans, the Millennium and the Future of Israel: Puritan Eschatology, 1600 to 1660* (Cambridge, UK, 1970).

'Torquato' ['Torquatus'], A., *Prognosticon Antonii Torquati de eversione Europae* (Antwerp, 1544).

Torquemada ['Turre Cremata'], J. de, *Tractatus contra principales errores perfidi Machometi et turcorum sive sarracenorum* (Paris, c.1510).

Trame, R. H., *Rodrigo Sánchez de Arévalo, 1404–1470: Spanish Diplomat and Champion of the Papacy* (Washington, DC, 1958).

Treves, P., 'The Title of Campanella's "City of the Sun"', *Journal of the Warburg and Courtauld Institutes*, 3 (1939–40), pp. 248–51.

Tuck, R., *The Rights of War and Peace: Political Thought and the International Order from Grotius to Kant* (Oxford, 1999).

Turbet-Delof, G., 'Jean Bodin lecteur de "Léon d'Afrique"', *Neohelicon: acta comparationis litterarum universarum*, 2 (1974), nos. 1–2, pp. 201–16.

Turgot, A.-R.-J., 'Plan du premier discours sur la formation des gouvernements et le mélange des nations', in *Oeuvres de Turgot et documents le concernant*, ed. G. Schelle, 5 vols. (Paris, 1913–23), i, pp. 277–98.

[Tyssot de Patot, S.,] *Voyages et avantures de Jacques Massé* ('Bordeaux', 1710).

Unghváry, A. S., *The Hungarian Protestant Reformation in the Sixteenth Century under the Ottoman Impact* (Lewiston, 1989).

Uomini, S., *Cultures historiques dans la France du XVIIe siècle* (Paris, 1998).

Ursu, J., *La politique orientale de François 1er (1515–1547)* (Paris, 1908).

Valensi, L., *Venise et la Sublime Porte: la naissance du despote* (Paris, 1987).

Valle, P. della, *The Pilgrim: The Travels of Pietro della Valle*, tr. G. Bull (London, 1989).

Vanel, C., *Abregé nouveau de l'histoire generale des Turcs*, 3 vols. (Paris, 1689).

Vanini, L. ['G. C.'], *Le Opere di Gulio Cesare Vanini e le loro fonti*, ed. L. Corvaglia, 2 vols. (Milan, 1933–4).

Varisco, D. M., *Reading Orientalism: Said and the Unsaid* (Seattle, WA, 2006).

Vasoli, C., 'A proposito della "Digressio in Nicholaum Machiavellium": la religione come "forza" politica nel pensiero di Botero', in A. E. Baldini, ed., *Botero e la 'ragion di stato': atti del convegno in memoria di Luigi Firpo (Torino 8–10 marzo 1990)* (Florence, 1992), pp. 41–58.

Vatin, N., and G. Veinstein, *Le Sérail ébranlé: essai sur les morts, dépositions et avènements des sultans ottomans, XIVe–XIXe siècles* (Paris, 2003).

Vaughan, D., *Europe and the Turk: A Pattern of Alliances, 1350–1700* (Liverpool, 1954).

Vaumas, G. de, *L'Éveil missionnaire de la France au XVIIe siècle* (n.p. [Paris], 1959).

Vella, A. P., *An Elizabethan–Ottoman Conspiracy* ('Malta' [Valletta], 1972).

Ventura, C., ed., *Tesoro politico in cui si contengono relationi, istruttioni, trattati, & varii discorsi, pertinenti alla perfetta intelligenza della ragion di stato* (Vicenza, 1602).

Venturino, D., 'Un prophète "philosophe"? Une *Vie de Mahomed* à l'aube des lumières', *Dix-huitième siècle*, no. 24 (1994), pp. 321–31.

Vermigli, P. M., *Loci communes* (London, 1583).

Vernière, P., 'Montesquieu et le monde musulman d'après *L'Esprit des lois*', in L. Desgraves, ed., *Actes du Congrès Montesquieu réuni du 23 au 26 mai 1955 pour commémorer le deuxième centenaire de la mort de Montesquieu* (Bordeaux, 1956), pp. 175–90.

[Verstegan, R.,] *A Declaration of the True Causes of the Great Troubles, Presupposed to be Intended against the Realme of England* (n.p. [Antwerp], 1592).

Vilfan, S., 'Die wirtschaftlichen Auswirkungen der Türkenkriege aus der Sicht der Ranzionierungen, der Steuern und der Preisbewegung', in O. Pickl, ed., *Die wirtschaftlichen Auswirkungen der Türkenkriege*, Grazer Forschungen zur Wirtschafts- und Sozialgeschichte, i (Graz, 1971), pp. 177–99.

Villalón, C. de, attrib., *Viaje de Turquía*, ed. A. G. de Solalinde (Madrid, 1965).

Villani, S., *Tremolanti e papisti: missione quacchere nell'Italia del Seicento* (Rome, 1996).

Villey, M., *La Croisade: essai sur la formation d'une théorie juridique* (Paris, 1942).

Viret, P., *L'Interim fait par dialogues*, ed. G. Mermier (New York, 1985).

Vismara, G., 'Limitazioni al commercio internazionale nell'Impero romano e nella comunità cristiana medievale', in *Scritti in onore di Contardo Ferrini*, 4 vols. (Milan, 1947–9), i, pp. 443–76.

——, *Impium foedus: le origini della 'respublica christiana'* (Milan, 1974).

Vitéz de Zredna, J., *Orationes in causa expeditione contra Turcas habitae*, ed. V. ['G.'] Fraknói (Budapest, 1878).

Vitoria, F. de, *Relectio de Indis*, ed. J. Pereña and J. M. Perez Prendes (Madrid, 1967).

Vives, J. L., *De Europae dissidiis, & republica* (Bruges, 1526).

——, *De concordia & discordia in humano genere, ad Carolum V. Caesarem, libri quatuor. De pacificatione, liber vnus. Quàm misera esset uita Christianorum sub Turca, liber vnus* (Lyon, 1532).

Vivo, F. de, *Information and Communication in Venice: Rethinking Early Modern Politics* (Oxford, 2007).

Vocelka, K., *Die politische Propaganda Kaiser Rudolfs II. (1576–1612)* (Vienna, 1981).

—— 'Das Türkenbild des christlichen Abendlandes in der frühen Neuzeit', in E. Zöllner and K. Gutkas, eds., *Österreich und die Osmanen—Prinz Eugen und seine Zeit* (Vienna, 1988), pp. 20–31.

——, 'Die diplomatische Beziehungen zwischen den Habsburgern und dem Osmanischen Reich in der Frühen Neuzeit', in B. Tremml-Werner and E. Grailsheim, eds., *Audienzen und Allianzen: interkulturelle Diplomatie in Asien und Europa vom 8. bis zum 18. Jahrhundert* (Vienna, 2015), pp. 171–83.

Volanus, A., *Paraenesis Andreae Volani, ad omnes in regno Poloniae, magnoque Ducatu Lituaniae, Samostenianae vel Ebioniticae doctrinae professores; eiusdem[que] ad noua Ebionitarum contra Paraenesin obiecta, responsio* (Speyer, 1582).

Voltaire [F.-M. Arouet], 'Projet secret présenté à l'Empereur Ottoman Mustapha III par Ali ben Abdallah, pacha du Caire . . . traduit du turc', in [Voltaire,] *Lettres à son altesse Monseigneur le Prince de **** sur Rabelais & sur d'autres auteurs accusés d'avoir mal parlé de la religion chrêtienne* ('London', 1748), pp. 109–14.

——, *Essai sur les moeurs*, ed. R. Pomeau, 2 vols. (Paris, 1963).

——, *Le Fanatisme, ou Mahomet le prophète*, in Voltaire, *Les Oeuvres complètes*, ed. N. Cronk et al., vol. 20B (Oxford, 2003), pp. 1–326.

——, 'De l'Alcoran et de Mahomet', ed. A. Gunny, in Voltaire, *Les Oeuvres complètes*, ed. N. Cronk et al., vol. 20B (Oxford, 2003), pp. 327–42.

——, *Textes sur l'Orient, i: L'Empire Ottoman & le monde arabe*, ed. J. P. Jackson (Tangier, 2006).

——, *Commentaire sur l'Esprit des lois de Montesquieu*, ed. S. Mason, in Voltaire, *Les Oeuvres complètes*, ed. N. Cronk et al., vol. 80B (Oxford, 2009), pp. 207–450.

Vrolijk, A., 'Sale, George (*b.* in or after 1696?, *d.* 1736), Orientalist', *Oxford Dictionary of National Biography* (http://www.oxforddnb.com).

Waddicor, M. H., *Montesquieu and the Philosophy of Natural Law* (The Hague, 1970).

Wagner, G., *Das Türkenjahr 1664: eine europäische Bewährung. Raimund Montecuccoli, die Schlacht von St Gotthard-Mogersdorf und der Friede von Eisenburg (Vasvár)* (Eisenstadt, 1964).

Watson, A., 'Systems of States', *Review of International Studies*, 16 (1990), pp. 99–109.

Webb, D., 'The Decline and Fall of Eastern Christianity: A Fifteenth-Century View', *Bulletin of the Institute of Historical Research*, 49 (1976), pp. 198–216.

Weber, B., *Lutter contre les Turcs: les formes nouvelles de la croisade pontificale au XVe siècle* (Rome, 2013).

Weil, F., 'Montesquieu et le despotisme', in L. Desgraves, ed., *Actes du Congrès Montesquieu réuni du 23 au 26 mai 1955 pour commémorer le deuxième centenaire de la mort de Montesquieu* (Bordeaux, 1956), pp. 191–215.

Weiss, C., ed., *Papiers d'état du Cardinal de Granvelle d'après les manuscrits de la Bibliothèque de Besançon*, 9 vols. (Paris, 1841–52).

Wengert, T. J., 'The Biblical Commentaries of Philip Melanchthon', in I. Dingel et al., *Philip Melanchthon Theologian in Classroom, Confession and Controversy* (Göttingen, 2012), pp. 43–76.

Westerink, K., 'Liever Turks dan paaps: een devies tijdens de Opstand in de Nederlanden', in H. Theunissen, A. Abelmann, and W. Meulenkamp, eds., *Topkapi & Turkomanie: Turks–Nederlandse ontmoetingen sinds 1600* (Amsterdam, 1989), pp. 75–80.

White, S., *The Climate of Rebellion in the Early Modern Ottoman Empire* (Cambridge, UK, 2011).

Wiegers, G. A., 'Muhammed as the Messiah: A Comparison of the Polemical Works of Juan Alonso with the *Gospel of Barnabas*', *Bibliotheca orientalis*, 52 (1995), pp. 246–91.

Winterhager, W. E., 'Ablasskritik als Indikator historischen Wandels vor 1517: ein Beitrag zu Voraussetzungen und Einordnung der Reformation', *Archiv für Reformationsgeschichte*, 90 (1999), pp. 6–71.

Wortley Montagu, Lady Mary, *The Complete Letters*, ed. R. Halsband, 3 vols. (Oxford, 1965–7).

Yaycioglu, A., *Partners of the Empire: The Crisis of the Ottoman Order in the Age of Revolutions* (Stanford, CA, 2016).

Yerasimos, S., 'Les Relations franco-ottomanes et la prise de Tripoli en 1551', in G. Veinstein, ed., *Soliman le Magnifique et son temps* (Paris, 1992), pp. 529–47.

——, *Hommes et idées dans l'espace ottoman* (Istanbul, 1997).

——, 'De l'arbre à la pomme: la généalogie d'un thème apocalyptique', in B. Lellouch and S. Yerasimos, eds., *Les Traditions apocalyptiques au tournant de la chute de Constantinople* (Paris, 1999), pp. 153–92.

Yurdusev, A. N., 'The Ottoman Attitude toward Diplomacy', in A. N. Yurdusev, ed., *Ottoman Diplomacy: Conventional or Unconventional?* (Basingstoke, 2004), pp. 5–35.

Zacour, N., *Jews and Saracens in the Consilia of Oldradus de Ponte* (Toronto, 1990).

Index